D0944924

D0903883

Italian Americans
New Perspectives
in Italian Immigration and
Ethnicity

Italian Americans
New Perspectives
in Italian Immigration and Ethnicity

edited by
Lydio F. Tomasi

1985
CENTER FOR MIGRATION STUDIES OF NEW YORK, INC.

*The Center for Migration Studies is an educational
non-profit institute founded in New York in 1964
to encourage and facilitate the study of socio-demographic,
economic, political, historical, legislative and pastoral
aspects of human migration and refugee movements.
The opinions expressed in this work are those of the authors.*

*This volume contains the proceedings of the
International Conference on the Italian Experience in
the United States held at Columbia University,
October 13-14, 1983. The Center for Migration Studies
gratefully acknowledges the financial support of the
Italian Embassy in Washington, D.C., for the
publication of these proceedings.*

ITALIAN AMERICANS
NEW PERSPECTIVES IN
ITALIAN IMMIGRATION AND ETHNICITY

First Edition
Copyright © 1985 by
The Center for Migration Studies of New York, Inc.

Center for Migration Studies
209 Flagg Place
Staten Island, New York 10304

ISBN 0-913256-69-2
Library of Congress Catalog Card Number 84-045348
Printed in the U.S.A.

TABLE OF CONTENTS

Introduction

His Excellency Rinaldo Petrignani
Ambassador of Italy, Washington, D.C.

I should like to open my remarks by conveying the warmest greeting of the Italian Government to all the participants in the Conference on the Italian Experience in the United States. I further wish to thank Columbia University for its perfect and hearty hospitality, and commend the Center for Migration Studies of New York and the Columbia University Center for Italian Studies for their excellent organization of such an outstanding endeavor.

The issues on the agenda are crucial and challenging: in the last two decades there has been an explosion of ethnic self-consciousness with a widespread impact on society, school, colleges, etc. It think it is now important to detect and to evaluate the new dimensions and trends emerging from the Italian emigration experience in the United States, to focus better on its original and enriching contribution in the progress of this country.

Indeed, the very fact that issues of this nature are at the core of this Conference shows how much the relations between our two countries are a two-way relationship, which thrives on a mutual give-and-take in enhancing a solid partnership. In this context it may be of considerable importance to American society that its interest in Italian ethnic culture be supported by a deep, inner knowledge of the new realities of modern Italy.

Within the consistent framework of its internal democratic system and of its pro-western foreign policy, Italian society has undergone an impressive process of change in these last 30 years. Italy has changed from a mostly agricultural economy into a highly industrialized one; millions of people moved from the South to the North and from the countryside to the cities; the crust of old traditions was broken; the patterns of social behavior have changed. A new Italian society has emerged, more open, more free. In essence we have made a new Italy, and yet much of the ancient profile remains. The diversity, the pluralism, the richness of the cities which are still the center of Italian life, the humanity of the individual, the quest for the classical sense of beauty and harmony, the enduring attachment to the family, all represent the continuity of a tradition of centuries. There is a striking combination in Italy of old and new. But undoubtedly the modernization of the economy has profoundly changed the way of life of the Italians, whose standards are today comparable to those of any major industrialized democracy in the world.

It appears then that, notwithstanding our historical and cultural differences, the Italian and American societies have many problems in common, those of the functioning of the welfare system for instance, or of the formation of a new youth culture. And it is in tackling such common and modern challenges that our two countries can join their efforts.

To give a wider and deeper meaning to our relations, we should extend the circulation of ideas and of knowledge from limited, though qualified, audiences, to an increasing number of participants. Only by fully including the American communities of Italian descent in such a dialogue can we in fact regain a cultural bilateralism and demonstrate the value of our overall relationship with the United States. The holding of this Conference, sponsored by the Italian Government, thus intends to remedy the previous neglect of such a relation, by trying to associate fully to the dialogue this indispensable partner represented by over 20 million Americans of Italian descent.

Don Luigi Sturzo used to say that the Italian Americans had to maintain their spiritual and cultural ties with Italy, in order to help build a post-war democratic society there. But there is also another reason: with your help, we will be able to make the new faces of Italian realities more familiar and more understandable to the American public. It is an effort which is worthwhile, because it concerns an industrial democracy of 56 million people, which is your friend, your partner, your ally. And, by strengthening the intellectual and spiritual bonds between Italy and the American communities of Italian descent, we should like to strengthen and to expand the influence of its values within the pluri-ethnic American society, in a stimulating double track enriching process.

In this context, the diffusion and the knowledge of the Italian language would seem to me a precious channel — other ways can be thought of, and you must tell us in which direction we have to move. On our side, we want to intensify and diversify the ways of collaboration through the wider spectrum of possibilities arising from the diffusion of cultural values in all their originality and complexity, going on to academic and student exchanges, to scientific and technological research, economic joint ventures, in short, to the multiplication of forms of integration and contacts at all levels.

Through such a process we should like to help the Italo-American community, at the very moment at which it is rethinking its emigration experience in the United States and is looking for its roots, to gain an increasing economical, political and social importance among the forces actively involved in the progress of the United States.

PART ONE

DATA AND PERCEPTIONS

1

A Sociodemographic Profile
of Italian Americans

Nampeo R. McKenney, Michael J. Levin and Alfred J. Tella [1]
U.S. Bureau of the Census

THE results of the 1980 U.S. Census show that about 12 million persons were reported as being solely or partly of Italian ancestry.[2] Italian was the sixth largest ancestry group in 1980, following English (50 million), German (49 million), Irish (40 million), Afro-American (21 million), and French (13 million). Table 1 shows that the Italians[3] constituted 5.4 percent of the total U.S. population in 1980, that is about 1 in every 20 people in the U.S. reported solely Italian or Italian in combination with another response. Almost 7 million persons reported Italian only, but more than 5 million reported Italian in combination with other ancestries.

This chapter will focus on the demographic, social, and economic characteristics of Italians in the United States and will show differences in the

---

[1] This chapter has benefited from the competent professional assistance of Nancy Sweet, Ethnic and Spanish Statistics Branch, Population Division. The authors also thank Diana Harley, Statistical Methods Division, for statistical review, and Emily Lennon, Population Division, for clerical assistance.

[2] The 1980 data on ancestry are derived from a new question, "What is this person's ancestry?" The ancestry question was based on self-identification, provided space for a write-in entry, and allowed for more than one ancestry response. People reported their ancestry either by specifying a single ancestry, for example, "Italian", or reported two, three, or more ancestry groups, for example, "Italian-Irish". Nonresponses to the ancestry question were not allocated; see "Technical Discussion" for more details.

[3] In this chapter, we use "persons of Italian ancestry" interchangeably with "Italian American" or "Italian".

Italian population by type of ancestry response and by generation in the U.S. Historical data will be used to assess some of the changes in the characteristics of the Italian community.

The 1980 census was the first census to collect data on Italians regardless of the number of generations removed from Italy; therefore, this is the first time we are able to compare the characteristics of Italians of all generations with persons born in Italy (first generation). Information on Italians was first collected using a question on birthplace asked in each census beginning with 1850. There were 3,679 persons born in Italy in that census (Table 2). The largest number of Italian foreign-born persons was enumerated in the 1930 census when 1,790,429 were counted (1.5 percent of the total population). This apex was the result of the large number of Italian immigrants (3 million) who immigrated between 1900-1914, the peak period of Italian immigration (U.S. Bureau of the Census, 1975:105), "the largest exodus of people ever recorded from a single nation" (Sowell, 1981:101). Sowell has noted that during this peak period of Italian immigration, "the number of people emigrating across the Atlantic from Italy to the Western Hemisphere was nearly equaled by the number immigrating to the other countries in Europe". Altogether an estimated 5.2 million Italians immigrated between 1820 and 1970 (U.S. Bureau of the Census, 1975:105). In the 1980 census only 831,922 Italian foreign-born persons were counted.

Distribution of Italian Americans

From the very beginning of their immigration, Italians settled primarily in urban communities. These ethnic communities have tended to be along the Eastern Seaboard, particularly New York and the cities of Rhode Island, Connecticut, Massachusetts, and New Jersey. The trend has continued into this century. The 1960 census, for example, showed that about 70 percent of first- and second-generation Italians were concentrated in the northeastern portion of America.

In 1980, more than one-half of all persons of Italian ancestry lived in the Northeast. Fewer than 20 percent of all Italians lived in each of the other 3 regions—North Central, South, and West:

Region	Number	Percent
TOTAL, United States	12,183,692	100
Northeast	6,929,876	57
North Central	1,995,424	16
South	1,555,340	13
West	1,703,052	14

Italian Population by State

New York, New Jersey, and Pennsylvania were major places of settlement for the Italian immigrants of the late nineteenth and early twentieth centuries. In 1980, these three states, along with California, had the largest Italian populations and contained 53 percent of all persons of Italian ancestry. Approximately 2.8 million Italians lived in New York State (Table 3). The Italians in New York were 23 percent of all Italians in the U.S.; that is, more than 1 in every 5 Italians in the U.S. lived in New York.

The next states with large numbers of Italians in 1980 were New Jersey, Pennsylvania, and California. New Jersey had about 1.3 million (11% of the total U.S. population of Italians), Pennsylvania about 1.2 million (10%), and California about 1.1 million (9%). The next 6 largest states (in rank order) were Massachusetts, Illinois, Connecticut, Ohio, Florida, and Michigan. The Italian population in these states ranged from about 750,000 for Massachusetts to 344,000 for Michigan.

Altogether the ten states shown in Table 3 contained 80 percent of the total Italian population in the United States.

Rhode Island (20%), Connecticut (18%), New Jersey (18%), and New York (16%) had the largest proportions of Italians in their total populations (Table 1). For most states, in fact, the farther the state was from New York State, the smaller the proportions of Italians in the state (Figure I).

The proportion of the population of the United States who reported a single response of "Italian" was 57 percent of all Italian ancestry responses; however, the proportions varied greatly from state to state (Table 1). The states in the Northeast had the highest proportion that responded with a single ancestry (*i.e.*, only Italian); for example, New York, with 69 percent single response, was the state with the highest proportion of single responses, followed by Rhode Island and New Jersey (each about 64 percent).

Italian Population by City

In 1980, about 1 million persons of Italian ancestry lived in New York City; they comprised 14 percent of the city's total population (Table 4). The next leading cities were Philadelphia (192,000 Italian persons who constituted 11% of the city's total population), Chicago (139,000 or 5%), and Los Angeles (107,000, or 4%). Three other cities—Boston, Massachusetts; Yonkers, New York; and Buffalo, New York—had over 50,000 Italians. The 1980 census showed that 23 cities in the Nation had 25,000 or more persons of Italian ancestry.

Of the 23 cities in Table 4, several had high concentrations of Italians. For instance, Cranston, Rhode Island, had the highest proportion—38 percent of the city's population was Italian. High proportions (25% or more) were also found in Waterbury, Connecticut; Yonkers, New York; and Providence, Rhode Island. The concentration in the New England cities is almost certainly the result of the large number of early immigrants who settled in that area.

Urban Rural Residence

Of the 12 million Italians in the U.S. in 1980, 91 percent lived in urban areas (Table 1). About 43 percent of the Italians lived in the central cities and somewhat less than 43 percent in the urban fringe of urbanized areas of New York State in 1980 (Table 5). Although the proportion of urban Italians was as large in New Jersey as New York, a smaller proportion of Italians in Pennsylvania lived in urban areas.

Among the multiple-ancestry Italian group in New York, about 78 percent were inside urbanized areas, with about 31 percent in the central cities of urbanized areas (Table 5). For the single-ancestry group, about 89 percent were in urbanized areas, with 49 percent in central cities. The proportion of total Italian urban dwellers was also high for both New Jersey (91%) and Pennsylvania (82%), but unlike New York, greater proportions of the population lived in urban fringes than in the central cities. In the past, Italians seem to have contradicted the melting pot theory. Glazer and Moynihan, who do not support the theory, have noted, for example, that "while the Jewish map of New York City in 1920 bears almost no relation to that in 1961, the Italian districts, though weakened in some cases and strengthened in others are still in large measure where they were" (1963:187). Italians have tended to live in tight-knit communities in urban areas and be much more reluctant to move to suburban and rural areas. In an early study of the Italian North End of Boston, for example, Firey (1947) showed that second-generation Italians were more likely to be suburbanites than the older first-generation Italians (1947:200-209).

The 1980 census showed that many of the Italian multiples were young families. These families may have been more likely to have moved to the suburbs to raise children, thus showing a continuation in the third generation of what Firey saw earlier. The Italian singles were older and more likely to have lived in central cities all their lives.

Demographic and Social Characteristics of Italians

Only limited 1980 census data are now available on all persons of Italian ancestry for the entire country (social and economic data are now available for selected states). Data for the entire country will be shown in the forthcoming Volume II report focusing on ancestry. We have used data from a special ethnic supplement taken in November 1979 Current Population Survey (CPS) to provide information on the characteristics of the total Italian population for the entire country. Refer to the "Technical Discussion" for a comparison of the sources and information on 1980 census tabulations and publications.

Nativity

Of the approximately 12 million persons of Italian ancestry in November

1979, approximately 800,000, or 7 percent, were born in Italy, and about 3 million, or 25 percent, were second generation (born in U.S., but having one or both parents born in Italy) (Table 8). Thus, about two-thirds of Italian ancestry persons were third or subsequent generations. This distribution by generation reflects the immigration from Italy to the United States which peaked in the early twentieth century, reaching over a quarter of a million annually during that period. In recent decades, immigration has continued, but at a much reduced level.

A smaller proportion of Italian ancestry persons (11%) than of the entire state population of New York (14%) was foreign born (Table 6). In 1980, about 15 percent of the Italian single-ancestry group in New York State were foreign born; in contrast to the Italian single-ancestry group, nearly all (99%) of Italian multiples were born in the United States.

In New Jersey, the 1980 proportion of Italian foreign born was 8 percent, and for Pennsylvania, 6 percent. The foreign born were found much more frequently among those who reported solely as Italian in these states.

Between 1870 and 1970 the census also asked about parental birthplace. This question helped identify persons who were born in the United States but had one or both parents born in Italy. In 1890, there were 66,964 persons who were native of Italian or mixed Italian parentage (Table 2). The number increased with each census until 1970 when 3,232,246 were enumerated.

Foreign born and native of foreign or mixed parentage persons comprise the "foreign birth or parentage population". Although the total persons born in Italy and native (born) with one Italy-born parent population was 249,544 in 1890, it increased to about 4.5 million in each census taken between 1930 and 1960 (Table 2). In 1890, the foreign born were almost three-fourths of the total Italian foreign birth or parentage population, but by 1920 they constituted almost one-half and were less than one-fourth of the total Italian foreign birth or parentage population in 1970. Since the proportion of second-generation persons had decreased, the question on ancestry added in 1980 replaced the question on parental birthplace. Therefore, 1980 data for second-generation Italians cannot be determined. As stated earlier, the Census Bureau counted all persons of Italian ancestry for the first time in 1980, regardless of the number of generations removed from Italy.

Age

Italians were a somewhat younger population than the entire population of this country. In 1979, the average (median) age of all persons of Italian ancestry was 27 years, compared to the 30 years for the entire United States population (Table 8). However, the median age for all persons reporting solely Italian in the November 1979 CPS was rather high at 42 years, significantly above the median age of about 18 years for Italians giving a multiple response. The age differential between persons who reported solely

TABLE 1

Total and Italian Population by Type of Ancestry and Urban Residence for United States and States: 1980

United States States	Total population	Italian						
		Total		Type of ancestry			Urban Residence	
		Number	Percent of total population	Single	Multiple	Percent single of total ancestry	Number	Percent of total population
UNITED STATES	226,545,805	12,183,692	5.4	6,888,320	5,300,372	56.5	11,077,966	90.9
Alabama	3,893,888	33,837	0.9	16,343	17,494	48.3	26,675	78.8
Alaska	401,851	8,678	2.2	3,967	4,711	45.7	6,192	71.3
Arizona	2,718,215	97,523	3.6	47,508	50,015	48.7	89,851	92.1
Arkansas	2,286,435	18,955	0.8	8,095	10,860	42.7	11,077	58.4
California	23,667,902	1,144,102	4.8	567,351	576,751	49.6	1,047,863	91.6
Colorado	2,889,964	116,361	4.0	51,637	64,724	44.4	98,179	84.4
Connecticut	3,107,576	561,542	18.1	346,053	215,489	61.6	478,020	85.1
Delaware	594,338	44,694	7.5	22,519	22,175	50.4	38,573	86.3
District of Columbia	638,333	8,977	1.4	4,881	4,096	54.4	8,977	100.0
Florida	9,746,324	461,757	4.7	274,202	187,555	59.4	418,935	90.7
Georgia	5,463,105	52,279	1.0	21,143	31,136	40.4	41,304	79.0
Hawaii	964,691	13,994	1.4	5,331	8,663	38.1	11,799	84.3
Idaho	953,935	16,264	1.7	6,583	9,681	40.5	9,950	61.2
Illinois	11,426,518	640,304	5.6	322,914	317,390	50.4	586,887	91.7
Indiana	5,490,224	86,040	1.6	33,674	52,366	39.1	64,840	75.4
Iowa	2,913,808	36,744	1.3	14,147	22,597	38.5	28,413	77.3

Kansas	2,363,679	28,692	1.2	10,713	17,979	37.3	22,147	77.2
Kentucky	3,660,777	36,001	1.0	14,125	21,876	39.2	25,252	70.1
Louisana	4,205,900	165,015	3.9	70,790	94,225	42.9	136,345	82.6
Maine	1,124,660	31,915	2.8	13,516	18,399	42.3	18,585	58.2
Maryland	4,216,975	185,253	4.4	85,695	99,558	46.3	160,961	86.9
Massachusetts	5,737,037	749,583	13.1	430,412	319,171	57.4	665,254	88.7
Michigan	9,262,078	344,402	3.7	170,740	173,662	49.6	287,422	83.5
Minnesota	4,075,970	64,545	1.6	20,853	43,692	32.3	54,671	84.7
Mississippi	2,520,638	23,098	0.9	10,534	12,564	45.6	15,747	68.2
Missouri	4,916,686	120,449	2.4	52,849	67,600	43.9	104,001	86.3
Montana	786,690	16,645	2.1	6,869	9,776	41.3	10,846	65.2
Nebraska	1,569,825	27,089	1.7	10,892	16,197	40.2	23,498	86.7
Nevada	800,493	53,698	6.7	28,132	25,566	52.4	46,667	86.9
New Hampshire	920,610	45,963	5.0	18,203	27,760	39.6	23,391	50.9
New Jersey	7,364,823	1,315,632	17.9	835,277	480,355	63.5	1,202,142	91.4
New Mexico	1,302,894	26,202	2.0	11,706	14,496	44.7	22,632	86.4
New York	17,558,072	2,811,911	16.0	1,937,791	874,120	68.9	2,562,068	91.1
North Carolina	5,881,766	52,540	0.9	22,185	30,355	42.2	34,569	65.8
North Dakota	652,717	3,722	0.6	1,370	2,352	36.8	2,608	70.1
Ohio	10,797,630	520,171	4.8	258,482	261,689	49.7	439,618	84.5
Oklahoma	3,025,290	30,062	1.0	11,469	18,593	38.1	23,402	77.8
Oregon	2,633,105	60,769	2.3	23,366	37,403	38.4	44,746	73.6
Pennsylvania	11,863,895	1,205,823	10.2	663,083	542,740	55.0	985,802	81.7
Rhode Island	947,154	185,080	19.5	118,966	66,114	64.3	167,127	90.3
South Carolina	3,121,820	28,474	0.9	12,462	16,012	43.8	20,929	73.5
South Dakota	690,768	4,126	0.6	1,528	2,598	37.0	2,802	67.9
Tennessee	4,591,120	41,554	0.9	17,915	23,639	43.1	31,752	76.4
Texas	14,229,191	189,799	1.3	78,592	111,207	41.4	167,507	88.2

TABLE 1 (continued)

Total and Italian Population by Type of Ancestry and Urban Residence for United States and States: 1980

United States States	Total population	Italian						
		Total		Type of ancestry			Urban Residence	
		Number	Percent of total population	Single	Multiple	Percent single of total ancestry	Number	Percent of total population
Utah	1,461,037	31,240	2.1	11,589	19,651	37.1	27,246	87.2
Vermont	511,456	22,427	4.4	8,769	13,658	39.1	10,012	44.6
Virginia	5,346,818	122,130	2.3	52,143	69,987	42.7	101,882	83.4
Washington	4,132,156	106,660	2.6	41,324	65,336	38.7	84,235	79.0
West Virginia	1,949,644	60,915	3.1	33,191	27,724	54.5	33,205	54.5
Wisconsin	4,705,767	119,140	2.5	46,588	72,552	39.1	91,804	77.1
Wyoming	469,557	10,916	2.3	4,853	6,063	44.5	7,666	70.2

Source: U.S. Bureau of the Census

TABLE 2
Persons of Italian Foreign Birth or Parentage: 1850-1980

Census Year	Total, foreign birth or parentage	Foreign born		Native of foreign or mixed parentage
		Number	Percent of total foreign birth or percentage	
1850	(NA)	3,679	(NA)	(NA)
1860	(NA)	11,677	(NA)	(NA)
1870	(NA)	17,157	(NA)	(NA)
1880	(NA)	44,230	(NA)	(NA)
1890	249,544	182,580	73.2	66,964
1900	738,577	484,027	65.5	254,550
1910	2,114,770	1,343,125	63.5	771,645
1920	3,361,204	1,610,113	47.9	1,751,091
1930	4,546,882	1,790,429	39.4	2,756,453
1940	4,594,780	1,623,580	35.3	2,971,200
1950	4,571,357	1,427,952	31.2	3,143,405
1960	4,543,935	1,256,999	27.7	3,286,936
1970	4,240,779	1,008,533	23.8	3,232,246
1980	(NA)	831,922	(NA)	(NA)

(NA) Not available.
Source: U.S. Bureau of the Census.

ITALIAN AMERICANS

TABLE 3

Rank of States with 300,000 or More Persons of Italian Ancestry: 1980

United States Selected States	Total			Single			Multiple		
	Number	Rank	Percent of total	Total	Rank	Percent of total	Total	Rank	Percent of total
UNITED STATES	12,183,692	...	100.0	6,883,320	...	100.0	5,300,372	...	100.0
New York	2,811,911	1	23.1	1,937,791	1	28.2	874,120	1	16.5
New Jersey	1,315,632	2	10.8	835,277	2	12.1	480,355	4	9.1
Pennsylvania	1,205,823	3	9.9	663,083	3	9.6	542,740	3	10.2
California	1,144,102	4	9.4	567,351	4	8.2	576,751	2	10.9
Massachusetts	749,583	5	6.2	430,412	5	6.3	319,171	5	6.0
Illinois	640,304	6	5.3	322,914	7	4.7	317,390	6	6.0
Connecticut	561,542	7	4.6	346,053	6	5.0	215,489	8	4.1
Ohio	520,171	8	4.3	258,482	9	3.8	261,689	7	4.9
Florida	461,757	9	3.8	274,202	8	4.0	187,555	9	3.5
Michigan	344,402	10	2.8	170,740	10	2.5	173,662	10	3.3

... Not applicable.

Source: U.S. Bureau of the Census.

TABLE 4

Cities with 25,000 or More Persons of Italian Ancestry: 1980

			Italian	
Rank of Italian population	Cities	Total population	Number	Percent of total population
1	New York City, NY	7,071,639	1,005,304	14.2
2	Philadelphia, PA	1,688,210	192,102	11.4
3	Chicago, IL	3,005,078	138,396	4.6
4	Los Angeles, CA	2,966,850	107,279	3.6
5	Boston, MA	562,994	68,962	12.2
6	Yonkers, NY	195,351	53,460	27.4
7	Buffalo, NY	357,870	50,429	14.1
8	Pittsburgh, PA	423,938	49,449	11.7
9	San José, CA	629,442	49,070	7.8
10	San Francisco, CA	678,974	41,875	6.2
11	Providence, RI	156,804	40,438	25.8
12	San Diego, CA	875,538	39,498	4.5
13	Phoenix, AZ	789,704	37,118	4.7
14	Rochester, NY	241,741	35,288	14.6
15	Jersey City, NJ	223,532	32,395	14.5
16	Waterbury, CT	103,266	31,610	30.6
17	Houston, TX	1,595,167	30,868	1.9
18	Detroit, MI	1,203,339	27,443	2.3
19	Cleveland, OH	573,822	27,054	4.7
20	Cranston, RI	71,992	26,967	37.5
21	New Orleans, LA	557,515	26,848	4.8
22	Syracuse, NY	170,105	26,749	15.7
23	Baltimore, MD	786,775	26,344	3.3

Source: U.S. Bureau of the Census.

TABLE 5

Total and Italian Population by Urban-Rural Residence for Selected States: 1980

State	Total persons		Italian				Percent distribution – Italian		
			Total						
	Number	Percent	Number	Percent of total persons	Single	Multiple	Total	Single	Multiple
NEW YORK									
TOTAL	17,558,072	100.0	2,811,911	16.0	1,937,791	874,120	100.0	100.0	100.0
Urban	14,858,524	84.6	2,562,068	17.2	1,814,369	747,699	91.1	93.6	85.5
Inside urbanized areas	13,793,214	78.6	2,411,079	17.5	1,727,369	683,710	85.7	89.1	78.2
Central cities	8,345,849	47.5	1,212,333	14.5	943,364	268,969	43.1	48.7	30.8
Urban fringe	5,447,365	31.0	1,198,746	22.0	784,005	414,741	42.6	40.5	47.4
Outside urbanized areas	1,065,310	6.1	150,989	14.2	87,000	63,989	5.4	4.5	7.3
Rural	2,699,548	15.4	249,843	9.3	123,422	126,421	8.9	6.4	14.5
NEW JERSEY									
TOTAL	7,364,823	100.0	1,315,632	17.9	835,277	480,355	100.0	100.0	100.0
Urban	6,557,670	89.0	1,202,142	18.3	776,790	425,352	91.4	93.0	88.5
Inside urbanized areas	6,291,944	85.4	1,166,160	18.5	755,785	410,375	88.6	90.5	85.4
Central cities	763,671	10.4	89,390	11.7	67,830	21,560	6.8	8.1	4.5
Urban fringe	5,528,273	75.1	1,076,770	19.5	687,955	388,815	81.8	82.4	80.9
Outside urbanized areas	265,726	3.6	35,982	13.5	21,005	14,977	2.7	2.5	3.1
Rural	807,153	11.0	113,490	14.1	58,487	55,003	8.6	7.0	11.5

PENNSYLVANIA

TOTAL	11,863,895	100.0	1,205,823	10.2	663,083	542,740	100.0	100.0	100.0
Urban	8,221,831	69.3	985,802	12.0	566,499	419,303	81.8	85.4	77.3
Inside urbanized areas	7,169,382	60.4	883,814	12.3	510,804	373,010	73.3	77.0	68.7
Central cities	2,995,527	25.2	327,950	10.9	207,825	120,125	27.2	31.3	22.1
Urban fringe	4,173,855	35.2	555,864	13.3	302,979	252,885	46.1	44.7	46.6
Outside urbanized areas	1,052,449	8.9	101,988	9.7	55,695	46,293	8.5	8.4	8.5
Rural	3,642,064	30.7	220,021	6.0	96,584	123,437	18.2	14.6	22.7

Source: U.S. Bureau of the Census.

TABLE 6

Selected Social Characteristics of Italians by Type of Ancestry for Selected States: 1980

Characteristic	New York				New Jersey				Pennsylvania			
	Total population	Total	Italian Single	Multiple	Total population	Total	Italian Single	Multiple	Total population	Total	Italian Single	Multiple
NATIVITY												
TOTAL	17,558,072	2,811,911	1,937,791	874,120	7,364,823	1,315,632	835,277	480,355	11,863,895	1,205,823	663,083	542,740
Native	15,169,134	2,507,972	1,643,219	864,753	6,607,001	1,207,948	731,584	476,364	11,462,879	1,134,225	593,502	540,723
Foreign born	2,388,938	303,939	294,572	9,367	757,822	107,684	103,693	3,991	401,016	71,598	69,581	2,017
Percent	13.6	10.8	15.2	1.1	10.3	8.2	12.4	0.8	3.4	5.9	10.5	0.4
AGE												
TOTAL persons	17,558,072	2,811,911	1,937,791	874,120	7,364,823	1,315,632	835,277	480,355	11,863,895	1,205,823	663,083	542,740
Percent	100.0	100.0	100.0	100.0	100.0	100.0	100.0	100.0	100.0	100.0	100.0	100.0
Under 5 years	6.4	6.6	3.4	13.9	6.3	6.9	3.1	13.4	6.3	7.8	2.5	14.2
5 to 14 years	14.8	15.8	9.7	29.3	15.1	16.4	9.3	28.8	14.6	16.8	7.4	28.3
15 to 24 years	17.8	19.1	15.3	27.6	17.4	19.1	14.5	27.1	18.0	20.8	14.6	28.3
25 to 54 years	38.4	36.5	41.0	26.6	38.6	37.1	42.3	28.0	36.8	35.0	41.5	27.0
55 to 64 years	10.4	10.9	15.0	1.8	10.9	10.5	15.6	1.8	11.4	10.3	17.4	1.6
65 years and over	12.3	11.1	15.7	0.8	11.6	10.0	15.3	0.9	12.9	9.4	16.6	0.7
Median age	31.9	32.0	40.3	17.1	32.2	31.1	41.0	17.4	32.1	28.9	44.4	17.4
HOUSEHOLD RELATIONSHIP												
Persons in households	17,109,174	2,770,432	1,911,072	859,360	7,229,311	1,302,434	826,674	475,760	11,566,626	1,181,031	650,504	530,527
Percent	100.0	100.0	100.0	100.0	100.0	100.0	100.0	100.0	100.00	100.0	100.0	100.0
Householder	37.1	33.7	41.0	17.3	35.3	32.3	41.2	16.9	36.5	32.3	44.6	17.3
Spouse	20.4	21.2	25.3	12.1	21.8	21.6	26.4	13.2	22.5	20.8	26.7	13.6
Child	35.1	39.6	27.8	65.9	36.0	40.6	26.4	65.3	34.6	41.3	22.4	64.5
Other relative	4.6	4.0	4.6	2.6	4.8	4.1	4.8	2.9	4.2	4.0	4.8	2.9
Nonrelative	2.8	1.6	1.4	2.0	2.2	1.4	1.3	1.6	2.2	1.6	1.6	1.7
FAMILY CHARACTERISTICS												
TOTAL families	4,468,031	723,591	613,089	110,502	1,942,108	338,989	275,069	63,920	3,147,809	300,782	228,892	71,890
Married couples	3,496,616	615,679	523,457	92,222	1,574,350	290,583	235,970	54,613	2,603,401	256,505	194,303	62,202
Percent of total families	78.3	85.1	85.4	83.5	81.1	85.7	85.8	85.4	82.7	85.3	84.9	86.5

With own children under 18	2,261,262	345,811	272,878	72,933	965,846	163,232	121,425	41,807	1,508,641	145,859	95,755	50,104
Percent	50.6	47.8	44.5	66.0	49.7	48.2	44.1	65.4	47.9	48.5	41.8	69.7
Persons under 18 years	4,688,845	795,991	333,746	462,245	1,992,299	385,729	136,744	248,985	3,125,534	369,106	88,202	280,904
Percent living with both parents	73.1	85.9	86.0	85.8	76.3	86.6	86.2	86.8	79.2	85.7	83.0	86.6
Persons 60 and over	3,000,883	452,135	438,828	13,307	1,227,327	194,193	186,620	7,573	2,165,368	169,232	162,197	7,035
Percent living in families	67.0	95.1	77.0	74.9	72.5	79.7	79.8	78.2	69.8	78.1	78.4	72.5
MARITAL HISTORY												
Ever married persons 15-54 years	6,002,681	948,186	729,951	218,235	2,628,315	459,066	330,129	128,937	4,192,466	408,455	260,007	148,448
Percent widowed	3.2	2.4	2.6	1.5	2.9	2.3	2.6	1.6	2.9	2.3	2.7	1.5
Percent divorced	17.0	13.3	12.3	16.9	15.8	13.7	12.8	16.0	16.8	14.5	13.4	16.3
FERTILITY OF EVER-MARRIED WOMEN												
Women 15-24 years	821	619	607	636	764	619	620	618	837	706	689	719
Women 25-34 years	1,599	1,472	1,492	1,433	1,552	1,400	1,425	1,364	1,650	1,493	1,498	1,489
Women 35-44 years	2,640	2,493	2,506	2,552	2,592	2,463	2,454	2,488	2,745	2,572	2,559	2,597
EDUCATIONAL ATTAINMENT												
Males 25 years and over	4,896,222	789,517	667,652	121,865	2,083,989	364,775	295,555	69,220	3,343,353	318,330	243,522	74,808
Percent	100.0	100.0	100.0	100.0	100.0	100.0	100.0	100.0	100.0	100.0	100.0	100.0
Elementary, 8 years or less	17.3	20.0	22.9	4.1	16.7	19.2	22.5	4.9	18.1	18.2	22.4	4.6
High school graduates	67.5	63.0	59.0	84.8	68.7	65.0	60.5	84.2	65.5	65.3	59.3	84.7
College graduates	22.2	16.5	14.5	26.9	23.8	19.6	17.5	28.6	17.4	17.1	14.7	24.9
Females, 25 years & over	5,824,790	854,802	720,869	133,933	2,420,258	393,623	315,373	78,250	3,896,891	340,845	256,851	83,994
Percent	100.0	100.0	100.0	100.0	100.0	100.0	100.0	100.0	100.0	100.0	100.0	100.0
Elementary, 8 years or less	19.1	23.5	27.2	4.0	18.5	22.1	26.7	3.8	18.6	20.7	26.1	4.1
High school graduates	65.2	59.7	55.1	84.5	66.2	62.1	56.4	84.9	64.0	62.6	55.5	84.5
College graduates	14.4	8.9	7.3	17.5	13.6	10.1	8.3	17.6	10.2	8.7	6.5	15.6

Source: U.S. Bureau of the Census.

TABLE 7
Selected Economic Characteristics of Italians by Type of Ancestry in Selected States: 1980

Characteristic	New York				New Jersey				Pennsylvania			
	Total population	Total	Italian Single	Multiple	Total population	Total	Italian Single	Multiple	Total population	Total	Italian Single	Multiple
LABOR FORCE												
Persons 16 years and over	13,519,262	2,127,067	1,659,156	467,911	5,651,301	922,440	720,718	201,722	9,170,050	885,780	590,604	295,176
In labor force	8,041,175	1,295,876	971,919	323,957	3,549,395	637,936	448,505	189,431	5,370,900	544,333	341,958	202,375
Percent	59.5	60.9	58.6	69.2	62.8	69.2	62.2	72.4	58.6	61.5	57.9	68.6
Female												
16 years and over	7,245,534	1,097,491	854,743	242,748	2,996280	506,038	370,051	135,987	4,865,881	454,515	301,239	153,277
In labor force	3,492,605	530,441	384,523	145,918	1,516,472	264,814	179,102	85,712	2,222,017	221,402	132,018	89,384
Percent	48.2	48.3	45.0	60.1	50.6	52.3	48.4	63.0	45.7	48.7	43.8	58.4
OCCUPATION												
TOTAL employed	7,440,768	1,210,401	911,723	298,678	3,288,302	575,807	420,489	175,318	4,961,501	503,679	319,125	184,554
Percent	100.0	100.0	100.0	100.0	100.0	100.0	100.0	100.0	100.0	100.0	100.0	100.0
Managerial	25.7	21.7	21.3	23.2	25.8	23.5	23.4	23.8	20.8	20.9	20.9	20.9
Technical	33.5	36.3	35.5	38.7	33.0	35.3	34.1	38.2	29.3	31.9	30.8	33.7
Service	13.9	12.8	12.5	13.5	11.6	11.6	11.4	12.1	12.6	13.1	12.7	13.8
Farming	1.3	0.8	0.8	0.9	0.8	0.8	0.8	0.8	1.6	0.7	0.7	0.7
Precision	10.4	12.8	13.6	10.5	11.7	13.0	13.8	11.2	13.3	13.7	14.9	11.7
Operative	15.2	15.6	16.4	13.2	17.1	15.8	16.5	14.0	22.4	19.6	19.8	19.2
WORKERS IN FAMILIES[1]												
TOTAL families	4,468,031	723,591	613,089	110,502	1,942,108	338,989	275,069	63,920	3,147,809	300,782	228,892	71,890
Percent	100.0	100.0	100.0	100.0	100.0	100.0	100.0	100.0	100.0	100.0	100.0	100.0
No workers	15.2	12.8	14.0	5.9	12.5	10.3	11.8	4.0	14.3	12.0	14.2	5.0
1	34.5	35.0	34.8	35.8	32.8	32.7	32.4	33.9	34.8	35.4	35.0	36.8
2	37.3	36.8	34.8	47.5	39.2	39.6	37.2	50.0	38.0	38.6	35.4	48.8
3 or more	13.0	15.4	16.3	10.9	15.5	17.4	18.6	12.3	10.9	14.0	15.4	9.4

FAMILY INCOME IN 1979[1]

TOTAL Families	4,468,031	723,591	613,089	110,502	1,942,108	338,989	275,069	63,920	3,147,809	300,782	228,892	71,890
Percent	100.0	100.0	100.0	100.0	100.0	100.0	100.0	100.0	100.0	100.0	100.0	100.0
Less than $5,000	8.2	5.0	4.9	5.5	5.9	4.0	3.9	4.1	6.1	4.9	4.7	5.7
$5,000 to $7,499	6.4	5.2	5.5	3.9	4.7	4.2	4.5	2.8	5.7	5.2	5.7	3.5
$7,500 to $9,999	6.6	5.7	6.0	4.3	5.4	4.9	5.1	3.8	6.6	6.2	6.9	4.2
$10,000 to $14,999	14.0	13.3	13.4	12.3	11.9	11.8	12.1	10.6	15.1	14.4	14.7	13.4
$15,000 to $19,999	14.3	15.2	15.0	16.4	13.6	14.6	14.5	15.1	16.6	17.2	16.6	19.2
$20,000 to $24,999	13.8	16.0	15.8	17.6	14.0	15.4	15.1	16.8	15.7	16.4	15.6	19.0
$25,000 to $34,999	18.9	22.0	21.7	23.6	21.8	23.7	23.2	25.9	19.8	20.9	20.3	22.8
$35,000 to $49,999	11.4	12.4	12.5	11.8	14.6	14.4	14.4	14.8	9.9	10.3	10.7	9.0
$50,000 or more	6.5	5.2	5.3	4.6	8.2	7.0	6.1	6.1	4.6	4.4	4.7	3.3
Median	$ 20,180	$ 21,738	$ 21,498	$ 21,886	$ 22,906	$ 23,420	$ 23,087	$ 23,972	$ 19,995	$ 20,617	$ 20,400	20,928
Mean	$ 23,683	$ 23,964	$ 23,933	$ 24,134	$ 26,336	$ 26,059	$ 26,019	$ 26,230	$ 22,634	$ 22,941	$ 23,042	22,619

POVERTY STATUS

TOTAL Families[1]	4,468,031	723,591	613,089	110,502	1,942,108	338,989	275,069	63,920	3,147,809	300,782	228,892	71,890
Families in poverty	647,767	44,707	36,423	8,284	199,121	23,978	19,228	4,750	346,089	26,775	19,580	7,195
Percent below poverty level	14.5	6.2	5.9	7.5	10.3	7.1	7.0	7.4	11.0	8.9	8.6	10.0
TOTAL Persons	17,558,072	2,811,911	1,937,791	874,120	7,364,823	1,315,632	835,277	480,355	1,863,895	1,205,823	663,083	542,740
Persons in poverty	3,090,315	211,244	144,264	66,980	931,981	109,947	73,393	36,554	1,683,766	132,391	74,535	57,856
Percent below poverty	18.1	7.5	7.5	7.8	12.9	8.4	8.9	7.7	14.6	11.0	11.4	10.9

[1] Families are classified by the ancestry group of the householder.

Source: U.S. Bureau of the Census.

TABLE 8
Selected Characteristics of Italians by
Type of Ancestry Response: November 1979 CPS
(Numbers in thousands)

Characteristic	TOTAL	Single	Multiple
Number:			
TOTAL persons	11,751	6,110	5,641
Foreign born	767	762	5
Second generation	2,984	2,672	313
Third or later generations	8,000	2,676	5,323
Percent			
TOTAL	100.0	100.0	100.0
Foreign born	6.5	12.5	0.1
Second generation	25.4	43.7	5.5
Third or later generations	68.1	43.8	94.4
MEDIAN AGE (Years)			
TOTAL persons	27.1	42.1	17.6
Foreign born	58.5	58.7	36.4
Second generation	54.3	55.6	33.7
OWN CHILDREN UNDER 14 YEARS OLD			
TOTAL persons in households	11,751	6,110	5,622
With own children			
under 14 years	2,721	568	2,153
Percent	23.2	9.3	38.3
TOTAL families[1]	2,867	2,134	733
No Children			
under 14 years old	1,695	1,383	312
Percent	59.1	64.8	42.6
MARITAL STATUS			
TOTAL persons, 14 years and over	8,914	5,519	3,395
Divorced	427	265	162
Percent	4.8	4.8	4.8
EDUCATIONAL ATTAINMENT			
Percent High School Graduates:			
TOTAL persons, 25 years and over	67.8	61.5	84.6
Foreign born	32.5	32.4	55.3
Second generation	60.2	58.7	76.2

TABLE 8 (continued)
Selected Characteristics of Italians by
Type of Ancestry Response: November 1979 CPS
(Numbers in thousands)

Characteristic	TOTAL	Single	Multiple
Percent College Graduates:			
TOTAL persons, 25 years and over	12.3	11.0	14.5
Foreign born	4.8	4.8	—
Second generation	9.7	8.8	19.8
LABOR FORCE			
TOTAL persons, 16 years and over	8,490	5,411	3,079
Civilian labor force	5,624	3,363	2,261
Percent	66.2	62.2	73.4
FAMILY INCOME IN 1978[1]			
Median Income:			
TOTAL families	$17,070	$16,457	$18,472
Foreign born	13,311	13,274	15,439
Second generation	16,852	16,527	20,712
Percent Income $10,000 or less:			
TOTAL families	15.1	16.4	11.8
Foreign born	29.7	29.9	—
Second generation	17.0	17.2	13.2
Percent Income $20,000 or more:			
TOTAL families	40.7	39.0	44.8
Foreign born	23.1	23.3	—
Second generation	40.9	39.8	55.5

— Represents zero or rounds to zero.
[1] Families are classified by the ancestry group of the householder.

Source: U.S. Bureau of the Census.

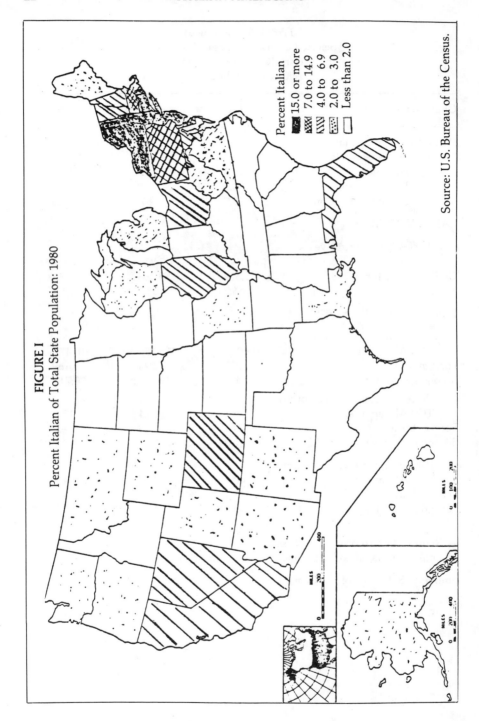

FIGURE I

Percent Italian of Total State Population: 1980

Percent Italian
- 15.0 or more
- 7.0 to 14.9
- 4.0 to 6.9
- 2.0 to 3.0
- Less than 2.0

Source: U.S. Bureau of the Census.

as Italians and those reporting a multiple response is due, in part, to the fact that the single-ancestry population included a higher proportion of foreign-born persons who tended to be older than native persons. In fact, in the November 1979 CPS, 56 percent of the persons responding as only Italian were either foreign born or of foreign or mixed parentage (13% were foreign-born). The average age of foreign-born Italians was 59 years and for second-generation persons, 54 years. The higher age for first- and second-generation persons reflects the very high levels of immigration of Italians in the early part of this century. About 6 percent of the Italian multiples were of foreign or mixed parentage (with only 0.1% of foreign birth).

The 1980 median age of Italians in New York State was 32 years (Table 6). The average age was 40 years for persons who reported only as Italian and 17 years for the multiple Italian ethnic group in New York. Multiple ancestry persons also had a younger median age than single Italians in New Jersey and Pennsylvania.

Family

The difference in the Italian singles and multiples by age and nativity also appears in information on household relationship and family type. Of course, most important in this analysis is the realization that there may have been a greater tendency for a multiple ancestry to have been reported for children whose parents had different ancestries.

In 1980, in New York State, for example, 41 percent of the single ancestry Italians in households were householders and 25 percent were spouses (Table 6). However, about 66 percent of the persons living in households with a multiple-ancestry householder were children, compared to 28 percent of those living in households with an Italian single-ancestry householder. The November 1979 data for Italians in the U.S. show that although only 9 percent of Italian singles were reported as own children under 14 years, 38 percent of the Italian multiples were in this category (Table 8). In 1979, although 65 percent of all Italian singles families had no children under 14 years, only 43 percent of the Italian multiple families were in this category.

"Marriage was essential for the southern Italian as a source of social identity, and family stability still seems to be relatively intact" (Femminella and Quadagno, 1975:73). Information from the 1980 census provides support for the hypothesis that family relationships are very strong among the Italian population. In New York, as well as in New Jersey and Pennsylvania, the proportions of families in 1980 that were married couples (both husband and wife present) were higher among the Italians than among the total population (Table 6). For instance, in New York, 85 percent of the Italian families were married couples, compared to 78 percent of families for the total state population. The proportion of persons under 18 years living with both parents was higher for Italians than the total state population (86% versus 73%). These differences hold true for both single and multiple Italian ancestry persons in all three states.

Also, the proportion of older persons living in families was higher among Italians than the total population 60 years and over of the states in this study. Ninety-five percent of Italians 60 years old and over were living in families, compared to 67 percent for the New York State population, supporting the literature showing strong family ties and evidently a pattern of caring for the older persons within the Italian family.

Although Greeley found that Italian American Catholics had the second lowest divorce rate (only 2.0 percent) of the ethnic groups he studied (1974:46), in 1979, the Italians' rate of divorce was not significantly different than the U.S. population as a whole (4.8 compared with 5.3 percent) (Table 8). In 1980, in New York, 13 percent of all ever-married Italians 15 to 54 years were divorced, with 12 percent for the single Italian group, but 17 percent for multiple Italians, which was also the figure for the entire state (Table 6). New Jersey and Pennsylvania showed similar distributions.

Fertility

In 1980, ever-married Italian women aged 35 to 44 in New York, New Jersey, and Pennsylvania had approximately 2.5 children, slightly below the U.S. average (2.8 children) (Table 6). Since the ancestry question was new in 1980, data or birthplace from previous censuses cannot be compared directly with the 1980 census data. However, the average number of children for ever-married between 45 and 54 years old who were born in Italy decreased from 6.0 in 1910 to 4.7 in 1940 and 2.6 in 1960 (U.S. Bureau of the Census, 1945 and 1971). For 1960, there were also 2.1 children per woman of this age who were born in the U.S. but who had one or both parents born in Italy. There were 2.2 children per woman for the 2 groups combined in 1960. "After having one of the largest size families among American ethnic groups, Italians are now tied with Jews for one of the smallest" (Sowell, 1981:124-125). Rosenwaite (1973:275) accounts for the change from the early part of the century by noting:

> Obviously very strong assimilationist pressures had been at work, for not only did the second generation Italian American women, on the average, have fewer than half the children of the immigrant generation; they curtailed their childbearing to a level below that of Americans of native parentage.

Educational Attainment

The November 1979 CPS showed that about 68 percent of the Italians 25 years and over had graduated from high school, compared to 69 percent for the U.S. as a whole. However, the proportions were very different for singles (62 percent) and multiples (85 percent) (Table 8). In New York and New Jersey in 1980, smaller proportions of Italian males and females than the total state population 25 years and over had graduated from high school (Table 6). For each of the three states and for both sexes, approximately three-fifths of single-ancestry Italians and about four-fifths of the multiple-ancestry Italians had graduated from high school.

According to the November 1979 CPS, 12 percent of Italians graduated from college. About 1 out of 3 Italian males attended college for 1 or more years, which is not statistically significantly different from non-Italian males. However, a smaller proportion of Italian females attended college than other females.

It is interesting, also, to note the change in proportions of college graduates by generation of Italian immigrants; in 1979, about 5 percent of first-generation Italians (those born in Italy) were college graduates, about one-half the 10 percent for second-generation Italians (Table 8). Similarly, about one-third of the first-generation Italians were high school graduates, compared to 60 percent of the second-generation Italians.

In New York, New Jersey, and Pennsylvania in 1980, smaller proportions of Italians of each sex than the general population had graduated from college, although the proportion of Italian males in Pennsylvania was similar to all males in the state (Table 6). The 1980 figures for New York State indicate that Italian women 25 years old and over had lower educational attainment levels than the total population. For example, about 69 percent of Italian women had completed high school compared to 80 percent of all women for the state. However, it is important to note that the women in the multiple-ancestry group have higher educational levels than the single ancestry woman in all three states.

ECONOMIC CHARACTERISTICS

Labor Force Status

The proportion of Italians in the civilian labor force in 1979 was 66 percent, slightly above the level of 64 percent for the entire population (Table 8). Among the Italian Americans, there was an inverse relationship between generation and participation in the labor force, that is, the later generations participated more fully in the labor force, but this is partly a reflection of age, since many of the persons born in Italy had already retired.

In New York State in 1980, the proportion of Italian Americans in the labor force was about 61 percent (Table 7). In New Jersey and Pennsylvania, the labor force participation rates were also somewhat higher for Italians than for the entire state. In each of the three states, Italians of multiple ancestry had higher labor force participation rates than those of single ancestry, reflecting the age differentials.

The 1980 data show that Italians have a lower proportion of families with no workers than the rest of the population in the three states. For example, in New York, 13 percent of the families maintained by an Italian householder had no workers; the figure was 15 percent for all families in the state. Italian families also tend to have higher proportions of families with 3 or more workers. However, among Italian families of multiple ancestries in New York, lower proportions had no workers, as well as 3 or more workers, than either the Italian single-ancestry population, the total Italian population, or the population of the state as a whole. Similar data were found for New Jersey and Pennsylvania.

Occupation

In 1980, Italians in New York were heavily engaged in technical, sales, and administrative occupations (Table 7). About 36 percent of all employed Italians were in occupations which included jobs such as salespersons, secretaries, stenographers, and typists. About one-fifth of Italians were in professional and managerial occupations, but this proportion was slightly lower than that of the total population. Similar occupational distributions were noted for New Jersey and Pennsylvania.

Family Income

Family income is an important measure of socioeconomic status. Family income in the November 1979 CPS tended to be lower than income data collected in the 1980 census, since income in the CPS collected data only for income intervals.

Nonetheless, the 1979 CPS data can give us a feel for the relative prosperity of particular groups, and by this measure Italian Americans are doing fairly well. Although the median 1978 family income, reported in November 1979, for the country as a whole was $15,800, Italian Americans (single and multiple combined) were earning about $17,100 (Table 8). Again, there is a direct correlation between generation and income of Italian Americans; first-generation Italian immigrants had a median of $13,300 per year and second generation made about $16,900.

Although 27 percent of the U.S. families had incomes of less than $10,000 in 1978, (from the November 1979 CPS) only 15 percent of the Italian families were in this category. Similarly, although 37 percent of all U.S. families earned $20,000 or more, this was true for 41 percent of Italian families. About 23 percent of the first-generation Italian families made $20,000 or more, while 41 percent of second-generation families were in this category; similarly, although 30 percent of the first-generation families made $10,000 or less, only 17 percent of the second-generation families fell into this category.

The 1980 census provides a better measure of income levels.[4] Income data for all Italians in the 1980 census have only been tabulated for New York, New Jersey, and Pennsylvania. The median income for Italian families in 1979 (based on the 1980 census) for New York State was $21,700 (Table 7). The median income for Italian singles was $21,500 and for Italian multiples, $21,900.

The 1979 median income for Italians ($21,700) in New York State was $1,500 higher than the median income of all families in the state (Table 7). Although 21 percent of New York's families had less than $10,000, 16 percent of the Italian families were in this category. Also, although 51 percent of all New York families earned more than $20,000, 56 percent of the Italians were in this category. It should be noted that since Italians in New York have more families with 3 or more earners than the total state population, that this may account, in part, for the higher income level.

Poverty Status

Lower proportions of Italians in New York, New Jersey, and Pennsylvania than the rest of the population were in poverty (Table 7). The poverty rate for 1979 (from the 1980 census) for Italian persons in New York State was 8 percent, compared to 18 percent for all persons in the state. Comparable relationships existed in New Jersey and Pennsylvania.

CONCLUSIONS

The data analyzed in this chapter show an overall Italian population that is similar to the rest of the population in this country. The overall figures for Italians mask vast differences between the Italians who reported solely as Italian (largely first- and second-generation) and those reported as multiples (almost entirely third-and subsequent generations) in the 1980 census. Any thorough examination must at least take into account these differences within the group. Also, a more complete evaluation would include comparisons with other ethnic groups (especially other European groups) and the total non-Italian population.

TECHNICAL DISCUSSION

The growth of the United States population has been sustained by immigration. The largest numbers of migrants came from Europe, with early migration

---

[4] In the census and surveys attempting to ascertain optimal estimates of total income, the individual responses to detailed sources of income questions for each family member are summed to obtain total income; then, total family income is derived by aggregating the total income of all family members.

from England, Ireland, and Germany, followed by later migration streams from Italy, Poland, and other areas. Throughout our nation's history, there has been a great deal of interest in the composition of the population, but there has been little consensus about defining ethnic subgroups in censuses or surveys.

The decennial census of 1850 was the first to gather information on the distribution of ethnic groups in the United States through a question on place of birth. Later in that century, and in all subsequent censuses, other specific questions were included to determine the birthplace of parents as well as mother tongue, reflecting changes in patterns of life in American society. The questions on parental birthplace and mother tongue were dropped before the 1980 census, but questions on current language and ancestry were added.

For Italians, as for most other ethnic groups, a new, more subjective ancestry question was used in the 1980 census to reflect the great majority of persons who identified themselves as belonging to a specific ethnic group but who were born, and whose parents were born, in the United States.

Ancestry, as used in the November 1979 CPS and the 1980 census, refers to a person's nationality group, lineage, or the country in which the person or person's parents or ancestors were born. The 1980 decennial census was the first to ask a question on ancestry regardless of the number of generations removed from the country of birth of respondents' ancestors. The responses to the ancestry question reflected the ethnic group or groups with which persons identified and not necessarily the degree of attachment or association the person had with the particular ethnic group(s).

All responses were coded manually by a procedure that allowed for identification of all single- and double-ancestry groups reported. In addition, 17 triple-ancestry categories were identified by unique codes, which were reported frequently in previous Census Bureau surveys. The triples were coded regardless of the order reported. All other multiple responses were coded according to only the first and second reported ancestry categories.

Persons reporting multiple ancestry groups were generally included in more than one category. For example, a person reporting as "Italian-English" was counted in both "Italian" and "English" multiple categories. A person reporting "Italian-American", however, would be recorded only once in "Italian", since "American" is not considered part of a multiple response. Also, persons reporting "Italian-Sicilian" or "Tuscany-Italian" would be recorded only once as Italian. Persons reporting one of the unique three-origin groups were tabulated in each of the 3 ancestry categories. Since persons who reported multiple ancestries were included in more than one group, the sum of persons reporting at least one ancestry or a multiple ancestry for all ancestry responses is greater than the population of the United States.

When an ancestry response was missing, the person's ancestry was tabulated as "not reported". Nonresponse to the ancestry question allows for the introduction of bias into the data since the ancestries of the nonrespondents have not been observed and may differ from those reported by respondents.

COMPARISON OF NOVEMBER 1979 CPS and 1980 CENSUS

The socioeconomic profile of the Italian population presented in this chapter is based upon two Census Bureau sources—the 1980 census and the November 1979 *Current Population Survey* (CPS).

Although demographic, social, and economic data for the United States and each state are available for persons who reported solely Italian in 1980, only limited 1980 census data are now available on all persons of Italian ancestry in the United States (These data will be published subsequently in 1980 census *Subject Report* on Ancestry of the Population). Therefore, we have used some data from a special ethnic supplement taken in November 1979 CPS to provide information on the social and economic characteristics of the total Italian population at the national level. A question on ancestry similar to the 1980 census question was asked in this special ethnic supplement. Also, the November 1979 CPS allows for an analysis using related ethnic variables, such as person's and parents' birthplaces, mother tongue, and current language. In this chapter, we also have analyzed the 1980 census data for the Italian population in New York, New Jersey, and Pennsylvania, since these were major areas of settlement for the early immigrants and were the 3 largest states in 1980.

The totals for the Italian population for the United States from the 1980 census and the November 1979 CPS are provided below.

	1980 Census (thousands)	Percent of Total Population	November 1979 (thousands)	Percent of Total Population
TOTAL population	226,546	100.0	216,613	100.0
Total persons of Italian ancestry	12,184	5.5	11,751	5.4
Single ancestry	6,883	3.0	6,110	2.8
Multiple ancestry	5,300	2.4	5,641	2.6
Percent Single ancestry	56.5	(X)	52.0	(X)

(X) Not applicable.

There is no statistical difference between the proportion Italian of the total population in the November 1979 CPS and in the 1980 census. The differences for singles and multiple reporting, however, are statistically significant.

There are several reasons why different estimates will be derived from the census and the CPS survey. The CPS estimates are based on population controls from the 1970 census which were updated for changes in the population since that time, and inmates of institutions and all members of the Armed Forces were excluded from the survey. Also, the CPS and the 1980 census used different procedures for collecting and processing the data. For example, the information in the CPS was obtained through personal interviews. However, the 1980 census was conducted primarily through self-enumeration; questionnaires were mailed to householders who were asked to fill in the required information. Differences between census and CPS data for the ethnic items were also affected by inconsistent reporting by respondents and differences in computer editing for unacceptable or missing data. Given all of these differences, it is remarkable that the data for Italians in the two sources are as analogous as they are.

For more discussion of the differences in reporting ancestry between the 1980 census and the November 1979 CPS, see the 1980 census *Supplementary Report* (PC80-S1-10), "Ancestry of the Population by State: 1980", and the paper "Direct and Indirect Measures of Ethnicity: How Different Definitions Affect the Size and Characteristics of Various Ethnic Groups" by Nampeo McKenney, Reynolds Farley, and Michael Levin.

CENSUS BUREAU PUBLICATIONS and TABULATIONS ON ITALIANS

The 1980 census *Supplementary Report*, "Ancestry of the Population by State: 1980" (PC80-S1-10), presents population size and geographic distribution (U.S., regions, divisions, and states) of more than 100 ancestry groups (including Italian) by type of response (single and multiple). Estimates for Italian ancestry persons (single and multiple separately) are shown in *Census Tracts* (PHC80-2) and *Congressional Districts of the 98th Congress* (PHC80-4).

We are currently publishing data on social and economic characteristics of persons of single-Italian ancestry for each state in our Volume I series, PC80-1-C report, entitled *General Social and Economic Characteristics*. Social and economic data for multiple-Italian ancestry persons will be presented in the PC80-1-C reports for New York, Pennsylvania, and Rhode Island. We will present data on age, fertility, household relationship and family composition, education, employment status, occupation, industry, income, as well as information on migration, military service, and other characteristics, for each PC80-1-C state report. In addition, the presentation of social and economic characteristics for Italian-ancestry persons is planned for our PC80-2 *Subject Report* focusing on ancestry.

As noted earlier, both single and multiple reporting were coded in the 1980 census. Tabulations are currently available for the number of persons of

Italian ancestry by states, standard metropolitan statistical areas (SMSAs), urbanized areas, places, congressional districts, counties, and census tracts. These data will be available on summary tape files, which can be obtained by special request from the Census Bureau.

Although the questions on parental birthplace and mother tongue were dropped for the 1980 census, questions on ancestry, current language, and English language ability were added. We asked questions on the birthplace of individuals, the language spoken in the home, and ability to speak English. The responses to these questions will permit us to determine for small geographical areas the number of Italian origin persons who are foreign born, the number reporting Italian as a current language, and the number who experience difficulty with the English language. These data will produce a wealth of information for persons of Italian ethnic origin in the United States.

2

Italian Migration to the United States 1966-1978 [1] The Transition Period and a Decade Beyond Public Law (89-236)

JOHN SEGGAR
Brigham Young University

In 1970, Joseph Velikonja reported his findings relative to Italian immigration into the United States for the early and middle 1960s. Velikonja noted "A new chapter of immigration history was opened by the new Immigration Act, which after a transitional period between December 1, 1965 and July 1, 1968, has replaced the national origin quota system with a new set of criteria, based primarily upon family relations and technical skills" (Tomasi and Engel, 1977:23).

Almost all serious students of the history of migration into the United States, as well as many lay persons are aware that Italy has been one of the leading contributors of immigrants to America. However, because of several international, social, economic, political, and diplomatic developments there have been shifts in foreign policy, philosophy, and procedures for admitting newcomers to the U.S. One such major change was the passage of the Immigration Act (Public Law 89-236). The purpose of the present analysis is to explore the extent to which Public Law 89-236 has influenced the trends in the pattern of Italian migration into the U.S. and nationalization.

This study utilizes data from the transitional period (1966-1968) and for ten years beyond, up to and including 1978. The data were gathered from the United States Immigration and Naturalization Service annual reports for the years 1966 through 1978. The report has three parts: Part One focuses on ad-

---

[1] Data for this research was derived from the Annual Reports of the United States Immigration and Naturalization Service, from 1966-78 inclusive.

mittance data; Part Two on naturalization data; and Part Three includes information about non-immigrant admittances.

PART ONE—ADMITTANCE DATA

In this part we are concerned with: 1) the relationship of Italian immigration to the U.S. and the total immigration into the U.S.; 2) admittances by gender and age; 3) admittance to geographic areas; 4) admittances by preferences; and 5) occupation of admitted immigrants.

Total Immigration and Italian Immigration

Since 1966, the first year of the transitional period from the national origins quota system, to the implementation and administering of the Immigration Act (Public Law 89-236) up to 1978 there has been an upward trend in the number of aliens admitted to the U.S. However, when one considers that the same annual report data summarized in Table One, one can see that there has been a steady decline of Italian aliens admitted. Table One indicates that during the transitional period 1966-1968 total immigration to the U.S. rose from 323,040 to 454,448 or an increase of 31 percent. In the same period, however, a downward trend began for the Italian immigrants which has continued to the present. The percentage the Italians contributed to total immigration to the U.S. in 1966 was 7.8 percent, by 1968 it declined to 5.1 percent. By 1978, total immigration was reported as 601,442 or 278,402 more

TABLE 1

Italian Migrant Percentage of Total Immigrants Admitted to U.S. 1966-1978

Year	TOTAL Immigrants to U.S.	Italians Admitted	Percentage
1966	323,040	25,154	7.8
1967	361,972	26,565	7.3
1968	454,448	23,593	5.1
1969	358,579	23,617	6.6
1970	373,526	24,973	6.7
1971	370,478	22,137	6.0
1972	384,685	21,427	5.6
1973	400,063	22,151	5.5
1974	394,861	15,884	4.0
1975	386,194	11,552	3.0
1976	398,613	8,380	2.1
1976[tq]	103,676	2,035	2.0
1977	462,315	7,510	1.6
1978	601,442	7,415	1.2

Source: Table 6. U.S. Immigration and Naturalization Service Annual Reports 1966-1978.

than in 1966 which represents an increase in total migration equal to 86.2 percent. During the same period Italian admittances dropped from 25,154 to 7,415, a loss of 17,739 or a decrease equal to 70.5 percent. In terms of contribution to the total in 1966 Italian immigrants comprised 7.8 percent whereas in 1978 they comprised only 1.2 percent.

The new chapter that Velikonja mentioned has shown that during the transition period and a decade beyond that Italian immigration to the U.S. has decreased to an all time low since 1946. In the 1966-1978 period Italy was not alone however, all the European countries had decreased in their contribution to immigrants to the U.S. except for Greece, Portugal, Romania, Spain, and the U.S.S.R.

Admittances by Gender and Age

In trying to make sense out of the age distribution figures, it was thought useful to consider the percentage that would probably be dependent on their families for support. Traditionally the Census Bureau uses the under 18 and over 65 years of age categories as the groups that combine to make up the dependent category. However, in the statistics reported by Immigration and Naturalization Service the categories do not allow for exact comparison to the 18 and 65 criteria. What they do permit is an under 20 and over 60 combination. While recognizing the lack of direct comparability, the under 20, and 60 and over can be a heuristic device that allows a determination of whether there has been a change in the age structure of migrants to the U.S. over the thirteen year period under examination.

Males. What one observes in Table 2 for the males is an erratic pattern from year to year but with a general decline in the percentage of males that could be labeled dependants. However, the fluctuation is slight, all within 4.7 percentage point range. The males are slightly more likely to be in the working age groups in 1978 than they were in 1966.

When the change is analyzed we find the decrease has resulted more from the decrease in the under 20 years of age category than the elderly group. In 1966, this young group contributed 36.8 percent, by 1978 it was contributing 28.9 percent. The 60 and over age group has actually increased in percentage from 1966 when it was 4.2 percent up to 6.4 in 1978. The thirteen year average was 5.6 percent.

Females. In 1966, the number of females admitted was 12,624. By 1978, the number had decreased to 3,719 or 29.5 percent of the 1966 figure. Again, as with the males, the females had an erratic pattern year by year but the trend was downward.

In terms of the modified "dependency" category, the trend was also downward in terms of percentages. The females in the combined under 20 and 60 and over category comprised 42.8 percent in 1966 and by 1978 had declined to 39 percent. Again, when the change is analyzed we see the similar pattern as the males, that is, young under 20 year old females declined from 37.5 in 1966 to 28.1 percent in 1978. The elderly 60 and over had an increase from 5.3 to 10.9 percent.

TABLE 2

Italian Male Immigrants Admitted by Age Categories 1966-1978

Year	Under 20	Percent	20-59	Percent	60+	Percent	TOTAL	Percent
1966	4,608	36.8	7,384	58.9	538	4.2	12,530	41.0
1967	4,629	33.8	8,325	60.8	742	5.4	13,696	39.2
1968	4,000	33.2	7,260	60.3	782	6.4	12,042	39.6
1969	4,071	34.0	7,181	60.0	721	6.0	11,973	40.0
1970	4,417	34.2	7,879	61.1	604	4.7	12,900	38.9
1971	3,946	34.0	7,106	61.2	559	4.8	11,611	38.8
1972	3,913	35.1	6,694	60.1	534	4.8	11,141	39.8
1973	4,115	35.8	6,866	59.7	515	4.5	11,496	40.3
1974	2,716	33.7	4,893	60.8	437	5.4	8,046	39.1
1975	1,889	32.4	3,609	61.8	339	5.8	5,837	38.2
1976	1,277	29.7	2,733	63.6	290	6.7	4,300	36.4
1976tq	375	35.9	607	58.1	62	5.9	1,044	41.8
1977	1,154	29.6	2,465	63.2	284	7.2	3,903	36.8
1978	1,069	28.9	2,388	64.6	239	6.4	3,696	35.3

Italian Female Immigrants Admitted by Age Categories 1966-1978

Year	Under 20	Percent	20-59	Percent	60+	Percent	TOTAL	Percent
1966	4,745	37.5	7,211	57.1	668	5.3	12,624	42.8
1967	4,461	34.7	7,577	58.9	831	6.5	12,869	41.2
1968	3,942	34.1	6,748	58.4	861	7.5	11,551	41.6
1969	4,185	35.9	6,663	57.2	796	6.8	11,644	42.7
1970	4,400	36.4	6,862	56.8	811	6.7	12,073	43.1
1971	3,794	36.0	6,096	57.9	636	6.0	10,526	42.0
1972	3,834	37.3	5,822	56.6	630	6.1	10,286	43.4
1973	3,923	36.8	6,097	57.2	635	6.0	10,655	42.8
1974	2,842	36.3	4,455	56.8	541	6.9	7,838	43.2
1975	1,976	34.5	3,315	58.0	424	7.4	5,715	41.9
1976	1,253	30.7	2,377	58.3	450	11.0	4,080	41.7
1976tq	308	31.1	583	58.8	100	10.1	991	42.2
1977	1,119	31.0	2,086	57.8	402	11.1	3,607	42.1
1978	1,044	28.1	2,271	61.1	404	10.9	3,719	39.0

Source: Table 9. U.S. Immigration and Naturalization Service Annual Reports 1966-1978.

Basically each year, as a general rule, there are slightly more males admitted than females. Furthermore, the percentages of females in the "dependency" category are anywhere from 1 to 6 percent greater than their male counterparts. In 1966, there were approximately nine times as many under 20 year-old males admitted than males 60 and over, but in 1978 their ratio was only about four-and-a-half to one, young for old. The young females in 1966 outnumbered the 60 and over females about 7 to 1 whereas in 1978 it had declined to 3 to 1. From this analysis it is clear that the age structure of the migrants is changing toward an older average age.

Admittances by Geographic Area

Because there was so much data in the master United States table for the thirteen year period it was decided for the sake of brevity and given the fact that ten states accounted for 94.1 percent of the total number of admittances that a summary table would suffice to present the admittances by geographical area data. Table 3 reports figures for the ten leading states admitting Italian immigrants to become permanent residents. Again, for the sake of brevity and also to dramatize the changes we calculated the averages for the 1966-1967 years and compared it to the 1977-1978 average. Using the two-year period allowed us to avoid the complication that would have resulted due to the change in the reporting year ending in 1976 from June to September.

TABLE 3
Top Ten States Admitting Italian Immigrants to
Become Permanent Residents 1966-1978

			Percent of TOTAL	1966- 1967	1977- 1978	Percent Decrease	Number Differ- rence
1.	New York	103,245	42.6	11,148	2,649	76.2	8,499
2.	New Jersey	32,557	13.4	3,284	956	70.9	2,328
3.	Illinois	19,578	8.1	2,181	554	74.6	1,627
4.	Massachusetts	16,844	6.9	1,811	453	75.0	1,358
5.	Connecticut	16,447	6.8	1,744	520	70.2	1,224
6.	Pennsylvania	13,398	5.5	1,680	359	78.6	1,321
7.	California	10,135	4.2	1,064	536	49.6	528
8.	Michigan	7,061	2.9	751	232	69.1	519
9.	Ohio	5,961	2.5	632	211	66.6	421
10.	Rhode Island	2,975	1.2	265	76	71.3	189
		228,201	94.1	24,560	6,546		18,014
	All others	14,226	5.9				
	TOTAL	242,427	100.0				

As can be seen here, with the exception of California, decreases are reported for the top ten states in terms of admitting Italian immigrants. The percentage decrease averaged 72.5 percent. Put another way, for those states admitting large numbers of Italian migrants and accounting for approximately 90 percent of the admission on the average they were admitting 1 in 1977-1978 for every 4 in the 1966-1967 period. Again, it is interesting to note that the Northeast accounted for 76.4 percent of the admittance during the study period. In Velikonja's report he noted that "The total of 72.5 percent of all the resident Italian aliens in January 1968 were registered in the Northeast" (Tomasi and Engel, 1977:23). So there does not appear to be very much change in the direction of geographical flows in terms of where the Italian migrants settle. Even though the extent of the flows are reduced.

Admittances by Preferences

It can be seen from Table 4 that during 1967 and 1968 there appeared to be a relative surge of Italians who were parents of U.S. citizens, admitted to the U.S. However, after 1968 there was a steady decline almost every year until 1978. It can also be observed that the number of wives of U.S. citizens being admitted decreased every year. The same basic trend is observable for husbands of U.S. citizens admitted to the U.S. with the exception of 1971-1972. The category that was most influential in the shrinkage was the children of U.S. citizens admitted. In 1966, this category represented 19.5 percent of those being admitted by family preferences and that was the highest proportion the children of U.S. citizen category had contributed since 1971. As one looks at the thirteen year trend it can be seen that while the actual percentage of the combined four family preferences has increased, numerically the reduction from 5,102 in 1966 to 1,653 in 1978 indicates there were 67.6 percent fewer admitted through family preferences (Preferences I, II, IV, V). This would suggest that families separated through migration will find it considerably more difficult to reunite their families by migrating to the U.S. if the present trend continues.

Table 5 allows us to explicate the preference data even further. The data indicates that the range admitted by relative preferences between 1966 and 1973 ranged from 15,103 to 19,521. In 1974, there was a sudden drop to 12,100, a decrease of thirty-five percent from the previous year. Then in 1975 there was another severe drop to 8,567 equal to another 29.1 percent from 1974 and again in 1976 a drop of 2,929 or 34.2 percent from 1975. Thereafter the decreases were not so dramatic. If one calculates the percentage contribution of each category for each year and then examines the trend over the thirteen year period the two most striking findings concern the fourth and fifth relative preferences. In 1966, the fourth preference, that is married sons and daughters of U.S. citizens and their spouses and children, contributed 7,166 or 42.9 percent of the total relative preference admitted. By 1977, the fourth preference accounted for only 369 or 7.9 percent of the total. This downward trend was sharp from 1966 to 1970, but then plateaued around 8 percent therafter.

With the fifth preference, that is brothers and sisters of U.S. citizens and their spouses and children, we see an opposite trend. In 1966 this preference only accounted for 3,040 or 18.2 percent of the total relative preferences, however, the number grew each year up to 1973 when this preference contributed 14,080 or 75.5 percent of the total relative preferences. Since that time the percentage has hovered around 68 percent.

The first thing that becomes apparent when one considers the occupational preferences is that over the thirteen years the proportionate contribution made by these admittances has decreased, the trend over the study period has been erratic but basically the pattern is one of decline. From 1966 to 1973 the steady, but seeming deliberate increase in family preferences appears to have been a priority. After 1973, the percentage has hovered between 85-90 percent. It appears that admittances through occupational preferences have been almost shut off. The probability of getting admitted to the United States to work if one cannot come in through a relative preference, is minute.

Occupations of Migrants Admitted

Though the members admitted through the occupational preferences have decreased the Immigration and Naturalization Service tracks the other migrants coming in through other preferences as to possible occupation status, so we can get some idea of the occupational structure change occurring. Table 6 shows that while the numbers declined, the percentages increased for the professional, technical, and kindred workers from a 2.1 in 1966 to a high of 5.2 percent in 1977. A similar pattern was observable for managers and administrators, also for sales and clerical workers, however in the sales and clerical cases the magnitude was smaller.

For craftsmen, the 767 admitted in 1978 represented only 24.4 percent of the number admitted in 1966. Of the migrants coming in to the U.S. the craftsmen have consistently contributed between 10 to 12 percent of the total. The same basic trend is also applicable for the operative category except between 1970 and 1973 when there was a slight gain that thereafter declined.

Over the thirteen years, the laborers declined not only in numbers, but also percentage wise. The 301 admitted in 1978 represent only 15.6 percent of the number admitted in 1966.

The number of service workers admitted in 1966 was 733. Throughout 1966-1973 the pattern was erratic in terms of numbers, but after 1973 the five year period up to 1978 was continually downward, but the percentage increased yearly from 1973 to 1978.

The household workers category has shown both numerical and percentage increases. For the thirteen year period it has historically contributed fewer than 3 percent to the total.

TABLE 4

Italian Immigrants by Classes Under the Immigration Laws and Country or Region of Birth 1966-1978[a]

Year	Number Admitted	Subject to Numerical Limitations	Exempt from Numerical Limitations	Parents of U.S. Citizens	Wives of U.S. Citizens	Husbands of U.S. Citizens	Children of U.S. Citizens	Others Classes	Special Acts	Four Familial Preferences TOTAL	Percentage
1966	25,154	19,135	6,019	941	1,840	1,324	997	165	523	5,102	19.3
1967	26,565	19,970	6,595	2,160	1,611	1,208	984	193	345	5,963	16.5
1968	23,593	17,248	6,345	2,127	1,524	1,176	1,10c	136	144	5,933	18.6
1969	23,617	18,494	5,123	1,634	1,397	979	91c	128	69	4,926	18.6
1970	24,973	19,739	5,234	1,644	1,388	1,280	775	132	15	5,087	15.2
1971	22,137	17,827	4,310	1,446	1,069	1,075	496	130	188	4,086	12.1
1972	21,427	17,620	3,807	1,304	919	947	329	131	177	3,499	9.4
1973	22,151	18,859	3,292	1,112	830	774	257	131	188	2,973	8.6
1974	15,884	13,235	2,649	909	684	600	208	102	146	2,401	8.7
1975	11,552	9,213	2,339	802	606	558	177	117	79	2,143	8.3
1976	8,380	6,202	2,178	721	566	534	135	103	119	1,956	6.9
1976*	2,035	1,462	573	158	160	142	43	32	38	503	8.5
1977	7,510	5,397	2,113	648	587	517	151	113	97	1,903	7.9
1978	7,415	5,089	2,326	646	784	529	171	84	112	1,653	10.3

[a] In 1966-76 the year ended June 30. July 1 to September 30 in 1976 was a transitional quarter; thereafter years end September 30.

* Transition quarter.

Source: Table 6. U.S. Immigration and Naturalization Service Annual Reports 1966-1978.

TABLE 5
Italian Immigrants Admitted by Preferences Under the Numerical Limitation of 170,000 for the Eastern Hemisphere (P.L. 89-236) 1966-1978

(Figures include adjustment of status cases. Numbers of visas issued and immigrants admitted will not necessarily agree. Differences may be caused by failure of aliens to make use of the visas issued or by immigrants who are admitted to the United States in the year following the one in which the visa was issued.)

Year	1966	1967	1968	1969	1970	1971	1972	1973	1974	1975	1976	1976^{tq}	1977	1978
TOTAL Immigrants	18,955	19,822	17,130	18,262	19,759	17,922	17,693	19,296	13,793	9,671	6,561	1,567	5,708	5,138
						Relative Preferences								
TOTAL Relatives Preferences	16,680	16,462	15,103	17,990	19,521	17,703	17,500	18,650	12,100	8,567	5,638	1,357	4,863	4,662
First Preference* Unmarried Sons and Daughters of U.S. Citizens and Their Children	.7	1.0	1.7	1.3	1.0	.8	.6	.4	.4	.4	.6	.9	.7	.7
	122	177	263	242	198	149	99	70	49	31	32	12	33	33
Second Preference Spouses, Unmarried Sons and Daughters of Resident Aliens and Their Children	32.3	29.7	31.7	26.0	23.6	24.0	21.6	17.7	23.0	23.6	25.6	24.5	22.0	23.4
	5,387	4,892	4,787	4,681	4,597	4,242	3,785	3,185	2,784	2,026	1,441	333	1,115	1,091
Fourth Preference Married Sons and Daughters of U.S. Citizens and Their Spouses and Children	42.9	39.4	31.5	23.1	15.9	12.3	8.1	7.0	7.3	8.1	9.8	6.1	8.0	7.9
	7,166	6,488	4,765	4,150	3,105	2,176	1,422	1,315	880	693	552	83	411	369
Fifth Preference Brothers and Sisters of U.S. Citizens and Their Spouses and Children	18.2	29.8	35.0	49.6	59.5	62.8	69.7	75.5	69.3	67.9	64.1	68.5	67.0	67.9
	3,040	4,905	5,228	8,917	11,621	11,126	12,194	14,080	8,387	5,817	3,613	930	3,304	3,169

Occupational Preferences

Total Occupational Preferences	2,232	3,305	1,913	179	163	151	132	516	1,451	588	315	56	199
Third Preference													
Immigrants in Professions	44	145	56	78	73	88	76	58	40	18	12	5	19
Spouses and Children	a	107	42	42	50	44	49	39	45	8	11	7	13
Sixth Preference													
Other Workers	289	1,431	756	27	8	4	3	212	602	264	137	20	92
Spouses and Children	a	1,622	1,059	32	32	15	4	207	764	298	155	25	75
Seventh Preference													
Admitted	10	37	48	39	48	38	38	97	54	12	7	2	11
Adjusted	—	—	—	1	2	1	2	—	9	7	—	—	—
Nonpreference Immigrants	33	18	66	53	25	29	21	33	179	497	601	151	635
Total Percentage Family Preference	87.9	83.0	88.2	98.5	98.8	98.8	98.9	96.7	87.7	88.6	85.9	86.6	85.2
Total Percentage Occupational Preference	11.8	16.7	11.2	1.0	.8	.8	.7	2.7	10.5	6.1	4.8	3.6	3.5

a 1966 reported these two categories combined for 1356.

* First preference in 1966 was special skills and there were 543.

Source: Table 7a. U.S. Immigration and Naturalization Service Annual Reports 1966-1978.

TABLE 6
Italian Immigrants Admitted by Major Occupational Group 1966-1978

Year	1966	1967	1968	1969	1970	1971	1972	1973	1974	1975	1976	1977	1978
Number Admitted	25,154	26,565	23,593	23,617	24,973	22,137	21,427	22,151	15,884	11,552	8,380	7,510	7,415
Professional, Technical, and Kindred Workers	2.1 / 520	2.6 / 690	2.1 / 499	2.1 / 501	2.3 / 595	2.6 / 570	2.3 / 489	2.1 / 474	2.9 / 460	3.6 / 420	3.9 / 324	5.2 / 388	4.8 / 357
Managers and Administrators, Except Farm	1.0 / 246	1.1 / 381	1.0 / 230	.8 / 308	1.0 / 260	1.2 / 273	1.3 / 275	1.3 / 290	1.6 / 251	2.1 / 240	2.8 / 237	3.6 / 273	3.3 / 247
Sales Workers	.4 / 98	.4 / 108	.4 / 90	.4 / 99	.5 / 128	.4 / 96	.3 / 72	.4 / 82	.5 / 82	.5 / 52	.5 / 44	.6 / 51	.8 / 65
Clerical and Kindred Workers	.9 / 222	1.1 / 290	1.1 / 261	1.0 / 245	1.2 / 308	1.0 / 227	1.2 / 259	1.2 / 259	1.2 / 196	1.2 / 133	1.3 / 109	— / 128	2.1 / 155
Craftsmen and Kindred Workers	12.5 / 3,146	14.3 / 3,810	13.2 / 3,113	11.2 / 2,638	11.8 / 2,942	11.5 / 2,535	11.2 / 2,399	11.5 / 2,554	12.6 / 2,000	12.2 / 1,412	11.5 / 966	9.9 / 740	10.3 / 767
Operatives, Except Transport	5.6 / 1,420	6.6 / 1,747	6.6 / 1,562	6.5 / 1,542	7.0 / 1,746	7.5 / 1,663	7.3 / 1,573	7.3 / 1,613	6.3 / 1,008	6.4 / 738	6.5 / 541	5.8 / 433	6.2 / 461
Transport Equipment Operatives	—	—	—	—	—	—	—	—	.8 / 133	1.0 / 116	1.0 / 80	1.0 / 74	.4 / 66

	%	No.	%	No.	%	No.	%	No.	%	No.	%	No.	%	No.	%	No.	%	No.	%	No.	%	No.	%	No.	%	No.
Laborers, Except Farm and Mine	7.7	1,929	7.0	1,847	4.7	1,695	6.6	2,033	8.6	2,344	8.6	1,894	7.9	1,700	8.2	1,832	6.7	1,063	3.7	429	3.6	301	4.0	303	4.1	301
Farmers and Farm Managers	2.9	721	2.8	741	2.3	551	3.9	925	4.4	1,093	1.4	317	.1	16	—	6	.1	19	1.1	129	1.3	112	.4	31	.0	19
Farm Laborers and Farm Foremen	2.9	752	3.0	790	4.6	1,087	2.5	598	1.9	471	4.9	1,090	5.7	1,225	4.9	1,093	4.2	672	3.5	404	2.6	216	3.5	266	3.3	251
Service Workers Except Private Household	2.9	733	3.1	828	3.1	730	2.7	627	2.8	701	3.1	681	3.1	664	3.1	681	3.6	576	3.9	450	4.8	406	5.0	372	4.7	347
Private Household Workers	1.7	440	1.6	425	1.3	300	2.3	535	2.7	674	2.0	441	1.6	345	1.6	362	1.6	250	1.0	121	1.2	104	1.3	94	1.5	108
Housewives, Children, and others with no Occupation Reported	59.3	14,927	56.5	15,008	57.1	13,475	57.9	13,666	55.7	13,911	55.8	12,350	57.9	12,411	58.2	12,905	57.7	9,174	59.8	6,908	58.5	4,904	58.0	4,357	57.6	4,271

Source: Table 8. U.S. Immigration and Naturalization Service Annual Reports 1966-1978.

Housewives, children, and others with no occupation have usually contributed about 55 to 59 percent of the total, but again, the number admitted in 1978 was only 28.6 percent of the number admitted in 1966.

The farmers, farm managers, laborers, and foreman categories combined have contributed only 5.6 percent of the total shown in Table 4. This is a drastic change in the masses of *contadini* that came when the migration waves from Europe were at their peak. Since 1971, the percentage for farmers and farm managers has dwindled to around one percent or less. The percentage for the farm laborers and foremen has ranged from a low of 1.9 percent to a high of 5.7 percent, but the pattern has been erratic.

Naturalizations

In this section the data are concerned with naturalizations as they relate to: 1) the contribution of Italian naturalizations to the total; 2) familial provisions; 3) occupational categories; 4) gender; 5) geographical areas; 6) longevity of stay; and 7) rural-urban settlement.

TABLE 7
Italian Percentage of Total Immigrants Naturalizing
1966-1978

Year	TOTAL Naturalizations	Italian Naturalization	% of TOTAL Naturalizations
1966	103,059	10,981	10.6
1967	104,902	10,572	10.1
1968	102,727	9,379	9.1
1969	98,709	8,773	8.9
1970	110,399	7,892	7.1
1971	108,407	7,637	7.0
1972	116,215	8,375	7.2
1973	120,740	8,902	7.4
1974	131,655	8,898	6.8
1975	141,537	8,798	6.2
1976	142,504	8,696	6.1
1976tq	48,218	2,173	4.5
1977	159,873	7,891	4.9
1978	173,535	8,180	4.7

Source: Table 39. U.S. Immigration and Naturalization Service Annual Reports 1966-1978.

Total Naturalization and Italian Naturalizations

The data in Table 7 indicate that between 1966 and 1971, between 98,000 and 110,000 immigrants from all countries naturalized annually. Beginning in 1972 and up to 1978 there was a continual upward trend in the total number from all countries. The pattern for the Italian immigrants naturalizing was not so clear. From 1966 to 1971 there was a continual decline from 10,981 down to 7,637. In 1972 the Italian trend followed the national upward trend and did so through 1973. Thereafter, however, there were three annual declines. In 1977-1978 the trend reversed slightly upward again. Probably what is more significant is that the contribution that Italians make to the overall total of all migrants naturalizing has generally declined from 10.6 in 1966 to 4.7 percent in 1978.

Naturalization and Familial Provisions

After 1969, as can be seen in Table 8 the range of the number naturalized by general and special provisions was most usually between 8,000 and 9,000. The general provision column indicates a fluctuating pattern within the 7,000-8,000 range except in 1970 and 1971. In these two years there was a drop of an average of about 1,000 to 1,200. The number in the married to U.S. citizens column indicates a fairly steady drop from 1,568 in 1966 to 362 in 1978. The 1978 figure represents 23 percent of the 1966 figure. While there are not so many involved, the children of U.S. citizens category shows a somewhat

TABLE 8
Former Italian Citizens Naturalized by General and Special Provisions
1966-1978

Year	TOTAL	General Provision	Married to U.S. Citizens	Children of U.S. Citizens	Military	Other
1966	10,981	8,485	1,568	892	33	3
1967	10,572	8,271	1,496	760	39	6
1968	9,379	7,509	1,256	572	41	1
1969	8,773	7,071	1,088	450	161	3
1970	7,892	6,017	1,049	389	435	2
1971	7,637	5,866	1,021	346	401	3
1972	8,375	7,024	773	249	322	7
1973	8,902	7,668	688	269	272	5
1974	8,898	7,711	717	234	233	3
1975	8,798	7,804	628	220	146	—
1976	8,696	7,815	542	211	126	2
1976tq	2,173	1,938	130	62	41	2
1977	7,891	7,148	441	195	105	2
1978	8,180	7,540	362	204	73	1
	117,147	97,867	11,759	5,053	2,428	40

Source: Table 38. U.S. Immigration and Naturalization Service Annual Reports 1966-1978.

TABLE 9
Former Italian Persons Naturalized by Major Occupation Group
1966-1978

Year	1966	1967	1968	1969	1970	1971	1972	1973	1974	1975	1976	1977	1978
TOTAL	10,981	10,572	8,773	7,892	7,637	8,375	8,902	8,898	8,798	8,696	7,891	8,180	
Professional, Technical, and Kindred Workers	2.6	2.4	3.0	2.6	3.6	3.7	3.7	3.7	3.3	3.1	3.3	3.5	3.9
	289	262	285	235	282	286	314	328	294	271	284	274	319
Managers and Administrators, Except Farm	1.7	2.2	2.0	2.5	2.6	3.4	3.2	2.7	3.6	3.8	3.9	4.6	5.0
	196	234	184	219	204	263	272	244	323	323	340	363	412
Sales Workers	.8	.9	1.1	1.0	1.1	1.2	1.4	1.4	1.3	1.4	1.5	1.5	1.6
	90	97	108	92	85	91	116	125	115	127	128	115	128
Clerical and Kindred Workers	4.1	4.7	5.9	6.0	6.1	6.0	5.8	5.4	5.7	5.7	5.7	5.4	5.4
	453	502	551	526	482	460	483	484	511	504	496	425	449
Craftsmen and Kindred Workers	16.0	15.8	16.8	17.0	16.7	17.2	17.0	17.6	17.2	17.6	16.0	15.3	15.3
	1,762	1,671	1,579	1,492	1,319	1,313	1,428	1,568	1,534	1,550	1,391	1,206	1,258
Operatives Except Transport	18.4	19.6	20.0	19.8	18.3	16.0	17.0	18.6	17.6	17.4	18.0	17.1	18.9
	2,028	2,074	1,877	1,733	1,441	1,225	1,425	1,652	1,563	1,539	1,563	1,349	1,547

Occupation													
Transport Equipment Oper.	—	—	—	—	—	—	—	—	71	95	88	68	1.1 / 91
Laborers, Except Farm	9.5 / 1,045	8.4 / 887	8.3 / 777	8.0 / 698	7.3 / 578	7.1 / 541	9.1 / 763	10.0 / 892	10.0 / 891	9.7 / 856	10.0 / 873	8.8 / 697	8.9 / 725
Farmers and Farm Managers	5	2	5	5	4	4	4	—	5	4	2	2	2
Farm Laborers and Farm Foremen	8	4	4	4	2	5	5	3	11	11	11	10	4
Service Workers, Except Private Household	8.2 / 899	7.7 / 818	7.9 / 743	9.5 / 834	10.0 / 792	8.9 / 679	9.2 / 775	8.2 / 738	7.3 / 649	7.4 / 650	7.8 / 681	9.0 / 712	8.9 / 729
Private Household Workers	.3 / 36	.4 / 41	.2 / 21	.3 / 27	.2 / 19	.2 / 16	.2 / 16	.2 / 24	.3 / 23	.1 / 10	.3 / 22	.2 / 18	.2 / 15
Housewives, Children, and Others with No Occupation Reported	38.0 / 4,170	37.6 / 3,975	34.6 / 3,245	33.1 / 2,098	34.0 / 2,684	36.0 / 2,754	33.1 / 2,774	31.9 / 2,844	32.7 / 2,908	32.5 / 2,858	32.4 / 2,817	33.6 / 2,652	30.6 / 2,501

Source: Table 40. Immigration and Naturalization Service Annual Reports 1966-1976.

parallel trend. The drop from 892 to 204 reduces the percentage to 22.8 percent of the 1966 figure. So basically there has been a rather considerable change in the provisions through which the Italians become naturalized. The military category had an upward trend pattern until 1970 but has declined fairly consistently to 1978.

Naturalization and Major Occupational Categories

Table 9 allows examination of the change in the occupational structure over the study period. It can be observed that for the professional and technical, managers, sales workers, and clerical workers that while there has been wave-like up and down fluctuations from year to year the overall pattern is one of slight numerical and percentage increases. For the craftsman, operatives, and laborers the numbers and percentages have been relatively stable. The category in which the most change is evident is in the decline of housewives, children, and those with no occupation reported. Since 1971, there has been a consistent percentage decline. Over the whole study period, the drop is 7.4 percent from 38.0 percent to 30.6 percent. The numbers for the farm related are so small that analysis is not made. Suffice it to say that we do not have the thousands of Italian agricultural workers we have had in earlier times.

TABLE 10
Numbers of Italian Citizens Naturalized by Sex
1965-1978

Year	TOTAL	Males	Percentage	Females	Percentage	Differential
1966	10,891	5,625	51.2	5,356	48.8	2.4
1967	10,572	5,107	48.3	5,465	51.7	3.4
1968	9,379	4,689	50.0	4,690	50.0	—
1969	8,773	4,500	51.3	4,273	48.7	2.6
1970	7,892	4,043	51.2	3,849	48.8	2.4
1971	7,637	3,906	52.2	3,731	48.9	2.2
1972	8,375	4,359	52.2	4,005	47.8	4.4
1973	8,092	4,711	52.9	4,191	47.1	5.8
1974	8,898	4,792	53.9	4,106	46.1	7.8
1975	8,798	4,804	54.6	3,994	45.4	9.2
1976	8,696	4,667	53.6	4,029	46.4	7.2
1976tq	2,173	1,209	55.6	4,029	46.4	11.2
1977	7,891	4,366	55.3	3,525	44.7	10.6
1978	8,180	4,433	54.2	3,747	45.8	8.4
	117,147	61,221		55,926		

Source: Table 41. U.S. Immigration and Naturalization Service Annual Reports 1966-1978.

Naturalization by Gender

As one can observe from Table 10 there has been a slight, steady increase over the study period for the male percentage naturalizing and a corollary decline for the females. The sex difference has ranged from basically none in 1968 to a high of 11.2 in the 1976 transitional quarter. Over the thirteen-year study period there have been 5,295 males than females representing 4.5 percent of the total 117,147.

Naturalization by Geographical Area

Again because there was so much data in the master state by state table we have resorted to a summary table. As can be seen from Table 11 the top ten account for 108,827 or 92.9 percent of the total. New York and New Jersey alone account for 54.4 percent of the total. There are three major regional areas: 1) the Northeast including New York, New Jersey, Pennsylvania, Connecticut, Massachusetts, and Maryland; 2) the Midwest including Illinois, Michigan, and Ohio; and 3) California. All the other forty states combine for 8,363 or 7.1 percent which is fewer than Illinois alone.

TABLE 11

Top Ten States Naturalizing Italians to Become United States Citizens 1966-1978

				1966-67 Average	1977-78 Average	Decrease
1.	New York	47,193	40.3	4,247	3,256	22.9
2.	New Jersey	16,514	14.1	1,471	1,327	9.8
3.	Illinois	10,067	8.6	838	625	25.4
4.	Pennsylvania	7,228	6.2	653	439	32.8
5.	Connecticut	7,207	6.1	656	480	26.8
6.	Massachusetts	7,087	6.0	728	504	30.8
7.	California	6,061	5.2	689	375	45.6
8.	Ohio	3,479	3.0	318	221	30.5
9.	Michigan	2,821	2.4	298	121	59.4
10	Maryland	1,170	1.0	122	80	34.4
		108,827	92.9	10,020	7,428	318.4
	All others	8,363	7.1			
	TOTAL	117,190	100.0			

Source: Derived from Table Fifteen.

Naturalizations within Ten Years of Entry

Table 12 was derived to determine whether there had been any changes in the frequency with which Italian immigrants became naturalized within ten years of their entry date. As can be seen in the table that while the number has vacillated from year to year there appears to be three periods. The first from 1966 to 1971 in which each year there was a numerical decline. From 1971 to 1975 there was an upswing but then in 1975 a decline began again which persisted to 1978. In looking at the percentages the pattern has been very unstable but the overall direction has been one of decline. Simply stated in 1966 approximately 68.5 percent of those naturalizing did so within 10 years of their entry date; by 1978 only 50.6 percent were naturalizing within 10 years of their entry date.

TABLE 12

Number of Former Italian Citizens Naturalized within 10 Years of Their Entry to the United States 1966-1978

Year	Number	Percentage of TOTAL Italian Naturalizers
1966	7,460	68.5
1967	7,141	68.1
1968	5,844	62.9
1969	5,352	61.8
1970	4,469	56.8
1971	4,187	55.3
1972	4,960	59.3
1973	5,067	57.2
1974	5,354	60.6
1975	5,419	61.9
1976	4,666	53.8
1976[tq]	1,214	56.0
1977	4,174	52.8
1978	4,130	50.6

Source: Derived from Table 44. U.S. Immigration and Naturalization Service Annual Reports 1966-1978.

Naturalizations by Rural-Urban Settlement

Historically Italian migrants from relatively rural or small town backgrounds settled in large cities in America. The data in Table 13 indicate that the historical trend has continued up through the study period from 1966 to 1978. Only around one percent of Italian immigrants coming to the United States appear to stay in the rural areas. The other 98-99 percent still appear to prefer the cities and usually between 60-65 percent of them prefer cities with populations over 100,000.

TABLE 13

Numbers and Percentages of Naturalizing Italian Aliens by Rural, Urban, Large City Designation 1966-1978

Year	Rural Number	Rural Percent	Urban 2,500-99,999 Number	Urban 2,500-99,999 Percent	Cities 100,000-over Number	Cities 100,000-over Percent	Not Reported	TOTAL
1966	226	2.1	3,762	34.3	6,973	63.5		10,981
1967	186	1.7	3,958	37.4	6,399	60.5		10,572
1968	147	1.6	3,450	36.8	5,767	61.5		9,379
1969	131	1.5	2,882	32.8	5,751	65.6		8,773
1970	143	1.8	2,554	32.4	5,188	65.7		7,892
1971	204	2.7	2,725	35.7	4,683	61.3	25	7,637
1972	120	1.4	3,165	37.8	5,069	60.5	20	8,375
1973	78	.9	3,743	42.0	5,056	56.8	25	8,902
1974	102	1.1	3,589	40.3	5,185	58.3	22	8,898
1975	94	1.1	3,388	38.5	5,302	60.3	14	8,798
1976	90	1.0	3,308	38.0	5,281	60.1	17	8,696
1976tq	27	1.2	754	34.7	1,390	64.0	2	2,173
1977	95	1.2	2,700	34.2	5,056	64.1	40	7,891
1978	87	1.1	2,822	34.5	5,246	64.1	25	8,180

Source: Table 42a. U.S. Immigration and Naturalization Service Annual Reports 1966-1978.

NON-MIGRANT ADMITTANCES

One of the surprising findings of this project was that given the fact that most of the tables have shown declines at almost every turn when we turn to non-migrants admittance there is an about face. The number admitted in 1966 was 95,428 compared to 220,016 in 1978. From 1966 to 1970 there were numerical increases anywhere from nine thousand to twenty-two thousand. Beginning in 1972 the number was usually between 178,000 and 185,000. In 1978, there was an all time high of 220,016. See page 52 for a summary table in rank ordering according to percentage change.

As one can observe from Table 13 the year by year comparisons are erratic but overall many general trends appear and these trends probably are more important than the year by year comparison anyway. Just to highlight the three categories of greatest percentage gain we have commented on the Treaty Traders and Investors, Returning Resident Aliens, and Temporary Visitors for Business.

The group leading the rank ordering percentage change was the Treaty Traders and Investors. Their numerical increase represented a 335.8% gain. Since 1969, the numbers in this category have exceeded 90,000 and in five of the years exceeded over 100,000. In 1978, there was a high of 126,927 reported.

Returning Resident Aliens were the group that had the second largest percentage gain. The difference between the 9,386 in 1966 and the 40,137 in 1978 represented a 327.6 percent gain. While the transition period averaged around 9,000 the 1969 reporting year indicated a sudden surge of Italians moving back after a visit to Italy. By 1972, the number shot up to an excess of 34,000 and has ranged to 42,000 plus since that time.

Third in rank order position in percentage change was the Temporary Visitors for Business category. Over the thirteen year period there was a 197.0 percent increase in those admitted temporarily for business purposes.

TABLE 14
Rank Ordering of Percentage Changes of Nonmigrants: 1966-1978

Returning Resident Aliens	+327.6%
Treaty Traders and Investors	+355.8%
Temporary Visitors for Business	+197.0%
Students	+136.3%
International Representatives	+129.6%
Temporary Visitors for Pleasure	+105.0%
Spouses and Children of Students	+100.0%
Representatives of Foreign Information Media	+ 89.3%
Foreign Government Officials	+ 70.1%
Spouses and Children of Exchange Visitors	+ 63.7%
Exchange Visitors	+ 60.1%
Transit Aliens	+ 47.9%
Temporary Workers and Trainees	+ 20.0%
NATO Officials	+ 4.1%

SUMMARY

In this study we have examined the extent to which changes have occurred relative to Italian migrant admittances, naturalizations, and non-migrant admissions. We have found that from 1966 to 1978 that 1) overall there has been a significant decrease in the number of Italians being admitted as permanent residents and that the population that they represent in relation to the total number of migrant admissions has declined; 2) there has been a shift towards older migrants; 3) overall there are fewer coming in on family preferences; 4) those coming in on occupational preferences are fast diminishing; 5) professional-technical percentage rose slightly, craftsmen stayed relatively constant but there were decreases in laborers, service workers, household workers, and farmworkers; 6) naturalizations have declined; 7) naturalizations for pro-tech, managers, sales workers, and clerical workers, craftsmen, operatives, laborers have been relatively stable and housewives, children, and those with no occupations are down; 8) generally, there are more males than females admitted and naturalized; 9) there are smaller percentages naturalizing within 10 years of entry than a decade ago; 10) Italian migrants continue to stay in large urban areas mostly in the N.E.; and 11) non-migrant admittances have been and continue to be on the rise.

CONCLUSIONS

It is obvious that the reasons for migration flows are complicated and it should be clear that in discussing the data of Italian immigration into the U.S. since Public Law (89-236) is in no way an attempt to suggest it as a simple factor explanation. What we have examined is descriptive, and not analytic from a theoretical standpoint. One of the major limitations here is that as in so many other migration studies the data may be inaccurate, irregular, and lacking in detail.

It is under to what extent decreases shown in this study are consequences of Public Law (89-236), or the general decrease in interest of Italians in emigrating to the U.S. given the fact that so many other opportunities have become available in common market countries in Europe. Salt has pointed out "that Italy is firmly embedded in the European common market's free movement system". Even though numbers of Italians to the U.S. has declined significantly, there have been anywhere between 50,000 and 83,000 Italians migrate within the principal European common market countries in the period 1973 to 1977.

I would suggest that while part of the decline is due to restrictive legislation in the U.S., opportunities 1) closer in proximity to Italy; 2) closer to family; 3) easier and cheaper transportation; and 4) either strong or fairly strong economies in Switzerland, West Germany, England and France have all combined to drain off some Italians who would possibly have been desirous of coming to the U.S. Historically much of the Italian migration to the U.S. was migrant labor rather than immigration per se. Now that the U.S. economy is tight and the demands for foreign labor are down, the migrant labor is moving to where the action is and it is more available in Western Europe. Italian migrant labor is still moving, but not to the U.S. In fact, the numbers that are permitted to come to the U.S. on occupational preferences are almost nonexistent. America, as most other countries, still allows some limited access for the purpose of family reunion, but even it has declined sharply.

Well so much for data and possible causes, the question now is "What will be the implications of such trends?"

Students of migration often use the term migration streams or flows. To

TABLE 15

Italian Nonimmigrants Admitted by Classes Under the Immigration Laws 1966-1978

(Data exclude border crossers, crewmen, and insular travelers. Students and others entering with multiple entry documents are only counted on the first admission.)

Year	1966	1967	1968	1969	1970	1971	1972	1973	1974	1975	1976	1976q	1977	1978
Number admitted	95,428	104,545	131,250	154,618	161,324	151,414	178,005	179,166	184,428	170,628	185,730	71,624	182,666	220,016
Foreign Government Officials	615	704	641	748	840	998	1,355	964	920	899	981	306	836	1,051
Temporary Visitors for Business	9,124	10,187	11,542	13,231	14,276	14,824	14,714	17,572	19,963	18,352	21,686	6,344	25,005	27,099
Temporary Visitors for Pleasure	61,910	70,431	88,465	103,823	103,743	103,400	107,088	97,367	99,331	91,787	101,249	38,747	98,371	126,927
Transit Aliens	11,511	15,345	16,439	13,739	15,266	13,965	15,876	16,546	16,108	16,103	16,777	3,864	15,131	17,028
Treaty Traders and Investors	449	504	656	644	783	878	918	999	1,227	1,258	1,427	663	1,621	1,957
Students	477	525	641	701	715	779	739	652	764	704	688	340	831	1,127
Spouses and Children of Students	30	23	36	45	49	45	68	58	50	71	37	26	52	60
International Representatives	300	395	342	357	419	387	483	431	545	645	633	190	658	689
Temporary Workers and Trainees	434	662	1,391	665	828	803	653	787	681	644	521	425	636	521
Spouses and Children of Temporary Workers and Trainees	NR	NR	NR	NR	4	51	80	84	109	99	120	63	140	117

Representatives of Foreign Information Media	169	160	304	242	322	334	306	269	236	299	334	124	310	320
Exchange Visitors	713	746	808	818	840	821	807	823	927	792	954	465	847	1,142
Spouses and Children of Exchange Visitors	262	266	333	333	329	303	359	292	264	283	359	140	439	429
Fiances (ees) of U.S. Citizens	NR	NR	NR	NR	—	202	195	220	154	148	129	22	123	109
Children of Fiances (ees) of U.S. Citizens	NR	NR	NR	NR	1	6	4	2	6	6	4	—	2	12
Intracompany Transferees	NR	NR	NR	NR	3	79	132	269	311	364	435	313	618	678
Spouses and Children of Intracompany Transferees	NR	NR	NR	NR	—	65	58	116	176	209	289	174	475	563
NATO Officials	48	49	32	44	55	35	53	65	75	77	85	19	41	50
Returning Resident														

continue this type of analogy, I would suggest metaphors in scale such as rivers, streams, and brooklets. Even in the 10 major recipient areas we see decline. In several states we see what were once rivers dwindling to streams and where there were once streams now brooklets or dry washes.

Decreased inflow is going to mean less vital life blood that sustains Italian culture in America. There now, and will continue to be, a decreasing number of native Italian speakers. Needs for Italian language press, both newspapers and magazines, will be fewer and we can expect to see fewer publications. We can expect to see the nature of Italian communities and neighborhoods change. Italian neighborhoods will become less clearly delineated, there will be fewer businesses owned by Italians catering to Italian cultural needs, and there will be fewer Italian first generation members in the churches. The impact of relatively close homogenous political blocs will become weakened. The voice of Italians in America will become a whisper drowned out by the clamour of others. Where neighborhoods are transient we can expect low-income minorities to come in where housing becomes vacated and this has the potential for increasing ethnic conflict. Needs for aid societies will decrease and either they will change their functions or become extinct.

If we project 100 years from now, the approximate number of Italians in America will be miniscule. If the current trends continue and only about 5,000 a year are admitted, the sustaining life blood will be almost nonexistent. Italian ethnicity may become symbolic. Herbert Gans pointed out in his preface to Crispino's book, *The Assimilation of Ethnic Groups*, that "Italian Americans are continuing to assimilate giving up Italian cultural practices, membership in Italian formal and informal groups and ethnocentric attitudes". If these trends are already happening, it is only logical to assume it will be accelerated if the opportunities to further sustain Italianess are diminished.

3

Comments on the Papers by Nampeo R. McKenney, Michael J. Levin, and Alfred J. Tella and by John Seggar

WILLIAM V. D'ANTONIO
Executive Officer
American Sociological Association

THE two preceeding presentations complement each other in several important ways. Together, they help us to understand the present and to project for the next twenty years the changing patterns of Italian ethnic identification in the United States. McKenney *et al.* remind us that the great majority of all those who identify themselves as at least partly Italian in ancestry live along the East Coast between Boston and Philadelphia. Thus, it is not surprising that Seggar reports that 3 out of every 4 Italian immigrants between 1966 and 1978 have located in this same area. While New York state reported the highest proportion responding "Italian" as their single ancestry, Seggar's data project a steady decline in the single ancestry category for New York and other urban areas as the rate of immigration drops off to a mere trickle.

An explanation for the decline in immigration from Italy is found in the new immigration laws of 1966 that base immigration on a preference system rather than a quota system. Given that the "overwhelming majority of Italian ancestry persons are third or subsequent generation" (McKenney *et al.*, p. 7), the family preference system can have only limited impact. Only a small proportion of U.S. Italians have parents, children, wives, husbands, brothers and sisters living in Italy who would be eligible to immigrate under the new law. In the ten years time since the law went into effect, the relatives who were eligible under this law have already immigrated. There is no large reserve pool to follow. As Seeger pointed out, Italian migrant workers are now moving back and forth within the Common Market countries.

These changing migration patterns pose challenges to traditional ways within Italian cities, towns and families. Migrants to the Common Market countries bring back to their villages and cities and to their families, bits and pieces of the new cultures which they have encountered in their migratory activity. And perhaps just as important, the new patterns of business and student contacts with American society not leading to immigration suggest another way that culture elements from American society may be diffusing to Italy. Since this pattern of increasing contact is so new, we can only hypothesize that there will be considerable impact on Italy even as Italy's impact on U.S. cities and families diminishes.

As Seggar makes clear, Italian American ethnicity will receive less and less support for its life blood from the immigration factor. Just as high migration rates help insure the vitality of ethnic neighborhoods, so low rates deprive neighborhoods of this kind of traditional tie with the past. Over the course of 20-25 years, it also may be expected to reduce the political clout that comes with tightly knit ethnic ghetto voting patterns. It will probably also affect at least gradually the small business economy that is built up around ethnicity. And traditional social clubs as well as old neighborhood churches will have difficulty retaining their membership.

But, we may ask, are these patterns of immigration decline followed by changing political, economic and social patterns not also occuring for the Irish, Poles, Greeks, French Canadians and other ethnic groups that came with the Italians in the late 19th and early 20th centuries? Does not the Immigration Reform Law of 1966 also affect their ways and have its noticeable impact there also within the next 20 years? How will it be different for the Hispanics?

The Census data reported by McKenney *et al.* now come into clearer focus. They note that Americans of Italian ancestry are already into their 3rd, 4th and subsequent generations. Unless there is a continuing strong migrant stream, many of the most salient features of Italian American ethnicity may well disappear. One interesting aspect of this phenomenon concerns traditional male-female roles and familial behavior. The traditional patterns are more evident in Italy than even in traditional older Italian neighborhoods in Northeastern cities. High rates of immigration by Italian young males in the past probably have meant continuing strength to these traditional family ways, especially given the fact that there are more women than men in the U.S., and the expectation that these males would be seen as desirable marriage partners.

On the other hand, a high female immigration might have meant a greater probability that these women would have confronted a social setting that would be less restrictive than Italy, and yet full of intergenerational strain. The decline in immigration not only shortens the life span of the ethnic ghetto, but also alters male-female relationships, perhaps even reducing the level of conflict between the sexes, given the rapid move toward educational and occupational assimilation by younger Italian American women.

Some other patterns need to be mentioned. As the migrant stream dries up, the general flow of the U.S. population is away from the East Coast to the South and West. Insofar as Italian migration in significant numbers would have continued to focus on the Northeast, such migration might be dysfunctional for them, as economic opportunities in the Northeastern cities continue to erode. Consider for example, the case of the heavy migration of blacks and Hispanics to these old industrial centers of the Northeast in the past 15 years. These people have come to the cities for jobs at a time when the old industries are collapsing. The industries that were there for our ancestors are no longer there for the newcomers, and they are trapped.

At the same time, it must be acknowledged that in the past 20 years, Italian American and other older ethnic groups have provided a degree of stability to many of these older cities, even as thousands of whites (of all ethnic identities) fled the urban centers. Does the end of the migrant stream (for other Europeans as well as for Italians) mean the further decline of urban white neighborhoods? What will be the social consequences of these changes? It seems fairly clear that the end of large scale immigration from Italy is having both positive and negative consequences for Americans of Italian ancestry as they become more and more tuned in to the ways of the larger American society.

The census data profile provided by McKenney *et al.* suggest that Italian Americans are indeed "making it" to use the colloquial phrase that so aptly describes upward social mobility. In terms of such significant measures as education, occupation and income, it appears that Italian Americans have more than closed the gap with the general U.S. population, a gap that was marked less than a generation ago. The 1980 Census will permit us now to carry out more refined comparisons between ethnic groups than was ever possible before. Thus, we may ask, how do Italian Americans compare on measures of occupation, education and income, with other ethnic groups, when such variables as single and multiple ancestry, and length of time in the United States are controlled for? These studies, which may be expected from McKenney and her colleagues in the coming months and years, will provide the basis for new and better understanding of the process of mobility and assimilation in this society.

Even as the data points up the notable achievement of Italian Americans, they provide solid evidence that there is substance to the widely-held belief in the cohesiveness of the Italian family. Italians have a higher proportion of married couples than are present in the general U.S. population, a lower divorce rate, and a higher proportion of families with children under 18 and both parents present. As expected, these patterns were more evident among single ancestry and older than among multiple ancestry and younger Italian

Americans. As with findings from a variety of earlier studies on many ethnic groups, marrying out leads to lower levels of stability as measured by these variables.

But, again, we may ask, how do Italian American families compare with those of other ancestries when such variables as single/multiple ancestry and length of time and generation in the United States are controlled for? Will we still find evidence of a particular holding power in the Italian American family? Or will some similarities appear among ethnic groups that can be explained by these and other variables?

And if we do find that there is something in the cultural ethos of Italian American life that manifests itself in the family, can we then isolate it? Will it be found in such social support mechanisms as caring, love, concern for the others, expressive signs of affection? Or will it be found in social control mechanisms that tie back to traditional ways: duty, obligation, authority, a highly particularistic collectivism? Evidence from our own experiences would suggest that it is some mix of the two, toegether with a more traditional role for women. In the context of a changing American society dominated by values of equality, freedom and achievement opportunities for men and women, what may be happening to these support/control mechanisms?

The data reported here and elsewhere show clearly now that Italian Americans have adapted well to the values and structures of American public life, while still retaining ways within the private sphere of the family that are warm and personally rewarding. An important challenge for future research is whether this pattern of public achievement and familial love and affection can serve as a model for the larger society.

4

Italian Americans: Media Perceptions

Stephen S. Hall

Every writer approaches the task of authorship with decisions of perfection. Unfortunately, an attitude like this leaves us open to one of two distressing fates. We can fail miserably, or we can fail in a slightly more admirable fashion. As a writer, I am constantly reminded of this, and constantly grateful for it too. But rarely have I been reminded of it in so vivid a fashion as last May when my article about Italian Americans appeared in the *New York Times Sunday Magazine*.

To start with, Phil Rizzuto, the New York Yankees baseball announcer, complained on the air—possibly to millions, on the basis of the calls I got—that he had not been mentioned in the article. One thing led to another and pretty soon the governor of New York State wrote Rizzuto a letter commiserating about this ghastly omission. That was read on the air during another broadcast.

Meanwhile, some folks in Washington felt a prominent local citizen had been unfairly omitted, and that prompted some wry comments in the local press. And, not surprisingly, a few complaints drifted in from other zip codes. But just to show that this isn't merely another tale about Italians complaining, I even caught a little heat from a cousin on my father's English-Scotch-Irish-German side—which is to say the non-Italian side—of the family. She pointed to the line that identified me as the grandson of Italian immigrants, looked at me accusingly, and demanded, "What about our side of the family?" When you can't even please your own family, that's failing miserably.

Now that I've dispensed with everyone else's perception of the media, I can turn the tables and proceed with the topic of my talk today, which is "Italian Americans: Media Perceptions". I am taking journalistic license with that title. I will proceed somewhat informally, and you will hear little that would require a footnote. I would simply like to make a few observations and describe my own experiences about life on what might be described as that frayed borderline where the media meets its subjects, be they Italian Americans or Hollywood celebrities or bureaucrats in Washington. I do this not with the presumption that my experiences are universally applicable. Rather, I offer them as pieces of a larger puzzle with the hope that they will intersect with someone else's impressions so our understanding of ourselves, and of these complex relationships, becomes clearer.

Our mutual point of reference is probably the aforementioned article in the *New York Times Magazine* (and I should mention at this point that I am a free-lance writer and am not now, nor have I ever been, employed by the *New York Times*). I can honestly say that, to this day, I have mixed emotions about the piece. The very fact that a story about Italian Americans appeared on the cover of what many people regard as the most influential and prestigious magazine in the country is, of course, an important moment in the recognition and acceptance of Italians in this country. Even though, I feel obliged to add, two pieces fairly similar in tone and thrust by Mario Puzo and Richard Gambino have appeared in that same magazine within the past 15 years.

One official active in Italian American affairs called it "a breakthrough piece". This, too, leaves me with mixed emotions. I am glad the article might be regarded as such, but I am a little troubled by the implication that so much power—and, more specifically, the power to approve—accretes to a single publication. The messenger—*The Times*, that is—is clearly more important than the message conveyed. I say that because I know that hardly a sentence in that story, hardly a fact, hardly an opinion or interpretation, had not been published or stated before. There was nothing terribly new or ground-breaking in the material (except perhaps that it was all collected under one roof, so to speak), and I suspect that is a fact much known to many people here in this audience today who invisibly lent a hand to the author with their insights and writings and indeed their life-work.

But, in journalism, as in other endeavors, timing is crucial. And in a certain sense, the timing has never been better than now for this type of article. Italian American values probably haven't changed dramatically in the past five years—or in the past fifteen years, for that matter—but the stature and visibility of the people who embody those values surely has. From the viewpoint of a writer, that is an important distinction, because values and ideas are best communicated to a general audience through respected individuals well-known to the public.

Just consider what a difference a few years makes. Five years ago, Mario Cuomo was not governor of New York State. Five years ago, Pete Domenici was not perceived as a leading figure on Capitol Hill, as he is today. Five years ago, Geraldine Ferraro was not touted as a potential vice-presidential candidate. Five years ago, things Italian—by which I mean everything from pasta to footwear to fashion—were popular, but I do not believe they were embraced with the same cultural affection and enthusiasm with which they are today. And five years ago, you did not see television commercials—which I believe are the single most reliable barometer of socially acceptable mainstream American images—showing Lee Iacocca as a symbol of competence and trustworthiness. Nothing is exactly different, yet the way America perceives Italian Americans—in politics and business as well as through advertisements—is now a whole new ballgame.

On the other hand, there were shortcomings in the article that I'd like to address as well. A few points will serve to illustrate problems that will always crop up in this business. They tend to be subtle and more philosophical than substantial, perhaps, but I believe they are important and worth mentioning.

Of all my regrets, probably the greatest regards the homogeneity with which Italian Americans were portrayed as a group. I quickly learned in my research that the term "Italian American" is a kind of semantic quicksand: he who is not careful will soon be up to his eyebrows in erroneous assumptions. Although many scholars warn against a monolithic interpretation of this or any other ethnic group, I know that magazine editors—and I was one myself—feel comfort and security when one explanation, like one size, fits all. It's not that we cannot handle ambiguity; it's just that we, like everyone else, would prefer not to. Complexity, subtle differences, contradictory evidence—these are all untidy concepts, particularly when you are dealing with the limited space of a print article or the even greater restraints of a broadcast report. It is always said that ambiguity confuses the reader, but sometimes we grievously underestimate the intelligence of the reader, too.

The fact of the matter is: we love to generalize. We love to stereotype. We love to reach conclusions. These are not media characteristics; these are human characteristics. These urges do not necessarily derive from ignorance or bias, but also from a need to process information as rapidly as possible in a world where there is already too much information and too little time to assimilate it.

We are all looking for shortcuts. And when I say "we", I include receivers of information as well as purveyors, because I believe there is a compact, a relationship, between writer and reader. If I were talking about Eskimos today, the chances are you would not want to know all the ways they are different from one another, but rather all the ways they are alike—in short, what makes them Eskimos.

But as I look back on it, the article in the *Times* made Italian Americans seem completely unique to themselves as an ethnic group, which probably isn't true, and utterly like one another within the group, which quite clearly is not the case. An immigrant from Lucca who settled in San Francisco in 1850 was worlds apart in experience and world view from an immigrant from Campobasso, like my grandfather, who arrived in America in 1911 and ultimately settled in Cleveland. To call them both Italian Americans is a little like capturing a duck and hummingbird in the same net and describing both of them as birds. Technically it's correct, but it's a distinction of no particular meaning or significance.

I prefer to think that Italian Americans will have really "arrived" when they are perceived by the media and the rest of the citizenry—and by themselves as well—not as a monolithic ethnic entity, not as "us" in an Us-and-Them social equation, but rather as a group of uniquely varied people who share certain (though often tenuous) ancestral similarities.

By doing that, we will perceive each person as an individual first and foremost, whose ethnic background is a character-shaping asset rather than a cultural straitjacket implying all sorts of generalized—and typically in-accurate—traits. This is the flip side of using those shortcuts that I mentioned before: they can create damaging and specious assumptions about the general character of an ethnic group.

This leads me, by circuitous route, to the Mafia, for this is the most pervasive stereotype weighing down on the Italians. If I had had my druthers—in a thoroughly unpragmatic and philosophical sense, I might add—I would not even have mentioned the Mafia in my article. Not because the Mafia isn't real and not because it isn't important. Simply because the point has been belabored so many times before, about so minor a segment of the Italian American community, that I thought it might be rather novel to talk about Italian Americans without this familiar shadow falling across the page.

That was wishful thinking on my part, of course. The sad point is that the Mafia issue has been trotted out so many times in the past that its absence now in any article about Italian Americans is most conspicuous. I do not feel equipped to comment on the historical legitimacy of those who argue that the media treatment of the Mafia—and by extension, Italian Americans—has been unjustified and unreasonably cruel, although there is significant and important evidence to support this view.

But I do know this: the connection is so firmly established in the popular imagination, and in the minds of people who bring information into our homes, that it is virtually impossible to discuss the Italian American ethos, at least with any claim to comprehensiveness, without referring to the problem of the Mafia. Not to do so, at least now, constitutes the kind of risk to credibility that most journalists are unwilling to take.

These attitudes have taken their toll. We have all become a little precon-ditioned to the Mafia issue, predisposed to compute that equation in our minds that says organized crime equals Italian Americans. It is a self-perpetuating fallacy. I recall an occasion when an editor with whom I was working insisted that organized crime was controlled by Italian Americans. When I expressed skepticism about this assertion, this is the answer I got:

"Oh, you know, whenever you see a story in the paper, the names are always Italian". This clearly is not a scientific method.

The fact is, we've trained ourselves to find what we expect to find. It takes rigorous intellectual integrity to resist these urges. Integrity is a word that looks good on paper, but it is an enormously difficult thing to maintain in the imperfect world of a newsroom, where noise and work pressures and space limitations and deadlines all conspire to usurp it. Similarly, the casual newspaper reader is not accustomed to questioning information—only absorbing it. And yet any astute reader should be able to conclude that organized crime, as has been stated before, is an equal opportunity employer, that Italian Americans hardly monopolize this world.

Perhaps the American perception of crime will change, too. Writers use words like "mob" and "syndicate" and "Cosa Nostra"—all with their sinister resonance and ring of threat and mystery—when we describe drug rings and prostitution rings and protection rackets. It's interesting, however, that when the president of American Airlines calls up the president of Braniff, as recently occurred, and tries to talk him into setting higher tariffs, it is described—both in court papers and in newspapers—as something called "collusive monopolization", which is a term designed to put everyone to sleep.

I do not mean to suggest that attempted price fixing—and this case did not result in conviction—represents the same degree of activity as drug dealing, for example. But I do think it is illustrative of how the selection of one or two words can dramatically change the tone and impact of a news report. Considering the fact that a magazine article may run anywhere from 2,000 to 8,000 words in length, that is a lot of words to choose, a lot of decisions to make. One adjective may seem like a mere pebble dropping into the lake, but when you consider that the ripples it makes can travel right on into posterity, it often seems like an awesome amount of responsibilty for a single individual. And yet greater responsibility, and greater sensitivity, is precisely what is needed.

As more writers and broadcasters take a critical position on the Mafia question and other issues regarding Italian Americans, the likelier it is that public perceptions on these points will change. Not by a lot, and not quickly—perceptions like that are slow to die, and it will take generations for such biases to be erased. But the change can be accelerated by judicious activity.

It has been my experience that, until recently, Italian Americans have not been particularly united nor particularly vigorous in pressing their case about perceived mistreatment. Complaining doesn't mean you get your way: more often it means you get your proverbial half a loaf. But it is also my experience that the squeaky wheel gets the oil. So I'll conclude with a brief bit of advice: if Italian Americans believe they are being unfairly portrayed in the media, it's about time they started getting seriously noisy about it. They might not be right, but they will be entering a dialogue that may help to desensitize them from the kind of sensitivity that Mr. Talese described, and that cannot be other than a healthy thing.

5

Italian Americans and the Media: An Agenda for a More Positive Image

JOSEPH GIORDANO
*Director, Center on Ethnicity, Human Behavior and Communications,
The American Jewish Committee*

BACKGROUND

WHEN I was an adolescent in the 1950s, my mother, sister and I glued ourselves to our seven-inch TV screen to see "Father Knows Best". Every week, we watched the Andersons, a white, Anglo-Saxon, surburban middle-class family, work out their many problems so very rationally.

While I felt a certain attraction to them, I also felt somewhat uneasy and frustrated with this model American family. The Andersons, and that other popular TV family, Ozzie and Harriet Nelson, bore little resemblence to what I was experiencing in my urban, Italian American, working-class home. Those people never fought or raised their voices. The fathers, Robert Young and Ozzie Nelson, handled every problem calmly and reasonably. I remember really disliking in particular, the teenage Bud Anderson.

What was I so attracted to? Did my family really want to be like the Andersons or the Nelsons? Were we in some way denying our own heritage and way of life? Not really. It was not denial, but tension. For Italian Americans, as well as members of other ethnic groups, there was and is a constant tug between the traditions we learn as we grow up and the dominant values of the larger society.

As a transmitter of society's values, the mass media have a tremendous impact on the shaping of our personal and group identities. Radio, TV, films and the print media can convey the rich textures of pluralistic society, or they can directly or indirectly (by omission) distort our perceptions of other ethnic groups and reinforce our defensiveness and ambivalence about our own.

Unfortunately, distortion of images of American ethnic groups by the mass media, particularly television and the movies, has a long history. Italians are depicted as lovable buffoons, blacks as criminals, Chinese as inscrutable, Mexicans as bandits, Jews as shylocks, and so on. While some of these stereotypes are not so prevalent as they once were, they are still all too often with us, as new stereotypes replace the older ones.

Some ethnic groups—blacks, Hispanics, native Americans and Asian—Americans—are generally ignored in films; and when they are included, they generally are treated as "faceless", reduced to a few customary ethnic or racial stereotypes.[1] They have fared equally poorly on television. According to "Television and Behavior", a 1982 National Institute of Mental Health report, they were cast in very few shows, mostly in situation comedies. In commercial programming designed for children, only 3.7 percent of all characters were black, 3.1 percent were Hispanic, 0.8 percent Asian—and exactly one American Indian appeared at all, according to a 1981 study by Professor F. Earle Barcus of Boston University. While 57.5 percent of characters with speaking parts were white, 33.8 percent were animals, robots or other non-humans. When an animal has a better chance than a black for a speaking role, Barcus concluded, it's time to take a closer look at what the children are watching[2] on TV.

More than any other communications medium, television plays a key role in providing information and entertainment. It shows us worlds we otherwise seldom see, determines which elements of those worlds to focus on, and presents them to us in a "good" or "bad" light. TV, in short, helps shape what we know, what we believe, and what we feel about the world.

The statistics say that 98 percent of American households have at least one television set, and that most children under 5 spend at least 23½ hours per week watching it. Older children watch an average of 30 hours per week and, by age 20, will have seen no fewer than one million commercials (In how many will an Italian American mother have screamed "Mangia!" as she

---

[1] See *Television and Behavior*, 1982 National Institute of Mental Health Report, Washington, DC; Fighting TV Stereotypes Action for Children's Television, Newtonville, Mass. 1983; *Minorities in the Media*, by Arthur Unger in a two part series, *The Christian Science Monitor*, May 9, 10, 1983; U.S. Commission on Civil Rights, *Window Dressing in the Set: An Update*, U.S.G. Printing Office, Washington, DC, Jan. 1979; testimony by Richard Gambino, *Civil Rights Issues of Euro-Ethnic Americans in the United States: Opportunities and Challenges*, Commission on Civil Rights, Chicago, Ill., December 3, 1979; *The Kaleidoscopic Lens: How Hollywood Views Ethnic Groups*, edited by Randall M. Miller, Ozer Publisher, Englewood, NJ., 1980; "What TV Teaches Children", Families Column by Joseph Giordano in *Attenzione Magazine*, December 1981.

[2] Action for Children's Television, *op. cit.*

shoves more pasta in front of her husband and children?). By the time a child has finished high school, he or she will have spent about 15,000 hours facing the tube, compared with 1,200 in a classroom. There are many children who spend more time staring at TV than in any other activity except sleeping.[3]

Yet TV simply does not reflect the variety of American life, although an essential part of being an American is to understand all aspects of the society, to learn to tolerate and appreciate differences. When individuals do not come into regular contact with members of other ethnic or racial groups, TV can contribute signficantly either to intergroup understanding or to prejudice.

TV is important also in shaping young people's self-image. I have observed in my clinical practice that many school age Italian Americans see themselves as "The Fonz," the leather-jacketed, rather "greasy", if likeable, star (Franchine, *Hertitage*, Oct. 1982; Steiner, *The Milwaukee Journal*, April 20, 1983). And for children and adults, negative stereotypes of Italian Americans as criminals,[4] dumb or racist have a heavy impact on our self-esteem.[5]

Study after study undertaken by the Center on Ethnicity, Human Behavior and Communications and other organizations reveals how crucial it is to mental health to feel at home with one's personal ethnic identity. Conversely, distorted and negative images of ethnic identity from the school system, the media or other sources can lead to self-doubt or feelings of inferiority — even, in some cases, to self-hatred or discrimination and aggressive behavior against other groups.[6]

These images were described by Richard Gambino, chairperson of the Italian Studies program at Queens College, in testimony to the United States Commission on Civil Rights regarding the impact of the media on Euro-ethnic Americans:

> Members of ethnic groups serve as conventional shorthand ways to evoke such qualities as criminality, stupidity, vengeance, anti-intellectualism, clannishness, working class primitivism, racism, over-sexuality, corruption, right-wing neofascism, and social and cultural backwardness.[7]

[3] *Ibid.*

[4] The FBI reports that 2 of every 10,000 Italian Americans are involved in organized crime.

[5] In conducting ethnotherapy groups I have observed that upwardly mobile Italian Americans will often internalize a definition of themselves by majority group standards. The result is a greater ambivalence about their own sense of Italian identity.

[6] The Center has for the past ten years been conducting studies on the relationship of ethnicity to self-esteem. See Center's *Jewish Identity and Self-Esteem: Healing Wounds Through Ethnotherapy* (1980) by Judith Weinstein Klein; *Ethnicity and Mental Health* (1973) by Joseph Giordano; *Ethno-Cultural Factors in Mental Health* (1978) by Joseph Giordano and Grace Pineiro Giordano; *Ethnicity and Family Therapy*, by McGoldrick, Pearce and Giordano, Guilford Press, New York, 1983; "The Ethnic Roots of Parenting" by Betty Washington *Chicago Sun Times*, August 8, 1983.

[7] Gambino, *op. cit.*

Italian Americans in particular have come to represent the darker and "lower" sides of American society. In a disproportionate number of cases, men are portrayed as criminals; the "good guys" often held low-income, low-status jobs; even likeable, successful Italian Americans are frequently portrayed as "lightweights" not to be taken seriously. And the Italian American woman, when shown at all, "lacks intelligence, is a slave to her household.... She somehow has passed on the same apron to her daughter and granddaughter so that we are still seeing the spaghetti sauce commercials today."[8]

In a comprehensive, well-documented study of 263 television episodes, Dr. Linda Lichter and Dr. Robert Lichter demonstrated that negative portrayals of Italian Americans outnumbered the positive two to one. This general trend held on all three major networks, in both dramas and comedies, and among stars and minor characters alike. In many episodes, an Italian American could not speak proper English; or held a low-status job, and one in six engaged in criminal activity. Only one in six was a woman (Lichter and Lichter, 1982).

In films, the Italian American has been a foil to the rugged, incorruptible Americanized hero; from Rico in *Little Caesar* to Don Vito Corleone in *The Godfather* (Golden, 1980) from the character "Luigi" on radio (and later TV) to "The Fonz" and "Laverne and Shirley" on television today, the stereotypes persist.

Recently, the stereotypical Italian American individual has sometimes given way to the stereotypical family, particularly in films. *The Godfather*, *Mean Streets*, *Rocky I* and *II*, *A Woman Under the Influence*, *Blood Brothers* and *Raging Bull* all have scenes in which men beat their wives, while the women are usually passive victims, dependent on men and otherwise not in control of their lives. The dominant message is that we deal with the world in a primitive way, express our frustrations in aggressive physical and sexual behavior. While some of these pictures are well-made and sometimes accurately capture certain aspects of our lives, they also legitimize and reinforce negative characterizations of supposed Italian American "types"; worse, they contribute to second- and third-rate imitations.

Stereotypes of Italian Americans are promulgated even by some of the country's leading newspapers and periodicals. For example, when Angelo Bartlett Giamatti was inaugurated as President of Yale University, the May 1, 1978 *Washington Post* described him thus:

> There certainly was something different about...Giamatti. He was flip, funny, iconoclastic... And he was, well, ethnic... With his dedicated public relations man, Stanley Fink, at his side, briefcase in hand, one could almost close one's eyes and hear him addressed as 'Don Giamatti'.

The flippant, patronizing stereotype implies that an Italian is not to be

---

[8] *Ibid.*

taken seriously—even when he becomes President of one of the most prestigious universities in the United States, or a prince of the Church. For when Joseph Bernardin was named Archbishop of Chicago, the Religion Editor of the *Sun Times* wrote: "Despite his Italian ancestry, he impresses many people as being somewhat reserved and self-contained".

In 1982, after Mario Cuomo won a gubernatorial primary over Ed Koch in New York City, a well-known broadcast reporter asked him if he planned to conduct a "vendetta" against the Mayor or then-Governor Carey, and whether he planned to wield a "stiletto" against his other political adversaries.

When such stereotypes are disseminated on radio or television, for instance, when Harry Reasoner of CBS' "Sixty Minutes" remarked, during a 1981 episode, that Sicilians have a "fascination with death and violence",—they are heard by millions. In newsprint, they would reach tens of thousands.

These stereotypes may also increase, or at least reinforce discrimination against Italian Americans in the business world. Although the education and income levels of Italian Americans have risen sharply in the past decade, the discrimination persists. According to a recent study by the Sons of Italy, of the chief executive officers and broad members of the 800 largest American corporations, only 3.2 percent are Italian Americans.[9] It must be remembered, however, that negative portrayals of ourselves in the mass media [has] to do with their general nature and, in particular, with the problem of its portrayal of all ethnic groups. In a 1982 lecture, Neil Postman, a professor of Media Arts and Sciences at New York University, discussed some of the inherent limitations of television:

> If it finds something of interest in an ethnic group—a food, a way of speaking, a point of view—it will instantly nationalize it into something resembling a peanut butter and jelly sandwich, in order to market it to a larger audience.[10]

Simplistic and negative stereotypes of ethnic groups are widely viewed as more "salable". At an April, 1983 conference on "Italian Americans and the Media", scriptwriter Philip DeFranco remarked:

> It is very painful to write a script on an Italian American family and to have some executive tell you that your show won't sell because it doesn't have blood, sex and violence... The negative material sells and it is very difficult to survive without selling out to the negative.[11]

Part of the reason, DeFranco went on to explain, is a technical limitation—

[9] *Survey of Forbes 800 Corporations*, Order of the Sons of Italy, Sept. 1982.

[10] Speech at *Conference Hard Times and Beyond: New Roles for Ethnic Leaders in School-Community Relations* sponsored by the Illinois Consultation on Ethnicity in Education, Chicago, June 4, 1982.

[11] Speech at *Italian Americans and the Media: Building a Positive Image*, sponsored by the Commission for Social Justice, Order of the Sons of Italy in America, and the National Italian American Foundation, Sheraton Center, New York City, April 9, 1983.

a built-in "shorthand" of TV and film, in which the...

> whole evolution of characters comes about because images... must be presented very fast. What tends to happen is that messages are telegraphed through compressed information and images,[12]

leaving too little room for historical background, social context, character development or historical nuance.

As a national medium, television in particular has little "feel" for ethnic culture; indeed the Heritage News Service's Media Panel concluded in a March, 1981 meeting that, media administrators usually do not think ethnicity is newsworthy.[13] They tend to think it is merely a transitional form of identity which precedes "Americanization", or perhaps does not matter at all to individual or group behavior. When ethnic news is considered uninteresting, it is sometimes called "parochial" or even "divisive"; emphasis on it is seen as a danger, a potential cause of America "balkanization".

When allusions to ethnicity do appear in the media, they are often very crude. TV entertainers in particular can be incredibly blind to ethnic sensitivities as they reach for the widest possible audience. For example, comedian Steve Allen permitted himself a carload of "Polack" jokes on the supposedly liberal and sophisticated Dick Cavett show several years ago. And TV executives can "stonewall" criticism of such ethnic slurs with legalisms. When TV critic Jean Bergatini Grillo complained to one of them about the one-dimensional portrayal of Italian Americans in a show, the official dismissed the charge, noting that the TV Code's "fairness doctrine" does not apply to entertainment programs.[14]

A partial reason for Italian Americana particular problems with the TV and film industries is their underrepresentation among professionals in these areas. They are also behind other groups—blacks, Jews and Hispanics come to mind—who have been lobbying and working with the media for some years. Finally, we have not worked enough with Italian American executives, writers, directors, producers, and actors already employed by the media. These people should be helped to appreciate how ethnic traditions in general, and "Italianism" in particular, continue to exert strong influences on family life, that they are a source of cohesiveness, and traditional contrast to many contemporary disentegrating forces. Understanding their tradition, and how it is expressed in the lives of second-, third- and fourth-generation individuals, is in the interest of Italian American media professionals, for it can provide them with broader repertoire of story ideas and authentic characters.

---

[12] *Ibid.*

[13] Consultation on *Ethnic Groups and the Media* sponsored by the Heritage News Service in Chicago, March, 1981.

[14] Remarks at Italian Americans and the Media Conference, *op.cit.*

WHAT HAS BEEN DONE

To date, the Italian American community has not devised a coherent strategy for dealing with the mass media. At times, we have protested portrayals of us as gangsters and other "heavies" through letters, newspaper ads, even demonstrations in front of studios. Carlos Cortez has written that Italian Americans as portrayed by Hollywood,

> were in the worst shape of any group. The protests have done a lot to change that. And there is always the possibility that once the pressure is off, they will be back on the hit list.[15]

Unfortunately, our pressure on the media has too often been *ad hoc*, a specific response to a specific offense, with little or no attempt to encourage positive images. In 1982, a prominent group including Congressman Mario Biaggi, then-Lieutenant Governor Mario Cuomo of New York, and John Volpe, former Governor of Massachusetts, and others met with CBS President William Leonard and *60 Minutes* producer Don Hewitt. They had come to protest a segment entitled "Welcome to Palermo", which projected Italian Americans of Sicilian ancestry as "fascinated by death and violence". The meeting, which was initiated by and included members of the Commission for Social Justice (CSJ) of the Sons of Italy, elicited an apology from the network, but had no strategy to encourage CBS to develop more positive programming.[16]

The Italian American community has "done its homework" in documenting the limited, usually negative, portrayal of our community in the media. But our communal leaders have only recently begun to discuss such matters with heads of television production companies. In late 1982, a small group headed by Ronald P. Quartararo, and Mat Nizza of CSJ, met in Los Angeles with the heads of Columbia TV, Twentieth Century Fox, Embassy Productions (Norman Lear's company) and four other producers[17] to discuss objections to specific characters and programs and — as important if not more so — make suggestions for developing new, more positive portrayals in existing shows, and for new characters and programs altogether.

Lea Stalmaster, Senior Vice-President of Programs at Twentieth Century Fox Television, told the CSJ delegation: "We have been visited by every group — Mexicans, blacks and others. Even the Arabs came in because they felt they were being stereotyped. Your group we never heard from, and we were wondering when you were coming in." On the other hand, Van Gordon

---

[15] *Ibid.*

[16] During this, my first meeting with the media on these issues I thought we needed to go beyond the "complaining stage" if we were to make a significant impact on changing negative stereotypes. Recorded minutes of the meeting January 6, 1982.

[17] The group also included Phil DeFranco of Los Angeles and myself.

Sauter, President of CBS-TV News, took the initiative for continuing dialogues with CSJ.

The Italian American community, has only begun to make contacts and create projects for generating more positive images in the media. At a CSJ meeting with two executives from the Aaron Spelling production, one of them promised to ask Gary Marshall, producer of "Happy Days" to do an episode in which "The Fonz" discovers his "roots". The Writers, Directors, Producers CAUCUS[18] offered to turn over one of its meetings to a discussion of Italian American life today and hoped for an ongoing relationship with community representatives. These experiences demonstrate the advantage of "cultivating" media professionals, learning about their concerns and bringing our own to their attention, of having some "input" into future programming, rather than just protesting offensive shows after they have been aired.

WHAT NEEDS TO BE DONE

To encourage the TV and film industries to present three-dimensional, positive images of Italian Americans, the community needs to: 1) better nurture its own creative resources, more generously and effectively; 2) create one or more instruments for regular meetings with media profesionals; and 3) work with other ethnic groups in monitoring and interacting with the mass media.

NURTURING ITALIAN AMERICAN CREATIVE RESOURCES

One reason why portrayals of Italian Americans on television and in the movies leave so much to be desired is that the community has not done enough to help our own scriptwriters represent our particular sensibility. One writer, John Furia, has expressed that sensibility in these terms:

> I have a certain volatility which I prefer to call energy. I have a powerful sense of family. Honor is important to me. I have a sense of the immigrant experience in that I want to make it myself in our society and I respect others who do the same. I was taught the great importance of courtesy, custom and tradition. I believe I have inherited that strange, and uniquely Italian, combination of spirituality and peasant toughness. Another unique combination is a sensibility and a tough determination in dealing with others.[19]

The black community has had its *Roots* on TV, the Jews a movie on *The Chosen*. We ought to be developing TV specials or films from such books as Richard Gambino's superb history, *Blood of My Blood*, Fred Mustard Stewart's *Century*, a moving saga of an Italian American family; Helen

---

[18] The members of the CAUCUS produced about 98 percent of what appears on television.

[19] Remarks at Conference on Italian Americans and the Media, *op. cit.*

Barolini's *Umbertina*, or Mario Puzo's *Fortunate Pilgrim* and there are others. To encourage these adaptations, we might follow Mico Dicastro's suggestion to establish a clearinghouse of information on our history and the positive aspects of our identity. The community also should take up his call for a general fund to support Italian American filmmakers and other artists, as well as Jean Bergentini Brillo's proposal that our ethnic community offer "substantial cash prizes" for short stories, novels, plays, and screenplays that most vividly portray our experience.

WORKING WITH THE MEDIA

As the CSJ delegation learned from its meeting with TV producers in late 1982, the media professionals are generally receptive to criticism and eager to hear about new approaches and ideas. One letter with a positive new suggestion, the group was told, is worth 50 responses to a program already aired.

What that means is that Italian Americans should work with the media as a special interest rather than as a pressure group. During the April, 1983 conference on Italian Americans and the Media Van Gordon Sauter explained the difference between the two approaches:

> A pressure group... seeks to alter program and news content so that they conform to the group's own set of beliefs, and to eliminate that kind of programming that is either contrary to or is offensive to the group's beliefs. A special interest group, on the other hand, does not attempt to alter programming or news in the form of suppressing, but rather to get its beliefs included in the programming or news inventory.[20]

To be an effective special interest group, we need an Italian American Media Institute, whose function would be to:

- form a network of prominent Italian Americans in media who will lend their expertise to bridging the concerns of the industry and of their ethnic community;

- sponsor research on, and monitor, the media's portrayal of the community on both the national and local levels;

- enter into periodic dialogues with media professionals on how to create authentic and entertaining portrayals of the Italian American experience;

- develop training seminars for professionals in the print, TV and film industries and prepare a manual on "do's and don'ts" for portraying our culture and concerns;

- conduct workshops for local Italian American groups on the best

[20] *Ibid.*

methods for reducing negative stereotypes and promoting positive images;

- organize a clearinghouse of information on Italian history, the Italian language and dialects, and program ideas for development by creative individuals might develop further;
- sponsor scholarships, grants and prizes to Italian American authors' quality works based on ethnic experiences;
- disseminate information on the Italian American experience through newsletters, newspapers and magazines, radio and TV programs and by other means; and
- join coalitions with other ethnic organizations concerned about authentic portrayals of their experience.

An Italian American Media Institute could not, of course, eliminate overnight all the negative or simplistic stereotypes of Italian Americans. A more realistic goal, as Irving Levine, Director of National Affairs for the American Jewish Committee, has pointed out, would be to make sure there is at least one hour of quality programming on our ethnic groups for every two hours of "schlock". In any case the creation of an Italian American special interest group to work with mass media professionals is long overdue.

COOPERATION WITH OTHER ETHNIC GROUPS

In a 1981 column, Philip C. Franchine, Editor of Heritage News Service, discussed two reasons why ethnic stories in general are under-covered in news reporting;

> Ethnics often fail to court media people with professional public relations methods. They don't bombard them with detailed, informative releases and aren't consistently available on deadline. They may tell their stories in narrow or parochial terms, not in "unifying" terms that explain how their activities benefit the rest of society.

> Reporters, like other professionals, are trained to deal with formal systems, on family, ethnic, religious, or neighborhood-based voluntary groups. Lacking training in this area, reporters may not link individual or group behavior to ethnicity. They may see ethnicity as a transitional stage through which one passes on the way to becoming fully "American". They see it as divisive and "un-American" (Franchine, *Chicago Tribune*, April 27, 1981).

It follows, then, that the Italian American community should work with other ethnic groups to encourage the media to provide more and better portrayals of each of them, and to show their common concerns. Such a coalition might "keep the media on their toes when they deal with ethnic stereotypes", in the words of a representative from the Greek American community at the April 1983 conference. It could sponsor research, conferences and publications on neglected aspects of our heritages, such as the role of women immigrants in making new lives in America, and of women writers and artists in recording our peoples' experiences.

Right now, a coalition could support the Biaggi Bill (H.R. 3015, 98th Congress), which calls for an Office of Ethnic Affairs within the Federal Communications Commission (FCC). The record shows that in the first quarter of 1983 alone, FCC received more than 22,000 complaints about radio and television broadcasts compared with 38,000 in all of 1982, and many of these concerned portrayals of ethnic and racial groups. The Office Biaggi proposes would hear complaints and serve as an information clearinghouse to carry out an education program to encourage better media treatment of ethnic groups and racial minorities, and conduct an annual conference designed to focus public attention on the way they are depicted on radio and TV.

The TV, radio and film industries are, respectively, over 30, 60 and 80 years old, so the problem of how Italian Americans are "seen" is far from new. As the 21st century rapidly approaches, we must at last devise a sophisticated, sustained strategy for dealing with the mass media. The tripartite approach suggested here—developing our own creative resources, building a community mechanism for interaction with media professionals, and entering coalitions with other groups—seems to me the best, in fact, the only way to go.

6

Italian Americans
In Contemporary America

HUMBERT S. NELLI
University of Kentucky

DURING the decades since the end of World War II more than 500,000 Italian immigrants have entered the United States. Nearly one-half (228,000) came in the decade following the passage of the 1965 immigration law, which gave all nations the same access to an overall quota but assigned priority status to immediate relatives of American citizens and resident aliens as well as for professional and skilled workers in short supply among the native population. The 1980 United States Census counted over twelve million Americans of Italian extraction and found them in every state in the Union, although almost 70 percent still resided in the heavily industrialized and urban Northeast.

Italian immigrants and their offspring no longer necessarily live in central city districts, but they still tend to live in or around major cities. In 1970 nearly 2.3 million first and second generation Italian Americans resided in only twelve metropolitan areas; one million of these lived in the New York Metropolitan area, the rest in Boston, Providence, Buffalo, Rochester, Philadelphia, Pittsburgh, Cleveland, Detroit, Chicago, San Francisco-Oakland, and Los Angeles-Long Beach (Louisville *Courier-Journal*, June 5, 1983; U.S. Census of Population, 1970).

Italian Americans have shared fully in the general prosperity the nation has enjoyed since World War II. Movement out of the ethnic districts slowed during the 1930s because of the depression and during the 1940s because of wartime housing shortages, but by the 1950s the process had accelerated, and the formerly heavy concentrations of Italians in immigrant neighborhoods has thinned. Thus although Chicago's Near West Side community continues in existence, its population is greatly reduced. The district held an Italian immigrant population of 12,955 in 1920; the same area contained a combined total of first and second generation Italians of 5,140 in 1960, and only 1,806 ten years later. In Boston's Italian district, the North End, the population decreased by 45.8 percent between 1950 and 1960, and by 40 percent in the next ten years. The decline, according to Spencer DiScala, is attributable "to younger people and couples moving out of the area". The general tendency has been "for more established persons to move out and for newer arrivals from Italy to take their place" (DiScala, 1977).

DiScala's observations illustrate the altered function of the limited number of core area ethnic districts still in existence. The typical community is largely a collection of the elderly whose ties to the area and advancing age discourages them from leaving; a residue of young adults, some single, some married with children, who remain to look after their parents; local businessmen; political patronage job holders; and a small number of recent immigrants for whom the neighborhood is a low cost area of first settlement in the city. Most of the ambitious members of the younger generation have left the colony to live in other parts of the city and the suburbs.

In recent years a new trend has emerged in such communities as Boston's North End and Chicago's Near West Side. While upwardly mobile Italian Americans continue to move out of the colony in search of a better life, non-Italian young upper middle class suburbanites are moving in. They are flocking "into the North End (and the surrounding waterfront) because it has become very fashionable to live there... Many of the old buildings are being purchased and renovated by developers." DiScala finds this process "disturbing" because after the rehabilitation has been completed, long-established Italian residents "can no longer afford to pay the high rents" and are forced to move (DiScala, 1977).

For the adventurous ex-suburbanites the core area is a pleasant and relatively inexpensive environment in which to live and raise their children. Ironically, even some third generation Italian Americans in search of their roots have been attracted back to the neighborhoods their grandparents and parents worked so hard to escape. In an article entitled "Young People Find a 'Good Deal', West Side Community Gets Second Chance", the Chicago *Tribune* on August 22, 1976 proclaimed the reclamation of Chicago's Near West Side Italian neighborhood, which just ten years ago was called a slum, an area which many had "written off" as one that could never be saved. "Today the Near West Side is a viable, healthy community of 10,000 persons getting an economic shot in the arm at every turn from both public and private capital." With the movement of middle class families into the area and the departure of low income residents, more than $20 million was poured into the community, "giving rise to shopping centers, apartment-condominium complexes, and restored and renovated apartment buildings". The new residents concluded that they had found the best of all possible worlds—"a social oasis, amid parks, schools, a hospital, and a score of ethnic shops" (Chicago *Tribune*, August 22, 1976). In addition, their new residences are located near the city's central business district, the Loop, where many of them work. By 1976 Chicago's Near West Side, like Boston's North End, was well on its way to becoming "chic". In this respect both locations were following a pattern similar to that in New Orleans. The French Quarter, which some 75 years ago contained the Crescent City's most miserable Italian slum district, Little Palermo, has long since become a fashionable residential community as well as the city's major tourist attraction.

The return migration from the suburbs of middle and upper income whites, especially young married couples, has played an important role in the break-up of some working-class Italian neighborhoods. Other Italian communities have dispersed because of the influx of blacks, Hispanics, and southern whites. Italians and other new immigrant groups applied to these low income newcomers many of the same attitudes that Anglo-Saxons and members of old immigrant groups had earlier exhibited toward them. Italians do not feel they are responsible for racism in America. In fact, they point out that during the immigrant era their parents or grandparents frequently were victims of racism. Prejudice against blacks has been tinged with envy and sometimes grudging respect for the effective use they have made of political pressure to gain economic and other benefits.

Recent demands by Italian Americans have significantly not included a return to the days of free immigration. The acrimony connected with the passage of the National Origins Act of 1924, which set up restrictive quotas, was in large measure related to the attitude that Italians and other Southern and Eastern Europeans were somehow less acceptable citizens than were arrivals from other countries. Rather than the system itself, what infuriated Italians was the pitifully small quota assigned Italians (3,845 per year). This is indicated by the fact that complaints dwindled with the enactment of the 1965 immigration law.

Among Italian Americans in the post war decades traditional immigrant community institutions have, with the exception of the Catholic Church fallen into disuse. Mutual benefit societies and the Italian-language press, vibrant and influential institutions during the immigrant era, had by the 1960s come on hard times. A survey of more than 300 Italian residents of Chicago's Near West Side found that none of the people interviewed belonged to an Italian fraternal organization and none read a foreign-language newspaper, nor did anyone else in their families. Many were not even aware of the existence of the two largest Italian fraternal groups: the Sons of Italy and the Italo-American National Union. A sizeable minority claimed to own life insurance policies, but with American companies. Only the Catholic Church continued to attract support: almost without exception residents claimed membership in one of the three Catholic Churches in the area, although religious observance appeared to be more common among the older generation than among their children.

The elderly still obtained news of events in Italy from Italian-language radio, and from a monthly paper, *Fra Noi*, which printed a summary page in Italian. *Fra Noi* is put out by a Catholic religious order, and during the mid-sixties was the only city publication written about and for Italian Americans. Later, the weekly *L'Italia* was started; by 1977 its circulation had reached 6,000. The Italian-language press is somewhat stronger in the East, where Italian immigrants continue to arrive and congregate. Yet only New York's *Il Progresso Italo-Americano*, which has a national as well as local edition, publishes daily. *Il Progresso's* circulation in 1977 was 68,637; the next largest Italian-language paper, the *Italian Tribune-News* of Newark, New Jersey, a weekly, had a circulation of only 14,500.

Italians remain loyal to the Catholic Church, although they do not exert a leadership within it in proportion to their numbers. In 1970 Nathan Glazer noted a basic factor responsible for the underrepresentation of Italians among the leadership of the Church: the number of Italian priests "remains small". While they drew high marks in several categories, including church attendance, support of parochial education, and acceptance of the Irish-dominated Church's cultural outlook, Italian Americans were found to lag "in one respect — they do not provide large numbers of priests". While this under-representation may change, "it seems likely that one reason for the small weight of Italians in the Catholic Church — aside from the influence of the superlative organizational and bureaucratic skills of the Irish — is the fact that so few of them enter the Church and are available for further advancement" (Glazer and Moynihan, 1970).

Multiethnic parochial schools, parishes, and church-sponsored social organizations have encouraged marriage with non-Italian Catholics. Inter-marriage among Italians in Buffalo, for example, increased from 12 percent in 1930 to 27 percent in 1950 to 50 percent in 1960. Intermarriage among third generation Italian Americans in the United States, according to a survey conducted in 1963-1964, was 58 percent. Even when they marry outside the group, however, Italians tend to remain within the Church and choose a mate of either Irish, German or Polish background.

Third generation Italian Americans are not only more likely than members of earlier generations to marry outside the ethnic group, they also are more readily disposed to dissolve unsuccessful marriages. Divorce is no longer an unthinkable and unacceptable option.

The contemporary Italian American family tends to resemble the smaller, more egalitarian, child-centered units typical of the American middle class. Even among the working class the third generation is only "slightly more patriarchal than other lower class families but still strives toward the 'demo-cratic family' ideal" (Ianni, 1961).

In keeping with the native American norm, the third generation Italian American husband "is likely to have a spouse who bears no resemblance to the old immigrant woman who considered herself dedicated to her husband's wishes and caprices, and he accepts this behavior as proper". Marital roles generally "are divided along sex lines, but there are many areas—including childrearing and discipline, cooking, cleaning—in which at times the two spouses exchange or complement roles". The family is "decidely child-centered. The children are deliberately instructed in the ways of the American middle-class." Thus education is highly valued. "Indeed, in reaction to the lack of education in the family background, the parents are often obsessively concerned with the success of the children in school." (Lopreato, 1970). If they do not already live in the suburbs one of the family's goals is to move, generally to an industrial suburb located adjacent to the city. Nevertheless, contact still is maintained with parents, grandparents, and friends still living in the old neighborhood.

Suburbanite Italian Americans also still drive in to core area neighborhood stores on shopping expeditions for olive oil, salami, cheese, artichokes, pepperoni, and other "authentic" food unavailable in the shopping center supermarket. They also return to "the old neigborhood" to participate in religious festivals and celebrations.

Italians and non-Italians alike flock to the San Gennaro, San Rocco, Santa Rossilia, and other feast days from remote parts of New York City and its suburbs and even from neighboring states. Many are attracted by the wide variety and high quality of the food stalls and local restaurants, little realizing or even caring that what they consume is not typical peasant fare. Food is also the main attraction at ethnic festivals held annually, if not more frequently, in various eastern and middle western cities.

What members of the third and fourth generations, most of whom "have never known anything but middle-class life... seek is the prestige that was denied their parents" (Acocella, Attenzione, July, 1979). Thus Italian Americans now concentrate on campaigns to eliminate real or imagined social prejudice and ethnic slurs against them as well as on opening up areas of economic, political, or cultural activity hitherto closed to them. In the American system benefits accrue through application of group pressure. During the era of the big-city machines, patronage jobs and other short-term benefits were the rewards of political power. Now that the Italian American group is moving into the middle class, promises of pick-and-shovel jobs and neighborhood conveniences like bathhouses and small parks have lost their attraction.

For Southern and Eastern European groups the immigrant era has long since passed. It has been fully a century since Southern Italians began to arrive in the United States in large numbers. The period of large-scale immigration lasted until the early 1920s when federal legislation severely restricted entry to America. In other words it has been six decades, or two generations, since the gates were closed to Italians and other Southern and Eastern Europeans. Thus discussions of the Italian American experience in the 1970s and 1980s generally refer to members of the third or fourth generations.

Perhaps because Italian Americans no longer are objects of the unyielding hostility and fierce prejudice that were encountered by new immigrants at the turn of the century, they feel free to proclaim their ethnicity and to search for their roots. One result has been the formation, in various urban centers, of organizations that in the late 1960s and early 1970s directed rallies and demonstrations to protest the Italian American image being projected in the media, especially television, movies, and newspapers.

Despite these extensive achievements the past two decades have been frustrating ones for Italian Americans. We have made good, even excellent progress in some respects; yet as a group we seem to feel that acceptance and respect are still tantalizingly out of reach.

Italian Americans have indeed achieved significant economic success. The general prosperity which the United States enjoyed in the postwar period and into the 1970s benefitted Italians as well as other Americans. Many veterans of World War II, the Korean conflict and Viet Nam used the G.I. Bill to finance college educations and take professional training; they obtained jobs in industry or started businessess of their own. A 1963-64 study of occupational patterns among Italian Americans found that 48 pecent of the respondents were employed in white-colar jobs and 52 percent in blue-collar jobs. In contrast, 26 percent of the fathers of the respondents held white-collar positions, 71 percent were in blue-collar jobs, and 3 percent were employed as farmers. Furthermore, Italians in working class occupations had shifted from unskilled to semiskilled and skilled jobs.

Based on reseach conducted by the National Opinion Research Center (NORC), of which he was Director, Andrew Greeley in 1974 stated that "Italians have reached the national average in the percentage of those who have become managers or owners or professional or technical workers". Referring to studies conducted by NORC over the previous several years, Greeley concluded that the evidence "leaves little doubt" that Italians "have moved rapidly into the upper middle class of American society during the last two decades" (Greeley, 1974).

In 1975 Greeley presented the findings of a survey NORC conducted for the Ford Foundation in the correlation between religion, ethnic background, and income. According to the NORC figures, Italian Catholic families ranked third from the top. With an average family income of $11,748, Italians followed Jews ($13,340) and Catholic Irish ($12,426). Interestingly, the lowest ranked of the 17 groups surveyed was the Baptists (with an average family income of $8,693), while several other Protestant groups also ranked in the lower level of the survey.

TABLE 1
Religion, Ethnic Background and Income

Religious/Ethnic Group	Average Family Income (1974 dollars)
Jews	$13,340
Irish Catholics	12,426
Italian Catholics	11,748
German Catholics	11,632
Polish Catholics	11,298
Episcopalians	11,032
Presbyterians	10,976
Slavic Catholics	10,826
British Protestants	10,354
French Catholics	10,188
Methodists	10,103
German Protestants	9,758
Lutherans	9,702
Scandinavian Protestants	9,597
Irish Protestants	9,147
Baptists	8,693

Source: Chicago *Tribune*, October 19, 1975.

In their move up the economic ladder Italians have followed, on a smaller scale and a generation later, a pattern noted among Jews, whereby "the children of storekeepers and small businessmen went to college and became professionals". Italians are attending college in ever increasing numbers. By the 1970s they comprised approximately one-third of City University of New York system and half of the student body at Fordham University. As a result of their stronger qualifications and better educational background, the grandchildren of Italian immigrants "are moving into the professions and the higher white collar fields" (Glazer and Moynihan, 1970). They are filling the great bureaucracies of government and business and they are also prominent in such glamor fields as advertising, sports, and entertainment.

Thus there is extensive evidence that Italian Americans are not doing badly. If this is true, why does there exist a pervasive and widespread feeling that recognition and acceptance are still beyond their grasp? This is, I believe, due in large part to two factors: the effects of public policy as well as the lingering negative image under which we, as a group, labor.

Many Italian Americans, particularly in the East, firmly believe that group members are passed over in favor of blacks and Hispanics who, because of federal laws and official pressure, are admitted to prestigious academic institutions or are given jobs for which Italian Americans are better qualified. Thus a study conducted in the mid-1970s found that in New York City, where Italian Americans composed 21 percent of the population, "less than five percent of the City University system had Italian American administrators, while 34 percent of the student body is Italian American". This is a bitter pill to swallow for, as Edward Miranda has maintained, "other American minorities have been protected by various Government agencies from just such job discrimination but, it seems, the Italian American plight has been largely ignored" (Miranda, *Identity*, July, 1977).

Still other studies have documented the fact that Italian Americans are seldom to be found in the executive suites of large, or even of medium-sized corporations. A study conducted by Chicago's Institute of Urban Life in the mid-1970s into the 107 largest corporations in that city found that Italian Americans comprised 1.9 percent of the corporations' board members and 2.9 percent of their officers. Furthermore, 75 of the companies (that is, 70 percent of the total) had not a single Italian American in any executive level position (Chicago, *Tribune*, September 14, 1976).

When viewed from the perspective of the black experience in the South or the Chicano in the Southwest, the discrimination Italian Americans and other white ethnics faced in the 1970s recedes in scale and importance. This fact, however, is not the significant point. White ethnics feel that for decades they played by society's rules—as formulated by the dominant WASP element—and just when they were on the verge of "making it" eonomically and socially, society changed the rules. According to the new rules, ethnic background—that is, color—takes on at least as much importance as hard work and other virtues which were formally extolled for society's welfare. Whether or not that was, or is, an accurate assessment of the intent and results of Civil Rights Legislation enacted in the 1960s, "the rude awakening", Columbia University Professor Fred Barbaro noted in 1974, led at least some "to seek affiliation with Italian American organizations although they may share little but a common ancestry" (Barbaro, *Italian Americana*, 1974).

As for the negative images that plague Italian Americans, I would say that they probably can be summed up in one word—Mafia—or, if you prefer two words, *Cosa Nostra*. Since at least 1890 Italians have been connected in the public's imagination with criminality and violence. I am not going to summarize the history of Italian identification with crime in the United States. The story is painfully familiar to most Italian Americans.[1]

The unfortunate fact is that there is truth in the claims that Italian Americans have been involved in crime. Obviously I am referring to a very, very small percentage of the total group, but since the 1920s this element has

---

[1] For those not familiar with the subject I suggest an examination of Joseph L. Albini, *The American Mafia: Genesis of a Legend* (New York, 1971) or Humbert S. Nelli, *The Business of Crime: Italians and Syndicate Crime in the United States* (New York, 1976).

played an extremely important role in the development of American syndicate crime.

In the process they have colored public perceptions of law-abiding Italian Americans, who, I emphasize, comprise the vast majority of the group. In a sense, all Italians are tarred by the brush of organized crime. We do, however, tend to lend some credence to the general view that every successful Italian American has criminal contacts if not criminal backing. We do this, or at least our spokespersons do, by vigorously denying the very existence of a syndicate. We have a terribly difficult time admitting any criminality at all, and in our denials we appear to the public to be ridiculous or implicated.

Fortunately, the heyday of the Italian American syndicates is probably past. Not all Italian Americans are, or perhaps, ever will be, out of syndicate crime, but the future appears to belong to other groups and individuals. This is already quite evident in the increasingly important illicit narcotics trade. In addition to Cubans, Columbians, blacks, and Orientals, even middle and upper class WASPS are moving into the business to reap the huge profits to be made.

So it would appear that in the future Italian Americans will be less and less important in the syndicate. A time could conceivably come when the American public and, perhaps, even Italian Americans will look back nostalgically on the Italian American syndicates of Capone and Costello and Gambino as we do to the gunfighters and bank robbers of the Old West. Actually, we are already beginning to do just this. During the evenings of August 28, 29, 30 and September 1, 1983, NBC Television devoted nine valuable prime time hours to yet another showing of *The Godfather*, and millions of Americans—including Italian Americans—eagerly followed the saga. Noted an Associated Press release: "*The Godfather* miniseries offered NBC a deal it couldn't refuse: first place in the Nielson ratings" for the week ending September 4 (Los Angeles *Times*, September 10,1983).Part Three of the miniseries was viewed in an estimated 15.5 million households. And this is despite the fact that the film, in various versions, has appeared on network and cable TV numerous times during the last decade.

Interestingly enough, the self-image Italian Americans hold—of meager achievement and limited acceptance—is not believed by the non-white ethnic groups such as blacks, Hispanics, native Americans (Indians), or even by many Asians. In their view we have made it. We are the part of the establishment with which they come in contact. When they look around, they find Italian Americans firmly entrenched as foremen, organized labor leaders, union members, school teachers, policemen, low and middle level white collar workers, and civil service employees. We have reached a level of achievement they hope and strive to achieve. Blacks and Hispanics would, of course dearly love to become corporation presidents but have little expectation of actually achieving that goal, at least in this generation. They can, however, entertain hopes of becoming, like Italian Americans, members of middle management.

This was brought home very forcefully to me at a conference in which I participated during May 1983 on the economic experience of several white and non-white ethnic groups. The groups were Poles, Italians, Irish, Jews, blacks, Hispanics, Japanese and native Americans. I found that because of the length of time Italians have been in the United States, our movement as a group up the socioeconomic ladder, and our status as members of the nation's white majority, we are viewed with envy and some degree of distrust and dislike by non-white ethnics. I must admit that I was shocked to find that I, as a representative of the Italian American group, was viewed and referred to as a spokesman of the establishment. I found that we and other white ethnics and not the WASPS are the ones who, in the view of non-whites, are limiting or preventing their movement up the socioeconomic ladder.

I believe that we Italian Americans have an obligation to help our fellows who are members of other ethnic groups. Instead of continuing to dwell on "the ordeal of the Italian immigrant", I should like to see us devote our attention to an examination of the lessons the Italian experience can offer to help blacks, Hispanics, native Americans and Asians adjust to urban-industrial America. Among the several other things we can do I hope that during the remainder of the 1980s Italian American groups will hold numerous conferences and meetings with various non-white ethnic groups, and not only in the East or Middle West.

To borrow a phrase from a phone company commercial—it is time for we Italian Americans to reach out and touch someone.

7

The Search for an
Italian American Identity
Continuity and Change*

RUDOLPH J. VECOLI
University of Minnesota

IN 1909, the novelist William Dean Howells, in a speech before the Society for Italian Immigrants confessed to misgivings when faced with the question how the half million Italians in New York City were to be assimilated. But on further reflection, he decided: "It was not for us Americans to have the misgivings, but for those Italians; it was not for us to assimilate *them*, but for them to assimilate *us*". While not oblivious to their defects, "too often passionate, jealous, revengeful, homicidal", Howells prized the Italians for their instinctive courtesy, their artistic temperament, their diligence and thrift. He, therefore, anticipated without anxiety the pending assimilation of New York City by the Italians.

> Is it indeed too much to ask, "Howells speculated," for that future nationality of ours which the Italians have so largely the charge of creating, that they shall glorify it with such names as have lent lustre to the Italy of our times, and that in the coming time, the Mazzinis, the Garibaldis, the Cavours, the Vergas, the Ferreros, the Mascagnis, the Marconis, shall all be Americans? (Howells, 1909, p. 28).

Howells was an Italophile and a cosmopolitan at a time when the immigrants from Italy were regarded as pariahs and the Melting Pot was in vogue. Now seventy-five years later his prophecy appears about to be fulfilled. In some sense, the Italians indeed appear to have assimilated America, rather than the reverse. The pizza has replaced the hotdog as the all-American snack. Italian names today adorn the offices of corporation presidents, governors,

---

* *Dedicated to the memory of John S. Crucciotti (1948-1983), Italian American by choice.*

senators, and university presidents. No less an authority than *The New York Times* recently confirmed that the Italian Americans were "Coming Into Their Own". Its *Magazine* of May 15, 1983 sported a cover with the portraits of such notables as Martin Scorsese, Mario M. Cuomo, Lee A. Iacocca, Joseph Cardinal Bernardin, and A. Bartlett Giamatti. If these are not quite American Mazzinis, Vergas, and Marconis, they will do for the time being.

The author of the article, Stephen Hall, himself the grandson of Italian immigrants, described "the quiet yet spectacular rise of Italian-Americans in the United States today". Previously regarded as slow to assimilate, they now "swell the ranks of the middle class, amass power and wealth and help set the decade's social and political agenda as never before" (Hall, 1983, p. 28ff). Hall is but the most recent of commentators who have hailed the coming of age of the Italian Americans. At the risk of being thought a nay sayer, such a roseate denouement of the Italian American saga leaves me dissatisfied. What of the majority who are still blue collar and low level white collar workers, employed (if they are so fortunate) in dying industries and living in decaying cities? More than two-thirds of the Italian Americans are located in the Northeast, the region most afflicted by "structural unemployment" and urban crisis. Such success stories also fail to examine the implications of upward mobility for the Italian Americans as an ethnic group. What is its meaning for ethnic identity? Is this the final step in an inexorable process of assimilation, and are we, in effect, celebrating the imminent disappearance of the Italian presence from American society?

I will not attempt a definition of the Italian American identity. I do not presume that such a thing exists. Given the enormous complexity of the population of Italian ancestry, the product of over a century of immigration, differentiated by generation, social class, regions of origin and destination, it is safe to assume a multiplicity of identities. What is indisputable is that over the past two decades there has been an intense search for an Italian American identity. The reasons for and the character of that search are the subjects of this inquiry.

In their quest for identity Italian Americans are behaving very American. Suffering from "future shock" as we move into post-industrial society, we, Americans, appear to be in the grip of a collective "identity crisis". The "rootsmania" of the seventies was a response to the disorienting traumas of the sixties. To the question, "Who am I?" the time-hallowed answer, "just a plain, red-blooded American", no longer sufficed. Philip Gleason has well expressed it:

> [The] profound crisis — social, political, and cultural — between the assassination of John F. Kennedy and the resignation of Richard Nixon...translated itself to the ordinary citizen as a challenge to every individual to decide where he or she stood with respect to the traditional values, beliefs, and institutions that were being called into question... [It] brought about a

reexamination on a massive scale of the relationship between the individual and society...and for the first time in American history, it seemed more attractive to many individuals to affirm an ethnic identity than to affirm that one was simply an American.[1]

The guru of the identity movement was psychoanalyst Erik H. Erikson, who had noted back in 1950 that the study of identity was "as strategic in our time as the study of sexuality was in Freud's time". Himself an immigrant, Erikson observed that the concept of "identity crisis" (a term he coined) "seemed naturally grounded in the experience of emigration, immigration, and Americanization".

> Identity problems, were in the mental baggage of generations of new Americans, who left their motherlands and fatherlands behind to merge their ancestral identities in the common one of self-made men (Erikson, 1963, 1968, 1975:43;).

The Eriksonian concept of identity views it as the product of a lifelong interaction between the individual personality and society. Erikson contended that the personality continued to be shaped and altered through its encounters with the external milieu thus allowing for the play of history and culture. Ethnic identity is "primordial" in the sense that it is deeply imbedded in the psyche of the child by the familial culture, but its later development in negative and positive forms is affected by the individual's life experiences. Since I am not a psychiatrist, I will not attempt to psychoanalyze the Italian Americans. But my Eriksonian assumption is that early personality formation in the Italian family, whether explicitly affirmed or denied in adulthood, is nonetheless the irreducible basis of an Italian American identity.

Who then are the Italian Americans? The 1980 U.S. Census, for the first time posed the question: "What is your ancestry?" Some twelve million answered "Italian".[2] Comprising 4.3 percent of the population, they constituted the sixth largest ancestry group. The responses were based upon self-identification. That twelve million claimed Italy as their land of origin is significant; they could just as easily have said "American". Doubtless some did. It is not an unreasonable estimate that the actual number of descendants of Italian immigrants number closer to 20 millions. We would dearly love to know more about these 12 million self-confessed Americans of Italian descent (I dare not call them Italian Americans). Of one thing we can be certain. The

---

[1] Philip Gleason, "Identifying Identity: A Semantic History", *Journal of American History*, March 1983, pp. 928-29. This is an excellent analysis of the origins and use of the concept of identity in American thought. *See also*, Gleason, "American Identity and Americanization", in *Harvard Encyclopedia of American Ethnic Groups*, Cambridge, MA: Harvard University Press, 1980, pp. 31-58; and Rudolph J. Vecoli, "Louis Adamic and the Contemporary Search for Roots", *Ethnic Studies*, Monash University, Australia, 1978, 2:29-35.

[2] U.S. Bureau of the Cenus, *1980 Census of Population. Ancestry of the Population by State: 1980* (Washington, D.C., 1983).

great majority is of the third generation or even further removed from their immigrant forebears.[3] This makes our task even more problematical since we know so little about these generations. Unfortunately the census taker did not ask his respondents: What does your Italian ancestry mean to you? How does it affect your values? your attitudes? your behavior? Are you an Italian-American?

Lacking both psychoanalytic and statistical evidence, we must turn to history for answers. Although our purpose is to understand the contemporary search for an Italian American identity, I believe we can do so only from a perspective which encompasses the experiences of three generations: the immigrant generation; the children of the immigrants; and the grandchildren of the immigrants. Between 1876 and 1924, over 4.5 million left Italy for the United States, but of these more than half returned. At its peak in 1930, the Italian foreign born population totaled almost 1.8 million. About three quarters of the immigrants came from the *Mezzogiorno*, but whether from the north or south, they were almost entirely *contadini* and *artigiani*. Young adults, their personalities had been molded by the traditional cultures of the *paesi* where everyone was known and named according to his family's reputation and status. Even the wrenching transplantation to America could not alter this basic identity. Chain migrations of relatives and *paesani* maintained the peasant culture and network of social relationships. Whether in the work gang or the neighborhood, the immigrant tended to remain with his own people. The mentality of *campanilismo* was expressed through the formation of *società di mutuo soccorso* and the celebration of the feasts of the patron saints. Separated as they were by dialects, customs, and prejudices, the immigrants from different regions or even paesi shied away from each other. They had little sense of a common nationality, of being Italian. Italy for them was a *matrigna* (stepmother) who had driven them from home in search of bread and work. Wary of *stranieri*, suspicious of institutions, they trusted only *la famiglia* or at most the circle of paesani.[4]

---

[3] In 1970, there were only a million foreign born Italians and 3.2 million second generation Italian Americans. Since their median ages were then 63 and 47 years respectively, many of them are now deceased. Also the net immigration from Italy in the 1970s was quite modest, totalling some 150,000.

[4] By now the works on the history of the Italian immigration are quite extensive. For my own writings, See, "*Contadini* in Chicago: A Critique of *The Uprooted*", *Journal of American History*, LI Dec., 1964, pp. 404-417; *The People of New Jersey*, Princeton, NJ: D. Van Nostrand Co., 1965; "The Coming of Age of the Italian Americans: 1945-1974", *Ethnicity*, 1978, 5:119-47; "Prelates and Peasants: Italian Immigrants and the Catholic Church", *Journal of Social History*, Spring, 1969, 2:217-68; "Cult and Occult in Italian American Culture", in R.M. Miller and T. D. Marzik, eds., *Immigrants and Religion in Urban America*, Philadelphia: Temple University Press, 1977, pp. 25-47; "Italian American Workers, 1880-1920", in S.M. Tomasi, ed., *Perspectives in Italian Immigration and Ethnicity*, New York: Center for Migration Studies, 1977, pp. 25-49; "The Italians", in June Holmquist, ed., *They Chose Minnesota*, St. Paul: Minnesota Historical Society; 1981, pp. 449-71; "The Formation of Chicago's 'Little Italies' ", *Journal of American Ethnic*

Their experiences in America confirmed the *contadini* in their paro-chialism. They quickly learned that they were hated and despised by the *Mericani*, which included all who had preceded them. While unaware of the vicious comments of Woodrow Wilson or E.A. Ross, they soon learned the meaning of "goddamn dago", "wop son-of-a-bitch", often accompanied by kicks and punches. During the pre-World War I years, the Italians, especially those from the south, were classified and treated as non-whites. Excluded from jobs, neighborhoods, and churches, they led a segregated existence. Nor did they have confidence in their would-be Italian leaders, the *padroni* and bankers, who more often than not swindled them of their hard-earned wages. Slow to naturalize and vote, reluctant to join labor unions, they remained distant from the mainstream of American life. Between the wars, the immigrants, by and large, remained in low-paying unskilled and semi-skilled jobs. Their highest ambition was to save enough money to buy a house with a bit of land. Isolated within the "Little Italies", they held tenaciously to the values and customs of their *paesi*. After decades in America, many spoke only a little broken English and some none at all. What they knew of this strange country often repelled them. From their perspective, the *Mericani* appeared a foolish people, without a sense of honor, respect, or proper behavior. Ideas of youthful freedom, women's rights, conspicuous consumption, they dismissed as *americannate*. Efforts on the parts of teachers and social workers to Americanize them and their children were resented as intrusions on the sovereignty of the family. The response of the *contadini* to discrimination and exploitation was to withdraw even more into their ethnic enclaves.[5]

The observation of Giuseppe Prezzolini, although reflecting class and regional bias, nonetheless has much truth to it:

> Non sono italiani, perchè non lo son mai stati. Hanno preso qui certe abitudini americane ma nel fondo son rimasti dei contadini meridionali, senza cultura, senza scuola, senza lingua, per cui, insomma, il momento della 'italianità' non e mai arrivato. Partiron dall'Italia prima di essere italiani. Son stati qui e non son diventati veri Americani.[6]

History, Spring, 1983, 2:5-20; "The Italian Immigrants in the Labor Movement of the United States from 1880 to 1929", in *Gli Italiani fuori d'Italia*, B. Bezza, ed. Milan: Franco Angeli, 1983, pp. 257-306.

[5] In addition to historical studies, novels and autobiographies offer valuable insights into the experience of Italian immigrants: Pietro di Donato, *Christ in Concrete*, Indianapolis: Bobbs-Merrill Co., 1939 and *Three Circles of Light*, New York: Julian Messner, 1960; Jerre Mangione, *Mount Allegro* (various editions); Marie Hall Ets, *Rosa: the Life of an Italian Immigrant*, Minneapolis: University of Minnesota Press, 1970.

[6] Giuseppe Prezzolini, *Diario, 1900-1941*, Milan: Rusconi, 1978, p. 470 (note of February 21, 1931) quoted in Nadia Venturini, "Le communitá italiane negli Stati Uniti fra storia sociale e storia politica", *Rivista di Storia Contemporanea*, XIII, Spring, 1984, p. 192.

Within the *colonie italiane*, there were those, like Prezzolini, who sought to promote a spirit of *italianità*. A colonial elite, composed of the educated few, professionals, teachers, and journalists, and the businessmen, from a mixture of self-interest and patriotism, exhorted the immigrants to think of themselves as Italians. These *prominenti* busied themselves with celebrations of *il giorno dello statuto* and *il venti di settembre*, and Columbus Day. They formed the *Società Dante Alighieri* and raised statues to Columbus and Garibaldi. Their nationalism expressed itself primarily in a never-ending round of banquets where bombastic rhetoric about *la madre patria* filled the air. But they did little to help the immigrants in their daily struggle for survival. Nor did they, with few exceptions, create institutions to nourish Italian language and culture among the unschooled *contadini*. Even before the Lateran Treaties, Italian priests also promoted Italian nationalism. Like the prominenti, they stood to gain from the development of an Italian identity which would overcome regional antagonisms. But their effectiveness was limited by the hostility of an Irish hierarchy and the anti-clericalism of the immigrants. Italian parochial schools were few; the parents, for the most part, preferred to send their children to public schools.[7]

World War I provided the nationalists with the opportunity to arouse a spirit of patriotism among the immigrants. Since Italy and the United States were allies, the Italians did not have a conflict of loyalties as did the Germans. Rallies, parades, impassioned orators, and the jingoist colonial press, did whip up some enthusiasm for the war in the "Little Italies". Some reservists did return to fight for *la patria* although the majority did not. Funds were raised for the Italian Red Cross. But there were counter-currents working against the nationalists. The war also inspired the movement for "One Hundred Percent Americanism" and intensified pressures were brought to bear upon the immigrants to assimilate. Great numbers of Italians served in the military forces of the United States. American patriotism vied for the allegiance of the immigrants and their children. The first World War, while stimulating the competing ideologies of Italian and American nationalisms, was a transitory phenomenon which did not basically alter the apolitical character of the immigrants.

Meanwhile, the Italian anarchists and socialists were waging a vigorous campaign against the war and nationalism of all kinds. These refugees from political represssion in Italy had for several decades carried on an intensive propaganda in favor of their radical ideas among the immigrant masses. Through their newspapers, *circoli di studi sociali*, theatre groups, they had won a minority to their revolutionary causes. They had led the Italian workers in scores of strikes, and had fought to break the power of the

---

[7] *See*, the studies cited in footnote 4, especially "Prelates and Peasants", and "The Italian Immigrants in the Labor Movement of the U.S.", and *Also*, Leonard Covello, *The Social Background of the Italo-American School Child*, Leiden: E.J. Brill, 1967.

prominenti and priests in the "Little Italies". But the ideal of working class solidarity made only limited inroads among the contadini. Now their anti-war stance brought down upon the *sovversivi* the full wrath of American government. Many of their leaders were imprisoned or deported during the "Red Scare". The culmination of this repression, the execution of Sacco and Vanzetti, rang the death knell for the Italian radical movement and sent a shudder of terror through the "Little Italies". Clearly a radical identity was not a viable option in the land of triumphant capitalism. (Vecoli, 1978c).

The most important development affecting the future of the Italians in America between the wars was the emergence of a second generation. Already by 1920, the American-born children outnumbered their immigrant parents, and by 1940, many of them had reached maturity. These Italian Americans, as we shall call them, were of two worlds: the little world of the family and neighborhood and the big world of America. Although the paese of their parents was to them but a legend, they imbibed the contadino culture with their mother's milk. As they grew older, they absorbed the ideas and dreams of America from the schools, the streets, and the mass media. Inevitably there was a clash of cultures and a conflict of generations: parents who demanded that their children abide by the ways of the paese; children who more than anything else wanted to be American. Before Erikson coined the term, the second generation suffered from "identity conflict". Its experience was one of marginality, not belonging entirely in either world, feeling constantly the tug-and-pull of opposed ways of life. These young *americanizzati*, in the exasperated phrase of their parents, learned from their teachers and peers that to be Italian was to be inferior. They were ridiculed for their melodic names, for their sausage and pepper sandwiches, for their patched clothing. They were taunted as "ignorant dago, dirty wop, and greaseball". They learned to be ashamed of their parents for their broken English and expressive manner. Mario Cuomo, now governor of the state of New York, recalls with pain how when he was fourteen he was embarrassed to bring his father to meet his teachers and other parents "because he didn't speak English well".[8]

Indeed, the second generation exhibited a classic case of self-hatred, having internalized the negative stereotypes of their antagonists. In his study, *Italian or American?* (1943), Irving Child noted reactions stemming from the rebels who rejected completely their Italian identity to those who became militantly pro-Italian. The first, often upwardly mobile, changed their names (from Falegname to Carpenter), married outside the Italian group, moved out of "Little Italy", and even stopped eating spaghetti. The latter embraced the

---

[8] Quoted in Andrew Rolle, *The Italian Americans: Troubled Roots*. New York: The Free Press, 1980, p. 43. *See also*, Covello, *The Social Background of the Italo-American School Child*. Although pretentious in its psychoanalytic approach, Rolle does address the issue of the second generation. *See also*, writing by second generation Italian Americans such as John Fante, Jo Pagano, and Michael De Capite.

Italian heritage, studied the language, and gloried in the achievements of ancient Rome and Fascist Italy. The majority fell somewhere between these extremes, keeping the contending elements within their personalities in an uneasy equilibrium. Such emotional conflicts took their toll in low self-esteem, lack of confidence, passivity, and delinquency. Most contadino parents were not equipped to handle such psychological problems, but then neither was the larger society (Child, 1943; Covello, 1967; Ware, 1935).

Actually there was a great deal of continuity between the first and second generations. The immigrant family for the most part held its children and inculcated in them the values of peasant Italy. Living at home until they married, most often to an Italian, and then establishing themselves in the neighborhood, the second generation kept close ties with their parents. Yet in their lifestyles, they aped the dress and manner of "real Americans" whom they knew primarily from motion pictures. The children pushed their parents to stop being "wops", to become citizens, and, most of all, to become consumers. To own a refrigerator, a radio, a car, was to consume yourself into an American identity. The sons and daughters overwhelmingly became blue collar workers, perhaps moving into skilled jobs. Their parents placed little value on education and were anxious to add their children's earnings to the family income. Low levels of academic achievement (few graduated from high school, to say nothing of college) and of occupational mobility were the hallmarks of this generation (Whyte, 1943; Gans, 1962; Lopreato, 1970; Vecoli, 1965).

Both as consumers and producers, the Italian Americans participated in creating the popular culture of their time, music, dance, sports, and less legal pastimes, such as gambling. The culture heroes of the second generation were the Joe DiMaggios, the Rocky Grazianos, the Frank Sinatras, and the Al Capones. (Capone, himself, was reported to have said: "I'm no Italian. I was born in Brooklyn".) Excluded from respectable careers in business and the professions, by prejudice as well as their own limited aspirations, not a few turned to crime as their "peculiar ladder of social mobility". Others found in the emerging labor movement opportunities for leadership. Working in factories and mills with Irish, Jews, Poles, Greeks, young Italian Americans developed a sense of working class comraderie if not class consciousness and played their part in the organization of the mass production industries in the thirties and forties. For this generation to be Italian American also meant to be working class. Their identities were a melange of Old World traits, workplace experiences, textbook ideals, Hollywood dreams, and popular culture (Rolle, 1981; Bell, 1962; Ewen, 1976).

Although written in a fit of pique at its negative reaction to Italy's entry into the war in 1940, the characterization of the second generation by Italian Ambassador Ascanio Colonna bears repeating:

Proveniente in gran parte dalla corrente immigratoria proletaria del meridione, non ha sentito dai genitori che descrizioni di una Italia misera e derelitta e ritenendosi, per una inqualificabile deformazione mentale, minorata nella lotta per la vita con l'America anglosassone cerca di sfuggire l'ambiente italiano e di rinnegare la propria origine.

Ma respinta dall'ambiente americano, fintanto almeno che non raggiunge la prosperità economica o il decoro di una professione liberale, esse si e rifugiata in un proprio mondo spirituale che e in fondo ugualmente distante dal mondo americano o dal mondo italiano e ha creato un suo strano folkore...a base di spaghetti e di "baseball" e un sua mitologia i cui heroi sono il sindaco Fiorello La Guardia, il giuocatore di palla Joe DiMaggio e el pugilista Tony Galento.[9]

The episode of Fascism has particular relevance to the second generation's search for an Italian American identity. Having been subjected to unremitting denigration of all things Italian, both the immigrants and their children derived a sense of pride from the admiration with which Fascist Italy was regarded by most Americans. It was said that Mussolini had made Italy respected and feared; very well, then, perhaps some of that would rub off on them. Philip Cannistraro has argued that the Italian Americans "identified with Fascism because it provided them with a recognizable and meaningful identity in the pluralistic society that was America" (Cannistraro, New York, 1977). The *prominenti* almost to a man became idolatrous supporters of *Il Duce*, but there was a generally pro-Fascist sentiment among the masses. The Italian anti-Fascists were a relatively small minority made up of the remnants of the socialist and anarchist movements reinforced by the *fuorusciti*. The Fascist regime mounted an intensive propaganda campaign directed at the Italian Americans, and through its consulates exerted control over most of the newspapers, radio programs, organizations, churches, schools, and cultural institutions.

Unquestionably there was a quickening of Italian nationalism among the immigrants. The Order of the Sons of Italy which since its establishment in 1905 had grown very slowly, soared to a membership of 300,000 in the 1920s. During the Ethiopian War, mass rallies of Italian Americans proclaimed their solidarity with Italy. Women contributed their wedding rings to the cause, but only a small number of men returned to fight for the new Roman empire. As John Diggins has put it, "rather than ideological true-believers, Italian Americans were sentimental fellow travelers".[10] Especially for the second

---

[9] Quoted in Philip V. Cannistraro, "Gli Italo-Americani di fronte all'ingresso dell'Italia nella Seconda Guerra Mondiale", *Rivista di Storia Contemporanea*, 1976, VII, p. 862.

[10] John P. Diggins, *Mussolini and Fascism: The View from America*, Princeton: Princeton University Press, 1972, p. 108. Diggins is the basic work on the response of Americans to fascism; however, for the Italian Americans, it should be supplemented by Salvemini, *Italian Fascist Activities in the United States*; Gian Giacomo Migone, *Gli Stati Uniti e il Fascismo*, Milan: Feltrinelli, 1979; and Nadia Venturini, "From Roosevelt and Mussolini to Truman and De Gasperi: The Politics of Italian American Leadership, 1930-1950", (unpublished master's thesis)

generation, Fascism was a balm for their wounded egos. One young woman explained the pro-Fascist sympathies:

> But you've got to admit one thing, [Mussolini] enabled four million Italians in America to hold up their heads, and that is something. If you had been branded as undesirable by a quota law you would understand how much that means (Ware, New York, 1971, pp. 50-55).

Salvemini, himself, estimated that only five percent of the Italian Americans were "out-and-out Fascists", another 35 percent were philo-Fascists, while ten percent were anti-Fascists. The other fifty percent were "concerned only with their own affairs" (Salvemini, 1979, p. 244). When Italy entered the war, the skindeep support for Mussolini was revealed by the alacrity with which Italian Americans, especially those of the second generation, repudiated the Fascist regime. Italian American voters did express their resentment in the election of 1940 against President Roosevelt who had accused Italy of "plunging the dagger" (an unfortunate metaphor) into its neighbor. December 7, 1941 put a definite period to the Fascist interlude in Italian American life. With almost complete unanimity, the Italian Americans, with the prominenti in the forefront, proclaimed their undivided loyalty to the United States (De Conde, 1971, pp. 225-48; Diggins, 1972, pp. 340-352).

World War II was in many ways a decisive watershed in the history of the Italian American ethnic group. The war provided, as Diggins said, "the fuel of the melting pot" for Italian Americans. Rumors of a "Fascist fifth column" initially caused them to be suspect. Although non-naturalized Italians, of which there were still 600,000, were declared enemy aliens, on Columbus Day 1942, they were removed from this category. Still fearful, Italian Americans disbanded societies and suspended traditional festivals. The teaching of Italian was abandoned in many schools. The latent conflict within the second generation's identity had erupted, and they rushed toward total Americanization. Yet the Italian Americans were treated gently compared with the German Americans in World War I and the Japanese Americans in World War II. They were not placed in camps, and only 228 Italian aliens were interned. Italian Americans served in the armed forces in great numbers, and the gold stars in the windows of "Little Italy" homes attested to the blood dues which were being paid to the American republic (*Ibid*). The war was especially bitter for the Italian Americans since it pitted them against their blood relatives; as Richard Gambino has remarked, it was "fratricide". In his novel, *Love and Pasta*, Joseph Verga has an Italian American soldier pondering his dilemma:

During those first days, I wondered how I would react if I was sent to Italy.

University of Minnesota, 1984; Fiorello B. Ventresca, "Italian Americans and the Ethiopian Crisis", *Italian Americana* (hereafter cited *IA*), Fall/Winter, 1980, 6:4-28.

Could I treat Italians as enemies...? Would I be able to pull the trigger if I saw one of Pop's *compa's* through the gunsight? (Gambino, 1974; p. 292).

The war also brought full employment and high wages, and the Italian Americans prospered as never before. Military service and work in war industries drew the young men and women out of the "Little Italies", threw them together with all kinds of Americans, exposed them to other parts of the world, and opened them up to new possibilities. Riding the economic boom of the post-war decades with an assist from the G.I.Bill of Rights, the second generation increasingly pursued the goals of Americanization and upward mobility. In growing numbers, they enrolled in colleges and universities, entered white collar occupations, moved into the mushrooming suburban developments, and married non-Italians, particulary Irish, German and Polish Catholics. The old neighborhoods appeared doomed by the bulldozers of urban renewal and the influx of blacks and Hispanics. The immigrant generation was passing from the scene, and there were few new immigrants to replace them. In the 1950s, it appeared that the Italian Americans were on the verge of blending into America, leaving little trace that they had ever existed. I believe it was this sense that we were a vanishing breed which impelled me to initiate my studies in Italian American history in the mid-fifties (Vecoli, New York, 1978c; Herberg, 1955).

But then came the 1960s, unexpected and unpredicted, a decade of conflict, violence and liberation. The society, which during the Eisenhower years appeared to be approaching an All-American middle class homogeneity, was suddenly rent by racial, ethnic, and class conflict. The war in Vietnam, racial injustice, and authoritarian institutions became the targets of civil disobedience, riots, and urban guerilla warfare. Society fragmented into hostile, particularistic groups; Arthur Mann has called this "the ungluing of America" (Mann, Chicago, 1979). The deadening climate of the Cold War years gave way to the countercultures of the sixties. A New Left movement swept many young people into revolutionary movements. Drugs, sexual freedom, rock music, bizarre clothing, all mocked traditional morality. Liberation was the password: black liberation, women's liberation, gay liberation. Underlying this chaos were two basic drives which appeared to animate these disparate movements: the search for identity and the search for community. Black nationalism inspired a general movement of ethnic affirmation. Everyone was coming out of the closet; bumper stickers and buttons proclaimed "Kiss me, I'm Polish", "I'm Proud to be a Ukrainian", and "Finnish Power". Everyone appeared to agree that the Melting Pot was another myth to be discarded. This was the beginning of what has been called the ethnic revival (Polenberg, New York, 1980; Greenbaum, 1974, pp. 411-40).

The Italian Americans responded to this turmoil in a manner consonant with their ethnic and class history. By and large, they came down on the conservative side of the barricades. Belonging to what was called euphemistically the lower middle class (*i.e.*, blue collar workers), wedded to traditional values, imbued with the "cult of gratitude", they viewed the violence, riots, draft-card burning, and bra-burning with bewilderment and growing anger. Americans, they had been taught, were not supposed to act that way. For their defense of family, neighborhood, and patriotism, the Italian Americans, along with other white ethnic groups of recent immigrant origin, found themselves denounced as Fascist pigs, racists, Honkies.

History cast the Italian Americans as opponents of the black thrust for housing, jobs, and integrated schools in the northern cities. The "Little Italies", it seemed, had not disappeared, rather they demonstrated amazing staying power. More than any other white ethnic group, the Italians clung tenaciously to their old neighborhoods. Retaining the contadino sense of place, they were rooted in the particular ambiance of homes, stores, churches, and social clubs where two generations had now lived. Often the only large white ethnic group left in the central cities, they perceived black demands as directed at their schools, their jobs, their neighborhoods. To Italian Americans, it appeared that they were being forced to compensate blacks for a history of oppression in which they had had no part. As one angry resident of Chicago's West Side "Little Italy", said: "My old man never owned no slaves". Of course, Italian Americans harbored racial prejudice (as part of their Americanization they had learned that a dark skin was a badge of inferiority), but as Gambino has pointed out, there was a basic conflict in values and lifestyles between Afro Americans and Italian Americans.[11]

In their own eyes, the Italian Americans were not only defending their property values; they were fighting for a way of life. In certain cities, they organized para-military groups led by strongarm men like Anthony Imperiale in Newark to defend their frontiers. But such tactics availed little against the federal government or city hall. Many Italian neighborhoods during these years were bulldozed to make way for freeways or public housing projects; some were abandoned in panic before the "blockbusting" techniques of unscrupulous realtors. But others were saved through community organizing, political clout, and a growing appreciation of the role of ethnic neighborhoods as a stabilizing factor in our cities. The "Hill" in St. Louis, Bloomfield in Pittsburgh, the "Little Italy" of Baltimore, all are examples of revitalized Italian American communities which have stayed the tide of urban blight. In these campaigns, the appeal to ethnic pride was central. Thus the struggle of these neighborhoods for survival itself contributed to the resurgence of an Italian American identity (Gans, 1981, 7:102-116; Fonzi, 1971, pp. 98-181).

Within the new climate of opinion, the Italian Americans aroused

[11] Although limited by its New York and Sicilian American perspective, Gambino's *Blood of My Blood* is an insightful and sympathetic portrayal of "the dilemma of the Italian Americans". *See also*, David K. Shipler, "The White Niggers of Newark", *Harpers Magazine* (August 1972), pp. 77-83.

themselves from their apathy and espoused a new style of ethnic militancy. Although they had played the old game of machine style politics, they learned from blacks the efficacy of direct action through rallies, demonstrations, and marches. The sixties saw the proliferation of Italian American organizations devoted to confrontation and protest. Other than the defense of their neigh- borhoods, the one issue on which Italian Americans could mobilize was their negative treatment by the media. Since the 1880s, the Italians had had a bad press; they were portrayed as ignorant, dirty, lazy, servile, superstitious, pagan, but most of all as dishonest, criminal, and bloodthirsty. Hollywood was quick to seize upon two Italian stock characters: the gangster and the buffoon. Chico Marx was the most loveable of the latter, while Edward G. Robinson made a career of playing Italian mobsters, beginning with *Little Caesar* in 1931. When television became the most influential medium in the fifties, in one of the most popular serials, "The Untouchables", Elliott Ness waged weekly war against the Mob, all of whom spoke with Italian accents. The program was known jokingly as "The Italian Hour" or "Cops and Wops". In 1950, the televised Kefauver hearings into organized crime paraded heavy-bearded, gravel-throated sinister characters before the camera, all with Italian names. And in 1963, Joseph Vallachi "sang" on television about the internal workings of "Cosa Nostra". The Mafia was kept before the public in an unending series of newspaper and magazine articles. Americans appeared to believe that all criminals were Italian, and that all Italians were at least potential criminals. There is no doubt that this media barrage has done grave injury to Italian Americans, both to their self-esteem and to their perception by others. Yet, as Harry Golden observed, although they were the most maligned group in American society, the Italian Americans simply shrugged their shoulders and kept on eating spaghetti and singing "O Sole Mio" (yet another stereotype!)(Papaleo, Juliani, Parenti, Monte, all in Miller, Phila- delphia, 1978; Afron, 1977, pp. 233-55; Szczepanski, 1979, pp. 196-204; Golden, New York 1959, pp. 139-40).

In the 1960s, the Italian Americans said: "Basta!" Taking a page from the Jews, they initiated vigorous anti-defamation campaigns. In fact, the Italian American Anti-Defamation League had to change its name to Americans of Italian Descent (A.I.D.) after a lawsuit by the B'nai Brith's A.D.L. New organizations like the A.I.D., the Italian American Coalition, the Columbian Coalition, the Joint Civic Committee of Italian Americans, and older ones such as the Order of the Sons of Italy, protesting the demeaning portrayals of Italian Americans in the media, went beyond letterwriting to direct action methods of picketing and boycotts. They brought pressure to bear on television companies, sponsors, and newspapers, with some effect.

This present movement culminated with Italian American Unity Day on June 29, 1970, which drew over 50,000 Italian Americans to Columbus Circle in New York City. The occasion was colorful and festive with green, red, and white banners, but angry voices demanded fair treatment for Italian Americans. This massive display of ethnic solidarity gave substance to the buttons which proclaimed: "Italian Power". Politicians and journalists were startled at this outpouring of repressed rage from an ethnic group noted for its quiescence. The rally was sponsored by the Italian American Civil Rights League which had even gone so far as to picket the New York offices of the F.B.I. because of its harassment of suspected Italian criminals. In response to these demonstrations, the Justice Department and even *The New York Times* agreed to drop the words Mafia and "Cosa Nostra" from their vocabularies.

The League's dominant figure, Joseph Colombo, Sr., was himself a reputed Mafia leader. At its second Italian American Unity rally, in 1971, Colombo was shot in an assassination attempt, presumably by rival gang leaders. What had begun as an impressive expression of Italian American militancy ended in a tragedy which simply confirmed most Americans in their prejudice. It was also a reflection upon the quality of Italian American leadership that it took a Joe Colombo to bring the Italian Americans out of their neighborhoods. While the League quietly slipped out of sight, the issue of defamation continued to be high on the Italian American agenda in the 1970s.[12]

Underlying these surface manifestations of an awakening Italian American identity were structural developments which were to transform the character of the ethnic group. Most important was the coming of age of the third generation and the emergence of a fourth generation, the grandchildren and great-grandchildren of the immigrants. As we have seen, by 1980 the great majority of Americans of Italian descent were of these generations. With them, we have embarked upon a new phase in the search for an Italian American identity. Innocent of the Italian language, even of the dialects, knowing their Italian ancestors only as curious, old people, growing up often in mixed ethnic neighborhoods, immersed in the youth culture of their peers, in what sense could these young people be considered or consider themselves Italian Americans? Still, the most important factor in their lives was their second generation parents (in 1980 a majority declared a single Italian ancestry), who we have seen were themselves ambivalent about their Italianness. Willy-nilly, these parents instilled into their own children many of the contadino values such as respect for authority, belief in hard work, loyalty to the family. Even if they rebelled against them, these traits were ingrained in the personalities of the third generation. But their parents also

[12] Nicholas Pileggi, "Risorgimento: The Red, White and Greening of New York", *New York*, June 7, 1971, pp. 26-36; Fred Barbaro, "Ethnic Affirmation, Affirmative Action and the Italian American", *IA*, Autumn 1974, 1:41-54. "The Mafia: Back to the Bad Old Days", *Time*, July 12, 1971, pp. 14-21. Cover story with photo of Joe Colombo, Sr.; Paul L. Montgomery, "Thousands of Italians Rally to Protest Ethnic Slurs", *The New York Times*, June 30, 1970.

inculcated American values of ambition, success, and individualism. Thus they received conflicting messages: "Get an education, but don't change"; "go into the larger world but don't become part of it". Richard Gambino has described the "lonely, quiet crisis", of the third generation Italian Americans:

> When the third generation person achieves maturity, he finds himself in a peculiar situation. A member of one of the largest minority groups in the country, he feels isolated with no affiliation with or affinity for other Italian Americans. This young person often wants and needs to go beyond the minimum security his parents sought in the world. In a word, he is more ambitious. But he has not been given family or cultural guidance upon which this ambition can be defined and pursued. Ironically this descendant of immigrants despised by the old WASP establishment embodies one of the latter's cherished myths. He rationalizes his identity crisis by attempting to see himself as purely American, a blank slate upon which his individual experiences in American culture will inscribe what are his personality and his destiny.[13]

The "identity crisis" of the third generation is exacerbated by the rapid upward mobility which it is experiencing. A variety of studies has shown that the grandchildren of the immigrants have made a quantum leap up the socioeconomic ladder. In education, occupation, and income, they have either equaled or surpassed the national averages. For example, the percentage of Italian American youth attending college rose from 21 percent in the 1940s to 45 percent in the 1970s. With higher education has followed their increasing entry into the professions and managerial positions.[14]

Italian Americans are to be found in top positions in major corporations and government. Of course, these grandsons of ditchdiggers are more likely to be automobile salesmen rather than company presidents, medical technicians rather than doctors, teachers rather than university professors. Yet this is a dramatic rise in two generations. Further this upward mobility appears to have been accomplished by a decline in prejudice. Social distance studies carried on over the course of fifty years which measure willingness to associate with individuals of other ethnic groups show Italians rising from a ranking of fourteenth in 1926 to fifth in 1977. In the latter year, the Italians were the only group among the first ten not of northern European background. Public opinion polls also indicate a growing favorable attitude toward Italian Americans. In March 1982, persons were asked whether they thought various

---

[13] Gambino, *Blood of My Blood*, pp. 36-37. This discussion draws heavily upon Gambino as well as my personal experience and observations. Vecoli, "Coming of Age of the Italian Americans".

[14] David L. Arnaudo, "The Status of Italian/American Families" (mimeograph, 1983). Arnaudo summarizes the findings of various studies; in a letter to me of March 9, 1983, the author asserts: "Certainly the Italian Americans have succeeded to the norms of the mainstream groups". *See also*, Fondazione Giovanni Agnelli, *The Italian Americans: Who They Are, Where They Live, How Many They Are*, Turin, 1980.

immigrant groups had been a good or bad thing for the United States: 56 percent thought the Italians had been good; only 10 percent bad. Again the Italians ranked fifth among the groups listed. Perhaps the most significant indicator of acceptance is that for the first time the names of Italian Americans, specifically Lee Iacocca, Geraldine Ferraro, and Mario Cuomo, have surfaced in discussion of possible presidential and vice-presidential candidates in 1984.[15]

Yet, there persists a widespread feeling among Italian Americans that they are still objects of bias and discrimination. In a recent study, over 25 percent of the respondents thought that there was a "great deal of prejudice" against Italians, and respondents with college educations and high status occupations felt this almost as much as did working class respondents.[16] There is evidence that they are not simply expressing ethnic paranoia. Need we be reminded that only a few years ago the then president of the United States had this to say about the Italians:

> They're not like us. Difference is they smell different, they look different, act different...Of course, the trouble is... you can't find one that's honest.[17]

Unfortunately for Richard Nixon he ran into two honest ones by the names of John Sirica and Peter Rodino. A woman was recently quoted in a national publication as saying about a neighborhood in Brooklyn: "There are no white families there; only Puerto Ricans and Italians". Old prejudices die hard. One can find at any newsstand, so-called "joke books" full of vulgar, revolting jibes at "Eye-talians". Such "Italian jokes" are also heard in country club locker rooms, executive suites, and faculty clubs. Of course, the Mafia stereotype is in greater vogue than ever thanks to *The Godfather*.

The rapid rise of the Italian Americans which makes them for the first time serious competitors with Anglo Americans, Irish Americans and other established groups has stimulated a heightened prejudice at the upper levels of American society. Rumors of Mafia connections have been used successfully by rivals to blight the careers of Italian American politicians and businessmen. Various Italian American organizations have argued that the underrepre-

[15] Hall, "Italian Americans: Coming Into Their Own"; Carolyn A. Owen, *et al.*, "A Half-Century of Social Distance Research: National Replication of the Bogardus' Studies", *Sociology and Social Research*, October, 1981, 66:80-98; "Public Opinion of Ethnics Surveyed", (Roper Organization, March 1982). Theodore H. White has described the Italian Americans as "the most important among the rising ethnic groups" and "the newest dynamic political force". *America in Search of Itself: The Making of the President 1956-1980*, New York: Harper and Row, 1982, p. 371.

[16] James A. Crispino, *The Assimilation of Ethnic Groups: The Italian Case*, Staten Island: Center for Migration Studies, 1980, p. 190. This is a narrowly based study of Italian Americans in Bridgeport, Connecticut, but its findings are suggestive.

[17] Quoted in *IA*, 4, Spring/Summer, 1978, 4:282.

sentation of Italian Americans in the management of major corporations is itself *prima facie* evidence of discrimination. An analysis of the top 800 companies in the United States found that only 3.2 percent of the officers and directors had Italian surnames. There also have been complaints and lawsuits by Italian Americans against alleged prejudice in employment and promotion by law firms, universities, and corporations (Ruffini, 1981, pp. 60-64, 1983, pp.40-44; Pane, Staten Island, 1983; U.S. Commission on Civil Rights, 1980, pp. 370-508; Barbaro, Albany, 1978).

Although Italian Americans appeared to have the green light on the highroad to success, they encountered obstacles along the way. Those who have been rejected and even some who have "made it", alienated by the impersonal, cold atmosphere at the top, have experienced a reawakening of ethnic consciousness. Memories of warm intimate relationships in the "Little Italies", even if imagined, have brought some home in search of community and identity. The upwardly mobile, seeking something they had lost, were even more involved in the ethnic revival that those who had never left. Marcus Lee Hansen, historian of immigration and second generation Scandinavian, formulated the law of third generation return (Hansen, Illinois, 1938). According to Hansen's law, what the son wishes to forget, the grandson wishes to remember. The grandchildren of the immigrants, secure in their Americanness and free of the inferiority complex of their parents, indulge their curiosity about their Old World roots. While some of the third generation seem to validate Hansen's law, others are impelled by an urgent need to assuage the sting of anti-Italian prejudice.

Certainly Italian Americans are still bombarded with negative stereotypes in the media. Television commercials portray the jolly, fat "Mama Mia" making sauce for her large, noisy family, or some swarthy character mimicking the broken English of the immigrants: "Thatsa soma spicy meatball". Among other characterizations are those of "Fonzi" of "Happy Days", a macho, tough "greaser" and LaVerne DiFazio of "LaVerne and Shirley", naive, wisecracking, and dumb. A recent study of the images of Italian Americans presented on television concluded that negative portrayals outnumbered positive ones by two to one, one out of six was engaged in criminal activities, most held low status jobs, and the majority did not speak English correctly (Robert and Lichter, 1982; Brizzolara, 1980, pp. 60-67). During the seventies, there was an explosion of Italian American talent in the film industry. As directors and actors, Martin Scorsese, Francis Ford Coppola, Michael Cimino, Robert DeNiro, Al Pacino, Sylvester Stallone, and John Travolta, created powerful images of Italian Americans on the screen. Some like *Mean Streets* and *Rocky* were sympathetic, if grimy, portrayals of working class life, while others like *Saturday Night Fever* were vile caricatures of Italian Americans (Mormino, 1982).

The cinematic event of the seventies, however, was *The Godfather I* and

II. Mario Puzo confessed that after writing *The Fortunate Pilgrim,* an excellent novel but a financial failure, he decided to write something that would make money. *The Godfather* became an international bestseller, and as a film, a box office success and Oscar winner. Puzo and Coppola combined their considerable talents to transform the trite theme of Italians in organized crime into the Saga of the Corleone Family. *Godfather I* is a eulogy of *la via vecchia,* in which personal loyalty and fillial piety make for order and justice in an amoral and chaotic world. In *Godfather II,* the old order is corrupted by greed, loss of discipline, betrayal, and indulgence, in short, Americanization. *The Godfather* in fact glorifies and enables the lives of crooks and killers. Such a Hobbesian view of the world suited the cynical mood of America following Watergate. Also, the strength and stability of the "honored family" appealed to Americans at a time when all institutions appeared to be a state of disarray. Of course, *The Godfather* has deeply imbedded in the American psyche the Mafioso as the Italian American stereotype. It has been shown on television five times with the disclaimer: "There is no intent to offend any ethnic group or to suggest that criminality is more characteristic of one group more than another". Its success has inspired a host of cheap imitations. Dwight Smith in a study he called "The Sons of the Godfather" identified 300 paperbacks which appeared between 1969 and 1975 exploiting the Mafia theme (Smith, 1975, pp. 191-208; Silversteen, 1974, pp. 105-116; Sinicropi, 1975, pp. 79-91; *Newsweek,* March 13, 1972, pp. 56-61; Puzo, New York, 1972, pp.32-69).

The response of Italian Americans to *The Godfather* was most curious. Some organizations protested and picketed the films, but for many it appeared to be the Italian American equivalent of Alex Haley's *Roots.* Many, especially among the younger generation, embraced the Corleone epic as a source of identity. One third generation student told me: "I was so starved for an ethnic identity that when *The Godfather* appeared, I latched on to it as my heritage". When a school in Providence, Rhode Island, was observing ethnic days, the Italian American students came dressed up like members of the Corleone clan. Godfather bars, restaurants, and pizzerias, owned by Italian Americans, are to be found throughout the country. The Godfather motif is used at Italian American festivals. Such self-caricature and self-denigration are a sad commentary on the lack of cultural resources upon which many Italian Americans have to draw in defining their identities.

In their search for a positive identity some Italian Americans have turned to Italy. Since the fiasco of their flirtation with Fascism, they have shown little interest in or understanding of Italian politics. Efforts to enlist them in a crusade against the Italian Communist Party have not had much success. There has been no international crisis akin to the issue of Cyprus for Greek Americans around which to mobilize. Yet the Italian American response to natural disasters which have afflicted the homeland reveals a bond of sympathy with their cousins in Italy. More important has been the high esteem in which things Italian have of late been held by Americans. The mental picture of the Italian as crude and vulgar has been replaced with the view of the modern Italian as stylish and sophisticated. Italian now evokes the names of Gucci and Pucci, of Sophia Loren and Luciano Pavarotti, of Alfa-Romeo and Necchi. The young hero of *Breaking Away* models himself after the Italian cyclist much to the dismay of his father who doesn't like "wop" food. *The New York Times Magazine* devoted to "The Italian Americans" carried a full page ad showing a chic, slim woman sipping Martini and Rossi on the rocks. The caption reads: "The Italian You Won't Forget. Winning, Worldly, Well Bred". We are a long way from the *cafone*.

In the seventies, two national magazines were launched, *I-AM*, which was shortlived, and *Attenzione*, which is still published, catering to well-to-do Italian Americans. Ostensibly aimed at encouraging ethnic pride, they were not only filled with advertisements for expensive and classy Italian products, but with articles devoted to whetting appetites for Italian wines, clothing, furnishings, etc. The problems of establishing an Italian identity through consumption is that everyone can drive a Fiat, wear Gucci, and sip Martini and Rossi. And, of course, now everyone cooks pasta. One can even take courses on "How to be an Italian". Many Italian Americans in their search for roots departed from the tourist itinerary and visited the paesi of their ancestors. While they enjoyed the warm hospitality of their *parenti*, their common reaction, as in my case, was to discover that they were not really Italians, but Italian Americans. We discovered that our identities were not to be found in Italy, but within ourselves, within our own history and culture.[18]

The making of an ethnic identity has become a complicated business for Italian Americans. I use "making" deliberately because unlike their immigrant ancestors who knew exactly who they were, the American-born generations have choices. For them, the question, "Who am I?" demands a conscious answer. The ingredients which they have at hand from which to assemble the Italian part of their identity are varied and incongruous. They include the contadino values of *la Nonna;* the media images of *The Godfather;* the classical heritage of Leonardo da Vinci; and the contemporary Italy of Federico Fellini. Folk, popular and high cultures, all meld in the miniature melting pot of the Italian American identity. Italian Americans, in greater or lesser degree, hold these discordant elements in their psyches, and it is the need to reconcile, to synthesize them which energizes their search for identity.

[18] Based upon a survey of readers, the editor-in-chief of *Attenzione* defined the objective of the magazine as "maintaining a lifestyle publication relating to things Italian, and at the same time serving a reader who is affluent, educated and sophisticated enough to use a variety of products and services, regardless of their origin", September, 1983, 4. For a humorous reflection on the search for ethnic roots: Anthony Mancini, "Ethnic Travel; When You Find Your Roots Eat Them", *The New York Times*, August 1, 1971.

In this, they are representative not only of ethnic Americans, but of all people who are making the transition from rural, traditional to modern industrial societies, from Gemeinshaft to Gesellshaft.[19]

If, like archeologists, we dig into the Italian American psyche, we find the different strata of identity formations which have accumulated over a century of history. *Campanilismo* persists in the *paesano* clubs, now composed of the post-immigrant generations, but which still restrict membership to persons originating in the same village or province. The most dramatic expression of this folkloric heritage is the celebration of the *feste dei santi*. This summer scores of feste, in honor of *San Gennaro, San Rocco, La Madonna del Carmine* were celebrated. Tens of thousands attend these feste, some of which have been observed for almost a hundred years. They scrupulously follow the traditional forms with statues borne in procession, brass bands playing triumphal marches, aerial bombs exploded. One of the most spectacular of these is the *festa di San Paolino* celebrated in Brooklyn by the paesani of Nola, which includes *il ballo dei gigli*. The significance of the festa was recently captured:

> In Brooklyn the celebration of the Feast of Saint Paulinus expresses religious commitment, family tradition, manhood, and the passage from childhood through maturity to old age. The exultation at the end of each day of dancing is...a remarkable display of pride in, and affection for, the men of all ages who, in dancing the *giglio*, have renewed for the community its sense of order, values and continuity (Posen and Sciorra, 1983, pp. 30-37).

The celebration of the feste is made possible by the survival of "Little Italies" long after their disappearance had been predicted. The spirit if not substance of the mentality of campanilismo is embodied in the ties which most Italian Americans maintain with family and neighbors. The suburbanization of ethnic populations was thought to be the final step in the assimilation process. Certainly this has not been true of Italian Americans who have tended to move together to new areas. Although in Chicago, the old "Little Italies" have been largely evacuated, the Italian Americans are highly concentrated in the northwestern districts of the city and adjacent suburbs. Then too there is the

---

[19] These observations are drawn from personal introspection as a second generation Italian American as well as attending scores of conferences, workshops, and meetings with other Italian Americans over the past two decades. In addition, *See*, "Italians Here Search for Their Identity", *The New York Times*, December 3, 1972. A report on a "consciousness-raising dialogue on ethnicity" in an Italian American community, it quotes Frank Arricale as saying "Sure, we'll have a special place in our hearts for Dante and Michelangelo and the others, but we have to learn to be proud of ourselves...We must remember we're not Italians. Our history began on Ellis Island". The conscious and complex character of this search is indicated by the establishment of groups to explore their Italian American identity. Joseph Giordano, a family therapist and director of the Center on Group Identity and Mental Health of the American Jewish Committee, directs a national project on research and training on Italian American identity.

phenomenon of the "weekend ethnics", the suburbanites who return to the old neighborhoods to visit relatives and friends, to shop in the Italian stores, to attend the Italian church, and to participate in the feste. Thus Italian American ethnicity survives in these intimate relationships of the "little community" (*The Sun Magazine*, Baltimore, 1970 pp. 6-9; Bryne, Chicago, p. 1-6; Pileggi, New York, 1959 pp. 14-23; Tricarico, New York, 1984; Juliani, 1983, pp. 133-46; Gallo, 1977; Wonk, New Orleans, 1983, pp. 10-15).

Perhaps the best symbol of the duality of the Italian American identity is the observance of Columbus Day. Cristoforo Colombo, who has been claimed as the spiritual father of all Americans of Italian descent (we are "the children of Columbus"), attests to the Americanness of their Italianness. Today, as in the past, October 12 is celebrated with banquets and parades. In a city like Chicago, the Columbus Day parade is a great pageant with bands, floats, celebrities, and dignitaries. Participation by politicians, especially presidential aspirants, is *de rigueur*. Everyone makes speeches extolling the virtues of the Italian people, invoking the names of Michelangelo, Garibaldi and Marconi. After a long campaign, the Italian Americans succeeded in having Columbus Day declared a legal holiday, over the protests of Scandinavian Americans. Such symbolic recognition takes on significance in the context of American ethnic politics.

A more recent manifestation of the Italian American presence is the metropolitan-wide celebration such as the *Festa Italiana* of Milwaukee. Attracting hundreds of thousands, including many non-Italians, these are mixtures of ethnic and popular cultures, of the sacred and the secular. Italian foods, Italian American pop singers and comedians, a mass and religious procession, folk dancing and strolling musicians, and a cultural exhibit ranging from "typical food stuffs of ancient Rome" to the modern "Art of Italian Automobile Racing", provide something for everyone. The profits of the Festa have been used to establish an Italian Community Center the purpose of which is "to unify the large factions in the Italian community into one cohesive whole".[20] Indeed, these citywide celebrations are expressions of the still incomplete process of creating an inclusive Italian American consciousness from the scatter of contending regional and provincial identities.

At another level, some Italian Americans are engaged in an intensive search for their family and ethnic heritage. Even before Alex Haley's *Roots*, many were pursuing genealogical studies. I have received poignant appeals for help from third generation persons who know only that their grandparents came from a village in the Abruzzi or Campania. Twenty years ago such

---

[20] *The Italian Times* (Milwaukee, Wisconsin) April, 1982; the issue of July, 1983 was devoted entirely to the sixth annual "Festa Italiana" which was described as "the largest and most successful Italian festival" in the country, expected to attract over 200,000 visitors. Its origins were traced to the first festa celebrated in 1905 in honor of the Holy Crucifix by immigrants from Santo Stefano di Camastra.

enthusiasm for tracing one's roots through steerage to humble paesi was unheard of; social-climbing Italian Americans then purchased coats of arms certifying to their noble lineage. Certainly today's attitude is much healthier than the shame-ridden second generation syndrome. Many local study groups, such as the Italian Cultural Society of Sacramento, California explore their heritage through lectures, art exhibits, concerts and tours. The study of Italian has increased modestly but steadily during the seventies while enrollments in other languages have fallen. A particularly fascinating development is the rediscovery of regional cultures. Arba Sicula, an international Sicilian ethnic and cultural association, was established some five years ago in response to "a felt need by an established [American] ethnic community...to define, preserve and disseminate our ancient heritage to assure its undistorted survival". Membership is limited to those who have at least one Sicilian grandparent, although honorary membership may be extended "to non-Sicilian ethnics under special circumstances". The society publishes a Sicilian language cultural and literary journal. This expression of ethnic pride among Sicilian Americans, the most maligned of the Italian Americans, is especially welcome.[21]

An important factor in the Italian American consciousness movement has been the emergence of an intelligensia among the second and third generations. These are scholars who have chosen to focus upon the Italian American experience in their studies. A generation ago such were rare indeed. If Italian Americans pursued humanistic studies it might be in the Renaissance or Risorgimento, far removed from their immigrant origins. As a result there were few works dealing with the history or sociology of the Italian immigration, and these few tended to be by non-Italians. Responding to the pluralist climate of the sixties, young Italian Americans, then entering the professoriat in modest numbers, began to write dissertations, books, and articles about "their own people". In his survey of doctoral dissertations on Italian American topics, Remigio U. Pane found that over half of them had been written since 1960, many by Italian Americans.[22] The formation of the American Italian Historical Association in 1966, dedicated "to an understanding of the Italian experience in America" reflected this new commitment. Unlike its predecessors, such as the Italian Historical Society of the 1920s, the A.I.H.A. was free of filiopietistic or political motives. Over the past seventeen years, through its conferences and publications, it has addressed many facets of Italian American history. Growing from a handful to several hundred

---

[21] Arba Sicula, the International Sicilian Ethnic and Cultural Association, publishes a journal by the same name and a newsletter, *Sicilia Parra*.

[22] Remigio U. Pane, "Seventy Years of American University Studies on the Italian Americans: A Bibliography of 251 Doctoral Dissertations Accepted from 1908 to 1977", *IA*, Spring/Summer, 1978, 4:244-73. For historiographical essays dealing with much of this literature *See*, Tomasi, ed., *Perspectives in Italian Immigration and Ethnicity*.

members, the Association has cultivated and legitimized this field of scholarship. Specialists in Italian American studies are now to be found in leading American universities and colleges. Their books and articles comprise a bibliography running to several thousand items. As one who was involved in launching this field of study, I sometimes feel as Max Müller did when writing to Giuseppe Pitre regarding the study of the popular traditions of Europe.

> Years ago, when that study was, if not despised, at least ignored, I spoke out as strongly as I could against its detractors. Now that I begin to feel old and tired, I find the trees which I helped to plant growing into such forests that I often feel tempted to cry out, enough, enough (Cocchiara, 1981, p. 293).

But upon reflection, I know that it is not enough. We have learned that the history of the Italian Americans is an enormously complex phenomenon; there are many parts of it about which we know little. The experiences of the second and third generations, for example.

Unfortunately the influence of this substantial and stimulating body of scholarhip upon the mass of Americans of Italian descent has been slight. Within the typical family, an anecdotal history of the paese, the immigration, and experiences in this strange land might have been passed down by word-of-mouth, although often the questions of the second generation encountered a wall of silence. Commonly the second generation chose not to transmit the mutilated fragments of oral tradition and folklore to their children. Thus the third generation exists in an historical vacuum. Yet when courses in Italian American studies have been offered at colleges they have been slow to enroll. That is, as Gambino has noted, because of their "shame-born-of-confusion condition". In their insistence that they are "just Americans", they are revealing their deep ambivalence about their identities. They have been denied the influences which would give them a positive sense of their ethnic background. For this, the Italian American community *in toto* is primarily responsible. Unable to create the linkages between neighborhood, political-economic leadership, and intellectual elite, it lacks the organizations, institutions, and publications by which dialogue and mutual education could take place among these levels. As Andrew Greeley has commented:

> When the time comes that the Italian American community provides the cultural marketplace that the Jewish community does and the larger society is willing to abandon its beloved stereotypes and listen seriously to what the Italian American experience is about, classrooms will be filled with young people in Italian-studies courses (Greeley, 1975, p. 245;. Gambino, p. 330).

It has been said that Italian Americans do not read, and there remains a good deal of truth in the observation. *Identity*, a monthly magazine devoted to a serious discussion of Italian American affairs, was established in 1977 and expired within the year. *Italian Americana*, a semi-annual journal, which treats the Italian American experience from a multi-disciplinary perspective, has a circulation of about 1,000 and struggles for existence. Clearly the "cultural marketplace" for literature dealing with Italian American life does not yet exist. One reason is an underlying anti-intellectualism, pronounced even among educated businessmen and professionals, which causes Italian Americans to keep "professors" at arms-length.[23]

There is no dearth of Italian American organizations with abundant resources which could underwrite programs in research, creation, and dissemination of publications, films, and exhibits about the history and contemporary status of Italian Americans, or which could sponsor classes, workshops, and summer camps for both adults and children. The Order of the Sons of Italy in America, UNICO National, the Italian American National Union, to name only a few, have the capacity to undertake such projects. But their activities are primarily social, and they would rather direct their philanthropy to medical research than to Italian American research. One finds little support for serious scholarship, intellectual debate, or critical self-examination among wealthy Italian Americans.[24] The National Italian American Foundation established in 1975, which promised to provide leadership in advancing the interests of all Italian Americans, has proven a disappointment. Its major function has been a biennial awards dinner at $ 125 a plate at which are assembled the most prominent Italian Americans and the Washington establishment. The failure of President Reagan to attend the dinner in 1982 cast a shadow over the event, and inspired mutterings of political revenge for this slight. The Foundation's lobbying effort has been directed at securing the appointment of Italian Americans to high government positions. With other Italian American organizations, it has opposed the media's negative image of Italian Americans and promoted a "positive image". These organizations, in their agendas, reflect upper and upper-middle class concern with "image" and status.[25]

Little attention is paid by Italian American organzations to the social

[23] For comments on the historical roots of this anti-intellectualism, *See,* Rudolph J. Vecoli, "The Italian American Literary Subculture: an Historical and Sociological Analysis", in John M. Cammett, ed., *The Italian American Novel,* Proceedings of the Second Annual Conference of the American Italian Historical Association, Staten Island, NY: A.I.H.A., 1970, pp. 6-10; and Anthony Pedatella, "Letters", *La Follia di New York,* February, 1983, p. 34-35.

[24] For a comprehensive list of Italian American organizations, *See,* Silvano M. Tomasi, ed., *National Directory of Research Centers, Repositories and Organizations of Italian Culture in the United States* (Turin: Fondazione Giovanni Agnelli, 1980), and Peter Sammartino, "National Italian American Organizations", in *The Family and Community Life of Italian Americans,* Juliani, ed., pp. 161-164.

[25] For the activities of the National Italian American Foundation, *See,* its *Washington Newsletter,* January-February, 1:1977. Typical of these activities is the conference jointly sponsored by the NIAF and the Order of Sons of Italy in America on "Italian Americans and the Media: Building a Positive Image", *La Follia di New York,* April, 1983, pp. 10-11.

and cultural needs of working class or poor Italian Americans. There are exceptions such as the Congress of Italian American Organizations (CIAO) and the Italian American Coalition of Organizations (AMICO) which have focused on the problems of the inner city ethnic neighborhoods, including the high rate of dropouts and drug addiction among youth, the plight of the elderly poor, and the inadequacy of social services. However, such organizations have been criticized by well-to-do Italian Americans for publicizing negative aspects of the ethnic group. The myth that, unlike other groups, Italian Americans care for their poor and needy through the family serves as a rationale for the relative paucity of philanthropy. Similarly the cultural and intellectual needs of the third and fourth generations are largely neglected by the ethnic organizations. As a group, Italian Americans are still handicapped by an elite which in its narrow vision and unenlightened self-interest resembles too much the prominenti of the past (Casalena, 1975; Arnold *The New York Times*, Sept. 29, 1972).

What then of the search for an Italian American identity? As this paper reflects, the subject is a vast one, encompassing millions of persons of various generations, spread over a continent, and situated from the top to the bottom of the American class structure. No easy generalization will suffice. Certainly there is a great deal of vitality, even a *risorgimento*, within the Italian American communities. From their mixed heritage of folk, popular and high cultures, many are engaged in the struggle to fashion whole and healthy identities which will bridge their past and present. Both at the interpersonal level of everyday life and at the level of consciousness we find a reaffirmation of ethnic community. But the fate of the third and even more the fourth generations remains problematical. Will they be finally absorbed into the anonymous American middle class bringing the saga of Italian American immigration to an end? Straightline assimilationists like Herbert Gans would have us believe so (Gans, preface to Crispino). Much depends, I believe, upon the Italian American community itself. Unlike our neighbor to the north, Canada, which in accord with its policy of multiculturalism susidizes the maintenance of ethnic languages and cultures, the United States follows a policy of cultural laissez-faire. It is up to each ethnic group to determine whether it will survive or vanish. The failure of the Italian Americans to create an infrastructure of institutions and organizations to define and sustain an ethnic identity gives us pause. But there is reason for hope. The very pluralistic structure of the society impels individuals, even the upwardly mobile, to seek community within their ethnicity. More fundamental is the basic hunger which all human beings have for identity which will validate their humanity, a hunger which is sharpened by the technological, bureaucratic society in which we live. Of one thing I am sure: the search for an Italian American identity will continue.

8

Comments on the Papers
by Stephen Hall, Joseph Giordano,
Humbert S. Nelli and Rudolph J. Vecoli

The Italian American Identity

FURIO COLOMBO
Professor of History, Columbia University Barnard

THE MELTING POT

WE were told by Glazer and Moynihan, in the 1960s, that the Melting Pot
dream had worked so well that the issue now was moving one step forward
and meeting the problem of a new, totally American image. Yet, the turmoil
of those same years, and the upheaval which accompanied the seventies
through to the present have proven to us that this was not the case.

Newly emerging groups and their just claims for identity (the blacks) and
language maintenance (the Hispanics) came forward proposing a new type of
America: a federation of different roots in which you harmonize and offer the
best of your old heritage, acquire the best of the new heritage, and give away
nothing of your original identity.

Groups that were already deeply involved in the American life, the
American dream, and the American identity were shocked at first and then
deeply affected by the new claims for roots and heritage. The Italians had
given so much away—some even their family name—to become American.
They were confronted, like so many European Jewish people, by the "as-
similation/separation" dilemma. Like many Jewish immigrants they chose
assimilation and paid full price for it. Customs were preserved in a discreet,
local way. Family ties, strong by nature and culture, remained strong (a
blessing which reinforced the survival of roots and heritage). Many other

European groups were lost and simply melted because there were no strong points of communal survival.

History had been harsh and demanding on the Italian American. They left a country which had not given them much. They were the children of the "difficult" parts of Italy, of "difficult" periods and of a glorious but troubled past. They came to America along with their memories, and were left alone even by their clergy, who seldom emigrated with them, unlike the Irish.

The Center for Migration Studies can tell you how much Italian heritage there is in American religion. The Italians had Irish churches to worship in, and English history to learn.

There were the years Italians couldn't care less for their brother immigrants. They who had remained in Italy also accepted, as everyone else in the world, the film and media cliche about these immigrants. And the new country allowed them to have the success they never had at home, at the price of total Americanization. What we, the Italians from contemporary Italy must remember and appreciate is that these Italian Americans did this by themselves, without help from any cultural establishment, either in Italy or the U.S. They created an Italian American culture which must be recognized and appreciated. For some time this culture and identity has been besieged by the Americans and ignored by the Italians. Yet, the special vitality of the Italian American identity has proved itself creative, strong and enduring. It was creative enough to establish links and to move toward the academy, politics and public life. It was strong enough and proud enough to become a partner to Italian cultural ventures in this country and it was enduring enough to be noticed and courted by presidents and the media.

Still, however, many problems remain.

1) *Language and cultural identity.* I know of at least one person who refuses to fill the census form because it was given to him in English and Spanish. He said: either in English alone, or you give it to me in Italian. It is not so much a political issue as it is a moral and cultural one. Language has something to do with identity. I do think the basic educational curriculum in this country is unfair to the children of Italian descent. I also think it can be corrected without interfering with the rights of the other American students. In fact, many groups would benefit by a new, more comprehensive vision of European history.

2) *Culture.* A stronger determination, from the Italian American point of view, in supporting cultural institutions, departments, colleges and places where Italian and Italian American culture is alive. The Italian American cultural network should be strong enough to orient the community independently from specific political choices. The image of the Italian American should be as visible as the one of other illustrious members of the American mosaic. We now know the strength of America is not the melting pot, but it is the capacity to create without destroying, to construct American without

dismembering pieces of other nationalities. The Italian Americans are strong enough to be fair and considerate and, let it be said, American enough to face these problems.

3) *Identity*. A sense of history should drive the Italian American away from Fascism, the death penalty, and the dream of being superior to other groups that are less fortunate. And they should address themselves to a new way to solve social problems without pressing onto others the burden of discrimination that has oppressed the Italian so long. A sense of compassion should assign a strong role in keeping high and alive that part of the American dream that is so beautifully inscribed in the Statue of Liberty and at the entrance of Kennedy airport.

A sense of healthy competition should motivate the Italian American never to abandon the real and symbolic places of their name, their culture, their image and—when possible—the preservation of their ancestor language. A sense of pride will guide the community to be, as it is, a strong and healthy part of the American mosaic. The Italian American must check the media, in a liberal and conscious way; reviewing school programs, especially at grade level; and be aware that too much celebration is just the other side of benign neglect. You don't want too much celebration. You want your real image reflected back to you.

The Italian Experience in the United States, October 1983

Virginia Yans-McLaughlin
Rutgers University

When a group of intellectuals from an ethnic group assembles to discuss the question of ethnic identity, it does, in fact, define ethnicity symbolically: in the words, concepts, theories, ideas and categories for discussion which we, as scholars, use. Imagine a visiting anthropologist from a foreign culture examining these presentations, hoping to create an ethnography of Italian Americans in 1983. A strange picture would emerge if our investigator examined only Mr. Hall's and Mr. Nelli's papers. A picture, I venture to say, which would not correspond with the nature and quality of Italian American life as most of us know it. The group, as these two papers define it, consists of upwardly mobile Italian males. This third-generation group has exchanged blue for white collars. Some are *mafiosi*. Others belong to baseball teams. A few hold political office. The Italian American version of Henry Ford pounds his chest, in some Pagliaccio-like gesture, on television. There is no working class in Mr. Nelli's and Mr. Hall's Italian America. If the group is doing well economically, its biological future stands in jeopardy: there are no women in these papers. And none of their authors seem to be concerned with women. It is interesting to observe that the earlier papers on the demographic characteristics of Italian Americans did not exclude women and the family from their discussion. The questions posed, the problems to be solved by demographers require reference to sex, fertility, family size and pattern. But, in this session, as our male authors seek to define Italian American identity, women have no place in it. There are no families, no homes, no neighborhoods, no religion. In fact, excepting Mr. Vecoli's paper, there is no mention of ethnic identity either. There is, instead, an obsession with success, with making it in America. So Lee Iacocca replaces Christopher Columbus in the new Italian American pantheon of gods.

It is clear this new symbolic definition of ethnicity belongs to the 1980s. One cannot imagine it emerging from such a conference held during the 1960s and 1970s, when conference participants held more romantic and more personal images of ethnic life. Then, unlike now, we discussed the family, the neighborhood, the work Italians did and the way they felt about their work. We talked about the novels they wrote and the political causes they championed. And, in that way, we created a different definition of Italian American ethnicity. That was ten or twenty years ago. Has the group changed or is it the way we, as a group, have changed the way in which we are thinking about ourselves that has changed? And if it is the latter, I leave it to you to determine which is the better measure of reality.

Comments on Papers by McKenney, Levin and Tella, and by Nelli and Vecoli

RICHARD D. ALBA
State University of New York at Albany

AT this conference, we are of course concerned with the signficance in our lives of having ancestors who came from Italy one of two or now three generations ago. Given this commonality, we tend to interpret our experiences from the perspective of being Italian, losing sight of the possibility that they may be far more general than that. We say, for example, that we're making it—and we are—but we imply that we are making it in a distinctive Italian way or that we can make it and retain an essentially Italian flavor in our lives.

I am convinced that these implications are not true. As I see matters, we are in a period of transition, one that is not simply affecting Italian Americans but all persons whose ancestors came from Europe. A profound transformation is underway, submerging ethnic boundaries among the former white ethnic groups and leading to a broad cultural convergence among them by eroding their once prominent cultural features. This process will have substantially reworked the nature of ethnicity in the United States by the end of the century, producing something approximating the hoary "myth" of the Melting Pot, at least for white Americans.

This claim is based on extensive analysis of census and other major survey data. I grant that if one looks today at Italians in the aggregate, the group still appears to be distinct from other ethnic groups (as the McKenney, Levin and Tella paper points out). But such appearances can be very deceiving because the group in the aggregate mixes together 70-year-olds who immigrated from the Mezzogiorno and youthful members of the third and even fourth generations. To trace the trajectory of change, it is necessary to determine the group by generation in the United States or by age, which is equivalent to the historical period in which a person matured. When such a detailed analysis is done, there are many indicators that a transformation is not only underway, but irreversible. A pointed instance involves the supposed lag of Italian American women behind other women. This is a problem to which previous speakers have referred, interpreting it as a reflection of the still vital family-centered culture of the group, which assigns an important family role to women but thereby handicaps them in achievement outside the home. Italian American women as a group do in fact have lower average educational and occupational achievement than women from core American groups, such as those with ancestry from the British Isles. But the picture changes dramatically when the group is analyzed by generation or by age. It then becomes clear that the gap is very large among older women or those from the first and second generations, but the youngest Italian American women, those born after World War II, have caught up with WASP women (and also, incidentally, with Italian American men). A process of convergence is underway. The same process is also evident among Italian American men. Its realm is not confined to education and occupation: the same convergence is visible for a broad range of cultural indicators (The evidence for these assertions is contained in my book on Italians, to be published in the summer of 1984 by Prentice-Hall.)

The most compelling evidence for the eclipse of ethnicity lies in the rise of intermarriage. Since World War II, the watershed for ethnicity in the United States, there has been a tremendous rise in the incidence of marriage across ethnic lines among whites (the same pattern does not hold, however, across racial lines). For example, analyzing recent census data, I have found that of Italians born since 1950, generally two-thirds to three-quarters, depending on the definitions employed, have intermarried. These figures are for individuals of wholly Italian parentage. Of those with only part Italian ancestry, close to 80 percent marry entirely outside the group. Nor are these intermarriages confined within a small circle of similar groups. Among Catholic groups, the Irish-Italian combination has become very common. But Italians also marry frequently across the Catholic boundary. According to national survey data, about 50 percent of the Italian American Catholics born since World War II have married non-Catholics (mostly Protestants). A sense of the impact of this surge of intermarriage on the Italian American group is given by the trend in mixed ancestry: very few older Italians have mixed ancestry (a mere 6% among those born before World War I); but the great majority of younger Italians do (almost 80% of those born after 1965). This trend implies a profound shift in the nature of the Italian group; by the end of this century, a majority of those who are Italian will also be something else.

The importance of the trends in intermarriage is not contained in some racial or genetic meaning; rather they speak to the social contexts in which individuals find themselves, contexts which are likely to constrain expressions of ethnicity. These trends and the earlier-mentioned convergence need not, of course, imply the complete disappearance of ethnicity. I, for one, do not believe that they will. But I do think they mean a fundamental change in its nature, which might be described with the metaphor of "twilight". I mean the word to suggest that there may still be some perceptible ethnic differences, but they will be much fainter and only intermittently visible. Ethnicity will no longer have the same life-organizing force that it has had heretofore.

I think these trends illuminate properly the nature of the much proclaimed revival of ethnicity. They indicate that this is not so much a revival of ethnicity in its most basic aspects as an increase in the degree to which individuals feel comfortable expressing ethnic sentiments and symbols in minor ways. The key notes of the revival are those of celebration and a quite-justified pride, a somewhat nostalgic focus on the bittersweet authenticity of the immigrant experience, and an attachment to ethnic symbols such as food and art forms rather than to the living culture itself. Its nature is occasional, undemanding, entirely consistent with social mobilty and easy intermingling with individuals from diverse ethnic backgrounds, and ulti- mately personal. This last is to say, it is left up to individuals to decide how they wish to be Italian, since they are less and less embedded in a matrix of ethnic communal life that might give common shape to their ethnic urgings. The essentially personal nature of ethnicity in the coming twilight era is nicely brought out in James Crispino's study of the Italian Americans of Bridgeport, Connecticut; the only thing his respondents could agree on is that it is not alright to change one's name to sound less Italian.

Those who wait for an ethnic renaissance will, in my view, wait in vain. The ethnic revival turns out not to disprove the twilight thesis but to be wholly consistent with it: ethnic pride is possible now precisely because ethnic differences have become so mild. It's finally alright to be a little ethnic in America, but just a little.

PART TWO
RESOURCES AND THEORIES

9

The State of Italian American Research Since 1976: Sources, Methodologies and Orientations in Italy

GIANFAUSTO ROSOLI
Editor, Studi Emigrazione, CSER, Rome

IF a compilation of the bibliography of a given topic implies its historiography, then in the case of Italian migration one may rightly assume that in Italy the lack of a valid history of emigration means the lack of an adequate bibliography. Thus any bibliographic attempt runs the risk of being a mere listing of titles. Moreover, to its many present-day economic, institutional, political and cultural problems, Italy adds also the problem of "its past" (When did the nation begin to exist? Its territorial dimensions? Its characteristics? Etc.). One becomes aware of this problem by analyzing the various debates arisen from the recent publications of Italy's histories (Einaudi, *La Nuova Italia*, etc.). But if there is an area in which the past has been completely erased and forgotten, due to a complex series of suspicions and gaps, this is the migratory field. Not only do we lack a worthy history of Italian emigration, and a school of higher studies—on a phenomenon affecting more than 26 million persons—but Italian migrants, in general, are seen as a body already separated from Italian history. This may mean that Italy does not yet consider its emigrants as its own and that migrant communities living abroad, in turn, are no longer feeling a vital part of Italian history. Speaking on more general terms, we must admit the difficult task of relating Italian history to the history of the host countries, due to the dominant historiographic trends.

This presentation will focus on sources published after 1976. As I stated earlier (Rosoli, 1977), Italian research on the United States, especially historical, has always been influenced by the national political debate. A deeper knowledge of American history was deemed necessary for a political comparison. The need was felt to examine carefully some experiences (the "founding" of the United States, constitutionalism, and later on the "New

Deal", etc.) comparable to the Italian ones. Moreover the strictly Eurocentered outlook, which had influenced this whole field of research, has been broadened only with the final decline of idealism and historicism and for a wider acceptance of American culture. In the 1960s the Italian Left dealt with a series of topics related to American populism, the "New Left", blacks and women's liberation movement. The labor experience of the I.W.W. was the main and compulsory field of research for all young scholars. But only the 1970s (and credit is due to some heads of history—such as Luraghi and Spini—for having convinced numerous young researchers to study American history) did Italian studies become more important and authoritative, offering new insights of great relevance (Bairati, 1978; Barié, 1978).

Nevertheless, considerable ideological and scholarly conditionings are still felt in this field of research. This is due to the very diverse scholarly backgrounds of the Italian Americanists. As for the research on Italian emigration to the United States and on Italian Americans, Italian scholars are still constrained by the following gaps: 1). insufficient or no interest on the part of academic structures on emigration; 2) misunderstanding of ethnic values seen as contrary to class values; 3) limited appreciation, until recently, of "minor" history, and local culture, because not politically active or backward and of the "American cafoni"; 4) the absence of an institution with the task of boosting and coordinating Italian research on Italian Americans (such as the American Italian Historical Association in the United States); and 5) poor originality of the studies in this area and their dependence on translations of the American "classics".

THE BICENTENNIAL EFFECT

Nevertheless it would be wrong to think that, notwithstanding all these gaps, research on Italian Americans has not made any progress in recent years. Evidence may be gathered from the numerous conferences and seminars on the United States and its relationship with Italy held from 1976 onward. Even though the topics have been mainly historical-political, they have had a positive effect on research on Italian emigration to the U.S.A.

We shall mention them briefly. I think it right to call to mind the two volumes edited by Spini in 1976. They constitute an interesting collection of essays, some original and important for their references to the migrant communities. In that same year R. Luraghi organized in Genoa an international historical conference in which Italian and American scholars faced each other. This "confrontation" was resumed in the Washington seminar (Luraghi, 1978; Tagliarini, 1976; Nelli, 1977). The political topics were always prevailing (*See*, for example, the volume on the Truman Administration and Italy, Aga Rossi Sitzia, 1976; 1979). In the following years, after a plentiful sociological production, the revolutionary labor movements and American radicalism drew the scholars' attention at the Second International Conference on North-American History (Milano, 1977), and at the 1980 Ferrara Conference (Bologna, *et al.*, 1977; Romero, 1981).

In those years even the political attitude of the Italian official institutions and the government was changing as a result of the National Conference on Emigration (CNE, 1974, 1975). The Conference was an event which drew national attention. It also showed signs of political inability in putting forward feasible proposals, notwithstanding the desire for a wider participation of the migrant communities. In fact, the immediate tabling of a migrants' representative body (as a plethoric organization and with uncertain responsibilities) and the predominance of the European components inside migrants' institutions represented put in second order the American communities. The Conference organized by the Ministry of Foreign Affairs and held in New York in 1977 to debate specific problems of the Italian migrant communities in North America, was once again—in the positive and the negative results—a proof of the changed political climate and of the feigned acceptance of the migrants' cultural needs.

The comparison between the cultural and institutional models of Italy and the USA and the search for more suitable ways for a reciprocal understanding animate the initiatives of the successive years, promoted by public organizations. This involvement of public institutions is relatively new in this scientific field. In 1978 and in 1979 the Ministry of Foreign Affairs and UNESCO organized workshops on Italian culture abroad and seminars on the comparison between Italian and American cultural organizations, history and ideologies (Bartile, 1980, 1981; Romano, 1979; Della Terza, 1982). In 1981 the problem of Italian publication with respect to the American publishing field was widely debated (MAE, 1982). Besides the various initiatives concerning history, promoted in particular by local bodies, regions and municipalities, we must recall the scientific activity of the Agnelli Foundation with its publications and seminars (Lange, 1979; Agnelli Foundation, 1979, 1980). The crossed analyses of Italian and American scholars in Florence (1978), such as De Felice, Farneti, Sarti, Matteucci, Barnes and Hoffman, deal with the sociological aspects of the cultural relationships between Italy and the USA, the political interpretations, the cultural ties and the diplomatic aspects. But the most original work in this field is the publication of a repertoire (edited by the Center for Migration Studies of New York) on Italian American cultural organizations. This allows us to get to the heart of the Italian American communities, following the cultural map of their institutions, various activities and networks: associations, newspapers, bulletins, teaching of the Italian language and archival sources (Tomasi, 1980).

Again in 1980, the historical-political Institute of the University of Florence organized a conference on the relationship between Italy and the

USA in the period 1943-1953 (Vezzosi, 1983). But only very recently, the AISNA (Associazione Italiana di Studi Nord-Americani) has at last promoted a conference on Italy and Italians in America with numerous contributions on the literary, artistic and human experiences of Italian Americans (Pinto Surdi, 1983; Massara, 1984).

THE PREDOMINANT TOPICS

Considering the nature of Italian studies on emigration and greater versatility of Italian scholars in political research, the best works on emigration published in Italy in recent years are overall and far-reaching analyses. The need for a synthesis at the national level goes along quite well with the most recent trend in regional studies, especially on the most typical areas of departure. Necessary and timely verifications of the general hypotheses are, in fact, needed and new fields of analysis are being sought (Di Nolfo, 1978; Migone, 1980; Lerda, 1981; Villari, 1977; Vaudagna, 1981a, 1981b; Valtz Mannucci, 1981; Margiocco, 1981).

Due to a revival of studies on emigration in the 70s, after a long pause, we meet with useful "tools" such as anthologies-collections of essays intended for general information and to stimulate further investigation. Even some useful translations fall into this category (Martellone, 1980, with an extensive introduction and a useful bibliography). On the same line we put the volume edited by Avagliano (1976) and also the two volumes by Ciuffoletti and Degl'Innocenti (1978). This latter work is a valuable tool for historians of Italian emigration. It reprints government and private organizations' documents and comments by scholars and politicians during the last one hundred years. The first volume starts with the parliamentary debate on emigration (1868) and ends with World War I; the second volume presents documents from 1915 to 1975.

Along this line, which offers some good general information and information on Italian emigration to the United States, we may add some collections of essays on the American labor movement. (Bock, et al., 1976). We recall the analysis by Paolo Carpignano (1976) on "immigration and degradation: labor market and ideologies of the American working class during the 'Progressive Era'". The Proceedings of the Naples Conference, held in 1974 (Assante, 1978) and the Salerno Seminar, held in 1976 (Dell'Orefice, 1979) offer a valuable framework and some contributions concerning the USA (E. Ginzburg Migliorino, "Italian immigrant pupils in Philadelphia's Schools"; A.M. Martellone,"An Outline of the Italian Left in the USA: trade unionists and reformists"). More original is the research coordinated by Renzo De Felice (1979), in particular the historical investigation of C. Belleri Damiani (1978) on the fascist migration policy and the complex and difficult relations with the American government.

But the most useful and important works are of a statistical-demographic nature (Rosoli, 1978a) or economic-political (Sori, 1979). The first book, the result of a collaboration of many Italian scholars, provides a quantitative analysis of Italian international and internal migration flows since the availability of statistical data in 1876. The contributors present a concise and complete picture of the volume of international and internal migrations, their structural causes of pathological dependency, regional imbalance in the Italian south and the persistent miopic government policies. An extensive annotated bibliography of official statistical publications, of international statistical sources and the most important statistical literature on migration in chronological sequence is also provided. Sori's volume is the most recent in-depth analysis on migration and is very useful for further research and studies with a rich bibliography at the end. The book is divided into three parts: 1) quantitative features of the phenomenon, 1861-1940; 2) economic causes and social consequences of mass migration, economic integration and class struggle, foreign labor markets and Italian experience abroad; and 3) the modification from out-migration to internal migration, 1915-40. (Cerase, 1976; Treves, 1976).

More recently, the economist L. De Rosa (1980) has analyzed migrants' remittances, and the policies pursued by the Italian banks in collecting and investing these funds (1896-1906). At a lower scientific level and with lesser accuracy, Briani's (1977; 1978) works on the Italian press abroad and the migratory legislations are nevertheless useful research tools.

With the revival of interest for the scientific study of migration we find, besides the traditional methods for research, new techniques and new approaches to the problem. Numerous social history researchers and the prevailing interest in the use of primary materials have put the migrant at the center of attention as the main focal point of the migratory process. The changed cultural and political climate, the incentives and the publishing successes on the experiences of Italian migrants living in Europe[1] or on the migrants' letters (Franzina, 1979) have produced, even in the case of the USA, results of great value. In particular we recall the autobiography of Antonio Margariti (1979). It is a life history of a Calabrese worker who migrated to Pennsylvania in 1911. The original form of this memoir containing dialect expressions mixed with American elements is published with a standard Italian translation. This autobiography presents the inner world, the expectations, moral values, political tensions and the cultural uprooting of a migrant worker in the USA. The result, not solely due to the oral history, is a search for a history from the grassroots, less abstract and automatic than that imposed in the past by some strict ideological prejudices.

---

[1] Castelnuovo Frigessi, *Elvezia, il tuo governo. Operai italiani in Svizzera.* Torino: Einaudi, 1977. Pp. cix-473; Rovere, Giovanni, *Testi di italiano popolare. Autobiografie di lavoratori e figli di lavoratori emigrati.* Roma: Centro Studi Emigrazione, 1977; Cavallaro, Renato, *Storie senza storia. Indagine sull'emigrazione calabrese in Gran Bretagna. Roma: Centro Studi Emigrazione, 1981.*

Searching for new fields of investigations, scholars have started exploring with doubtless usefulness, even on the part of historians, the fields of minor literature, law, ideologies, oral history and folklore applied to the migration field. As proof of these interests we find the monographic issue of the journal *Movimento operaio e socialista:* "Dall'Italia alle Americhe: storie di emigranti e immagini dell'emigrazione" ("From Italy to the Americas: Migrants' Histories and Migration Images", 1981). We find bibliographic critical essays (Molinari, 1981), interviews of some protagonists of the Italian American emigration (P. Ortoleva, 1981, "A voice from the choir: A. Rocco and the Lawrence strike of 1912"; N. Fasce, 1981, on the oral testimony of Italian migrants in the USA at the beginning of the century). Interesting also are the analyses of the propaganda contained in the guidebooks for migrants and the literature on successful migrants centered upon the topics of departure, journey and homeland (Lupi, 1981). A. Traldi (1976) had already analysed in depth the literature and the prevailing topics of the Italian American novelists and Massara (1976) masterfully presented the Italian travelers to the U.S., 1860-1970 and the literary image of the U.S. in Italy (1984).

More recently this analysis has been resumed with more interpretative sophistication by an American professor teaching in Venice. He analyzes autobiographies, or rather self-critical artistic analyses, of Italian American writers such as C. Panunzio, P. D'Angelo, E. Carnevali and J. Mangione within the more general framework of migrants' autobiographies in the USA. (Boelhower, 1982; *See,* the new journal *In Their Own Words,* 1983 and the 1981 issue of *Letterature d'America*).

Even the traditional research areas which deal directly or indirectly with migration has been resumed in recent years. Suffice it to think of the implications in the migratory field contained in the research by Dinucci (1979) on the expansion ideologies pursued by Italy at the end of the last century. Of interest are some references to the intellectual history and the influence of ideas between Italian and American writers (Ottaviano, 1981, 1982; Villari, 1980).

Always qualified and well represented are the studies on Italian socialists and anarchists in the USA (Vanzetti, 1977; Fiori, 1983) and in particular on the work of the anti-fascists (Haupt, 1976; Salvadori, 1978; Dadà, 1979, 1982; Papa, 1982; Spadolini, 1982; Valiani, 1982) with references to individual personalities and events, interpretations or evaluation overviews.

Among the abundant recent literature of political history, some new and important contributions on US-Italy political involvements have been brought forth. The activity of antifascist personalities or institutions and of Italian diplomats during and immediately after World War II are recurrent themes (Varsori, 1976, 1980; Miller, 1976; Canavero, 1979). The study of Italian communities abroad and of their elites is a key passage in studying group contrast and political conflicts (Cannistraro, 1976; Miller, 1980; Killinger,

1981). The utilization of new materials reveals an ignored complexity of factors and connections (Sartori, 1979; Filippone Thaulero, 1979).

Some outstanding political personalities, who lived for a time in the U.S. such as centenarian Prezzolini, attract the interest of Italian historians. De Felice (1982) presented a special portrait of Prezzolini between war and the affirmation of Fascism. On the same topic, E. Gentile is working to complete a general and definite biography, including Prezzolini's experience as Director of the Casa Italiana in New York.

THE ITALIAN AMERICAN COMMUNITIES

The "classic" field for well trained American researchers is the study of the Italian American communities, either urban or rural, their living conditions and institutional and group peculiarities. Even today American expertise is confirmed; in fact the most valid contribution on this topic is the Italian translation of the American anthology edited by Pozzetta (1981) on Little Italies in North America. Moreover, American historians published more frequently in Italian journals than their Italian counterparts. For example, Caroli (1976) studied the formation of American restrictionism and the Italian attitude, Di Pietro (1976) considered the role of language as a marker of Italian ethnicity, Loatman (1977) studied a small Italian community in a rural environment of upstate New York where Italian characteristics resist better to the dominant way of life. De Marco (1980) analyzed the Italian community of Boston's North End and the persistence of an ethnic enclave tinged with regional connotations. On the topic of return migration from the USA, we must indicate the interpretive model of Gould (1980), while Cinel (1981, 1982) considers social conditions and personal expectations bound with return, intended as a necessary step in migratory project.

Some Italian contributions on Italian American communities have also been produced during these years: Migliorino's (1976) study on a Philadelphia community, Loverci's (1980) essay on "Risorgimental" emigration in California and Calvi's (1980) considerations on modifications of Italian Americans "from paesani to citizens". But the most in-depth research is Salvetti's (1982) essay on the Italian community of San Francisco during the 1930s and 1940s. The rise of Italian Fascism led to a deep and pronounced split within the community. The role played by the Italian press, as well as the Italian voluntary associations and institutions, are analyzed both in terms of their influence within the community and the city of San Francisco itself. A remarkable transformation of the Italian community occurred in the post-war period not only within the community but also in its relationship with the mother country. The same researcher is now completing a detailed portrait of an Italian community of New York's Greenwich Village through an analysis of Our Lady of Pompei records (1984).

On the role of the ethnic church among Italian American communities, some new investigations have been carried out during these years, both as general overview (Rosoli, 1979) or as monographic contributions. Among them, in a special issue of *Studi Emigrazione*, are Tomasi's (1982) essay on the role of the Prelato per l'emigrazione Italiana in the U.S., Vecoli's (1982) description of Italian religious organizations in Minnesota and Mormino's (1982) research on the Italian parish in St. Louis, Missouri. We must also acknowledge Vannicelli's (1978) research on Italian parishes in Boston and Philadelphia and Di Giovanni's (1983) work on Bishop M.A. Corrigan and the Italian immigrants in New York, 1885-1902. With particular reference to Europe during Fascism, the presence of the Church in the political discussions on Italian emigration and the Vatican dissent with Fascist programs have been analyzed (Cannistraro and Rosoli, 1979).

One of the most interesting topics recently analyzed regards the role of Italian immigrant women in the North American society (Calvi, 1981; Tirabassi, 1982; Cetti, 1983).

REGIONAL VERSUS NATIONAL HISTORY

Even though in Italy we lack far-reaching interdisciplinary research projects on emigration, studies on emigration at a regional or local level have sufficiently increased. They have succeeded, generally speaking, in overcoming merely local interests. Thus we are forming a national mosaic, multifaceted and for the great part unknown before. Each Italian region, in fact, possesses its own migratory "tradition", with its own temporal, spatial and sociocultural variables (Calice, 1982). To traditional out-migration regions, which in past years had provided matter for fundamental studies, new contributions have been added in recent years concerning other regions. This is also a consequence of the revival in the study of local history and the support of local institutions, municipalities and regional bodies in promoting seminars and conferences on emigration.

Veneto and the Southern regions hold supremacy in the field of migration research. For the Veneto region, Franzina's (1976, 1979, 1982) publications on the workers' movement and the use of primary sources and the most recent book by Lazzarini (1981) constitute points of reference because they are in-depth and valuable researches, which analyze almost all aspects of local history tied to the migratory phenomenon — such as economic conditions and causes, demographic variables, social classes, local elites' behaviour, political components, economic, cultural and political influences upon the migratory phenomenon, etc. Other scholarly essays were also published in journals and dealt with the various aspects of the Veneto emigration. They analyze some unaccustomed social roles, such as those of the emigration agents (Brunello, 1977) or the migration flows during the Fascist regime (Scarzanella, 1977) or social organizations working on behalf of migrants in such areas as Friuli-Venezia Giulia (Micelli, *et al.*, 1982).

Besides, some seminars on local history, such as the one sponsored by the Treviso municipality in October 1981 (*Society and Emigration in Contemporary Veneto, XIX, XX Centuries;* have acted as incentives for investigations into new topics, such as the role of welfare agencies for migrants, secretariats and charitable institutions, local surveys on emigration, peculiar aspects on popular literature, health problems, etc. (Franzina, 1983).

Even in regions with a low rate of out-migration, such as Umbria, research on migration is carried out. We recall in particular the recent publication of Luciano Tosi (1983), researcher at Perugia University, on the Umbrian migration during Giolitti's period.

Analyses of the southern regions have often appeared in different journals. In particular we recall the essays concerning Calabria (Izzo, 1977; Nobile, 1977), and especially the seminar promoted by the Deputazione di Storia Patria per la Calabria entirely dedicated to the Calabrese emigration from Italy's unification to the present time (Polistena, Rogliano, December 6-8, 1980; Borzomati, 1982). In the proceedings we find some very relevant historical and sociological essays on some Calabrese communities hit by the emigration phenomenon (Polistena, S. Pietro in Guarano, Delianuova). We find contributions on certain aspects of newspaper controversies, on the interventions of the political forces, the Socialists and the Catholics, including also the actions of Propaganda Fide in favor of the Italian migrants in the USA (Vannicelli, 1982). Of particular interest is Arlacchi's original interpretation reaffirmed in an ad hoc publication. The author maintains that the Calabrese emigration hit especially the small farm owners rather than the day laborers working in the latifundia (Arlacchi, 1980). Piselli (1980) analyzes the kinship networks and states that at times they are reinforced through the migration experience. Among the numerous regional essays, we must recall Remigio Pane's study (1982) on the experience of the Calabrese migrants in the USA. It is, as far as we know, the first monographic research, but others are planned such as the one on the Venetian migration to the USA.

Some micro-social surveys on emigration have been promoted by associations which, traditionally, deal with people on the move, such as the union of historical demography. *See,* for example, the recent seminar held in Assisi (April 26-28, 1983) on the *Italian demographic evolution in the 19th century: continuity and changes (1796-1914).*

To conclude this section on seminars and conferences, it will be useful to recall the conference promoted by the Brodolini Foundation. Proceedings are now available (Bezza, 1983). This conference on *Italians outside Italy: Italian migrants in the workers' movement of the host countries, 1880-1940* has offered very interesting contributions on different countries and institutions, but also on more general points of view. Suffice it to recall here F. Grassi's essay on migration policies pursued by the first Crispi' government, Sori's on the political debate and Franzina's on police control over extremists living abroad. Among the contributions more specifically concerning the USA are the important presentations by R.J. Vecoli on the Italian immigrants in the United States and Labor Movement from 1896 to 1929, Cartosio on Italian migrants and the Industrial Workers of the World and A.M. Martellone on the presence of the Italian ethnic elements in the USA political life: from non-participation to post-ethnicity.

ARCHIVAL RESEARCH AND THE PROBLEM OF SOURCES

The archival sector and, more generally, the primary sources for the study of the phenomenon of migration are clearly proliferating and have in store for us bigger surprises than in the past. If we compare the present situation with the situations of up to twenty years ago—when the first Italian publications on migration were beginning to appear—we find much progress has been made in preserving archival materials, in cataloguing them, and in discovering new and original sources (especially in private institutions) that are useful for understanding migration. Even informational and bibliographic tools have improved or are coming into being (Formez-CSER, 1976; Bonazzi, 1976; Centro Studi Americani, 1981; Franzina, 1978; Rosoli, 1978b, c; Tomasi, 1979). We have only to think of Bettini's contribution on the anarchic press (Bettini, 1976) to get an idea of the scientific rigor of this scrupulous research. But, for scope of research (comprehending a whole century), for archival and documentary completeness and accuracy, and for steadfastness (covering a 20 year period), the catalogue edited by Professor Pietro Russo (1983) of the University of Florence is preeminent: *Catalogo collettivo della stampa periodica italo-americana (1836-1980)*. (Comprehensive Catalogue of the Italian American Press (1836-1980) to be published by the Center for Migration Studies of New York. This catalogue is an indispensable tool for gauging the quantity and quality of this migration press (over 2300 titles)—a press that was very much alive and constantly reviving, though divided and chauvenistic. But the catalogue is indispensable also for studying the impact of the Italian American press on the immigrant communities and on sur-rounding American society.

It is a well known fact that Italy was late in discovering the value and importance of the archival and library documentation it possesses throughout the country, one of the richest in the world. Only in recent years has Italy begun to make a comprehensive inventory of its artistic and cultural riches. We can easily understand why this immense effort to collect and catalogue has not made much of a dent on more recent documentation. Still, the Ministry for Cultural and Environmental Goods has initiated a multi-volume work: the *Guida generale degli Archivi di Stato italiani* (General Guide to the

Italian Government Archives). So far, the first two volumes have appeared (up to the letter M). These are supremely useful work tools and are enriched with copious archival and bibliographic information which will help even researchers in the field of migration.

Unfortunately, archival material on migration is scattered throughout various collections, public and private, central and local; hence, even a simple catalogue is impossible. Published archival inventories are rare, especially for private institutions (among the few recent ones, see that of the Propaganda Fide: T. Kowalsky, Metzler, 1983). As a result, a study of them is almost impossible. Certain aids—containing references to relations with foreign countries—provided by the General Administration of the archives can be of some use[2] (Gencarelli, 1979). But, to date, we still do not have—for the United States—a guide to historical sources like the one for Latin America, edited by Lodolini (1976).

The various collections on migration have already been listed in certain studies (Ostuni, 1981). Besides the two main ones—ACS and ASMAE—we must point out those of the House and the Senate, of the Museum of the Risorgimento, of various banks, especially those of the Banca d'Italia, the Banco di Napoli and the Banca Commerciale Italiana, the archives of the various steamship companies, of the Lega Navale, of the Confindustria, as well as the archives of institutions important in the field of migration assistance, like the Umanitaria of Milan, the many benevolent societies throughout the length and breadth of Italy, the Dante Alighieri (active in promoting Italian language and culture abroad); finally, the private archives of certain people, like Salvemini.

The Archivio Centrale dello Stato (Central State Archives) in Rome—which is undoubtedly the richest and most important source, has emigration material in the collections of PCM, the Interior Ministry (especially in the press section), in the Duce's private Secretariate—NUPIE, as well as in the well known CPC collection (Casellario Politico Centrale) and in that of the Polizia Internazionale.

ASMAE (Archivio storico-diplomatico del Ministero degli Esteri) has various collections. Besides the P series (Politica, the most consulted and endowed even with printed catalogues that go up to 1950), one can find the collections of the Italian embassies and consulates abroad, the most important

---

[2] See, in particular: Casucci, C. (ed.), Archivi di "Giustizia e Libertà" (1915-1945). Inventario. Roma: Istituto Poligrafico dello Stato, 1969; D'Angiolini, P. and C. Pavone, "Gli archivi". In Storia d'Italia, vol. V: I documenti 2. Torino: G. Einaudi, 1973. Pp. 1659-1691; Piccialuti Caprioli, M., Radio Londra, 1940-1945. Inventario delle trasmissioni per l'Italia. Roma: Direzione generale degli archivi di stato, 1976, vol. 2. Gencarelli, E., Gli archivi italiani durante la seconda guerra mondiale. Roma: Quaderni della 'Rassegna degli Archivi di Stato', 1979. Ministero per i Beni Culturali e Ambientali, Garibaldi nella documentazione degli Archivi di Stato e delle Biblioteche statali. Roma: 1982.

of which have catalogues. There is a separate collection for the archive of the cabinet of the General Commissariate for Emigration and of the General Administration for Italians Abroad, for which CSER prepared the catalogues (Ostuni, 1978, 1980); of special importance are the relations of the General Commissariate for Emigration and other government agencies with the Italian steamship companies. But many administrative, consular and commercial papers are not in order and often there are not even the analytic registers of documents deposited. Of importance is the collection of the Polizia Internazionale, as well as series Z Affari Privati (Private Affairs), which contains much material of the international legal department as a result of incidents to the detriment of Italian citizens. This material documents very well the Italian government's attitude toward foreign governments in the matter of migration and the protection of Italian workers abroad.

How this archival material, intelligently used and cross-referenced with the printed material from parliamentary and political debate, can make an original contribution is illustrated by the work of Loverci (1977) on the first Italian ambassador to the United States, Baron Saverio Fava. The portrait of the ambassador, who represented Italy in Washington for an unusually long time (from 1881-1901) emerges with distinct contours by studying the political and migration events he had to cope with *vis-a-vis* the American government during the period of American expansionism.

The need to better understand the institutional aspects of Italian diplomatic representations abroad and the history of each mission (number, quality and mobility of the personnel, the tasks performed, etc.) was the reason for recently beginning the *Storia della diplomazia italiana* (History of the Italian Diplomatic Service). Professor Fabio Grassi, of the University of Lecce, is coordinating the work. This research is extremely important for understanding many aspects of diplomatic activity regarding Italian emigrants.

The material of the diplomatic and consular representations in the United States needed to be set in order. To cope with this problem and make this material available in the shortest time, the General Administration of Emigration of MAE, in agreement with the Superintendency of the archive, decided to entrust CSER with the job of ordering and classifying these collections, beginning in 1983. Though this work is long and tedious, it is nonetheless beginning to give the first results and first inventories for each consulate. But not all the consulates in the United States are represented. To date, the only archival material conserved at ASMAE deals with just six consulates: New York, San Francisco, Chicago, New Orleans, Cleveland and Denver. To these we must add the vast and highly interesting material of the Embassy in Washington, which has material predating the Unification of Italy (from 1860).

Material from the consulates is much more recent: in effect, it dates from the 1920s and is mostly administrative—namely, material dealing with various tasks the consulate performed for the Italian community or for local authorities. But it is not ongoing. Moreover, we don't find the same material in every consulate. But we can point to certain constant blocks of material that can lend itself to a new kind of research: lists of names with some demographic and economic data and information on regional origin, etc. We are referring to registers of passports issued by the consulates, registers of aid given to Italians in financial difficulties, registers of succession (for San Francisco alone over 2000 documents of succession for the 1930-1950 period are on file), dossiers for sending students to Italy, scholarships, etc. Material on the numerous Italian associations abroad and on the Italian schools abroad is copious and interesting.

We can easily see, therefore, that the prospects are promising for further research and eventual collaboration, especially with American scholars who, because of their knowledge of the material in question and the American sources, can fruitfully cross-reference them with what is presently becoming available in Italy.

10

The State of Canadian Italian Research in North America

CLIFFORD JANSEN
Associate Professor of Sociology,
York University

AT the end of the second World War, there were 113,000 persons of Italian origin in Canada. By 1981, there were over 800,000. This massive increase in the numbers of Italo-Canadians has been accompanied by a corresponding growth in the socioeconomic literature on Italians in Canada.

In the years immediately following the war, little was written about the group. It was not until the end of the 1960s that studies began to appear, about both their current situation and their history in Canada. By 1971, Italians had become the fourth largest origin group in Canada, after the British, French and German origin groups. But Italian immigration to Canada seems to have reached its term; relatively few Italians have immigrated to Canada since the beginning of the 1970s.

Reviewing the literature on Italo-Canadians since 1975, several themes can be discerned. First, attempts have been made to reconstruct their history. Second, a number of general descriptive studies have appeared. Those of a demographic-statistical nature were made possible by availibility of 1971 census data on a 1 percent sample basis. Thus, persons of Italian origin could be compared to those of other origins. Third, the literature has covered themes of particular importance to Italo-Canadians, namely, social stratification and social mobility, educational levels, relationships with Canadians, family relations and sex-roles.

HISTORY

The most important attempt to reconstruct the history of Italians in Canada has been carried out by Robert F. Harney, continuing a tradition he started in the early 1970s. The most comprehensive works include "Italians in Canada", (1978c) and an article, "The Italian Community in Toronto" (1979a). Both works give a comprehensive, well documented history of Italians and their relations with the wider Canadian society. They underscore the evolution in attitudes towards Italians, from hostile racist attitudes in the early part of the century to a more accepting attitude in recent decades. Harney also focuses on particular problems in the history of Italian immigrants such as the commerce of migration, the system of *padronism*, being treated as a *sojouner* rather than as a member of Canadian society and how immigrant men survived without their wives and families.

Recently, similar studies of Italians in Montreal have appeared. Since 1979, a group of researchers have begun work on reconstituting the social history of Italians in Montreal. Among publications already available are *The Italians of Montreal: From Sojourning to Settlement, 1900-1921* (Ramirez and Del Balso, 1980) and "Montreal's Italians and the Socio-Economy of Settlement 1900-1930: Some Historical Hypotheses" (Ramirez, 1981).

Very little is available about the history of Italians in other parts of Canada, particularly the west. Vancouver has over 40,000 Italians, but little is known of their history (a 1971 publication, *Strangers Entertained: A History of Ethnic Groups of B.C.*, by John Norris refers to important Italians in the history of British Columbia).

A publication by the Italian Ministry of Foreign Affairs, covering Italian emigrants in several countries, gives an overview of the salient points in the history of Italians in Canada (Briani, 1975). Recent articles in the Journal *Polyphony* give insight into the Italian press in Canada since the Second World War.

GENERAL DESCRIPTION

In 1978 the Italian National Congress published the results of a study of Italians across Canada. The main theme of the study was that Italians in the rest of the country did not feel that they belonged to a national organization directed from central Canada, *i.e.*, Toronto-Ottawa (Augimeri 1978).

A demographic profile of Italians in Toronto is among descriptive studies in a specific location (Tomasi, 1977). A study of Italians in western Canada focused on the establishment of an Italian center in Vancouver. Written by an ex-Italian consul (Germano, 1978) it is amply illustrated with pictures. Published in Florence, the text is in both English and Italian. A study of the Italian community of Vancouver based on the theme that ethnic groups only appear homogeneous to the outside observer, while there are numerous bases for differentiation giving rise to rival sub-groups and leaders within, was published in 1981 (Jansen, 1981b). The same author published an article focusing on the community organization of Italians in Toronto in 1977.

While not focusing exclusively on Italians, two studies (Trovata and Burch, 1980 and Trovato, 1981) compare fertility ratios across Canada for several ethnic groups using census data. They find that Italians are among groups with low fertility patterns in Canada.

Other general descriptive studies appear in a high school text book on Canadian studies (Doughty et al., 1976); in a relatively short book called The Italian Canadians (Mastrangelo, 1979); in The Culture of Italy: Medieval to Modern (Chandler and Molinaro, 1979); and in a book entitled From an Antique Land: Italians in Canada (Hardwick). A study of Italians in a northern Ontario town, Timmins, is published under the title: They Live in the Moneta: An Overview of the History and Changes in Social Organization of Italians in Timmins, Ontario (DiGiacomo, 1982).

In an attempt to bring together as much data as available on Italians in Canada for reference purposes, Jansen and La Cavera published a Fact-Book on Italians in Canada (1st edition) in 1981. It includes tables and maps and covers total numbers of Italians in Canada, provinces and major metropoolitan areas. It identifies Italian provinces from which Canada and the U.S. received most immigrants in the period 1962-1971 and presents other migration data. The 1971 census of Canada is used to compare characteristics of Italians to those of the total population and to those of other immigrant groups. Maps of Canada's three major cities (Montreal, Toronto and Vancouver) identify settlement patterns. The degree of satisfaction of Italians in any specific areas and with life in general is compared to national trends. A bibliography on Italians in Canada contains over 120 references.

A fairly long report on Quebec Italians was made available in manuscript form in October, 1981. It covers Italian immigration to Quebec, the history, social structure, leadership and associations, family, sex-roles and politics of Italians in Quebec (Painchaud and Poulin, 1981).

In addition to the census as a source of data on ethnic groups in Canada, several studies have been carried out at the national and local levels which allow comparisons of Italians to others. Among the most prominent of these are: The Non-Official Languages Study (1973-National) focusing on retention of non-official languages and the survival of ethnic groups; The Majority-Minority Study (1976-National) which analyzes interethnic attitudes; The Social Change in Canada Project (repeated nationwide in 1977, 1979 and 1981) which focuses on the degree of satisfaction experienced by Canadians, and the Pluralism Study (1977-Toronto) focusing directly on survival of ethnic groups. All of these studies can be accessed through the Institute for Behavioral Research, York University, Toronto, Canada.

STRATIFICATION, SOCIAL MOBILITY, EDUCATION

There is little doubt that the majority of post-war Italian immigrants were persons of low socioeconomic status. This is reflected first in the proportion of Italian-origin labor force immigrants destined for the lowest status jobs in Canada between 1962 and 1977—76 percent. Similar proportions for some other origins were: Greeks—58 percent; Portuguese—54 percent; East Indian—34 percent; British—32 percent; Chinese—21 percent; Japanese—18 percent and Americans (U.S.A.)—13 percent. It is also reflected in the fact that in 1971, while 17 percent of the Canadian labor force were in high white-collar (professional) jobs, this was 7 percent of the Italo-Canadian labor force. While 37 percent of the Canadian population (15 years and over) had only completed elementary school, this was 66 percent for those of Italian origin (Jansen, 1981a, Chapter 2).

Following on John Porter's *The Vertical Mosaic* (1972), which demonstrated a link between ethnicity and social class, Darroch in a 1980 study shows that over time the occupational structure of specific origin groups becomes similar to that of the Canadian structure as a whole. Among exceptions was the Italian origin labor force, which became even more dissimilar from the overall structure between 1961 and 1971, tending to over-representation in the lowest status jobs. This is not to say that there has been no upward social mobility for Italians in Canada. Richmond and Kalback, in an analysis of the 1971 census, conclude that "... the Canadian born of Italian origin showed remarkable upward social mobility ..." (p. 253). This was mainly due to the fact that, while their immigrant parents had extremely low levels of education, and Italo-Canadian school children were obliged to remain in school until ages 15 or 16 (obligatory school age), there was a big jump in highest levels of schooling for children compared to their parents. This fact is reflected in the high proportion of second generation Italians in low white-collar (clerical, sales, service—44 percent compared to the Canadian average of 41 percent.

Yet when considering post-secondary (non-obligatory) education, which usually leads to the professions, the proportion of Italians attending was still below average. While 11 percent of the total population ages 18 years and over were still at school, this was 8 percent for those of Italian origin. Other non-English, non-French groups, also had 11 percent (Jansen, 1981a).

Several studies have considered the aspirations and achievements of minority group children, including Italians. Among these are studies by Anisef (1975), Danziger (1979), Denis (1978), Maykovich (1975) and Wilkinson (1981). The principal theme of these studies is that the aspirations of children of Italian origin for higher education and professional careers is no different, and in some cases is higher, than that of the average Canadian school child.

However, when asked if they feel they will realize their aspirations, most Italians feel that they will not.

A combination of factors are offered as explanations for this situation. A majority are starting from very low levels; thus even completing secondary school is a great achievement. School authorities tend to stereotype the Italian school child as one who does not aspire to higher education. There is great difficulty in getting parents involved in their children's education. This is partly because of their own low levels of education and their lack of fluency in Canada's languages and partly due to their belief that the schools have sole responsibility not only for educating but also for disciplining their children. Canadian schools do not adequately reflect the multicultural composition of society, so that role models are often those of Anglo-Saxon society. Many Italian leaders believe that the only solution is complete assimilation to the core-group values (Jansen, 1981a).

RELATIONSHIPS WITH CANADIANS

Canada is committed to a policy of cultural pluralism in which specific groups are encouraged to preserve their own culture and identity, while participating formally in Canadian life. The policy known as multiculturalism encourages maintenance of ethnic culture, intercultural encounters and acquiring at least one of Canada's official languages.

The French and the people of Quebec, however, are not as devoted to the idea of mulitculturalism as is the federal government and many other provinces. Some feel that it relegates the French culture to the same status as that of other minority groups.

With the election of the Parti Quebecois in 1976, a policy of assimilation to French culture was endorsed. This led to friction between minority groups and the French. Most minority groups in Quebec are located in Montreal and most were assimilating to the English rather than the French in that city.

In an interesting analysis of the 1971 census of Canada, Ares (1975) shows that of all minority groups living in Montreal, Italians were the only ones who were more likely to use French rather than English when not using their own language. Also, when asked how well they knew either English or French, only 15 percent of Italians said they knew English only, while this was 45 percent or more for other minority groups. However, Italians strongly resented the imposition of French language schools (Troper and Palmer, 1976) and many English leaders in Montreal took up the cause of minorities like Italians, defending their rights to choose the language of instruction for their children.

Italians not living in Quebec were caught in a dilemma. They wanted to side with their fellow Italians in Quebec, but they saw the French as a group which has always held a minority position in English-French relations. In a study of Italian media personnel in and around Toronto, they expressed their ambivalence. A typical response was: "The Quebecois reaction is expected. It happens in all societies where minorities are oppressed. The same thing—being left behind culturally and economically—could happen to my (Italian) community" (Jansen and Gallucci, 1977).

In most other communities in Canada, Italians as a group appear to be well accepted and are often wooed by rival political parties when elections are held. While generally seen to support the Liberal party of Trudeau, Italian candidates have run for all official parties in recent elections. They form important pressure groups at the time of elections (Jansen, 1979).

As for relationships with Canadians at the unofficial level, a few recent studies indicate the degree to which they have been accepted. In a 1977 study by Berry *et. al.*, when respondents were asked for their perceptions of Italians in Canada, they were significantly above average in describing Italians as hardworking, wealthy and tending to stick together. It is interesting that Italians are thought of as being wealthy when they have below average incomes. But the fact that large numbers own their homes could be a cause for this belief. In the same study, Italians were considered to be significantly below average with respect to being important, Canadian, clean, similar to the respondent, likeable and interesting. In other words, respondents still felt that Italians stood out as a group (Berry *et. al.*, Appendix 5.1).

Other studies focusing on Italians and other Canadians include articles by Driedger and Mezoff (1981) in which it is told that Italian and Jewish high school students in Winnipeg reported frequent incidences of prejudice and discrimination; Robert D. Day (1981), where the author points out that despite the fact that London (Ontario) soccer clubs were orginally formed to retain a sense of cultural identity, they now promote assimilation; a study about the role of Canadian media in assimilating the Italian community (Battistelli, 1975); and a study showing that a higher degree of assimilation was being experienced by Italian adolescent girls (Colalillo, 1979).

THE FAMILY

A 1975 study described the difficulties faced by the new immigrant in Canada (D'Antini, 1975). Because of his or her feeling of disorientation, insecurity and anxiety, the Italian immigrant resorts to a greater dependence on immediate family and kin. Since the family represents a direct link to the original culture, the immigrant tries to reinforce family traditions and values and maintain a tighter control on the behavior of his or her children who are exposed to the more individualistic patterns of behavior in Canadian society. Thus, kin and home become the focal points of the Italian immigrant's life. While one could have expected a threat to family unity, since all members did not immigrate together, Ziegler (1977) confirms that family ties were not only maintained but were reinforced through migration.

The theme of the role of the family in easing the adaptation of new immigrants is repeated by Sturino (1980) who points out the number of ways in which the new immigrant is helped in the process. Once families were reunited in Canada, the role of the father was clearcut: he had to maintain or improve upon the status of his family. The wife was responsible for the upbringing of the children. In those cases where the wife held a job as well, she could not neglect her duties at home. Parents were judged by the success of their children who were encouraged to succeed and children showed their gratitude by the respect they paid to their parents. Even after marriage, children stayed in close or in constant contact with their parents.

Sturino (1978) also gives a good illustration of how a particular southern Italian family can be traced from their origins in 1935 to their present-day situation. He shows a combination of social and geographical mobility of the initial immigrant and his descendents within the city of Toronto. He also shows how post-war immigrant utilized pre-war immigrant kin ties in their efforts to gain desirable employment and how these ties influenced settlement patterns.

In a study of Italian immigrants in Quebec, Ramirez (1982a) points out that, given the expectations of the new society, it was only within the family that immigrants could continue to preserve their Italian traditions. Here, they could "... express their sentiments by words and actions that would be totally incomprehensible to a Canadian" (p. 135). So, in a sense, the family became the guardian of traditional Italian values.

SEX-ROLES

In October 1977, a conference entitled *The Italian Immigrant Women in North America* was held in Toronto (Caroli, *et. al.*). Among papers on Italian women in Toronto, one compared Italian women in Toronto to those in Italy in their involvement in trade union movements (La Vigna, 1979). The author argues that North Americans were not any more liberal or progressive in their dealings with women, and that involvement in unions in Italy was inspired more by economic and political ideals than by a feminist attitude. A second study (Pautasso, 1979) considered the situation of Italian women in Toronto during the Fascist period in Italy. According to the then Italian consul in Montreal, there was a misconception on the part of Italo-Canadians that under the Fascist government Italian women were considered to be politically and morally inferior. To this end, the consul's wife was organizing a cycle of conferences in English and in French to put the record straight.

A third paper presented at the conference (Parry, 1979b) referred to a study carried out in 1976 of 227 Italian families in Toronto. The author points out that the most desirable role for females was that of wife and mother. If an Italian girl remained a spinster, it was usually because she had taken on the responsibility of caring for elderly parents. But in the eyes of the community at large, she was considered to be somewhat of a failure, even if she was involved in an important career.

In "The Acculturation of Italian Immigrant Girls", Danziger (1976) argued that while parents had high aspirations for their sons and encouraged assimilation of Canadian values of success, girls were protected from acculturation by 1) imposition of an excessively rigid pattern of feminine role specialization; 2) allowing daughters less autonomy than sons; and 3) having a less permissive attitude toward them. The study was based on Italian and non-Italian boys and girls in high schools in Toronto.

One table in the *Fact-Book on Italians in Canada* (Jansen and La Cavera, 1981, Table 4.3), compared characteristics of males and females of Italian origin in 1971. There were relatively few strong differences, except that 8 percent more females than males knew neither English nor French and 5 percent (15 years and older) had below secondary education. The big difference, however, was found in comparing occupations and incomes. While there was 7 percent each of males and females in high white-collar jobs (professional), there were 19 percent more females than males in low white-collar jobs (clerical, sales, service) and the male proportion in blue-collar jobs was 21 percent higher than that of females. Yet, when considering average income from wages, the male average was $ 6,208 while the female average was $ 2,963.

CONCLUSION

In reviewing the literature on Italians in Canada since 1975, it is obvious that the attention paid to this group has increased considerably. Nonetheless, there appears to be some important areas which have been given scant attention. The first, is the effect on the relative importance of the group of the fact that Italian migration to Canada has literally stopped, while newer groups with higher levels of education and occupational skills have begun entering the country. Second, the changes taking place among Italian females should be studied. In the past decade, more and more Italian females have been continuing on to post-secondary education and to universities in particular. How will this affect the traditional roles of females and values of the Italian family? What happens to these females upon graduation? Do they revert to the 'expected' role of wife and mother? Third, the question of whether Canadian images of Italians are changing with the facts should be examined. While the group has experienced considerable upward social mobility, old stereotypes about the laborer and construction worker tend to persist.

11

Italian Americans in the East and West Regional Coverage in Italian American Studies, 1975-1983

JOSEPH VELIKONJA,
Department of Geography,
University of Washington, Seattle

THE documentation of the Italian American experience in the United States has been, for a long time, dominated by emphasis on the history and evolution of "Little Italies" in major Eastern cities. The regions and communities outside the east coast megalopolis have received less attention although their roles in the evolution of the American society and culture are neither less prominent nor less commendable.

This essay reviews the geographical coverage of the Italian American presence in published and unpublished studies of the last eight years, between 1975 and 1983. The period covers approximately the time from my earlier statement (Velikonja, 1977) on the Italian experiences where I outlined numerous topics for future research.

The harvest of studies is commendable. The revived enthusiasm for ethnic heritage awareness associated with Bicentennial celebrations, the acceptance of multicultural society as a viable alternative to the homogenizing "melting pot" and the financial resources of the federal and state agencies contributed to renewed research activity. The increased number of scholars and associations lend support and encouragement to research and publication. This period has also seen the appearance in print of earlier studies in the American Ethnic Groups — The European Heritage series of the Arno Press.[1]

---

[1] The Arno Press series, edited by F. Cordasco, include previously unpublished doctoral dissertations on the Italians in Rhode Island, Gabriel, 1980; Newark, NJ, Churchill, 1975; Philadelphia, Juliani, 1982a; Cleveland, Ferroni, 1980; New Orleans, Scarpaci, 1980; San Francisco, Scherini, 1980. The dissertations served as bases for the published monographic studies of Cleveland, Barton 1975; San Francisco; Cinel, 1982a; Buffalo, Yans-McLaughlin, 1977; Kansas

The pioneering work of Andrew F. Rolle (1968) forced many researchers to take notice of the America beyond the Mississippi River and to acknowledge the achievements of European immigrants in shaping the vast extents of the American interior and of the West. The absence of a comprehensive regional bibliographical inventory shares the responsibility for an inadequate recognition of the Italian Americans. Regional coverage has been included in earlier bibliographical aids (Cordasco, 1974, 1978; Velikonja, 1963; Briani, 1979); they are found in selected biographical aids to historical, geographical and sociological studies often without an easy regional identification (Bentley) 1981; Byrne, 1983; Miller, 1976; Wasserman and Kennington, 1983).[2] The recently published bibliography of the Italian American studies in the *Italian Americana* (D'Aniello and Porcari, 1983) is a welcome addition to the established bibliographical coverage in the *Italica,* both without regional references. H. Nelli's (1980) chapter on the Italians in the *Harvard Encyclopedia of American Ethnic Groups* recognizes the Italian achievements outside the East Coast, but the meager bibliographical references dictated by the format of the volume offer little help. References are often relegated to notices in newsletters, ethnic periodicals or national newspapers. For the purpose of the present survey, an effort was made to identify appropriate items from books and monographs where the reference to the Italians cannot be detected from the titles (LaPin *et al.*, 1982; Locati, 1978; Kathka, 1977; Swiderski, 1977; Levitov, 1976; Notarianni, 1980; Kessner and Caroli, 1981, and others); newsletters and newspaper articles are not included in this review.

The studies published in the last eight years reveal an encouraging departure from the once dominant syndrome of the East Coast experiences by expanding research on centers and regions of the Italian settlements further west. While more than two-thirds of all Italian Americans reside in the northeastern part of the United States, the studies of the communities in the region account for one-third of recently published research. Several years after Nelli (1970) and Iorizzo (1970) reviewed the Italians in the countryside and in the cities, and after Betty Boyd Caroli (1977) and the present writer (1977) argued for the revised and more extensive coverage, there is some evidence that the calls were not completely ignored. Olha della Cava's report of 1977 reviewed studies in progress in the mid 1970s. Some of them have subsequently appeared in print, others remain incomplete.

Progress has been made in numerous fields outlined in my review of seven years ago. In this assessment the focus is confined to the territorial

---

City, Rochester, and Utica, Briggs, 1978; Greenwich Village, Tricarico, 1984; Bridgeport, Crispino, 1980; St. Louis, Mormino, 1984; San Francisco, Cinel, 1982a; and New York, Tomasi, 1975.

[2] Earlier general or specialized bibliographies (*See,* Cordasco, 1974, 1978) do not provide regional arrangement of included items. The examination of individual items is necessary to determine the extent of their regional coverage.

coverage. Little attempt is made to analyze the content and define the substance of the sociological, historical or geographical contributions. Assuming that the totality of ethnic experiences and its time dimensions are reviewed by historians, the mechanisms of societal functioning by the sociologists, the political participation and institutional behavior by political scientists and the assessment of cultural heritage and its transformation   by anthropologists and folklorists, the territorial assessment of achievements and failures remains the domain of geographers (Brown, 1980; Raitz, 1979; Ward, 1982; Thompson, 1973).

The geographical attitude toward uniqueness of experiences and the universality of principles has been debated for many decades and has produced enthusiastic supporters as well as eloquent critics. It would be fruitless to search only for universalities unless derived from the evidence of diversities of existence, be it for the Italian as well as non-Italian migrants, be it in the East as well as in the West of the United States, for the Italians in the United States or for those in Switzerland or in Argentina, for the 1880 settlers in Mendoza in Argentina as well as for the 1980 residents of Columbia, the new city in Maryland (Fandetti and Gelfand, 1983).

We are not yet at the point at which we could formulate definitive historical principles. We are still at the stage of accumulation of documentation for local and regional experiences which could contribute to the formulation of general principles, nor do we have sufficiently weighted analyses of sectoral and topical processes of transformation that would retain general validity regardless of specific time, location and participating group. Nevertheless, the decade witnessed major steps forward. The process of ethnic maintenance, survival and revival; the assimilation, adjustment and integration; language maintenance and language transformation; neighborhood formation and preservation; the role of agents and agencies; and the significance of formal and informal organizations, both ethnic and non-ethnic, are all experiences at different locations and different times. They involve people who are identified as Italians, those who came more than a century ago as well as those that came only recently. The commonality of characteristics and processes is often assumed but not verified. The research that has been produced so far has been unable to prove the extent by which the Italian experiences are unique or common to all or many migrants. Nor do they answer convincingly the question of the uniqueness of the Italian experience as a response to conditions of the home country and home society, or maybe as a response to specific conditions in a specific locality in the United States: is the specific nature of Roseto (Bianco, 1974) in Pennsylvania a reflection of the original Roseto in Italy, or is it more a reflection to social and environmental conditions in an American setting? The elements are detectable, but not the integrated total.

The voluminous literature on the role of American Italians in organized crime (Nelli, 1976; Graebner-Anderson, 1979) has not yet answered the question of the Italian or non-Italian monopoly in it, nor provided an assessment of how its westward spread relates to the Italian migration. Similarly the documentation of the *padrone* system (Iorizzo, 1970) does not exhaust the history of the Italian rural settlements.

The ethnic research is by its nature multi-cultural. The common attitude that the investigation of one group leads to conclusions on group behavior and activities of all groups and of the total society is not particularly convincing. The host society does not consist of an amalgamated and integrated multi-racial, multi-cultural assembly, but an assembly of often detached and not integrated social complexes or fragments (for an assessment of immigrant experiences in England, *See*, Sibley, 1981). The studies of ethnic communities face the challenge to compare and contrast their behavior imprints with the host society. For a Polish immigrant research, the non-Polish society appears to be diverse but nevertheless cohesive and includes also the Italians; the Italian research more often than not refers to the total host society which also includes the Poles. Only occasionally the comparative studies deal with two such groupings, like the study of the Italians and the Jews, or the Poles and Ukrainians. Recent comparative studies are Barton's (1975) book of the Italians, Rumanians, and Slovaks in Cleveland; Bodnar, Simon and Weber's (1982) study of blacks, Italians and Poles in Pittsburgh; Stack's (1977) review of the conflict between the Irish, Italians and Jews in Boston; Bayor's (1978) examination of the Irish, German, Jewish and Italians in New York City; and Kessner's (1977) study of the Italian and Jewish immigrant mobility in New York. Comparative analysis of Italians in three cities: Kansas City, Utica and Rochester is evident in the admirable study by Briggs (1978).

Empirical studies of geographers and non-geographers tend to stress the uniqueness of experiences, focusing on significant personalities, events and locations. Such is the study of the Italians in San Francisco (Cinel, 1979, 1982a; Scherini, 1980; Baccari and Canepa, 1981-82; Gumina, 1978), the review of events in Denver (De Rose, 1977), new experiences in Phoenix (Martinelli, 1977, 1983), the Italian activities in Cortland (Vanario, 1980; Wilson, 1983), Newark (Churchill, 1975) and New Orleans (Scarpaci, 1975, 1977), the settlements of Arkansas (Guida, 1980, 1981, 1982) and in Duluth (Moran, 1979) and many others. Although unique, they nevertheless share commonalities of processes that are neither confined to the Italians as a unique group, nor to selected locations as exceptional places and neighborhoods.

Geographical studies of recent years have been severely handicapped by the scarce and capricious inventory of statistical information. Although the 1980 census for the first time assembled more comprehensive ethnicity data, the reconstruction of earlier assemblages of "ethnics" beyond the second generation is often speculative. There is no substitute to detailed field recordings and investigation which, however, with the demand for time and financing, is seldom done in a large scale.

A noticeable achievement in numerous recent studies is the extensive use of primary documentations, archival material, original records, personal diaries, manuscript census returns, travel manifests, naturalization records and the use of documentation provided by contemporaneous reports and notices. The systematic collecting of archival material which at one time was relegated to rare institutions greatly expands and enables investigations that were beyond reach only a decade ago (Cummins and Jeansome, 1982).

The use of primary sources is much in evidence in the studies of the "Hill" in St. Louis (Mormino, 1977, 1980, 1981a, 1981b, 1982a, 1982c, 1982e), the activities in Tampa (Pozzetta, 1979, 1980, 1982; Mormino, 1982b, 1982d), the comprehensive history of the Italians in Minnesota (Vecoli, 1981, 1982), the activities in Duluth, Minnesota (Moran, 1979), and labor issues in Colorado and Utah (Notarianni, 1975, 1976, 1980a, 1980b), the story of the Italians in San Francisco (Cinel, 1982a), Cleveland (Barton, 1975; Ferroni, 1980), Kansas City (Briggs, 1978), Boston (Stack, 1979), Buffalo (Yans-McLaughlin, 1977) and New York (Tomasi, 1975), to mention the most prominent.

My own published and unpublished research convinced me that the persistence of ethnicity survives far beyond the first or second generation; the survival is not limited only to large clusters, it is evident also in small communities.

Studies of the smaller Italian settlements and communities, similar to my earlier assessment of Tontitown and Rosati (Velikonja, 1972) are evident in the study of Krebs, Oklahoma (Brown, 1975; Matthews, 1982), Rock Springs, Wyoming (Kathka, 1977), Helper, Utah (Notarianni, 1980; Notarianni and Raspa, 1983), Walla Walla, Washington (Locati, 1978) Lake Village, Arkansas (Guida, 1980), Cherry, Illinois (Caroli, 1980), Cortland, New York (Vanario, 1980; Wilson, 1983) and many others. These studies imply or document the existence of a fundamental support system for the survival of the communities; the persistence of formal and informal networks through institutions of churches and parishes, newspapers and periodicals, fraternal organizations and annual festivals, where the numerical size of an ethnic community is less significant than existence and maintenance of social ties. The Italian behaviors in this respect are similar to those of other south and central Europeans: Greeks, Hungarians, Croats, Slovenes, Czechs and Slovaks.

The territorial coverage of these studies recognizes the achievements of recent research and calls attention to major gaps that still exist. It is obvious that the studies which do not refer to specific geographical areas do not make part of this assessment. New York City and the Italian communities in the New York metropolitan area are included in the bibliography but are not discussed in this review.

The studies cover twenty-two states and fifty odd locations in thirty states. Although writings on specific communities often include references to the Italian experiences elsewhere in the state and the research on specific states often covers only a selected location, a more refined analysis of the coverage was not attempted at this time.

The prominent states with four or more studies are: New York, Rhode Island (due to the small size of the state the studies dealing with Providence are often titled as the studies of the Italians in Rhode Island), California and Louisana. Major blank areas extend from the edge of Minnesota to the Pacific in the north and leave blank a large portion of the south. The most researched cities and communities are in ranking order: New York City (24), St. Louis (12), San Francisco (10), Philadelphia (8), and Tampa (8), Boston (6) and New Orleans (6).   Over sixty percent of the studies of specific locations are the only recent works on those locations. This means that there is little duplication either for location or for the topic. The three most researched cities, New York, St. Louis and San Francisco, received more attention (46 studies) than thirty-four other centers represented each by a single study. St. Louis stands out prominently due to Mormino's prolific writing (seven of the twelve studies).

The regional inventory demonstrates significant coverage of the eastern United States, especially the state and communities in New York, Connecticut and Rhode Island with less comprehensive portrayal of Massachusetts, New Jersey and Pennsylvania. Noticeable is the lack of studies of Italian communities in upper New England (except a study of an unidentified community in New England by Swiderski, 1977). The Italian communities in New Jersey that received some attention include Newark (Churchill, 1975), Paterson (Carey, 1979), Jersey City (Stokvis, 1979) and Trenton (Peroni, 1977, 1979). New England is represented by Lawrence (Vecoli, 1980), Worcester (Thompson, 1980, publication of 1971 dissertation) and Boston (Stack, 1977, 1979; Di Scala, 1977; DeMarco, 1980, 1981; Gesualdi, 1982). It also includes Rhode Island (Roche, 1977, 1982; Gabriel, 1980) with Providence (Bardaglio, 1975) and several communities in Connecticut — Bridgeport (Allen, 1980; Crispino, 1980), Hartford (Allen, 1980) and New Haven (Allen, 1980; Peach, 1980). Numerous communities in the state of New York outside New York City were investigated — Mechanicsville near Albany (Loatman, 1977), Utica (Briggs, 1978; Hartman and McIntosh, 1978), Rome (Carlin , 1978), Oswego (Iorizzo, 1981), Rochester (Briggs, 1978), Cortland (Vanario, 1980, Wilson, (1983), Rochester (Briggs, 1978) and Buffalo (Yans-McLaughlin, 1977; Lotchin, 1976). Pennsylvania is represented by studies conducted in Philadelphia (Juliani, 1978, 1980; Migliorino, 1976; Verbero, 1975; Passero, 1978; Belfiglio, 1982) and Pittsburgh (Krause, 1978; Simons, Patti and Herman, 1981; Bodnar, 1982, Weber, Bodnar and Simon, 1982; as well as by the studies of communities in southwestern Pennsylvania (Bruman, 1979 and

FIGURE I

ITALIAN-AMERICAN RESEARCH   1975-1983

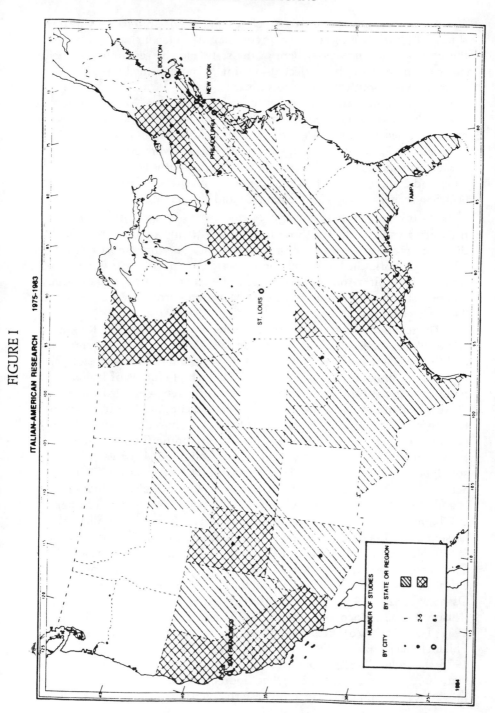

Ambridge, northwest of Pittsburgh (Serene, 1980). The new city of Columbia in Maryland and the behavior of the Italians there is a topic of recent investigation by Fandetti and Gelfand (1983). Virginia and Southern Appalachia are examined in the studies of Wolfe (1977, 1979). The major history of the Italian communities in the area remains, nevertheless, unrecorded. The Great Lakes region with the host of Italian communities has been researched selectively: Cleveland (Barton, 1975; Ferroni, 1980, Alissi, 1978); Detroit (Re, 1979; Cannistraro, 1975); South Bend (Fotia, 1975) and Chicago. The major project of the Italians in Chicago, supported by the National Endowment has produced pamphlets, expositions, festivals and displays; has accumulated a sizeable archival collection, and is to be used as a stepping stone for serious future investigation. Earlier studies of Campisi (1942, 1947), Vecoli (1963) and Nelli (1970) remain unsurpassed. The upper Midwest received attention in the study of Vecoli for Minnesota (1981) and the thesis of Moran (1979) for Duluth. The Italian communities in Hurley and Irontown and the experiences in upper Michigan (Calumet, Houghton, Red Jacket) wait to be exposed and documented. Similar needs remain for further studies of the Italians in southern Illinois where the report on Roanoke (DeJohn, 1983) and the study of the Cherry mine disaster (Caroli, 1980) do not exhaust the topic.

St. Louis is the focus of attention for numerous studies by Mormino. Except for these and the study of Kansas City (Briggs, 1978), the state of Nebraska (Levitov, 1976) with Omaha (Fimple, 1978) and Iowa (Schneider, 1982), work on the Italian settlements in Wisconsin, Missouri and Kansas remains to be done. Similarly, Kentucky and Tennessee remain uncovered. This is not surprising in view of the somewhat dispersed presence of the small number of Italians.

The South is prominent primarily by the continuous research of the Italian past in Tampa (Pozzetta, 1975, 1979, 1980, 1981, 1982; Mormino, 1982b, 1982d, 1983) and the Italian communities in New Orleans and in nearby Louisiana (Scarpaci, 1975, 1977, 1980; Gambino, 1977; Giordano, 1978, 1979; Haas, 1982). The Arkansas Delta received recent attention by Ernesto Milani (unpublished) and Louis Guida (1980, 1981, 1982), as did Alabama (Cinel, 1982b) and the Italian community in Birmingham (Norello, 1981). The coverage of the South is the work of a few enthusiasts. The first references to the Italians in Oklahoma (Brown, 1975, 1980; Matthews, 1982) are slowly closing the gap in the map of the United States. Galveston, for many decades the gateway for entering immigrants, waits to be discovered.

The West and Southwest appeared recently on the scene as an area of investigation. The introductory survey of Wyoming (Kathka, 1977), the sketchy references to the Italians in Denver (DeRose, 1977) and southern Colorado coal fields (Notarianni, 1980b), are to be added to recent studies of Arizona and Phoenix (Martinelli, 1977, 1978, 1983) and the series of investigations conducted by Notarianni on Utah (1975, 1976, 1980a, 1980b, 1983).

What remains to be explored is how the Italians adjusted to the colossal changes in Montana, especially in Butte and Anaconda, faced with the recent closures of mines and smelters; little has been written about the Italian experiences in northern Idaho and northeastern Washington (Spokane). The enthusiasm of a single person (Locati) gave us the story of the Italians in Walla Walla. We do not have one yet for the Puget Sound area of Seattle and Tacoma. Equally, a brief history of Portland (Gould, 1976) does not exhaust the somewhat different experiences of the Italians in Oregon and northern California. In the same category is the lack of coverage of Reno, Nevada, an early center of Italian activities in the West. Cofone's work on Nevada (1982) is a promising beginning.

It would be misleading to believe that California's Italian experiences have been exhausted by the studies of Scherini, Gumina, Cinel and others. While the San Francisco Italian community has been and remains the most prominent, the Italian presence is not confined to the Bay area. References have been made to the early participation of the Italians in the Gold Rush, but the event has not been explored nor thoroughly documented. The obvious recognition of the Italian origin of California's wine industry is not yet balanced by a comprehensive study of the Italian contribution. The fragmented records of Asti (Gumina, 1975), Napa, Gallo, Italian Swiss and Petri, and brief references to the prominent Ghirardelli chocolate and Giannini Bank of Italy call for the need for recognition of the Italians in Eureka and Crescent City, the history of the Italians in Weed and Dunsmuir, their role in Monterey and Fresno, and many, many others. Los Angeles is almost untouched. Just like Martinelli had identified the Italians among the recent arrivals to Phoenix, recent migration to Southern California warrants some attention. Except for the published study of Richardson (1981) on the Italian fishermen in San Diego, various unpublished theses cover local topics (such as Crosby), but the sketchy information prevents adequate bibliographical reportings.

Three features warrant special comments: the expansion of the established frame of American Italian ethnic studies by content and by format.

The first is the behavior of ethnic immigrants in the planned new city of Columbia, Maryland, half way between Washington and Baltimore, is not constrained by the historical neighborhood, by the remnants of traditional local institutions and surviving community ties. The Italian newcomers are partners in the population of this new city; their behavior is identifiable and different than the behavior of the remaining society. Fandetti and Gelfand (1983) opened new ground with their investigations.

The second new phenomenon is the resettlement of Italian Americans in new communities in Florida, Southern California and the Southwest. Only Phoenix has been examined so far by Martinelli (1977, 1983). Neither Southern California, a major pull region of recent migration, nor Florida, the destination of older populations from northern cities, have been investigated, though the evidence of migration is at hand: the periodicals of New Britain and Hartford, Connecticut, continue their series by being published in Hollywood-Ft. Lauderdale in Southern Florida (Russo, 1983).

The third aspect is the appearance of studies on Italian Americans in geographical publications in Italy (Cortesi, 1981; Mori, 1977), a welcome expansion of traditional publication outlets.

In summary, the survey of studies, collated with the inventory of earlier research, shows a major expansion of regional coverage and the intensified deepening of investigation for previously studied communities and regions. Some major gaps, nevertheless, persist.

The coverage of upper New England where the Italian communities are spread in cities and centers from Portland, Maine to Barre, Vermont and numerous places in between is sketchy. Earlier studies do not exhaust the topic.

The research reports regarding the Italian communities in the New York area, be it in the city of New York, or in the metropolitan area, as well as the centers in upper New York, have received much attention. The studies, however, are still fragments of the total. The difficult task of collating them into a comprehensive mosaic is facing the scholars.

The Appalachia was once the dominant region of ethnic communities. Its historic evolution, the rise and decline of ethnic clusters, has not been investigated. The general aim to review the successes might have prevented assessing the decline and disappearance of the Italian communities as a segment of the total Appalachia history. The immigrant in the mines, including the Italians, fill volumes of the Dillingham Report of 1911. Recent publications do not touch their demise or survival.

Gaps persist regarding Italian communities outside major cities of the East: Cincinnati and Columbus, Ohio; Louisville, Kentucky; and Memphis, Tennessee. The Italians in Chicago were prominently portrayed in the recent project, but the public display and awareness did not contribute much to basic research.

The upper Michigan communities, Calumet and Marquette, the centers on the Michigan-Wisconsin border, received little attention, unlike the Finns and Scandinavians who shared the life in the communities with the Italians. Minnesota was admirably researched and portrayed by Vecoli (1981); studies are not yet produced for the whole region along the Canadian border. The Italians in the Black Hills, the settlers in Montana, the miners in Idaho, the railroad workers in Washington wait to be discovered. Earlier studies do not provide much assistance. The sketchy coverage of Nebraska and Wyoming (Kathka, 1977; Levitov, 1976) is just the beginning. The secondary movement of the Italians into scattered farms in Kansas and eastern Colorado, the communities in Wisconsin, Iowa, Montana and further west remain unrecorded. Southwestern Kansas, Pittsburgh and surrounding mining centers need a researcher to examine the Italian community life and its share in the radical movement.

The South, from Florida to the Mexican border, has two major gaps: the secondary migration of the Italians to southern Florida and the Italian presence in Texas. The multicultural and multiethnic composition of Texas has been extensively studied, but most studies do not include the Italians. The record of Italian newspapers points to the important gateway of Galveston for the entering of new immigrants. Neither earlier nor recent studies cover the phenomenon.

In the Southwest the recent focus is limited to Phoenix, but the history of Italian communities in the mining districts of New Mexico and Arizona is still missing.

The intermountain region is represented by the studies of Utah, leaving sizeable gaps for once prosperous communities in southwestern Wyoming, the interior of Nevada, and in peripheral regions of Utah. Even when the present life of communities is less than vigorous, and the historical investigation has been restricted to the exploration and missionary stages of the region, the settlement stage is not covered. Malcom Comeau's (1981) recent geography of Arizona refers to the presence of the Italians, but not more than that. Equal casual reference to the immigrants appears in Brown's geography of Wyoming (1980); the Meagerville in Butte, Montana described by Rolle (1968) vanished with the open pit mine, now closed. The Italians — where are they now?

The West Coast has a major gap in the dispersed Italian presence in Southern California contrasted by territorially more cohesive Italian communities in the Bay area. It is, therefore, not surprising that the San Francisco Italians received more attention than those in Los Angeles and San Diego, nor is it surprising that the communities in other California cities go unrecognized except for San Jose (Matthews, 1977).

Ethnic history research of the life and death of Italian ethnic communities throughout the United States, from East to West, is a challenge and program for future investigations. The field is wide and complex. There is much room for everybody. As the pioneers opened the American West for new settlers, small groups of research pioneers provided the opportunity for numerous followers to discover, explore documents, analyze and explain the massive imprint left by the Italians throughout the country. The present review attempted to identify what has been done so far and what can be added in the future.

TABLE 1

Italian American Studies — Regional Coverage

	State	Region	No. Locations	No. Studies
Alabama	1		1	1
Arizona	1		1	2
Arkansas	1	3	1	1
California	4	2	4	13
Colorado	1		1	1
Connecticut	1		3	5
Florida	1		1	8
Illinois			3	7
Indiana	2		1	1
Iowa	1			
Louisana	6		3	8
Maryland			2	2
Massachusetts			3	8
Michigan			1	3
Minnesota	2		1	1
Missouri			1	14
Nebraska	1		1	1
Nevada	1			
New Jersey	3		4	5
New York	4		11	38
Ohio			1	4
Oklahoma	1		1	
Oregon			1	1
Pennsylvania	1	1	5	15
Rhode Island	4		1	2
Texas	1			
Utah	3		2	3
Virginia	1			
Washington			1	1
Wisconsin			1	1
Wyoming	1			
Other Regional Units		3		

Bibliographical References 1975-1983

Alissi, Albert S. (1978)
Boys in Little Italy: A Comparison of their Individual Value Orientations, Family Patterns, and Peer Group Associations. San Francisco: R & E Research Associates, Inc.
Pp. 119   Cleveland, Ohio

Allen, Irving Lewis (1983)
"Variable White Ethnic Resistance to School Desegration: Italian-American Parents in Three Connecticut Cities, 1966". In William C. McCready (ed.) *Culture, Ethnicity, and Identity.* New York: Academic Press. Pp. 1-16.
Bridgeport, Hartford, New Haven, Connecticut

Aquino, Salvatore A. (1978)
"The Third of Twelve", *Italian Americana.* 4(1), 65-71.   New York City

Baccari, Alessandro and Andrew Canepa (1981-82)
"The Italians of San Francisco in 1865: G.B. Cerutti's Report to the Ministry of Foreign Affairs", *California History.* 60(2):350-369.
San Francisco, California

Bardaglio, Peter W. (1975)
"Italian Immigrants and the Catholic Church in Providence, 1890-1930". *Rhode Island History.* 34(2):46-57.   Providence, Rhode Island

Barton, Joseph S. (1975)
Peasants and Strangers: Italians, Rumanians, and Slovaks in An American City, 1890-1950. Cambridge, MA: Harvard University Press. Pp. 217.
Cleveland, Ohio

Batinich, Mary and Ellen Mancina (1978)
"The Interaction Between Italian Immigrant Women and the Chicago Commons Settlement House, 1909-1944". In Betty Boyd Caroli, R.F. Harney, and Lydio F. Tomasi, *The Italian Immigrant Woman in North America.* Toronto: The Multicultural History Society of Ontario. Pp. 154-167.   Chicago, Illinois

Bayor Ronald H. (1978)
Neighbors in Conflict: The Irish, German, Jews and Italians in New York City, 1929-1940. Baltimore: Johns Hopkins University Press. Pp. 232.
New York City.

Belfiglio, Valentine J. (1982)
"Italian Culture in Eighteenth Century Philadelphia", *Italian Quarterly.* 23(87):
73-83.   Philadelphia, Pennsylvania

Bodnar, John E. and Michael P. Weber (1982)
Lives of Their Own: Blacks, Italians and Poles in Pittsburgh, 1900-1960. Urbana: University of Illinois Press. Pp. 286.   Pittsburgh, Pennsylvania

Briggs, John W. (1978)
An Italian Passage. Immigrants to Three American Cities, 1890-1930. New Haven: Yale University Press. Pp. 348.

Kansas City, Missouri; Rochester, New York; Utica, New York

Brown, Kenny L. (1975)
"Peaceful Progress: An Account of the Italians of Krebs, Oklahoma". *Chronicles of Oklahoma.* 53(3):332-352.

Krebs, Oklahoma

Brown, Kenny L.(1980)
The Italians in Oklahoma. Newcomers to a New Land Series. Volume 4. Norman: University of Oklahoma Press. Pp. 96.

Oklahoma

Bruman, John F. (1979)
"Ethnic Adaptation in a Southwestern Pennsylvania Coal Patch, 1910-1940". *Journal of Ethnic Studies.* 7(3):1-24.

Southwestern Pennsylvania

Byrne, Donald E., Jr. (1981)
"Maria Assunta: Berwick's Italian Religious Festival". *Pennsylvania Folklife.* 30(3): 124-141.

Berwick, Pennsylvania

Cannistraro, Philip V. (1975)
"Fascism and Americans in Detroit, 1933-1935." *International Migration Review,* 9(1):29-40.

Detroit, Michigan

Carey, George W. (1979)
"The Vessel, the Deed, and the Idea: Anarchists in Paterson, 1895-1908", *Antipode. A Radical Journal of Geography.* 10:3 and 11:1 (double issue), pp. 46-58.

Paterson, New Jersey

Carlin, Marianne B. (1978)
"Education and Occupational Decision of the Children of Italian and Polish Immigrants to Rome, New York, 1900-1950." Ph.D. Dissertation, Cornell University. Pp. 105.

Rome, New York

Carlson, Alvar W. (1982)
"Recent European Immigration to the Chicago Metropolitan Area". *International Migration.* 20(1-2):45-64.

Chicago, Illinois

Caroli, Betty Boyd(1980)
"Italians in the Cherry, Illinois Mine Disaster". In George E. Pozzetta, *Pane e Lavoro: The Italian American Working Class.* Toronto: The Multicultural History Society of Ontario. Pp. 67-79.

Cherry, Illinois

Cavaioli, Frank J. (1983)
"Chicago's Italian American Rally for Immigration Reform". In Richard N. Juliani (ed), *The Family and Community Life of Italian Americans.* Staten Island: American Italian Historical Association. Pp. 35-46.

Chicago, Illinois

Cassidy, Robert (1975)
"The Hill Builds for Tomorrow". *Planning (ASPO).* 41(7):16-18.

St. Louis, Missouri

Churchill, Charles W. (1975)
The Italians of Newark: A Community Study. New York: Arno Press. Pp. 173 + 36. Ph.D. Dissertation, New York University, 1942. Newark, New Jersey

Cinel, Dino (1979)
"Conservative Adventurers: Italian Migrants in Italy and San Francisco." Ph.D. Dissertation. Stanford University. Pp. 385. San Francisco, California

Cinel, Dino (1981)
"Between Change and Continuity: Regionalism Among Immigrants from the Italian Northwest". *Journal of Ethnic Studies.* 9(3):19-36. San Francisco, California

Cinel, Dino (1982a)
From Italy to San Francisco: The Immigrant Experience. Stanford, CA: Stanford University Press. Pp. viii + 347. San Francisco, California

Cinel, Dino (1982b)
Italians in Alabama, 1980-1930. AIHA meeting, St. Paul, Minnesota.
Alabama, Georgia

Cofone, Albin J. (1982)
"Themes in the Italian Settlement of Nevada". *Nevada Historical Society Quarterly.* 25(2):116-130. Nevada

Cohen, Miriam (1977)
"Italian-American Women in New York City, 1900-1950: Work and School".In Milton Cantor and Bruce Laurie, eds. *Class, Sex and the Woman Worker.* Westport, CT: Greenwood Press. Pp. 120-143. New York City

Cohen, Miriam J. (1978)
"From Workshop to Office: Italian Women and Family Strategies in New York City, 1901-1950". Ph.D. Dissertation, University of Michigan. Pp. 360.
New York City

Cohen, Miriam (1982)
"Changing Educational Strategies Among Immigrant Generations: New York Italians in Comparitive Perspective". *Journal of Social History.* 13(3):443-466.
New York City

Cooper, Eileen M. (1980)
"Whiskey Run: Where Coal Dust Mixes with Murder". *Pennsylvania Heritage.* 6(2):15-19. Whiskey Run, Pennsylvania

Cortesi, Gisella (1981)
" 'The Hill': un'enclave italiana nella città di St. Louis". *Rivista Geografica Italiana.* 88(4):457-473. St. Louis, Missouri

Crispino, James A. (1980)
The Assimilation of Ethnic Groups: The Italian Case. Staten Island: Center for Migration Studies. Pp.205 Bridgeport, Connecticut

Crosby, Rosalind (n.d.)
"Italians in Southern California". n.d. M.A. Thesis, San Francisco State.
California

Cummingham, Barbara, ed. (1977)
The New Jersey Ethnic Experience. Union City, NJ: W.H. Wise. Pp. xi + 466.
New Jersey

D'Antonio, William V. (1975)
"Confessions of A Third Generation Italian American". *Society*. 13(1):57-63.
Connecticut

DeJohn, Dominick, Wayne DeJohn (1983)
"Italians in Illinois: A Memoir of an Ethnic Mining Community". *Italian Americana*.
7(2):27-32.   Roanoke, Peoria, Illinois

D'Emilia, Alfonso F. (1983)
"The Baricellis: Clevelands' Foremost Italian Professional Family". In Remigio U.
Pane. *Italian Americans in the Professions*. Staten Island: American Italian Historical
Association. Pp. 153-164.   Cleveland, Ohio

DeMarco, William M. (1980)
"Boston's Italian Enclave, 1880-1930". *Studi Emigrazione*. 17(59):331-359.
Boston, Massachusetts
DeMarco, William (1981)
Ethnics and Enclaves: Boston's Italian North End. Ann Arbor, MI: UMI Research
Press. Pp. 176.   Boston, Massachusetts

DeRose, Christine A. (1977)
"Inside 'Little Italy': Italian Immigrants in Denver". *Colorado Magazine*. 54(3):
277-293.   Denver, Colorado

Di Leonardo, Michaela (1984)
"La Vita Nuova: Class, Work and Kinship Among Italian American Women in
Northern California". Ph.D. Dissertation (in progress), University of California,
Berkeley.   California

DiScala, Spencer (1977)
"The Boston Italian American Community". In Humbert Nelli, ed., *The United States
and Italy: The First Two Hundred Years*. Staten Island: American Italian Historical
Association. Pp. 228-236.   Boston, Massachusetts

Devita, James J. (1976)
"Italy, Italians and Indiana", *La Parola del Popolo*. Chicago, Special Number 68, Vol.
26, Sept-Oct. Pp. 112-123.   Indiana

Devita, James J. (1983)
"The Italians in Indiana", *Italian Americana* 7(2):77-90.   Indiana

Ewen, Elizabeth W. (1979)
"Immigrant Women in the Land of Dollars, 1890-1920". Ph.D. Dissertation, State University of New York, Stony Brook. Pp. 709.   New York

Fandetti, Donald V. and Donald E. Gelfand (1983)
"Middle-Class White Ethnics in Suburbia: A Study of Italian-Americans". In William C. McCready, ed. *Culture, Ethnicity and Identity*. New York: Academic Press. Pp. 111-126.   Columbia, Maryland

Ferroni, Charles D. (1980)
The Italians in Cleveland: A Study in Assimilation. New York: Arno Press. Ph.D. Dissertation, Kent State. Pp. 288.   Cleveland, Ohio

Fichera, Sebastian (1981)
"The Meaning of Community: A History of Italians of San Francisco". Ph.D. Dissertation, UCLA. Pp. 291.   San Francisco, California

Ficile, Enzo (1975)
Storia degli Itraliani di New York. New York: Italian-American Center for Urban Affairs. Pp. 128.   New York City

Fimple, Kathleen L. (1978)
"Midwestern Mosaic: A Study of the Homogeneity of Ethnic Population in Omaha, Nebraska, 1880". M.A. Thesis (Geography), South Dakota State University.
                          Omaha, Nebraska

Fotia, Elisabeth R. (1975)
The Italian-Americans of the South Bend-Mishawaka Area. South Bend: Indiana University Ethnic Heritage Studies Program, n.p.
                          South Bend -Mishawaka,Indiana

Furio, Colomba M. (1979)
"Immigrant Women in Industry: A Case Study. The Italian Immigrant Women and the Garment Industry". Ph.D. Dissertation, New York University. Pp. 520.
                          New York City

Gabriel, Richard Alan (1980)
The Irish and Italians: Ethnics in City and Suburb. New York: Arno Press. (Ph.D. Dissertation, University of Massachusetts, 1969. Pp. 294.   Rhode Island

Gambino, Richard (1977)
Vendetta: A True Story of the Worst Lynching in America, the Mass Murder of Italian Americans in New Orleans in 1891, the Vicious Motivation Behind It, and the Tragic Repercussions That Linger to This Day. Garden City, NY: Doubleday. Pp. xi + 198.
                          New Orleans, Louisana

Garibaldi Centennial Committee of San Francisco (1982)
Garibaldi and California (pamphlet).   California

Gesualdi, Louis (1982)
"Research Note: A Note on Boston's Racial Problems". *Sociological Inquiry*. 52(3): 255-257.   Boston, Massachusetts

Giordano, Paul Anthony (1978)
"The Italians of Louisiana: Their Cultural Background and Their Many Contributions in the Fields of Literature, the Arts, Education, Politics, Business and Labor." Ph.D. Dissertation, Indiana University. Pp. 256.   Louisiana

Giordano, Paolo (1979)
"Italian Immigration in the State of Louisiana: Its Causes, Effects and Results". *Italian Americana.* 5(2):160-177.   Tangipahoa Parish, Louisiana

Gould, Charles F. (1976)
"Portland Italians, 1880-1920". *Oregon Historical Quarterly.* 77(3):239-260.
                                                                   Portland, Oregon

Guida, Louis (1980)
"The Italian Farmers of Lake Village", In *Uncertain Harvest: The Family Farm in Arkansas.* Eureka Springs: Ozark Institute.   Lake Village, Arkansas

Guida, Louis (1981)
"Immigrant Farmers: Italians in the Arkansas Delta". Unpublished paper, American Italian Historial Association Conference,   Arkansas

Guida, Louis (1982)
"The Rocconi-Fratesi Family: Italianità in the Arkansas Delta". In Dierdre LaPin, Louis Guida and Lois Pattillo, *Hogs in the Bottom.* Little Rock: August House. Pp. 86-100.   Arkansas

Gumina, Deanna Paoli (1975)
"Andrea Sbarboro, Founder of the Italian Swiss Colony Wine Company". *Italian Americana,* 2(1):1-17.   Asti, California

Gumina, Deanna Paoli (1978)
The Italians of San Francisco, 1850-1930. Staten Island: Center for Migration Studies. Pp. 230.   San Francisco, California

Haas, Edward F. (1982)
"Guns, Goats and Italians: The Tallulah Lynching of 1899". *North Louisiana Historical Society Journal.* 13(2-3):45-48.   Tallulah, Madison Parish, Louisiana

Haller, Herman (1979)
"Linguistic Interference in the Language of 'Il Progresso Italo-Americano' ". *Italian Americana.* 5(1):55-68.   New York City

Harney, Robert F. and Vincenza Scarpaci eds. (1981)
Little Italies in North America. Toronto: Multicultural History Society of Ontario. Pp. 310.   Philadelphia, Pennsylvania; Baltimore, Maryland;
              New York; Tampa, Florida; St. Louis, Missouri; Oswego, N.Y.

Harrison, I. Glenn (1979)
"A Geographical Analysis of the Northwest Arkansas Grape District". M.A. Thesis (Geography)University of Arkansas.   Indiana

Hartman, Peter and Karyl McIntosh (1978)

"Evil Eye Beliefs Collected in Utica, New York". *New York Folklore*. 4(1-4): 60-69.   Utica, New York

Hartman, Sharon Strom (1978)
"Italian American Women and Their Daughters in Rhode Island: The Adolescence of Two Generations, 1900-1950". In Betty Boyd Caroli, Robert F. Harney and Lydio F. Tomasi. *The Italian Immigrant Woman in North America*. Toronto: The Multicultural History Society of Ontario. Pp. 191-204.   Rhode Island

Henderson, Thomas M. (1979)
"Immigrant Politician: Salvatore Cotillo, Progressive Ethnic". *International Migration Review*. 13(1):81-102.   New York

Iorizzo, Luciano and Salvatore Mondello (1975)
"Origins of Italian Criminality: From New Orleans through Prohibition". *Italian Americana*. 1:217-234   (New Orleans, Louisiana).

Iorizzo, Luciano (1981)
"The Italians of Oswego". In Robert F. Harney and J. Vincenza Scarpaci, *Little Italies in North America*. Toronto: The Multicultural History Society of Ontario. Pp. 165-182.   Oswego, New York

Juliani, Richard N. (1978)
"The Settlement House and the Italian Family". In Betty Boyd Caroli, Robert F. Harney, Lydio F. Tomasi. *The Italian Immigrant Woman in North America*. Toronto: The Multicultural History Society of Ontario, pp. 103-123.
                                                                           Philadelphia, Pennsylvania

Juliani, Richard N. (1981)
The Social Organization of Immigration: The Italians in Philadelphia. New York: Arno Press, Ph.D. Dissertation, University of Pennsylvania, 1971. Pp. xxxi + 229.
                                                                           Philadelphia, Pennsylvania

Juliani, Richard N. (1981)
"The Italian Community of Philadelphia". In Robert F. Harney and J. Vincenza Scarpaci. *Little Italies in North America*. Toronto: The Multicultural History Society of Ontario. Pp. 85-104.   Philadelphia, Pennsylvania

Kathka, David (1977)
"The Italian Experience in Wyoming". In Gordon Olaf Hendrickson, ed. *Peopling the High Plains. Wyoming's European Heritage*. Cheyenne: Wyoming State Archives and Historical Department. Pp. 67-94.   Wyoming

Kessner, Thomas (1977)
The Golden Door: Italian and Jewish Immigrant Mobility in New York City, 1880-1915. New York: Oxford University Press. Pp. 224.   New York City

Kessner, Thomas and Betty Boyd Caroli (1978)
"New Immigrant Women at Work: Italian and Jews in New York City, 1880-1905". *The Journal of Ethnic Studies*. 5(4):19-31.   New York City

Kessner, Thomas (1981)
"Jobs, Ghettoes and the Urban Economy 1880-1935". *American Jewish History.*
71(2):218-238.   New York City

Kessner, Thomas and Betty Boyd Caroli (1981)
"I Didn't Choose America, I Chose New York". In Thomas Kessner and Betty Boyd
Caroli. *Today's Immigrants, Their Stories.* New York: Oxford University Press.
Pp. 205-232.   New York City

Krase, Jerome (1978)
"Italian-American Female College Students: A Generation Connected to the Old". In
Betty Boyd Caroli, Robert F. Harney, Lydio F. Tomasi. *The Italian American Immigrant
Woman in North America.* Toronto: The Multicultural History Society of Ontario.
Pp. 246-251.   New York City

Krause, C.A. (1978)
"Urbanization Without Breakdown: Italian, Jewish, and Slavic Immigrant Women In
Pittsburgh, 1900-1945". *Journal of Urban History.* 4(3):291-306.
                                                        Pittsburgh, Pennsylvania

LaGumina, Salvatore, ed. (1982)
"Ethnicity in Suburbia: The Long Island Experience". By the author. Pp. 104.
                                                             Westbury, New York.

LaGumina, Salvatore (1983)
"Marconiville, USA. The Rise of an Italian-American Suburban Community".
Richard N. Juliani. *Family and Community Life of Italian Americans.* Staten Island:
American Italian Historical Association. Pp. 81-93.   Marconiville, New York

LaPin, Deidre, Louis Guida, Lois Pattillo (1982)
Hogs in the Bottom. Little Rock: August House.   Arkansas

Levitov, Betty (1976)
"Italians: La Famiglia". In Nebraska Curriculum Development Center. *Broken Hoops
and Plains People.* Lincoln: Nebraska Curriculum Development Center. Pp. 337-
368.   Nebraska

Loatman, Paul J., Jr. (1977)
" 'Contadini' in the New Work 'Paese' ". *Studi Emigrazione.* 14, 45:68-84.
                                                         Mechanicville, New York

Locati, Joe (1978)
The Horticultural Heritage of Walla Walla County, 1818-1977. Walla Walla.
Pp. 283.   Walla Walla, Washington

Lotchin, Roger W. (1978)
"Ethnic Continuities in Sicilian Buffalo". *American History.* 6(3):373-378.
                                                             Buffalo, New York

Loverci, Francesca (1979)
"Italiani in California negli Anni del Risorgimento". *CLIO.* 15(4):469-547.
                                                                  California

MacNab, John B. (1977)
"Bethlehem Chapel: Presbyterians and Italian Americans in New York City". *Journal of Presbyterian History.* 55(2):145-160.

Greenwich Village, New York

Margavio, Anthony V. (1978)
"The Reaction of the Press to the Italian Americana in New Orleans, 1880 to 1920". *ItalianAmericana.* 4(1):72-84. New Orleans, Louisiana

Margavio, A.V. and Jerome Salomone (1981)
"The Passage, Settlement, and Occupational Characteristics of Louisiana's Italian Immigrants". *Sociological Spectrum.* 1(4):343-359. Louisiana

Marolla, Ed (1978)
"Horicon, Wisconsin, The Veneto and Aosta". *Italian Americana.* 4(1): 127-137.

Horicon,Wisconsin

Martinelli, Phylis Concilla (1977)
"Italy and Phoenix".*Journal of Arizona History.* 18(3):319-340.

Phoenix, Arizona

Martinelli, Phylis Concilla (1978)
"Italian Immigrant Women in the Southwest". In Betty Boyd Caroli, Robert F. Harney, Lydio F. Tomasi. *The Italian Immigrant Women in North America.* Toronto: The Multicultural History Society of Ontario. Pp. 324-336. Arizona

Martinelli, Phylis Concilla (1983)
"Beneath the Surface: Ethnic Communities in Phoenix, Arizona". In William C. McCready, ed. *Culture, Ethnicity, and Identity.* New York: Academic Press. Pp. 181-194. Phoenix, Arizona

Mathias, Elisabeth and Angelamaria Varesano (1978)
"The Dynamics of Religions Reactivation: A Study of a Charismatic Missionary to Southern Italians in the United States". *Ethnicity* 5(4):301-311.

Philadelphia, Pennsylvania; New Jersey; New York; Pennsylvania

Matthews, Glenne (1982)
"An Immigrant Community in Indian Territory". *Labor History.* 23(3):374-394

Krebs, Oklahoma

McIntosh, Karyl (1978)
"Folk Obstetrics, Gynecology, and Pediatrics in Utica, New York". *New York Folklore.* 4(1-4):49-59. Utica, New York

Migliorino, Ellen Ginzburg (1976)
"Il Proletariato Italiano di Filadelfia all'Inizio del Secolo". 1976. *Studi Emigrazione.* 13(41):23-40. Philadelphia, Pennsylvania

Mondello, Salvatore A. (1980)
The Italian Immigrant in Urban America, 1880-1920, As Reported in the Contemporary Periodical Press. New York: Arno Press. Ph.D. Dissertation, New York University, 1960. Pp. 254. General

Moran, Jacqueline R. (1979)
"The Italian Americans in Duluth". M.A. Thesis, University of Minnesota -Duluth.
(Unpublished).   Duluth, Minnesota

Mori, Alberto (1977)
"Pescatori Italiani a San Francisco". In Carlo della Valle, ed. *Scriti Geografici in Onore di Riccardo Riccardi*. Vol. 2, Pp. 509-524. Roma: Società Geografica Italiana (1974).   San Francisco, California

Mormino, Gary Ross (1977)
"The Hill Upon the City: An Italo-Amerian Neighborhood in St. Louis, Missouri, 1880-1955". Ph.D. Dissertation, University of North Carolina, Chapel Hill. Pp. 505 (to be published by University of Illinois Press).   St. Louis, Missouri

Mormino, Gary Ross (1980a)
"A House on the Hill: Mobility Patterns in an Italian Neighborhood". *Maryland Historian* 11(2):13-23.   St. Louis, Missouri

Mormino, Gary (1981a)
"The Immigrant Editor: Making a Living in Urban America". *Journal of Ethnic Studies*. 9(1):81-85.   St. Louis, Missouri

Mormino, Gary (1981b)
"The Hill Upon a City: The Evolution of an Italian-American Community in St. Louis, 1882-1950". In Robert F. Harney and J. Vincenza Scarpaci. *Little Italies in North America*. Toronto: The Multicultural History Society of Ontario. Pp. 141-164.
                                                              St. Louis, Missouri

Mormino, Gary (1982a)
"The Church Upon the Hill: Italian Immigrants in St. Louis, Missouri, 1870-1955. *Studi Emigrazione*. 19, 66. Pp. 203-224.   St. Louis, Missouri

Mormino, Gary R. (1982b)
"Tampa and the New Urban South: The Weight Strike of 1899". *Florida Historical Quarterly*. 60(3):337-356.   Tampa, Florida

Mormino, Gary Ross (1982c)
"The Playing Fields of St. Louis. Italian Immigrants and Sports, 1925-1941". 1982c. *Journal of Sport History*. 9(2):5-19.   St. Louis, Missouri

Mormino, Gary (1982d)
" 'We Worked Hard and Took Care of Our Own': Oral History and Italians in Tampa". *Labor History*. 23(3):395-415.   Tampa, Florida

Mormino, Gary (1982e)
"La Collina Sulla Città: Evoluzione di una communità a St. Louis, 1882-1950". *Storia Urbana*. 4(Giugno):97-122.   St. Louis, Missouri

Mormino, Gary and George Pozzetta (1983)
"Immigrant Women in Tampa: The Italian Experience". *Florida Historical Quarterly*. 61(3):296-312.   Tampa, Florida

Moss, Leonard (1983)
"Family and Community: Voluntary Association in South Italy and Detroit". In Richard Juliani. *The Family and Community Life of Italian Americans.* Staten Island: American Italian Historical Association. Pp. 11-22.   Detroit, Michigan

Nelli, Humbert (1976a)
"Italian Immigrants and Criminals in New Orleans". In Humbert Nelli. *The Business of Crime: Italians and Syndicate Crime in the United States.* New York: Oxford Press, Chapter 2. Pp. 24-46.   New Orleans, Louisiana

Nelli, Humbert S. (1976b)
"The Hennesey Murder and the Mafia in New Orleans". *Italian Quarterly.* 19. Pp. 75-76, 77-95.   New Orleans, Louisiana

Norell, Jeff (1981?)
The Italians from Bisacquino to Birmingham. Birmingham, AL: Birmingfind. Pp. 25.   Birmingham, Alabama

Notarianni, Philip F. (1975)
"Italian Fraternal Organizations in Utah, 1870-1934". *Utah Historical Quarterly.* 3(2):172-187.   Utah

Notarianni, Philip F. (1976)
"Italianità in Utah: The Immigrant Experience". In Helen Z. Papanikolas, ed. *The Peoples in Utah.* Salt Lake City: Utah Historical Society. Pp. 303-332.   Utah

Notarianni, Philip F. (1980a)
"Tale of Two Towns: The Social Dynamics of Eureka and Helper, Utah." Ph.D. Dissertation, University of Utah.   Helper, Eureka, Utah

Notarianni, Philip F. (1980b)
"Italian Involvement in the 1903-04 Coal Strike in Southern Colorado and Utah". In George Pozzetta, ed. *Pane e Lavoro: The Italian American Working Class.* Toronto: The Multicultural History Society of Ontario. Pp. 47-65.
                    Colorado, Utah

Notarianni, Philip F. and Richard Raspa (1983)
"The Italian Community of Helper, Utah: Its Historic and Folkloric Past and Present". In Richard N. Juliani. *The Family and Community Life of Italian Americans.* Staten Island: American Italian Historical Association. Pp. 23-33.   Helper, Utah

O'Leary, Timothy and Sandra Schoenberg (1977)
"Ethnicity and Social Class Convergence in an Italian Community: The Hill in St. Louis". *Missouri Historical Society Bulletin.* 33(2):77-86.   St. Louis, Missouri

Passero, Rosara Lucy (1978)
"Ethnicity in the Men's Ready Made Clothing Industry, 1880-1950: The Italian Experience in Philadelphia." Ph.D. Dissertation, University of Pennsylvania. Pp. 380.   Philadelphia, Pennsylvania

Peach, Ceri (1980)
"Which Triple Melting Pot? A Re-Examination of Ethnic Intermarriage in New

Haven, 1900-1950". *Ethnic and Racial Studies*. 3(1):1-16.
                                            New Haven,Connecticut

Peroni, Peter A. (1979)
The Burg: An Italian American Community at Bay in Trenton. Washington, D.C.:
University Press of America.   Trenton, New Jersey

Peroni, Peter Aloysius, II (1977)
Chambersburg: Its Enculturative Process. Ph.D. Dissertation. Rutgers University.
Pp. 321.   Trenton, New Jersey

Pitkin, Thomas Monroe and Francesco Cordasco (1977)
The Black Hand: A Chapter in Ethnic Crime. Totowa, NJ: Littlefield, Adams. Pp. 274.
                                                        New York City

Pizzo, Anthony P. (1981)
"The Italian Heritage in Tampa". In Robert F. Harney and J. Vincenza Scarpaci. *Little
Italies in North America*. Toronto: The Multicultural Society of Toronto. Pp. 123-
140.   Tampa, Florida

Pozzetta, George E. (1975)
"A Padrone Looks at Florida: Labor Recruiting and the Florida East Coast Railway".
Florida Historical Quarterly. 54(1):74-84.   Florida

Pozzetta, George E. (1979)
"Immigrants and Radicals in Tampa, Florida". *Florida Historical Quarterly*. 57(3):
337-348.   Tampa, Florida

Pozzetta, George (1980)
"Italians and the Tampa General Strike of 1910". In George Pozzetta, ed. *Pane e
Lavoro: The Italian American Working Class*. Toronto: The Multicultural History
Society of Ontario. Pp. 29-46.   Tampa, Florida

Pozzetta, George (1981)
"The Mulberry District of New York City: The Years Before World War I". In Robert
F. Harney and J. Vincenza Scarpaci. *Little Italies in North America*. Toronto: The
Multicultural History Society of Ontario. Pp. 7-40.   New York City

Pozzetta, George E. (1982)
"Italian Radicals in Tampa, Florida: A Research Note". *International Labor and
Working Class History*. 22:77-81.   Tampa, Florida

Re, V. (1979)
History of the First Italian Presbyterian Church in Detroit. Detroit: Ethnic Studies
Division. Pp. 37.   Detroit, Michigan

Richardson, William C. (1981)
"Fishermen of San Diego: The Italians". *Journal of San Diego History* 27(4):213-
226.   San Diego, California

Roche, John Patrick (1977)
Ethnic Attitudes and Ethnic Behavior: Italian Americans in Two Rhode Island Suburban

Communities. Ph.D. Dissertation, University of Connecticut. Pp. 292.
                                                                    Rhode Island

Roche, John Patrick (1982)
"Suburban Ethnicity: Ethnic Attitudes and Behavior among Italian Americans in Two
Suburban Communities". *Social Science Quarterly* 63(1):145-153.
                                                                    Rhode Island

Rudnicki, Ryan (1979)
Peopling Industrial America: Formation of Italian and Polish Settlements in the
Manufacturing Heartland of the United States. Ph.D. Dissertation, Pennsylvania
State University (Geography).   Eastern United States

Rusich, Luciano G. (1979)
"The Marquis of Sant'Angelo, Italian American Patriot and Friend of Texas". *Italian
Americana.* 5(1):1-22.   New York; New Orleans; Texas

Russo, Nicholas John (1975)
"From Mezzogiorno to Metropolis: Brooklyn's New Italian Immigrants". In Francesco
Cordasco, ed. *Studies in Italian American History.* Totowa, NJ: Rowan and Littlefield.
Pp. 118-131.   Brooklyn, New York

Salvetti, Patricia (1982)
"La communità italiana di San Francisco tra italianità e americanizzazione negli anni
'30 e '40". *Studi Emigrazione.* 19, 65. Pp. 3-39.   San Francisco, California

Sansone, Carmela (1983)
The Relationship between Ethnic Identification and Self Acceptance in Third Generation
Italian-Americans. Ph.D. Dissertation, New York University. Pp. 152.
                                                          Brooklyn, New York

Scarpaci, Jean Anne (1975)
"Immigrants in the New South: Italians in Louisiana's Sugar Parishes, 1880-1970". In
Francesco Cordasco, ed. *Studies in Italian American Social History.* Totowa, NJ:
Rowan and Littlefield. Pp. 132-152.   Louisiana

Scarpaci, Jean (1977)
"A Tale of Selective Accommodation: Sicilians and Native Whites in Louisiana".
Journal of Ethnic Studies. 5(3):37-50.   Louisiana

Scarpaci, Jean Ann (1980)
*Italian Immigrants in Lousiana's Sugar Parishes: Recruitment, Labor Conditions, and
Community Relations, 1880-1910.* New York: Arno Press. Ph.D. Dissertation, Rutgers,
1972. Pp. vii + 333.   Louisiana

Scarpaci, J. Vincenza (1981)
"Observations on an Ethnic Community: Baltimore's Little Italy". In Robert F. Harney
and J. Vincenza Scarpaci. *Little Italies in North America.* Toronto: The Multicultural
History Society of Toronto. Pp. 105-122.   Baltimore, Maryland

Scherini, Rose Doris (1980)
The Italian Community of San Francisco A Descriptive Study. New York: Arno Press.

Ph.D. Dissertation, University of California, Berkeley, 1976. Pp. vi + 246.
San Francisco, California

Schoenberg, Sandra P. (1980)
"Community Stability and Decay in St. Louis: The Ethnic Factor in Two Urban Neighborhoods". *Ethnicity*. 7(4):404-419.   St. Louis, Missouri

Schwieder, Dorothy (1982)
"Italian Americans in Iowa's Coal Mining Industry". *Annals of Iowa*. 46(4):263-278.
Iowa

Serene, Frank H. (1980)
"Paesano: The Struggle to Survive in Ambridge". *Pennsylvania Heritage*. 6(4):15-19.
Ambridge, Pennsylvania

Shankman, Arnold (1977-78)
"The Menacing Influx: Afro-Americans on Italian Immigration to the South: 1880-1915". *Mississippi Quarterly*. 31(1):67-88.   South

Simons, William, Samuel Patti and George Herman (1981)
"Bloomfield: An Italian Working Class Neighborhood". *Italian Americana* 7(1): 103-116.   Pittsburgh, Pennsylvania

Smith, Judith E. (1980)
Remaking Their Lives: Italian and Jewish Family, Work, and Community in Providence, Rhode Island, 1900-1940. Ph.D. Dissertation, Brown University. Pp. 317.
Providence, Rhode Island

Sowell, T. (1981)
Ethnic America. New York: Basic Book Publishers. Pp. 353.   General

Spengler, Paul A. (1980)
Yankee, Swedish and Italian Acculturation and Economic Mobility in Jamestown, New York, from 1860 to 1920. New York: Arno Press, 1980. Ph.D. Dissertation, University of Delaware, 1977. Pp. iii + 385.   Jamestown, New York

Stack, John Francis Jr. (1977)
The City as a Symbol of International Conflict: Boston's Irish Italians and Jews, 1935-1944. Ph.D. Dissertation, University of Denver. Pp. 360.
Boston, Massachusetts

Stack, John F., Jr. (1979)
International Conflict in an American City: Boston's Irish, Italians, and Jews, 1935-1944. Westport, CT: Greenwood Press. Pp. 181.
Boston Massachusetts

Starr, Dennis J. (1984)
The Italians of New Jersey: A Research Guide. In press.   New Jersey

Stokvis, Jack R. (1979)
" ' Salute' to Jersey City". *Planning (ASPO)*. 45(10):21-23.
Jersey City, New Jersey

Stout, Robert J. (1977)
"Can't You See That We're Home?" *Westway.* 69(11):24-27.   California

Swiderski, Richard W. (1977)
"Main Street and Church Road: Ethnic Relations in a New England Town". In George
L. Hicks, Philip E. Leis. *Ethnic Encounters: Identities and Contexts.* North Scituate,
MA: Duxbury Press, 1977. Pp. 119-135.
                                                    Unidentified town in New England

Thompson, Bryan (1980)
*Cultural Ties as Determinants of Immigrant Settlement in Urban Areas: A Case Study
of the Growth of an Italian Neighborhood in Worcester, Massachusetts, 1875-1922.*
New York: Arno Press, 1981. Ph.D. Dissertation, Clark University, 1971. Pp. ix+191.
                                                              Worcester, Massachusetts

Tomasi, Silvano (1975)
Piety and Power: The Role of the Italian Parishes in the New York Metropolitan Area.
New York: Center for Migration Studies. Pp. 201.   New York

Tomasi, Silvano (1982)
"L'Assistenza religiosa agli italiani in USA e il Prelato per l'Emigrazione italiana:
1920-1949". *Studi Emigrazione.* 19,66, pp. 167-190.   Various locations

Tricarico, Donald (1983a)
"The Restructuring of Ethnic Community: The Italian Neighborhood in Greenwich
Village". *The Journal of Ethnic Studies*, 11(2)61-77.
                                                    Greenwich Village, New York

Tricarico, Donald (1983b)
"The Italians of Greenwich Village: The Restructuring of Ethnic Community". In
Richard N. Juliani. *Family and Community Life of Italian Americans.* Staten Island:
American Italian Historical Association. Pp. 133-146.
                                                    Greenwich Village, New York

Vanario, Louis M. (1980)
"St. Anthony's Day in Cortland: 'La Festa' in Central New York". *New York Folklore.*
6(3-4):161-170.   Cortland, New York

Vecoli, Rudolph J. (1978)
"The Coming of Age of Italian Americans: 1945-1974". *Ethnicity.* 5(2):119-147.
                                                                        General

Vecoli, Rudolph (1980)
"Anthony Capraro and the Lawrence Strike of 1919". In George Pozzetta, ed. *Pane e
Lavoro: The Italian American Working Class.* Toronto: The Multicultural Society of
Ontario. Pp. 3-27.   Lawrence, Massachusetts

Vecoli, Rudolph J. (1981)
"The Italians". In June Holmquist, ed. *They Chose Minnesota: A Survey of the State's
Ethnic Groups.* St. Paul: Minnesota Historical Society. Pp. 449-471.
                                                                      Minnesota

Vecoli, Rudolph J. (1982)
"Italian Religious Organizations in Minnesota".*Studi Emigrazione*. 19, 66. Pp. 191-202.
Minnesota

Venturelli, Peter J. (1981)
Acculturation and the Persistence of Ethnicity in a Northern Italian-American District. Ph.D. Dissertation, Chicago (History).
Chicago, Illinois

Venturelli, Peter J. (1983)
"Tuscan-American Families". In Richard N. Juliani. *Family and Community Life of Italian Americans*. Staten Island: American Italian Historical Association. Pp. 69-80.
Chicago, Illinois

Verbero, Richard A. (1975)
"The Politics of Ethnicity. Philadelphia's Italians in the 1920's." In Francesco Cordasco, ed. *Studies in Italian American Social History*. Totowa, NJ: Rowan and Littlefield. Pp. 164-181.
Philadelphia, Pennsylvania

Veronesi, Gene P. (1977)
Italian Americans and Their Communities of Cleveland. Cleveland: Cleveland State University. Pp. ix + 358.
Cleveland, Ohio

Weber, Michael, John Bodnar and Roger Simon (1981)
"Seven Neighborhoods: Stability and Change in Pittsburgh's Ethnic Community, 1930-1960". *Western Pennsylvania Historical Magazine*. 64(2):121-150.
Pittsburgh, Pennsylvania

Wilson, Diana Vecchio (1983)
"Assimilation and Ethnic Consolidation of Italians in Cortland, New York 1892-1930". In Richard N. Juliani. *Family and Community Life of Italian Americans*. Staten Island: American Italian Historical Assocation. Pp. 183-191.
Cortland, New York

Wolfe, Margaret R. (1977)
"The Rural and Small-Town Experience: With Commentary on Italians in Southern Appalachia, 1900-1920". In Humbert Nelli, ed. *The United States and Italy: The First Two Hundred Years*. Staten Island: American Italian Historical Association. Pp. 162-172.
Southern Appalachia

Wolfe, Margaret Ripley (1979)
"Aliens in Southern Appalachia, 1900-1920: The Italian Experience in Wise County, Virginia". *Virginia Magazine of History and Biography*. 87(4):455-472.
Virginia

Yans-McLaughlin, Virginia (1977)
Family and Community Italian Immigrants in Buffalo, 1880-1930. Ithaca, NY: Cornell University Press. Pp. 286.
Buffalo, New York

(These additional titles are not analyzed in the review).

Alba, Richard D. (1984)
Italian Americans Into The Twilight of Eternity". Englewood Cliffs, NJ: Prentice-Hall, Inc. Pp. 182.   General.

Baily, Samuel L. (1983)
"The Adjustment of Italian Immigrants in Buenos Aires and New York, 1870-1914". *The American Historical Review.* 88(2):281-305.
                                                                                       New York City

Belfiglio, Valentine (1983)
Italian Experience in Texas. Austin, TX: Eakin Press. Pp. 264.   Texas

Calomiris, Ellen (1983)
"Conflict, Cooperation, Acceptance: The Italian Experience in Delaware". *Delaware History.* 20(4):269-290.   Delaware

Candeloro, Dominic (1981)
"Suburban Italians: Chicago Heights, 1890-1975. In Peter d'A. Jones and Melvin G. Holli. *Ethnic Chicago.* Grand Rapids, MI: W.B. E. Erdmans.   Chicago, Illinois

Carini, Mario A. (1984)
Milwaukee's Italians: The Early Years. West Allis, WI: Italian Community Center. Pp. 14.   Milwaukee, Wisconsin

Center for Migration Studies of New York, Inc. (1981)
Images: A Pictorial History of Italian Americans. New York: Center for Migration Studies. Pp. xix + 328.   General

Cinel, Dino (1981)
"Between Change and Continuity: Regionalism among Immigrants from the Italian Northwest", *The Journal of Ethnic Studies,* 9(3):19-36.   San Francisco, California

Crispino, James A. (1980)
The Assimilation of Ethnic Groups: The Italian Case. New York: Center for Migration Studies. Pp. 205.   Bridgeport, Connecticut

Di Comite, Luigi and Ira A. Glazer (1984)
"Socio-Demographic Characteristics of Italian Emigration to the United States from Ship Passenger Lists: 1880-1914". *Ethnic Forum.* Vol. 4,(1-2) Pp.78-90.
                                                                              Philadelphia, Pennsylvania

di Leonardo, Micaela (1984)
The Varieties of Ethnic Experience: Kinship, Class, and Gender Among California Italian-Americans. Ithaca and London: Cornell University Press. Pp. 262.
                                                                                          California

Ficile, Enzo, (1975)
Storia degli Italiani di New York. New York: Italian American Center for Urban Affairs. Pp. 128.   New York City

Gabaccia, Donna R. (1984)
From Sicily to Elizabeth Street: Housing and Social Change Among Italian Immigrants, 1880-1930. Albany, NY: State University of New York Press. Pp. 174.
New York

Jackson, Peter (1983a)
"Vito Marcantonio and Ethnic Politics in New York". *Ethnic and Racial Studies.* Great Britain, 6(1):50-71.   New York City

Jackson, Peter (1983b)
"Ethnic Turf: Competition of the Canal Street Divide". *New York Affairs.* 7(4): 149-158.   New York City

LaGumina, Salvatore J. (1979)
The Immigrants Speak: Italian Americans Tell Their Story. New York: Center for Migration Studies. Pp. 209.   General

Lissak, Rivka (1983)
"Myth and Reality: The Patterns of Relationship Between the Hull House Circle and the 'New Immigrants' on Chicago's West Side, 1890-1919". *Journal of American Ethnic History.* 2(2), Pp. 21-50.   Chicago, Illinois

McCoy, Maureen and William Silag (1983)
"The Italian Heritage in Des Moines: Photographs". *Palimpsest* 64(2):58-68.
Des Moines, Iowa

Salvemini, Gaetano (1977)
Italian Fascist Activities in the United States. New York: Center for Migration Studies. Pp. 300.   General

Schwieder, Dorothy (1983)
Black Diamonds. Life and Work in Iowa's Coal Mining Communities, 1895-1925. Ames: Iowa State University Press, Pp. 203.   Iowa

Stephenson, Sally S. (1981)
Michael A. Nusmanno: A Symbolic Leader. Carnegie-Mellon University. Ph.D. dissertation.   Pittsburgh, Pennsylvania.

Tomasi, Lydio F. (1978)
The Italian in America: The Progressive View (1891-1914). New York: Center for Migration Studies. Pp. xvi-309.   General

Tomasi, Silvano M. and Edward Stibili (1978)
Italian Americans and Religion: An Annotated Bibliography. New York: Center for Migration Studies. Pp. 225.   General

Tomasi, Silvano M. ed. (1980)
National Directory of Research Centers, Repositories and Organizations of Italian Culture in the United States. New York: Center for Migration Studies. Pp. 255.
General

Torrieri, Nancy K. (1982)
Cultural Change and Residential Dispersal: The Survival of Italian-American Culture

in Baltimore. Ph.D. Dissertation (Geography), University of Maryland. Pp. 251.
                                                            Baltimore, Maryland

Tricarico, Donald (1984)
The Italians of Greenwich Village: the Social Structure and Transformation of an Ethnic Community. New York: Center for Migration Studies. Pp. xx + 181
                                                            New York City

Vecoli, Rudolph J. (1983)
"The Formation of Chicago's Little Italies". *Journal of American Ethnic History.*
2(2), Spring. Pp. 5-20.   Chicago, Illinois

Venturelli, Peter J. (1982)
"Institutions in an Ethnic District". *Human Organization.*41(1):26-35.
                                                            Chicago, Illinois

Veronesi, Gene P. (1977)
Italian Americans and Their Communities of Cleveland. Cleveland: Cleveland State University. Pp. ix — 358.   Cleveland, Ohio

12

Ongoing Research
in Italian American Studies: A Survey

DIANA ZIMMERMAN
Librarian, Center for Migration Studies

FROM February through July of 1983, the Center for Migration Studies (CMS), in keeping with its commitment to explore and document the Italian American experience, conducted a survey of the ongoing research in Italian American studies. Approximately 1700 questionnaires were distributed to members of the American Italian Historical Association, to departments of Italian Studies and to individuals and groups who were identified as having an interest in the field. The survey solicited the following information: 1) a title and brief description of the respondent's current research and future research plans in Italian American studies; 2) a description of relevant studies being conducted by other researchers known to the respondent; 3) a list of repositories in the respondent's geographic area that hold primary documentation on Italian Americans; and 4) a list of courses in Italian American studies taught by the respondent or his/her colleagues.

GENERAL DATA

Survey questionnaires were returned by 135 respondents (8% rate of return). Of this group, 123 provided information about current research projects. Approximately one-third (36%) of the research dealt with the Italian experience in a specific community or region. Cultural topics and studies dealing with Italian American women were next in reported frequency with 11 percent and 9 percent respectively. The remaining projects were distributed among nine subject categories: labor, politics, education, linguistics, immigration history, ethnic press, mass media, mental health and religion. Each received between 2 and 6 percent of the reported research. Approximately 9 percent of the projects did not fall under one of the above topics and were grouped together in a thirteenth category labeled special studies.

In addition to obtaining data on current research in Italian American studies, the survey provided information about the future research plans of forty-nine respondents. This group reported seventy-three potential research projects. Community studies represented 25 percent of the planned research. Italian American woman accounted for another 9 percent whereas immigration history, mental health studies and cultural studies received 8 percent each. The categories of education and labor were reported by 5 percent of the respondents. The remaining studies spanned a wide array of topics with 4 percent or less falling into any one category. It is interesting to note that more than one-half of the forty-nine respondents intend to continue work on their current research topic.

In processing the CMS data, every attempt was made to conform as closely as possible to the categorical system used in a similar survey conducted by the American Italian Historical Association (AIHA) in 1976 (della Cava, 1977, pp. 165-172). The AIHA categories were specific and provided the reader with a clear view of the broad scope of research in Italian American studies. Equally important, adherence to the same categorical system provided a means of comparison between the surveys.

TABLE 1

Percentage of Reported Research in Italian American Studies
by Selected Categories[a]

Categories of Studies	Surveys [b]		
	Percent of Current Research Reported in the AIHA Survey 1976	Percent of Current Research Reported in the CMS Survey 1983	Percent of Planned Research Reported in the CMS Survey 1983
Community or Regional Studies	35	36	25
Cultural Studies	11	11	9
Italian American Women	11	9	9
Labor	14	6	5
Politics	5	6	5
Religion	7	4	2
Linguistics	4	4	1
Family	4	0	0
Socialization	9	0	3
Other	0	24	41
TOTAL	100	100	100

Note: a Data is only presented for categories common to both surveys.

b These percentages are based on 55 reported studies in 1976, 123 reported studies in 1983, and 73 planned research projects reported in 1983.

When comparing the results of the two surveys, several interesting findings come to light. First, the 1983 CMS survey reported more than twice the number of current projects than did the AIHA survey (122 and 55 respectively). It is unclear as to whether the gain can be attributed to the larger mailing or increased interest in Italian American studies, and is more likely an interplay of both factors.

Of the 55 ongoing studies reported in the AIHA survey, 35 percent were devoted to community or regional studies. As was previously indicated, similar percentages occurred in the recent CMS survey. Furthermore, the data on future research plans of CMS respondents indicated continued research interest in this area. Clearly, a substantial body of research is accumulating on Italian American community life which could, in the future, lead to valuable comparative studies.

Apart from community studies, comparable results occurred between the surveys in four additional categories: Italian American women, politics, linguistics and cultural studies. In 1976 and 1983, projects dealing with Italian American women represented approximately 10 percent of the reported research.Moreover, 9 percent of the CMS respondents who provided information about their future research plans intend to conduct studies in this area. Given the current emphasis on women's studies in general, it appears most likely that this area of Italian American studies will experience future growth.

The percentage of reported research dealing with Italian American political behavior has remained constant, albeit low, in 1976 and 1983. In both surveys, approximately 5 percent of the respondents reported current research on topics related to Italian Americans and politics. The same percentage was registered for the CMS data on planned research.

The categories of linguistics and cultural studies also reported uniform results across the two surveys. However, the data regarding research plans of CMS repondents indicated a decline in research interest for these fields. Research on linguistic topics represented 4 percent of the current studies in 1976 and 1983, but only 1 percent of the future research projects. In both surveys cultural studies received 11 percent of the reported research whereas planned research in this area dropped to 8 percent.

Apart from the five categories that produced comparable results, there were four categories in which the findings reflected a clear change in research interest. Labor and religion attracted less research attention in the CMS survey. In 1976, 14 percent of the current research dealt with labor issues and 7 percent focused on religion, whereas in the 1983 survey, 6 percent and 4 percent respectively were reported for these areas. The data on respondents' future research plans indicated further decline. Approximately 5 percent of the respondents intend to conduct research on labor-related subjects and 2 percent on Italian Americans and religion.

Decline in research interest was equally marked for the areas of family and socialization. They had registered 9 percent and 4 percent respectively in the 1976 AIHA survey, but there were no current studies reported for either in the CMS survey.

To summarize briefly, several observations can be drawn from the comparative data. The 1983 CMS survey involved more than twice the number of studies than were reported in the 1976 AIHA survey. However, the categorical distribution of the research was similar for both. Of the nine categories for which comparative data was available, five entailed comparable percentage for the two surveys: community studies, cultural studies, Italian American women, politics and linguistics. Of these five categories, community studies, cultural studies and Italian American women comprised the higheset percentages of current research. The future research plans of CMS respondents indicates that research activity in these areas will continue at or near their present level. In contrast, interest in the topics of religion and labor declined in the 1983 survey, and no research was reported in the categories of family and socialization.

Finally, the data points to increased diversity in research on Italian Americans. In Table 1, the category labeled "other" indicates that 24 percent of the ongoing research and 41 percent of the planned research reported in 1983 were devoted to topics that were not covered by the original nine AIHA categories. The additional categories in the CMS survey were mental health, mass media, ethnic press and immigration history. A fifth category labeled "special studies" subsumed a wide range of topics for each of which there was only one reported study. These data suggest that, overall, the scope of the research in Italian American studies is expanding.

In conclusion, it should be noted that in using a categorical system that allowed for a comparison of the results of the 1976 AIHA and 1983 CMS surveys, certain problems were inherent. The categories, although narrow, were not mutually exclusive, and many of the categories had too few studies to be considered reliable indices. Despite these problems, the results provide the reader with a substantive overview of the current research as it was reported in 1976 and 1983, and point to future trends in the field of Italian American studies.

CURRENT RESEARCH

Respondents to the 1983 CMS survey reported ongoing research in twelve areas of Italian American studies: community and regional studies, women, politics, labor, education, culture, linguistics, immigration history, ethnic press, mass media, mental health and religion. Under a thirteenth category, special studies, are grouped a wide range of topics for which there was only one reported study each.

Community and Regional Studies - West

Community and regional studies dominated the reported current research. Eight survey respondents have focused on the Italian population in western communities. Peppino Ortoleva (University of Bologna, Italy), is studying Italian immigration to San Francisco from the Ligurian region, particularly the Fontanabuona area around Genoa. His research will include an analysis of the village structure in Italy and its influence on the San Francisco emigrant *colonia*.

Early Italian Settlers in San Francisco is the title of a forthcoming book by Augusto Troiani and the Societa' Italiana di Mutua Beneficenza of San Francisco. It is a commemorative publication marking the Society's 125th anniversary and includes a history of the organization and biographical data on its original officers and supporters.

The Italians are one of twenty-two major ethnic groups in the greater Sacramento area selected for an indepth survey by the Sacramento History Center. Bruce Pierini, Assistant Director of the survey, is conducting the research on the Italian community. The results of the survey will be incorporated into the Community Gallery of the Sacramento History Center.

Italians in a rural California *paese* are the focus of an inter-generational study being conducted by Paola Sensi-Isolani (St. Mary's College, Monaga, CA), whereas Italians in urban California have been investigated by Rosalind Giardina Crosby (San Francisco, CA) in her recently completed masters thesis,"Italians of Los Angeles, 1900". Denzil R. Verardo's (Pacific Grove, CA) current research deals with the Italian experience in World War II California.

Phylis Cancilla Martinelli (Arizona State University, Tempe) has completed the data collection for her doctoral dissertation on ethnic identity among Italian Americans who have migrated to Phoenix since World War II. Independent of this effort, she is gathering information, primarily through oral histories, about Italian emigration to Arizona mining towns.

Texas Italians have been dealt with comprehensively in Valentino J. Belfiglio's (Texas Woman's University) recently published book "The Italian Experience in Texas". He is now preparing biographical sketches of prominent Italo-Texans and a short history of the Italians in Texas for the Texas Historical Society's "Handbook of Texas".

Joseph Velikonja's (University of Washington, Seattle) research on the Italian immigrants in the American West will include a detailed assessment of the Italian communities west of the Mississippi.

Midwest

In the Midwest, Dominic Candeloro (Italian Cultural Center, Stone Park, IL) is engaged in research on the Italians in the Chicago area, and Mario A. Carini

(Italian Community Center of Milwaukee, WI) is recording the Italian experience in Metropolitan Milwaukee. Carini intends to document the migration of Italian nationals to that city from 1880 to 1930 and to trace the development of three Italian colonies established during that time period. Carini also reported research-in-progress on the history of the Italian Protestant Mission in Milwaukee and the ill-fated community "Villa Marconi" which the Mission's pastor had attempted to settle.

Michigan's Italian American heritage is being investigated by Leonard W. Moss (Wayne State University, Detroit, MI) and Russel M. Magnaghi (Northern Michigan University, Marquette). Moss is studying the Italian American voluntary associations in Metropolitan Detroit whereas Magnaghi is focusing on the Italians in the Upper Penninsula region. Magnaghi has accumulated a wealth of source material, including some 400 photographs, 150 oral history tapes, miscellaneous artifacts and published materials from Italian communities throughout the Upper Penninsula.

James J. Divita (Marian College, Indianapolis, IN) is continuing his research on the Italian experience in Indiana, and looks toward completing the first book on the topic.

South

In the southeastern sector of the United States, George E. Pozzetta (University of Florida, Gainesville) and Gary R. Mormino (University of South Florida, Tampa) are analyzing the interaction between the Italians, Cubans and Spaniards in Tampa, Florida from 1885-1930. Drawn by employment in the cigar industry, these three groups established very close ties during the period under investigation. The Pozzetta and Mormino studies are examining the nature of these relationships and the historic events which forged them and eventually led to their dissolution.

Anthony V. Margavio (University of New Orleans, LA), Paul Giordano (Rosary College, River Forest, IL) and doctoral student Roselyn Boneno (Louisiana State University, Baton Rouge, LA) are conducting research on the Italian experience in Louisiana. Margavio is interested in the social and cultural history of Louisiana Italians and is giving particular attention to immigration and settlement patterns, occupation distribution and the effect of family structure on economic achievement and fertility patterns. Giordano has published a number of articles on the Italian presence in Louisiana and is currently preparing a book length manuscript on the topic. Boneno's dissertation concentrates on the Italians in New Orleans and southwestern Louisiana between 1880 and 1910.

Italians are one of the ethnic groups represented in a book being written by Randall M. Miller (St. Joseph's University, Philadelphia, PA) entitled, "Immigrants in the American South". This is a study of European and Asian immigrants to the American South in the nineteenth and twentieth centuries, with particular emphasis placed on the impact of the new immigration on southern culture.

In the border state of Kentucky, doctoral student Gregory Stanley (University of Kentucky, Lexington) is conducting research on the Italian and Jewish communities of Louisville for his dissertation project.

Northeast

Research focusing on the Italians in the Northeast accounts for approximately one-half of the reported community studies. Dennis Starr (Trenton, NJ) and Robert E. Immordino (American Italian Historical Association, Central New Jersey Chapter) have collaborated on a project to identify materials and repositories important to the study of Italians in New Jersey. Their findings have been compiled in a forthcoming book entitled, "Italians in New Jersey: A Research Guide". The social and cultural activities of the Italian Americans in Trenton (NJ), 1885-1940, is a topic of continuing interest to Erasmo S. Ciccolella (American Italian Historical Association, Central New Jersey Chapter). He recently co-edited, with Mary Nicoli Ferre, a volume of essays by Joseph LoBue entitled "Italian American Vignettes". LoBue was a native born resident of Trenton) and his essays examine Italian American community life in that city from the vantage point of an "insider". The Italians in the Newark Ironbound Colony, 1870-1920, are being studied by doctoral student William Bolen (Rutgers University, New Brunswick, NJ) for his dissertation project.

Gennaro J. Capobianco (Italian American Historical Society Greater Hartford, CT) has done extensive research on the Italian presence in the greater Hartford area and now intends to organize the material into a book length manuscript.

New York City and State reported a considerable amount of research activity. "The Italians of Greenwich Village" is the title of a recently published book by Donald Tricarico (Queensborough Community College, Bayside, NY). It is a study of the adaptations made by second and third generation Italians in that community, with a particular focus on institutional changes in the areas of family, religion, politics, economics and social life. Special attention is given to the effects of dwindling population and the expansion of the Soho artist community on Italian neighborhood life.

The Center for Italian American Studies at Brooklyn College, under the direction of Jerry Krase (Brooklyn College, Brooklyn, NY), has involved students at both the graduate and undergraduate levels in an active program of research. Current projects include demographic research on Brooklyn's Italian American neighborhoods and the development of family history and photographic archives of Brooklyn's Italian Americans.

Salvatore J. LaGumina (Nassau Community College, Garden City, NY) is preparing a social history of the Italians in Long Island (NY) and Howard R.

Weiner (College of Staten Island, NY) is tracing the development of the Italian community in Staten Island.

The New York Central Chapter of the American Italian Historical Association has begun an oral history project to record the experiences of **family members and other Italian Americans in the central New York region. The Broome County Immigration Project (Robeson Center for Arts and Sciences, Binghamton, NY) continues its work collecting, preserving and** interpreting local ethnic history sources. Current research is focused on the Triple Cities area where the majority of newly arrived immigrants first settled. The Project has already developed impressive photo and oral history archives that are substantially Italian American.

In 1974, a group of interested citizens, headed by Fr. Joseph Beatrini, began the process of documenting the Italian American heritage in Seneca Falls, NY. They have been collecting oral histories and photos and have gathered information from the Senaca Falls census, church and county records and local Italian American organizations. These efforts have culminated in a forthcoming publication entitled "The Early Italian Immigrants to Seneca Falls, New York", which details the experiences and contributions of the Italian Americans in that city.

Studies were also reported by Salvatore Mondello (Rochester Institute of Technology, Rochester, NY), Michael M. Miller (Marconi Lodge #154, OSIA), Louis M. Vanaria (State University College at Cortland, NY) and Diane Vecchio Wilson (Cortland, NY). Mondello is continuing his research on the Italian community in Rochester while Miller is studying the Italians of Corning (NY). Among his many projects, Miller is writing the history of both the Marconi Lodge and the Italian American Women's Lodge of Corning. **Vanaria and Wilson have concentrated their research efforts on Cortland's Italians. Wilson has organized a pictorial exhibit entitled "The Immigrant Experience of Italians in Cortland".**

One research project was reported for the District of Columbia. Howard Gillete, Jr. (George Washington University, Washington, DC) is studying the evolution of Washington's Italian American Community, 1890-1980.

Women

Research dealing with Italian American women is being conducted by eleven survey respondents. Two doctoral students, Mary Jane Capozzoli (Lehigh University, Bethlehem, PA) and Dorothy M. Balancio (Mercy College, Dobbs Ferry, NY) have chosen the changing role of the Italian American women for their dissertation research. Capozzoli is tracing the lives of three generations of Italian American women in Nassau County, NY and is examining the effects of social, economic and political forces on their education, work, religious upbringing, sexual mores and leisure time activities. Balancio's project is also an intergenerational analysis. It deals with the changing identity of Italian American women and the evolution of the Italian American community.

Research is also being conducted by Pauline F. Fusaro (Mercy College, Dobbs Ferry, NY), Carmela E. Santoro (Rhode Island College, Providence), University of Florida graduate student Helen T. Smith and University of Turin (Italy) graduate student, Elizabeth Vezzosi. Fusaro is collecting data on **Italian American women in the Belmont community of Bronx (NY) and in Westchester County (NY), whereas Santoro is gathering information about Italian immigrant women entrepreneurs in Rhode Island. Smith is doing a comparative study of Cuban, Spanish and Italian immigrant women in** Tampa, Florida in the early 1900s. Vezzosi is focusing her research on the adaptation process as it relates to the Italian immigrant woman in early 20th century America.

"World of our Mothers" is a project being conducted by sociologists at the State University of New York at Stony Brook. Their research is focused on Italian immigrant women from Southern Italy and Jewish immigrant women from Eastern Europe who came to the United States prior to 1927 at the age of 13 or older. Through extensive taped interviews, the sociologists are recording the personal accounts of these unique women whose experiences offer documentation of the historic 'great migration' from the perspective of the female immigrant.

Four respondents reported books-in-progress. Co-authors Rita and Rose Calvano (San Diego, CA) have begun work on a book depicting the varied experiences of Italian women throughout the United States. Lucia Chiavola Birnbaum (American Italian Historical Association, Western Regional Chapter) has just completed a book, "Italian Feminists", and intends to finish the final draft of "Earthmother, Godmothers and Companions: The Heritage of Sicilian American Women", in the near future. Helen Barolini's (Ossining, NY) most recent work, "Italian American Women Authors", is slated for 1984 publication. It is an anthology of literary writings in all genres preceeded by an introductory essay placing each author in historical and cultural context.

Labor

The involvement of Italian Americans in the U.S. labor movement is of research interest to seven survey repondents. Rudolph J. Vecoli (University of Minnesota, St. Paul) is focusing on the Italian immigrants who entered the American labor force during the 1880-1940 period and their relationships with American labor organizations such as the United Mine Workers, the I.W.W. and the A.F. of L. trade unions. His study will consider the impact of autonomous labor activities, such as the socialist, anarchist and syndicalist movements on the Italian immigrant workers, and the eventual radicalization of a segment of this group.

Other studies in progress on Italian radicalism in America were reported by Eugene Miller and Gianna Panofsky (Illinois Labor and History Society, Chicago), Robert D'Attilo (Medford, MA) and doctoral student Concetta Tuttle (University of Arizona, Tucson). Miller and Panofsky are collaborating on a book entitled, "Italian Political and Labor Radicalism in Chicago", and D'Attilio and Tuttle are investigating the Italian American anarchist movement.

Doctoral research on Italian American workers in the International Ladies Garment Workers Union is being conducted by Charles A. Zappia (University of California, Berkeley). His dissertation is planned as a social history of Italian locals 48 and 89 of the I.L.G.W.U.

Kenneth Waltzer's (James Madison College, Michigan State University, East Lansing) forthcoming book on the American Labor Party will include an indepth discussion of Vito Marcantonio and the politics of East Harlem.

Politics

Seven survey respondents are conducting research on the involvement of Italian Americans in the U.S. political system. Frank J. Cavaioli (State University of New York at Farmingdale) is studying the broad spectrum of Italian American political behavior while Ralph Riverso (Federation of Italian American Organizations) is focusing on Italian Americans in government and commerce at the executive and policy making levels. Former Massachusetts governor John Volpe is the subject of a biography by Kathleen Kilgore (Mattapan, MA). The emergence of an Italian American political leadership is being researched by Nadia Venturini (University of Turin, Italy) whereas Elizabeth Vezzosi (University of Florence, Italy) is conducting an investigation of the Italian Socialist Federation in the United States, 1910-1930.

Two respondents are writing on the topic of Italian American fascism. Vincent M. Lombardi (Adelphi University, Garden City, NY) is preparing an article-length manuscript that analyzes the social, economic and cultural backgrounds of Italian fascist sympathizers while Philip V. Canistraro's (Drexel University, Philadelpohia, PA) book-in-progress deals with Italian anti-fascist exiles in the United States, 1939-45.

Education

Research on Italian Americans and higher education is being conducted by Francis X. Femminella (State University of New York at Albany), William Egelman (Iona College, New Rochelle, NY) and the Center for Italian American Studies (Brooklyn College, Brooklyn, NY).

Culture

A broad range of projects spanning the fields of literature, fine arts and folklore fall into the category of cultural studies. In the area of fine arts, Museo Italo-Americano (San Francisco) is developing a collection of artists files which provide biographical information and slides exemplifying the work of individual Italian and Italian American artists. Furthermore, Regina Soria (College of Notre Dame of Maryland in Baltimore) is compiling a comprehensive dictionary of Italian American artists, 1776-1914, while Carlo A. Scalfani's (Westchester Community College, Valhalla, NY) research focuses on the specific contributions of this group.

The field of literature is represented by Rose Basile Green (Cabrini College, Radnor, PA) and Joseph Fioravanti (State University Agricultural and Technical College, Delhi, NY). Green is completing two articles for publication, entitled, "The Italian American Literary Patrimony" and "Contemporary Italian American Creative Writing", and is preparing a new edition of her book *The Italian American Novel.* Fiorvanti is writing a fictional account of the impact of American culture on a representative community of Italian immigrants living in New York City during 1900-1920.

There are several respondents examining the customs, music and folkways of Italian Americans. Doctoral student Marcello Sorce-Keller (University of Illinois, Urbana) is conducting a survey to uncover what remains of the Northern Italian musical traditions in the Italian communities of Chicago (IL) and Clinton (IN). Particular attention is being devoted to the repertoire of ballads, to popular songs of the early twentieth century and to the repertoire remembered by immigrants who migrated from the Trenton area.

The musical culture of the Italian community of Hartford (CT) is being studied by Anthony T. Rauche for his dissertation research. He is concentrating on three topics: 1) the role that musical activity plays in maintaining an ethnic identity among Hartford's Italians; 2) the impact that recent immigrants have had on the community's interest in contemporary Italian culture and music; and 3) the future of traditional musical activity and festival life in Hartford.

The Italian Cultural Society (Sacramento, CA) is developing a collection of records, pamphlets, photographs, oral histories and memorabilia that document the Italian presence in the Sacramento area.

The Philadelphia Food Project has generated a series of studies which explore the relationship between foodways and Italian ethnicity. Among them are Janet S. Theophano's (University of Medicine and Dentistry of New Jersey) dissertation entitled "It's Really Tomato Sauce But We Call It Gravy": A Study of Food and Women's Work" (University of Pennsylvania) and Karen A. Curtis's (Temple University) dissertation, "I Can't Go Anywhere Empty Handed: Food Exchange and Reciprocity in an Italian American

Community".

Giovanni Allen Cicala (Folklore Institute, Indiana University, Bloomington) is also conducting a food study for his doctoral research. He is comparing the style, method of preparation, creativity and presentation of ordinary and ceremonial meals of two Italian American women; one Sicilian and the other San Marinese. Apart from this project, Cicala is completing an edition of Italian American narratives which he collected from Detroit (MI) Italians. The publication will include an analysis of the Italian American narrative and a short history of the Italian Community of Detroit.

Linguistics

"Italian American Language in the Greater New York Metropolitan Area: A Study of Sociolinguistic Behavior" is an interdisciplinary project directed by Fiorenza Weinapple (New York University). It joins a linguist, a dialectologist, a sociologist, an anthropologist and an historian of Italian language in a collaborative effort. They seek to determine, through a series of interviews: a) the degree of retention and interference between English and Italian in three successive generations; and b) the socioeconomic factors that influence these processes. The final product of this two year project will be a volume that addresses theoretical as well as practical issues of bilingualism.

Herman W. Haller's (Queens College, Flushing, NY) current research project, "Linguistic Aspects of Italian Language Mass Media", is a sociolinguistic analysis of Italian in the news media in the United States during 1983. It presents both quantitative and qualitative analyses of Italian programs and news articles. Furthermore, Haller is continuing his study of the sociolinguistic behavior patterns of Italians in the United States.

Research in linguistics was also reported by John Perrotta (Washington, D.C.) and Joshua A. Fishman (Yeshiva University, NY). Perotta is studying "code-switching" (switching between Italian dialect and English) among Italian Americans in Baltimore (MD). Fishman continues his work in the area of language maintenance among American ethnocultural minorities.

Immigration History

Historical works dealing with the phenomenon of Italian migration at the global or country-wide levels were reported in progress by F. Robert Pascoe (Charles Warren Center, Harvard University, Cambridge, MA), Patrizia Audenino (University of Turin, Italy) and Vittorio Re (Italian American Cultural Society, Grosse Point City, MI). Pascoe is writing a social history of Italian immigration that is expected to comprise three volumes: one covering the United States, another for Western Europe and the Mediterranean, and a third dealing with Canada, Latin American and Australia. Audenino is gathering information on the migration to the Unites States from Biella, Italy.

Her research is part of a larger project sponsored by SELLA Foundation of Biella (Italy) to document the phenomenon of Biellese migration world-wide. Re's study deals with the Italian immigration to North America in 1650 as a means of escaping the tyranny of Spanish rule.

Ethnic Press

The forthcoming publication, "Italian American Periodical Press, 1836-1980: A Comprehensive Bibliography" represents twenty years of research by Pietro Russo (University of Florence, Italy). The catalog lists and annotates 2,344 periodical press and serial publications which appeared in the United States from 1836 to 1980. Included are newspapers, journals, bulletins and other serials which conform to the following criteria: 1) all or part are in Italian; 2) they are published by Italians or their descendents with an interest in things Italian; 3) they are substantially about Italian American communities; 4) they have regular sections or articles on Italian Americans; and 5) they deal essentially with Italy or Italo-U.S. relationships.

Italian American periodical press is also the focus of Joseph Velikonja's (University of Washington, Seattle) current rearch. He is concentrating on three interrelated topics: 1) the territorial diffusion of the Italian periodical press from entry points such as New York and San Francisco, to the interior cities; 2) the directional flows of the press and their correlation with the establishment of communities, with the development of a transportation system and with industrialization; and 3) the time lapse between the arrival of the immigrants and the establishment of the Italian press.

Carlo Dondero, pioneer Italian language journalist in San Francisco, is the subject of a biography being prepared by Francesca Loverci (University of Rome, Italy).

Mass Media

Projects dealing with the mass media have been reported by six survey respondents. Salvatore Primeggia (Adelphi University, Garden City, NY), Carlos E. Cortés (University of California, Riverside) and the Commission of Social Justice (West Hempstead, NY) are conducting research on the stereotyping of Italian Americans in motion pictures and television. Joseph Giordano (Center on Ethnicty and Mental Health, Institute on Pluralism and Group Identity, American Jewish Committee) is developing strategies which will enable the Italian American community to work with the media in creating a more positive Italian American image.

Mental Health

Increased awareness of the relationship between ethnicity and mental health among Italian Americans is reflected in the reported current research. Social psychiatry and its implications for Italian Americans is being studied by

Francis X. Femminella (State University of New York at Albany). Joseph V. Scelsa (New York Association for Clinical Mental Health Counselors) is investigating the cultural issues inherent in the psychosocial conflicts experienced by Italian Americans while doctoral student Lisa Mann (Columbia University, NY) is exploring the use of ethnotherapy with Italian Americans for her dissertation research.

The Center on Ethnicity and Mental Health (Institute on Pluralism and Group Identity, American Jewish Committee) is supporting a number of studies relevant to Italian Americans. Among them are Carmela Sansone's study entitled "The Effects of Ethnic Identification on the Self-Esteem of Third Generation Italian Americans", as well as a Center study aimed at determining the effectiveness of clinical group experiences in understanding the many facets of the Italian American identity.

Religion

The role of religion in Italian American life is a topic of research interest to five survey respondents. Alessandro Baccari (Baccari Associates, San Francisco) and Vincenza Scarpaci (American Italian Historical Society, Western Regional Chapter) are preparing a commemorative history marking the 100th anniversary of Sts. Peter and Paul Church (San Francisco). The church was established by the Salesian Fathers as an Italian parish for North Beach residents. The Italian American Baptist Movement is the subject of an on-going study being conducted by Salvatore Mondello (Rochester Institute of Technology, Rochester, NY).

Mary E. Brown's (Columbia University, NY) dissertation to be entitled "Churches and Communities: Italian immigrants and the Archdiocese of New York, 1850-1940" is focused on five "Little Italies" within the New York Archdiocese. She is studying the evolution of the Church's ministry in these communities as they moved through various stages of assimilation. She is particularly interested in the ways in which the immigrant laity shaped their parishes to meet their own specific needs. Lydio F. Tomasi (Center for Migration Studies, Staten Island, NY) has completed his investigation of the institutional role of the church in the adjustment process of Italians in Metropolitan Toronto (Canada) and a 1984 publication date is expected for the work.

Special Studies

Forming a category apart are nine one-of-a-kind research projects spanning a wide range of topics. Among them is John Appel's (Michigan State University, East Lansing) collection of paper ephemera that depict Italian Americans. Post cards, trading cards, magazine illustrations, cartoons and vaudeville jokes are some of the items of interest to him.

Also included in this category are projects reported by Joseph Giordano (Center for Ethnicity and Mental Health, NY), Sr. Margherita Marchione (Salvitore Center for Mazzei Studies, Fairleigh Dickinson University, Morristown, NJ), Alesandro Baccari (Baccari Associates, San Francisco) and Vincenza Scarpaci (American Italian Historical Association, Western Regional Chapter). Giordano is preparing a resource catalog to assist Italian Americans in determining those aspects of their heritage they wish to maintain, and to provide helpful hints on how to do it. The catalog will cover subjects such as history, family and traditions. Sr. Marchione has completed a three volume work entitled "Selected Writings and Correspondence of Philip Mazzei". The forthcoming edition will be published in both English and Italian. Baccari and Scarpaci are collaborating on a pictorial history of the Italians in the fifty states, the District of Columbia and Canada. The text and historical photos will document the period from 1880 to 1940.

Italian Americans are one of the ethnic groups included in Kenneth Waltzer's (James Madison College, Michigan State University, East Lansing) study of second generation immigrants in 20th century urban America, and in Richard K. Lieberman's (La Guardia Community College, Long Island City, NY) history of the Steinway piano workers.

The Commission for Social Justice (West Hempstead, NY) is conducting a "Survey of Italian American Businessmen" for the purpose of studying Italian American representation on the boards of America's largest corporations. Apart from this, the Commission is engaged in another project aimed at assessing Italian American representation in the history textbooks used in New York State schools.

Other current projects include Andrew M. Canepa's (American Italian Historical Association, Western Regional Chapter) research on the Italian American freemasonry in California, John E. di Meglio's (Mankato State University, Mankato, MN) study of organized crime and Stanley H. Balducci's (State Social Services, Richmond, VA) genealogical research.

COURSE OFFERINGS IN ITALIAN AMERICAN STUDIES

Respondents to the CMS survey provided the following information about courses in Italian American studies.

ADELPHI UNIVERSITY, Department of Sociology, Garden City, NY. Salvatore Primeggia teaches an undergraduate course entitled "The Italian American Experience".

BROOKLYN COLLEGE, Department of Sociology, Brooklyn, NY. "The Italians in America" is an interdisciplinary course taught at the undergraduate level. A seminar in the sociology of the Italian American community is taught at the advanced undergraduate level.

LEHIGH UNIVERSITY, Department of Urban Studies, Bethlehem, PA. David Amidon teaches an undergraduate course on Italian Americans.

MERCY COLLEGE, Dobbs Ferry, NY. Pauline Fusaro teaches two courses in the Department of Italian entitled "Italian American Culture" and "Italian American Literature". Dorothy M. Balancio is teaching a course in the Sociology Department entitled, "The Ethnic Woman: The Case of the Italian Americans".

QUEENS COLLEGE, Department of Romance Languages, Flushing, NY. Herman W. Haller teaches courses at the graduate and undergraduate level on Italian dialects, dialect literature and on linguistic aspects of contemporary Italian in Italy and the United States. The courses are cross-listed with the program of Italian American Studies.

COLLEGE OF STATEN ISLAND, Department of History, Staten Island, NY. Howard R. Weiner teaches an undergraduate course in "Italian American History".

STATE UNIVERSITY OF NEW YORK AT ALBANY, Department of Hispanic and Italian Studies. A course entitled, "The Italian American Experience" is taught at the undergraduate level.

UNIVERSITY OF SOUTHERN CALIFORNIA, Los Angeles, Anthropology Department. Italian Americans are one of the ethnic groups covered in a course entitled, "Special Ethnic Studies in American Culture".

UNIVERSITY OF WASHINGTON, Department of Geography, Seattle, WA. Joseph Velikonja teaches a course on "Immigrants and the American West", which includes the Italian immigrant experience.

REPOSITORIES OF PRIMARY DOCUMENTATION

Both the 1976 AIHA survey and the 1983 CMS survey sought information about repositories of primary documentation for the study of Italian American experience. The following list combines the information gathered from both surveys.

ARIZONA

ARIZONA STATE UNIVERSITY, Hayden Library, Tempe.
UNIVERSITY OF ARIZONA, Tucson.

CALIFORNIA

JESUIT ARCHIVES, California Province, Los Gatos. Materials on Italians and Italian Jesuit missionaries in Southern California.
MUSEO ITALO AMERICANO LIBRARY.
SAN FRANCISCO PUBLIC LIBRARY, Main Branch, American Italian Historical Society Depository.
UNIVERSITY OF CALIFORNIA, Berkeley, Bancroft Library, Berkeley.

FLORIDA

UNIVERSITY OF FLORIDA, Gainesville, P.K. Yonge Library of Florida History. Among their holdings are the Italian language weekly newspaper, "La Voce della Colonia", a large number of cigar union newspapers, labor union manifestos, pamphlets and handbills (pre-1930).
UNIVERSITY OF SOUTH FLORIDA LIBRARY, Division of Special Collections, Tampa. Collections include Tony Pizzo papers, Joe Avallanal papers.
UNIVERSITY OF WEST FLORIDA, Pensacola.
YBOR CITY FEDERAL WRITERS PROJECT, Ybor City.

CONNECTICUT

CONNECTICUT HISTORICAL SOCIETY, Hartford.
HARTFORD PUBLIC LIBRARY.
UNIVERSITY OF CONNECTICUT, Storrs. Ethnic Heritage Culture Center Project on "Peoples of Connecticut".

INDIANA

INDIANA HISTORICAL SOCIETY LIBRARY, Indianapolis.

ILLINOIS

ARCHIVES OF THE SERVERITE ORDER, Chicago. A typescript guide (3 p.) to the materials on Italian Americans has been prepared.
CHICAGO HISTORICAL SOCIETY LIBRARY, Chicago. there is a substantial amount of material dealing with Italian Americans, including an unpublished guide to materials on ethnic neighborhoods in Chicago.
UNIVERSITY OF ILLINOIS ARCHIVES, Chicago.

MARYLAND

LOYOLA-NOTRE DAME LIBRARY, Baltimore.

MASSACHUSETTS

ANDOVER-HARVARD THEOLOGICAL LIBRARY, Cambridge. Papers of George la Piana.
BOSTON PUBLIC LIBRARY. Aldino Felicano Collection and other important materials on

Italian American radicals.
BOSTON UNIVERSITY LIBRARY. Papers of Max Ascoli, Italian American journalist.
HARVARD UNIVERSITY LIBRARY, Cambridge. Lawrence A. Lowell Collection, includes materials on Sacco-Vanzetti case.
MASSACHUSETTS HISTORICAL SOCIETY, Boston.

MICHIGAN

DETROIT PUBLIC LIBRARY, Burton Historical Collection, Giuliano Family papers.
MARQUETTE COUNTY HISTORICAL SOCIETY, Marquette.
MICHIGAN TECHNOLOGICAL UNIVERSITY ARCHIVES, Houghton.
WAYNE STATE UNIVERSITY, Walter Reuther Library, Archives of Labor and Union Affairs, Detroit. Among their holdings are the personal papers of many Italian American labor leaders. The collection includes oral history tapes.
WAYNE STATE UNIVERSITY, Purdy Library, Folklore Archive, Detroit.

MINNESOTA

MINNESOTA HISTORY AND RESEARCH CENTER, University of Minnesota, St. Paul. Their holdings include a substantial number of archival collections dealing with the Italian immigrant and ethnic experience.
MINNESOTA HISTORICAL SOCITY, St. Paul.

NEW JERSEY

RECORDS OF THE MERCER COUNTY COURT HOUSE, Trenton.
TRENTON PUBLIC LIBRARY.

NEW YORK

AMERICAN BAPTIST HISTORICAL SOCIETY, Rochester. A guide to sources on Italian American Baptists.
ADELPHI UNIVERSITY, Garden City.
ARCHIVES OF ST. BONAVENTURE UNIVERSITY, St. Bonaventure.
ARCHIVES OF ST. ANTHONY CURIA, New York City.
CENTER FOR ITALIAN AMERICAN STUDIES, Brooklyn College, Brooklyn Family History and Visual History Archives.
BROOME COUNTY IMMIGRATION HISTORY PROJECT, Roberson Center, Binghampton.
CENTER FOR MIGRATION STUDIES, Staten Island. Numerous collections documenting the Italian American experience. Published guides available for all processed collections.
COLUMBIA UNIVERSITY LIBRARIES, Division of Special Collections, New York City.
CORTLAND COUNTY HISTORICAL SOCIETY, Cortland.
INTERNATIONAL LADIES GARMENT WORKERS UNION ARCHIVES, New York City. Correspondence of I.L.G.W.U.'s General Secretary, Luigi Antonini. Unpublished inventory available.
MERCY COLLEGE LIBRARY, Dobbs Ferry.
NASSAU COUNTY MUSEUM and REFERENCE LIBRARY. Eisenhower Park, East Meadow, Long Island.
NEW YORK PUBLIC LIBRARY, Manuscript Division. Collections include the papers of Fiorello La Guardia and Vito Marcantonio.
NEW YORK STATE EDUCATION DEPARTMENT LIBRARY, Albany.
NEW YORK UNIVERSITY, Tamiment Library, New York City. The papers of Gerolamo Valenti, Italian American socialist and newspaperman.
QUEENS COLLEGE LIBRARY, Flushing.
SENECA FALLS HISTORICAL LIBRARY, Seneca Falls.

STATEN ISLAND INSTITUTE, Richmondtown, Staten Island.
SYRACUSE UNIVERSITY LIBRARY, Manuscript Division, Syracuse. Edward Corsi papers, inventory available.
STATE UNIVERSITY OF NEW YORK AT ALBANY, Manuscript Division.
WESTCHESTER COMMUNITY COLLEGE LIBRARY, Valhalla.

OHIO

THE WESTERN HISTORICAL SOCIETY, Cleveland.

OREGON

OREGON HISTORICAL SOCIETY LIBRARY, Portland.
UNIVERSITY OF OREGON LIBRARY, Eugene.

PENNSYLVANIA

BALCH INSTITUTE FOR ETHNIC STUDIES, Philadelphia. Among their holdings are the papers of Leonard Covello, prominent Italian American educator.
CABRINI COLLEGE, Cabriniana Room, Radnor.
DUQUESNE UNIVERSITY, Pittsburgh. Papers of Judge Michael Angelo Musmanno, defense counsel for the Sacco-Vanzetti trial.
STUDY CENTER FOR AMERICAN MUSICAL PLURALISM, University of Pittsburgh.
TEMPLE UNIVERSITY, Paley Library, Urban Archives, Philadelphia.
UNIVERSITY OF PITTSBURGH LIBRARY, Archives of Industrial Society.

RHODE ISLAND

RHODE ISLAND COLLEGE, Special Collections.
PROVIDENCE COLLEGE, Providence. Papers of John O. Pastore, U.S. Senator from Rhode Island.

TEXAS

SOUTHERN METHODIST UNIVERSITY, Fondren Library, The Texana Collection, Dallas.
TEXAS STATE LIBRARY, State Archives and Library Bldg., Austin.
UNIVERSITY OF TEXAS AT AUSTIN, Barker Texas History Center.

VIRGINIA

VIRGINIA HISTORICAL SOCIETY, Richmond. The papers of the Adams family include material on Philip Mazzei and Italian immigration to the state.

WASHINGTON

ARCHIVES OF THE SOCIETY OF JESUS, Oregon Province, Crosby Library, Gonzaga University, Spokane. Contains papers and manuscripts of pioneer Italian Jesuits who worked in the Pacific Northwest of Alaska.

WASHINGTON, D.C.

CATHOLIC UNIVERSITY. A large collection of Catholic diocesan press on microfilm.

WISCONSIN

DOMINICAN ARCHIVES, Sinsinawa. Included are the papers of Father Samuel Mazzuchelli, **O.P. (1806-1864), Italian-born pioneer missionary to the Wisconsin lead mining region and founder of an order of native American teaching sisters now known as the "Sinsinawa Dominicans".**

ITALIAN COMMUNITY CENTER OF MILWAUKEE. Ted Mazza Collection.

MARQUETTE UNIVERSITY, Milwaukee.

MILWAUKEE COUNTY HISTORICAL SOCIETY, MILWAUKEE. Among their holdings are the papers of Angelo Cerminara, Italian consul in Milwaukee (1916-1940); papers of Hasso R. Pestalozzi, the city's chief truancy officer; scrapbook of Mrs. William Hauerhas, a Protestant missionary who worked in the Italian Third Ward; the letter file of Gaetano Trentanove, sculptor; and the Stefano Carini Collection.

MILWAUKEE PUBLIC LIBRARY, the Italian file.

UNIVERSITY OF WISCONSIN, Milwaukee. Italian American press titles.

WISCONSIN STATE HISTORICAL SOCIETY, Madison. Italian American press titles.

13

The Future of Italian American Studies: An Historian's Approach to Research in the Coming Decade

SAMUEL L. BAILY
Rutgers University

ITALIAN American studies have come a long way during the past two decades, especially in recent years. Even a casual reading of some of the bibliographies in the field and the works they list reveals that not only is there quantity, but that the quality and intellectual sophistication of many publications is high (D'Aniello and Porcari, 1983; Cordasco and LaGumina, 1972; Cordasco, 1974 and 1981). Surveys and interpretive essays provide various overviews. Monographs, articles and dissertations contribute hard data on and analysis of practically every conceivable theme. We have investigations of the Italian context, urban and rural immigrants, permanent and return migrants, labor, crime, the press, politics, education, the family, residence, mobility, assimilation, chain migration, culture and ethnic conflict. Geographically these studies cover most areas of the country from New York to San Francisco and from Chicago to New Orleans.

Others have reviewed and evaluated these accomplishments. My concern is to look ahead and to suggest an answer to the question: given the current state of Italian American studies, where do we go from here? What kinds of research should we and our graduate students pursue in the future? What approaches will be most effective in increasing our understanding of the Italian American experience?

The answers to these questions will inevitably vary among us. The subject matter is large and complex. We differ in terms of scholarly disciplines, ethnic origins, generations, sex, regions of the country, and ideological perspectives. The variety of answers, however, should stimulate us to re-examine our own views and hopefully to contribute to a systematic and coordinated effort to formulate the most fruitful approach or approaches for the future.

A review of the literature published during the past two decades provides important indications of where we might go in the future. One of the most noticeable changes in this literature is the shift in assumptions scholars make about the nature of the Italian migration process. Where twenty years ago most assumed the inevitabliity of assimilation, the primacy of the host environment, and the passivity of the immigrant, now many scholars have rejected these assumptions and adopted new ones. Assumptions fundamentally influence the way we define problems and research strategies and the approaches we use. Therefore, before we proceed to a discussion of approaches to future research, we must discuss briefly some of the more important new assumptions upon which they will be based.

At least five new assumptions have emerged from the literature (*See*, for example, Barton, 1975; Bell, 1979; Briggs, 1978; Yans McLaughlin, 1982; Bodnar, Simon and Weber, 1982; Cinel, 1982; Baily, 1983). First, Italian migration is a complex and dynamic process. To explain the process we must look to a number of interacting social, cultural, psychological, political and economic variables which continually change with time, place and specific individuals and groups. We must, therefore, reject mono-causal explanations such as those which, for example, focus solely or primarily on labor markets or the new environment. Second, Italian migration is an open-ended process. There is no one outcome nor does the process necessarily terminate after any given period of time. The direction is not inevitable nor irreversible. Third, the Italian background is essential to an understanding of what happens to the migrant in the United States as well as to why he/she migrated in the first place. We need to examine the economy, the social structure and the culture of the Old World if we are to understand how individuals and groups of migrants adjusted to the New World. Fourth, the immigrant is an active participant who has influenced the nature of the migration process and not just a helpless, passive pawn whose fate has been determined by larger impersonal forces. The immigrant made meaningful choices throughout his/her life based upon a careful evaluation of the options available. He/she also influenced the host society as well as being influenced by it. And finally, both change and continuity are at the same time part of the migration process. Previously most scholars focused on one to the exclusion of the other, rather than looking at the varying interaction between the two. Yet some aspects of the migrants' traditional culture, values and behavior persist while others change in response to the new situation. It is the recognition of the simultaneous operation of both change and continuity that is important.

The growing consensus on multi-causal dynamic explanations, the open-endedness of the migration process, the crucial nature of the Italian context, the migrant as an active participant and the simultaneous operation of change and continuity provides a basic cluster of assumptions upon which to build an approach for the future study of Italian Americans. This approach, which focuses on process and structure, includes at least three components: the micro-historical method, a dialectical framework and a comparative perspective.

The micro-historical method is not new. Social historians in particular have been using it for more than a decade. Anthropologists have used it even longer. Scholars of the Italian American experience, however, have only recently begun to adopt it in any number (*See*, Cinel, 1982; Bell, 1979; Sturino, 1981; Baily, 1982; Piselli, 1981; Arlacchi, 1983; Douglass, 1984). This shift to micro-history by some is the result of a number of factors. Certainly the emergence of the cluster of assumptions discussed previously, especially the assumption of the active migrant, is important. In addition, it has become increasingly clear from our studies that the general structural characteristics of the areas of origin and settlement, and of the whole migrant group, affected individuals and families differently and produced divergent results. Some Italians migrated, but others did not. In any given region or province there were villages that sent out migrants and also many that did not. Within villages there were those who emigrated and those who stayed at home. Individuals from the same village went to different cities in the United States and to different countries in Europe, the Americas and Australia. Even those who came from the same village and went to the same city in the United States settled in different areas of that city. Some immigrants married members of the host society, others married non-Italian foreigners, and still others married Italians from their own village or from other parts of Italy.

Generalizations based on macro-levels analysis frequently have obscured the complexity of the process, the variation in individual and sub-ethnic patterns and the causes for variation. It is not very useful to generalize about Northern or Southern Italians, about Italians from a specific province or region, about Italian Americans or even about urban Italian Americans. Italian migration has been a village, sub-village and family phenomenon from the outset and has continued as such for a considerable period of time.

What we then need is a "village outward" approach focusing on individuals and families in specific villages and following them and their offspring in the New World context or contexts. There are some studies that do in fact tie specific villages in Italy with specific cities in the United States and we need more of them (Cinel, 1982; Sturino, 1981; Baily, 1982). We also need studies that trace migrants from a specific Italian village to their various destinations in Europe, the Americas and Australia. To my knowledge no study has yet appeared, although I know of one forthcoming study by Franco Ramella of the Biellese to their multiple destinations in parts of the United States, Argentina and Brazil.

There are potential weaknesses in the micro-historical approach. Most importantly there is the danger of restricting the analysis to the micro level and in so doing ignoring the broader structural factors in the process. Good history must deal with the macro as well as the micro issues and must place the micro-level analysis in the general structural contexts on both sides of the Atlantic. There is also the danger of generalizing on the basis of a few examples. If we study only a few villages we cannot assume that they are necessarily representative of other villages. We do not need to study every village in Italy, but we need to study many more before we can generalize with confidence. Even now, however, the micro-historical method is a highly effective means with which to test and refine existing generalizations and theories.

To carry out micro-level studies scholars will have to rely on different sources, as some already have done, and there may be difficulty finding and using these sources. We will have to use village records — birth, death and marriage certificates as well as family and passport records. In the United States we will have to consult naturalization and parish records, manuscript census returns, interviews and membership records of mutual aid societies and other immigrant institutions. We will, of course, continue to consult Italian language newspapers, aggregate statistical data, government reports, published personal accounts and secondary sources, but they must be used along with the individual local data.

The second component of the approach I am suggesting is a dialectical framework of analysis. This framework is a logical extension of the assumptions that the migration process is complex and dynamic and that it encompasses simultaneous change and continuity. Several decades ago, scholars generally explained the migration process in terms of the host environment. In 1964, Rudy Vecoli's pioneering article, "Contadini in Chicago: A Critique of The Uprooted", stimulated a reevaluation of the environmentalist interpretation and resulted in the emergence of a series of works which concentrated on the persistence of pre-migration culture and values as explanatory variables (See, Barton, 1975; Briggs, 1978; Yans-McLaughlin, 1982). In the past few years, several scholars have begun to focus systematically on the interaction of premigration culture and the host environment and to set forth explicitly what I am calling a dialectical framework of analysis.

In their 1982 study, Lives of Their Own: Blacks, Italians, and Poles in Pittsburgh, 1900-1960, John Bodnar, Roger Simon and Michael P. Weber view "the urbanization of working-class families within an interactional framework in which traditional cultures and structural realities confront each other to produce distinct patterns of adjustment". They then apply this framework to areas of importance to the immigrants themselves: jobs, the family, neighborhoods, mobility and homeownership.

Similarly, in his 1982 study, From Italy to San Francisco: The Immigration Experience, Dino Cinel examines the nature of continuity and change in the migration process both in Italy and in the United States. He rejects the notion that continuity and change are mutually exclusive categories and seeks to demonstrate how both were operating at the same time. Thus, he concludes, "explaining the dialectical relationship between change and continuity may be more rewarding than studying either by itself".

My own recent article, "The Adjustment of Italian Immigrants in Buenos Aires and New York City, 1870-1914", (1983) also adopts a dialectical framework. In it I attempt to explain the varying adjustment processes by analyzing the interplay between the characteristics of the immigrants at the time of arrival and the characteristics of the receiving environments which, in turn, produced a new set of characteristics of the developing communities in the New World. The interaction of these three categories of variables is crucial to an understanding of the Italian adjustment process.

The dialectical framework, as applied to the Italian American experience, is in its conceptual infancy and therefore needs to be developed and refined. Yet the effort to relate systematically the dynamic processes of continuity and change both in Italy and abroad is, in my opinion, an important step forward and should be pursued in the future.

The third component of the proposed approach, which also emerges especially from the assumptions that the migration process is complex and dynamic and that it encompasses simultaneous change and continuity, is the comparative perspective. The use of the comparative perspective is not new in Italian American studies. Robert F. Foerster's 1919 book, *The Italian Emigration of Our times*, stands as a pioneering, if not very systematic, effort to examine the Italian migration experience in its varied contexts throughout the world. In recent years a number of scholars have used the approach with excellent results. Josef Barton, Thomas Kessner, Ronald Bayor, John Bodnar, *et al.* and Miriam Cohen compare aspects of the Italian experience with those of other ethnic groups in the same city of the United States. John Briggs and the Australian scholar Robert Pascoe compare the experience of the Italians in different cities of the United States. Dino Cinel compares the Italians from different communes and from different villages within some of these communes both in Italy and San Francisco. My own work (1983) compares the experience of the Italians in the United States city (New York) and in a foreign city (Buenos Aires). Ginny Yans-McLaughlin and others use occasional comparisons in their studies of Italian Americans.

The comparative perspective has proved useful to historians in identifying problems, determining uniqueness, formulating generalizations, establishing controls by which to test conclusions, and in helping establish causal explanations. Theda Skocpol and Margaret Sommes (1980) provide the most sophisticated and useful analysis of the comparative perspective. They set forth three "distinct logics" of comparative history: comparative history as the parallel demonstration of theory; comparative history as the contrast of contexts; and comparative history as macro-causal analysis (*See also*, Grew, 1980; Morner, Fawaz de Viñuela and French, 1982; Skocpol, 1979; Frederickson, 1981). The deductively-based parallel demonstration of theory logic is least useful to historians wary of grand theory and universal hypotheses. The other two logics, however, are important to historians of the Italian American experience. The contrast of contexts logic is an effective way to clarify the unique features of each case examined. Most importantly, the macro-causal analysis enables us to make inductively-based inferences about structures and processes. But what specific kinds of comparative studies might we most fruitfully pursue in the Italian American field in the future?

Several areas of potential systematic comparative investigation imme- diately come to mind. One is the Italian urban ethnic enclave. There are a great many studies of Italian urban enclaves of different sizes, in different locations, with different characteristics, (*See*, DeMarco, 1981; Tricarico, 1984; Cinel, 1982; Baily, 1983; Barton, 1975; Briggs, 1978; Kessner, 1977) including eight case studies presented in a recent work, *Little Italies in North America*. The editors of this work, Robert Harney and Jean Scarpaci, recognize the need for systematic comparison of the similarities and differences of their cases both in terms of process and structure, but in this work they do not attempt it. Although there is an abundance of data on the subject, there is, to my knowledge, no existing comparative study of Italian urban enclaves.

A second area which, in my opinion, deserves attention is the comparison of the Italian experience in United States cities with that of Italians in foreign cities. Such a comparison will enable us to control for certain variables in these experiences while exploring the effects of other variables on the process. For example, my study of Italians in Buenos Aires and New York controls for Italians while investigating the differing impact, among other things, of host cultures. A study of San Francisco and Buenos Aires would enable us to refine this analysis by controlling for Northern Italians, as opposed to Italians in general, while looking at the influence of the host cultures. Many other cities in the United States, Argentina, Brazil, Canada and Australia could be compared for the purpose of establishing controls for some variable in order to understand the working of others.

The approach I am suggesting combines three equally important compo- nents: the micro-historical method, a dialectical framework and a comparative perspective. What remains to be discussed is how this approach will lead us to an increased understanding of the Italian American migration process. Certainly the approach will lead us to focus on neglected aspects of the experience. Perhaps more importantly it may help us rethink our concepts and theories. Scholars of Italian American studies and of migration in general have made considerable progress in developing what Charles Price labels classifications of migration — classifications of typologies, classifications of differences, and especially sequential classifications — but not in constructing formal theory with the power to predict events in other places and at other times. (*See,* Price, 1969). I am not suggesting that we put our efforts into developing a general theory of the Italian migration process. That I think, is a long way in the future and may well be impossible. Nevertheless, we need to strengthen and refine our conceptual schemes and to postulate and test middle-range hypotheses if we are to understand the working relationships of the various aspects of the migration process.

One of the most useful and important concepts to emerge from the study of Italian migration in the past two decades, and one that flows logically from the assumption of the active migrant and from the micro-historical method, is that of chain migration. Set forth and developed primarily by the post World War II generation of Australian scholars (MacDonald and MacDonald, 1964), the concept has been used extensively by others and has been subject to somewhat differing interpretations. Yet most agree that in essence the concept refers to personal relationships among family, friends and *paesani* in both the sending and receiving communities which influenced destination, settlement, occupations, mobility and social interacting (*See also*, MacDonald and MacDonald, 1970; Price, 1963; Baily, 1982).

Nevertheless, most scholars have used the concept as formulated two decades ago without attempting to develop or refine it. At least two problems exist with the concept which can be fairly easily resolved. The first problem is, as my colleague Rudy Bell (1981) pointed out recently, the metaphor of the chain is not entirely appropriate or accurate. A chain implies direct contact of one link to only two other links in the sequence. Yet the empirical studies show that individuals may well be linked to a number of other individuals in the sequence who are not next to them. Most scholars recognize this and use the metaphor very loosely to indicate a personal network or cluster of individuals in the sending and receiving societies. The metaphor is valuable and should not be abandoned lightly because it immediately and dramatically communicates the long distance personal linkage of migrants in Italy and abroad. At the same time if we found a more neutral term, such as Migrant Networks, we would gain in accuracy of conceptualization. The least we can do is to use the term "chain migration" in quotes and to make it clear exactly what we mean when we use it.

Whether or not we adopt a new terminology or continue using "chain migration", we need to refine and specify the workings of the concept. I find the work of Jeremy Boissevain conceptually very suggestive. In his 1974 book, *Friends of Friends: Networks, Manipulators and Coalitions*, Boissevain sets forth a series of interactional and structural criteria that determine the nature and functioning of such networks. His interactional criteria include: the diversity of linkages, the transactional context, the directional flow and the frequency and duration of interaction. The structural criteria are size, density, degree of connection, centrality and clusters. His scheme may in some cases be difficult to apply, but the effort to utilize his approach will force us to clarify our own understanding of the operation of migrant networks and will make the results of our work more useful to other scholars.

There are other problem areas regarding our understanding of migrant networks. We are uncertain how to determine who actually and potentially is in a given network either in Italy or in the receiving community, why and how they migrate, how the network operates specifically to help its members adjust in the receiving community, how long a period of time it continues to operate, and what exactly is the nature of forward and backward linkages.

Some progress has been made in a few of these areas in recent years and we can build on these studies as we approach the future. For example, a number of people have been working on the concept of social space and how it determines the extent of the networks in Italy. In his study of the Rende area of Cosenza, Frank Sturino (1981) found that "there existed a unit of socioeconomic interaction, often face-to-face, roughly bounded by a ten-kilometer radius from Rende" including the eight surrounding communes which comprised the social space of the inhabitants and defined the extent of the migrant network. (See also, Piselli, 1981; Arlacchi, 1983; Bell, 1979; Ianni, 1958). Josef Barton (1975) however, found that marriage records for several towns in Southern Italy indicated a rather larger geographical base for the migrant network. Both are certainly correct for their specific areas, but the difference suggests the need to refine the nature of social space as it relates to the migration networks.

Similarly, we need to determine the nature of the social space of the village networks in the receiving communities. Cinel's (1980) study of San Francisco and my study (1982) of networks in Buenos Aires begin to do this. Gabaccia's study (1982, 1984) of Italians from Sicilian agro-towns to the Sicilian neighborhood on Elizabeth Street in New York City suggestively develops the concept by looking at the changes that took place in household and neighborhood membership.

What ultimately is compelling about the concept of "chain migration" or migration networks is that it is the closest thing we have to a theory of Italian migration. It is possible to predict with some accuracy that if an individual from a given town in Italy, at the turn of the past century, decided to emigrate, he would most likely go to a specific town in the New World, follow a specific route to get there, live in a particular area of the city, and join a specific mutual aid society. In addition we might speculate with some confidence that he would work in certain establishments where his fellow *paesani* already worked and marry a woman from his home town or social space (See, Baily, 1982). The concept of migration networks has already served us well and with a little more attention will serve us even better in the future.

The purpose of this essay is to stimulate the systematic evaluation of our collective goals and priorities for the coming decade. I have tried to delineate a three-part approach to the study of the Italian American experience based on some of the new assumptions emerging from the existing literature. This proposed approach will also hopefully help us refine and develop our concepts and theory and especially the idea of "chain migration". It is the starting point for an ongoing debate.

14

Comments on
the Paper by Samuel L. Baily

ANDREW ROLLE
Occidental College

PROFESSOR Baily has done a workmanlike survey of the changes that have come over Italian American studies in the past few years. Without saying so specifically, he infers that we have come a long way from the partisan fileopietistic approach that existed when some of us first began to write books and articles on the experiences of Italians in America. Baily does a good job of fashioning an inventory, particularly of the micro-historical emphasis that threatens to take over the entire field of immigration study. Related to social history and anthropology, this approach is not really new; historians have simply been slow to adapt it to their discipline.

There are other aspects of immigration history, or "ethnic studies", if you prefer that term, in which historians have been "frozen in the moulds of the past." This accusation was orginally made by William Langer in his presidential address to the American Historical Assoication in 1957. And I happen to agree with his criticisms (Langer, 1958, pp. 284-285).

Because this is a session devoted to "new approaches", I want to focus on an emerging field in which I have become interested. Toward the beginning of his paper, Baily mentions assumptions that have surfaced in recent years. In explaining these he uses the term "psychological", but then goes on to describe other approaches. If we are to understand how immigrants (and not only Italians) either affected or were themselves influenced by the new environment, we cannot afford to shun the whole field of psychiatry and psychoanalysis. To do so is to cut ourselves off from an established literature that had already impoverished even some of the most modern structural studies which Baily admiringly mentions.

Sociological generalizations are no substitute for understanding important internal, sometimes unconscious, mental processess that affected the lives of the courageous persons, young and old, who once ventured forth into a brave new world. Activity on the surface of immigrant life was not always indicative of what went on underneath. The "village studies" which Baily calls for can be most useful in understanding intrapsychic forces that guided immigrants in the old country as well as in the new. Fusion of many approaches is possible, however inconvenient and uncomfortable.

Admittedly, the emerging discipline that has come to be called "psychohistory" is a fragile one. Some of the research that has characterized this delicate new field runs from good to hopeless. But this is no reason to turn our backs upon an entire approach which most historians—untrained as they are in it—simply do not understand. Their own critiques of work derived from psychiarty and psychoanalysis usually verges upon the puerile and naive.

While crossing the Atlantic, millions of persons approached more than a melting pot or the Statue of Liberty. A psychological barrier of differentness also lay across the foamy sea. Ever since these newcomers streamed down the splintered gangplanks along the American waterfront, they (and we) have been perplexed by what they saw and thought.

Finding the right niche in America included confronting poverty, hunger for success, feelings of exclusion, and all those internal hatreds directed against one's foreignness. These disabilities were reflected in clashes within the immigrant family that appear and reappear in the writings of Italo-American novelists.

Former peasants who suffered lost feelings of anomie scarcely realized that part of their unease also lay in the provincial life from which they had only recently emerged. Deprivations suffered in Italy's Mezzogiorno had masked insecurities that came alive in new forms within America's so-called melting pot.

I should make it clear that countless immigrants were not disturbed. They showed tenderness and a healthy strength in support of their families. However, mother-centered and father-dominated, the Italian family resembled a tossing ship plowing its way through the unfamiliar shoals of American life. Occasionally a bit of prow got nicked or the vessel careened as in a storm. Its passengers hoped they would survive the journey. But at first they could not be sure of how to combat prejudice.

One such prejudice Italian Americans would like to rid themselves of forever is the stigma, odious and quite unfair, of the Mafia. I know of no better method than to use the principles of dynamic psychiatry. Psychoanalysts have found that a group often displaces anxieties about itself onto a minority. The technique is known as scapegoating. Of course this is not to say that "troubled roots" did not exist in the background of ethnic crime figures. But stigmatizing an entire minority because of the transgressions of sociopaths among them is immoral. Psychoanalysis can help the Italian Americans to "call a spade a spade" — instead of resorting to the use of denial, an ineffective mechanism for the defense of ego.

Some sociological studies continue to maintain that poverty and unemployment are the root causes of ethnic crime. Actually, most poor people turn out to be law-abiding, not criminals. Ethnicity is also a dubious major cause of criminality. Insufficiently supportive parenting would seem to offer a better explanation. This does not mean that a child who always gets his way will not be a criminal. While the ghetto is not an ideal environment in which to rear children, whatever their genetic background, most people do not become even ordinary hoodlums, let alone violent criminals. Any discussion of the Mafia has to be tied to various clichés about what people think are the root causes of crime. The liberal myth that poverty breeds criminals grossly simplifies complex psychological issues.

The immigrant children who left their own families behind to enter Mafia-like groups could be called pseudo-sociopaths who hid out within the protection of a new "family" based upon fear and economic gain rather than love. True sociopathy has childhood origins that are closer to psychotic, rather than neurotic, behavior. True sociopaths, whether they murder their brothers or rape their sisters, have no remorse; they wish to push the order of things out of shape. The Mafia weeds out true sociopaths; they are too dangerous and too destructive to group discipline.

It is too easy to explain criminality and delinquency as a natural response to discrimination alone. The emotions that churned beneath the surface in the lives of immigrants were not those that have appeared in the record. this is because we reveal mostly the history of our outer life. Family turmoil is not a subject that most Italians discuss openly. Instead, the outer record shows that Italians have a genius for dealing with babies, that they are hyperloyal to family, and that its harmony exists because children subordinate their wills to those of parents.

Not all children went down the road to delinquency or despair. It was the exceptionally deprived ones who stole cars and motorcycles to work out unresolved conflicts. Others found models in teachers or in the corner policemen.

I believe that a part of the human mind, which psychoanalysts have identified as the ego, was placed under maximal pressure as confused former peasants sought to mediate between the extremes of the American environment. To preserve self-esteem they understandably employed a number of defense maneuvers. Historians have never really looked at how such immigrants were searching for an identity within themselves. Of course, they also sought economic opportunities not available in their former homeland.

Historians who have followed in the footsteps of Oscar Handlin continue to examine the immigrant record almost exclusively in urban settings and along economic lines, characterizing the foreigner's past as primarily "a history of alienation and of its consequences". According to this archaic interpretation, the bulk of America's immigrants were of peasant origin, remaining downtrodden, backward-looking, ghettoed and changeless — enslaved by a pessimism characteristic of eastern Europe. Yet, millions of immigrants were never inside a steel mill or a big factory. Not all pounded city pavements in search of jobs. Some were brutalized by industrial jobs and anomie. Others were not.

The line of least resistance is to perpetuate the old-style immigration history. Based upon names, dates, election statistics and other hard "facts", that type of history brushes over the softer data, the internal feelings of individuals and groups. As Langer inferred, many historians (especially immigration specialists) do not really welcome tentative new findings. In seeking consenses, too often they deal in stereotypes.

It is more comforting to respond in the usual cheery way to the clichés that portray Italians as either romantic, happy, carefree, lovable and gluttonous, or greasy, dark-skinned, lazy and insensitive.

Today it takes much less courage for the descendents of immigrants to claim an inheritance that their grandfathers either denied or repressed. Likewise, new patterns of historical interpretation have a chance to supercede old ones. We may at last write histories of minorities that do more than repeat clichés about racial melting pots or leave unexplained desolation and disillusionment. Today's ethnic history breathes less of the spirit of apology or of the nativist bigotry of the past.

It is a paradox that only in the 1970s did America discover the word "ethnicity". By then most persons of Italian background were well on the way to being alchemized and blended into the dominant society. Yet, as blacks and Chicanos reminded us, roots were suddenly something to be treasured as a primary source of sustenance and means of survival. Though one can never fully put into parentheses the country in which one's family originated, Jerre Mangione has expressed what happened to him: "I had learned how to... cope with the ever-recurring sensation of being a foreigner in my native land." (Mangione, 1978).

Finally, were immigrants upraised, uprooted, defeated or assimilated? Rather than Handlin's "uprooting", some immigrants were like a plant that needs daily watering. The temporary shock of replanting led to an accomodation that was not total. The Italians have not been entirely assimilated. They have, however, been changed by the American experience. It is natural that they should seek to obscure their failures, sufferings and the reversals of life itself. Oscar Wilde once said that our lives were not really the life which we secretly live (Rolle, 1981).

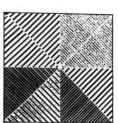

PART THREE
DIMENSIONS OF THE
ITALIAN AMERICAN EXPERIENCE

15

Circles of the Cyclopes: Schemes of Recognition In Italian American Discourse

ROBERT VISCUSI
Humanities Institute, City University of New York

IF I begin by disclosing that the conclusion of this essay uncovers the source and prospects of an innovation in political language, possibly an important innovation, then I may be excused if I open the discussion with an innovation in literary language. In this essay, there is one word coined for the occasion, and I think both the word and its existence need some preparation.

Literary people have the notion still that an essayist ought to avoid new coinages, either his own or those of another. The "literary artist", as Walter Pater most definitively has expressed the rule, "will feel the obligation of those affinities, avoidances, those mere preferences, of language, which through the Associations of Literary History have become a part of its nature, prescribing the rejection of many a neology, many a license, many a gypsy phrase, which might present itself as actually expressive".[1] I confess that this formula has always, for me, held the force of law. When I employed a neology, I felt the paradoxical emotions of one who commits a misdemeanor. Editors and professors of English who examined my work made it clear to me that newfangled lingo is, in the prose of an essay, an offense. Over the years, I acquired a style of intricate avoidance, replacing the polysyllable with a circumlocution in plain English, hoping this conveyed a sense of grace and power in the sentences. Perhaps I had some doubts as to whose grace and power were in question. I repressed these doubts. Grace and power in a writer's words belong, I thought, to the writer.

But do they?

Pater's law, if we look back at it, is specific on this point. It is the Associations of Literary History which prescribe the rejection "of many a

---

[1] Walter Pater, "Style", in *Appreciations, with an Essay on Style* (London: Macmillan, 1908), p. 10.

neology, many a license, many a gypsy phrase which might present itself as actually expressive". The Associations of Literary History is a phrase that I used to read, as perhaps I was meant to do, as an allusion to Godwin's psychology: pleasure in the language of a given text depends upon what it recalls to mind of other texts, texts well-established by the traditional pleasures of one who reads the books prescribed by literary history. But in such words here as established, traditional, and prescribed, a new meaning forces its way into the reading. The Association of Literary History (if we write in this way; we clearly see) are not mental phenomena. They are groups of people, real persons, in real buildings holding real jobs and having very clearly visible group interests. They exclude the "gypsy phrase" because they exclude the gypsy.

This essay is precisely about the "gypsy phrase", its history, its prospects. What becomes of the language of a great mass of outsiders as they labor painfully, generation after generation, to work their way inside? That is my theme, and in the spirit of it, I have decided to allow myself a neology. This is not an act of bravery, however. Rather, it is one of imitation. Most students of Italian American literature respect the Associations of Literary History, but when I wrote this essay, I had been reading the work of one who had allowed himself to use to good effect, some remarkable and even startling neologisms.[2] The spectacle of license temped me. I succumbed.

My new word is awkward but, I think, precise. It is *heteroglossolalia*, and it means the production of meaningless speech in another tongue. It has the advantage of being at first sight an example of the very phenomena it names, but that is not why I am introducing it.[3] Rather, it specifies an interruption in systems of communication which occurs as a result of large-scale migration into a nation with foreign language, customs, and political institutions.

[2] Straightforward prose and comprehensive research combine to make, for example, Rose Basile Green, *The Italian-American Novel: A Document of the Interaction of Two Cultures* (Rutherford: Fairleigh Dickinson University Press, 1974), the standard work in this field. William Boelhower, *Immigrant Autobiography In The United States: Four Versions of the Italian American Self* (Verona: Essedue Edizione, 1982), certainly acepts "many a neology" "as actually expressive". Boelhower's use of the coinages of Mikhail Bakhtin is both surprising and valuable.

[3] *Heteroglossolalia* is a typical coinage. Bakhtin's term *polyglossia* refers to the presence in the community of two or more languages; it is defined in "From the Prehistory of Novelistic Discourse" in *The Dialogic Imagination: Four Essays by Mikhail Bakhtin*, trans. Karl Emerson and Michael Holquist (Austin: University of Texas Press, 1981), pp. 50-51; Bakhtin's term *heteroglossia* refers to the "diversity of social speech types which constitutes novelistic discourse, and is defined in "Discourse in the Novel" in *The Dialogic Imagination*, pp. 262-263. Both of these concepts underlie the notion of *heteroglossolalia*, which also employs the term *glossolalia*, familiar from the New Testament as the name for would-be-significant nonsense. The joining of these three concepts is meant to specify the particular problem of a minority discourse attempting to create a literary tradition in a majority language.

Words or other signs that enter one language from another in the form of nonsense — such an expression as *moo goo gai pan*, familiar to many Americans who only rarely can define it[4] — are the clearest examples of this phenomenon. Signs which change their meaning radically in the new language so that they are understood in mutually exclusive senses by the migrants and the natives also fit this category. A wide sample of such signs occurs in Lou D'Angelo's book *How to Be an Italian*, where much of the gestural vocabulary of Italian face-to-face communication is explained for American readers in various burlesque ways which would have little meaning, and give less pleasure, to native employers of this dramatic language.[5]

The production of sense in any community is a result of a double process of cognition and recognition. One knows certain patterns and recognizes, even creates, them in observed phenomena and received messages. I am going to examine one such *schema*,[6] important in many systems and particularly in Italian discourse: the figure of the circle. Mediterranean mythology offers this figure as one which may either close communication off or open it up widely. What is more striking is that both of these meanings are attached to the same figure, that of the one-eyed giants, the Cyclopes. Two models of Cyclopes summarize the relationships between success and failure in making sense across a linguistic divide.

The Homeric Cyclopes

The circle of the single eye which lacks perspective and the hole of the cave where each of these monsters lives correspond to the more ancient legend which paints the Cyclopes as wall-builders who erected the ring of stones around the Acropolis at Mycenae; for each Homeric Cyclops is entirely cut off from the world outside his cave. "They have no laws nor assemblies of the people" Odysseus says, "but live in caves on the tops of high mountains; each is lord and master in his family, and they take no account of their neighbors".[7] In our terms, the only circle the Cyclops can recognize with his monocular vision is the family circle. This makes him perfect prey for Odysseus'

---

[4] Of twenty New York professionals questioned, all but two recognized this as the name of a Chinese dish; four knew it contained chicken; two added vegetables; but none was more precise than that. I myself, though I have eaten it on several occasions, remember *moo goo gai pan*, as a nonsense phrase which sounds like baby-talk rather than as a particular dish, whose contents must always be explained to me again when I visit a restaurant which serves it.

[5] (Los Angeles: Price/Stern/Sloan, 1968).

[6] On *schema-theory See*, John R. Anderson, *Language, Memory, and Thought* (Hillsdale, N.J.: Lawrence Erlbaum Associates, 1976), and *Cognitive Psychology* (San Francisco: W.H. Freeman and Company, 1980), pp. 128-160.

[7] Homer, *The Odyssey*, trans. Samuel Butler (Chicago: Encyclopedia Brittania, 1952), pp. IX, 111-116.

intricate sense of the play of diplomatic language, and the hero in fact tricks the Cyclops Polyphemus with a sophisticated pun worthy of a Jesuit. When Polyphemus asks the hero his name, he responds, *Outis*, which means no-man in Greek but sounds close enough to a cognomen for "Odysseus" that it is not precisely a lie;[8] to the Cyclops, who speaks with very few people, only the literal meaning occurs, so that his curiosity is provoked in a very different direction from the hero's actual name, which indeed was famous enough after the Trojan trick Odysseus had invented that it would have put Polyphemus on his guard. When Odysseus blinds him, Polyphemus cries out for help, the other Cyclopes ask, "Who is trying to kill you?" He replies, "*Outis* (No one) is trying to kill me". Odysseus is able to carry off this heteroglossolalia exactly because the Cyclops' communicative network is not secure outside his own family circle. That circle encloses, shuts off, and isolates.

The Vergilian Cyclopes

Though they are also one-eyed, Vergil's Cyclopes are Romanized monsters, part of a system of divine bureaucrats who trade favors like any network of cousins in modern Campania. Not alone, they live in the Lipari islands north of Sicily and work as forgers and smiths for the god Vulcan. When Venus desires armor for her son Aeneas, she seduces Vulcan to obtain it. He gives the order to his monsters and they produce a great circular shield in which the entire history of Rome is portrayed in advance.[9] Here the circle is exploited as a tool of extension both inward and outward: inward extension is suggested by the proleptic accuracy of the shield, and the Cyclops' single eye becomes a sign of literal in/sight; outward extension is suggested by the concentric circles of the shield which, added one to another, take in eventually a total historical range. As a poetic figure, the shield of Aeneas is correlative to the reduplicating tactic of Roman imperium, which recreated its own temples, altars, and other focal institutions everywhere it went. Focus, or hearth, which in the Homeric Cyclopes excluded or simply ate outsiders alive, here becomes a device for making them part of a single circuit of communication which can convey messages of every kind.

These two models suggest with considerable force the conditions of migrants, first, enclosed by the nonsense-effect of their language, and second, after they have learned to overcome these effects. I will offer three examples of each type.

[8] *Odyssey*, IX, 367. *See,* also George E. Dimock, Jr., "The Name of Odysseus", in Charles H. Taylor, Jr., ed., *Essays on the Odyssey* (Bloomington: Indiana University Press, 1969), pp. 54-72, for a survey of the linguistic play around the hero's name, which does not, however, include the pun discussed here, despite the currency given it by the Jesuitical James Joyce; *See,* Richard Ellmann, *Ulysses on the Liffey* (1972; New York: Oxford University Press, 1979), p. 112.

[9] *Aeneid*, VIII.

The Martana family in Lou D'Angelo's *What the Ancients Said* lives according to a set of proverbs worthy of Polyphemus. "All neighbors are werewolves". "The neighbor is a serpent; if she doesn't see you, she'll hear you". "*Michelune lassa dittu: Cu fa bene e maledittu*".[10] A magic circumference of such protocols is drawn in the first chapter of the book, entitled "The Ancients". The partriarch of the family offers these laws with the authority of those ancients; and the action of the novel centers around the attempts, mostly failures, of his children and grandchildren to cross the lines inscribed around them and make contact with the larger world outside. Since they expect it in advance to be full of werewolves and serpents and so approach it with a code that turns into nonsense every message they receive, they have a very difficult time of it indeed. D'Angelo's second novel, *A Circle of Friends*, takes up a similar theme, portraying a young man so tied to his mother and sister that the "circle" in the title refers to no real society, but instead a garland of women who populate his masturbation fantasies.[11]

Masturbation, indeed, is a Cyclopean theme. It certainly has a place important in the Cyclopean work of Vito Acconci, an Italian American poet who late in the nineteen-sixties turned to conceptual or performance art as a practice. His most famous piece was entitled "Seedbed". At the Sonnabend Gallery on Lower Broadway for several days in January of 1972, Acconci hid under a false floor masturbating for six hours at a stretch, fantasizing into a microphone about the people walking above, who could not of course see him but could hear his fantasies through loudspeakers.[12] This piece is harmonious in theme with yet more evidently Cyclopean works such as an album composed entirely of snapshots of Acconci's mother written over with expressions of his desire to see her continue living,[13] or clearest of all, a performance entitled "Claim", where the artist blindfolded himself and stood for three hours at the foot of a stairwell with an iron bar in his hands threatening to kill anyone who came near him.[14] These works represent a sophisticated exploitation of Cyclopean isolation, showing by their very form how a wall or a floor or a blindfold takes the discourse of the artist, which is meaningful to himself in a way as absolutely direct as are one's masturbation fantasies or his good wishes towards his mother or his desire to protect his territory, and turns such discourse into a set of meanings almost

[10] Lou D'Angelo, *What the Ancients Said* (Garden City: Doubleday, 1971), pp. 11, 14. D'Angelo, p. 14 translates the last of these, "Michelune left it said: Who does good is damned".

[11] (Garden City: Doubleday, 1977).

[12] The most complete account of Acconci's early years as poet and performance artist is Mario Diacono, *Vito Acconci: dal testo-azione al corpo come testo* (New York/Norristown/Milano: Out of London Press, 1975); "Seedbed" is documented, pp. 168-70.

[13] Vito Acconci, *Pulse (for My Mother)*, Paris: Michel Durant, 1973.

[14] "Claim", in Diacono, pp. 162-165.

nonsensical to his desires, and even more anomalous to the audience, which is expected to react to these avant-garde outrages with the surprise and confusion traditionally associated with successful crossings of the boundaries of common sense.[15]

My final example is Jerre Mangione's *Mount Allegro: A Memoir of Italian American Life*.[16] The narrator plays constantly upon the difficulties the immigrants have in recognizing a pattern of communication in their new setting. The family circle of his relatives, fortunately for them, is not confined to a single household, but it directs its gaze pretty thoroughly inward. "My relatives were constantly seeking each other out to celebrate the existence of one another", the narrator remarks,[17] in a nostalgic aside considerably complicated by an ironic distance which is in fact the most pronounced heteroglossolalic effect in the book. I give it this name because Mangione's irony precisely rises from the mutual incomprehensibility of his account to the Sicilians who are its theme and the Americans who are its audience. The narrator mediates beteen these two discrete circles with that Homeric wit belonging to a commentator whose vision can accommodate comfortably conflicts which might inspire sadness in a lesser mind.[18]

He straightforwardly explains this heroic ability: "My mother's insistence that we speak only Italian at home drew a sharp line between our existence there and our life in the world outside. We gradually acquired the notion that we were Italian at home and American (whatever that was) elsewhere".[19] In practice, this gave him a very full spectrum of duplicities, double versions of the same phenomena, versions which tended less to contradict than mutually to exclude one another. His parents had notions of religion, politics, education, and, indeed, all the conventions of extrafamilial life, which bore little relationship to those institutions as the boy encountered them in the streets of Rochester. As these two circuits, familial and political, often confronted one another, there are innumerable instances in this account of heterglossolalic communication, frequently exploited as comedy, sometimes as pathos or mere observation. The nonsense ran in both directions. The

[15] On the interdependence of sense and nonsense and the boundary conditions which define them, *See*, Susan Stewart, *Nonsense: Aspects of Intertextuality in Folkore and Literature* (Baltimore: Johns Hopkins University Press, 1978).

[16] Jerre Mangione, *Mount Allegro: A Memoir of Italian American Life*. (New York: Columbia University Press, 1981). *Mount Allegro* has been through several widely differing editions since its first publication in 1942; the Columbia edition most fully represents the author's textual intentions and includes a valuable epilogue ("Finale", pp. 287-309), written in 1981.

[17] *Mount Allegro*, p. 24.

[18] Or might be considered in a more gloomy light, as for example, by John Fante in *Ask the Dust* (New York: Stackpole Sons, 1939). *See*, R. Viscusi, "The Text in the Dust: Writing Italy across America", *Studi Emigrazione*, p. 19 (Marzo 1982), pp. 127-130.

[19] *Mount Allegro*, p. 52.

Italian spoken by the immigrants included such terms as *storo* for store, *barra* for bar, and *baccauso* for bathroom, — a word which mystified Sicilians, Mangione says, when he used it in Italy, "a nation without backhouses".[20] But even more frequently, Americans were mystified by the immigrants' attempts to make themselves understood in English. These attempts run from the idiosyncratic, such as the father's decision to use she as the only pronoun in English and the present as the only tense, to the semiologically startling and symptomatic, as when Mr. Michelangelo, who can speak no English, wishes to express his disapproval of his neighbor, a Canadian woman who dislikes the narrator and other boys who play ball in the street. She confiscates any balls that land in her yard. Mr. Michelangelo shouts at her in Sicilian, a frightening performance which only increases her intransigence. She whips a boy who comes into her yard after a ball. Mr. Michelangelo tells the police she should be taken away and electrocuted, but the police do not understand Sicilian. Unsatisfied with this inefficient communication, Mr. Michelangelo, the boys helping him, builds a huge brick wall between his house and hers. "In two weeks' time, the brick wall was up and painted, a strong white monument to the old man's dislike for the old woman",[21] the narrator says, to which we may add that it was a strong white monument standing in the place of a common verbal medium which might have allowed, at the least, for a satisfying invective, and, at best, for a successful negotiation with the Canadian lady. And she might, indeed, had there been a shared language, have had a more precise identity than Mr. Michelangelo could ever find for her. He called her simply *la Strega*, the witch.

Mangione's memoir chronicles a great deal of this kind of short-circuited communication. Readers who are tempted to make of *Mount Allegro* an utopian vision ought to pause over the long list of courtships that founder, jobs that are lost, lies that are told by child to parent and parent to child, along the borders of two languages in this work. And particularly should such readers reflect upon Mangione's flat assertion in his recent epilogue to the book that "Mount Allegro no longer exists as a neighborhood".[22] Failing to create a wider circle around it own center, Mount Allegro survives only in

[20] *Ibid.*

[21] *Mount Allegro*, p. 45.

[22] *Mount Allegro*, p. 287. Willial Boelhower, "A New Version of the American Self", in *Immigrant Autobiography in the United States: Four Versions of the Italian American Self* (Verona: Essedue Edizioni, 1982), pp. 179-218, argues that Mangione achieves a "transindividual subject", writing, in effect, the "autobiography...of the group's collective consciousness" (p. 217). Such a merging of narrator and group seems to Boelhower necessary if Mangione is not "to be caught in cross purposes" (p. 185), because the narrator's path of "mobility and acculturation" differs radically from the groups' folkloric world view". It is true that these are cross purposes"; but it is equally true that Mangione manages both of them without confusing their identities, producing a narrative considerably more intricate and ironic than Boelhower's (nonetheless very ingenious and useful) account suggests.

Mangione's account, a work of which we can say that few wider circles have ever been drawn, for it surrounds the little network of relatives with a commentary intricately alert to the messages received in both directions that, reading it, one breathes a slightly higher air than most of us can ever attain without this kind of help.

THE VERGILIAN CYCLOPS AS IMMIGRANT

Attempts to make the family circle into the pattern of an every-widening concentricity are not uncommon in Italian American discourse. Mangione himself engages in such a process, beginning with the autobiographical narrative that binds together his account of Mount Allegro, and expanding its range considerably in the circular journeys described in *Reunion in Sicily*,[23] *A Passion for Sicilians: The World Around Danilo Dolci*,[24] and *An Ethnic at Large: A Memoir of America in the Thirties and Forties.* But I will suggest the ubiquity of this theme by turning to the texts of other works here.

The first is paradoxical. The family of Demetrio Lyba, in Louis Forgione's novel of 1928, *The River Between*,[26] is Cyclopean and Homeric to a very dark degree. Isolation, paternal tyranny, a phlegmatic stiffness which only can express itself in great outbursts on melodramatic occasions, incest, fear, half-blindness, primeval superstition, and a life devoted to building with stones are only a few of the Cyclopean motifs which enclose the unhappy existences of the characters in this book. The paradox here is that Forgione, working in the mythological manner made fashionable in the 1920s by T.S. Eliot and James Joyce, presents all of this precisely in terms not of the Homeric but of the Vergilian Cyclopes. Demetrio Lyba comes from the very island where Vergil's Cyclopes worked. The crisis of the action turns upon a picture which, like the shield of Aeneas, has magical powers. The daughter-in-law whom Demetrio, unknown to himself, passionately desires, is presented as "a true daughter of Aphrodite" — that is, an avatar of the goddess Venus whose impulse is the efficient cause of the shield. I will not pause over the machinery of Forgione's allegory. Only its point need preoccupy us. Following a poetic logic he never quite succeeds in dramatizing, Forgione attempts to make the suppressed mutual love of Rose and her father-in-law Demetrio the model of a new kind of freedom. At the novel's end, Demetrio is completely blind. Rose has been driven from the family home by her husband's unconscious ferocity and her father-in-law's unconscious desire. Though she has tried to live a glamorous life as the mistress of an American jazz composer, the codes of this existence are beyond her, and she ends as a prostitute. Blind Demetrio does

[23] (Boston: Houghton, Mifflin Co., 1980.)

[24] (New York: William Morrow, 1968.)

[25] (New York: G.P. Putnam's Sons, 1978.)

[26] (New York: Dutton, 1928.)

not recognize her at all when she finds him wandering homeless and destitute on the Lower East Side and takes him in to what we are left to suppose is a kind of unconscious mother-and-child reunion, Venus and Aeneas, Demeter and Demetrio, living in a preconscious libidinal utopia beyond the reach of confusion, sight, or even language itself.

Forgione's book, as this awkward Freudian algebra must suggest, needs a more patient deciphering than this if its full force is to be experienced — or, at least, explained. In the absence of such a reading, one must suspend evaluation of *The River Between*. But we may assert with some assurance that Forgione's instincts were excellent, for the translation of the Cyclopean immigrant family into a utopian pattern of itself is the bold stroke of genius which makes Pietro di Donato's *Christ in Concrete*[27] the sacred text it has become in the history of Italian American discourse. There are two simple movements in this novel. The first is the blinding, castration, and death of the immigrant Cyclops, the ill-fated father Geremio, who falls into the absolute isolation and aphasia of the concrete which swallows and kills him as the last indignity in the long process of humiliations and losses which, for Geremio as for so many other immigrants, constitutes the ritual of migration.[28] The second movement is the transfiguration of this same Geremio as the type of Christ. Di Donato's Christian Communist theology is absolutely flawless. The worker-Christ dies alone, calling vainly upon God in heaven. Not only does he die on Good Friday; not only is he raised out of the tomb on Easter Sunday; not only do the *paesani* draw these parallels; not only does the event draw them together in the shared allegory of the Holy Family which has been one of Rome's most enduring inventions. But Geremio's resurrection as a Christ endows them with precisely the opposite of heteroglossolalia. The *paesani*, and the narrator along with them, can now speak in tongues, a gift called in the New Testament by the name *glossolalia*. Glossolalia enabled the apostles at Pentecost to transcend differences of language in the throng assembled at Jerusalem for Sh'vuit. No longer afraid, the apostles shared their gospel with any and all; and, what was more miraculous, any and all understood them. The *paesani* are endowed with a similar power. Confronted by the incomprehension, greed, and prejudice of the bureaucrats at the compensation board, the lawyers,and the police, the immigrants at first seem driven to a hopeless isolation. But then, in the sort of dialectic move which takes the place of a plot in this novel, there occurs a wedding scene where they suddenly realize all the possible promise of their improvised community, expanding for the occasion into utopian demigods, offering one another care, love, and especially, food

---

[27] (New York: Bobbs Merrill, 1939.)

[28] *See*, R. Viscusi, "The Semiology of Semen: Questioning the Father", unpublished paper read at the American Italian Historical Association, XV Annual Conference, St. John's University, October 31, 1982, for a discussion of these themes in *Christ in Concrete*.

and drink in a love feast that surely counts as one of the more opulent beggars' banquets on record; it unfolds at the ritual pace of a high mass at midnight in a cathedral painted in the polychrome glory of a baroque cornucopia, without ever quite realizing the ugly question of who paid for what or got what in return. The language of this scene, as of the whole novel, makes nonsense into high poetic sense, turning all the peculiar heteroglossolalia of the American Italian into an idiosyncratic eloquence which has no exact parallel in the English language.[29] This epic vernacular supports the dialectic image of the wedding feast; and the powerful growth of the family circle in this scene, to the point where it includes not just relatives but friends and even neighbors who are not Italian, has a place in the history of Italian American no less crucial than that of the Mayflower Compact in Anglo-American discourse. For it represents the first achievement of a universal Roman — or, if you like, Roman Catholic — vision for the future of American life.

Time has already shown the power of this poetic construct. The Italian American family has in American folklore long since assumed and equivalence with stability, generosity, and good internal communications which has been exploited gleefully by such popular ideologues as the advertising man who invented Aunt Millie and the ambitious gambler who wrote *The Godfather*. The most exquisitely Vergilian use of this trope, however, appeared in the recent discourse of a Catholic rhetorician with a Roman name, Mario Cuomo. When he marked his inauguration as Governor of the State of New York by offering the allegory that the government should work as a family does,[30] Cuomo spoke in the mythological and visionary tradition of Vergil, Dante, and di Donato. The focal image which can, at the same time, see *multum in parvo* and *parvum in multo* offers genuine promise for a political discourse which has tended to avoid, thanks to its passage through the Presbyterian Enlightenment, the harmonious imagery of the family circle which the Romans, emperors and popes alike, have used with such long success in the administration of vast and disparate territories. The great American political allegories of the past — John Winthrop's image of Massachusetts as "a city set upon a hill", Jefferson's creation of a God who is also a civil-rights lawyer, Lincoln's portrait of the fight for the union as a

---

[29] *See*, R. Viscusi, "*De Vulgari Eloquentia*: An Approach to the Language of Italian American Fiction", *Yale Italian Studies*, I, 3 (Winter, 1981). Pp. 21-38.

[30] "Transcript of Gov. Cuomo's Inauguration Address at the Empire State Plaza," *New York Times*, January 2, 1983, B-19. Cuomo drew a direct line from the arrival of his mother, "alone and afraid", at Ellis Island and his father's prearrival "looking for work", to "What our imperfect but peerless system of government has done for those two frightened immigrants from Europe", and he drew this moral: "Those who made our history taught us, above all things, the idea of family mutuality, the sharing of benefits and burdens fairly for the good of all... We must be the family of New York". The whole speech merits analysis.

heavenly battle between good and evil, Roosevelt's figure of the president as a card-sharp issuing a fresh deal — all seem theoretical and bloodless next to Cuomo's vivid reinvention of an old idea.

It is a long way from the Cyclopes to the vision of the nation, people and government together, as one large family. What gives the vision force at this moment is the long struggle of Italian American discourse to deal afresh with a nightmare which has haunted Europe at least since Odysseus visited the Cyclopes and discovered to his horror that they had no laws.[31] One must linger over the stories of Demetrio Lyba and Vinnie Martana or the wall of Mr. Michelangelo, to assess at fair value the collective heroism and cognitive energy which could produce *Christ in Concrete* or enable an American son of and Italian immigrant to ask, as the Governor recently did, "What is there in our society more important than the rule of law? What has meant more to this country?" Or to answer, as he did, "Of course there have, from time to time, been abberations — but overall the direction of the Law is forward and upward toward the light. Over all, our Lady of the Law has proven stronger than the sins of her acolytes".[32] I suspect that the recognition of antique and hard-won truths which supports these statements will continue to find grateful attention in American political discourse. Sense and nonsense are cognitive problems and political problems at the same time. True, "Our Lady of the Law" may be too Roman a prosopoeia for the moment, but there is every reason to suppose that the American Italian allegory which transforms familial isolation into a scheme of universal recognition will prosper. If it does, it may be that the churches of our civil religion may yet assume a brighter coloration, a more personal set of faces and figures, and that government of the father, by the mother, and for the children shall not perish from the United States of America.

---

[31] The crucial importance of the Cyclopean image and the implicit consequences of speech and law in Western tradition, from Socrates to Marcuse is the subject of an excellent essay by James L. Kinneavy, "Restoring the Humanities: The Return of Rhetoric from Exile", in James J. Murphy, ed., *The Rhetorical Tradition and Modern Writing* (New York: The Modern Language Association of America, 1982), pp. 19-30.

[32] *Address to the Fordham Law Alumni Association, March 5, 1982, cited in "Mario Cuomo: Advocatus Advocatorum", Fordham*, 16, 4 (July, 1983), p. 18.

16

Italian American Experience through the Arts: "The Metamorphosis Continues"

ROBERT VOLPE
International Art Consultant, New York

To appreciate the present and properly guide the future, we must take from the past. As we observe the evolution of the Italian American in the arts and literature, we can trace a heritage filled with greatness. A culture that in the year 80 A.D. could erect a Coliseum that would seat fifty thousand and stand proudly 1900 years later. A culture that gave us a Michelangelo Buonarroti, whose gifted hands created the "Pieta" and later would carve the statue of "David" from a damaged and discarded chunk of marble; to a culture that produced a Leonardo di Vinci, who's brilliant mind conceived man's flight in helicopters, and submarine travel, in addition to the machine gun, steam engine and the multiple gear and an assortment of other inventions that would not be a reality for generations to come and as if that were not enough, he then created the "Mona Lisa"; to the great families of the Renaissance, the Bellinis, Bossanos and Rossellinos who alone gave us over a dozen artists and sculptors; to the Angelicos, Botticellis, Canalettos, Fetis, Mellis, Pontis, Rossis, Tintorettos, Titians, Vasaris, and Zuccaros of the past, we owe the future.

The Italian American, more than any other culture in history is so evident in today's American society. In the late 1800s when the first great waves of Italian immigrants reached these shores they, like most who came, were not the aristocrats of the culture, but rather those who were seeking a dream in this land of opportunity.

Coming to a strange land, unable to speak its language this dream might well have become a nightmare, if it were not for the spirit of the Italian soul, and the strength of its family structure. Where there was no employment for the Italian, there soon stood Italian American businesses which from humble beginnings grew to great enterprises.

But it was during these years of building and establishing ourselves in our new homeland, that it became a time of sacrifice and a time to place one's personal dreams aside, and, possibly, one's cultural heritage to survive, to provide and to achieve.

Today one only need to look to see the positive impact of Italian influence in the American society. It is apparent that Italian Americans, need not be standing in front of an easel painting, or carving a slab of marble to be considered artists: Italian Americans at work bring an inborn artistry to whatever task at hand.

It is with pride that we turn to the creativity, individuality and artistry of the Italian American. The Mario Cuomos and John Volpes of politics, the Coppolas, Scoreses, DePalmas of cinema, the DiMaggio image in sports, the style of the Pacinos, Stallones and Sinatras of the screen. The Lee Iacoccas of business and an endless list of others in as many varied fields.

We can look with pride at those who have taken their place among the notables of the arts and literature, the Fasenellas, Stellas, DiModicas, and the Taleses, Mangiones and Puzos.

As one continues to observe, he will also see the evolution continues. Over the past years if I were to site an example of change, using the New York art district of SoHo, as a microcosm of the art world, I would tell a story of my first walk on West Broadway, and seeing a small electric shop bearing the name of Volpe nestled among the newly emerging art galleries. Its facade appearing like a poor relative among the new glamor of today. Although there was no known blood relationship, I still looked with pride at seeing the family name.

It would only be another few years of walking in the area, until I would be able to only look across the street to see the name of Volpe, once again. This time it was on the facade of one of the finest art galleries of SoHo. Today the electric shop is gone and the gallery remains. But we have in no way completed the evolution.

We are the descendants of the great artisans of the world. Now that we have realized the American dream many times over and achieved stations equivalent to our ancestors, it is time once again to seek new directions and dreams.

With this heritage of which I speak, comes a feeling of confidence and pride, but also an even greater responsibility. That we as Italian Americans should not live off the inheritance of our past in the arts, but should enrich the treasury by continuing and adding new and greater riches, by directing new generations to again pursue the arts.

Too often we consider art and literature as frivolous endeavors, rather than as the passions of the soul — as a hobby rather than a calling.

One must stop and think that if only one Michelangelo, or diVinci has been lost to the world since we have arrived on these shores, it would be culturally a human catastrophe.

In conclusion, I should like to take a moment to extend a thank you to those Italian Americans whose sacrifices and contributions helped build this great land.

But a special thank you to those sculptors who labored as brick layers, to the prima ballerina who waited tables, to the fashion designer who toiled as a tailor, and the artist who chilled his soul while carrying ice blocks up tenement stairs.

Most important of all, a thank you must go to the artist, writers, poets, dancers and musicians who put aside their dreams to be called "mother" and gave birth to another generation of Italian Americans.

17

Italian American Experience through Literature and the Arts

REMIGIO U. PANE
Professor of Italian Emeritus, Rutgers University

FIRST of all I would like to present some figures in support of Mr. Tella's report that the 1980 Census indicates that Italian Americans are now better educated than previously, in preparation for the AIHA Conference on the "Italian Americans in the Professions" I checked the letter M in the 1978-79 edition of *Who's Who in America* and found 117 Italian Americans listed. For this meeting I checked the same letter M in the 1982-83 edition and found that 85 out of 117 were still listed, 32 had either died or were dropped, but 68 new names appeared for a total of 153 Italian Americans whose name begins with M. This represents a substantial increase of 53 percent in the four-year period 1978-1982.

And now for my comments on the presentations on Literature and the Arts. Mr. Volpe concluded that "now that we have realized our dreams we must share our riches with our fellow Americans, as our ancestors have done over the centuries". Almost all writers on the Italian American Experience make brief allusions to the arts and ignore the abundant actual evidence. Stephen Hall in his excellent *New York Times* article under the heading THE ARTS has the brief statement: "The influence of Italian Americans pervades the nation's culture on an almost daily basis" followed by pictures of six representatives of the arts as follows: "Michael Bennet, Choreographer of *Dreamgirls;* Francis Ford Coppola, moviemaker; Frank Sinatra, singer, movie star, legend; Gay Talese, author of *Thy Neighbor's Wife;* Jack Valenti, Motion Picture Association of America; and Robert Venturi, architect, father of postmodernism". In the few minutes allotted me I can only outline briefly some of the accomplishments of contemporary Italian Americans in Arts and Letters which we are already sharing with our fellow citizens. Let me begin with Italian Americans in the Media.

MEDIA

Newspapers: John Peter Giuggio is Executive Vice President and General Manager of *The Boston Globe*. Thomas Michael Tallarico is Executive Vice President and General Manager of the *Chicago Sunday Times*. William Montalbano is Bureau Chief for Knight-Ritter Newspapers in Peking, China. A.J. Maro is Washington, D.C. Bureau Chief for *Newsday*. Philip Gialanella is Publisher and Vincent Spezzano President of *U.S. Today*.

Magazines: Four bureau chiefs of *Time* are Italian Americans: Bonnie Angelo in London, Erick Amfitheatrof in Moscow, Jordan Bonfante in Paris, and Roland Flamini in Bonn. Marie Cherichetti is general manager and Walter Guzzardi, Jr. is a member of the Board of Editors of *Fortune*. Joseph P. Bonsignore is publisher of *Smithsonian*. Sam R. Spoto is vice president and Elaine M. Matteo secretary of *The New Yorker*. Joseph Barbieri is president and Charles Buccieri publisher of *Stagebill*. Anthony Mazzola is editor in chief of *Harper's Bazaar* and Grace Mirabella is editor in chief of *Vogue*.

Book Publishers: *Arno Press:* Joseph Consolino, president; Louis Boccardi, executive vice president and chief operating officer. *Farrar, Strauss & Giroux:* Michael di Capua, literary editor. *Houghton Mifflin:* Jonathan Galassi, literary editor. *Little Brown:* Robert Ginna, Jr., editor in chief. *American Express Publ. Corp.:* Pamela Anne Fiore, editor in chief and executive vice president.

Television: John Severino is President of *ABC*, Tony Malara is President of *CBS*, and John Bonanni is Vice president of *WABC*, but the most amazing successful Italian American T.V. executive is Mother M. Angelica (Francis), founder and chairman of the Board of Catholic Cable Network EWTN (Eternal Word Television Network) of Birmingham, Alabama.

Journalists: Next I should like to mention six journalists who became outstanding writers of fiction and non fiction and will begin with Gay Talese born in Ocean City, N.J. in 1932. He worked as a reporter for the *New York Times* from 1953 to 1965 when he decided to devote his full time to writing books. He is considered a pioneer in the new journalism and his articles published in *Esquire*, *The New York Times Magazine*, *Harper's*, the *Reader's Digest*, and other periodicals, are considered classics of the genre. He has published many books based on intensive and extensive research, his latest being *Thy Neighbor's Wife*.

    Another author who has been much in the news recently is Philip Caputo, born in Chicago in 1941. He served as an officer with the U.S.Marine Corps. in Vietnam from 1965 to 1967 before becoming a reporter for the *Chicago Tribune* and winning a Pulitzer Prize. As a foreign correspondent he worked in Rome and Beirut before returning to Vietnam in 1975 to cover the fall of Saigon. His personal experience in Vietnam as a soldier and later as a journalist was the basis for his 1977 book *A Rumor of War*, which made the bestseller list for non-fiction. In 1977 Mr. Caputo resigned his post as correspondent in Moscow to devote full time to writing and in 1980 he published a novel about soldiers of fortune in Ethiopia with the title *The Horn of Africa*. His second novel, *DelCorso's Gallery*, has recently been published.

Barbara Grizzuti Harrison, who was born in Brooklyn in 1934, has been writing articles and reviews on contemporary problems, people and ideas which have attracted a strong following of readers and excellent praise, especially for her most recent book, *Off Center*.

Len Giovannitti, born in New York City in 1920, is the son of the poet and labor leader Arturo Giovannitti who was involved in the Lawrence, Massachusetts strike of 1912. Len was a labor journalist from 1946 to 1958. He joined NBC in 1962 as a writer, director and producer of NBC News and later was producer, writer and director of *NBC White Papers* and won the Lasker Medal for journalism in 1969 and the Peabody Award in 1975. Between 1948 and 1977 he wrote a biography of Sidney Hillman, a history of the dropping of the first atomic bomb, and three novels.

The political journalist Richard Rovere was born in Jersey City in 1915 and died in Poughkeepsie, New York in 1979. He served as Washington correspondent for *The New Yorker* for more than thirty years and was the creator of the expression: "The American Establishment". He was one of the most respected political writers in America, and was visiting professor at Columbia, Yale and Vassar, and was awarded honorary doctorates by Bard College (1962 and Grinnell College (1967). In addition to his many columns and articles in the *New Yorker* and other magazines he wrote nine books which illuminate American political history.

The most successful journalist was the great sports writer, columnist and editor for the *New York Daily News* from 1922 to 1936, Paul Gallico, born in New York City in 1897 and died in Monte Carlo, Monaco in 1976. He left the *Daily News* to dedicate himself entirely to writing fiction and published forty-one books and about 200 short stories scattered in periodicals such as *The New Yorker, The Saturday Evening Post, Argosy, Cosmopolitan, Good Housekeeping*, and many others. His writings include fiction, children's literature, fables, ghost stories and biographies. He also wrote nine screen plays and two television spectaculars.

ITALIAN AMERICAN WRITERS

I propose that the time has come at our Conferences when we must consider not only Italian Americans who have written of the Italian Experience in America, but also those who have achieved success in the writing profession regardless of their subject matter, and with your permission I will cite some examples in each category reserving the full bibliographical information of the works of each author for the reference section.

Of the writers dealing with the Italian American experience, first, of course, is Pietro di Donato (1911 —) bricklayer, novelist, playwright, biographer and short story writer whose novel of 1938 *Christ in Concrete* is a classic. And his story of Aldo Moro published in *Penthouse* won the 1978 Overseas Press Club Award.

John Fante (1911-1983), novelist and Hollywood scenarist, wrote of Italian family life and his native Colorado in his first novel, *Wait Until Spring, Bandini;* and of the family's experiences in California in his later novels. *Dago Red*, his collection of family sketches, is considered his best work.

Guido D'Agostino (1906 —), novelist and short story writer, was born in New York City's "Little Italy" and wrote of the adjustment problems of immigrants. His first and best known novel *Olives on the Apple Tree* came out in 1940.

The life of Sicilian immigrants in Rochester, N.Y. is faithfully and artistically rendered by Jerre Mangione (1909 —) in his autobiographical chronicle: *Mount Allegro*, first published as fiction in 1943 and reissued in 1981 by its fifth publisher with the added subtitle *A Memoir of Italian American Life*, a new final chapter by the author entitled "Finale", and an introduction by Herbert J. Gans who defines the book as "a classic of American ethnic literature".

Another Sicilian American who has written of life both in Sicily and in America in three novels is Ben Morreale, born in New York City in 1924 and currently professor of history at SUNY College at Plattsburgh, N.Y.

The experience of life in a small Sicilian village, Palazzo Adriana, and in Standing Pine, Mississippi is the subject of the book *A Highly Ramified Tree* by the poet and novelist Robert Canzoneri, a Mississippian cousin of the former lightweight boxing champion of the world Tony Canzoneri.

Mario Puzo's (1920-) great success as a novelist was the subject of a cover story in *Time* which featured his picture with the title "The Godfather of the Paperback Boom". Puzo's experience of growing up during the Great Depression in New York's "Hell's Kitchen" resulted in his second novel. *The Fortunate Pilgrim* and contributed to the material included in his *Godfather*.

Recent Italian Immigrant Writers

There are three Italian Americans who are well known as writers of fiction both in their native Italy and in the United States, where they emigrated around or after World War II.

Niccolò Tucci (1908-), novelist, short story writer, and playwright, came to America in 1938. He worked several years for the U.S. State Department and in 1944 became a free-lance writer. He has published three books in Italy, three in the United States, and has written nearly a dozen plays.

Pier Maria Pasinetti (1913-) came to America in 1946, earned doctorates in Italy and at Yale, and since 1949 has been on the faculty of UCLA. He has written seven novels in Italian published in Italy. Four of them he translated into English and published in the United States. He also writes film scripts and contributes articles and reviews to journals both in Italy and the United States.

Arturo Vivante (1923-) is the son of philosopher Leone Vivante and grandson of poet Adolfo de Bosis. He practiced medicine in Italy before emigrating to the U.S. in 1958, when he became a full-time writer. He has seven volumes of fiction and has contributed over fifty short stories to *The New Yorker*.

Main Stream Novelists

Don DeLillo (1936-) was born in the Bronx of immigrant parents from Molise province. He graduated from Fordham University with a B.S. in communication arts in 1958 and spent five years working for an advertising agency before devoting his full time to writing. From 1971 to 1982 he published seven novels which have received excellent reviews and have established him as a master of style and language.

Joseph DiMona was born in Haddonfield, N.J., graduated from law school and passed the bar examination and then turned to writing. His first assignment was to cover the Mitchell-Stans trial for *New York Magazine*. He has written four very successful novels, a book about court martial, and ghosted four books for various authors from Ann Corio to R.H. Haldeman.

New York born novelist and university English professor George Cuomo (1929-) taught in Arizona, British Columbia, and California before joining the faculty of the University of Massachusetts at Amherst in 1973. His literary production includes seven novels, a collection of short stories, and a book of poems. He also regularly contributes stories, poems, and articles to many magazines and journals.

Francis Pollini (1930-), born in West Wyoming, Pennsylvania and now living in Norwich, England, is, according to Rose Basile Green, "one of the most representative Italian American writers to emerge during the past decade (the sixties)". He has published seven novels in England and in the United States, and a collection of plays.

Mass Production Writers

Mystery: Certainly the most published Italian American and perhaps the most prolific writer in America is Michael Angelo Avallone, Jr. born in New York City in 1924, one of seventeen surviving children of stone mason Michael Angelo and Marie Antoinette Antonelli Avallone. In the thirty-year period 1953-1983 Mr. Avallone has published, under his own name and sixteen pseudonyms, more than one thousand works, including 186 novels with some forty million copies still in print. He has written mysteries, science fiction, occult, sex and juvenile novels and novelizations of movies and television shows. In his first novel, *The Tall Dolores* he created the character of detective Ed Noon, who proved so popular that it has lasted through thirty-eight novels.

Evan Hunter, son of Charles P. and Marie Coppola Lombino, was born in New York City in 1926 and attended Cooper Union for one year, receiving a B.A. from Hunter College in 1950. He is one of America's most prolific writers, and has published some twenty novels under the name of Evan Hunter, including *The Blackboard Jungle* (1954) which became a very successful movie. He also published thirty-seven mystery novels in "The 87th Precinct Series" under the pseudonym of Ed McBain and several more under the pseudonyms of Hunt Collins and Richard Marsten. He wrote, under the name of Evan Hunter, three plays and television scripts for the Columbia Broadcasting series *The Chisholms* (1979-80).

The third Italian American prolific mystery writer is the Californian Bill (William John) Pronzini, born in 1943 the son of a farm worker. Between 1971 and 1980 Pronzini published twenty-two novels under his own name and two pseudonyms: Jack Foxx and Alex Saxon. He also edited a dozen anthologies and has published over two hundred short stories. His books have been translated into nine languages and published in fifteen countries.

Science Fiction: Benjamin William Bova, born in Philadelphia in 1932, is the prolific author of books, anthologies and articles in the genres of science fiction and science for popular reading. He was editor of *Analog Science Fiction-Science Fact Magazine* from 1971 to 1978 when he became Editor of *Omni Magazine*. Since 1981 he has been its editorial director and vice president. He began his science fiction writing with the novel *The Star Conquerors* (1959) and up to 1981 he had published 24 novels. In the non-fiction field of science popularization he published *The Milky Way Galaxy* in 1951 and by 1981 had published nineteen additional novels. In 1971 he published: *The Many Worlds of Science Fiction*, the first of his ten anthologies of science fiction.

Biography: The biographer *par excellence* Frances Winwar (Francesca Vinciguerra) was born in Taormina, Sicily in 1900 and was brought to New York City in 1907. She attended the city schools, Hunter College and Columbia University, was co-founder of the Leonardo da Vinci Art School and was its executive secretary from 1923 to 1930. During her forty-year career as a writer (1927-1967), she published seven novels, and in 1933 published the first of her thirteen biographies, *Poor Splendid Wings*, which won her the $5,000 non-fiction prize from the *Atlantic Monthly*. As a translator she excelled with the best translation into English ever made of

Boccaccio's *Decameron* (1938) and translated the librettos of Verdi's *La Traviata* and *Don Carlos* and Donizetti's *Lucia di Lammermoor* for the Metropolitan Opera. She also wrote the works of history: *The Monument in Staten Island, Meucci, Garibaldi and the Telephone* and *Italy and Her People* and five juvenile books.

Children's Books - Authors and Illustrators

Valenti Angelo (1897-) was brought to California from his native Tuscany at the age of eight in 1905. He had only two years of elementary school and at fifteen was working in a paper mill. Later he worked as a laborer in rubber, steel and glass factories. Three years in a photoengraving plant directed him toward his future profession as book illustrator, which began in 1926 when he illustrated his first book for the famous Grabhorn Press. In 1933 he became a free-lance artist and throughout his forty-year career illustrated hundreds of books ranging from Walt Whitman's *Leaves of Grass* (1930) to Hawthorne's *Twice-Told Tales* for the Limited Editions Club (1966). Thirty-seven books illustrated by Angelo were included in the American Institute of Graphic Arts "Fifty Books of the Year" Exhibits. From 1938 to 1966 Mr. Angelo wrote and illustrated sixteen children's books based on his own experience as a child immigrant growing up in America.

Leo Lionni, born in Amsterdam in 1910, was an architect, designer, painter, and free-lance writer in Italy before coming to America in 1939. Here he worked as art director for a Philadelphia advertising agency (1939-47), as design director for Olivetti Corporation of America in San Francisco (1949-59), and as art director for *Fortune* magazine (1949-62). He has won numerous awards and honors and has had many one-man shows of his paintings and sculptures in leading museums and galleries. Since 1959 he has written and illustrated twenty-three children's books.

Leo Politi (1908 —) was born in California, but at the age of seven he was brought to Italy when his family returned there. Young Leo studied for six years at the Art Institute of Monza, near Milan, before returning to California in his early twenties. In Los Angeles he was a sidewalk artist and also painted murals and carved wooden figures before starting his successful career as writer and illustrator of children's books. In addition to illustrating his own books, Polliti has illustrated many children's books and textbooks written by others. In 1950 he won the Caldecott Medal of the American Library Association for best illustrated book of the year.

Tomie (Thomas Anthony) de Paola (1934-) was born in Meriden, Connecticut, has a B.F.A. from Pratt Institute (1956) and an M.F.A. from the California College of Arts and Crafts (1969). He has taught art in New England and California colleges for twenty years, is a painter, muralist, designer of theater sets, and writer and illustrator of children's and juvenile books. He has received many awards, honors, and prizes for his book illustrations in America, Europe and Japan. Between 1975 and 1983 he published forty children's books with his own texts and illustrations. He also has illustrated sixty-two children's books written by other authors and published between 1965 and 1980. Of his own books the following five deal with Italian subjects or legends: *Strega Nona* (1975); *The Legend of the Old Befana* (1980); *The Prince of the Dolomites* (1980); *Francis: The Poor Man of Assisi* (1982); *Giorgio's Village* (1982).

Scholarly and Professional Writers:

Sociology: Professor Leo Buscaglia of the University of Southern California, where he teaches a very popular course on LOVE, published his first book in 1973 consisting of his lecture notes on the course's lectures. *Love* gathered momentum and catapulted its author into the national limelight "as an enormous draw on the lecture circuit", and a very popular lecturer in a regular series on Public Television. He published *Personhood* in 1978, *Living, Loving and Learning*, in 1982, and *The Fall of Freddie the Leaf* also in 1982. By the fall of 1982 *Love* had had two more editions in paperback and had more than 1.5 million copies in print, and by April 17, 1983 Buscaglia had become a publishing phenomenon by having four of his seven books on the *New York Times* Bestseller Lists: *Living, Loving and Learning* was #5 on the "Non-Fiction" list of 15 titles and had been on the list for the previous fifty-two weeks, while *The Fall of Freddie the Leaf* was #12 on the same list and had been on it for twenty-two weeks. The other two titles were on the "Paperback Best Sellers". *Love* was #15 on the "Mass Market" list, and *Personhood* was #9 on the "Trade" list. The other three books published by Buscaglia are: *The Way of the Bull, Because I Am Human,* and *The Disabled and Their Parents.*

The sociology professor Peter Henry Rossi was born in New York City in 1921 and was educated at the City College and Columbia. Before joining the faculty of the University of Massachusetts at Amherst, where he is Director of the Social and Demographic Research Institute, he was at Johns Hopkins and at the University of Chicago where he directed the National Opinion Research Center. Alone or in collaboration he has published fourteen books and is editor of *Social Science Research* since 1974.

Psychiatry: Dr. Silvano Arieti (1914-1981) was born and educated in Pisa, Italy and emigrated to New York in 1939 in the wake of the Fascist racial laws. He became Professor of Clinical Psychiatry at the New York Medical College for twenty years and maintained a private practice from 1952 to his death. He published eight books and nearly one hundred articles and was editor in chief of the seven-volume *American Handbook of Psychiatry.* His *Interpretation of Schizophrenia* won him the 1975 National Book Award in the field of the Sciences.

Dr. Richard C. Robertiello (1923 —) was born in Brooklyn and was educated at Harvard and Columbia. He practices psychiatry and psychoanalysis in New York City and since 1956 has been Supervising Psychiatrist on the New York City Community Guidance Service. He has published eight books and is editor of the *Journal of Contemporary Psychiatry.*

Religion: Professor Joseph Politella was born in Roccamonfina, Caserta, Italy, in 1910 and was brought to America in 1919. He received the B.A. (1933) from the University of Massachusetts, the M.A. (1935) from Amherst College, and the Ph.D. from the University of Pennsylvania in 1938. From 1946 to his retirement in 1973 he was professor of philosophy and religion at Kent State University in Ohio and has published extensively on world religions, especially the Far Eastern religions.

Politics: Former Secretary of Health, Education and Welfare in the Carter Administration, Joseph A. Califano, Jr., has contributed to political science with the publication of his two books *A Presidential Nation* and *Governing America: An Insider's Report from the White House and the Cabinet.*
    The journalist Robert Caro won a Pulitzer Prize and Francis Parker Prize for his celebrated 1200 page biography of New York's legendary bridge builder Robert Moses: *The Power Broker: Robert Moses and the Fall of New York* (1974). Caro is now working on a monumental biography of the late president Lyndon B. Johnson. The first of the projected three volumes, *The Years of Lyndon Johnson: The Path to Power,* was the Book of the Month selection for December 1982.

Literary Criticism: The New York born Matthew J., Bruccoli (1931 —)is currently professor of American Literature at the University of South Carolina and president of Bruccoli-Clark Publishing Company, founded by him in 1972. Dr. Bruccoli is one of the country's foremost authorities on American fiction writers and has published eleven volumes in the field. He is editor of the Literary Works of F. Scott Fitzgerald and series editor of *Pittsburgh Series in Bibliography,* 1971-; *Lost American Fiction,* 1972-; and *Dictionary of Literary Biography,* 1978-.

Film Criticism: Another New Yorker, James   Monaco (1942-) has carved himself a very successful career as an educational administrator-chairman of the University Center SEEK Program, a teacher of literature, film, drama, and media- at the City University of New York and the New School for Social Reserach and through his many publications he has established himself as one of the top authorities on all phases of film making and media. Some of his books deal with "The New Wave", 1976; "The Media as Image Maker", 1978; "Alain Renais", 1978; "American Film Now", 1979.

Poetry

The first Italian American poet to gain national recognition for his poetry written in English was Arturo Giovannitti (1884-1959). He was born in Campobasso, Abbruzzi, and emigrated to Canada in 1900 where he spent several years attending McGill University and working for a period in a railroad gang. He came to New York and worked at several jobs and attended Columbia University. After a brief excursion to Pennsylvania working as a coal miner he returned to New York where he joined the Italian Socialist Federation and became the editor of its newspaper *Il Proletario*. In 1912 he accompanied labor organizer Joseph Ettor to Lawrence, Massachuetts where the textile strike led by the IWW was in progress. Both Ettor and Giovannitti were arrested, under false charges, and kept in jail for almost a year before they were brought to trial and found innocent. While in jail Giovannitti wrote a number of poems that were published in literary journals all over the country. In 1914 these poems were gathered and published in the volume *Arrows in the Gale*. The appearance of the volume established Giovannitti as the most important Italian American poet of his time and of his masterpiece "The Walker" the poet and critic Louis Untermeyer wrote "As an art work it is the most remarkable thing our literature can boast". In 1962 E. Clemente, the editor of *La Parola del Popolo*, published a definitive edition of Giovannitti's poems with an introduction by Normas Thomas.

Rosa Zagnoni Marinoni (1888-1970) was born in Bologna, Italy, and emigrated to Fayetteville, Arkansas in 1908 where she married Antonio Marinoni (1879-1944), a professor of Italian and later chairman of the Department of Romance Languages, at the University of Arkansas. They remained at Fayetteville, he teaching and she bringing up a family and acculturating herself to the point of writing poetry in English reflecting the local and regional land and people. The first of her fourteen books of poetry she published had the title of *Pine Needles* and her last was *Whoo-Whoo, the Howl of the Ozarks Says: Think and Wink!* She wrote short stories reflecting local and relgious legends and many serials, one of which "Ozark Flint and Star Gold" was serialized in *Household Magazine*. Her poems and short stories appeared under her name as Rosa Zagnoni, Rosa Marinoni and under the pseudonyms of Rosca, Dawn Star and The Jester in 159 periodicals all over the world. By act of the same legislature she became Poet Laureate of Arkansas and was also Poet Laureate of the Ozarks.

Poet and critic John Ciardi (1916—) was born in Boston and raised in Medford where he graduated from Tufts before going to the University of Michigan. He taught English at the University of Kansas City for three years, at Harvard from 1946-53, and at Rutgers from 1953-61 before devoting full time to writing and lecturing. He was director of the Bread Loaf Writers' Conference from 1955 to 1972 and was poetry editor for the *Saturday Review of Literature* from 1956 to 1972. He has won numerous awards and prizes for his poetry and has received seven honorary doctorates from colleges and universities throughout the country. He published fourteen volumes of poetry between 1940 and 1979, in addition to miscellaneous essays, anthologies and textbooks. As his three children were growing, Ciardi wrote verses for them and this led him to write and publish 14 volumes of juvenile poetry between 1959 and 1975. His major work is his verse translation of Dante's *Divine Comedy*. Ciardi's life-long interest in language has resulted in his most recent publication: *A Browser's Dictionary and Native's Guide to the Unknown American Language*.

The poet and novelist Gilbert Sorrentino was born in Brooklyn in 1929 and attended Brooklyn College. He worked at a great variety of jobs until 1965 when he became an editor at Grove Press where he worked for five years. Since 1976 he has been teaching writing at the New School for Social Research and writing poetry and prose. From 1960, when he published his first volume of poetry *The Darkness Surrounds Us*, to 1981 when he published *Selected Poems 1958-1981* he published ten volumes of poetry, six novels, and one play. His last two novels *Mulligan Stew* and *Aberration of Starlight* received very good reviews. His literary work has been recognized nationally with awards and grants from the Guggenheim Foundation in 1973, the National Endowment for the Arts in 1974, the Samuel S. Fels Award in 1974, a Creative Arts Public Service Grant in 1975, and the National Endowment for the Humanities in 1979 (*See, Who's Who in America*, 1982-83 editions.

Professor Joseph Tusiani (1924-) is a recent immigrant (1947) who has combined a college teaching career with the writing of poetry and has been eminently successful in both. As a poet he had published widely in Italian and in his native dialect of the province of Foggia. He has also published many poems in Latin in journals in Europe and in America which he is now collecting in a volume to be published., He has published three collections of poems in English: *Rind and All, The Fifth Season*, and *Gente Mia and Other Poems*. Tusiani's greatest contribution to Italian American culture consists of his poetic translations of many Italian classics into English including *The Complete Poems of Michelangelo*, Tasso's *Jerusalem Delivered*, and a three-volume anthology of poets from the thirteenth to the twentiety century. Tusiani has received many awards and prizes for his literary and poetic achievements including the Greenwood Prize from the Poetry Society of England in 1956 and the Alice Fay di Castagnola Prize from the Poetry Society of America in 1968 (*See, Joseph Tusiani: A Bibliography*).

The most widely known and published Italian American poet is Lawrence Ferlinghetti (1920-). He was born in Yonkers, N.Y. and has a B.A. from the University of North Carolina, an M.A. from Columbia, and a doctorate from the Sorbonne in Paris.

In 1951 he moved to San Francisco where he founded the City Lights Bookshop in 1953, which, with his publishing firm City Lights, founded in 1955, became the center for writers and artists of the "beat generation".

Ferlinghetti, who is also a painter, book designer and graphic artist, edited City Lights' Pocket Poets Series which began in 1955 with the publication of his first verse collection, *Pictures of the Gone World*, (the second book published in the series is Allen Ginsberg's *Howl* in 1956). This resulted in Ferlinghetti's arrest because of the book's alleged obsenity, but he was found not guilty and released.

From 1955 to 1981 Ferlinghetti wrote hundreds of poems published in journals, books, and newspapers all over America and Europe, particularly in France. He also became more famous for his public readings of his poems which attracted large crowds wherever he went. He published a dozen volumes of his poems, about a dozen experimental plays, a surrealist novel, essays, and many articles. His most successful book of verse is *A Coney Island of the Mind*. His latest volume is *Endless Life: Selected Poems* consisting of poems chosen by the author from his entire production.

The other Italian American poet associated with the "beat generation" is New York born Gregory Nunzio Corso (1930 –). He had a difficult childhood living with five different foster parents and attending only grammar school. He spent three years in prison (1947-50) and worked in three different jobs the next three years. In the mid-fifties he attracted a great deal of attention with a series of poetry readings throughout the East and Midwest before traveling extensively in Mexico, the United States and Europe and devoting himself to writing. A number of his poems were inspired by and written at the places he visited. His first book published, *The Vestal Lady on Brattle and Other Poems* reflects his extended stay "for free" with friends at Harvard in Cambridge. His second volume, *Gasoline*, was written while traveling in Mexico, while his third and fourth volumes of verse, *Happy Birthday of Death* and *Long Live Man*, were written while traveling back and forth from America and Europe and the poems are about America and Europe. Altogether, Corso published some ten volumes of poems, two novels, two plays, and collaborated in screenplays and filmscripts (*See, Contemporary Authors*, Vol. 7-8).

THE THEATER

As in fiction and poetry, the Italian presence is evident and growing in the American theater and drama on the stage, screen, and television. Mario Fratti (1927-) came to New York in 1963 from Italy as a drama critic for Italian newspapers and became an American citizen. Since his arrival Fratti has been writing and producing plays in English at the rate of two or more a year, in addition to writing and publishing some in Italian. Since 1967 he has been teaching playwriting at Hunter College and in 1979 he won the Eugene O'Neil Competition for Composers and Librettists with his adaptation of the text of Fellini's *Eight and Half* for the Broadway musical *Nine*, and in 1980 he won the Richard Rogers Award for the same libretto.

Albert Innaurato, the best known Italian American young dramatist, was born in Philadelphia in 1948, graduated from the Yale School of Drama in 1974, and in 1977 he had three of his plays running simultaneously in New York! Best known for his play *Gemini* which started Off Broadway in 1977 and moved to Broadway, running for five years and becoming one of the longest-running plays in Broadway history. The author has received Guggenheim and Rockefeller grants and has been in residence at New York's Public Theatre and at the Circle Repertory Company. Six of his plays have been published in a paperback volume under the title *Bizarre Behavior*.

Julia (Julie) Ann Bovasso, born in Brooklyn in 1930, is a playwright, actress on stage, screen, and T.V., and a director. She wrote, directed and acted in *The Moon Dreamers*, 1969; *Gloria and Esperanza*, 1969 and for this she received a Triple Obie Award for Playwriter-Actress-Director. She wrote and directed *Standard Safety*, 1974, *The Nothing Kid*, 1974; *Shubert's Last Serenade*, 1971 and *Monday on the Way to Mercury Islands*, 1971. She also wrote *Down by the River Where Waterlillies are Disfigured Every Day* 1972-73. In 1975 she toured Latin America for the U.S. Department of State. She received Obie awards for best acting, best experimental theater, and for introducing the Theater of the Absurd in the United States.

Another successful director-producer is Carmen Charles Capalbo (1925 —), born in Harrisburg, Pennsylvania and a product of the Yale School of Drama. He directed and co-produced nine plays including *Juno and the Paycock*, *Dear Brutus*, *The Threepenny Opera*, *The Potting Shed*, *A Moon for the Misbegotten* and others. He directed five plays including *A Connecticut Yankee* and produced for T.V. *The Power and the Glory*. He is also director and producer of two hundred radio plays. He received Tony and Obie awards in 1956.

Lewis John Carlino, born in New York City in 1932, is a well known playwright and movie director. He specialized in one-act plays and in the early sixties he won the Vernon Rice and Obie Awards when he had three plays, *Cages*, *Telemacus Clay*, and *Doubletalk*, simultaneously on the New York stage. He has written the screenplays of a number of films he directed, including the recent *The Great Santini* and *Resurrection* in 1980.

Joseph Pintauro's three one-act plays *Cacciatore I, II*, and *III* were produced at the Actors Repertory Theater in New York in 1977 and his three-act play *Orchid* was produced by the Circle Repertory Company in 1982.

William Mastrosimone (1948 —) the Trenton, N.J.-born playwright has had two successful plays in New York recently, *The Wool Gatherer* in 1979 at the Circle Repertory Theater and *Extremities* at the Westside Arts Center on 43rd Street, which Walter Kerr of *The New York Times* called "Electric". Two other plays of his were produced in New Jersey: *Ham*, and *Devil Take the Hindmost*.

There are many other successful Italian American playwrights whose works are produced regularly on Broadway or Off, or Off Off Broadway, but time permits me to mention briefly some names and cite one or two works for each. Leonard Melfi (1935-) *Bird Bath, Night Taxi Tales.* Louis La Russo II (1936-) *Knockout, Marlon Brando Sat Right Here, Lampost, Wheelbarrow Closers, Momma's Little Angel.* Joseph Bologna (1938-) together with his wife Rene Taylor write and act in their plays. *Lovers and Strangers,* 1968; the film *Made for Each Other,* 1971; the play *It Had To Be You,* 1981; television shows *Acts of Love* and *Other Comedies,* 1973, *Paradise,* 1974 and also the T.V. series *Calucci's Department.* Anthony Giardina, *An American Tragedy,* 1980; *The Child,* 1981; *Living at Home,* 1978. Richard Vetere, *Rockaway Boulevard,* 1980. George Rubino, *The Last Tenant,* winner of the ABC Theater Award of $10,000 and presented over Channel 7 on June 25, 1978.

In its August 1983 issue the *Smithsonian* magazine featured (in a well-illustrated cover story) the Sicilian Marionette Theater brought to New York in 1919 by Agrippino Manteo and continuously operated at 109 Mulberry Street,until today by three generations of Manteos with the same original title of "Papa Manteo's Life-Sized Marionettes" (*See also*, article by Harold C. Schoenberg).

Broadway Musicals

Four of the best musicals currently on Broadway have a strong Italian American connection *42nd Street* is a stage version of the 1933 screen musical with the same title and music by Harry Warren (1893-1981), who was born Salvatore Guaragna in Brooklyn, the eleventh of twelve children of Calabrian immigrant shoemaker Anthony Guaragna and his wife Rachel De Luca, who had immigrated in 1885. Before going to Hollywood in 1932, Warren had written songs for the hit Broadway musicals *Sweet and Low* and *Crazy Quilt* produced by Billy Rose and for Ed Wynn's *Laugh Parade.* Warren's first assignment at Warner Brothers in Hollywood was to write the music for *42nd Street.* During his fifty-nine year career Warren composed more than 380 popular songs for over fifty Hollywood films. He won three Academy Awards for "Lullaby of Broadway", 1935; "You'll Never Know", 1943; and "On the Atchinson Topeka and Santa Fe", 1946.

The libretto of *Nine* was adapted from the Italian text of Federico Fellini's film *Eight and a Half* by playwright Mario Fratti.

Producer, director, choreographer, and writer Michael Bennett, born in Buffalo in 1943 the son of Mr. and Mrs. Salvatore Di Figlia, is responsible for the two award winning musicals *A Chorus Line* and *Dream Girls.*

New York City born Frank Corsaro (1924-) is a graduate of the Yale School of Drama and is a most respected director of both theater and opera. On Broadway he directed *A Hatful of Rain, The Night of the Iguana,*

Treemonisha, Whoopy, Knockout, and others. Since 1958 he has directed some thirty operas at the New York City Opera and forty or fifty more at opera houses and festivals in Washington, D.C.; Houston, Texas; St. Paul, Minnesota; Ottawa, Canada; and Glyndebourne, England.

Franco Zeffirelli, born in Italy in 1923, is a brilliant director and stage designer of drama, opera and film and operates both in Europe and in the United States. He has directed opera at La Scala, at Covent Garden, and at the Metropolitan. He has written, designed and directed the exceptional film version of Verdi's *LaTraviata* shown in New York this year.

BALLET

The Italian influence on the ballet in America began right after the Civil War when three Italian ballerinas from La Scala in Milan came to dance at Niblo's Garden in New York. Maria Bonfanti (1845-1921) and Rita Sangalli (1849-1909) came in 1866 to dance the principal roles in *The Black Crook,* a very popular musical show that set a record as the longest running play in American theatrical history up to that time. Giuseppina Morlacchi (1843-1886) came in 1867 to perform in *The Devil's Auction.* Sangalli returned to Europe in 1870 to become the *prima ballerina absoluta* at the Paris Opera. Morlacchi and Bonfanti married Americans and spent the rest of their lives performing and promoting dance in America. Morlacchi married an Indian scout, Texas Jack, and with him and Buffalo Bill, she toured in western dramas dancing and portraying a variety of characters. After her husband's death in 1880 she returned to her home in Lowell, Massachusetts where she taught ballet to the local mill girls. Bonfanti married George Huffmann of a socially prominent family in New York and continued her dancing. From 1888 to 1894 she was the *prima ballerina* at the Metropolitan Opera and in 1896 she opened a dance school for professionals and society pupils in New York City, where Ruth St. Denis was one of her pupils. These three ballerinas, through their work in both popular entertainment and opera and ballet, and their high personal and professional standards, were instrumental in laying a foundation for the Americanization of ballet.

Today ballet in America has achieved prominence and New York City is the dance capital of the world. A number of Italian Americans are contributing to its success as directors, choreographers and dancers, and some enjoy leading positions.

Louis Falco (1942-) is a New York-born dancer, choreographer and director of his own Louis Falco Dance Company. He has an international reputation and regularly tours the United States, Canada, Mexico and Europe. He has choreographed works for the La Scala Opera Ballet and six episodes for RAI Television in Italy.

Gerald Arpino (1928-) who was born in Staten Island, danced with the Ballet Russe and appeared on television and in Broadway musicals before joining the Robert Joffrey Ballet when it was founded in 1953. Arpino is now Associate Director and chief choreographer of the company.

Edward Villella (1936-) born on Long Island, was principal dancer of the New York City Ballet for many years and is currently artistic director of the Eglevski Ballet and choreographer for the New Jersey Ballet. In 1978 Mayor Koch appointed him chairman of the New York City's Commission for Cultural Affairs.

Dan Siretta is choreographer for Goodspeed Opera House Theater in East Haddam, Connecticut. Chicago-born Paul Sanasardo is a dancer, choreographer and director of the Paul Sanasardo Dance Company which operates in New York City. Matteo Vittucci is director of his own Ethno American Dance Theater. Gus (August T.) Giordano (1923-) is choreographer, dancer and director of his own Gus Giordano Jazz Dancer Chicago Company since 1958. He has been touring the U.S. and Europe yearly since 1975. Ronn Guidi is Artistic Director of the Oakland, California Ballet. Elisa Monte is a dancer and choreographer who has her own company, Elisa Monte and Dancers, and also choreographs works for the Alvin Ailey American Dance Theater. Other ballet companies or troupes are: Merle Marsicano Dance Company, Anthony La Giglia Dance Theater, Linda St. Ambrogio Dance Troupe. The dance critic for *The New Yorker* is Arlene Croce who is author of two volumes consisting of her collected articles and reviews.

MUSIC

The Italian contribution to American and world music is well known and well documented. Here I will briefly mention some achievements and contributions by Italian Americans both immigrants and native born. It being the 100th anniversary of the founding of the Metropolitan Opera it is appropriate to recall that for its first season of 1882-83. Conductor Augusto Vianesi (1837-1908) was brought over from Italy and he assembled an orchestra consisting of 50 musicians from the *Fenice* opera house of Venice, 15 from the *San Carlo* of Naples and 18 from the leading opera houses of London, Leipzig and Brussels (*See*, Giovanni Schiavo). Baritone Antonio Scotti (1866-1921) sang there from 1902 until his death. The Golden Age of the Metropolitan Opera began in 1908 with the arrival, from *La Scala* of Milan, of Giulio Gatti- Casazza (1869-1940) as general manager, and Arturo Toscanini (1867-1957) as chief conductor. Gatti-Casazza "reigned" as general manager for twenty- seven years (1908-35), Toscanini left in 1915 as World War I was expanding. During the seven seasons of the Gatti-Toscanini teamwork seventy-two operas were given at the Met; fifty-nine Italian and 13 German. During these past hundred years of continuous operation of the Met, Italians have contributed greatly to its success from the pioneers Scotti and Caruso to Giovanni Martinelli (1885-1961) to Rosa Ponselle (1897-1981) and today's Luciano Pavarotti. The most frequently performed operas over the century are Verdi's *Aida* with 631 performances and Puccini's *La Boheme* with 599. Toscanini conducted the New York Philharmonic from 1926 to 1936 and the National Broadcasting Orchestra, especially created for him, from 1936 to 1946. In an article entitled "How American Culture Has Been Shaped by the Artist in Exile", Donal Henahan, chief music critic of *The New York Times*, wrote "most magnificently, there was the coming of Toscannini, who changed the art and craft of conducting in America beyond recognition" (September 2, 1979, section 2, p. 1).

In 1905 another opera impresario, Alfredo Salmaggi (1886-1975) arrived in New York and spent the next sixty years popularizing opera in New York by staging performances at stadiums and Madison Square Garden for large crowds and charging as little as twenty-five cents for admission. Even today, Maestro Vincent La Selva, born in Cleveland, Ohio of immigrant parents, with his New York Grand Opera Company is performing opera for the people in Central Park (The New York Times, Arts and Leisure Section, July 24, 1983).

Alfredo Antonini (1901-1983) for a quarter of a century conducted the Columbia Broadcasting System Symphony for radio and television and was guest conductor with the major American symphony orchestras. Carlo Maria Giulini currently conducts the Los Angeles Philharmonic, while Riccardo Muti conducts the Philadelphia Orchestra, John Mauceri the Kennedy Center Opera House Orchestra in Washington, D.C., Nicola Rescigno the Dallas Opera and John Giordano the Fort Worth, Texas Symphony.

Composers

The dean of Italian American composers is Giancarlo Menotti (1911-) who came to America at age 17 and graduated from the Curtis Institute of Music at Philadelphia in 1933, a composer, librettist, playwright, scriptwriter and director, has composed some twenty operas including *Amahl and The Night Visitors* shown over NBC television on Christmas Eve of 1951, and *The Saint of Bleeker Street* (1954). In addition to producing his own and other operas and composing music in various fields, he founded, in 1958, the *Festival of Two Worlds* at Spoleto, Italy and its American counterpart at Charleston, South Carolina in 1977.

Vittorio Giannini (1903-1966) a second generation Italian American born in Philadelphia the son of tenor Erruccio Giannini, founder of the Italian opera house Verdi Hall, and brother of world famous soprano Dusolina Giannini (1900 —), taught composition at various conservatories and composed twelve operas and several symphonies, concertos and choral and chamber works.

Thomas Pasatieri (1945 —) born in New York City and a graduate of the Juilliard School of Music, has composed sixteen operas and has set over 500 art songs.

Dominick Argento (1927—) born in York, Pennsylvania, graduated from the Peabody Institute and the Eastman School of Music and has been a professor of music at the University of Minnesota since 1958. He has composed nine operas, song cycles, choral and orchestral works.

One of America's most respected composers is Norman dello Joio (1913-) born in New York City, where his father Casimir was an organist, studied at Juilliard and Yale and has received five honorary doctorates in music. He has taught music at various conservatories and is a prolific composer in all fields of music. He received the Pulitzer Prize in 1957.

The third generation Italian American composer Walter Piston (Pistone) (1894-1946) was born in Belmont, Massachusetts, and attended Harvard and later taught music there from 1926 to 1959. He composed eight symphonies and won the Pulitzer Prize for the third in 1937. He has also written other orchestral works, chamber and choral music and a ballet.

Vincent Persichetti (1915—) was born in Philadelphia and graduated from the Philadelphia Conservatory and the Curtis Institute of Music where he became a teacher. Since 1963 he has been chairman of the Composition Department of the Julliard School of Music. He is an active composer, pianist, conductor, lecturer and critic. He has written more than 130 works including symphonies, piano sonatas, songs, band works, quartets, quintets, chamber and choral works and organ pieces.

John Corigliano, Jr. (1938-) is a third generation Italian American whose father was a violinist with the New York Philharmonic Orchestra for 47 years (1919-1961), twenty-three of them as concertmaster, He graduated from the Manhattan School of Music and has taught compositon and is president and founder of "Music for the Theater" a rental library of music tapes and scores for radio and television stations. He has written in various fields including concertos for various instruments including piano, clarinet, flute and oboe. His composition for flute "Pied Piper Symphony" was performed by the internationally famous flautist James Galway with the Los Angeles Symphony Orchestra on February 4, 1982. Recently he was commissioned by the Metropolitan Opera to write an opera for the centennial celebration. It is an opera based on the third play of Beaumarchais' triology which follows the fortunes of Figaro twenty years after the events of Mozart's *Le Nozze di Figaro* (The Marriage of Figaro) (*See*, Bernard Holland, *The New York Times Magazine*, January 31, 1982, p. 24).

David Del Tredici (1937-) was born in California, got his B.A. at Berkeley and an M.F.A. at Princeton. He is a composer, recital and symphony pianist and teacher at Harvard, 1968-1972, at the University of Buffalo and at Boston University since 1973. His most important works have been a series of compositions based on Lewis Carrol's *Alice In Wonderland:* "In Wonderland", "Illustrated Alice", "An Alice Symphony", "Vintage Alice", "Adventures Underground", "Final Alice" commissioned for the United States Bicentennial of 1976 and performed by eight major symphony orchestras throughout the country, and "Child Alice (In Memory of a Summer Day)" (Tim Page, "The New Romance with Tonality", *The New York Times Magazine*, May 29, 1983, p. 2); John Rockwell, "Del Tredici — His Success Could Be A Signpost", *The New York Times*, October 26, 1980, p. D23).

Peter Mennin (Mennini) (1923-1983) composer and president of Juilliard School of Music for the last twenty years, was born in Erie, Pennsylvania and studied at the Oberlin Conservatory and the Eastman School of Music. He composed nine symphonies, instrumental concertoes and music for chorus and orchestra as well as chamber and choral music.

Henry Mancini was born in 1924 in Cleveland and is now living in California where he has composed music for more than 100 films including "Breakfast at Tiffany" and "The Glenn Miller Story", and prize winning songs "Moon River" and "Days of Wine and Roses".

Salvatore Martirano (1927-) was born in Yonkers, N.Y., and studied at Oberlin Consevatory and Eastman School of Music. Currently he teaches at the University of Illinois at Urbana. His compositions are considered avant-garde.

New Jersey born Donald Martino (1931-) is both a producing composer and a respected teacher, was chairman of the Composition Department at the New England Conservatory, 1969-80, and is now Professor of Music at Brandeis University. A very prolific composer, he won the Pulitzer Prize in 1974 for his "Notturno".

Jazz, Rock, Pop Music

In addition to their full participation in the development of classical music, Italian Americans have been involved in the composition and performance of popular music, through its various phases of jazz to today's Video Rock Music. Some leading figures in the various music fields, beginning with the early days of New Orleans, are: Nick (Dominic) La Rocca (1899-1961) born in New Orleans of Sicilian immigrants, cornettist, trumpeteer, composer and conductor, was one of the best known jazz exponents in the country between the two World Wars. He was the leader of the "Original Dixieland Band" moving from New Orleans to Chicago and eventually to New York. Some of his compositions became jazz standards.

Another jazz-leader and composer is Louis Prima (1911) born in New Orleans in a family of jazz players — his brother Leon became a well known trumpeteer, and his sister Mary Ann a pianist. At the beginning of the swing era he recorded under the title of "Lousi Prima and his New Orleans Gang". He also moved to Chicago and New York where he formed his own band and made many film appearances.

Joe (Giuseppe) Venuti (1904) came to New Orleans at age 12 and became a jazz violinist. He played in New Orleans with another famous Italian American jazz guitarrist Eddie Lang (Salvatore Massaro) (1902-1933), and the Lang-Venuti duo became famous in New Orleans in 1925. They continued playing in New York with the Paul Whiteman Orchestra. Lang died young and Venuti continued to play in big bands and then as a soloist in nightclubs and on Broadway. In 1944 he moved to Hollywood and became an MGM musician appearing in many films. He led his own band and sold thousands of records. Venuti participated in the 1968 Newport Jazz Festival, and in 1969 he was in the London Jazz "EXPO". He is still playing today and is considered the greatest jazz violinist ever.

Chuck (Charles Frank) Mangione (1940 —), nephew of Jerre Mangione, graduated from the Eastman School of Music and taught there before dedicating himself to composing jazz and pop music and playing the flugelhorn with his own quartet. His sound track album "Children of Sanchez's" won the 1979 Grammy Award for best Pop Instrumental Performance.

Chick (Armando) Corea (1914-) born in Chelsea, Massachusetts, is a composer, pianist and bandleader, who is at home with both classical and jazz music. He has cut many records and albums that have sold phenomenally well and have gained him a national reputation (*The New York Times Magazine*, June 2, 1983).

Tav Falco is the leader of the rock band *Panther Burns* which specializes in Pop Jazz music in New York.

One of the best known exponents of Pop music is Frank (Francis Vincent, Jr.) Zappa (1940 —) born in Baltimore and living in California. He is lyricist, composer, performer, record producer and actor in his own films. He founded the group *Mothers of Invention* in 1964 and they have produced and sold innummerable records and albums. With his daughter Moon Unit Zappa he wrote "Valley Girls" in 1982.

Glenn Branca has emerged recently as the most prominent composer in the field of Rock avant-garde experimentation. The three Porcaro brothers: Jeff, Mike and Steve are half of the sixman group Toto, which won five Grammy Awards in 1982. Ray Caviano is president of the disco division of Warner Brothers Records. Bob Giraldi is the director producer of Video Rock Music and Advertising Commercials. He produced the Paul McCartney-Michael Jackson video *Say Say Say* and directed Diana Ross's *Pieces of Ice*. Giraldi's *Beat It* was one of the *Top 20 Videos* chosen by *Time* magazine, December 23, 1983, as was *Love Without Anger* by Gerald V. Casale.

Band Music

Musical bands were organized by immigrants in small and large towns and held Sunday and holiday concerts in churches and halls for their celebrations, and in public squares and parks for the entire communities on special occasions and national holidays. Many Americans were introduced to Italian classical and popular music through the thousands of free concerts given by Italian bands across the country.

The tradition of Italian bands in the United States goes back to the beginning of the nineteenth century, when president Jefferson imported Italian bandsmen for a national band. In 1805 fourteen of these formed what later became the United States Marine Corps Band and, since then, most of its directors have been Italian Americans, notably Francis Scala (1819-1903), who led the band from 1855 to 1871 (Paul Joseph LeClair).

The Italian musician Felix Vivatieri (1834-1891) came to the United States in 1859, served in the Civil War and in two post-war regimental bands and later led a band in the Dakota Territory. He composed three operas and 71 pieces for wind bands or wind and string bands (James Richard Gay).

Another Italian-born musician, Leonard Falcone (1899—) came to America in 1915 and served as director of bands at Michigan State Univesity for thirty years (Myron Delford Welch).

Another immigrant musician was Achille La Guardia, Fiorello's father, who came to Greenwich Village in 1880 and shortly after, joined the U.S. Army as a bandmaster assigned to Arizona. Maestro Tommaso Venetozzi was the leader of the *Banda Bianca* of Utica, N.Y. from 1911 to 1930 (John Thomas Venetozzi). Frank J. Cipolla is currently director of university bands for the State University of New York at Buffalo.

There have also been many large commercial bands directed by Italian Americans. Here I will mention only Giuseppe Creatore (1870-1952) who was perhaps the most famous and acknowledged master of the large-bandleaders.

As representative of the many ballroom bands of recent times I mention the late Guy Lombardo (1902-1977) who, with his Royal Canadians, for 48 years, 1929-1977, broadcast and televised the New Year's Eve program from the Grill Room of the Roosevelt Hotel while millions in Times Square and many more millions at home throughout the continent heard or watched the "Ball" come down to announce the New Year.

Individual Performers

There are so many excellent instrumental and vocal performers who are so well known that here I will only mention four: Frank Sinatra (1915—), Perry Como (1912-), Tony Bennett (Anthony Dominick Benedetto) (1926-), and Vic Damone (Vito Farinola) (1928-).

THE MOVIES

After World War II Italian film makers established a world-wide supremacy which continues today. In the United States a number of Italian Americans have contributed significantly to the art of film making, beginning with director Gregory La Cava (1892-1952) who started his career as a cartoonist for *The New York World* and *The New York Sun*, then pioneered in producing animated cartoons in 1915, and in 1926 began to direct regular films, featuring W.C. Fields in his first one.

Frank Capra (1897 —) is the acknowledged master of all American film makers and producers.

Albert Broccoli (1909 —) since 1962 has produced twelve James Bond films and had produced twenty-seven other films before the Bond series. Vincente Minnelli (1910-) has had a brilliant career as theater and stage director and producer before producing his first of many brilliant films in 1943.

The current Italian American film directors are in the news daily and here I list chronologically six that come to mind first: Alan Alda 1936-; Francis Ford Coppola 1939-; Brian De Palma 1940-; Martin Scorcese 1942-; Michael Cimino 1943-; Sylvester Stallone 1946-. I have not mentioned any of their films because they are so well known to you.

There are many outstanding Italian American performers and actors in both the film and the stage, but for brevity's sake I will mention only Robert De Niro, Al Pacino, Frank Langella, Anne Bancroft (Italiano), Liza Minnelli and Kay Ballard (Catherine Gloria Balotta).

ART

As in the field of Music, the Italian American experience in art begins with the early 1800s when President Thomas Jefferson imported a number of Italian artists to decorate the Capitol in Washington. The most famous of these Italian artists who worked in the Capitol was the Fresco painter Costantino Brumidi (1805-1880) who became known as "the Michelangelo of the U.S. Capitol". A brief history of "The Art of the Italian Artists in the United States Capitol" was written by Charles E. Fairman, curator of art of the Capitol, and inserted in the *Congressional Record* in 1930 by Fiorello La Guardia, then Congressman from New York, who stated in his introduction that "its publication is warranted for the purpose of preservation of these facts of history never before published and constituting an important addition to the history of the United States Capitol" (*Congressional Record-House*, January 29, 1930 p. 2630 and January 18, 1925, pp. 2606,2608). To discuss adequately the Italian American experience in art in the twentieth century we would need an entire conference devoted to it. Here I must limit myself to the mentioning of only a very few names in each field of art:

Architecture: Pietro Belluschi (1899 —) is one of America's most respected architects. He designed the Juilliard School of Music at the Lincoln Center and has been Dean of Architecture at the Massachusetts Institute of Technology 1951-1965.

Robert Venturi was born in Philadelphia in 1925 and heads his architectural firm there. He is a theorist as well as a builder and his book of 1966 *Complexity and Contradiction in Architecture* has greatly influenced contemporary architecture.

Architect and city planner Paolo Soleri (1919-) has been building *Arcosanti* in Arizona, a community for 5,000 people as well as other buildings in Arizona and New Mexico.

Sculpture: Mark di Suvero (1938—) is the best known of contemporary sculptors. In 1975-76 the Whitney Museum with the City of New York held a show of sixty-five works of Mr. di Suvero. Ranging from table tops to steel structures five stories high, to be viewed inside the museum and scattered in the parks and streets of New York.

Italo Scanga (1932—) came to the United States in 1947 and has acquired a national reputation teaching in a number of universities from the University of Wisconsin to the University of California and has exhibited his sculpture in twenty-five one-man shows.

Frank Gasparro (1909—) retired in 1981 from the United States Mint in his native Philadelphia where he had been chief sculptor-engraver and has designed many coins and medals including the official bicentennial medal and the Mint's presidential medals from Johnson to Carter.

Another sculptor-engraver is Caesar Rufo, a medalist who served more than eleven years as senior sculptor at the Franklin Mint. He designed the Metropolitan Opera's Centennial Medallion.

Painting: It is appropriate to recall Joseph Stella (1879-1946) this centennial year of the Brooklyn Bridge because he painted six versions of its view. Stella participated in the famous Armory Show of 1913 in New York and painted his famous *Battle of Lights, Coney Island.* For two decades Stella was an acknowledged leader among the progressive painters in the United States (*See*, John I.H. Baur).

O. Louis Guglielmi (1906-1956) was born in Egypt of Italian parents and came to America in 1914 with his family, settling in Italian East Harlem. The poverty he saw and experienced is reflected in his surrealist paintings which hang in many American museums. In 1980 the Rutgers University Art Gallery held a retrospective exhibition of his paintings which traveled to Brown University, SUNY Albany and the Whitney Museum (John Baker).

Gregorio Prestopino (1907-1984) was born in New York City and studied at the National Academy of Design. After suffering through the Great

Depression he became successful painter whose canvases hang in the Whitney and Hirshorn museums and others. He has been living in the art colony of Roosevelt, New Jersey for a long time.

Ralph Fasanella (1914-) born in New York City, became a labor organizer in the thirties and forties and began painting on his own without any formal training. To devote more time to his painting, he left his union job and opened a gas station to survive. His paintings represent the workers and working conditions as he knew them. He recently spent three years studying, on location, the textile strike of Lawrence, Massachusetts, called the "Bread and Roses Strike" (1912). He painted twelve large scenes depicting the strike, the buildings, the crowds and the suffering.

Frank Stella (1936—) today, is a classic. In 1970, when only 33, he became the youngest painter ever to be given a retrospective by New York City's Museum of Modern Art. In 1983 he was chosen by Harvard University to deliver the six celebrated Charles Eliot Norton lectures. He was born in Malden, Massachusetts, son of a medical doctor of Sicilian descendence. (There is no relationship between Frank Stella and Joseph Stella who came from Muro Lucano, Lucania.)

At this point I will call your attention to the many Italian Americans who, in their daily work have added to the enrichment of life in America. Representative of all folk artists is Simon Rodia (1873-1965). He spent years building, in his front yard in the Watts section of Los Angeles, three towers 99, 97, and 55 feet tall. These towers which were covered with a mosaic of broken glass, shells, pieces of pottery and bottles, were recently declared "a monument to be protected" by the Los Angeles Cultural Heritage Commission (*Smithsonian*, August 1983).

Stage and Scenic Design: Beni Montresor is one of the very best stage designers. He has designed more than thirty operas for the Metropolitan Opera, the New York City Opera, the Festival of Two Worlds and other opera houses. A retrospective show of his designs during his first twenty years of work was held in 1981 at the Lincoln Center Library for the Performing Arts.

Cartoonists: Gregory LaCava (1892-1952), the movie director, began his career as a cartoonist for *The New York World* before World War I. Currently John Fischetti (1916-) is a Pulitzer Prize winning political cartoonist with the *Chicago Daily News*; Vic Cantone (1933-) has been editorial cartoonist for the *New York Daily News* since 1959, and since 1980 he is a syndicated political cartoonist and caricaturist and winner of many awards: Charles Barsotti is cartoonist for the *New Yorker*; Carlo Rambaldi is the creator of E.T. and many other film characters.

Fantastic Art: The most popular fantasy artist of our time is Frank Frazzetta (1928—). Comic book and comic strip artist, he created the *Buck Rogers* series. Frazzetta worked on *L'il Abner* before dedicating himself completely to painting fantastic art. His albums have sold hundreds of thousands of copies.

PATRONS OF THE ARTS:

In conclusion I would like to tell you that Italian Americans not only have produced writers and artists that enrich America's cultural patrimony with their works but we are now producing art patrons, like Florence had during the Renaissance.

Four examples are: Daniel James Terra (1911-) a Philadelphia-born chemist, president and chairman of the board of the company he founded, Lawter Chemicals in Chicago. In 1982 he purchased, for $3.25 million, Samuel Morse's 1832 painting *The Gallery of the Louvre* to place in his Terra Museum of American Art in Evanston, Illinois. Since 1981 Dr. Terra has been, by appointment of President Reagan, Ambassador-at-Large for Cultural Affairs, Department of State.

On October 22, 1983, the College of William and Mary in Virginia opened the Joseph and Margaret Muscarelle Museum of Art, built with money donated by Joseph Muscarelle, an alumnus of the college in the class of 1927.

Arthur Julius Decio (1930-) has donated, this year, $6.2 million to the University of Notre Dame in Indiana for the construction of a faculty office building which will house 250 College of Arts and Letters professors and the University's Helen Kellogg Institute for International Studies. Mr. Decio is president, chairman of the board and executive officer of Skyline Corporation of Elkhart, Illinois since 1959.

George Thomas DeLacorte (1894—) chairman of the board of Dell Publishing Co., Dell Books, Laurel Books, DeLacorte Press, and twenty-five magazines. He is the largest comic book publisher in the United States, owning at various times, over 200 magazines. He donated to New York City the DeLacorte Theater, which shows free Shakespeare plays in Central Park.

In closing I apologize for the length of this paper and more so for its sketchiness. The length was necessary to prove Stephen Hall's statement that "the influence of Italian Americans pervades the nation's culture on an almost daily basis". But the cultural achievements of the Italian Americans are so extensive that I could only present to you a sketchy outline at this time and hope that a future Conference will be devoted entirely to the important subject of ITALIAN AMERICAN CULTURE.

18

The Italian American Periodical Press, 1836-1980

Pietro Russo
University of Florence

The beginnings of the Italian American periodical press date to 1836, when an exile of the *Risorgimento*, Marquis Orazio De Attellis of Sant'Angelo resumed publication in New Orleans of a Spanish language newspaper entitled *El Correo Atlantico*, which he had initated the year before in Mexico with a section in Italian. Writings of Italian residents and passages in Italian had appeared earlier in periodicals printed in the United States, but they had been sporadic cases of outside collaboration with the journals of immigrants of other nationalities, or pages of the classics quoted in their original language.

Over 150 years about 2,500 titles have existed which — completely or in a substantial part — concern Italy and the experience of her emigrants in the United States. In this long span of its history, Italian American journalism has passed through various stages, which can be grouped into three principal periods: 1) from the beginning to 1880; 2) from 1880 to mid-twentieth century; and 3) from mid-twentieth century to the present.

FROM THE BEGINNING TO 1880

In 1849, the first newspapers printed entirely in Italian were founded: *L'Europeo Americano, L'Esule Italiano* and *L'Eco d'Italia*.

The first newspaper rapidly ceased printing, leaving only a few copies and scanty evidence. The last and certainly the most important paper up to the 1880s is even very useful as a source of information about the other Italian American periodicals, either because it announced the publication of its *confratelli* (fellow papers) or because it drew attention to the presence of Italian members of the editorial staffs of bilingual periodicals or those written in other languages. The director himself, Secchi De Casali, cooperated with

American journals and newspapers, which usually followed the Italian movement for independence and the work of Italian exiles in the United States while showing solidarity.

News of these newspapers reached Europe immediately.[1] In Italy they were quickly drawn to the attention of the public, because they were considered an integral part of the *stampa nazionale* (national press), centers of industriousness for the benefit of the new Italy. There was also the intention to break the *cospirazione del silenzio*, by which the leading classes attempted to blot out the memory of Italian immigrants by ignoring their newspapers, in so far as they were word and tool of the people recreating their history. From then until the 1870s the Italian American press — even if small in number and circulation — acquired continuity, improved its quality, and was no longer limited to one city. It was an important instrument of information for the Italians in America, a link with their fellow-countrymen in Italy and elsewhere and a means of integration in the country of adoption. Today the Italian American press is the most precious source for the study of the Italian American experience in that period.

In the last quarter of the nineteenth century, the formation of Little Italies as a result of the intensification of the inflow of immigrants from the Italian Peninsula and the favorable conditions for the prospering of journalism created the premises for the development of the Italian American press, not only as a private initiative, but also as an organism of social importance. The Centennial celebration of the Declaration of Independence and the Exposition at Philadelphia in 1876 were the occasion to make the Italian American journalists appear as protagonists of various roles: spokesmen for their community, intermediaries with the authorities and the Italian agencies, interpreters of America for the immigrants, and correspondents for Italian newspapers.

FROM 1880 TO MID TWENTIETH CENTURY

The year 1880 can be indicated as a milestone in the progress of Italian American journalism. The initiative to found a daily paper in Italian had lasting success for the first time with *Il Progresso Italo-Americano* of New York, which, indeed, became the most important in the community and the most long-lived among those in a foreign language in the country. In the period which goes roughly from 1900 to World War II, the Italian American press reached the height of its expansion, both for number and variety of publications, as well as for diffusion and circulation. It made itself known as the pre-eminent sector of the Italian press abroad and found a place in the

[1] Mazzini, G., *Scritti editi ed inediti*, XLIV (Epistolario XXIII), letter MMCMXCV (Geneve Oct. 26, 1850); *ibid.*, letter MMCMXLIII (Geneve Sept. 21, 1850). Cironi P., *La stampa nazionale italiana 1828-1860*, Prato 1862 (repr. 1980).

foreground of the press of all immigrants in the United States. In particular during the first twenty years of the century countless periodicals of every kind and frequency were founded or continued to live. Some were very influential and prestigious. They played remarkable political and cultural roles of social and economic promotion, of conservation of traditions, of the strengthening of ties with Italy, and of the integration of immigrants into American society. Above all, they were an interesting expression of an Italian American reality now mature and echoed the original and creative commitment, with which Italian Americans sought to make the most of their experience, counting almost exclusively on their own forces. Even from a financial point of view, the Italian American press became a considerable phenomenon, both as a whole, and in specific cases — as, for example, *L'Opinione* of Philadelphia — in which the heading represented a sound investment.

During the last decade of the nineteenth century, major attention was given in the United States to the Italian American press, not so much for its intrinsic importance, but rather because it was part of the foreign language press, which was then assuming vast proportions, and was a manifestation of the "new immigration". The headings and the principal data were registered in directories, which also offered indications about circulation, advertising and political learning. Evidently these newspapers were even a good deal and were anything but extraneous to American life, as it is clear from their very pages.

The pretty satisfactory *modus vivendi* that had been established between the Italian press and the American public opinion, broke down in the 1890s. The xenophobic positions — which with highs and lows had always been present in America — took the upper hand and concentrated on the recent immigrants, in particular on the Italians. Their press was accused of obstructing the process of assimilation, of being miseducating and corrupted. The negative opinions became still more frequent and harsh in the early 1900s, because of the preoccupying dimensions that the press was reaching and in particular of the weight of the revolutionary press.

Positive evaluations were also emerging. Private managers and then some institutions — as for example the International Institutes — considered it a necessary go-between to establish relations with the immigrants, to better fit them into the company, to accelerate the process of Americanization. The editors of foreign language papers gave birth to an association and to their own gazzette;[2] in addition, they could count on the support of American organizations of which they were part — such as unions and political parties—overcoming the barriers which had kept the immigrant workers separated from one another and from the native born.

The hyphenated press lived one of its most difficult moments during

[2] American Association of Foreign Language Newspapers: "The American Leader", New York 1912-1918.

World War I, when the reaction of political authorities and of public opinion was unleashed against the unpatriotic and revolutionary press. Unlike that in the German language, and with the exception of that of the left wing, the Italian American press was favored by the fact that Italy was an ally of the United States. Altogether, the opinions regarding it remained anything else but flattering, even from Italian Americans, as well as from some journalists.

Until the end of the nineteenth century, only *vaga notizia* of Italian journalism abroad reached Italy.[3] Some scholars under the care of government offices, however, began to take note of it in appendices to repertories of Italian periodicals.[4] The embitterment of the phenomenon of emigration after 1870 had *divenuto argomento quotidiano di conversazione per gli uomini di stato, e soggetto di ardenti polemiche per il giornalismo*.[5] However, the interest in the Italian American press did not develop before the beginning of the twentieth century, when emigration began to be considered even from the side of the country of destination and in its manifestations abroad, among which were precisely the Italian American newspapers.

In 1906, at the Exposition of Milan, an autonomous committee organized an Exhibit of Italians abroad, in which 60 newspapers were displayed. Among the various publications appearing on that occasion or suggested by it, the most notable is certainly that of Fumagalli. Not only does it offer an exhaustive summary outline of the Italian press abroad, with precise data of headings, many first hand, but even now remains one of the few — and doubtlessly the most fundamental and exemplary — up to our days.[6]

On the other hand, as we have seen, on non-official and popular levels, from mid nineteenth century there were latent threads that carried the echo of its newspapers abroad back to the Italian Peninsula. Magazines with a wide circulation often made use of these publications — especially *L'Eco d'Italia* — and of the correspondences of their editors, whether to give news of curiosities and facts of news items in America, or for services on happenings of importance. This flux of information came to side with that which was reaching Italy from European countries — first France and England then, following the Triple Alliance, from Germany and Austria. In turn the Italian American newspapers used those in Italy and in other countries (they often had a wide range of them at their disposition) to keep the emigrants updated on facts and trifling matters of the mother country.

[3] Buonvino O., *Il giornalismo contemporaneo*, Milano 1906.

[4] Bernardini N., *Guida della stampa periodica italiana*, Lecce 1890, Pp. 721-739; *Ministero di Agricoltura industria e commercio, Direzione generale della statistica, Statistica della stampa periodica*, Roma 1881; *Annuario statistico italiano per l'anno 1881; Annali di statistica*, VIII (1883).

[5] Carpi L., *Statistica della emigrazione all'estero...*, Roma 1878, Pp. 7-8.

[6] Fumagalli G., *La stampa periodica italiana all'estero*, Milano 1909.

On the waves of migrants many things from America were transported and diffused in Italy, from savings to myths; and vice versa. This is a field of investigation — until now generally neglected by academic scholars — which opens interesting perspectives for reinterpreting the relations between Italy and the United States; to understand more completely how a public opinion of America was formed and why it has been scarcely damaged by twenty years of anti-American propaganda; to show the impact that emigration had from abroad on contemporary Italy. The attitude of Americans toward Italy however, came to depend mostly on the presence of its emigrants and on the image that they gave of it.

The 1920s seemed to herald the disappearance of the foreign language press in the United States. In fact, there was a period of crisis in 1929, which hit even the Italian American press. This was caused particularly by the political repression following World War I, the restrictive immigration laws and the Americanization movement of the immigrants. Various factors however contributed to re-launching the vitality of the Italian American periodicals, which prospered for yet another quarter of a century, adapting to the changing requirements (for example, by using the English language to attract the second generation) and adjusting to the new situation in which they worked (for example, by dedicating more space to American issues and to the internal facts of their community). Many of them could even count on the contribution of services from American agencies responsible for the immigrants' press — such as the Foreign Language Information Service — and on that, even financial — of various Italian and Italian American organizations. World War I had made, felt more than ever, the daily presence of specific organs of information for Italians in every zone of the United States. In addition, institutions, organizations and groups of different leanings—syndicalists, socialists, anarchists, Catholics, nationalists and prominent leaders — felt the need to have at their disposal independent instruments in defense of their own political, economic, social, cultural and religious interests.

Various motivations backed the press, such as coping with discriminations, established powers, and competition from other ethnic groups. Italian periodicals were revitalized to maintain their own identity and to enlarge their sphere of influence; to be of greater importance in American political parties; and to carry out an original role even with regard to Italy. With the exception of daily newspapers and a few others, however, the periodicals rarely succeeded in being very successful among the general public. Even in sectors nearer to them, they were not popular because of ideological or other motives. More than a professional and suitable answer to an effective request by potential readers, they were often emissions from centers of power, of organisms or individuals essentially not connected with the Italian American public opinion or, at least, with the real life both of the first and the second generation. Even more so, they were not connected with the culture and daily problems of the rest of the population. In a considerable number they were tentatives of social self-promotion, or even of earning a living, on the part of persons who did not have any experience in journalism, of scarce and outdated culture, incompetent and, in some cases, to say the least, of doubtful morality. Still, there was ample space to occupy and for several decades great and small, good and mediocre editors could reap the rewards — both those who were searching for personal gratification, and those who were animated by ideal outbursts, as well as those who were only interested in what they could get out of it.

Journalism was one of the few fields — the most fertile, or perhaps the easiest — for persons of lower or middle class origins, who had come from Italy firmly determined to raise their social status, but who did not know or did not wish to follow the hard life that the work market offered. Analogously the press was the means to which those who wished to continue or begin a revolutionary action or renewal had to resort, barred in their native land by the persecutions or the rigidities of the social structures. In America there were concrete opportunities of initiative and success within the reach of everybody, particularly in this field, which was neglected by American newspapers. For more than two decades, Fascism and anti-Fascism were determining elements in the launching of renewed editorial undertakings, by reviving the debate, confrontation, or collaboration, between Italian Americans and the others. During the 1920s and even longer afterwards, many periodicals had scholars and journalists as directors and collaborators, in greater number and proportion than their predecessors and in a way that would not be possible after the war until recent times.

During this period the foreign language press steadily passed from behind the scenes into the public eye. It could no longer be considered merely a foreign product of importation temporarily present in the country. Whether or not it was destined to disappear in the future, it could not be ignored; rather it had to be taken care of with zeal and comprehension: it was no longer a foreign body, and it was there to stay. As already populated with a variety of ethnic groups and considering the contrasting tendencies to the right and to the left together with an emerging isolationist mood, the United States had to impede these periodicals immediately from becoming the tools of foreign nations, and insure instead that they become Americanized and hence Americanize their readers. The problem was real, but was focused within an historical vision of the problem of immigration and in a strategy that regarded especially the second generation of the "new" immigration. Besides political and ideological motives, there were also economic interests: the immigrants' communities represented a not negligible market, but one largely monopolized by its own members and by foreign concerns. The moment had come for Americans to make it their business also. The immigrants, on the other hand, had not carried only illnesses to cure. In half a century America had been transformed in an extraordinary manner. One had only to pass through 40 blocks of her larger cities to go "round the world" and to realize that there was something new in history. One felt the need to bite into the press, which was the expression of it, and to utilize it to broadening national life and culture, in a mutual giving and taking of contributions between natives and foreign born, recognizing the duplicate function "to interpret the immigrant to America and America to the immigrant". This recognition was not only formal. The immigrants' press was constantly collected and analyzed with the aid of reliable editors to know, if anything else, what was boiling in the melting pot. Consequently, the archives and the publications of the Foreign Language Information Service and of the agencies which carried out the work on it are extremely valuable. Also, the printed and handwritten materials of the Works Progress Administration, Federal Writers Project, which are the result of direct investigations, are very important. Some treat the press especially, others treat it only in part.

References, information and comments on Italian American newspapers can be found in numerous works of various kinds and subjects appearing between the two World Wars: bibliographic indexes, civic guides, studies on journalism, on local history, on churches, memoirs, biographies, etc. The hunt is tiring and often frustrating, because it is necessary to consult thousands of volumes, many of which are quite rare. On the other hand, this is the only way to trace data and indications of headings not given in specific repertories, as for example single numbers and small local papers that ceased shortly after their foundation. It must be noted that rarely had authors seen the periodicals directly; therefore, they give information which is not very reliable and requires further investigation.

As always, Italian American periodicals are the most important sources, especially because they report news of other periodicals in the same city or category. Since there were often controversies among them, they mutually shed light on each other, although of a menacing type. The Italian American documentation deals for the most part with facts and people of the time. Already in the period under examination, the Italian American press was beginning to look at the Italian American experience from an historical point of view, considering it an aspect of modern Italian civilization and of the progress of the New World. Some — first among them Giovanni Schiavo — devoted themselves to a keen pioneering work of research of data and collection of documents, thus bringing to light even headings of which the traces had been lost, as in the case of the first ones.

During the Fascist period the Italian American press came under the spotlight of the Italian government as it had never been in the past and as it would never be afterward. Already at the beginning of the regime, the *Commissariato Generale dell'Emigrazione* started a census of the Italian press abroad, publishing various lists which were incomplete and not always precise. The aim was to make use of the press of the emigrants as a resonance box and instrument of penetration for the Fascist politics abroad. This objective was reached easily — and with results quite superior to the profuse diligence on the part of the Fascist government. It met with the interests of the majority of Italian American journalists and corresponded to their way of thinking. On the relations between Fascism and Italian Americans various studies have already been published. It is a field that merits other works that could shed light on new aspects of the relations between nationalism and Fascism, and perhaps on the very origins of Fascism. The emigrants' press and their archive papers, in fact, contain an interesting documentation not only on the favorable reactions that Fascism had in America, but exactly on the relations and on the cooperation that was — at least at the beginning — enthusiastically offered on the part of Italian Americans. A notable example of this cooperation is Agostino De Biasi, who deluded himself that the Fascist revolution was truly a revolution, and that the Italians abroad would have had a role as protagonists in making it universal. Helpful materials on Italian American journalism can be found in the State Archives; the publications appearing in Italy during the regime, however, are less useful than one would expect, considering the close ties that the editors had with Italy.

Just as precious, for another reason, are the periodicals and manuscripts of the Italian American anti-Fascists. These periodicals shed some light on the relations of Italian American anti-Fascists with the Italians who were political exiles in Europe. While it would seem that who was in Italy around 1920 was not very interested in the collaboration offered by comrades in America, during the 1930s and 1940s the anti-Fascists in the United States played an important role in joining and supporting together, those who had been exiled in other countries.

The declaration of war by Italy to the United States in 1941 imposed a political change upon the newspapers which had been pro-Fascist, but in general did not bring about an immediate crisis for the Italian American press. However, it made a change of tactics inevitable. For many, having broken off with the others, the time had come to change the subject and even the content, to review their position and to commit themselves to re-evaluate their presence in America. On the other hand, the war — above all after the Armistice of 1943 — was the long awaited occasion of the anti-Fascists to become the representatives of the community and its spokesmen with regard to the Administration, assuming an influential and prestigious role in liberated Italy. For Italian Americans — except that is, but not always, the Italian exiles who lived in the United States, awaiting to return home — the future of the mother country was an aspect of the clash between personalities and power groups to maintain or change the existing situation, and plan for their future. As always the internal polemics prevailed over the other problems and were an essential motivation of their press, which was followed with greater attention by American and Italian authorities.

FROM THE MID-TWENTIETH CENTURY TO THE PRESENT

The conditions which had previously made Italian American journalism valid did not lose ground in the post-war period. The Little Italies were again a reality. Considering the scarce coverage in American newspapers, the request for news which directly concerned them remained high. As a matter of fact, the problems of the political, economic, social and institutional reconstruction of Italy further confirmed the function of the newspapers for the immigrants and their descendents during the 1940s.

The resumption, however limited, of immigration renewed the possibilities of success for new titles, and slowed down, but did not impede, the decline of Italian American journalism during the 1950s. MacCarthyism made the difficulties worse, emarginating for good what remained of the left, accentuating in it the moderate tendencies and recreating a terrain favorable for conservative and reactionary publications. The renewal of relations between Italy and the United States, on the other hand, re-established contacts and exchanges between the editors and their Italian contributors. The crisis became evident in the 1960s. With the disappearance of the old generations, the rapid reduction of the number of readers of newspapers in Italian was not compensated by the more diffuse use of the English language. The publications were hardly able to survive because they did not answer the needs of the second and third generations, who at the same time did not care about launching new titles. Once again the death knells sounded for the Italian American periodical press. Indeed, within a span of a few years almost all the headings disappeared or were forced to merge; nor did a better fate await the new ones. The years when the sun seemed to be setting on the Italian American press, were also those in which arose new initiatives of various kinds regarding it and, with the birth of numerous publications with different characteristics, it seemed to be born to a new life.

A symptom and stimulus of the renewal was the flourishing of associations, largely a product of the second generation. Italian associations had already existed from the middle of the last century by the thousands, of every type and wherever a group of immigrants settled. Although usually consisting of a few dozen members and lacking cultural interest, they were an important support for the life and diffusion of many periodicals. Many publications which are still alive or begun in the last twenty years, are organs of societies, for the greater part bulletins and newsletters. Particularly significant are those edited by university institutions and other cultural centers, which sought to re-evaluate the Italian American experience — both past and present.

There are numerous aspects and results to be noted, whether directly relevant to the publications, or to the work of the centers. Among the organizations that chiefly have contributed to the gathering and to the study of the Italian American press, the foremost are the American Italian Historical Association, the Center for Migration Studies of N.Y., and the Immigration History Research Center of the University of Minnesota at St. Paul. They are well known to those interested in immigration. In addition to their publications, they must be remembered as well for the promotional work they have been carrying out since the 1960s.

Today a more emphasized tendency toward specialization is noticeable. Many periodicals limit their interests to a determined sector — cultural, geographical or of other kinds. Consequently, editors and contributors are competent in the field — by learning or by personal experience. Even bulletins without pretensions can offer quite useful contributions for the understanding of the Italian American experience. Today as before, the Italian American press is an occasion and a stimulus to study, to write, to make known what has been found to be interesting in life.

The existing interrelationship between the scholarly world and the rest of the Italian American community is one of the most vital aspects of one part of the contemporary Italian American periodical press. Among the contributors to the periodicals — as among the members of the associations which support them — there are at the same time university faculty members, self-taught persons and uneducated persons, managers and clerical workers, together with pensioners. From this bridging of social groupings and from the union of learning and experience is derived the original character of numerous publications. In other cases the periodicals serve more as documents of an actual situation than for the analysis of facts.

If on one hand the Italian American press is today still a product of its communities, animated by a lively ethnic conscience and by the will to affirm its own identity, on the other hand it is also more closely connected than before with the rest of society in America. Institutions and scholars who are not of Italian origin consider it an integral part of the country and of its culture, even if there are positions remaining which echo the discriminating interpretations of the past.

Similarly, Italian American relations with centers and scholars of other nationalities have become closer and more cooperative. This is due to the intertwining of relations with those of other foreign countries and because the parallel paths on which ethnic groups move in search of the past or of the prospective future, often intersect and have many points in common.

The exchange of experiences and the cooperation among editorial offices of different periodicals as well as scholars and correspondents — is one of the latest trends with positive consequences. This stimulus to converge and consult came from practical and urgent motives, including the opportunity to seize the moment and remain current with other ethnic groups, and the necessity of making their own action more efficient by including it in a common organization. Furthermore, such a cooperation was made possible because of the overcoming or, at least, the weakening of ideological, political, religious, and regional contrasts. In particular, it was due to the fact that Italian Americans no longer felt the effects of the consequences of what was happening in Italy, as before World War II. Also, ideologies counted less in stating the terms of their problems.

As the Italian American community is composed almost entirely of American born, so the periodicals are mainly in English and the topics refer above all to the Italian American experience itself. For the majority of the second and third generations, the country of origin is no longer connected with their daily life and remote enough from their culture that they know little or nothing about it — not even the language: somewhat as the Latin world is for modern Italians.

In another way a series of circumstances has favored the development of interests, acquaintances and relations with Italy, and *vice versa*. All this is reflected in the press in various forms, such as the cooperation with Italian newspapers (for example, the recent change of hands of *Il Progresso Italo-Americano*).

By studying their own past from their point of view, moreover, Italian Americans focused on Italian culture and events which are closely connected with their experience and tradition: emigration seen from the popular level more than from the level of "official Italy", and from where they stood in the American system.

For a series of circumstances, the rebirth of studies in the United States corresponds to analogous initiatives in Italy, where after World War II there was a rediscovery of America and of the Italian American press. This expression would seem less strange if we consider, on one side, the gushing desire to know the new world after twenty years of Fascist dictatorship and the happenings of the war; and on another, the fact that Italian libraries had never provided for acquiring the emigrants' periodicals and possessed very little documentation on American history; and on yet another, that for the Italian academic spheres, America — particularly the Italian American experience — was almost *terra incognita*.

Almost a decade had to pass before notice was taken of the Italian press abroad. In starting the research there was a notable convergence on the part of scholars of the two countries, and it is significant that geographers (Joseph Velikonja in the U.S. and Giuseppe Barbieri in Italy) had parallel interests and contacts before historians did (Rudolph Vecoli and the author of this presentation and the Scalabrinian fathers, Silvano and Lydio Tomasi and Gianfausto Rosoli).

The founding in 1964 of the Istituto di Studi Americani in Florence was the starting point for the research and the collecting of the Italian American press. This was the principal basis which helped to develop other studies and establish a positive collaboration that had, as its first manifestation, the symposium on "Gli Italiani negli Stati Uniti" organized in Florence in 1969. Unfortunately the projects which were then launched were not so successful in Italy as those in America. As a consequence of the policy change of the Biblioteca Americana of Florence, its Italian American press collection became, if not precisely a ghost town, something resembling a museum. Even other initiatives undertaken by Italian American and Italian government organs during the 1970s (such as the World Congresses of the Italian press abroad) also fell through. This renewal of tentatives is however an indication of the modernity of the topic. In order to achieve the hoped for results, it is necessary to have both a solid cooperation between Italian Americans and Italians, as well as a renewal of methods and a re-examination of the very concept of the Italian American press.

PRESERVATION OF THE ITALIAN AMERICAN PRESS

It is not the task of this presentation to draw an outline for the revival of the Italian American press, even if we can not remain indifferent to its destiny. There is another problem, however, about which the scholars of the Italian American experience have the right and the duty to call to the attention of those who have the responsibility and the power to intervene. The Italian American press is a valuable cultural patrimony (not only for Italian Americans) which must be saved. This requires a long-range operation, coordinated and with adequate means to:

1) trace the periodicals still in the possession of private citizens and have them deposited in libraries which are able to guarantee their preservations;

2) proceed at the same time to the microfilming of materials of which the existence is known, beginning with those which are in poor condition;

3) integrate the series of periodicals in such a way as to form collections as complete as possible and place them at the disposition of researchers for a relaunching of the studies.

An analogous plan was already formulated almost twenty years ago, when those interested in such matters seemed pioneers. In America these initiatives have already become numerous and organized, and have given life to a flourishing production. Hopefully, as an Italian American journalist feared, this path will not be marked only by crosses.

19

Comments on the Paper by Robert Viscusi "Circles of the Cyclopse: Schemes of Recognition in Italian American Discourse"

JERRE MANGIONE
Director, Italian Study Center
University of Pennsylvannia

THE brilliancy of Dr. Viscusi's paper tends to blind us to what I assume is its basic tenet: the vagaries of communication when short-circuited by human insularity, particularly in its application to the Italian American immigrants.

As a full-blooded Sicilian (born in Rochester, N.Y.), at first I found it somewhat disquieting, though fascinating, that Dr. Viscusi, whose astuteness as a literary critic cannot be disputed, chose as his principal and most negative metaphor those one-eyed Sicilians of prehistoric Sicily—Homer's Cyclops. But, despite the unflattering implication that those creatures might be counted among my antecedents, I soon realized that there is nothing wrong with his choice of metaphor, for who can deny that Cyclopean minds of limited vision have always transcended geographical boundaries, and continue to be omnipresent? Witness, for example, the "heteroglossolalian" logic and lingo in the rhetoric of the superpowers as they threaten to transform the world into a vast crematorium.

The Italian immigrants were certainly made aware of Cyclopean mentality on their arrival in the early decades of the century. Despite the welcoming words on the base of the Statue of Liberty, they were made to feel like intruders. Their dialects, understandable only to some of their *paesani*, as well as their physical features, immediately set them apart from the rest of society and made them targets of derision. Sensing the hostility of the host society, they huddled together for mutual protection in crowded enclaves which the Americans misnamed "Little Italy" ("Little Sicily", "Little Naples", "Little Calabria", *etc.* would have been more precise), away from the strangers who could not speak their language, away from their curious customs and habits, away from their anger.

The meaning of such words as "wop", "dago", and "guinea" was beyond their comprehension, but their perjorative intent was unmistakable to the immigrants. They were not surprised; they had already been forewarned by their *paesani* immigrants who preceded them. The first supposedly American word many of my relatives learned even before they landed in the United States was *ghirarahir*, meaning "get out of here". The immigrants were advised to shout this word at any stranger in America who approached them, for it was emphasized that if a Sicilian should be identified as a *greenhorno*, some American would surely try to rob him of his money and belongings.

Although the immigrants suspected all Americans (anyone who was not Italian was considered an *Americano*, particularly if he spoke no foreign language) of extraordinary shrewdness and dishonesty, they often preceded the word *Americano* with the Italian word *fesso*, meaning stupid and naive. The more contemptuous immigrants referred to them as *Merdicani*. But the phrase heard most commonly in Italian immigrant families, almost as commonly as *Porca miseria*, was *Mannagia La Merica*—rather mild expletive (akin to "Damn America") which was used indiscriminately in response to a wide variety of annoyances and disappointments.

We need not go so far back as Homer for symbolic situations that engender hostile and misunderstood communication among peoples who feel threatened by newcomers. We have only to examine the history of American immigrants. With the exception of the earliest American settlers, who received a friendly enough welcome from the primitive Indians, every succeeding immigrant group was pelted with Cyclopean insults and assults by the immigrants who preceded them. The Irish suffered badly in the hands of the Yankee settlers; the Germans were denigrated and attacked by the Yankees and the Irish. Then all three of these groups vented their bigotry and hatred on the immigrants from eastern and southern Europe, especially the Jews and Italians. Alas, the process continues with Italian Americans expressing low opinions of Puerto Ricans and Hispanics. And now the Asians are under general attack. Yes, Dr. Viscusi's metaphor of Homer's one-eyed Cyclops is quite apt, and it suggests a perverse version of the American success story: the evolution of its immigrant groups into positions of social superiority that provide them with the perogative to deride the most recent immigrant groups.

Dr. Viscusi illustrated some of his points with references to several books about the Italian American experience, among them Forgione's *The River*

Between, Lou D'Angelo's *What the Ancients Said*, Pietro DiDonato's *Christ in Concrete*, and my own book, *Mount Allegro*. I should like to take this opportunity to lament the apparently general indifference to many other literary works that are important to an understanding of the Italian American experience which have been virtually forgotten, and are difficult to find. Especially valuable are those written by the offspring of immigrants during the thirties and forties. The writers that quickly come to mind are Garibaldi Marto Lapolla, the author of several novels, the best of which is *The Grand Gennaro;* John Fante, who died only a few months ago, two of whose works deserve to be read as long as there is any interest in the saga of Italian Americans: *Dago Red*, a collection of short stories which includes his classic commentary on the problem of the search for identification, "The Odyssey of a Wop", and his finest novel, *Wait Until Spring, Bandini;* Jo Pagano's *Golden Anniversary;* Mary Tomasi's *Like Lesser Gods;* Guido D'Agostini's *Apples on the Olive Tree;* Michael DiCapite's *Maria*, the first of a cycle that was interrupted by his death. Pietro DiDonato's *Christ in Concrete* and *Mount Allegro* belong in this group; as do Rocco Fumento's *The Tree of Dark Reflection*, and Mario Puzo's best work, *The Fortunate Pilgrim*, even though Fumento and Puzo belong to a more recent generation.

All these writers experienced the cultural shock of being caught between the world of their immigrant parents and the American world into which they were born—a shock which impelled them to record their observations, conflicts, and dreams with all the truth and poetry at their command. Collectively, their books project the unique experience of the Italian Americans during a time when they were trying to come to grips to the foreign world around them. Yet as indispensable as the books are to teachers and students of the Italian American saga, all but three of them (*Mount Allegro, Christ in Concrete*, and *The Fortunate Pilgrim*) have long been out of print and are known to relatively few scholars.

Several of the previous speakers have implied that the nation abounds with affluent Italian Americans. We all know that some of them are leaders in Italian American organizations that profess a concern about the culture and the image of their people. Yet, as far as I know, nothing is being done to resurrect such books as I have mentioned, nor to promote a strong enough constituency of Italian American readers that will change the negative attitude most publishers have toward the saleability of good books dealing with the Italian American experience. This is not, of course, the only cause in the field of Italian American culture that cries for support and assistance from individuals and organizations that are in a position to provide it. I find it shocking, for example, that in no American university is there an endowed chair related to Italian or Italian American studies. Isn't it time that affluent Italian Americans do more than pay lip service to the love they profess for their Italian heritage?

Dr. Viscusi's paper triggers one more comment on the general theme of insularity and communication. I am bothered by the continued presence of the hyphen in the phrase "Italian-American", which, from both a linguistic and psychological point of view, has considerable significance. For too many decades the hyphen separating "Italian" from "American" has literally indicated a bar between Italian Americans and all other Americans. Some years ago, I resolved the problem for myself by simply deleting the hyphen, thereby reducing the word "Italian" from noun to adjective. Several Italian American groups, I've been pleased to note, have done the same in recent years. Yet, as we all know, the hyphenated phrase is still very much with us.

As long as Italian Americans kept within "Little Italy" enclaves, fearful of venturing into the American mainstream, the hyphen in the phrase "Italian-American" accurately expressed their situation—right up to the start of World War II when there were more than 600,000 Italian residents who had not yet become American citizens (the largest non-citizen group in the nation). But we have come a long way since then, *bambini*. A large and increasing number of Italian Americans are well into the American mainstream. In retrospect the hyphen was an expression of self-imposed segregation and Cyclopean insularity. It is time to relegate it to the junkpile of history.

20

Generoso Pope and the Rise of Italian American Politics, 1925-1936

PHILIP V. CANNISTRARO
Professor of History
Drexel University

ON Thursday, May 17, 1906, the *SS Madonna*, having sailed from Naples via Marseilles, arrived in New York harbor.[1] Among the several hundred steerage passengers that disembarked and went through immigration clearance was a fifteen year old Italian boy from Arpaise, a small village of less than 2,000 people in the province of Benevento.[2] He had $10 in his pocket, and could neither read nor write English.[3] The boy went immediately to East Harlem and entered the anonymous, crowded world of Little Italy. Within a few days he found a job hauling water to laborers working inside the Pennsylvania Railroad tunnel that would soon connect New York with New Jersey.[4] Thus began the self-defined *via crucis* of Generoso Pope.[5]

---

[1] *New York Times*, May 16, 1906, indicates the ship's arrival as May 15; it may have been delayed, since immigration records give May 17.

[2] *Censimento della Popolazione del Regno al 10 febbraio 1901* (Rome, 1901), 8.

[3] National Archives and Records Service, Washington, D.C. (hereafter NA), U.S. Department of Justice, Immigration and Naturalization Service (hereafter INS), "List or Manifest of Alien Passengers", *SS Madonna*, May 17, 1906, T-715, Roll 711, page 57.

[4] *New York Times*, April 29, 1950; *Il Progresso Italo-Americano* (hereafter PIA), April 29, 1950.

[5] Ario Flamma, ed., *Italiani di America* (New York, 1936), 271. Pope was born on April 1, 1891. He anglicized his name from the original "Papa" sometime between 1906 and 1910. He died on April 28, 1950.

Thirty years later, on February 15, 1937, the forty-six year old Pope was having lunch with the president of the United States. He had been invited to the White House by Franklin D. Roosevelt as part of a delegation of two dozen ethnic leaders of the Democratic National Committee. Pope was there in his capacity as the chairman of the committee's Italian Division, and therefore presumably as one of the principal architects of FDR's second term election victory.[6]

In less time than it took some Italian immigrants to adjust to the cultural shock of their new environment, Pope had carved out for himself an astoundingly successful piece of the American dream — as a millionaire building contractor with offices at Rockefeller Center (his Colonial Sand and Stone Company was the largest supplier of building materials in the country); as the owner of *Il Progresso Italo-Americano*, the nation's largest circulation Italian-language newspaper; and as the most important and politically influential Italian American leader of his generation.

Pope's life was often controversial. His enemies made a variety of unfounded charges about his business affairs, and that in the tough, often violent world of New York's construction business he had overcome his competition with methods that were not part of the Harvard Business School curriculum.[7] In the late 1920s Pope was a friend of Mayor James J. Walker and Tammany Hall, and prospered greatly during that period of urban growth and political corruption.[8] Still another cause of notoriety was the fact that from the early 1930s until Pearl Harbor, Pope's name was closely associated with Mussolini and the Italian Fascist regime, whose glories were spread through Pope's newspapers. Anti-Fascists saw him as the *bête noire* of Fascism in the United States and as a major cause of the respectable image that Mussolini enjoyed both among Italian Americans and in official circles.[9] This study deals with one phase of Pope's biography — his role as an Italian American leader in the context of ethnic politics during the period from 1925 to 1936. It argues that Pope was a key figure in the development of the techniques and institutional structures that characterized Italian American political behavior in the interwar period.

Pope's success was no doubt due in large measure to hard work and an intense inner drive. While still in his teens he worked as a shoveler in the Glen

[6] NA, Franklin D. Roosevelt Library, Hyde Park (hereafter FDRL), "Foreign Language Citizens Committee", PPF 603.

[7] U.S. Department of Justice, Washington, D.C., Federal Bureau of Investigation (hereafter FBI), Generoso Pope file, report dated April 13, 1944; "Generoso Pope, His Paper and His Politics", undated typescript (ca. 1941), Immigration History Research Center, University of Minnesota (hereafter IHRC), *Cupelli Papers*, box 1, folder "Pope". *See* also *New York Times*, December 31, 1931.

[8] FBI, reports dated April 13 and October 3, 1944.

[9] Max Ascoli, "Salvemini negli Stati Uniti", *La Voce Repubblicana*, December 20-21, 1967.

Head (Long Island) pits of the Manhattan Sand and Gravel Company; in 1912, when he filed a declaration of his intention to become a citizen, he described his position as "foreman" with the recently formed Colonial Sand and Gravel Company.[10] Two years later his petition for naturalization indicated his occupation as "superintendent".[11] In September 1915, four months after Italy entered World War I, Pope applied for U.S. citizenship, which he received in December.[12] By then his prospects with Colonial must have already seemed good; in any case, he preferred American citizenship to the nationalist war appeal that was to draw other young immigrants back to Italy.

The next year the Colonial company was threatened with bankruptcy and Pope saw his opportunity—he persuaded its owner and creditors to give him two years to make the company solvent, in return for a half interest in its stock and the corporate presidency. Operating out of a small "office" shack at 50th Street and Twelfth Avenue, Pope worked long hours to build up the business and fend off his competition. In 1920 he bought out his partner. Over the next five years he expanded into coal, and formed associations with several other builing supply companies.[13] Through Colonial, Pope became a key figure in the New York City construction industry.[14] Eventually the company had more than three hundred modern diesel trucks in operation and gross sales of $6,500,000 a year.[15] By the mid-1920s Pope had and interest in the Arex Real Estate Company and was a board member of a New York bank (*New York Times*, May 11, 1926). Reputedly "the wealthiest Italian in New York City", he is considered to have been the first Italian American millionaire.[16]

When Pope expatriated in 1906, during a peak year of Italian emigration, more than 358,000 Italians arrived in the United States, a quarter of whom came from Pope's region of Campania.[17] Clearly, certain qualities of character accounted for Pope's rising above his fellow immigrants so quickly and

[10] INS, "Declaration of Intention" no. 1641, April 29, 1912; FBI, report dated November 8, 1943.

[11] INS, "Petition of Naturalization" vol. 34, no. 7559, August 7, 1914.

[12] INS, "Certificate of Naturalization" no. 640585, December 13, 1915; FBI, report dated November 8, 1943.

[13] FBI, report dated July 8, 1941.

[14] *New York Times*, April 29, 1950; PIA, April 29, 1950; FBI, report dated July 8, 1941; Colonial Sand and Stone Company, Inc., *Annual Report, 1966*, 3.

[15] FBI, reports dated August 21, 1941 and October 4, 1944.

[16] FBI, reports dated August 21, 1941, and May 10 and August 21, 1941, and October 4, 1944. The FBI identified 59 bank accounts owned by Pope in 1944. *See* also Andrew Rolle, *The Italian Americans* (New York, 1980), 147.

[17] The year 1906 saw the second largest number of Italians emigrating to the United States for the period 1901-1915. For these and other statistics *see* Gianfausto Rosoli, ed., *Un secolo di emigrazione italiana, 1876-1976* (Rome, 1978).

spectacularly. Certainly he was intelligent, ambitious, and tough; a shrewd sense of survival combined with an egocentric but fragile self-image to drive him to the accumulation of money, influence, and prestige. As *Fortune* magazine commented in 1940, "Since coming to this country in 1904 [sic], Pope has never changed his aim, which was to get to the top" (*Fortune*, November 1940) Pope always retained the instincts of the street fighter but he developed the largesse of a self-made man who dispensed patronage and influence in exchange for respect and recognition.

But what made him the archetype of a new form of Italian American leader was the fact that he wielded considerable power beyond the confines of America's "Little Italies" through channels that he himself created. Pope deliberately stimulated and played on a new ethnic militancy, and acted as self-appointed advocate for his fellow ethnics in the wider area of American society. He was never completely removed from his Italian roots and immigrant self-perception, and his most consistent ambition was to be the supreme power broker of the ethnic community. He defined his life essentially as an Italian who made good in America, and without his ethnic identity he would no doubt have remained a successful but unknown businessman. In the pattern of Italian leadership that evolved in the United States, Pope held an unusual position for which there had been no real precedent. No other contemporary Italian American figure, with the possible exception of Fiorello LaGuardia, reached so prominent a place in national politics before the Second World War. Unlike those judges and state assemblymen who played lesser roles in the political system, Pope never held an elected or appointed office. His status as the most important Italian leader in the country was unique and clearly of his own making, and at once both subtle and ubiquitous.

Pope developed his political power at a time when ethnic indentification was fast becoming a crucial element in the political life of large American cities. In New York during the two decades before World War I, Tammany Hall's Timothy D. ("Big Tim") Sullivan dominated the political life of the city below Fourteenth Street. For years Irish leaders there used Italian and Jewish lieutenants to deliver the ethnic vote. Reliance on these groups increased steadily as the Irish and Germans began to move out of their old neighborhoods and were replaced by hoards of New Immigrants from southern and eastern Europe. Sullivan's ability to control patronage, charities, licenses, and city services, to say nothing of his alliances with gangsters, served to assure Tammany uninterrupted election victories in districts where the Irish had become a minority. Yet political power and representation remained in Irish hands. Tom Foley's 2nd Assembly District in the lower east side of Manhattan was typical: there Michael A. Rofrano was his lieutenant in the Italian neighborhoods, and from 1908 to 1933 every candidate for alderman, state senator, and state assemblyman was Irish in an area that was 60 percent Jewish, 24 percent Italian, and only 5 percent Irish. When Rofrano tried to revolt against Foley because he was refused a Congressional nomination, a long and bitter struggle ensued which resulted in Rofrano's defeat (Henderson, 1976).

Tammany's ability to maintain the voting loyalty of the New Immigrants began to show signs of weakening on the eve of World War I. After Sullivan's death in 1913, no one wielded quite the same degree of personal power; moreover, an array of new political forces that included Progressives, Socialists, and Fusionists, had begun to compete with the Democrats for the votes of some immigrants, especially of the Jewish workers. Most important, however, was the fact that improvements in the socioeconomic status of the Italians and Jews had resulted in their dispersal throughout the city, especially northward to East Harlem (Kessner, 1977). The breakdown of the cohesiveness of the old neighborhoods not only eroded Tammany's authority there, but also its ability to deliver patronage in the new areas. East Harlem Jews and Italians showed themselves to be much more independent, especially as higher literacy and voter registration were generally accompanied by an increased cultural consciousness and a new ethnic militancy. In 1912 East Harlem's more than 60,000 Italians (out of a total population of about 114,000) showed their new ethnic self-awareness by electing Salvatore Cotillo as the first Italian to serve in the New York State Assembly. Cotillo's victory was the result of two factors: between 1900 and 1912 the Italian vote in the area had nearly doubled, and dozens of local Italian organizations pressured local Tammany boss Nick Hayes into backing Cotillo (Henderson, 1979).

The First World War acted as a major catalyst of ethnic political attitudes, and for the Italians it served especially to ignite nationalist pride and dissolve some of the divisive effects of an ever present *campanilismo* (Salvemini, 1977 ; Diggins, 1972; Henderson, 1976) Despite — and perhaps because of — the fact that Italian voters appeared to be developing an interest in having Italian candidates to vote for, Tammany's Irish leaders showed little inclination to open its political doors to all the "New Immigrants". In 1916 the boundaries of New York's A.D.s were redrawn in such a way as to divide and dilute the Italian vote. Although in the 1920s Tammany was to accommodate itself to Jewish voters by letting their leaders into the machine, it was not until 1931 that the first Italian district leader was nominated.

When Pope began taking an active interest in politics in the early 1920s the Italians in New York represented a large proportion of the foreign born population of the city.[18] Yet politically they lacked an equivalent influence because they were divided and unorganized. If, between 1916 and 1920, the number of Italian voters increased more than 30 percent (Henderson, 1976)

---

[18] From a foreign born population of 12,000 in 1880, the Italians had grown rapidly to 145,000 in 1900 and to 391,000 in 1920. *See*, Kessner, *Golden Door*, 15, 17. The 1930 census revealed a total of 1,070,355 Italians in the city. William B. Shedd, *Italian Population in New York* (Casa Italiana, 1934), 3.

they still had low literacy and nationalization rates, and one of the lowest voter registration records of any ethnic group. In the two Italian sections of lower Manhattan, where the Church and mutual aid societies were the dominant neighborhood institutions, only 13 percent of the males were members of political clubs (Henderson, 1976). Of the two major Italian American dailies, the *Bollettino della Sera* was Republican and anti-Tammany and *Il Progresso* generally Democratic; Luigi Barzini's *Corriere d'America*, founded in 1922, was a nationalistic paper run by an editor who viewed himself as an Italian.[19] Before World War I, the owners of these papers represented the only real leadership that transcended the narrow limits of ward politics and gave a city-wide focus to Italian interests. While they sometimes advocated political unity and the creation of an Italian voting bloc, they failed to sponsor the kind of local organizational work necessary to achieve this purpose. Newspaper publishers like Pio Crespi and Carlo Barsotti were entrepreneurs whose interests and values had little in common with the vast majority of working class Italians, and their relationship to the mass of poor immigrants was still defined largely in terms of the *padroni* tradition that had characterized the early period of Italian immigration.

In the 1890s a network of *padroni* or "bosses", actively recruited Italian immigrant laborers and exploited their willingness to take the most difficult and lowest paying jobs in America's burgeoning construction industries. Even after assimilation began, they acted as intermediaries in a variety of ways for immigrants, and some developed a clientele system while advancing their personal affairs in local communities.[20] When Pope arrived in the United States in 1906, the padroni were already disappearing. After World War I there began to emerge, in place of the padroni, a group of individual leaders whose success in business or the professions had earned some measure of recognition in American society. But these so-called *prominenti*, who constituted an emerging Italian American upper middle class, were largely without any form of institutional organization until Pope began to shape an identity for them through his political strategy.

In Italian American usage, prominenti denoted important, powerful, and influential — hence "prominent" — leaders in the ethnic community. Conveyed by the term was the sense that the prominenti's prestige extended into the mainstream of the larger American society in which immigrants

---

[19] A useful survey of the Italian American press is Pietro Russo, "La stampa periodica italo-americana," in *Gli italiani negli Stati Uniti* (Florence, 1972), 494-546. Russo's complete catalog is not yet available.

[20] The *padroni's* role in Italian American history has undergone significant revision. *See,* especially Humbert S. Nelli, "The Italian Padrone System in the United States", *Labor History,* V.2 (Spring 1964), 153-67; Luciano J. Iorizzo, "The Padrone and Immigrant Distribution", in *The Italian Experience in the United States,* ed. S.M. Tomasi and M.H. Engel (New York, 1970), 43-75; the same author's "A Reappraisal of Italian Leadership", in *Gli italiani negli Stati Uniti,* 207-32.

lived.[21] But to the Italians of the 1920s and 1930s the prominenti represented a decidedly different form of leadership than the padroni of an earlier generation. The success and authority of this Americanized group had more cultural meaning and held greater promise for immigrants. Correctly or not, the prominenti were regarded as defenders and advocates, not so much of individual interests, as of a larger common Italian community.[22]

In the years after World War I the ranks of the Italian American professionals and businessmen who constituted the prominenti were growing rapidly. Manhattan alone counted about 250 Italian religious and civic societies (Mangano, 1917) and the Order of the Sons of Italy claimed 590 lodges and 125,000 members throughout the country (Aquilano, 1925). While it is impossible to estimate how many of these could properly be considered prominenti, a national survey by *Il Progresso* in 1931 listed 60,000 Italian Americans in the following professional categories: 24,000 lawyers, 17,000 pharmacists, 14,500 doctors, 2,000 engineers, and several thousand businessmen, teachers, writers, and artists.[23]

Pope was the pivotal figure in the coalescence of the prominenti. By the mid-1920s, his business success moved him into the circle of New York's Italian American elite, a fact highlighted in the Spring of 1926 by the first important public recognition he received. On May 11, Mayor Walker presided at a reception in Pope's honor and, on behalf of the Italian government, presented Pope with the Order of the Knights of the Crown of Italy. The

---

[21] The word "prominenti" already had some currency before 1920 in this sense. Antonio Mangano, *Sons of Italy: A Social and Religious Study of the Italians in America* (New York, 1917), 123, described them as "those who have influence with the powers that be".

[22] Richard Gambino, in *Blood of My Blood: the Dilemma of the Italian Americans* (Garden City, 1974), 318-20, seriously underestimates the influence of the prominenti on the Italian Americans.

If the prominenti of the interwar years were regarded more positively by working class immigrants than had been the earlier *padroni*, the developmental links and functional similarities between them did not go unnoticed. Because so many prominenti, including Pope, embraced Fascism enthusiastically before World War II, they became the target of anti-Fascists and leftwing critics. Writing during the war, the anti-Fascist exile Gaetano Salvemini was particularly bitter: "Italian emigration has always been accompanied by parasites of one sort or another — most of whom belong to those intellectual lower middle classes that are the curse of Italy; people without the will or the power to work, who have always lived off the poor, and who call themselves intellectuals because they have been educated above their intelligence. The humble, illiterate Italian laborers in America were the predestined prey of these parasites. Padroni (recruiters of manpower), local politicians, directors of the small mutual aid societies, liaison officers between the Italians and the outside world, too often abused without pity the good faith of the immigrants. The wealth nowadays enjoyed by not a few prominenti ("Prominent persons") or sons of prominenti of Italian extraction has been the fruit of vicious rape". Salvemini, *Italian Fascist Activities*, 7-8.

[23] PIA, April 23, 1931. The 1936 edition of Flamma, *Italiani di America*, listed approximately 1,000 names, which can be assumed to have represented the most "prominent" Italian Americans.

medal, the first of many which Pope and his fellow prominenti would receive from Fascist Rome, was intended to acknowledge his "philanthropies" and the "credit he has reflected upon his native land" (*New York Times*, May 11, 1926). Officially, the decoration was issued by King Victor Emmanuel III, but Pope's award was part of a general effort by the Mussolini regime to establish ties with and solicit the loyalty of the most important Italian leaders in America. By 1927 he was among the most prominent on a list of some 200 Italian American leaders that included A.H. Giannini and the Paterno brothers.[24] Pope's wealth naturally enabled him to exercise great financial power inside the ethnic community, where he made generous gifts to Italian charities and social causes. His many business enterprises which hired Italian workers almost exclusively, were also a source of considerable job patronage that spilled over into political influence.[25]

Like other Italian leaders before him, Pope began working to bring out the vote for the predominantly Irish machine, and established an intimate and life-long alliance with Tammany Hall. For a variety of reasons, however, his relationship with Tammany was different. Pope never coveted elected or appointed public office for himself, so that he could concentrate on enhancing his status as a power broker who operated as middle-man between Tammany and his constituency and remain impervious to the whims of the electorate. Moreover, because Tammany's grasp over Italian voters was no longer so secure as it once had been, a leader who could deliver their electoral support was now more vital than ever before (Henderson, 1976). Part of Pope's deliberate strategy, however, would be to stimulate a greater sense of Italian American self-pride and political consciousness — the more vocal and important the Italians became in politics, the more powerful would be his own role as arbiter of Italian strength.

Pope's strategy was eminently successful, for New York politicians came to regard him increasingly as a spokesman and leader of the city's Italian American voters, a role he deliberately cultivated both because city contracts were good for business and because the psychological impact of his rags-to-riches experience drove him to covet such a role.[26] This political function was crucial to his early financial success, but once having made his

[24] Balch Institute for Ethnic Studies, Philadelphia, *Leonard Covello Papers*, box 98, folder 10, "Leaders -1927".

[25] William F. Whyte, *Street Corner Society: The Social Structure of an Italian Slum*, enlarged edition (Chicago, 1955), 200, explains how until the end of the 1920s old ward bosses placed great emphasis on using private companies for patronage jobs. *See also*, Humbert S. Nelli, *From Immigrants to Ethnics: The Italian Americans* (New York, 1983), p. 97.

[26] FBI interviews with people who knew Pope agreed that his psychological drives and character demanded such recognition. *See*, reports dated May 10, July 19, August 21, 1941. His own statements, scattered over a twenty year period, are also remarkably consistent in confirming this interpretation.

fortune, politics became his real passion. In this regard, the 1925 mayoralty election was a turning point for Pope. Tammany's candidate, James J. Walker, won handsomely, and Pope could claim to have contributed to the victory through liberal gifts to Walker's campaign chest and informal support among Italian Americans. Pope had already established connections with the Hall, but hencefoth these connections became more intimate and were to be solidified through a close personal friendship with the new mayor and a host of Tammany politicos (*New York Times*, April 29, 1950). On one public occasion in 1931, Walker said he and Pope were made of the same experience, comparing his own youth as an ethnic boy growing up in the city streets with Pope's early years as a newly arrived immigrant (PIA, May 17, 1931).

During the Walker era there flourished, just below the surface of New York's public life, a complex network of men whose activities reached into machine politics, labor corruption, and racketeering. Pope stood close to the edge of that network, connected through a number of private businesses that operated in the grey area between legitimate enterprise and machine politics. At the end of 1925, for example, Pope joined the board of directors of the Federation Bank and Trust Company. His entry into the bank came through Salvatore A. Cotillo, Tammany's first Italian justice of the New York State Supreme Court. The fact that Pope replaced Cotillo on the board (Cotillo had been a member since its founding in 1923 as the Federation Bank of New York) reveals the extent to which he was already regarded as an influential leader of the Italian community.[27] Although documents on the bank's actual operations are lacking, it is nevertheless safe to assume that it provided a useful channel through which such men could redirect cash made in other ventures and provide each other with loans for a variety of business purposes. For Pope, membership on the board also served to cement and extend his political contacts.[28]

Pope's fellow directors were a facinating group of men that included William J. McCormack, Joseph P. Ryan, Jeremiah T. Mahoney, and Matthew Woll (*Rand McNally Bankers Directory and Bankers Registry*, January 1926 and *Moody's Manual of Investments*, 1928). "Big Bill" McCormack, whose Penn Stevedoring Corp., Jersey Contracting Co., and United States Trucking Co. had exclusive loading contracts on ten piers, was czar of the New York waterfront and had been deeply enmeshed in the violence of the early

[27] *Rand McNally Bankers Directory and Bankers Register*, 95th ed., *July 1923* (Chicago, 1923), 2517; *Polk's Bankers Encyclopedia*, 62nd ed., *September 1925* (Detroit and New York, 1925), 1688. In 1920-21 Cotillo had been an advocate of regulations to protect savings and transfers to Italy, and subsequently he had the Bank of Naples and Bank of Rome as clients of his law practice. *See*, Henderson, "Immigrant Politician", p. 87.

[28] Jeffray Peterson, *Sixty-Five Years of Progress and a Record of New York City's Banks* (New York, 1935), p. 54. In October 1931 the Superintendent of Banks closed Federation; it reopened a year later with a reorganized administration and without Pope.

teamster unions (Local 449). His influence in the labor movement was such that by the mid-1920s he began to assume the role of strike fixer, especially on the piers and in the city's transit system, while known gangsters on his payroll kept workers under control in his own enterprises. Franchises and contracts from the city (later investigated by the New York State Crime Commission) made his other companies highly profitable, while his Tammany connections — Al Smith served as chairman of United States Trucking — brought him rewards that included appointment as New York State Boxing Commissioner (Reid, 1953; New York Times, July 13, 1965). Joseph P. Ryan, a close friend of McCormack, was a major figure in labor corruption. A Tammany Democrat, since 1918 Ryan served as president of the Atlantic Coast District of the International Longshoremen's Association and vice-president of the ILA. From 1927 until 1953 (when the ILA was expelled from the AFL for corruption), he was president of the International Union, a period distinguished by his obsessive anti-Communism and the infiltration of organized crime into the waterfront union (Nelli, 1976; Fink, 1974). Matthew Woll, a labor organizer and attorney, was president of the International Photo-Engravers Union from 1906 to 1929 and vice-president of the AFL. Although he usually supported the Republican Party, Woll shared with Ryan a virulent and instinctive anti-Communist mania and was one of the most conservative labor leaders in America. He was also president of the Union Labor Life Insurance Company (Fink, 1974).

Along with these tough and somewhat disreputable labor figures, Pope sat on the board with the affable Tammany politico Jeremiah T. Mahoney. A life-long Democrat, he was an intimate of Robert F. Wagner (with whom he established a law firm), a member of Tammany's executive committee, and a frequent delegate to his party's state and national conventions. In addition to having served on the New York State Banking Commission, Mahoney was on the board of Woll's Union Labor Life Insurance Company. From 1923 to 1929 he was, like Cotillo, a justice of the State Supreme Court. In 1937 Mahoney ran as Tammany's candidate for mayor against La Guardia, supported by a small Trades Union Party organized by his labor friends. Pope served as head of the Italian Finance Committee for Mahoney's campaign (New York Times, June 20, 1970; Who's Who in America, 1970-71; Bayor, 1978).

Although the Federation Bank was an important element in his enterprises, Pope concentrated his efforts in the building materials business, on which his fortune rested. The construction business was fertile ground for profit during the Walker administration, and his profits grew rapidly in this area. Colonial, of which Pope was sole owner, was the jewel in his financial crown, and through a combination of mergers, partnerships, tough dealings with his competitors, and political influence, Pope managed to secure a virtual monopoly of the city's sand, gravel and cement markets. When

Walker was elected, Colonial and five other firms dominated the business: Goodwin-Gallagher Sand and Gravel, Norton-Keating Sand, Manhattan Sand, Lenox Sand, and Ready-Mix Concrete. By 1928, Pope had absorbed, taken over, or secured an interest in each of them, [29] a process facilitated by the fact that rival companies found themselves losing money when they could no longer win municipal contracts.[30] The 1931-32 Seabury investigations into municipal corruption would record the ways in which city officials conspired with contractors, building supply firms, excavators and others in the construction industry for licenses, permits, and contracts.[31]

Pope's business and political relationship with Bill McCormack carried over from banking into the construction industry. In 1927, McCormack disolved his Ready-Mix Concrete Company and, with Pope and Samuel R. Rosoff, set up the Transit-Mix Concrete Company. Together the three men made a powerful business alliance. Rosoff, like Pope, was a poor immigrant turned self-made millionaire whose numerous enterprises made a fortune through city contracts. In 1925 "Subway Sam" was awarded the job of building ten blocks of subway tunnel under St. Nicholas Avenue, and subsequently the Rosoff Subway Construction Company received more than $50,000,000 in such contracts.[32] Pope acted as president of Transit-Mix until 1935, but thereafter continued to hold shares in the very profitable company. By the end of the 1930s, McCormack, Rosoff, and Pope were the principal figures behind a combine that controlled 80 percent of the sand and gravel sold wholesale in New York (Reid, 1953). By the following decade, however, Pope and McCormack had become fierce competitors.

It was politics, rather than business, that induced Pope to move into publishing during this same period. In the spring of 1927 Carlo Barsotti, founder of *Il Progresso Italo-Americano*, died and his estate put the paper up for sale. It was a valuable prize, for its circulation of more than 100,000 copies a day made it the second largest foreign-language paper in America.[33]

---

[29] On Pope's business dealings in the mid-1920s, *see*, FBI, reports dated July 8 and July 31, 1941 and April 13, 1944; *New York Times*, May 11, 1926.

[30] Contemporary testimony on this point is widespread. *See*, especially: FBI, report dated April 13, 1944; A.J. Muste, letter to *The New Republic* (January 27, 1932), 298; Paul J. Kern, "Fiorello La Guardia", in J.T. Salter, ed., *The American Politician* (Chapel Hill, 1938), 9; *Fortune* (November 1940), 112; "Generoso Pope, His Paper and His Politics", cit.; *New York Times*, April 29, 1950.

[31] These findings are scattered throughout the volumes of hearings. *See*, New York State, *Joint Legislative Committee to Investigate the Administration of Various Departments of the Government of the City of New York* (July 1931-December 1932), 24 vols., New York Public Library.

[32] *New York Times*, April 10, 1951. Rosoff operated the Omnibus Bus Co. and the East Side Comprehensive Bus Corp., which McCormack actually controlled.

[33] Barsotti founded *Il Progresso* in 1880. Circulation figures vary: Nelli, *From Immigrants*, 124, cites 110,000 by 1921, and the FBI, report dated July 8, 1941, gives 95,000 at the time of its

Pope grasped at once that control of *Il Progresso* would substantiate his role both as spokesman and molder of opinion for the Italian American community, to say nothing of the political clout it would give him in the struggle for the ethnic vote unfolding in New York[34]

Among those interested in acquiring the paper were the Hearst syndicate, the International Paper Company, Luigi Barzini (editor of *Il Corriere d'America*), and several Italian American investors, one of whom was Pope. Behind the scenes, Mussolini's diplomatic agents in New York were deeply concerned over the fate of the paper and worked hard to see that its new owner would be friendly to the Fascist regime. Emanuele Grazzi, Consul General since October 1927, explained to the Italian Ambassador that "it was of the upmost interest to us to insure that the paper would stay in the hands of those faithful to the Italian nation" to guarantee "the continuation of a strong Italian line and of support for the national government". Grazzi arranged an understanding between Angelo Bertolino (the paper's business manager and a Barsotti estate trustee whose permission was necessary for the sale) and Italo Falbo (*Progresso*'s editor) that agreed to Pope's purchase of the paper. He also secured a guarantee of financial support from A.P. Giannini of the Bank of America although it was not needed; finally, Barzini was persuaded to drop out of the competition.[35] Pope bought *Il Progresso* on September 28, 1928 for more than $2,000,000.[36] Four months later the Italian government awarded Pope a second decoration — Commendatore della Corona d'Italia — at a ceremony attended by more than 1,000 people. Consul Grazzi, Mayor Walker, and Judge Cotillo hosted the affair (*New York Times*, February 6, 1929).

Over the next several years Pope added three other newspapers to his holdings. Immediately after the purchase of *Il Progresso*, Barzini announced his intention of selling *Il Corriere d'America*, which had a circulation of about 60,000, and Pope indicated his desire to buy it. Once again Italian officials intervened, but now to inform Pope that Rome did not want to see one person control a monopoly of the Italian American press.[37] But Pope was determined

investigation. Two earlier attempts to buy the paper are known: in 1920, by the prestigious *Corriere della Sera* of Milan, and in 1922, by the journalist and publisher Luigi Barzini. *See* Valerio Castronovo, *La Stampa italiana dall'unità al fascismo* (Bari, 1970), 252, 422-23.

[34] When Pope took over the paper, its masthead began to carry the motto, "The spokesman of Italian immigrants and American citizens of Italian origin."

[35] Emanuele Grazzi to Giacomo de Martino, October 3, 1928, Italian Records (hereafter IR), World War II Collection of Seized Enemy Records, NA, T586, roll 430.

[36] *New York Times*, September 30, 1928; FBI, reports dated July 8 and 23, 1941. *See also,* Castronovo, *La Stampa*, 426-2

[37] Foreign Minister Dino Grandi to de Martino, October 15, 1928, IR, roll 430. The ambassador actually arranged for the Order of the Sons of Italy to buy the paper, but the agreement fell through. *See,* Castronovo, *La stampa*, 427. In 1926 the *Bollettino della Sera* was bought by *Il Corriere d'America*, so that the major Italian evening paper was also involved.

to create just such a monopoly. In the summer of 1929 he left for his first visit to Italy since his emigration to the United States, taking with him a personal letter of introduction to Mussolini from Mayor Walker.[38] Pope had little need for an introduction, for the Fascist government was delighted with his visit. He was feted grandly, met King Victor Emmanuel III and Pope Pius XI, was hosted by an array of Fascist Party officials, and was honored at a dinner given by Piero Parini, director of the Fasci all'estero (New York Times, July 4, 1929). The high point was a private interview with Mussolini, selected details of which Pope proudly described in Il Progresso and for the American press (New York Times, July 6, 1929; PIA, June 27, July 2, 4, 5, 6, 1929). What he did not make public was that during this meeting,Pope gave Mussolini written assurance that if he were permitted to buy Il Corriere, the editorial policies of his newspapers would support Italian policies.[39] Upon his return to the United States, financial discussions with Barzini and Crespi went forward and the legal transfer of ownership to Pope was completed.[40] In April 1930 the Italian government bestowed still a third honor on him—the prestigious Grande Officiale della Corona d'Italia (New York Times, April 3, 1930).

Armed with the influential Progresso and bolstered by the prestige of his political friends on both sides of the Atlantic, Pope set out to build the foundation of an Italian American political organization throughout the city. In 1929 he began, with the help of Paul P. Rao, to promote a string of Democratic political clubs amid New York's Italian neighborhoods, using his financial resources to fund them and his newspapers to publicize their activities (PIA, April 12, 1931). His connections with the Tammany machine provided a trained leadership and workers in each of the city's sixty-two Assembly Districts and the hundreds of wards, and frequently also the meeting places in regular Democratic club houses. Unlike many of the splinter clubs continually formed and disbanded during this period in opposition to Tammany, Pope's clubs were designed to strengthen and extend the machine's power in the relatively unchartered waters of Italian voters.

The rallying cry of these clubs was not reform, but rather a demand for recognition and patronage for the Italians, a theme repeated over and over in the pages of Il Progresso. Pope's writers delighted in pointing out that along with the increasing number of Italian residents in New York had come an important growth in the number of registered voters, who threatened to challenge both political parties should they fail to ignore this powerful new constituency. "250,000 voters of Italian extraction", Edward Corsi warned in 1929, were "watchfully waiting" (PIA, July 14, 1929; April 23, 1931). Pope

---

[38] Max Ascoli to Gaetano Salvemini, June 24, 1941, Gaetano Salvemini Papers, Rome.

[39] Copy of telegram from Piero Parini to de Martino, August 7, 1929, IR.

[40] The Corriere d'America discontinued publication in April 1943. For details of the business aspects of Pope's newspapers, see, FBI, reports dated July 8 and 23, August 1 and 12, 1941.

continually pressured Democratic district leaders and borough bosses to make Italian appointments, and when they did so he celebrated their political wisdom rather than their generosity. When Isilius A. Gardella became alderman from Staten Island, Pope announced his success as evidence of the "continual political progress of the Italians of Greater New York", and added that Richmond's Democratic boss David Rendt had finally "recognized the force of the Italian vote" (PIA, January 6, 1931).

The first real test of Pope's political influence came in the 1929 mayoralty race. Despite his public insistence that Italian Americans should vote for their own ethnic candidates, Pope stood solidly behind Walker and against La Guardia. With the help of Tammany Judges John Freschi and Albert H. Vitale, Pope organized and publicized a pro-Walker Italian American committee that worked hard to defeat the Republican Fiorello La Guardia (Mann, 1959; Kearn, 1938). On the eve of the election, Il Progresso came out for Walker (PIA, November 1, 3, 10, 1929). Although La Guardia did well in the Italian American assembly districts, in the end he lost to a Tammany landslide. Walker's victory was also Pope's. On the other hand, when Pope tried to repeat his success in the 1930 congressional election, he found that his forces were not yet sufficiently organized to defeat La Guardia in East Harlem's 20th A.D. There, in the heart of La Guardia's electorial strength, Il Progresso sponsored Vincent H. Auleta, but he won only 42.8 percent of the vote (Mann, 1959; Congressional Quarterly, Guide to U.S. Statistics, 1975). Pope would therefore have to redouble his efforts over the next several years.

Despite the 1930 setback, success in stimulating Italian political cons-ciousness and developing a network of regular Italian Democratic clubs was rapid. A study conducted in 1930-31 identified 750 ethnic political clubs in New York out of a total of 2,819. Among the 302 ethnic clubs studied, by far the largest number—130—were Italian, of which 110 were Democratic.[41] While some of these were reform-minded anti-Tammany groups, the bulk were regular clubs. By 1934, the author of the study contended that "Today, although still grossly under-represented in the party organization, the Italians have the most thoroughly-regimented and closely coordinated system of political clubs in the area" (Peel, 1935).

Besides organizing clubs, Pope developed a wide circle of friends among the established Italian American politicians, most of whom held Tammany appointments. Among the city and state judges, Thomas A. Aurelio, Cotillo, Freschi, F.X. Mancuso, Ferdinand Pecora, Vitale, and Louis A. Valente all regarded Pope as a useful ally, whose endorsement and support they came to value. In his efforts to cultivate these men, Pope used his wealth to put on innumerable banquets and ceremonies at fashionable New York hotels, and

[41] Roy V. Peel, The Political Clubs of New York City (New York, 1935), p. 265 and Appendix. The second most numerous ethnic clubs were Jewish (31), followed by Polish (25) and black (22) clubs.

his "beefsteak dinners"—often eaten before he took his guests to important boxing matches—became a "Gene" Pope trademark.[42] When Freschi was elected judge of the Court of General Sessions in 1932, Pope organized a lavish dinner in his honor at the Biltmore for almost 1,000 people. The program announced Pope as toastmaster and chairman of the executive committee, and the honorary committee included more than 300 names that read like a who's who of the New York political establishment—congressmen, senators, mayors past and present, judges, municipal and state officials, and every important Tammany leader in the city.[43]

Pope also took it upon himself to sponsor many of the younger generation of Italian American lawyers who were just entering the political arena in the late 1920s. Paul Rao, Samuel DiFalco, James Lanzetta, Louis Pagnucco, Vincent Auleta, and Dolores Facconti all regarded Pope as something of a patron, and a special monthly column in *Il Progresso* celebrated them as Italian Americans who had "made good" in America. Each year since 1934, Pope also held an annual dinner at the Commodore Hotel honoring Italian American college and law school graduates. Sometimes they already owed him an obligation even before graduation, since he often contributed to scholarship funds in metropolitan area universities, and on more than one occasion secured Italian government fellowships for them. This was obviously good public relations for Pope, but it also enabled him to identify bright, ambitious young men and women interested in politics. Although it may be an exaggeration to speak of the emergence of a Pope political dynasty, clearly many of the rising generation of Italian American professionals saw Pope as their power broker. It may have been more than idle day-dreaming that led Pope to speculate in public that perhaps one day his own son would be mayor of New York.[44]

In implementing his strategy between 1929 and 1934, Pope kept a low profile in ward and assembly district politics, preferring to operate on higher ground as the disinterested patron of Italian American unity. Where he did intervene directly was in the civic life of New York's Italian community. There the Italians had developed an extraordinarily large number of social, religious, and fraternal clubs in their neighborhoods long before Pope's entry into politics, but he rapidly made his influence felt. In the early 1930s he began making countless appearances at ceremonies and social functions throughout the city, often speaking with prominent local politicians on the same platform,

---

[42] Pope sponsored a number of popular Italian boxers, and his ability to get large blocks of tickets for important fights was no doubt helped by his friendship with Bill McCormack and James A. Farley, both of whom were New York State Boxing Commissioners. PIA, November 16, 1930, April 8, 1931.

[43] A copy of the Freschi dinner program, June 4, 1932, is in the Balch Institute for Ethnic Studies, *Leonard Covello Papers*, box 98, folder 31, "Freschi". *See also*, PIA, June 4, 1932.

[44] FBI, report dated July 31, 1941; PIA, May 17, 1931, April 29, 1950.

donating flags and insignia, and making contributions to fund-raising campaigns. Pope's ties to the Mussolini government were especially useful, for not only was he invited to all public ceremonies of the New York consulate and the Washington embassy, but he was often able to bring Italian officials with him to neighborhood functions.[45] In 1934 he attempted to institutionalize his influence over these diverse groups by sponsoring an umbrella organization known as the National United Italian Associations (NUIA). Representing 188 societies with a membership of about 50,000, NUIA was headquartered at 225 Lafayette Street,[46] New York, and was run by Captain Vincent Rossini. Pope was its honorary life chairman.[47]

Along with his political and civic activities, Pope launched a much publicized campaign to combat the popular stereotypes of Italians as criminals and gangsters. With more than a touch of irony, this campaign "in defense of the good Italian name" was conducted in the spring of 1931, when the streets of New York were riddled with bloody violence during the climax of the so-called "Castellammarese war" between rival mob factions.[48] But while Pope's press campaign may not have been unrelated to the wave of violence, it was clearly part of his overall effort to project himself as defender of the Italian community. He engaged the assistance of prominent Democratic judges Ferdinand Pecora and John J. Freschi, and sent some 5,000 letters to public officials across the country, including President Herbert Hoover (PIA, April 5, 7, 8, 12, 19, 1931). From the outset, the political implications of the campaign were clear: Italians, Pope announced, "have a numerical and a qualitative importance" which no longer allows them to be "looked down upon by anyone... they demand equality of treatment with all other ethnic groups in the great American melting pot... We have today a respectable electoral force which in New York alone is more than half a million voters." (PIA, April 23, 1931). The campaign closed in May with a lavish banquet at

---

[45] Salvemini, *Italian Fascist Activities*, is the best record avialble—besides the innumerable notices that appeared in Italian American newspapers, from which Salvemini drew his material— of such civic clubs. Many of Pope's appearances are also documented by Salvemini, who would certainly have agreed with Peel's description, in *Political Clubs*, of them as "quasi-political" associations. *Il Progresso* offered to send a photographer free of charge to the social functions of all Italian civic groups. PIA, June 30, 1929.

[46] 225 Lafayette Street was the center of a large number of Italian organizations, most of which were officially connected to the Italian government or were Fascist front groups. Salvemini called the building a "beehive of Fascist activities". Salvemini, *Italian Fascist Activities*, p. 97; *Fortune* (November 1940), p. 108; *Il Mondo* (June 1942), p. 11

[47] Salvemini, "Transmission Belts", unpublished typescript, *Michele Cantarella Papers* (Mimeograph in authors's possession), pp. 25-28; *The New Italian* (August-September 1938).

[48] PIA, March 15, 1931. On the Castellammarese war *see*, Nelli, *Business of Crime*, pp. 199-205; Joseph Bonnano with Sergio Lalli, *A Man of Honor: The Autobiography of Joseph Bonnano* (New York, 1983), pp. 59-143; Fred J. Cook, "The Purge of the Greasers", in Nicholas Gage, ed., *Mafia, U.S.A.* (Chicago, 1972), pp. 80-99.

the Hotel Biltmore—amid patriotic music and a cheering crowd, Pope and Mayor Walker appealed for an end to ethnic prejudice and showered each other with effusive praise.[49]

While the anti-defamation publicity was at its greatest, Pope moved toward the unification of his chain of political clubs. In April 1931, Rao presided over a meeting of the principal groups in the "Italian American Democratic Clubs of Manhattan", and discussed plans for bringing together the clubs in the entire New York area. Acknowledging their patron, the assembled leaders "enthusiastically applauded the interest taken by Generoso Pope in this great meeting and in the development of all the Italian American Democratic clubs of the city".[50] A few weeks later, Pope organized a huge convention in Atlantic City touted as a general meeting of the clubs of Greater New York. Its main participants were the Italian American Tammany politicos with whom Pope had established a relationship: Paul Rao served as honorary head of the convention; Michael Laura of Brooklyn sat as chairman; former Judge Albert H. Vitale and Vincent H. Auleta acted as vice-president;[51] Judge Freschi was honorary president. Among the non-Italian guests who came at Pope's invitation were Congressman William I. Sirovich of Manhattan, Brooklyn Democratic Party boss John H. McCooey, and Queens boss John Theofel. After the adoption of resolutions regarding immigrant rights, the convention voted its unanimous endorsement of Mayor Walker, whose administration was then under fire from the Seabury investigations (PIA, April 16, 18-20, 1931).

By the end of 1932, it was possible for an astute observer of the New York scene to acknowledge that an Italian American political substructure was emerging. Its component elements were by no means connected with each other in a clearly discernable way, and the full extent of Pope's influence in its development was half-hidden behind his deliberately self-cultivated image as the benefactor of the ethnic community. "It is difficult to say", shrewdly noted a contemporary political scientist, "where the real leadership lies. Perhaps with Commendatore Generoso Pope, the weathly newspaper

[49] PIA, May 15, 16, 17, 1931; New York Times, May 15, 1931. Herbert Lehman sent Pope a letter of support for "a subject in which I have always been deeply interested, and which similarly affects many other races of our population". Pope to Lehman, April 29, and Lehman to Pope, May 8, 1931, Herbert Lehman Papers, Columbia University, Special File #720, "Pope".

[50] Among the clubs represented at the meeting were Ralph Stabile's Loyal Boys Democratic Club of Harlem, John Orofino's Italian American Democratic Club (IADC) of the upper east side's 16th A.D., Charles Vallone's IADC covering the 6th and 8th A.D.s of the lower Easts Side, Salvatore Titolo's IADC of the west side 7th A.D., and Albert Rolandelli's IADC of the east side 12th A.D. Together these clubs covered the major centers of Italian American population in Manhattan. PIA, April 13, 1931.

[51] Vitale was removed from the bench in 1930 because of his association with known criminals. Denis T. Lynch, Criminals and Politicians (New York, 1932), pp. 87-94.

publisher and contractor. He, at least, derives the most profit from the political strength of the Italians at the present time." (Peel, 1935). In the four years since his purchase of *Il Progresso*, Pope built the basis for a unique political machine of remarkable endurance. The fact that it was able to withstand the shattering defeats suffered by Tammany Hall in the early 1930s was due to Pope's skill in maneuvering between the constraints of traditional machine politics and the opportunities afforded by a new politics of ethnicity.

Walker resigned as mayor in September 1932 in the wake of Judge Samuel Seabury's revelations of municipal corruption.[52] Self-interest demanded that Pope remain loyal to Tammany on the local level, but he realized that the winds of political change were blowing, especially on the state and national levels. In the city itself, the challenge was represented by Fiorello La Guardia, who was doubly dangerous in Pope's eyes because the irrepressible Republican congressman combined a serious commitment to reform with a shrewd ability to capitalize on his own ethnic identity. La Guardia's electoral base was in East Harlem's 20th A.D., where Italian voters had repeatedly given him a plurality. When La Guardia decided to oppose Walker in the 1929 mayoralty race—on a defiantly anti-Tammany platform—Pope had been forced into the uncomfortable position of supporting the non-Italian candiate. Determined to avoid the dilemma again, the next year Pope unsuccessfully sponsored Vincent H. Auleta against La Guardia's bid for reelection to Congress.

Auleta's defeat demonstrated La Guardia's vote-getting power as well as his organizational strength in East Harlem, and Pope took the lesson to heart. Working through Jack Ingegnieros (who was on the staff of *Il Progresso*), in January 1931 Pope fostered the so-called Sunset Political Club in La Guardia's district. Its aim, ostensibly, was to unite the Italian Amerians of the area in their common interest, for which purpose a school was established to teach immigrants English and provide instruction in attaining citizenship. The club, soon rebaptized as the Sun Ray Democratic Club and affiliated with Rao's IADCs, was also active in registering voters.[53] When La Guardia ran for reelection in 1932, the club—and Pope—supported James J. Lanzetta. Born and raised in the district, Lanzetta was a charming, ingratiating young attorney who, with Tammany backing, had been elected to the Board of Aldermen the previous year. During the congressional campaign, the full weight of Tam-

---

[52] The best study of the Seabury investigations is Herbert Mitgang, *The Man Who Rode the Tiger: The Life and Times of Judge Samuel Seabury* (Philadelphia & New York, 1963).

[53] On Ingegnieros and the clubs, see PIA, June 9, 1942; Flamma, *Italiani di America*, 183; Salvemini, "Transmission Belts", p. 15. Ingegnieros settled in the United States in 190_; from 1920 to 1922 he was in Italy, where he participated in the March on Rome and helped organize the Fascist movement in the Italian capital.

many's ward methods—repeat voting, machine-paid election inspectors, violence and intimidation—was unleashed against La Guardia, while *Il Progresso* portrayed Lanzetta as the rising new Italian star in city politics. La Guardia was unseated by 1220 votes (Flamma, 1936; La Gumina; and Mann, 1959).

The importance of Pope's victory against La Guardia was somewhat blurred by wider events. Tammany was unable to secure the nomination of candidates for the New York governorship or the presidency, and Pope had to accomodate himself to Herbert Lehman as the Democratic candiate for governor and Franklin D. Roosevelt for president (Moscow, 1948). Pope's approach, therefore, was to separate local politics from state and national issues and carefully steer an independent course between a continuing loyalty to Tammany in municipal affairs and support for the emerging New Deal coalition. Pope became a "Roosevelt man" and threw *Il Progresso*'s support behind both FDR and Lehman. [54] With an eye toward seizing the opportunities of the moment, Pope determined to extend his Italian American Democratic organization to the state level. In June 1932, Ingegnieros, now operating out of headquarters at 225 Lafayette Street, established the Federation of the Italian American Democratic Organizations of the State of New York, with Pope as its honorary life president (PIA, June 9, 1942; *Il Mondo*, June 1942). Its declared aims were similar to those of the Sun Ray Club, as well as to further the interests of the Democratic Party. Ingegnieros was especially intent on advancing Italian American politicians, who in turn were expected to follow the will of the Federation—and hence, Pope's leadership. It also came out for Lehman and Roosevelt. [55] Over the next several years it developed a powerful network of state-wide political clubs claiming a membership of between 100,000 and 150,000 voters. [56] Typically, after Lehman's election, Pope telegraphed the new governor, "Italian Americans overjoyed your splendid victory". [57]

If the 1932 elections had been difficult for Pope, the mayoralty race of the following year was even more so. Once he secured the nomination from the Republicans and the Fusionists, La Guardia appeared to have the edge. Tammany's official candidate, John P. O'Brien, was a lackluster figure whose voter strength was sapped by a third candidate, Joseph V. McKee. Bent on breaking Tammany's opposition to Roosevelt's New Deal, Bronx Democratic

[54] "Generoso Pope, His Paper and His Politics", cit; Lehman to Pope, December 19, 1932, *Herbert Lehman Papers*, Columbia University, Special File #720, folder "Pope".

[55] "Dove vanno quando arrivano?" *L'Agente Elettorale* (organ of the Federation), October 1935, in Charles Poletti Papers, Columbia University, folder "Ingegnieros".

[56] *Il Grido della Stirpe* (May 18, 1940) claimed 100,000; the WPA Federal Writer's Project, *The Italians of New York* (New York, 1938), p. 97, gives 150,000.

[57] Pope to Lehman, November 8, 1932, *Herbert Lehman Papers*, Columbia University, Special File #720, folder "Pope".

boss Ed Fynn and James A. Farley endorsed McKee to divide the Democratic vote, thus contributing significantly to La Guardia's victory. Perhaps more important for Pope, the La Guardia forces were making a systematic effort to capture the Italian constituency, which one observer described as in "a mood for revolt against the dominant machine".[58] A pro-La Guardia Italian committee, led by Edward Corsi, Vito Marcantonio, and Leonard Covello, left no stone unturned to secure endorsements from ethnic organizations, civic groups, and newspapers, and the candidate himself played heavily on his own Italian heritage. Ironically, Pope's strenuous efforts over the years to stimulate Italian consciousness contributed to the Italian landslide that was building behind La Guardia. Sensing that New York's Italians were ready to jump party affiliation to ensure the victory of one of their own, Pope could not afford to damage his credibility by backing a non-Italian candidate as he had done in 1929.[59] He therefore decided to follow the logic of his political strategy by avoiding questions of candidates and parties in favor of capitalizing on the wave of ethnic solidarity sweeping the Italian community. Celebrating the fact that fourteen candidates for municipal posts were running, *Il Progresso* gave prominent coverage to each, and reported the campaign without taking a clear position.[60] On the eve of the election, Pope even printed cheers of "Viva il nostro Fiorello!" (PIA, April 16, 18-20, 1931). La Guardia won 90 percent of the 345,000 Italian votes cast in the election, and the mayoralty (Peel, 1935) In a contest of ethnic loyalty, Pope's Tammany friends required no explanation of his position.

Pope's skillful maneuverings had not gone unnoticed by his anti-Fascist enemies, most of whom had supported La Guardia. They ridiculed his "impartiality", accused him of "opportunism", and assaulted his self-appointed role as "monopolizer of Italianità". Commented Girolamo Valenti's *La Stampa Libera*, "La Guardia's election represents a resounding slap in the face of...Mr. Pope's ugly newspapers" (*La Stampa Libera*, November 1, 5, 7, 9-11, 1933). Presenting La Guardia's victory as a blow against Tammany and the supporters of Fascism, Valenti proclaimed that "Mr. Pope and his Fascist cohorts undergo a change of heart. They bitterly fought La Guardia at all times before his election...Now they are 100 percent for the successful former congressman and even claim the credit for his victory." (*La Stampa Libera*, December 2, 1933). Behind Valenti's charges lay a desire to strike a blow against Pope's very successful attempt to appear as the spokesman for Italian Americans.

[58] Wallace S. Sayre to Samuel Seabury, July 18, 1933, cited in Arthur Mann, *La Guardia Comes to Power, 1933* (Philadelphia and New York, 1956), p. 78.

[59] It should also be noted that the Italian Associations of New York had voted to boycott any Italian newspaper that opposed La Guardia. *La Stampa Libera*, November 9, 1933.

[60] PIA, October 22, 1933. Mann, *La Guardia Comes to Power*, pp. 137-38, says that La Guardia's managers persuaded Pope to remain neutral, but he hardly needed to be convinced.

On December 31, *La Stampa Libera's* headlines read: "Is Mr. Pope a Defender of the Italians in the United States?... Tammany Hall Contractor a Vicious Foe of Prominent Italians Such as La Guardia and Cotillo".

Valenti's attacks had little effect outside anti-Fascist circles, and indeed La Guardia himself, who never lost his sense of political reality, was to make his own accomodation with Pope once in office. Both Pope and La Guardia, each for his own reasons, preferred to leave Fascism out of their political relationship, at least until 1940. For the rest of the decade, each implicitly avoided directly attacking the other, remaining political opponents but publicly joining forces under the banner of Italian American unity. In future city elections, Pope supported Jeremiah T. Mahoney and William O'Dwyer against La Guardia. Not until Italy's entrance into World War II did the Little Flower find the opportunity to settle the score; then, with Pope's Fascist activities coming under increasing criticism, La Guardia persuaded Roosevelt to order an FBI investigation of Pope's sympathies.[61]

Between 1934 and the end of 1936, Pope's attention was focused mainly on two closely intertwined issues—Italian foreign poicy and American presidential politics. Mussolini's success in convincing the world that he had rejuvenated Italy and made her a great power had a major impact on Italian Americans. In a society in which Italians were still the poorest and least influential of the New Immigrants, many of them identified with Mussolini's "greatness"—just as they had identified with La Guardia in 1933—and his achievements tended to give them a sense of greater self-worth in dealing with the pressures of acculturation and assimiliation (Cannistraro, 1977). When Mussolini attacked Ethiopia in October 1935, therefore, a great number of Italian Americans rallied enthusiastically behind Italy's bid for empire.[62] But officials in Rome were concerned that Roosevelt's reactions against Fascist aggression—he had called for a "moral embargo" against Italy—might result in assistance to the beleaguered Ethiopians, and they turned to Pope to lead the battle in the United States. For this purpose, the Italian government increased the free cable allowance of 9000 words a month with which to telegraph official information from Rome.[63] Besides supporting the official Italian line in *Il Progresso*, Pope also launched a drive that eventually raised more than a half-million dollars for the Italian Red Cross (PIA, March 25,

[61] J. Edgar Hoover to Henry Morgenthau, Jr., July 2, 1940, FBI.

[62] In the summer of 1935, as Italian-Ethiopian relations deteriorated, *Il Progresso* published strongly pro-Italian editorials. *See*, for example, PIA, June 14, July 6, 7, 14, 18, 21, August 23, 1935.

[63] Angelo Flavio Guidi to Emanuele Grazzi, October 8, 1935, and memorandum dated October 25, 1935, IR, roll 429. The cable allowance had originally been granted at a lower rate to *Il Progresso* before Pope purchased the paper. Pope's pro-Fascist reporting of the war was attacked almost at once. *See*, Eleanor Clark, "The Italian Press, New York", *The New Republic* (November 6, 1935), pp. 356-57.

1936; Diggins, 1972; Salvemini, 1977; *Il Mondo* July 1941).

More important still, Pope orchestrated a massive effort among Italian American clubs and societies to pressure Washington into maintaining a strict neutrality that would favor the Italian war effort. Over a million letters flooded senators, congressmen, and the White House, with the result that the president began to back down from his anti-Italian position. Alarmed by the Italian American response, the administration was clearly worried about the possible effects of the Italian vote in the forthcoming presidential election, and both Pope and Roosevelt knew it (Kanawada, Jr., 1982). The president therefore ignored anti-Fascist charges that Pope was acting as a Fascist agent and began to place domestic political constraints on the formation of foreign policy.[64]

Pope realized that this delicate situation offered him a unique opportunity to seize a measure of influence on the national level that he had not anticipated. He moved carefully between continuing pressures from Rome and political requirements in Washington. In January 1936 Congress began to debate neutrality policy and Roosevelt asked for authority to withhold any commodities he deemed important from a belligerant power which was prolonging war. Intense Italian American pressure against that proposal mounted, and on January 30 Pope, together with his Tammany friend Congressman William I. Sirovich, went to Washington. There he received statements of support from John McCormack and other congressman and senators who opposed the neutrality bill. Pope then went to the White House and spoke with Roosevelt for almost an hour about how Italian American pressure was sure to defeat the president's legislation. Roosevelt assured Pope that America wanted to remain neutral and that Italy would be free to buy any goods it desired except war contraband. "Tell the Italians", Roosevelt urged Pope, "that our neutrality will never imply a discrimination against Italy in favor of other nations". Given Roosevelt's response, Pope suggested that the existing neutrality law might simply be extended in place of the proposed bill, and the president appeared to agree.[65]

Pope next went to the State Department to talk with Secretary of State Cordell Hull, who tried to convince his visitor that he was an enthusiastic admirer of Italy. Hull also agreed that an extention of the current neutrality law was desirable. After the meeting, Hull realized that Pope might publish an account of their conversation, and when newspapers in Italy actually carried the interviews later that month, he ordered a repudiation prepared in case they also appeared in the English-language press. Hull understood, however, that if the administration published the repudiation, "the Democrats

[64] Telegram from an anti-Fascist committee to Roosevelt, October 31, 1935, NA, Record Group 59, Department of State, 811. 00F/227.

[65] The quotation and description of the meeting is in Kanawada, *Franklin D. Roosevelt's Diplomacy*, p. 86.

would probably lose most of the Italian American vote in the forthcoming election".[66] The Italian American lobbying campaign continued unabated, with the result that "practically no member of Congress who had any considerable number of Italian Americans in his district dared to proceed with the bill". [67] In the face of political reality, Roosevelt at last abandoned his proposal for a new neutrality law, an event that Pope had openly predicted (PIA, February 6, 1936). His triumph was complete when, following the successful conclusion of the war in May, Mussolini telegraphed personal thanks to Pope for his work on behalf of the Italian nation.[68]

As a result of his role during the Ethiopian War, Pope had scored perhaps the greatest political coup of his career. His meeting with Roosevelt not only determined the outcome of the entire neutrality issue, but to Italian Americans Pope had been the man who stood up to the president. Moreover, in Roosevelt's mind it established Pope as national spokesman for a vast Italian electorate. *Il Progresso* underscored the point by reminding its readers of their new-found political strength and of his own role in their victory (PIA, February 20, 1936).

As the Democrats geared up for the presidential election, Roosevelt's campaign managers organized an all-out effort to make the ethnic vote an integral part of the New Deal coalition (Bayor, 1978; Gerson, 1964). The Democratic National Committee (DNC) therefore established a Foreign Language Citizens Committee to work for Roosevelt's reelection among more than two dozen ethnic communities. "Gene", the president's new friend and alley, was named chairman of the Italian Division of the Democratic party.[69]

Pope moved into action to press home his usefulness to the president. In July, Jack Ingegnieros informed Roosevelt that the Federation of Italian American Democratic Organizations would hold a state convention in the early fall "to pledge the New Deal and Govenor Lehman's candidacy, of which we are sure of victory". When the White House, not familiar with Ingegnieros' name, asked the DNC for information, Roosevelt was told that "Mr. I. is highly regarded by the New York State Democratic Organization...

---

[66] *Ibid.*, p. 87. Hull's repudiation draft is in NA, Record Group 59, Department of State, 765.84111/79.

[67] Joseph C. Green to Carleton Savage, July 27, 1934, Kanawada, *Franklin D. Roosevelt's Diplomacy*, p. 74.

[68] *Ibid.*, May 5, 1936. At the conclusion of the war, Italian officials in Rome convinced Pope to push for an immediate revocation of Roosevelt's neutrality proclamation of November 1935. Pope obliged not only in a series of articles in *Il Progresso*, but also by pressuring Democratic Party chairman Jim Farley. Ambassador Augusto Rosso to Foreign Ministry, Rome, June 8, 1936, Archivio Centrale dello Stato (Rome), *Ministero della Cultura Popolare*, busta 163, fascicolo 18/8.

[69] FBI, report dated August 21, 1941.

and is entitled to the full confidence of the President."[70] On August 11, the Italian American Democratic Clubs endorsed Roosevelt's candidacy.[71] A few weeks later Pope wrote to the White House that his newspapers were at Roosevelt's complete disposal and that they "will spare no effort to give their readers all the information in news and editorials in English and in Italian in your behalf".[72] On September 12, the state convention of the Federation voted unanimously to support the president's reelection. Throughout the next two months, *Il Progresso* spared no rhetoric in selling Roosevelt to the Italian Americans.[73] As the man whom the DNC believed could swing the Italian vote of New York — and thus perhaps the election itself — to Roosevelt, Pope had overnight become a pivotal figure in American politics.

Viewing Pope's remarkable career between 1925 and 1936 in retrospect, three essential elements stand out: his connection with the political-business life of New York's Tammany machine; his "discovery" of the potential strength of Italian American ethnic consciousness; and his relationship with the Italian Fascist regime.

In the years from 1925 to 1928, this poor immigrant-turned millionaire became involved in the powerful network of influential men who indirectly controlled much of the political and economic life of New York. That early experience, played out in an atmosphere of widespread political corruption that flourished during the Walker era, resulted in Pope becoming "one of the best connected men in New York City", [74] and gave him an abiding taste for politics and for power.

Despite his wealth and influence, however, Pope always remained a product of the Italian immigrant experience. Although shrewd and intelligent, there was a strong "Italian boy makes good" bent to his personality that thirsted for recognition, not only from the prominent figures of the day, but especially from his less able or fortunate fellow immigrants. Almost by instinct, then, Pope turned back to the ethnic community out of which he had come. He recognized, before most of his contemporaries, that the huge Italian population of the largest city in the nation was without leadership and

[70] Ingegnieros to Roosevelt, July 2, 1936; Preston McGoodwin to the White House, July 18, 1936; Roosevelt to Ingegnieros, August 6, 1936, FDRL, PPF 3778, "Federation of Italian American Democratic Organizations". In March 1941 a State Department ONI report observed that "There is no question that he [Ingegnieros] is Pope's political 'alter ego'". NA, Record Group 59, Department of State, 800.01811.

[71] "Resolutions adopted September 12, 1936," FDRL, PPF 3778, "Federation of Italian American Democratic Organizations".

[72] Pope to Roosevelt, September 1, 1936, FDRL, of 233A. *See also,* Diggins, *Mussolini and Fascism,* p. 282.

[73] Ingegnieros to Roosevelt, August 9, 1936, and "Resolutions adopted", FDRL, PPF 3778, "Federation of Italian American Democratic Organizations".

[74] "Generoso Pope, His Paper and His Politics", cit.

organization. He knew also that the harsh realities of immigrant life had obscured and eroded the immigant's sense of self-worth. Driven partly by his own need for affirmation and partly by a will to power, Pope thought to create the institutional basis of a political movement that he hoped would mobilize and focus Italian identity. In the process, he also built a unique instrument of personal authority. That his efforts were tied to the Tammany Democratic machine was logical; that they joined forces with Roosevelt's New Deal was the result of circumstance and a keen aptitude for political judgment.

Pope's talent for sensing the opportunities of the moment led him into an alliance with Fascism that would one day almost prove his undoing. He had little understanding or interest in the ideology of Fascism; rather, he was captivated by Mussolini's appeal to instincts of national pride and greatness — an appeal, it should be stressed, that had meaning for Pope in the context of his American life. For most of the 1930s, he rode the crest of Mussolini's popularity among Italian Americans, reaping personal glory and immense political advantage from the dictator's aggression. Mussolini's greatest moment of success—the conquest of Ethiopia—also belonged to Pope, who must have been secure in the knowledge that he shared the fruits of tragedy with the president of the United States.

Soon after his invitation to lunch with Roosevelt at the White House in 1937, Pope left for a second, triumphal visit to Italy. Heralded by Fascist officials as a heroic son returning to his native soil, he received from the hands of Foreign Minister Galeazzo Ciano a prestigious decoration, Commendatore dell' Ordine dei Santi Maurizio e Lazzaro. Pius XI and Mussolini granted him private audiences.[75] But it is difficult to escape the feeling that in Pope's mind the high-point of his tour was his visit to the small town of Arpaise, where he had been born not quite a half-century earlier: there, surely, his immigrant memory was stirred and he drank deeply of the waters of affirmation.

---

[75] A detailed account of Pope's 1937 visit is in a release by the anti-Fascist Italian News Agency, "Mr. Pope's Triumphal Visit to Italy", Arents Research Library, Syracuse University, *Edward Corsi Papers*, box 27, "Corrrespondence of Others". *See also*, PIA, June 6-18, 1937; *Il Giornale d'Italia* (Rome), June 16, and *Il Corriere della Sera* (Milan), June 12, 1937.

21

"La Questione Sociale", an Anarchist Newspaper in Paterson, N.J. (1895-1908)

GEORGE CAREY
Professor of Urban Studies
Rutgers University

ON July 15, 1895, an Italian language anarchist newspaper, *La Questione Sociale* was launched from editorial offices located at 325 Straight Street, Paterson, New Jersey. It was sponsored by an affinity group which called itself the *Right to Existence Group*, largely composed of Northern Italian textile workers employed in the silk mills—principally as skilled weavers and dyers.

Max Nettlau, the chronicler of fín-de-siècle anarchism listed seventeen newspapers in the world which he felt were authoritative organs of anarchist thought in 1900. These included *La Questione Sociale* of Paterson along with *L'Anarchie* of Paris and *Freedom* in London (Nettlau, 1924).

During its thirteen year history it published many articles of substantial intellectual content written by anarchist theoreticians of the caliber of Elisée Réclus, Peter Kropotkin, among others. Among its editors were persons of international distinction within world radical circles. The foremost of whom was Errico Malatesta, the distinguished protégé of Michael Bakunin who became the leading figure of Italian anarchism after his mentor's death in 1976 (*La Questione Sociale*, [*LQS*], 1895-1908, *passim*).

In fact, the influence of Malatesta was decisive among the paper's founders. The very name *La Questione Sociale* had been the designation of two previous papers. The first appeared in Florence from 1883-84, the second in Buenos Aires in 1885. Malatesta had founded both, the second while in exile (Richards, 1965).

The anarchism which Malatesta accepted, embraced the Marxist critique of capitalism, while rejecting the Marxist program for social change. Libertarian and voluntaristic in tone, the anarchists tended to reject all coercive aspects of government and to endorse a concept of revolution aimed at the simultaneous overthrow of the state, the power of the church and the capitalist system, thus setting the stage for an anticipated reorganization of society from below, through the voluntary federation of grass roots communes. In this they opposed the Marxist doctrine of overthrow to capitalism through a vanguard party's seizure of the state. They feared that a Marxist group who might seize state power would be corrupted by it and become an oppressive force like those capitalists whom they supplanted (Malatesta, *LQS*, Sept. 9, 1899).

Some anarchists, especially in France, carried their opposition to the state to the extreme of opposition to all formal organization. In Italy, the movement divided into the *organizzatori*, whom Malatesta sought to shape into an effective social force, and the *anti-organizzatori*, led by a younger generation of activists disillusioned with the ineffectuality of their elders in the face of conservative power and police repression.

Masini has said that the anti-organizzatori position could lead in only one tactical direction—toward the *attentat*, the deed of terrorist violence.

> Deny the party, deny the work of organization, of consultation, of the elaboration of policy, deny the participation of the trade union,... there remains as the only available means of struggle and of political pressure the individual act—the *attentat* or whatever other form of violent protest—is made the pivot of revolutionary commitment (Masini, 1969).

The Right to Existence Group of Paterson belonged to the organizzatori tendency of Malatesta. Only a few miles away, in West Hoboken, New Jersey, Giuseppe Ciancabilla was to assume a leadership role among an anti-organizzatori group which included Gaetoni Bresci. Both groups eventually sought to control *La Questione Sociale*.

By 1895, a rash of terrorist acts in Europe, culminating in the assassination of President Carnot in France by an anti-organizzatori Italian, Sante Caserio had resulted in the wholesale oppression of anarchists in France and Italy of whatever tendency. As a consequence, a small group of anarchist emigrès gathered in London in that year. Among them were Malatesta and his friend Pietro Gori—a 29 year old lawyer, playwright, poet and orator who had achieved distinction in the legal defense of accused anarchists in Italy (Galleani, 1930; Masini, 1969).

While in London, Gori received an offer from Francesco Saverio Merlino to travel to the United States on a lecture tour. Merlino, a friend of Malatesta, and—at that time still an anarchist—was editor of a paper, *11 Grido Degli Oppressi*, at 116 Bleeker Street, New York (Nattlau, 1924).

Gori arrived in New York in 1895, exhausted after working his passage as a sailor on a sailing ship. He was met by Pedro Esteve—a friend of Merlino,

Emma Goldman and Malatesta. Esteve, a printer and compositor by trade was a Catalan intellectual who had met Malatesta during the course of the anarchist rising in Barcelona of 1892 (Fabbri, 1936; Paterson Evening News, Aug. 3, 1900; and Goldman, 1970). He fled immediately after to Brooklyn where he worked among Spanish- and Italian-speaking anarchists.

Merlino, Esteve and Gori organized a round of public meeting and conferences in Paterson during the latter half of 1885 in order to publicize the founding of a bi-weekly newspaper *La Questione Sociale*. In this effort, Gori served as a fund-raising speaker, and contributor to the paper, while Esteve served as the practical editor, publisher and production manager.

By October, 1895, the paper was sustaining itself and the Right to Existence Group sponsored a coast-to-coast speaking tour for Gori. He first toured the Boston area, speaking to the stonecutters of Barre, Vermont, and to the laborers of the Massachusetts and New Hampshire mill towns. By March 15, 1896, he was in San Francisco, having spoken in St. Louis, Kansas City, Denver, and Salt Lake City to receptive Italian audiences. His return was via Arizona and New Mexico, where communities of Italian speaking miners were to be found, then Cincinnatti, Pittsburgh, Philadelphia, Baltimore and Washington. He detoured to make return appearances in Kansas City and St. Louis.[1]

Exhausted and always frail in health, he returned to Paterson in 1896, having accumulated sufficient resources to sustain a paper which now had a readership of about 3,000, of whom about 1,000 were local, while the balance were nationally and internationally distributed (LQS, April 7, 1900).He found awaiting him a request from Malatesta that he return to Europe as his representative at the International Socialist Congress, London, 1896. Gori accepted, resigned his editorship and returned to Europe. Esteve took over the paper as interim editor while the Right to Existence Group sought new leadership (LQS, July 15, 1896).

The Group were largely skilled Italian textile workers, predominantly from northern Italian textile districts. Altarelli, a knowledgeable contemporary, tells us that from an insignificant number in 1879, the Paterson Italian population rose to nearly one fifth of the city—18,000—by 1911. Some of these people were from the Italian northwest and were as comfortable in French as in Italian.

> After 1892 a constant stream of Northern Italians, mainly from Biella in Piedmont and Como Lombardy began to pour in attracted by the higher wages then paid to operatives. Those of Lombardy, on account of their well known ability as silk dyers, advanced rapidly to good positions and good wages.[2]

[1] *LQS*, July 1895 through March 1896, contains a continuing chronicle of Gori's activities.

[2] Carlo C. Altarelli, *History and Present Conditions of the Italian Colony of Paterson, N.J.*, Paterson, N.J., duplicated, 1911. The paper was a master of arts thesis at Columbia University, p. 3.

The core affinity group of the anarchists among them came to number about 90 to 100.

While this number may not appear to be significant, we must bear in mind that under anarchist principles of decision-making, concensus rather than majority vote was the rule. Thus, before people were acceptable in an affinity group, they had to be accepted on a basis not only of shared commitment to anarchist goals, but also on the basis of a concensual subjective judgment about their compatibility in the group's working processes. For this, and other reasons as well—such as anarchism's emphasis on small scale grass roots, non-hierarchical organization—affinity groups tended to be very small. A group of twenty was already considered fairly large. In these terms, therefore, the Right to Existence Group was actually unusually large in anarchist terms. As to its influence, with a circulation hovering about 1,000 in a linguistic community of 18,000—bearing in mind that it is reasonable to suppose that each copy of the paper was likely to be read by more than the subscriber alone—it is fair to conclude that it reached a not inconsiderable number of Paterson's Italians. This surmise is supported by the actual influence which the anarchists manifested in the labor organizing and industrial strike activities in Paterson during their greatest period of influence 1895-1908.

The downtown of Paterson near the Bartholdi Hotel on Straight Street was a focus of settlement for the early Italians. It was a neighborhood of poor dwellings interspersed among massive brick silk mills. The Italian workers brought with them not only their skills, but also their politics, and so it was to be expected that an anarchist group, among others, would establish itself. The Right to Existence Group near the turn of the century numbered about ninety active members. Leaders—outside of such itinerant luminaries as Gori, Malatesta and Luigi Galleani, included Esteve, and his companion Maria Roda, a feminist and friend of Emma Goldman who was active as early as 1897 in an effort to organize and establish propaganda groups in favor of unionism among mill workers—many of whom were women. She attempted to link these efforts with those of Louise Reville in Paris (May, 1900) calling for the formation of an international group organized around the periodical *Feminist Action*. Esteve himself was a frequent speaker on the topic. Ernestina Cravella, a bilingual worker of the Paragon Mill, assumed the role of spokesperson for the group before the English speaking press, and helped guide the group through the stormy aftermath of the slaying of King Umberto I by Gaetano Bresci of the Hamil and Booth Silk Mill, and the red scare which followed the ensuing assassination of MacKinley. Francis Widmar, a multi-lingual Tyrolean acted in the capacity of business manager and fund raising speaker for the group. Antonio Guabello, a union advocate, was active in organizing the silk weavers. He led his workers into a successful strike against the Victoria Silk Company with the help of the IWW in November, 1905. By March 4, 1906, the weavers became one of the first locals to affiliate with the infant IWW. The dyers followed suit by mid-April. Beginning with the March 24, 1906 issue, the IWW logo appeared on *La Questione Sociale's* masthead (*LQS, passim*).

From the beginning, therefore, the activities of the Right to Existence Group focused upon union organziation and workers' issues. Much of its effort went to sponsoring propaganda which advocated a class conflict theory of union militancy in which the goals of workers and managers were held to be largely incompatible. This was in contrast to the Gompers view of non-political bread and butter unionism predicated on the assumption of compatible goals between workers and managers. Ultimately the latter position came to dominate American unionism.

Also, unlike the socialists who put such questions on the tactical back burner in 1907, the group clearly had women among its leaders, and espoused a feminist position advanced for its day, conventional wisdom concerning the role of women in Italian American culture to the contrary notwithstanding (*LQS*, Sept. 15, 1897; May 5, 1900).

The group committed a serious error in their choice of Gori's successor for editor in chief, however. During the latter part of 1898 Giuseppe Ciancabilla was given the post. A young man of twenty-seven, he had been personally recruited as an anarchist from the ranks of the socialists by Malatesta in a railway station in Ancona, Italy, while Malatesta was being sought by the police. Neither Malatesta (imprisoned on Lampedusa in 1898) nor Esteve and the group realized, however, that during his residence among French anarchists in exile he had assumed extreme individualistic views, which put him in the anti-organization camp. He had in fact, become an admirer of the work of Max Stirner and Max Nordau (*Avanti*, Oct. 3, 1897. Fabbri, 1936).

Immediately, he began to publish extremist articles in *La Questione Sociale* under the pseudonym "Atomo". The group was thrown into consternation, but the West Hoboken anti-organizzatori group, whom Ciancabilla cultivated, was delighted. It appeared as though the paper might be captured by them (*LQS*, Jan. 28, 1899).

Throughout 1899, articles by Guabello, Della Barile, Pallavinci and Esteve appeared contesting the views of "Atomo" on theory and tactics. Those of the Right to Existence Group whose central concern was the creation of a militant union contended that a rhetoric of individualistic terrorism and violence alienated rather than inspired the millworkers. They felt that Ciancabilla's view was acceptable only to a small fringe coterie of intellectuals who identified with European oriented vulgar interpretations of such philosophers as Nietzsche and Max Stirner (*LQS*, Jan. 28, 1899; Sept. 2, 1899).

In a letter, Ernestina Cravella even accused Ciancabilla of saying that anarchists should withdraw from the "... sterile battle of the Workers' Unionism..." and using as authorities Jean Grave and Sebastian Fauré (*LQS*,

Jan. 28, 1899).

The crisis came when Malatesta escaped from Lampedusa on May 9, 1899. He traveled via Malta, Tunisia and London—reaching Paterson in August 1899 (LQS, Aug. 26, 1899). He received a hero's welcome at a public meeting in the last week of that month and became the editor in the September 2 issue of the paper by virtue of a vote of 80 to 3 of the Right to Existence Group (LQS, Sept. 2, 1899). Ciancabilla withdrew to West Hoboken where he founded an anti-organizzatori journal L'Aurora.

The spilt of the two factions was decisive and acrimonious. In early November 1899, Malatesta was invited to speak at the Tivoli and Zucca saloon in West Hoboken. After his appearance, he was shot at, and possibly slightly wounded by one of the West Hoboken group. Ironically, he later credited Bresci, then present, with defending him (Frappi, 1936; Petacco, 1969; Borghi, 1930).

Even more ironically, when Bresci, affiliated with the anti-organizzatori group, assassinated King Umberto in the following year, La Questione Sociale, the Right to Existence Group and Malatesta were widely blamed for the deed and subjected to the heaviest kind of public sanction. By that time, however, Malatesta was back in Europe, having accomplished the transfer of the paper back into organizzatori hands. Once again led by Esteve, the editorial emphasis shifted to the organizing of workers into a militant union movement, while themes central to European radical debate were de-emphasized. Ciancabilla moved his activities westward, ultimately to San Francisco, where he died, age 33 on September 11, 1904, editing the individualist paper La Protesta Umana (Fedeli, 1956).

The silk strike of 1902 posed a second crisis to the interests of the group. Following a catastrophic winter marked by the devastating Paterson fire, a record breaking flood and a paralyzing ice storm which wrecked the downtown—especially the Italian neighborhood—economic paralysis forced mill shutdowns with attendant layoffs. When it became evident that the spring demand for silk would be robust, the silk dyers struck for higher wages as the mills sought to get back into fall production. A tragic strike began on April 22, 1902, which deadlocked the industry until mid-July.

The strikers had to organize themselves by language. Committees required Italian, German, Dutch, French and English speaking membership. Of these lingusitic provinces, the Italian and German groups had a particularly strong anarchist component who sought broader class struggle goals than bread-and-butter issues, but the majority followed the more moderate leadership of James McGrath and Paul Breen of the Federation of Labor. By May 19, the policies of the moderates had collapsed in the face of management intransigence coupled with a system of subcontracting textile orders to nonstriking mills in Pennsylvannia. The anarchists stepped into the leadership vacuum.[3]

[3] For accounts of the strike, see, the Paterson Daily Press (PDP) and LQS for the period.

Luigi Galleani was to become—as Altarelli describes him "...the soul of the famous silk strike of 1902". Galleani described the dye-workers milieu in unforgettable language.

> The dyeworks were real hell pits in which the life of the poor worker wasn't worth an old cigar butt. For the most part they were squalid barrack like structures or underground vaults without light or air in which the suffocating stench of acid, the lethal emanations of the dye-baths, the perennial high humidity diminished even the youngest and most robust of constitutions, and gave the men who worked there a squalid and pitiful appearance after only a few months (Fedeli, 1956).

La Questione Sociale had turned over the editorship to Luigi Galleani barely six months earlier. At the age of forty-one, he just escaped from the penal island of Pantelleria. A Genoese lawyer, and a gifted orator, Galleani was equally able to harangue the Italian and French speaking workers. He was joined by the Austrian Rudolph Grossman and the idealistic friend and disciple of William Morris, the Scotsman William McQueen who was equally fluent in English and German.

The lynchpin to success in the strike was the participation of the weavers alongside the dyers. Silk weaving being more concentrated in Paterson than dying, the subcontracting strategy would be harder to apply and the manufacturers would have to yield ground (*PDP*, April 25, 26, 1902; May 6, 1902). Grossman and McQueen were essential to the anarchist effort to penetrate the weavers because of the smaller presence of Italians and French Canadians among them (*PDP*, June 7, 1902). These efforts failed. As a last ditch tactic, a giant rally was organized on Wednesday, June 17. An estimated eight thousand were present at Belmont Park. The theme was one which had gained great influence over European anarchists: the power of a general strike.

Following speeches by McQueen and Grossman which failed to arouse enthusiasm, a rhythmic chant "Vogliamo Galleani" was heard. Galleani's speech was fiery, bitter and emotionally charged. A French journalist, present at the scene recorded it. This is from his account:

> A clique, a thirst for gold and human blood, has been exploiting your labor for many years, comrades. For them; wealth, luxury: for you; misery, shame. And while your veins are drained, the coffers of your bosses fill with money. With that hoard, your masters build other fortunes; and if it transpires as it has always transpired, alas! they buy the consciences of these miserable (scabs) whom they pay to slit your throats. Will you let them slit your throats?"

A shiver ran through the audience; but Galleani continued:

> Look at your wives; they were pretty, brimming with health. The work to which the bosses have condemned them has made them pale, emaciated, anemic. Look at your children: you dream of seeing them grow up handsome, affectionate, intelligent: the factory is there to brutalize them. Look at yourselves.

Weren't you full of hope as you left a homeland crushed beneath a medieval tyranny? Alas! In this country of so-called progress, you are equally forsworn to another tyranny equally crushing (Ghio, 1903; Fedeli, 1956; Galleani, 1907).

Several thousand people broke away from the crowd and went on a riotous rampage through the mill district. In addition to many thousands of dollars worth of property damage, there were numerous persons wounded by pistol and shot-gun fire, including Galleani. It was decisive for the weavers who turned their backs on the desperate strikers. The city was placed under martial law—from June 21 to July 2. The strike was smashed, the union was in fragments. Galleani first, then Grossman fled prosecution. McQueen remained to face charges of inciting to riot. Convicted, he languished in prison until 1907 when, shattered in health, he was permitted to return to England, over the personal objections of President Roosevelt, where he died in 1909 (*LQS, PDP;* Wishart, 1905).

It took *La Questione Sociale* three years to recover from the 1902 fiasco, under the leadership of Esteve. Finally it succumbed in March 1908—a victim of the anti-red campaign of that year. The president and Republican reform Mayor McBride cooperated to remove the paper's mailing privileges—under obscenity statutes (*N.Y. Times,* March 22, 24, 1908; *Paterson Morning Call,* March 23, 24, 1908. *LQS,* last edition, undated, about April 1, 1908.

During its brief history, it was continually caught between the interests of its local group of constituents in improving the conditions of their lives through local union related activities, and leadership imported from abroad—however distinguished—which sought blindly to apply to American conditions formulae forged in the European context. In a sense, therefore, the 1908 *coup de grace* came to a group which had outworn its social relevance. Leadership such as that manifested by Galleani in the 1902 strike simply caused the group to self-destruct.

And yet we may learn much of interest from the pages of *La Questione Sociale.* First and foremost was the heterogeneity of belief and subcultural difference which existed among the Paterson Italians. We see that here was a substantial constituency for women's rights and social justice in the group. However, misguided tactically the leadership may have been, they were cultivated, well-informed, well-read and articulate—even eloquent.

We see how—in the hysteria of the Bresci affair—the English language press pursued sensationalism to the extent that the deed of a single person belonging to a splinter faction of the Italian anarchist minority came to afflict, through guilt by association, not only the *organizzatori* anarchists of the Malatesta tendency, but also the Italian community as a whole.

The Right to Existence anarchists nevertheless contributed to the raising of workers' consciousness, and the growth of the union movement in the region. As the silk workers moved into the fold of the IWW, leadership among them shifted from an anarchist base to one in which socialist thought predominated. The tragic Paterson strike of 1913 was important in the collapse of that alternative. In a sense, therefore, the failure of the anarchists was the closing off of one development route, that of the socialists another. The union movement which did in fact develop was to some extent constrained by these failures.

The history of this group also reveals to us the functioning of a close-knit network of intellectuals in Italy, France, Argentina, Spain and elsewhere who interacted significantly with immigrant Italian populations not only in Paterson, but also throughout the United States. It may thus be argued that the study of the Italian American experience requires that attention be paid to the continuous series of interactions between Italy and America which characterized the operation of such networks as the anarchist. It would seem that study of the American context in the absence of the Italian is insufficient.

As to the anarchist program, its economic advocacy of decentralist communal socialism fell upon barren soil in the Paterson region. On the other hand, the tradition of distrust of government, repudiation of bureaucratic authority and the cherishing of local self-government in loosely federated small political jurisdictions remains deeply rooted in the particularist localism of northern New Jersey politics. Modern movements like the Libertarian Party show us that the anti-governmental attitude of the anrachists—if not the economic—is alive and well in the region today.

22

Comments on the Papers by Philip V. Cannistraro, George W. Carey and Miriam Cohen

Dimensions/The Italian American Experience II

RONALD H. BAYOR
Professor of Social Sciences
Georgia Institute of Technology

A full understanding of the Italian expereince in the United States can only be provided through a comprehensive analysis which takes into account both the leadership and rank and file elements of that community. The presentations in this chapter, taken together, attempt such an analysis and indicate the varied range of Italian American studies today.

Philip Cannistraro's essay on Generoso Pope provides a good preliminary look at the career of this influential individual and is intended to serve as a cases study of Italian American leadership particularly in the era between the two world wars.

By preliminary, I mean that the author provides the basic narrative of Pope's career and the events of the Fascist-anti-Fascist conflict of that period, but has not at this point probed deeper into Pope's actions and motivations nor delineated all the pertinent happenings of the complex times of the 1930s and 1940s.

For example, Pope's attachment to Fascism should be explained in more detail. As it appears now, Cannistraro gives the impression that Pope was won over by a few medals and other honors. Many Italian Americans, as well as other Americans, reacted favorably to Mussolini and his Fascist regime. Il Duce was respected in the United States and was seen as furthering the prestige of the Italians in America. Pope, who gave evidence on a number of occasions of his concern with the enhancement of the Italian American group, probably was drawn to Fascism, like many of his co-ethnics, for non-ideological, ethnic prestige factors. Although the author does note that "it is doubtful that Pope ever developed a sophisticated understanding of Fascist ideology", he does not pursue this line of thought or provide any evidence to support this claim. Pope's willingness, for example, to reject Mussolini's anti-Semitic decrees in 1938 could be cited to indicate his non-ideological approach to Fascism.

His motivation can also be understood by looking at New York City politics during the 1930s. Even though closely allied with Tammany, *Il Progresso* supported La Guardia for mayor in 1933 as part of its endorsement of all Italian candidates. In 1937 and 1941, the newspaper, under pressure from the Democrats to endorse their non-Italian mayoral candidates, remained neutral rather than come out against La Guardia. But after the election, *Il Progresso* noted with satisfaction that La Guardia's election indicated growing respect for Italians. Pope's motivations for his Fascist sympathies must be discussed within the context of ethnic pride and loyalty.

Also Cannistraro overstates the role and impact of the anti-Fascist leadership in causing Pope to shift his position. *Il Mondo* and the Mazzini Society were certainly active and were partly responsible for his change of mind. However, missing from this presentation is any sense of world events and American public opinion. By focusing narrowly on Pope, the author ignores the broader scene—the world outside the Italian American community—which certainly had a significant impact.

Pope's shift to a public anti-Fascist position, similar to many Italian Americans, came during a period of insecurity and fear for this community after Italy entered the war on the side of Germany. Concerned with an anti-Italian response in the United States, Pope, although slowly, changed his views during 1941. The fear of an anti-Italian crusade, as well as the work of the anti-Fascists and the role of Roosevelt, seemed to cause this shift. Cannistraro must acknowledge and explain all the factors of this complex story.

Finally, and this is more of a suggestion for a possible larger essay on Pope, there must be more information on the Italian community. If Cannistraro's work is to serve "as a case study in ethnic leadership" and is an attempt "to understand what aspects of his [Pope's] life may be extended to the Italian American experience" then we must know more about this ethnic group.

George Carey's study of the anarchist movement in Patterson, New Jersey provides basically a descriptive account. We learn about the founding of the paper, the Right to Existence Group and the conflicts within the anarchist community over tactics.

What the presentation does not address and does not answer is, I feel, more significant. Little is said about the paper's readers—the Northern Italians who helped support the paper and the Right to Existence Group. To say that "the Italian workers brought with them not only their skills, but also their politics, and so it was to be expected that an anarchist group among others, would establish itself" is not saying enough about these workers or their Italian or American experience. Why the Right to Existence Group had only 90 active members near the turn of the century in a city with an increasing and substantial Italian population should also be discussed and analyzed. Furthermore, I would have liked to have seen more on the I.W.W. connection and also on his reference to support for women's rights in the Right to Existence Group. Was this support only on a leadership level? Did the rank and file readers of the paper and members of the Group also support it fully.

This was a difficult presentation to deal with mainly because it is lacking depth and substance which I hope is provided in the larger study from which it seems to be drawn.

Miriam Cohen's paper concentrating on the high school years and changing career goals of Italian girls during the 1930s and 1940s raised a number of questions for me. Her paper also sent me scurrying around my house looking for my old high school yearbook to see if her findings are true for a later period in a neighborhood Bronx high school with a mixed Italian-Jewish student population.

Cohen suggests that Italian girls stayed in high school and looked forward to different careers than earlier generations. The lives of the young women graduating in 1944 and 1949 were different in some ways and the same in some ways from their mothers and older sisters. The new high school lifestyle for increasing numbers of Italian girls and the new career goals were observed as early as the late 1930s and were due to demographic and employment changes. Although different in pursuing office work careers and enjoying high school extra-curricular activities, the girls maintained traditional family roles and entered work to aid the family as had their mothers and older sisters. "White collar work did little to liberate second-generation Italian women from their families at mid-century."

I don't dispute Cohen's conclusions, but I also do not see the necessary research to support some of her generalizations. Actually it appears to me that she is correct. My quick survey of my Bronx high school indicated that Italian and Jewish young women were noting either business or teaching as career goals. However, just as I would not base a generalization on the career choices at my high school, Cohen should not have looked at only Julia Richmond High School in Manhattan. Richmond High may not have been a good choice and might be an atypical school. For example, it was not a neighborhood school but rather drew from all of Manhattan—perhaps including a more adventurous student willing to go to school outside the neighborhood. I would like to see comparisons among different schools—Julia Richmond, one in a predominantly Italian neighborhood and one in a mixed ethnic neighborhood. Also a comparison of schools in different class neighborhoods would be informative. There might be differences between a high school in a poor neighborhood and one in a middle class neighborhood. And as Cohen herself states, since Richmond was a general school the "proportion of Italian girls who planned on college may well be higher than the Italian population at large".

Moving beyond the career choices to discuss the actual work situation, Cohen notes the lack of satisfaction on the job and the inability to express individualism. In other words, securing white collar jobs, although they were cleaner and safer than factory work, did not represent a real break with the past. She is probably right, but I do not see any significant evidence noting attitudes of Italian women towards their jobs. Also she states that "the majority of Italian women in 1950, unlike many of their Jewish counterparts, could not yet afford to be individualists, but, rather, had to take jobs where they were on call to do whatever supervisors demanded". I doubt many Jewish women, many of whom probably went into teaching, were able to express their individuality. For that matter that Italian women may not have found job satisfaction is not surprising at all since most people, male or female, cannot afford to be individuals and are under the direction of supervisors. I would also say that most jobs are probably not satisfying.

I do think Cohen has an important topic and her book might answer the questions I have raised; nonetheless judging simply on the basis of this presentation, I would say that significant points, at least to my thinking, need more verification.

In all, the three papers provide a good beginning on some important topics and hopefully will eventually be the basis for some signficant research presentations.

23

Michael Augustine Corrigan and The Italian Immigrants: The Relationship Between The Church and The Italians in the Archdiocese of New York, 1885-1902

Rev. Stephen M. DiGiovanni, H.E.D.

ABBREVIATIONS[1]

AANY	Archives of the Archdiocese of New York
WIA	Archives of the Diocese of Wilmington
AUND	Archives of the University of Notre Dame
ACMS	Archives of the Center for Migration Studies
ANAC	Archives of the North American College in Rome
AGS	Archives of the Generalate of the Congregation of the Missionaries of St. Charles Borromeo (Scalabrinians)[2]
AMSH	Archives of the Generalate of the Missionary Sisters of the Sacred Heart
APall	Archives of the Pious Society of the Missions (Pallotines)

[1] The language in which all original documents were written is indicated after the archival citation. For instance, a document written in Italian will be cited: (orig. Ital.). Those documents without any language citation are those originally in English.

[2] Francesconi, *Inizi della Congregazione Scalabriniana (1886-1888)*, Rome 1969. *Storia della Congregazione Scalabriniana*, vol. 2, Rome 1976. These works contain reproductions of much of the archival holdings of the Roman Scalabrinian Archives.

ARSI   Archives of the Roman Curia of the Society of Jesus
ACS   Archives of the Society of the Salesians of St. John Bosco

Archives of the Sacred Congregation for the Evangelization of Peoples, or *de Propaganda Fide*:

ACTA   The *Acta* of the General and Particular Congregations of the Sacred Congregation *de Propaganda Fide*

APNS   The "New Series" of the Archives of the Sacred Congregation *de Propaganda Fide*, 1893-1922.

S.C.   *Scritture Riferite nei Congressi. America Centrale dal*
Amer.   *Canada all'Istmo di Panama* of the Sacred Congregation
Cent.   *de Propaganda Fide.*

S.O.C.G.   *Scritture Originali Riferite nelle Congregazioni Generali, 1622-1892,* of the Sacred Congregation *de Propaganda Fide*

Collegi   Collegi d'Italia of the Sacred Congregation *de Propa-*
d'Italia   *ganda Fide*

Udienze   Audiences of the Sovereign Pontiff of the Officials of the Sacred Congregations *de Propaganda Fide*

ASV   The Secret Vatican Archives:
Sdis   Archives of the Secretariat of State in the Secret Vatican Archives
Del   Archives of the Apostolic Delegation in the United States
ApUSA   in the Secret Vatican Archives

n.d.   No date given in a document or letter referred to.
n.p.   No place of origin given in a document or letter referred to.

The mass immigration of the Italians began during the last twenty years of the nineteenth century and continued through the 1920s.

Of the estimated 9,391,200 immigrants who arrived in the United States during the years 1880 through 1900, nearly 1,000,000 were Italians.[3]

For the individual city and state governments, such an enormous number of arrivals provided practical headaches. However, the institution most immediately affected by such an unexpected onslaught was the Roman Catholic Church.

---

[3] U.S. Bureau of the Census, *Historical Statistics of the United States: Colonial Times to 1957,* Washington D.C., 1960, pp. 56-57.

In 1880 the estimated total white population of the United States was 43,403,000, with an estimated Catholic population of 6,259,000. By 1900 the total white population was approximately 66,809,000 of which 12,041,000 were Catholics: the Catholic population had nearly doubled in 20 years time (*See*, Shaughnessy, *Has the Immigrant Kept the Faith?* 1925, pp. 166-172).

For a church which was desperately trying to present itself as being in harmony with American institutions, such an immense increase in membership, made up primarily of the foreign-born, could do little more than confirm the anti-Catholic accusations that the Church of Rome was a dangerous, foreign threat to the country.[4]

The Church had been persecuted in most of the original thirteen colonies, its members being deprived of basic rights to own property, vote, and in some colonies even to exist. During the first half of the nineteenth century the Church in the United States began to grow, resulting from natural increases, and immigration. The hierarchy had been established in 1790 with the consecration of John Carroll as the first American bishop, thus allowing for the start of normalized Catholic life in the United States and leading to the increase in the number of dioceses and Catholic institutions.

However, the battle for acceptance as an institution which could truly live in harmony with the American Republic haunted the hierarchy and the American Catholics of the nineteenth century. Of all the Catholic immigrants which arrived in the United States during those years, that group which posed the greatest pastoral problems for the Church and which seemed to confirm the anti-Catholic accusations that the Church was foreign, anti-American, superstitious and incompatable with the principles of liberty and freedom, was the Italians.

In a stinging editorial of March 5, 1882, the *New York Times* wrote:

> There has never been, since New York was founded, so low and ignorant a class among the immigrants who poured in here as the Southern Italians who have been crowding our docks during the past year... They are of the provinces South of Naples whose principle export to foreign countries is rags... There is often a grave suspicion that they have been forwarded to this port by the Italian municipalities who were glad to get rid of them (*New York Times*, March 5, 1882, 6-3).

The *Times* applauded the efforts of the Children's Aid Society which was striving to save the Italians by educating them and exposing them to the best of American Protestant influences.

---

[4] *New York Times*, April 14, 1880, 7-7: The Church was a constant menace to freedom, especially since its foreign population would undoubtedly double over the subsequent twenty years: "They will constitute a terrible power". *New York Times*, December 15, 1884, 4-4: Billington *The Protestant Crusade: 1800-1860. A Study in the Origins of American Nativism*, Chicago 1964.

By the 1880s the American hierarchy found itself divided along clearly delineated battle lines as a result of various issues, one of which was the pastoral care of the Catholic immigrants.

The so-called "liberals" were united around John Ireland, the fiery Archbishop of St. Paul, who counted James Cardinal Gibbons of Baltimore; John Lancaster Spalding, Bishop of Peoria; John Keane, Bishop of Richmond; Denis O'Connell, Rector of the North American College in Rome as his cohorts and supporters. This group was supported by the Paulists who employed their periodical, *The Catholic World* to defend the liberal cause.

This group favored the immediate assimilation of the Catholic immigrants to American life by means of forced acceptance of customs, habits and language of their new country.

One observer described the liberal philosophy as follows:

> They were convinced that the institutions, the customs and the mentality of the United States was the best in the world, and that their country was destined to illumine old Europe... Catholicism would rise to new heights of religion, without, however, losing any of its American character... creating a new form of Catholicism, purer, more enlightened, more charitable than it has ever been before (*See*, Soderini, *Leo XIII and the United States of America*, (undated manuscript), in Aund (Eng. trans. of Ital. orig.).

Such a goal could be achieved only if every vestige of "foreigness" had been removed from the "American Catholic".

The opposition party, the so-called "conservatives", was led by Michael Augustine Corrigan, Archbishop of New York, and joined by Bernard McQuaid, Bishop of Rochester; Patrick Ryan, Archbishop of Philadelphia and the German bishops of the Mid-West.[5]

These prelates favored a more natural Americanization of the immigrants. the preservation of the immigrants' Catholic faith was of greater importance to them than was the defense of the "Americanability" of the Roman Church. The customs, languages and individual national religious practices of the various national groups needed to be respected, according to the conservatives, lest the immigrants become demoralized and lose their Catholic faith.

It is an interesting observation that the position of the conservative Catholics of the last century concerning the Americanization and pastoral care of the immigrants; the use of foreign languages in worship; education and counseling; has now become the position held by the liberal Catholics of this century.

Since the majority of the Italian immigrants to the United States entered

---

[5] *See*, Barry, *The Catholic Church and German Americans*, Milwaukee, 1953. This is the most detailed work to date of the German Catholics in the United States during the last century. The stronghold of German Catholicism in America was an area known as the "German Triangle", extending between the cities of Milwaukee, St. Louis and Cincinnati.

by way of New York City during the latter nineteenth century, the Archdiocese of New York became a type of testing ground for the application of the various pastoral decisions made by the Vatican and the American hierarchy in regard to the Catholic immigrants in general and the Italian immigrants in particular. This brief study, therefore, deals primarily with those pastoral efforts of the Church in favor of the Catholic Italian immigrants in the Archdiocese of New York under the leadership of Michael Augustine Corrigan, who served as Archbishop of New York from 1885 until his death in 1902.

In 1979 the archives of the Vatican and of the Sacred Congregation for the Propagation of the Faith were opened to students. These contained much information relating to the question of Italian immigration to the United States during the reign of Pope Leo XIII (1878-1903). The opening of the archives of the Holy See; the use of the Roman archives of various religious congregations; and of archives here in the United States have contributed greatly to the clarification of the Vatican's call for special pastoral care in favor of the Italian immigrants and the efforts actually made in this country by Church officials in response to those decisions.

Until 1909 the United States was considered to be mission territory by the Vatican and as such was under the jurisdiction of the Propogation of the Faith. All decisions concerning the Church's life in the United States were referred to Rome; the pastoral care of the Italians was no exception.

By the tenth and fifteenth anniversaries of the fall of Rome to the Savoyard troops in September of 1870, the Vatican authorities had become very much aware of the sorry spiritual and material state of the growing number of Italian immigrants.[6]

The Church in Italy had suffered from Garibaldi's victory and from the anti-clerical policies and laws which brought exorbitant taxes; the confiscation of ecclesiastical properties; savage accusations and calumnies from the government of United Italy against the Church and against its ministers.

The growing Italian emigration from Italy seemed to the Church to be the perfect opportunity to regain the Italians' respect and trust. Since the Italian government did precious little to remove the causes of emigration or to protect the emigrants by way of legislation (See, Dore, La Democrazia Italia e l'Emigrazione in America , Brescia 1964, p. 56; Foerster, The Italian Emigration in Our Times, 1919, p. 474; Perotti, La Società Italiana di fronte alle prime migrazioni di massa, in Studi Emigrazione, Febbraio-Gigugno 1959, Anno V, n. 11-12, 15, nt. 3), the Church would step in.

Since the Vatican staunchly refused to recognize the government of

[6] New York 20-lv-1882 Cav°. Binsse to Jacobini, in S.O.C.G. 1887, vol. 1027, f 772r-774r (orig. Ital.): New York 8-viii-1882 John Card.McCloskey to Simeoni, in above ref., f 770r-771r (orig. Ital.); n.p. 1-ii-1883 Mr. Raimondi to Propagation, in above ref., f 762r-766v (orig. Ital.); Carroll, MD. 10-x-1883 Rev. Luca to Propagation, in above ref., f 778r-781r (orig. Ital.); Jersey City 12-x-1883 Msgr. Gennaro DeConcilio to Leo XIII, in above ref., f 782r-785v (orig. Ital.).

United Italy, so too would it refuse to nourish any nascent nationalistic sentiments which might exist in the hearts of the expatriate Italians.

Permission to use individual dialects; to celebrate familiar feasts; to employ religious customs; and to establish national churches was all part of a practical concession to the Catholic immigrants for the salvation of souls, designed to bolster their Catholic faith in their new homeland.

The Italians received all these concessions along with the special attention of the Vatican officials, so anxious to preserve the Catholic faith of the Italians while proving the loyalty of the Pope to these poor individuals who were at once his fellow countrymen and his spiritual sons and daughters.

The obligation and the opportunity to assist the Catholic immigrants was made very clear to the Church by the work of two men: Peter Paul Cahensly, a merchant from Limburg, and Giovanni Scalabrini, Bishop of Piacenza.

Cahensly had devoted his life and energies to assisting German Catholic immigrants, and had founded the St. Raphael Society in 1871 for the protection of German Catholic immigrants.

Scalabrini hoped to interest the Roman authorities in a similar project dedicated to the Italian Catholic immigrants. The *Società San Rafaelo* was approved by the Vatican in November of 1887, as was Scalabrini's plan for an institute of Italian missionary priests who would attend to the needs of the Italians in the New World.[7] The institute was to be under the patronage of St. Charles Borromeo, and would have a strong influence on the Italian communities in the United States.

The Vatican's approval of Scalabrini's plans was part of a larger study into the entire question of Italian immigration to the Americas commissioned by the Pope in June of 1887, completed and presented to the authorities of the Propagation in November of that year.[8]

The Vatican had decided to oversee all pastoral efforts in favor of the Italian immigrants. However, an important classification was to be made concerning the Church's efforts; the work of the Church for the Italian Catholic immigrants was grounded primarily in a desire to preserve their Catholic faith and not to inspire any nationalistic sentiments. The Church could not enter into nationalistic disputes or favor any one national group

---

[7] Piacenza 16-ii-1887 Scalabrini to Simeoni, *Progetto di un Associazione allo uopo di provvedere ai bisogni spirituali degli Italiani emigranti nelle Americhe,* in Collegi d'Italia, vol. 43, f 1416r-1425v (orig. Ital.); Udienze 1887, vol. 225, f 2978r. The missionary institute was approved with the Papal Brief, *Libenter Agnovimus,* November 25, 1887 which may be found in *Acta Sanctae Sedis,* Romae 1887, vol. 20, 305; *Osservatore Romano,* December 1, 1887.

[8] *Rapporto sull'Emigrazione Italiana con Sommario,* in Acta 1887, vol. 257, f 507r-529r (orig. Ital.): The Pope had also ordered that a cleric be sent to America to examine the state of the Italians and of the Church; that the bishops of Northern Italy be ordered to send priests for the Italian immigrants, and that the American bishops be notified of their obligations toward the Italian immigrants arriving within their countries and dioceses.

over another in America.

The Roman authorities had learned rather quickly that the nationalistic tensions between the various immigrant groups in the United States were very strong and very volatile. The Germans, the Irish and the French Canadians had made that painfully clear by means of open hostilities and political maneuverings for national bishops and parishes in the United States.[9]

The Church had to tread very carefully in the area of the faith and nationalism of the various Catholic immigrants. The Church, therefore, could not support any individual national group since such support might endanger the unity of the Catholic Church in the United States. The Church could tolerate the use of the languages and religious customs of the respective national groups only in so far as such usage might prove helpful in the presentation of the immigrants' Catholic faith.[10]

In April, 1887 the Vatican approved the formation of national parishes, established for individual national groups, distinct from and independent of territorial parishes (*See, Relazione con Sommario e Voto Intorno all'Elezione [sic] di quasi-parrocchie distinte per Nazionalità negli Stati Uniti d'America*, in Acta 1887, vol. 257, f 186r-217v (orig. Ital). Such parishes were granted as

[9] Three petitions from the German-Catholic immigrants in the United States played a major role in this decision of 1887: LaCrosse 7-iv-1885 Bp. Kilian Flasch to Simeoni, in S.O.C.G. 18857, vol. 1026, f 943r-944v (orig. Latin): Flasch asked for a clarification of the relationship between national churches (those established for individual national groups) and territorial parishes, and the freedom of the immigrants to attend the church of their choice; n.p. 28-ix-1886 Rev. Peter Abbelen to Propagation, in above ref., f 904r-942v (orig. Latin): The Abbelen Memorial had the approval of a number of Mid-western German bishops who felt that the ecclesiastical rights of German clergy and laity were being thwarted in the United States by various "Irish" (really Americans of Irish descent) bishops, among whom were John Ireland and James Gibbons. Abbelen's memorial made numerous demands which were nothing more than an elaboration of Flasch's original questions. The memorial sparked furious attacks on the Germans by the American press, much of the furor having been produced by John Ireland who widely publicized Abbelen's memorial as a secret mission designed to undermine the "American Church". Rome simply sat back and watched. The nationalistic fervor of the Americans would explode once more in 1891 when Cahensly submitted the "Lucerne Memorial" to the Pope, calling for national bishops and claiming that the Church in the United States had lost 10,000,000 souls: in S.C. Amer. Cent. 1892, vol. 58, f 1037r-1050r (orig. French).

[10] *Rapporto sull'Emigrazione Italiana con Sommario*, in Acta 1887, vol. 257, f 512v (orig. Ital.); *Istruzione speciale a Msgr. Delegato Francesco Satolli an. 1892*; Folder: *Persico to Satolli, Pres. Acad. Eccles.* Tit. Sheet: *Pel Visitatore Apostolico dell'America del Nord...*, in ASV del ApUSA, 3a (orig. Ital.); Rome 30-v-1893, Ledochowski to Satolli, in ASV DelApUSA, Emigrazione Italiana, 1 (orig. Ital.): The first Apostolic Delegate in the United States was instructed by the Vatican Secretary of State concerning Satolli's unwise interference in the closure of a bankrupt Italian national parish in New York City. The Secretary of State wrote Satolli: "I believe that similar questions (concerning immigration) should be treated with extreme delicacy, since, while ample means of spiritual culture by which to preserve the faith should be provided the immigrants of various nations, yet one should avoid giving too national a direction and color to the various churches, which, as a result, could do not a little harm to the proper homogeneity and good course of the Church in America, as experience has shown us in other countries".

temporary provisions, since the reason for their establishment would no longer exist once immigrants were born in America.These churches were to exist only so long as the local bishops deemed them useful for the salvation of souls (*Ibid*, f 190r).

The Vatican, therefore, established a seemingly workable plan for the pastoral care of the Italian immigrants in the Americas: a special institute of missionary priests had been founded by Scalabrini; Italian bishops were to be notified and urged to send their priests to join the work in America; other religious congregations were urged to help by also sending priests and religious; American bishops were to assist the work as much as possible, establishing schools and churches while providing the financial assistance necessary for the project's success.

The plan, however, had not adequately considered the true religious state of the majority of the Italians. The plan was designed primarily for a church-going people, or at least for a people well-disposed toward the Church, having a modicum of religious education, common religious customs and heritage and a common language. Since the Italian immigrants were far from a united people — politically or culturally — this plan was impractical from the outset.

The religious education of the arriving Italians had been minimal, while the faith of many was a home brew of local superstition and Catholic doctrine. It was often a practical religion, based on a view of the world as populated by saints, demons and evil spirits (*See*, Rosoli, *Chiesa e communità Italiane negli Stati Uniti* [*1880-1940*], in *Studium*, Roma I-1979, 28; *also*, Williams, *South Italian Folkways in Europe and America*, New York, p. 146ff), who threatened or blessed; assisted or hindered the Italians' life and family. Such a faith was described as "...some peculiar kind of spiritual condition fed on the luxuries of religion without its substantials (*See*, Lynch, *The Italians of New York*, in *The Catholic World*, XLVII, 1888, p. 70).

The manner of worship in America was radically different from that of the Italians who, so accustomed to *feste* and lavish, public religious displays, found American Catholics to be too staid and self-conscious in their puritanical, intellectual approach to worship, religion and God (*See*, New York 13-xi-1895 Giorgio Cerio to Corrigan, in AANY, G-6 (orig. Ital.) New York 29-vi-1900 Lorenzo Antoni to Abp. Martinelli, in ASV DelApUSA, N.Y., 57).

The regional and provincial loyalties of the Italians also posed problems to the Church authorities in America. Northern and Southern Italian immigrants oftentimes refused to worship together, fought over special honors for local patron saints and societies, and spoke only in their local dialects, requiring a priest who spoke their dialect as a prerequisite to their church attendance (*See*, Newburgh 8-v-1889 Corrigan to Scalabrini (photo), in ACMS SRSR, #005, Box 1 (orig. Ital.) NY 16-v-1888 Rev. Marcellino Moroni to Simeoni, in AGS, D,I,2 (orig. Ital.) Poughkeepsie 1-i-1889 Rev. James Nilan to

Corrigan, in AANY, C-22).

The Church in the United States was primarily supported by the contributions of the faithful. The Italians, for the most part poor, were neither accustomed nor willing to contribute to the Church, especially when they were supporting their families, either in Italy or America, and were often heavily indebted to their *padroni* for their passage and for their livelihood (*See*, Iorizzo, *The Padrone and Immigrant Distribution*, Silvano, Engel, (ed.), *The Italian Experience in the United States*, New York, 1970, pp. 52-58).

Added to this was a pervasive anti-clericalism and religious indifference among the Italian immigrants. Their distrust of the Church in Italy had been successfully honed to a fine edge by an anti-clerical Italian government (*See*, Halperin, *Leo XIII and the Roman Question*, in Gargan, (ed.), *Leo XIII and the Modern World*, 1961. *See also*, Martina, *La Chiesa nell'Età del Totalitarianismo*, Brescia 1978, pp. 9-14), whose officials and representatives, both in Italy and in America, continued to work against the Church.[11]

To the American Catholic, the Italian immigrant was an antipapal heathen;[12] to many American ecclesiastics, a headache; (*See*, Lynch, The Italians in New York, in *The Catholic World*, XLVII, 1888, pp. 67-73); to the American Protestants, a poor wretch in need of delousing by a good dose of American Protestantism (*See*, 18-xii-1884 Corrigan to Bp. Thomas Becker papers, Box 1, 1884-85. *New York Times*, March 5, 1882, (6-3). *See also*, Mangano, *Sons of Italy: A Social and Religious Study of Italians in America*, 1917, p. 201, Palmieri, *Italian Protestantism in the United States*, in *The Catholic World*, CV11, 1918, pp. 177-189); to his fellow countrymen, a foreigner from the Abruzzi, or Naples, if not his mortal enemy (*See*, Chapman, *Milocca: A Sicilian Village*, 1971, p. 27. Newburgh 8-v-1889 Corrigan to Scalabrini, (photo), in ACMS, SRSR, #005, Box 1 (orig. Ital.).

The Church in the United States also found it difficult to throw itself headlong into the apostolate to the Italians. Obliged by church legislation to build parochial schools (*See*, *Acta et Decreta Concilii Plenarii Baltimorensis Tertii A.D. MDCCCLXXXIV*, *Baltimorae* 1886, tit. v., 155; tit. vi., 199);

---

[11] New York 11-v-1893 Corrigan to Satolli, in ASV DelApUSA, Emigrazione Italiana, 1 (orig. Ital): The Italian government subsidized Protestant schools for the Italians in New York City. Kansas City, MO 11-iv-1896 Prof. G. Lancieri to Rev. Zaboglio, in above ref. (orig. Ital.): A representative of the Italian government had urged the Italians in the area to vote in the local election for the representative of the American Protective Association—a rabidly anti-Catholic organization. Brandi, *Civiltà Cattolica*, Roma 1903, vol. IX, Series 18, 750: the Italian government donated pictures of the king and queen along with a substantial library to the Italian Evangelical Church on Broome Street in New York City.

[12] *Fiat Lux sullo Stato Morale e Materiale—Religioso d'Italiani Sbarcati a New York in Questi Ultimi Anni: Cause e Remedi*, New York 1888. A copy may be found in ASV DelApUSA, Emigrazione Italiana, 1. Hoboken 17-ix-1887. Rev. Domenick Marzetti to Corrigan, in AANY, C-13.

strapped for priests and funds to provide services for native American Catholics, as well as providing for the numerous immigrant Catholics (*See,* New York n.d. Corrigan to Countess Teinitzel (copy), in ACMS, #019, Box 1), the program of special care for the Italians set out by the Propagations' decision[13] seemed nearly impossible to execute.

New York City received the majority of the Italian immigrants who arrived in the United States. Because of this the city became a type of pastoral testing ground for the Italian apostolate during the years of Corrigan's administration. Even though the "Italian problem", as it came to be called, was located in America, the Propagation authorities in Rome were in charge of the apostolate with Scalabrini acting as the Vatican's champion for the Italian immigrants — an ocean away. As a result of this, Corrigan himself would find it difficult at times to work, and was oftentimes hampered by decisions made in Rome which were based on misinformation about the New York situation.[14]

The immigrant colonies of New York City presented a great pastoral challenge to Corrigan upon his succession as Archbishop in 1885, but none as acute or difficult as that posed by the Italian colonies. Theirs was a Catholicism and an identity which, unlike those of the other nationalities, were not strongly bound up with national sentiment.

Corrigan had no authority in the archdiocese during his years as coadjutor to McCloskey. It was during these years that he had the opportunity to study the material and religious conditions of the Italian immigrants in New York.[15] Once convinced of their needs, and once he succeeded McCloskey in 1885, Corrigan began a program of pastoral concern for the Italians which was unequaled by any other American bishop of that period, employing much of his time, patience, archdiocesan and personal funds to bolster the faith of the Italians in his archdiocese.

[13] *Quam Aerumnosa,* December 10, 1888, in *Acta Sanctae Sedis,* Romae 1888, vol. 21, 258-260: Pope Leo XIII reinforced the decision of the Propagation with this letter to the American hierarchy, emphasizing the importance of the Church's work for the Italian immigrants.

[14] Digiovanni, "Michael Augustine Corrigan and the Italian Immigrants: The Relationship between the Church and the Italians in the Archdiocese of New York, 1885-1902" (unpublished doct. dissert.), Romae 1983, 403-430: A classic example of this was the untimely sending of Mother Cabrini and her sisters to New York in March, 1889. Despite Corrigan's frequent protests to Rome that the project of an Italian orphan asylum in New York was not yet sufficiently thought out or financially secure enough to support religious sisters, Scalabrini had secured Rome's permission for the project and sent the sisters — a decision based on erroneous information sent him by his missionary priests then working in the city.

[15] New York 17-xii-1884 Corrigan to Bp. Thomas Becker, in WIA Becker papers, Box 1, C-2. New York 18-xii-1884 same to same, in above ref., Box 1-1884-85. New York 23-xii-1884 same to same, in above ref.: Becker had been chosen by the fathers of the Third Baltimore Council to compose a letter to the Roman authorities concerning the Italian immigrants; Corrigan was the source of Becker's information.

For Corrigan the answer to the pastoral challenge of preserving the faith of the Italian immigrants was to be found in the provision of good, zealous Italian priests, national parishes, and education in the basics of religion.

New York was not particularly deprived of Italian priests during Corrigan's years as archbishop. The need, rather, was for good priests who would be willing to dedicate themselves to the welfare of their expatriate conationals. The Italians, unlike most other Catholic immigrants, did not bring their priests with them from Italy. Those who did come were usually far from desirable to either bishop or faithful.

Corrigan wrote to Rome as early as 1884 (*See*, New York 4-viii-1884 Corrigan to Simeoni, in Collegi d'Italia, vol. 43, f1442r-1444v [orig. Ital.]) complaining about Italian priests who had fled Italy because of crimes or immoral behavior, and had come to America, many bearing good letters of recommendation from their ecclesiastical superiors, only to begin profligate if not criminal lives in America. Many of the Italians were very wary of clerics and of the Church. The presence of such priests did in no way prove their distrust to be false (*See*, New York 17-xii-1884 Corrigan to Bp. Thomas Becker, in WIA, Becker papers, Box 1, C-2. Philadelphia 5-vii-1895 "Roman Catholics of the Italian Tongue" to Ledochowski, in APNS [1895]).

To rectify this situation, Corrigan frequently petitioned Rome for more stringent controls and penalties which might check the wanderings of such clerics, and assist him in obtaining the release of zealous Italian priests from their respective bishops and religious orders (*See*, New York 6-iii-1885 Corrigan to Simeoni, in S.O.C.G. 1887, vol. 1027, f 791r-792v [orig. Ital.]).

Corrigan also communicated with Italian bishops and religious superiors, by means of letters, personal visitations, and representatives, asking for assistance that the Italian immigrants in the United States might not be lost to the Church.[16] His efforts secured the sending of numerous religious, especially Jesuit,[17] Pallotine,[18] Scalabrinian,[19] and Salesian priests [20] along with diocesan priests to join in the work among the Italians in New York.

[16] New York 25-i-1884 Corrigan to Simeoni, in S.C. Amer. Cent. 1884, vol. 40, f 303 rv (orig. Ital.). New York 28-iii-1884 same to same, in above ref., f 501r-504v (orig. Ital.). New York 16-ix-1884 same to same, in S.C. Amer. Cent. 1884, vol. 41 f 467r-468v (orig. Ital.). New York 3-iii-1885 same to same, in Collegi d'Italia, vol. 43, f 1480r (orig. Ital.). New York 23-iii-1885 Corrigan to *Emo. e Rev. Signore* (copy) in AANY, G-33 (orig. Ital.). New York 4-11-1886; Corrigan to Simeoni, in S.C. Amer. Cent. 1886, vol. 44, f598r-599v (orig. Ital.). New York 20-iv-1886 Corrigan to D. Jacobini, in above ref., f 1120r (orig. Ital.). New York 23-viii-1887 same to same S.C. Amer. Cent. 1887 vol. 47, f196r-197v (orig. Ital.). New York 29-iii-1887 Corrigan to Simeoni, in S.C. Amer. Cent. 1887, vol. 46, f 531r-532v (orig. Ital.). New York 31-iii-1887 Corrigan to Ella Edes, in above ref., f 533r (Ital. trans. of Eng. orig.). Paris 8-iii-1888 Rev. Charles McDonnell to Corrigan, in AANY, C-19, New York 3-viii-1888 Corrigan to Simeoni, in S.C. Amer. Cent. 1888, vol. 49, f 255r-256r (orig. Ital.). New York 22-xi-1889 Corrigan to Fr. Gen. of the Redemptorists (copy), in AANY, C-31.

[17] New York 14-xii-1888 Corrigan to Rev. Antonius Anderledy, S.J., in ARSI, Prov. Maryl, 1888-1897. New York 15-xii-1888 Rev. Thomas Campbell, S.J. to Anderledy, in above ref. (orig.)

Corrigan also wrote to Italian bishops concerning the possible establishment of a seminary exchange program in which American and Italian seminarians would train in both Italy and the United States for eventual work among the Italians in America.[21] The plan was never carried out because of lack of funds and the Vatican's disapproval of the plan.

Corrigan instead insisted that all New York seminarians studying in the archdiocesan seminary be required to study Italian; to speak only Italian at table; to restrict refectory readings to either Latin or Italian; and to attend classes on the pastoral care of the Italian immigrants taught by an Italian priest (See, *The Catholic Church in the United States of America; Undertaken to Celebrate the Golden Jubilee of His Holiness, Pope Pius X*, 1934, vol. III, 301. New York 16-x-1899 Corrigan to Abp. Martinelli (copy), in ACMS, SRSR, #005, Box 1).

The number of New York seminarians attending the North American College in Rome increased during Corrigan's years in New York. This provided a substantial force of American priests able to speak and understand Italian,

---

Latin). The Jesuits eventually began the Italian mission of Our Lady of Loretto on Elizabeth Street in New York City, which opened in August, 1891.

[18] Rome 6-xii-1884 Rev. William Whitmee to Corrigan, in AANY, C-17: Corrigan had met with the procurator general of the Pallotines while he was in Rome in the Fall of 1883. The Pallotines took over the Italian mission of Our Lady of Mt. Carmel in Harlem in late May, 1884 with the arrival of the Rev. Dr. Emiliano Kirner.

[19] New York 29-iii-1887 Corrigan to Simeoni, in S.C. Amer. Cent. 1887, vol. 46, f 531r-532v (orig. Ital.). New York 16-xii-1887 Corrigan to Scalabrini (photo) in ACMS, SRSR, #005, Box 1 (orig. Ital.). New York 10-ii-1887 Corrigan to Scalabrini (photo), in above ref. (orig. Ital.). The first missionary priests of the Congregation of St. Charles Borromeo arrived in New York in October, 1887, and established three Italian missions in New York City: St. Joachim on Roosevelt Street; Most Precious Blood on Baxter Street;and Our Lady of Pompeii on Bleecker Street. They also assumed the responsibility of the port mission for the Italian immigrants.

[20] Rome 15-xii-1883 Corrigan to Don Bosco, in ACS, 38, N.Y. Corresp., 1883-1898 (orig. Ital.): Corrigan met with Bosco in Turin in the Fall of 1883. New York 7-iii-1884 same to same, in above ref. (orig. Ital.). New York 16-ix-1884 Corrigan to Simeoni, in S.C. Amer. Cent. 1884, vol. 41, f 467r-468v. Rome 21-v-1887 Rev. Vincent DeParocco to Corrigan, in AANY, C-13. New York 1-ii-1888 Rev. Edward Paroco to *Revmo e Carmo. Sig. Vicario*, in ACS 38, N.Y. Corresp. 1883-1898 (orig. Ital.). New York 26-x-1897 Corrigan to ?, in above ref. (orig. Ital.). New York 30-ix-1897 Corrigan to Rev. Michele Rua, in above ref. (orig. Ital.). New York 24-ii-1898 same to same, in above ref. (orig. Ital.). New York 13-iv-1898 same to same, in above ref. (orig. Ital.). New York 25-xi-1898 same to same, in above ref. (orig. Ital.). The Salesians arrived in New York in November, 1898, and eventually took over Transfiguration Chruch on Mott Street, and opened other Italian missions in Manhattan.

[21] New York 23-viii-1887 Corrigan to D. Jacobini, in S.C. Amer. Cent. 1887, vol. 47, f 196r-197v (orig. Ital.). New York 16-xii-1887, Corrigan to Scalabrini (photo). in ACMS, SRSR, #005, Box 1 (orig. Ital.). Cremona 4-i-1888 Bp. Geremia Bonomelli to Corrigan (copy), in S.C. Amer. Cent. 1890, vol. 54, f 891r-802v (orig. Ital.). New York 19-i-1888 Corrigan to Simeoni (?), in above ref., f 803r (orig. Ital.).

who were also familiar with some Italian customs.[22]

With the assistance of various religious congregations, and especially with the approval of Scalabrini's missionary institute in 1887, the establishment of Italian national churches in New York was somewhat plausible. Practical problems, as outlined above, were compounded by a distinct lack of funds and the not too covert opposition to such churches by many of the "Irish" pastors of the archdiocese (New York 13-v-1888 Corrigan to Scalabrini(photo), in ACMS, SRSR, #005, Box 1 (orig. Ital.).

Many such ecclesiastics saw the granting of national churches to the Italians as a mistake and a threat, since such churches would be within the territorial boundaries of their parishes, but would be independent of their jurisdiction.

The opposition of some of these pastors was motivated, in part, by a sense of prejudice towards these "new immigrants". But more than that, they were motivated by a fear of the loss of their own authority and an inability to adapt to the changing complexion of their parishes.

In many of these city parishes the surrounding neighborhoods were changing rapidly. The American and Irish families — the builders and pillars of many territorial parishes — were fleeing the old neighborhoods in face of the Italian onslaught.

With their prosperous congregations moving away and being replaced by poor, sometimes superstitious and unfriendly Italians, the pastors' last stand could only be to fight for the maintenance of their territorial jurisdiction, thus securing the little financial contributions which might be forthcoming from the Italians to help secure their churches which the pastors had worked so diligently to build.

Many of these pastors had allowed the local Italian immigrants to worship in the basements of their churches, thus assuring the fact that they would be subject to the pastors' jurisdiction. To allow an Italian church, indepedent of the local territorial church would herald the end. These proud city pastors of once prosperous American congregations were faced with the difficult reality that they might soon find themselves in charge of debt-ridden "inner city" churches populated by foreigners. It was a difficult change, and one which many could not face up to, deciding rather to oppose any program which might rob them of their life's work (*See,* New York 16-v-1888 Rev. Marcellino Moroni d'Agnadello to Simeoni (copy), in AGS, D,I,2 (orig. Ital.). New York 19-vii-1888 Rev. Franceso Zaboglio to Scalabrini, in AGS, D,1,3 (orig. Ital.).

Upon Corrigan's appointment as the ordinary of New York there was only one so-called Italian church in the city — St. Anthony's on Sullivan

---

[22] ANAC Student Register, 1859-1935: From 1885 until 1902 Corrigan supported 55 ecclesiastical students at the North American College in Rome, 41 of whom were ordained priests and returned to the archdiocese.

Street, which was staffed by the Franciscans. In reality it was a mixed congregation of Italians, Irish and Americans. Between 1885 and 1902 Corrigan established twenty-two churches and chapels within the archdiocese for the Italians (*See, Official Catholic Directory*, Milwaukee 1903, pp. 98-109), six of which were exclusively Italian national churches.

Parish religious and mutual aid societies were developed in these churches to draw the Italians together within the Church itself, to celebrate local feasts, to promote frequent reception of the sacraments, and to offer minimal assistance to families in time of need, illness, family disaster or death.

The work of the Italian priests and religious women within the various Italian churches in New York affected the Italian immigrants in more than merely sacramental ways. In spite of the staunch provincialism; overwhelming poverty; distrust of the Church and anti-clerical sentiments of many of the Italian immigrants, the Church proved itself to be the only institution in America truly interested in the well-being of the Italian immigrants.

Italian priests and religious showed themselves to be of great value to the Italians. Since few city officials spoke Italian, the immigrants could only turn to either their priest or *padroni* in time of trouble or need. The priest was the only individual formally associated with any institution, and because of this slowly began to fulfill many of the functions once performed by the padroni, if not always as effectively, at least with requirements less costly and dangerous to those assisted.

Italian and American priests and religious involved in the Italian apostolate assisted immigrant children who had no families (*See*, New York 17-ix-1903 T. Riordan to Rev. Anthony Demo, in ACMS, O.L. Pompei, Box 14); counseled those unjustly convicted or in need of legal assistance [*See*, New York 1-v-1899 Rev. Bonaventura Piscopo, O.S.F. to Corrigan (photo), in ACMS, #019, Box 2]; comforted those Italians who were imprisoned [*See*, New York 9-xii-1901 Corrigan to Mr. Pickett (copy), in AANY, G-16]; watched over young men and women released from correctional and charitable institutions (*See*, New York 14-vii-1903 T. Riordan to Rev. Anthony Demo, in ACMS, O.L. Pompei Box 14. New York 14-xii-1903 same to same, in above ref.); visited the sick and aided them in the city hospitals [*See*, New York 29-ix-1888 Rev. Felice Morelli to Corrigan, in S.C. Amer. Cent. 1890, vol. 52, f 1011r (orig. Ital.)]; worked in the city port assisting the arriving Italian immigrants, protecting their legal rights and helping them to locate family, lodging and jobs [*See*, Piacenza 20-xiii-1891 Scalabrini to Simeoni, in S.C. Amer. Cent. 1891, vol. 57, f 578r-579v (orig. Ital.). *Relazione della Societa Italiana di San Raffaele in New York*, Piacenza 1892, in ASV DelApUSA, Emigrazione Italiana, 1. New York 4-vii-1894 Corrigan to Simeoni (copy), in AANY, G-33 (orig. Ital.). New York 11-ii-1902 Corrigan to Thomas Fitchie, in AANY, G-18]; assisted the newly arrived Italian immigrants to adjust to their new homes [*See*, Castellonchio di Berretto

7-ix-1902 Rev. Giuseppe Bonfanti to Rev. Anthony Demo, in ACMS, O.L. Pompei, (orig. Ital.)]; took charge of orphans of the immigrants [*See*, Memorie dello Casa i Bassa Citta, April 21, 1889, f 59, in AMSH (orig. Ital.)]; and tried to better the lives of the immigrants by educating them and their children.

The education of Catholic children was of particular interest to the Church in nineteenth century America. Every parish was to strive to build its own school in an effort to assure every Catholic child in America a place.

For Corrigan this legislation of Baltimore III was to extend to the Catholic immigrants as well. The Italians' posture towards the education of their children, however, was somewhat different than that of other immigrants, basically for two reasons. The first and most immediate was the poverty of many of the Italians which made for a constant lack of sufficient funds on both the parochial and archdiocesan levels, thus prohibiting the construction, operation and maintenance of Italian parochial schools [*See*, New York 18-xii-1888 Corrigan to Simeoni, in S.C. Amer. Centl. 1888, vol. 54f844r-845v (orig. Ital.). New York 3-iv-1894 Rev. Luigi Monsella to Corrigan (photo), in ACMS, #019, Box 1, O.L. Mt. Carmel, New York 16-ix-1899 Corrigan to Abp. Martinelli (photo) in ACMS, SRSR, #005, Box 1]. The second reason was that many of the Italian immigrants took the education of their children for granted, preferring that they work, rather than attend school [*See*, New York 11-v-1893 Corrigan to Satolli, in ASV DelApUSA, Emigrazione Italiana, i (orig. Ital.). New York 16-1-1896 Rev. Luigi Monsella to Corrigan (photo), in ACMS, #019, Box 1. New York 16-x-1896 circular letter of Corrigan to clergy and laity, in AMCS, Scal. Frs. in N. Amer., Box 10].

Since many of the arriving Italian immigrants had received only rudimentary religious instructions, the primary need was to supply religious classes, if nothing else. However, the same obstacles to the establishment of Italian parochial schools hindered the establishment of a religious education system for the children of the Italian immigrants [*See*, New York 11-v-1893 Corrigan to Satolli, in ASV Del ApUSA, Emigrazione Italiana, 1 (orig. Ital.)]

Some schools were established, but the effect was minimal. Most parishes had catechism classes which did affect a large number of Italian children, especially through classes preparatory to the reception of the sacraments (See, ACMS, Box 21: "Miscellaneous").

All of this aided at least in laying the foundation for a closer relationship of the Italian immigrants with the Catholic Church in America.

The Italian immigrants' relationship with the Catholic Church was radically different from that of other Catholic immigrant groups whose faith was bound up with their national sentiments.

For many Italians, when they left Italy they also left the Church behind. In order to attract many of the Italians who had immigrated, the Church had to prove itself, in some way, to be different in America than the Church which they had left in Italy.

For many Italians their relationship with God and the saints was a practical, if not purely utilitarian one. The Church, if it was the instrument of that same God, needed to prove itself as useful and practical to the Italian immigrants in the new world.

If the Church was to be believed it could not hamper its work by favoring any individual national group. It needed to show itself to be truly Catholic, working for the good of the Italians and not for their exploitation as was feared by many of the Italian immigrants [*See*, New York 17-xii-1884 Corrigan to Bp. Thomas Becker, in WIA. Becker papers, Box 1, C-2. Wilmington *Idibus Ianuariis* [*sic*] 1885 Bp. Thoms Becker/James Card. Gibbons to Simeoni, in S.O.C.G. 1885, vol. 1023, f 848r (orig. Latin)].

The Pope, so recently without temporal power or lands, needed to prove himself to be God's man, interested and dedicated to the spiritual well-being of his co-nationals and co-religionists. This interest could be manifested only by his earnest pastoral solicitude seen in the actions of the local American bishops and priests in favor of the Italians [*See*, Philadephia 2-1-1889 Antoni Vitas to Abp. Martinelli (copy), in ASV DelApUSA, Emigrazione Italiana, 1. New York 29-vi-1900 Lorenzo Antoni to Abp. Martinelli, in above ref.]

The majority of the Italian immigrants found life in the new world to be extremely difficult. They were faced with problems, both practical and emotional, which could never have been imagined, either by them or by the Roman and American ecclesiastical authorities, prior to the phenomenon of mass migration during the last century.

The immigrants brought with them their beliefs, customs, superstitions, faith, provincial and familial loyalties, prejudices and suspicions which they tried to insert into their new foreign environment which held only poverty and dreams.

The Church had to overcome all of this in order to win the Italians to the Church. In many ways the Church was not successful The sincere efforts made by Corrigan and the priests and religious women working with him in the archdiocese of New York did not cure the religious indifference so pervasive among the Italian colonies of the city [*See*, New York 11-v-1893 Corrigan to Abp. Satolli, in ASV DelApUSA, Emigrazione Italiana, 1 (orig. Ital.)].

They did succeed in weakening some of the anti-clerical sentiments held by many of the Italians by means of the practical assistance offered them by the Church in the form of parishes, charitable Catholic institutions, and the personal assistance granted them by so many priests and religious women dedicated to their welfare.

However, it would not be until the children and grandchildren of those Italian immigrants who arrived in America during the final twenty years of the last century — not until the subsequent generations of Italo-Americans had set aside many of the prejudices and fears of their parents and godparents, and were themselves ready to accept the Church, that the foundations of the Italian apostolate in New York, established by the pastoral zeal and personal generosity of Archbishop Corrigan, would finally be built upon.

PRINTED SOURCES

Acta et Decreta Concilii Plenarii Baltimorensis Tertii A.D. MDCCCLXXXIV, Baltimorae 1886.

Acta Sancta Sedis 20 (1887), 305; 21 (1888), 258-260.

The Catholic Church in the United States of America; Undertaken to Celebrate the Golden Jubilee of His Holiness, Pope Pius X, III, New York 1914.

Fiat Lux Stato Morale e Materiale-Religioso d'Italiani Sbarcati a New York in Questi Ultimi Anni: Causi e Rimedi, New York (Agosto) 1888.

LYNCH, B.J. *The Italians in New York*, in *The Catholic World*, 47 (1888).

MANGANO, A., *Sons of Italy: A Social and Religious Study of the Italians in America*, New York 1917.

Official Catholic Directory, Milwaukee 1903.

PALMIERI, A. *Italian Protestantism in the United States*, in *The Catholic World*, 107 (1918), 177-189.

RIIS, J. *How the Other Half Lives*, New York 1926.

U.S. BUREAU OF THE CENSUS, *Historical Statistics of the United States; Colonial Times to 1957*, Washington, D.C. 1961.

SECONDARY SOURCES

BARRY, C.J. *The Catholic Church and the German Americans*, Milwaukee. 1953.

BILLINGTON, R.A. *The Protestant Crusade: 1800-1860. A Study of the Origin of American Nativism*, Chicago 1964.

CHAPMAN, C.G. *Milocca: A Sicilian Village*, Cambridge, 1971.

DIGIOVANNI, S.M. *Michael Augustine Corrigan and the Italian Immigrants: The Relationship Between the Church and the Italians in the Archdiocese of New York, 1885-1902*, Rome 1983.

DORE, G. *LaDemocrazia Italiana e L'Emigrazione in America*, Brescia 1964.

FOERSTER, R.F. *The Italian Emigration of Our Times*, Cambridge, MA, 1919.

GARGAN, E. (ed.) *Leo XIII and the Modern World*, New York 1961.

MARTINA, G. *La Chiesa nell'Eta del Totalitarianismo*, Brescia 1978.

SCANLAN, A.J. *St. Joseph's Seminary, Dunwoodi, New York, 1896-1921*. New York, 1922.

SHAUGHNESSY, G. *Has the Immigrant Kept the Faith? A Study of Immigration and Catholic Growth in the United States, 1790-1920*, New York, 1925.

TOMASI, S. *Piety and Power, The Role of the Italian Parishes in the New York Metropolitan Area, 1880-1930*, New York, 1975.

TOMASI, S., M.H. ENGEL, eds. *The Italian Experience in the United States*, New York 1970.

WILLIAMS, P.H. *South Italian Folkways in Europe and America*, New York, 1966.

ARTICLES

PEROTTI, A. *La Società Italiana di fronte alle Prime Migrazioni di Massa: Il Contributo di Mons. Scalabrini e dei Suoi collaboratori alla Tutela degli Emigranti*, in *Studi Emigrazione*, 11-12 (1968) 1-481.

ROSOLI, G. *Chiesa e Communità Italiane negli Stati Uniti (1880-1940)*, in *Studium* 1 (1979) 25-47.

NEWSPAPERS

New York Times
L'Osservatore Romano

24

The Greenwich Village Italian Neighborhood: The Emergence and Eclipse of an Ethnic Communal Forum

DONALD TRICARICO
Queensborough Community College,
City University of New York

THE magnitude of Italian settlement in New York City between 1890 and 1920 gave rise to a number of Little Italies of varying sizes. Through these years the Italian neighborhood became a salient feature of the New York City landscape and a major component of the Italian American experience. Unfortunately, urban Italian communities in New York and elsewhere have received relatively little attention from social scientists. There has been a conspicuous neglect of community organization beyond the period of mass migration. In the case of New York City, first settlement areas have demonstrated a "surprising endurance" (Glazer and Moynihan, 1963:187). They have also shown a capacity to absorb social and cultural changes in effecting new communal adaptations.

The area of Greenwich Village south of Washington Square Park has been the site of one of the city's best known Italian neighborhoods.[1] It is certainly one of the oldest; the first Italian national parish in the city was established in the South Village in 1866. Only the East Harlem and Mulberry Street Italian communities were larger; prior to World War I, some 50,000 Italians were living in South Village tenements (Ware, 1965:156).

---

[1] This paper is based on a study of the Greenwich Village Italian American community published by the Center for Migration Studies.

After the war, the Italian population of the Village declined sharply as families moved away and quotas were imposed on immigration. In her classic study of Greenwich Village in the 1920s, Caroline Ware depicted an Italian community that was "socially disorganized", primarily owing to the effect of "American ways" on the second generation. In Ware's view, this "undermined" the Old World foundations of Italian community in the Village, in particular the traditional family and the solidarity of immigrant *paesani* (*i.e.*, an identification based on place of origin, such as a village or province, and distinguished by a peculiar dialect, customs, and history). She specifically ruled out the restructuring of community along other lines (Ware, 1965: 152-202).

However, from a longer view and without the theoretical assumptions that encumbered Ware's position on ethnicity and community in modern urban society (Stein, 1960), it is apparent that the Village Italian community was fundamentally restructured in the period following World War I. A sizeable Italian population remained in the area; four census tracts that comprised the heart of the South Village Italian community contained 24,918 people in 1930 (Laidlaw, 1935). At the same time, an increasing proportion of the population was American-born (Ware, 1965:281) and communal life came to reflect their interests and needs. New urban institutions were appropriated or developed in place of immigrant frameworks like the mutual aid society and the *padrone*, although major ethnic patterns were retained or modified. The paesani distinctions that fragmented the immigrant colony were leveled or sublimated by common acculturation experiences in the second generation (*e.g.*, growing up in the city instead of the *paese*, speaking English instead of dialect). A new solidarity came to be based on an expanded concept of ethnicity (*i.e.* being Italian or Italian American) in a city where nationality background informed major social divisions.

A RESTRUCTURED COMMUNITY

The family was at the center of a restructured ethnic community; in fact, its significance for community organization became greater as the number and proportion of immigrant male sojourners declined. Although the second generation had fewer children and patriarchal elements were modified (Ware, 1965:178-202), family life was informed by traditional values pertaining to a household division of labor and the solidarity among family members. A kinship network materialized in the second generation and became embedded in the neighborhood; in a case that was not uncommon, one neighborhood family group (in 1955) spanned 13 distinct households and four generations. Common family tradition were the basis of a moral consensus which distinguished Italians from other groups (*e.g.*, "The Americans", bohemians, the middle class). On a more concrete level, neighborhood families effected a solidarity based on the respects exchanged on the occasion of life-crises rituals. To this extent, the South Village was a community of families; indeed, residents have referred to it as a "family neighborhood" (*i.e.*, family group life imparted its basic rhythms, values, and morality). The ethnic neighborhood and its communal familism furnished a supportive milieu for the family's "little tradition" (Covello, 1967), countering acculturative pressures.

Perhaps the most authoritative work on the urban Italian American community is Gans' study of the West End of Boston in the mid-50s (1962). For West End Italians, meaningful social experience was collapsed within the family-centered peer groups; in Gans view, the community was "relatively unimportant" and was discussed only from the standpoint of the family-centered peer group. In Greenwich Village, on the other hand, there were levels of community beyond the family and relations among families.

Whereas the paesani group served as the communal context for immigrant Italians, in the second generation this function was taken over by the Italian neighborhood. Solidarity with neighbors was a function of the physical constraints of tenement life (Suttles, 1968) as well as a common ethnic culture. The boundaries separating the tenement flat from the neighborhood were rather permeable; the hallway, the rooftop, and the street were extensions of the home. Localized interaction made it possible to know, or at least "know of", a large number of individuals and families in the neighborhood, gossip chains supplied information about those who shared the same life-space.

Although traditional Southern Italian kinship was "an inclusive social world" (Covello, 1967:149), the second generation formed intimate ties to peers that were the basis of a social neighborhood. Males elaborated a classic streetcorner pattern for which there was a precedent in *dolce far niente* and the *passegiatta*. More than just vehicles for sociability, streetcorner groups exercised informal control, especially by keeping a watchful eye on "strangers". Females also had a peer group life, although it was more encumbered by traditional concerns like household chores, responsibilities to children and kin, and religious obligations. In lieu of paesani societies, there were opportunities for formal group memberships in social/athletic clubs, VFW and American Legion chapters, mothers' clubs at the local settlement houses, and business and professional men's clubs. These organizations had a purposeful aspect and gave expression to status distinctions within the ethnic community.

In addition to the family and social neighborhood, there were institutions that had a more encompassing, community-wide significance: the parish, district political organizations, and a "Mafia" syndicate. Although actuated by special interests and organizational objectives, they furnished the community with material advantages and leadership. Linked to hierarchical structures that transcended the local Italian community, they mediated ties to the larger society.

Two Catholic parishes were established in the South Village in 1866 and

1893 respectively. Although they preceded the bulk of Italian immigrants in the area, the parish does not appear to have figured prominently in the early Italian settlement. One factor was the assimilationist policies of an Irish Catholic hierarchy; a consequence of this was the banning of the religious feste which continued to be celebrated by the immigrant societies outside the Church (Vecoli, 1969; Tomasi, 1970). In the older (national) parish, the inclusion of Irish families who lived in the area seems to have alienated Italians; the Irish played a leading role in early parish affairs while Italians were invited to worship in the church basement.

Matters changed after World War I. In the older parish, Italians became the dominant force as Irish families continued to move away. Whereas single male sojourners may have been indifferent, families had greater need of parish services. Moreover, in the second generation, there was some absorption of Irish Catholic patterns (Russo, 1970). Finally, both parishes were moving closer to the younger, second generation Italians (Ware, 1965:312). They built halls and gymnasiums to house social and recreational programs; a 1941 parish yearbook makes it clear that this was intended to counteract the popularity of settlement houses and the "danger" of Protestant missions. Parish facilities became an important resource in the tenement neighborhood. Parish schools (including a two-year commercial high school for girls) were well-attended by Italian children. Italians supported the parish financially (local businessmen and politicians made generous and conspicuous gifts) and volunteered their services to run parish affairs. Parish priests were regarded with respect and affection; the pastor played a major civic role which brought him into contact with community power brokers. In a number of respects, the Italian American parish came to resemble its Irish American counterpart.

South Village Italians were not only influenced in their political adaptation by the Irish, they actually took over political frameworks that had been dominated by the Irish. Irish politicians backed by Tammany Hall maintained control over the two election districts that split the South Village into the thirties, in part through the practice of gerrymandering. Italians made headway against the Irish as the second generation began taking the "business of politics" seriously (Ware, 1965:281). In 1931, Al Marinelli was elected Democratic district leader with the help of Italian mobsters; Marinelli was the first Italian district leader inside Tammany Hall. In the other district, Carmine DeSapio succeeded "Bashful Dan" Finn in 1943 as the Democratic district leader; DeSapio was socialized into machine politics by the Finn family which had dominated the Village political scene since the end of the 19th century. This succession meant that political patronage was more open to local Italians, especially those who were affiliated with Democratic clubs. District leaders were the new padrones; they performed favors for loyal constituents and occasionally became involved in community-wide issues like the proposed urban renewal of the fifties.

A local Mafia syndicate also had a significant role in the South Village Italian American community (the term "Mafia" follows local usage; moreover, prominent members have been identified as such by national law enforcement authorities). Initially a ritual brotherhood and secret society, an American Mafia assumed the characteristics of the urban street gang in the second generation, while responding to a changing structure of opportunity (Ianni, 1972). In the South Village a criminal syndicate attained prominence during Prohibition (Ware, 1965:55-62). With the repeal of Prohibition, it maintained an "underground" economy, providing goods and services like bootleg cigarettes and numbers gambling to local consumers. Neighborhood men were employed in a variety of capacities (e.g., runners, bookies); syndicate capital was invested in neighborhood businesses and real estate. On the whole, however, the syndicate maintained a predatory stance toward the local economy, for example by "selling protection" or imposing a business relationship on merchants. To secure its illicit operations, syndicate interests coopted official authority (who "looked the other way") and stifled civic initiative. They became an invisible government, except to local Italians, propped up by intimidation and force. However, since syndicate activities contributed to the maintenance of a defended neighborhood, Italians have been able to rationalize syndicate tyranny to a degree.

THE SOUTH VILLAGE IN THE PRESENT

Unlike other urban Italian neighborhoods (Nelli, 1970), the Italian South Village has persisted well beyond the period of initial settlement. This has been predicated on a complex of ecological, structural and cultural factors. The South Village has not experienced an expansion of business or industry, urban renewal, or an invasion of unacceptable groups; it has remained, until recently, a "zone of transition". Rents stayed low while the quality of housing improved, tenement flats were renovated and families moved to more spacious apartments, reflecting a rise in living standards. Moreover, a South Village location offered convenient access to blue-collar jobs throughout the city. Within this framework, South Village Italians actualized cultural preferences and values, including the importance of staying close to the family and living in an ethnic community.

While Italians have not been pressed to leave the South Village, they have left at their own pace; in 1980, 4,160 persons in four South Village census tracts with a total population of 19,476 claimed Italian ancestry (an additional 697 identified themselves as "Italian and other"). They have left for a combination of economic and cultural reasons. The tenement neighborhood has precluded home ownership and related amenities — the cornerstone of a suburban life-style that Italian Americans have enthusiastically embraced; a recent *New York Times* survey (November 4, 1978) found that Italians were the single largest ethnic group in suburban New York City at 19 percent of the total. Moreover, the ethnic neighborhood — Italian or otherwise — is insular and provincial with its comparatively restricted indentification with kin and ethnicity. To this extent, there have been limits on the ability of the community to absorb social and cultural changes. In particular, it has not been able to accommodate mainstream, middle-class life-styles. Leaving the neighborhood, then, has typically been perceived as entailing a status passage and cultural leap.

Presently, there is still an Italian American community in the South Village, although the latter is no longer an Italian neighborhood. Italians are being replaced by upper middle class professionals in town houses and apartment buildings, and by young aspiring professionals and Portuguese immigrants in tenement walk-ups. While the middle-class has been reclaiming the Village since World War I (Ware, 1965), the latter is a more recent phenomenon. The impact of the Portuguese has been relatively slight (986 were enumerated by the 1980 census. However, the influx of young professionals has thoroughly transformed the character of the South Village. It is directly related to the emergence of the SoHo artists community in the adjacent manufacturing districts; in 1971, the Department of City Planning legalized loft residence for working artists in the area. SoHo, which stands for South of Houston Street, overflowed its official boundaries and has absorbed the Italian neighborhood. In fact, the South Village is now widely regarded as part of SoHo, except among Italians. The latter remain in the interstices, largely thanks to the city's rent control law which protects them from suddenly inflated real estate values. Nevertheless, the influx of newcomers, together with a dwindling population, determine the parameters of Italian American community life in the present.

Families that stayed into the second or third generation have left in the third or fourth. With relatives living elsewhere, there are now only fragments of families. Young couples and families with school-age children are rare; elderly family members (*e.g.*, parents and grandparents) comprise an increasingly large segment of the community. Although interaction with kin, especially between parents and adult children, is considerable and is accorded special significance, there is the perception that "families are not as close as they used to be". Moreover, kinship interaction is no longer focused on the neighborhood. As families move away, interfamilial solidarity has eroded; neighborhood wakes are only sparsely attended as "obligations" between family groups lapse. The waning of a "family neighborhood" is especially lamented by older South Villagers who are unable or unwilling to meaningfully reorder their lives. Social service programs, including senior citizen centers instituted by the parish and local settlement houses, have attempted to take up some of the slack.

A social neighborhood has also withered. Social/athletic clubs have disappeared. Groups of cornerboys are smaller and fewer in number; they look out of place in SoHo where gourmet shops and boutiques have replaced candy stores and "members only" clubs. Since newcomers are regarded as "strangers" with different life-styles and values, they do not qualify as replacements for those who moved away. If anything, they are identified with the loss of community (young cornerboys have reacted belligerently to what they perceive as an encroachment on their turf). Fraternization with the young aspiring professionals is inhibited by status distinctions. However, tensions have been tempered by the social and physical benefits of "gentrification". SoHo has given Italians who stayed in the ethnic neighborhood a respectable address, an irony that mobile South Villagers have difficulty comprehending.

Without cornerboys and housewives leaning out their kitchen windows, burglaries and street crime have become more prevalent. SoHo has transformed the South Village into a neighborhood of "strangers" (categories that informed a cognitive map of the city have been rendered meaningless). The young aspiring professionals have only "limited liability" to the local community; their cosmopolitan life-styles and values are not conducive to a "defended neighborhood" (Suttles, 1968, 1972). Art galleries and fashionable restaurants have opened the neighborhood to the city.

The status of the two Italian parishes in the South Village in recent years has been determined by various strategies for survival. The loss of parishioners has reached a dangerous point and created a persistent fiscal crisis. An early response was the cultivation of ties to mobile parishioners. In the forties, the older parish held radio broadcasts of weekly novenas; a street festival in honor of the parish patron was introduced in the fifties primarily with former South Villagers in mind (the appropriation of the "feste", although purged of some of its peasant aspects and increasingly commercialized, is significant in light of the erstwhile "Italian Problem"). The event has since attained city-wide significance and is responsible for a major share of parish revenues; it now warrants extensive preparation, including sophisticated media exposure (each year, news reporters from local television stations eat sausage sandwiches and calzones on camera). The other parish has reluctantly exploited the revenue potential of a "festa Italiana" as well. Staging commercial events like the feast are part of the trend away from institutional programs and religious services oriented to the local population.

The small Portuguese community has benefited the older parish, although not so much as anticipated. The immediate result was a parish within a parish consisting of a native friar, Portuguese language masses, and a devotion to Our Lady of Fatima — a development resented by Italians and of some concern to the pastor who moved to incorporate the immigrants within the main congregation. SoHo has not provided a significant infusion of new parishioners. Although the parish has been friendly to the artists and middle class groups (*e.g.*, by making facilities available for meetings and a day care center), it is not an integral part of their world. In SoHo, the parish is just another civic institution and property owner (in recent years, there has been considerable opposition among the newcomers to the feast on the grounds of its inconvenience to local residents and alleged syndicate involvement — that the parish was acting as a front for "Mafia" interests). However, the parish has made some influential new friends. Recently, an internationally famous opera singer who lives in the neighborhood staged a concert in the church to raise funds for damages it sustained in a fire.

The dominance of Italians in district politics was short circuited by demographic shifts that have been transforming the entire lower west side of Manhattan into an area for the affluent. This was signalled in 1961 when Carmine DeSapio was defeated by reform interests (which included the present Mayor Ed Koch) reprsenting the views of middle class groups. Although a second generation Italian survived the coup and has retained the assembly seat from the district, his politics are shaped by liberal, middle class constituents. Italians have held on to positions in the other district. However, it is now more than ever, dominated by the East Side Italian neighborhood. Moreover, SoHo portends radical changes for what has been referred to as a "wasteland for reformers".

Over the years, syndicate interests were being directed to more lucrative ventures outside the Italian neighborhood. Along with other South Village Italians, syndicate members moved their families to the suburbs and commute to work. While traditional operations like numbers gambling and loansharking have remained, the scale is much smaller. Although artists and young professionals have generated little demand for these services, gentrification has offered new investment opportunities, for the most part in legitimate areas. In contrast to Italians, the newcomers are only vaguely aware of the syndicate's presence. However, there is a widespread belief that "The Mafia keeps the neighborhood safe".

THE ITALIAN SOUTH VILLAGE
IN PERSPECTIVE

There has been an Italian community in Greenwich Village for more than one hundred years. However, there have been major social, cultural, and economic changes since the period of initial, large-scale settlement. In particular, a new institutional structure crystallized following World War I. A restructured community reflected the common acculturation experiences of second generation Italians, including the institutional capital available to them at a particular historical juncture (Kramer and Leventman, 1969, pp. 21-34). This is noteworthy because the sociological and historical literature portrays the urban Italian neighborhood as an artifact of the immigrant experience — as "Little Italy". As such, it precludes significant communal development beyond immigrant patterns (paesani socieities, the immigrant church, the padrone, etc.. Perhaps a reason for this is the acceptance of "straight-line" assimilation models (Sandberg, 1974; Crispino, 1980; Steinberg, 1981) which emphasize the "decline" rather than the variable nature of ethnicity and ethnic group life (Royce, 1982; Horowitz, 1975; Barth, 1969; Yancey, et al., 1976). Another and more subtle factor may be the pervasive assumption that Italian familism has worked to inhibit community (Muraskin, 1974), although in the South Village common ethnic family traditions were an important basis of solidarity with other Italians (Covello, 1967).

Like the immigrant colony, this restructured, neighborhood-based Italian American community is historically specific. It is limited by ongoing processes of acculturation and social mobility (the new immigrant settlements and Italian American neighborhoods in outlying residential areas have different configurations).

Presently, institutions that structured a neighborhood community for the second generation are either withering away (the localized kinship group and interfamilial solidarity, a streetcorner society, the defended neighborhood), increasingly disengaged from the community (the mobile family, the Mafia syndicate, the prestigious businessmen's clubs, or else oriented to new groups that have staked a claim to the South Village (district politics, the parish, the Mafia syndicate, social settlements, the neighborhood economy). The Italian population continues to contract; with relatives and friends living elsewhere, there is a powerful sense of being left behind. A large segment of the community can be defined by some setback or constraint such as old age, poor health, or the death of a spouse. The ascendance of a "problem" constituency has elicted new communal responses, as with senior citizen programs initiated by local parishes and settlement houses with the aid of grovernment grants. However, bureaucratic resources have tended to supplement existing freameworks, rather than effect another restructuring of community. The family group, in particular, is still the most important social capital of South Village Italians. The elderly, for example, rely primarily on adult children.

Although a neighborhood-based Italian American community is in eclipse, selected aspects of the Italian heritage in the South Village have become more prominent. As the neighborhood becomes less Italian, sights and attractions conducive to an ethnic experience have become available to publics outside the South Village. Thus, The New York Times "Weekend Section" (August 26, 1983) called attention to a local pasta maker and the Romanesque architecture of one of the Italian churches (the same article directs the consumer of urban culture to Federal Period row houses on Charlton Street and a kosher deli on the lower East Side). The old Italian church has become quite self-conscious in its display of the ethnic heritage; in a 1966 yearbook, it saw itself competing with the Greenwich Village bohemian quarter for tourists. More recently, South Village merchants have been giving patrons the ethnic ambiance they seem to desire; an unassuming luncheonette was transformed into a "casa di cafè" and a corner tavern installed facilities for the "al fresco" trade. This stylization and commercialization of the Italian heritage is superimposed on the social worlds of local Italian Americans, although the animated cornerboys and the old women in black coats have inadvertently become part of the "cultural scene" (Irwin, 1977) that entertains and enriches cosmopolitan urban residents.

As an ethnic quarter, the South Village is at a distinct disadvantage relative to the nearby Mulberry Street/East Side community. The latter has recently been designated as a "special landmarks district" and "symbol of Italian life in New York", (New York Department of City Planning, 1974) and has received the city government's commitment to programs that would restore its Italian character. This made official the East Side's status as "Little Italy", although the ensuing "risorgimento" is almost entirely commercial. While this has overshadowed the South Village (and other Italian neighborhoods), its restaurants, shops and street festivals are still capable of generating a representative ethnic scene (the relative advantage of Mulberry Street should be qualified in light of the ongoing expansion of Chinatown).

The initial settlements like the South Village and Mulberry Street have also attained a special significance for mainstream and higher status Italian Americans. Hitherto, the old neighborhood has been a measure of how far they have come socially and economically; ties had to be severed to resist cultural backsliding and consolidate status gains. With the qualified acceptance of ethnicity, and the increasing respectability of Italian American ethnicity in particular (Tricarico, 1984), the old neighborhoods have been regarded in a new light. For mobile Italian Americans, "the neighborhood" is able to mediate a meaningful connection to a cherished ethnic past; the annual festa Italiana, al fresco cafès, Italian bakeries, etc., furnish opportunities for the situational expression of ethnicity. As such, one can be Italian American without disrupting or compromising — and now, perhaps, even enhancing — mainstream, middle class identities (Tricarico, 1984). Although they have transcended it socially and psychologically, the Italian neighborhood can be experienced on the level of "symbolic ethnicity" (Gans, 1982).

25

Italian Americans on Long Island: The Foundation Years

SALVATORE J. LAGUMINA
Nassau Community College
Garden City, New York

FOR years it has been my consuming interest to trace ethnicity among Long Island's population by focusing on Italian Americans, the largest of the area's ethnic groups. Inspired by such classic studies as *Beyond the Melting Pot*, by Daniel S. Moynihan and Nathan Glazer, I became convinced that the alchemetic effect of the intense and unprecedented mixture of ethnic groups in the United States still had not blotted out the Italian Americans' sense of heritage, and that a blending of groups into a standardized mass has not yet occurred (Femminella, New York, 1968). Above all I was convinced that the story of the Italian American contribution to the quality of life on Long Island has not been told. For too long there has been media preoccupation with the asocial aspects of Italian American life — especially with the activities of the Mafia or Cosa Nostra. In the latter instances when Long Island was mentioned, it frequently was in connection with the demise of a reputed "family head" in a comfortable home in Nassau County.

The story of Italian Americans on Long Island is, in truth, a tale much richer and more wholesome than that of organized crime. It is the story of a hard-working people struggling to earn a decent living for themselves and their families, an account of upward mobility which has been a dramatic rise to power, as in the case of Senator Alphonse D'Amato, for example. But success has had its price — the price of sacrifice and deprivation, of ostracism and discrimination, of poverty and neglect. Not all have been able to overcome these adversities of life, to be certain, but a significant number have risen from the depths of society to a point where they can affirm by their successes fulfillment of the American dream.

While it is beyond the scope of this presentation to write a comprehensive history, (this will be accomplished in a forthcoming book) an overview of their presence on Long Island for the better part of a century is possible. The best available evidence is that they represent about thirty percent of the population of Nassau and Suffolk Counties or about 750,000, a significant number when it is realized that it is a greater aggregate figure than that of Italian Americans in most states and cities in the nation and that it constitutes the densest Italian American concentration of any two counties in the nation (New York State Manuscript Census, Nassau County, 1914, 1925; U.S. Census Schedule of the Population Tracts, 1900). New York City's Italian American population may be greater; however it is spread over five counties.

The large numbers involved do not themselves make an identity, of course. When and why did they arrive? How is an Italian different from other Americans? How does he feel about his heritage? How has his residency in our midst influenced the social, political, and economic forces in Long Island? These are only a few of the many questions which abound.

As students of American immigration have shown, mass immigration from Italy began approximately one hundred years ago, that is by the 1880s and it was within a few years of the onset of this massive migration that Long Islanders would see them settling amongst them. However, long before this era individual Italians came to live on Long Island and thereby merit a place as pioneers of Italian immigration into this region. Undoubtedly the first was Pietro Cesare Alberti who came to New Amsterdam during the period of Dutch settlement and built a home in what is now Brooklyn in 1639 (Pyrke, 1943). Whether he set foot in Nassau is unknown but the historical record does indicate that his descendants did reside in Nassau and Suffolk counties, particularly in Hempstead and Oyster Bay. The family name was later altered to a Dutch facsimile, since it seems to have in fact been assimilated into the predominant Dutch society on Long Island.

One American of Italian descent from Long Island who deserves mention is Francis Spinola, the first Italian American elected to Congress (LaGumina, New York, 1982). Spinola was born in Stony Brook in 1821, gained fame as a brigadier general during the Civil War and subsequently held a string of public offices including that of alderman and supervisor of New York City, New York State assemblyman, state senator and United States congressman from 1887 to 1891. His public career existed largely before the great tide of Italian immigration to this country and therefore, probably could not be considered an Italian American politician in the sense of reflecting the aspirations of a distinct immigrant minority striving to obtain a position of importance and prestige. Nevertheless, during his congressional tenure Spinola openly confessed pride in his ethnic background and displayed a warm disposition toward immigrants then entering the country, of which Italians began to predominate.

The story of Alberti and Spinola were isolated if interesting examples of individual Americans of Italian descent who could be considered among the first of their ethnic background to reside in Long Island. The masses of Italian immigrants, however, came into the region during the latter part of the 19th century when emigration from southern and eastern Europe began to approach epic proportions. The historical record indicates that the first-comers of the mass immigration era were attracted by the then prevailing economic opportunities usually in the capacity of cheap laborers. For example, the Belmont Race Track, which was constructed in 1902, utilized considerable numbers of Italian laborers to clear the lands of trees preparatory to the creation of the race track (Winsche, 1964). As one historian described it, hundreds of Italians, because they worked for low wages, were employed in the construction and housed in a large shed which accommodated 370 of them when laid side by side. In those days laborers were not accorded much esteem, as could be seen by newspaper references which identified them with numbers. For example, one item read, "No. 2398, a laborer who was crushed to death...". It was apparently sufficient to deny the unfortunate victim even the dignity of his Christian name on the occasion of his death.

By the turn of the century a number of Long Island communities attracted Italian immigrants, several of which will be cited in the examples which follow. According to the United States Census Bureau there were 204 Italian immigrants in Inwood, a hamlet located in the southwest corner of Nassau County and adjacent to Queens County in New York City. This figure rendered Inwood the largest Italian enclave on Long Island at the time. Part of the Rockaways, Inwood, along with its sister communities in the vicinity, was gaining popularity with New York City residents as a nearby and desirable place, in which to enjoy recreational opportunities afforded by a bountious nature. Accordingly, the latter part of the nineteenth and the early part of the twentieth centuries found the area in need of manpower to work the estates and recreational facilities.

Indications are that the native inhabitants in the community were uneasy about the Italians in their midst whose number increased yearly as Italian names replaced non-Italian ones as homeowners and small businessmen. Most of the Italians who settled in Inwood by 1910 were from Calabria and Sicily. Reservations about the desirablity of the ethnic group can be gleaned in the newspaper accounts, which dealt with Italian Americans in the first two decades of the century. Without question, local newspaper preoccupation was with criminal, violent and anti-social behavior perpetrated by Italian Americans either against native Americans or other Italians. The researchers cannot help but be impressed with the numerous and detailed accounts of criminal assaults and violence given extensive and unwanted publicity, frequently as front page matter. The only other activities of the Inwood Italian community which merited similar coverage in this area were on occasions of feast day celebrations such as St. Cono's Day, and the creation of an ethnic parish — Our Lady of Good Counsel.

For Port Washington, situated on a peninsula off the north shore on the Long Island Sound, it was sand which served as the improbable catalyst for the presence of Italians in the community in 1900 (Carucci, 1981; Williams, 1983). Coming primarily as laborers into the burgeoning sand and gravel mines which operated in the town and its vicinity, Italians were employed by the hundreds in what was one of the very few large-scale industries on Long Island at the time. The importance of the sand industry can be ascertained by reference to the fact that it accounted for most of the sand necessary for the construction of New York City's first subway, Fort Schuyler, and numerous skyscrapers.

Although there was a mixture of nationalities, clearly Italians emerged as the largest single ethnic group in the workforce. Most of the early Italian arrivals to Port Washington were from the province of Avellino with the result that many of their descendants still reside there to this day. Virtually all came as laborers although some quickly moved beyond that status becoming sand and gravel entrepreneurs themselves. James Marino, who emigrated from Avellino in the mid-1880s is a case in point. Correctly gauging the potential in the sand industry, he became a pioneer in the field through management of the Crescent Sand and Gravel Bank. Parlaying his access to the large Italian labor pool to good advantage, by persuading fellow Avellinesi to move to the sand pits, he was also a *padrone*, even if a benevolent one, operating a grocery store, a boarding house and a saloon which his workmen were expected to patronize. By 1900 he had married and begun to raise a large family, while also boarding twenty-four "day-laborers", mostly recent arrivals from Italy. Marino subsequently became deputy sheriff, a successful real estate promoter and a leading figure in the community. The John Marino Sons of Italy Lodge in Port Washington — Nassau County's second largest lodge, is named after his son who lost his life while in the American Army during the first World War.

Westbury represents another long-standing Italian American community in Nassau County (LaGumina, 1980). When Joseph Posillico and James Razzano left Durazzano, a mountain town near Naples, for the United States in the 1880s, they began an influx of generations of immigrants from their home town to the Long Island location — a migration which perdures to the present. Italian immigrants from Durazzano, and nearby Saviano and Nola came to work on the developing estates then being constructed in Westbury for some of the nation's wealthiest members of the establishment: the Whitneys, the Winthrops, the Phipps. They also came to work in local nurseries which employed hundreds of workers at the turn of the century.

The Westbury Italian American community established some of the oldest ethnic organizations on Long Island. For example, the Dell'Assunta

Society, a mutual aid society organized in 1911, boasts of sponsoring the oldest and most continuous feast day celebration in the metropolitan area — even older than the famed San Gennaro feast. The Durazzano Society, a similar organization, founded in 1929, continues to limit membership to those born in Durazzano or their descendants. In addition, there are a few other functioning Italian American organizations for the ethnic group in Westbury.

When Vito Capobianco, a stonecutter from Sturno, left for Glen Cove, it was the beginning of a large migration of Italians to that North Shore community — a movement which occurred about the same time as that of Westbury. Capobianco and others from his village who joined him found employment in the estates then emerging in the vicinity of Glen Cove, one of them being that of the banking tycoon J.P. Morgan, while another was that of the Woolworth family. These jobs provided steady work but low pay (*Glen Cove Echo*, 1913-1960; *Glen Cove Record*, 1934-1976 *passim*).

A poetess tried to capture the impact of the growing Italian population in a poem written in later times. Although romanticized, it gives some insight into the impression made:

With the tide of immigration
Strangers came from Europe's shore,
Seeking freedom like those others'
Of three hundred years before,

Dark-eyed, dark skinned gay Italians,
Joined the immigration throng,
Tillers of the farm and vineyard
Master of the minstrel song,
Of at evening time their neighbors,
Listened as their songs were sung,
For love stories set to music,
Knows no barriers of tongue,......

One ideal of how rapid the increase was can be gleaned by a look at the enrollment lists of Glen Cove's St. Patrick Church in 1895 which listed not more than one or two students out of an enrollment of some 400 with identifiable Italian names. In 1911, however, the community's Italian population had founded the San Rocco Society, a mutual aid society which was committed to building an Italian parish with its own school. This latter development came to pass in 1937 as St. Rocco's Church was completed on land provided by the society (*First Souvenir Journal of St. Rocco's Parish*, January, 1937).

Another mark of the identifiable Italian background lies in the formation of the oldest Nassau Sons of Italy lodge established in 1920; an institution which has been functioning as a fraternal order ever since. In 1950 a new building housing the lodge was dedicated to Guiseppe Nigro, who for many years proved to be a tireless promoter of the Sons of Italy throughout Long

Island. His biography mirrors that of a number of other Italians from Glen Cove. Emigrating as a poor teen-age immigrant also from Sturno, Italy, Nigro earned his first money working on truck farms in Glen Cove and eventually entered the building business, prospering by building homes for immigrants who were moving from New York City into the suburbs in the periods following the first World War.

To further illustrate the coming of the age of Italians in Glen Cove a final item will be mentioned. When Luke Mercadante ran and won the office of mayor in 1947, it marked the first time an Italian American was nominated for the post despite the fact that the Italians then comprised 30 percent of the community's population. The fact that Mercadante defeated a Scot for whom he once caddied at the golf course made the victory even sweeter. Mercadante's election began a succession of six mayors of Italian descent (including the current mayor Alan Parente).

Elmont is still another community in western Nassau which has acquired a substantial population of Americans of Italian descent. Thus today the school district offers at least one bilingual Italian American course to accommodate the Italian-speaking newer immigrants. But Italian movement into the community commenced most likely at the time when they worked to build the famous racetrack which previously was mentioned. Although the early period is sketchy, it appears that Elmont's population began to grow in the post-World War I period as a result of the entreprenuership of a Brooklyn realty firm which aggressively promoted land sales advertising "Ideal attractive home site on high fertile ground". Its proximity to the city and the availability of mass transportation rendered it an unusual attraction.

One of the most interesting examples of Italians upward mobility in Elmont is the story of Anthony Barbiero, who moved into the community after his marriage in 1940 — his house constructed on the site of a former farm. The old farm name subsequently was changed to Alden Terrace. Barbiero became very active in the community and in 1954 was elected school board president.

A look at the DePaola family of Elmont offers another insight into a cross-section of Italian American minor entreprenuers. Leonardo DePaola, born in 1899, came to New York City in 1919 and lived in the Hell's Kitchen neighborhood, an area made famous by Mario Puzo in his book *The Fortunate Pilgrim*. De Paola married Rosa Tota in a bethrothal which was arranged in 1924. After a few years he and his wife returned to their home town in Bari, Italy, only to emigrate to America once more, this time for good. He worked in the ice business in New York City, a business into which a considerable number of Barese entered, especially in Brooklyn. As the age of refrigeration expanded and the ice business declined, DePaola decided to enter another field and invested his money in the purchase of 12 acres of land on Dutch Broadway. As a result of his membership in many Italian American organizations he learned that most of them sought a place outside New York City where they could celebrate the feast days of their saints. They sought some land which could be turned into a chapel. In 1938, together with a member from one of the groups with which he associated, DePaola opened a small bar and restaurant, placed picnic tables where he had room, and proceeded to rent the space to the Italian American organizations from Brooklyn, Manhattan and the Bronx. For many of these people it was the first time they had ever been to Long Island. And many of them eventually came to live there so that today Elmont, which was originally settled by colonies of German immigrants, contains one of the largest Italian American populations on the island. The DePaolas originally lived in six rooms over what became the chapel and from which they ran the small business; today they have graduated to proprietorships of several businesses run by various members of the family.

The late nineteenth century saw Italian immigrants entering Suffolk County communities mostly as laborers, construction workers and gardeners. Once again, although the record is scanty, several items indicate their presence in these capacities during these years. One is a newspaper article dated April 27, 1894 which told of 200 Italians employed on an extension of the Long Island Railroad between Port Jefferson and Wading River (Seyfried, 1966, Garden City). The article related a story of these workers striking over a failure to receive wages due them — the company had apparently paid the labor contractors who had not paid the Italian workers. In the course of time this incident produced a widespread strike in the industry as hundreds of other Italian railroad laborers joined in the strike. Eventually the dispute was resolved, albeit only partially satisfactorily so far as the Italian employees were concerned. This historical event was not an isolated instance, but rather one of several in which Long Island Italian immigrant workers undertook strike action to promote their cause. As such they warrant attention as a positive force, thereby counterbalancing the prevailing stereotypes of Italian anti-unionism during that period.

In the early years of the twentieth century, at a time when the majority of Italian immigrants worked and lived in the industrial cities of the Northeast, localizing the neighborhoods of cheapest rent, not a few of them longed for a chance to replicate the lives they knew in the old country — namely lives in which they worked the soil here in America. Some of these city inhabitants held on to that dream tenaciously, saving their money until they could buy some land in the country. This was the background to the establishment of an Italian colony in Patchogue and its vicinity approximately 70 miles from New York City.

Working either in construction or gardening or as truck farmers on their own lots, the number of Italians in the Patchogue area grew in the early twentieth century. Early in the century a Sons of Italy lodge was established in East

Patchogue (then called Hagerman), and masses for ten to twelve Italian Catholic families were celebrated there. In the pre-World War I years, in recognition of the feast of St. Joseph, celebrated by the Italians, St. Joseph Patron Church was constructed. Apparently dissatisfied with the local non-Italian Catholic clergy who knew neither their language and cutoms, nor their religious mentality, the growing Italian community of Patchogue proper determined to build a national parish of their own in 1919. While the church was being built, Italian laborers, their wives and children attended masses at a make-shift church in a local garage for three years. The first pastor of the Italian parish was Monsignor Rapael A. Cioffi of New York City who was succeeded by a continuous string of Italian pastors. The results of the endeavors was the building of Our Lady of Mount Carmel, one of the truly first national Italian parishes on Long Island. For nearly forty years the parish membership remained exclusively Italian, celebrated familiar Italian saint days several times a year and carried out other distinctive Italian customs. This uniqueness as a national parish continued until 1965 when, in recognition of a more heterogenous population, especially the growing Hispanic portion then entering the community, Our Lady of Mount Carmel was designated a territorial parish by the diocese of Rockville Centre. Although the Italian immigrant era of Patchogue seems to be over, its Italianita can still be seen in such landmarks as an Italian language movie theater, Italian bakery and fish stores on its main street.

The Suffolk Community of San Remo is an interesting example of Italian impact on Long Island. A small community tucked away in the North Shore of the Nissequogue River, it had its origins in the 1920s when Generoso Pope, publisher of *Il Corriere* and *Il Progresso-Italo-Americano*, along with some builders bought 194 acres of land in the vicinity of the Smithtown Harbor. As speculators, Pope and his associates focused on attracting Italians from New York City, correctly gauging their desires to own their own land where they could eventually build their own homes, plant fruit trees and enjoy the verdant surroundings. In an effort to attribute their holding some of the best of the old country images, the developers named their property San Remo after the famed resort town in the Italian Riviera. The property was then divided into city-size plots with city lot designations and advertised in Pope's newspapers.

To induce the New York City Italians to consider purchasing this land the developers treated prospective buyers to a trip on the Long Island Railroad, whereupon reaching the San Remo destination, they would be met by an agent of the company and provided with sandwiches and beer as he showed them 20' x 100' lots which he tried to sell for the price of $300 per lot. At the time the area was bereft of electricity and running water and had no streets. The absence of these facilities notwithstanding, quite a number of Italians purchased lots and began to enjoy limited use such as camping on their grounds during the summers when they could make use of the nearby beach. Eventually a number of them began to build homes, mostly for summer use, although a few could be utilized year round. The Great Depression interrupted the development, however, forcing a number to give up their lots for failure to pay taxes. A smaller number of stalwart families held on returning on weekends and summers over the years and gradually developed their lands. These latter people formed the nucleus of the on-going Italian element in the area and not a few of them and their children became prosperous as proprietors of important businesses in and around the community. San Remo has changed over the years as homes were built on small narrow plots which leave little room for the fruit trees and tomato patches of yesteryear. Nevertheless Italian names still predominate.

Without a doubt Copiague is one of the most interesting and most unique of Italian American communities on Long Island. All one has to do to sense its *Italianità* is to drive through its streets and see street names like Mazzini Boulevard, Garibaldi Boulevard, Dante Boulevard and Marconi Boulevard, among others. These names were not coincidences but in fact reflected genuine Italian roots.

Located on the southwestern shore of Suffolk County, this community came into its own in 1895 when it received official designation as Copiague therby distinguishing it from Lindenhurst and Amityville, two nearby and better known towns. During is infancy years Copiague constituted a sleepy country villlage existing anonymously amidst more popular communities and known primarily for its large trees and gardens and as a place where a few individuals maintained summer homes. In 1903 it was assigned its own post office and shortly afterwards elicited the interest of a number of Italian immigrants attracted by the bucolic setting. Most of the early Italians to settle in Copiague were from the northern part of Italy especially from the province of Emilia-Romagna — people who had previously settled in the Italian Belmont section of the Bronx. By the outbreak of the first World War, the northern part of Copiague, where the Italians lived, came to be known as Marconiville, named after the famous inventor of the wireless. Guglielmo Marconi did in fact visit the Long Island village on at least two occasions in 1917 and 1921, stopping at a hotel which was also named after him. The occasions of his visits were the result of a friendship with a former classmate John Campagnoli, a northern Italian engineer from the University of Bologna who had turned into a real estate developer and who deserves credit as the catalyst for Italian settlement of Copiague. In this capacity Campagnoli advertised the lots of land he had for sale in Italian American newspapers and proceeded to sell either building sites or homes primarily to Italian Americans. Indeed his advertisements emphasized Marconiville as an "Italian" community. While many of his initial customers purchased Marconiville property in a desire to partake of the kind of living they loved, "working under the sun in planting vegetable gardens and tending wine-producing grape vines".

Marconi's visits to the Long Island community which bore his name were usually carried on in conjunction with inspections of wireless stations in nearby towns. These visits became instances of high honor and pride for the local Italian community which showed up in its entirety, clear indication of the inventor's popularity among his fellow ethnics. Campagnoli's effort to render "Marconiville" the official name of the community, including recognition by the Town of Babylon board, unfortunately failed, due, in considerable part, to opposition from the WASP and other non-Italian groups in the vicinity. Later developers in Copiague continued to utilize Italian identification in attempts to lure prospective home buyers. Thus one development replete with canals, picturesque bridges, and the lions of Venice mounted on tall pillars, was dubbed the "American Venice". Weekend visitors from the city would be regaled by music emanating from a bandstand as they were taken on tours of the community on board gondolas manned by colorfully dressed gondoliers.

Copiague's Italian roots are also visible in the establishment of an Italian parish — Our Lady of the Assumption (Golden Jubilee Journal, August 1977). The first mass was celebrated in 1928, but the parish's growth over the next decade was slow. It took thirteen years before the basement church was covered with superstructure which would house the real house of worship. In 1940 a young priest, Fr. Francis Del Vecchio, was assigned to the parish and succeeded in energizing the community to complete the building of the parish plant including the church, parish hall and rectory, performing much of the work himself as he donned overalls and plastered walls. By the time his tenure in the parish was over, it had become a strong functioning entity. Although subsequent changes in the population have altered the almost exclusive Italian membership — so that it can no longer be considered a strictly Italian parish — nevertheless, Americans of Italian descent continue to be the predominant group.

What has been related is a brief description of the founding of Italian enclaves on Long Island. The survey format utilized, however, while offering a glimpse into ethnic group life, precludes comprehensiveness and thereby fails to do justice to reflections of *Italianità* in other Long Island locations such as Valley Stream and Shirley, for example. Nor has it been possible, within the space limitations of this presentation, to explicate interaction regarding many other topics such as the role Italian Americans have played as builders, contractors, gardeners, landscapers, caterers, writers, artists, clergymen and politicians in the life of Long Island. Nevertheless, what has been presented, it is hoped, is the beginning of an acknowledgement that Americans of Italian descent have been an integral part of a century. It is hoped that this presentation demonstrates a preference for the possibilities of home ownership more available in the suburbs than in the central cities at the earlier stage of Italian immigration. It is hoped, too, that this presentation indicates a selection for working the soil on the part of suburban home-seekers, for experiencing a milder degree of discrimination from the host society as well as from within the ethnic community (for example, *padronismo*).

Finally, it is hoped that this account of Italians in suburbia demonstrates that a minority of these immigrants took advantage of the option of settling in the less-congested areas of the country almost from the beginning of their sojourn in America. In so doing they paved the way for the presence of a large corporation of contemporary Italian Americana in the nation's suburban localities.

Concord and Discord:
Italians and Ethnic Interactions
in Tampa, Florida, 1886-1930

GARY R. MORMINO,
University of South Florida

GEORGE E. POZZETTA,
University of Florida

DURING the past twenty years our knowledge of the Italian immigrant experience has greatly expanded. We now have at hand a variety of community studies more specialized examinations of selected aspects of Italian migration (the family, crime, mobility, etc.), and analyses which provide a conceptual framework to assist in understanding the wider implications of this great folk movement. What we should like to examine today is one aspect of this tapestry that perhaps has not received the scholarly attention it deserves. We are referring to the interactional dimensions of the immigrant experience in America. Using the Italian community in Tampa, Florida as a case study, this preliminary exploration suggests some of the questions present in an inquiry of this sort and proposes some hypotheses that may be useful to other community studies.

With some notable exceptions, scholars have not addressed in a systematic way questions dealing with the adaptations and interrelationships resulting from the coming together of diverse immigrant groups in North American urban centers. This is true despite the fact that immigrants often came into initial and most immediate contact with other immigrant groups, rather than with some idealized "American" society. As one important study of ethnic interactions pointed out, most scholarly analysis has been conducted "in terms of majority-minority relations" or, more recently, along the lines of comparative group experiences (Juliani and Hutter, 1975, p. 42). Although these efforts have resulted in important advances, gaps remain in our understanding of how groups interact with one another. This is particularly true of the non-confrontational, more ordinary patterns of life in multi-ethnic neigh-borhoods. An examination of such interactional situations, sociologists Richard Juliani and Mark Hutter remind us, is necessary "to understand minority-minority relations as another normal and enduring part of the social structure of complex, pluralistic societies" such as our own.[1] Moreover, it is important to see how these relationships related to the wider urban context and how they evolved over time.

Our brief remarks will deal with Tampa, Florida, an important manufac-turing center situated along the Gulf Coast of Florida. More specifically, they will focus on Ybor City, a multi-ethnic, multi-racial enclave located in the northeast sector of the city. Ethnicity in Ybor City was shaped in important ways by the interactions taking place among four distinct groups (Italians, Cubans, Spaniards, and Afro-Cubans), and, on a different level, by the relationships existing between these immigrants and the host society. The nature of these relationships, both structural and social, changed over time and place, but they remained central to defining what it meant to be "immigrant" (and later "ethnic") in Tampa.[2] By examining the nature of these contact points we can perhaps gain insight into the processes by which groups in such multi-ethnic situations sorted out their New World orders for themselves. There exists also the opportunity to explore the dynamics by which the wider context of ethnicity was arranged in a bustling, urban-industrial center.[3]

Tampa played a key role in the history of the Florida frontier, first as a fort and later as a trading post and commercial hub of a region open to exploration in the 1840s. Change came slowly to South Florida, and as late as the 1870s, economic stagnation, political paralysis, and yellow fever forestalled growth. As in other areas of the "New South", city fathers in the late nineteenth century combined an aggressive entrepreneurial spirit with bouyant boosterism to spur development. Yet, almost unique in the southern experience

---

[1] Richard Juliani and Mark Hutter, "Research Problems in the Study of Italian and Jewish Interaction in Community Settings", in Jean A. Scarpaci, ed., *The Interaction of Italians and Jews in America* (American Italian Historical Association, 1975), pp. 42,43; Ronald Bayor, *Neighbors in Conflict: The Irish, Germans, Jews, and Italians of New York City, 1929-1941* (Baltimore, 1978) deals primarily with conflict situations, but does have material on neighborhood developments.

[2] Gary R. Mormino, "Tampa and the New Urban South: The Weight Strike of 1899", *Florida Historical Quarterly*, 60, January, 1982, pp. 337-56. A very insightful essay by D.R. Middleton, "The Organization of Ethnicity in Tampa", *Ethnic Groups*, 3, 1981, pp. 281-306, has informed the arguments of this paper.

[3] We should add here that each group possessed an interior history of its own that could be investigated with profit and pleasure. Thus, this essay is not to deny that there were aspects of each groups' adaptations that belonged very much to its own inner strategies, cultural imperatives and personalities.

Tampa's expansion was powerfully linked to the inflow of foreign immigration (Mormino and Pizzo, 1983, pp. 60-76; Long, 1971, pp. 31-44).

Numbering only 720 residents in 1880, Tampa awakened from its economic slumber in 1884 when railroad magnate Henry Bradley Plant wove the city into his transportation network. Small discoveries of phosphate near the city added to the commercial activity, which, up to that point, had consisted mainly of the sale of fish, cattle and citrus from the hinterland. By 1885 Tampa contained fewer than 1,000 inhabitants (U.S. Census, 1900, p. 214; Long, 1971, pp. 333-345).

This equilibrium was profoundly altered when an enterprising Spanish industrialist, Don Vicente Martinez Ybor, decided to move his cigar manufacturing operations to Tampa in that same year. Embroiled in bitter labor disputes with his fractious workforce and seeking a more competitive location, Ybor was attracted to Tampa. The newly formed Tampa Board of Trade lured him with free grants of land and pledges to protect the cigar industry from disturbances. In a section of unincorporated land to the northeast of Tampa, Ybor laid out an industrial community with workers' homes, factories, streets, and wooden sidewalks (Westfall, 1977, pp. 55-75; Muniz, 1976, pp. 6-14). Native Tampans welcomed this addition to their municipal fortunes, but very early exhibited a set of ambivalent attitudes toward the cigar workforce, which was composed almost entirely of Cubans, Afro-Cubans, Spaniards, and later Italians. They quickly employed the word "Latin", a term of generalized ethnicity when referring to these immigrant workmen, a label that simplified for them a confusing blend of peoples and cultures. Immigrants countered with the equally inclusive, but more accurate, term of "Anglo" when referring to Tampans [(the notable exception here being American blacks, who were given specific identities by each immigrant group) (Federal Writer's Project, n.d., p. 186; American Guide Series, p. 42)]

The economic fortunes of Tampa soared as more and more cigar factories relocated to this emerging cigar manufacturing center. "The cigar industry is to this city what the iron industry is to Pittsburgh", exclaimed the *Tampa Morning Tribune* (July 30, 1896). By Ybor City's first anniversary, some 3,000 immigrants were settled into the community and engaged in producing high quality, hand rolled cigars. By 1890 the city counted 5,500 individuals, with more than 50 percent of the population composed of foreign born immigrants connected in some capacity with the cigar industry. Census takers in 1900 listed over 15,000 residents (almost surely an undercount), 5,000 of whom were cigarmakers. By 1910 the city numbered nearly 40,000 inhabitants, including almost 21,000 foreign born. Ethnic development followed almost parallel lines in West Tampa (incorporated in 1895 but remaining separate from Tampa until 1925, which, by the end of the new century's first decade possessed more than 8,000 residents, only 626 of whom were native born, of native parentage (U.S. Census, 1910, Washington, 1912, pp. 330-32; Muniz, 1963, pp. 335-336; Long, p. 341).

During the period 1886-1910, the cigar industry accounted for 75 percent of the city's entire payroll and the percentage of foreign born employed in the industry never dipped below 70 percent. By 1895 Tampa had some 130 factories of various sizes, with more constructed monthly, and in 1909 the value of tobacco products accounted for nearly 82 percent of the city's manufacturing effort. The cigar trades and ancillary industries, therefore, dominated the economic structure of Ybor City (U.S. Senate, pt. 14, 1911, p. 87; *Tampa Morning Tribune*, Dec. 18, 1911; Rerrick, 1902, p. 222). It should be mentioned, however, that though Tampa was a one industry town, it was not a one company town. This fact allowed for a substantial amount of diversity within the ranks of owners and it also encouraged the efforts of enterprising immigrants to begin small-scale *chinchales* [(operations employing a handful of individuals)(Rabb, 1938; Scaglione, 1933, pp. 7-10)].

The cigar industry arriving in Tampa in 1886 was characterized by skilled workers who possessed a special work ethos. Dominated by a pre-modern craft mentality and possessing a full compliment of artisan work styles and outlooks, it created an industrial environment governed by the rhythms of the individual. There existed within factories a clear occupational hierarchy, which in the early years was organized along ethnic lines. The first major division existed between salaried and piecework employees. The former category included foremen, managers, skilled clerical staff, salesmen and accountants, most of whom typically were Spaniards. The salaried staff also included *selectores* (selectors), trained men who selected the tobacco on the basis of color, maturity and texture. Spaniards filled these ranks exclusively. Below this level were skilled cigarmakers, who ordered themselves by status in relation to the size, complexity, and particularly the rate of return attached to the type of cigar produced. Next in the hierarchy were banders, strippers, box makers and packers, and the like. Here the Spanish generally held the higher level positions of skilled craftsmen, with Cubans ranking below. At the bottom of the occupational ladder rested those individuals who did not work directly with tobacco, but merely dealt with the physical tasks of sweeping, hauling, portering, etc. Cubans and early arriving Italians usually filled these positions (Campbell and McLendon, 1939; Leon, 1962, pp. 76-83).

Skilled cigar workers followed distinctive work styles. Cigarmakers typically had no formal schedule. They came and went as they pleased, often taking extended coffee breaks at neighboring cafes catering to immigrant artisans. Cigarmakers also enjoyed the privileges of taking home free cigars at day's end, and of smoking as many cigars during working hours as they desired.[4] A complicated system of apprenticeship also served to order the workplace,

---

[4] Interview with Fermin Souto, Federal Writer's Project (Tampa, n.d.), pp. 3-5; Muniz, *Los cubanos*, p. 89. A short strike was occasioned by an effort to deny workers free cigars. *See*, *Tampa Morning Tribune*, September 23, 28, 29, 30, 1911.

with its own panoply of relationships, privileges, and perquisites. In general, Spanish owners maintained a set of pre-modern, *Patron* attitudes toward their workers, reflective of an older style of work management. Ybor exemplified this tradition by providing kitchen utensils for workers' homes at his expense and sponsoring numerous banquets and musical performances for his factory staff (Westfall, pp. 118, 130; Federal Writer's Project, Tampa, p. 18; del Rio, Tampa, 1950, p. 11).

Most symbolic of the special *ambiente* of the industry was the presence of *el lectore*, the reader. The practice of reading from a raised platform (the *tribuna*) in the workroom had been a Cuban tradition. Cigarmakers paid the lector's fee and also selected the items to read. During the course of a typical day, the lector read selections from the labor press and excerpts from the great radical masters (Marx, Kropotkin, Malatesta, Fanelli, etc.). Among the works of fiction read, those featuring proletarian themes of the class struggle found particular favor [(Hugo, Gorky, Zola, etc.) (Perez, 1975, pp. 443-44; Gallo, 1936; Interview with Coniglio, May 2, 1976)]. "When in 1902 I landed in Tampa", reminisced Angelo Massari (who became a banker), "I found myself in a world of radicals". The lectura, therefore, provided an underpinning for a militant labor movement that took root in Ybor City. This fact was not lost on the owners, who waged an unremitting war to abolish the system of reading and gain control of the workforce and workplace (Massari, New York, 1965, p. 107; New York, 1959; Stelzner and Bazo, 1965, pp. 124-31).

The importance of the reader extended beyond factory walls, as the information disseminated from the tribuna filtered outward into the wider immigrant community through a series of informal networks. Family and friends at the evening meal discussed readings of the day thus extending the range of contacts. Early Italian arrivals established a loose system of meetings among fellow immigrants to allow those few who had gained access to factories to pass on news gleaned from the daily readings (Interview with Provenzano, Tampa, March 13, 1982; Interview with Longo, June 1, 1979).

The cigar industry also influenced residential patterns. The groupings of factories close by each other — and the constellation of workers' homes about them — resulted in a high degree of residential concentration (but relatively low density because of a relative absence of multifamily units). Remarkably for a city rooted in the deep South, Afro-Cubans resided in integrated neighborhoods in Ybor City.[5] In the early years, the very low cost of housing and rentals, coupled with the frontier-like quality of the surrounding area, limited the possibilities for wider dispersal. The mere clustering of

[5] Interview with Juan Maella, August 1, 1983, Tampa; Interview with Francesco Rodriguez, July 15, 1983, Tampa; Tampa City Directories, 1900-1930, Special Collections, USF Library, Tampa. The remarkable insurance maps of the Sanborn Company show the clustering effect. They are available for Tampa from 1884 onward (with some missing years) and are located at the University of Florida.

housing, of course, did not in itself make for social contact as even close neighbors can be invisible. Yet individual and group contacts appear to have been frequent and fervent.[6]

The topography of the enclave added its own distinctive flavor to the evolving immigrant society. The land lay very flat and few buildings were more than one story in height (the exception being the factories and the club buildings). Hence, the opportunities for mutual sharing of such functions as parades, picnics and festivals were enchanced. Unlike residents of the canyons of New York's lower East Side, few individuals in Ybor City could avoid notice of their neighbors' public lives.

It is impossible in this short space to do more than suggest the differences characterizing the migration streams that flowed into Tampa. These divergent patterns, however, did play important community roles in determining the nature and extent of the interactions that followed.

SPANIARDS

The Spanish community consisted almost entirely of immigrants who came from the three northern provinces of Asturias, Galicia, and Catalonia (areas of Spain long noted for traditions of migration and immigration). The great majority had spent time in Cuba working in the cigar industry centered in the capital city of Havana. Generally, they followed a pattern of migration which was characterized by the flow of skilled labor and mercantile activity and long periods of sojourner status. Indeed, many Spaniards in the New World "commuted" between Spain and the Americas for extended time periods, maintaining separate households on both sides of the Atlantic. Persistently high ratios of males to females characterized the Spanish presence, as did the heavy use of boarding houses, very low rates of English language usage, and a continued adherence to regional identifications until well into the twentieth century. Also indicative of the strength of Old World connective tissues were the unusually large numbers of Spanish radicals (especially anarchists) who found Tampa a congenial home. Yet, because of the large number of wealthy factory owners among Spaniards, they occupied, as a group, the apex of the immigrant status pyramid (Gomez, 1962, pp. 59-77; Federal Writer's Project, Tampa, pp. 2-5).

CUBANS

Above all, the geographic proximity of Ybor City to Cuba facilitated the process of migration and the peripatetic nature of Cuban movement. The

---

[6] Joan Marie Steffy, "The Cuban Immigration to Tampa, Florida, 1886-1898", (Unpublished M.A. thesis, University of South Florida, 1975), pp. 14-15; Westfall, pp. 82-85. Ybor owned the Ybor City Land and Improvement Company, which controlled much of the early housing.

continuing struggle for independence on the island also profoundly shaped the Cuban community. For the most part, Cubans regarded themselves as exiles, long awaiting *Cuba Libre*. Movement most commonly involved families, in large part due to the unsettled conditions in Cuba. Depending on the fortunes of the cigar industry and the revolution, Cubans shifted between the island and the mainland. After 1898 they diverted their energies to labor militancy and radical activities (Perez, 1978, pp. 129-140; Steffy; *Tampa Morning Tribune*, June 23, 1895).

AFRO-CUBANS

Afro-Cubans tended to live on the periphery of Tampa and Ybor City. They similarly occupied marginal postitions in the economic structure of the community, although Afro-Cuban women appear to have been engaged in a relatively wide range of jobs. They followed essentially the same migration patterns as white Cubans, who courted them during the patriotic struggle against Spain. After 1898, however, Afro-Cubans increasingly assumed separate identities. They constituted roughtly 10 percent of the Cuban population throughout the period under review (*Tampa Times*, Sept. 14, 1977; Muniz, 1982; Cordero, 1982).

ITALIANS

Italian immigrants initially followed classic sojourning patterns, featuring single males seeking seasonal employment. Five Old World villages in west-central Sicily supplied the migrants who made their way to Florida. Two streams branching through New Orleans and St. Cloud, a sugar plantation in east-central Florida, brought individuals first to Tampa. The sojourner stage was very short, however, as the lynching incident in New Orleans (1891) and the suppression of the *fasci* in Sicily (1894) forced a rapid movement into the family stage.[7] Although the latest of the immigrant groups to arrive, by 1894-95 the Italian community already possessed a rough institutional framework and numerous family groups.

Interactions during the initial years of settlement and community formation were principally shaped by events surrounding the struggles in Cuba. The independence movement among Cubans spawned intense organizing activities in Ybor City and West Tampa in support of *Cuba libre* and splintered the city's Spanish-speaking population. Only the Spanish anarchists broke ranks to denounce Spanish colonial policies and support Cuban demands for independence. As the 1898 war approached, relations deteriorated badly

[7] Interview with Rosalia Cannella Ferlita, May 18, 1980, Tampa; Interview with Philip Spoto, June 30, 1979; Interview with Joe Valenti, April 18, 1980; Calogero Messina, *S. Stefano Quisquina: Studio critico* (Palermo, 1977). The villages were Santo Stefano Quisquina, Allessandria della Rocca, Bivona, Cianciana, and Contessa Entellina.

and there were frequent shootings, knifings, and fights between the two groups. Even such a respected figure as Ignazio Haya, an early Spanish industrialist active in the founding of Ybor City, was stoned by Cubans while walking with his wife (Federal Writer's Project, Tampa, p. 177; Steffy, pp. 66-67; *Tampa Morning Tribune*, Dec. 27, 1895; Westfall, p. 119). Indeed, it was Haya who played a key role in forming *Centro Espanol* (the first major immigrant club of Ybor City) as a place of refuge (Interview with Balbontin, Tampa, 1939, pp. 48-54; Bagley, 1948; Middleton, pp. 288-89).

Cubans were the most volatile element of the Latin community as they struggled with the problems of independence and conflicts generated by the local labor movement. They came most often into direct confrontation with other Ybor City groups and the host society. For their part, native Americans often experienced conflicting pulls as they attempted to relate to the Cuban presence. Americans generally supported ideals of freedom and independence, but they feared any disruption of the cigar industry that Cuban activism might bring. Their attitudes, therefore, tended to whipsaw widely.[8]

Within the Cuban immigrant group, the independence movement eroded color distinctions and generated numerous occasions for interracial contact. One must be cautious with easy generalizations about racial harmony, however, as conflicting evidence exists suggesting that racial distinctions remained important throughout.[9] Similar doubt surrounds the opinions Anglos had of Afro-Cubans. At times natives were clearly confused by the curious mix of color and culture that Afro-Cubans possesssed, but they usually solved any dilemmas by simply referring to them as niggers or "Cuban" niggers. The fact that Afro-Cuban residences tended to border these sections of the city normally occupied by native blacks seemed to give added validity to the characterizations (Middleton, p. 290; *Tampa Morning Tribune*, Oct. 29, 1895; September 14, 1977; Steffy, pp. 46, 143).

The first large-scale arrival of Italians occurred in an atmosphere of conflict and confrontation existing between Cubans and Spaniards. This situation affected the multi-layered adaptations Italians faced. On an economic level, Italians encountered obstacles to an easy entry into the cigar factories. Lack of skills and the hostility of Spanish owners and foremen emerged as the most important impediments (U.S. Senate, 1911, pp. 204-05; Westfall, pp. 116-117). Cubans tended to have ambivalent attitudes. They sensed the economic threat that Italians posed, but they were anxious to use these new arrivals as challenges to the Spanish. Hence, they often taught Italians

---

[8] Strike situations most often brought out the widest variations in attitudes. See, *Tampa Morning Tribune*, December 20, 1910 and January 26, 1911, for during-strike and post-strike opinions.

[9] Interview with Jose Ramoń Sanfeliz, Federal Writer's Project (Tampa, 1939), 7; Steffy, pp. 44-45, 46-49. Sanfeliz claimed that the early Cuban Club was characterized as being like "rice and black beans" (with whites and blacks).

cigarmaking skills and frequently patronized Italian stores and shops (Ginesta, Tampa).

Italians squeezed into areas of the occupational structure where vacuums existed and competitive advantages could be forged. Such a strategy, at least in the initial years, promised less overt conflict with immigrant neighbors. Thus, Italians gravitated to street trades, small shops, truck farming, and dairying. One 1909 report detailing street trades, for example, found that of 115 licenses granted, 102 were given to Italians.[10] Yet, these immigrants were not blind actors on the stage of economic structure; there was a range of choice and individual initiative.

Many Italians shop owners went into small businesses that served groups of *paesani*. Others supplied services that aimed at different immigrant clientele. Each large cigar factory spawned a satellite formation of small cafes, shops, and stores. Italians quickly delved the potential markets existing in this situation and learned to supply the necessary services. They opened cafes that specialized in Cuban coffee, others that featured Spanish pastries and meats, etc. These shops were often used to expand the range of contacts for entry into factory jobs and to forge the lingusitic tools needed for entry into the wider Ybor City society. Italians appear also to have almost exclusively shown an inclination to open small groceries in Tampa's Afro-American community (Interview with Scaglione, Tampa, 1980; with Longo, 1979).

A wide variety of middlemen arose in the Italian community to provide the brand of services mandated by Tampa's pluralistic society. Individuals to teach Spanish, contact persons to supply the right types of foods for small cafes and groceries, intermediaries to interact with the Anglo community, etc. all found ample need for their services. This pattern was clearly seen in the nature of the early community leadership — the men who guided the destinies of Italian Tampa came heavily from this adaptable element.[11]

Just as Italians adeptly shaped their small businesses to the demands of the wider ethnic landscape, so too did they manipulate the variety of ethnic labels available in Ybor City to their advantage. The Cuban War crystallized national identities in Tampa and energized them with significance. The strong sense of "Cubanness" and "Spanishness" existing in Ybor City pushed later-arriving Italians to shape an identity for themselves. Italians defined themselves according to context and contest. In family and kin situations, individuals embraced the security of *campanilismo*, thus one grasped the exclusivity of Stefanesi or Alessandrini. In the wider neighborhood, residents preferred "Sicilian", a label which served the purpose of separating the small non-

---

[10] *Immigrants in Industries*, p. 205. Among the trades, Italians totally dominated fruits and vegetables, ice cream, peanut vending, oyster and clam sales, and street bear exhibitions.

[11] Interview with John Grimaldi, November 9, 1978; Interview with Nick Nuccio, June 10, 1979, Tampa. Leaders of radical groups and labor unions did not come from this element.

Sicilian contingent of the Italian population (Interviews with, Cacciatore, March 2, 1982; Palermo, March 6, 1982; Grimaldi, Nov. 9, 1978, Tampa). To immigrant Tampa, the term "Italian" was most used because this was the designation most familiar to non-Italians and it carried with it possible rewards to Sicilians (e.g., the exploitation of favorable stereotypes regarding Italian expertise as fruit peddlers and merchandizers). In reference to cigar manufacturers from New York City who transferred to Tampa after 1900 and often did not distinguish between different kinds of "Latins", Spanish-speaking Italians sometimes utilized that designation to gain factory employment (Interviews with Adamo, April 19, 1980, Palermo, March 23, 1979, Tampa; Tampa Morning Tribune, July 4, 1897).

Italians did make concessions to local conditions (they learned Spanish, accepted Latin labels, participated in Spanish medical programs, and acquired cigarmaking skills), but they continued to manifest their own particular cultural preferences. In work choices, for example,men typically used factories as springboards to other occupational niches, not as permanent choices. Italian women entered cigar factories in greater numbers than men, usually starting work in the stripping rooms. Males normally worked a few years, built nest eggs for investment in business or property and left the cigar trades. Women, and to a lesser degree children, provided steady wages until these ventures matured. By 1909 cigar industry reports showed that Italian women actully earned more than Italian men on average.[12] Because of their greater presence in factories they also learned Spanish quicker, English slower, and participated slightly more often in militant unions. Though Spanish and Cuban families were not adverse to allowing women to work in factories, male cigarworkers always predominated among them (Interview with Italiano, April 16, 1980, Tampa; U.S. Senate, 1911, Table 150, p. 218).

Italian men tended to view the cigar industry as too volatile to suit their conservative family goals. As cigarmaker-turned-grocer Frank Setticasi explained, "the cigarworkers were too crazy — too many radicals, too many strikes" (Interview with Setticasi, July 1, 1979, Tampa). Italian strategies made them more able to survive the disruptions recurring strikes brought to Tampa. Indeed, for Italians these occasions often brought opportunities, as Cubans often left Tampa in search of employment and sold their possessions at a loss. Italians also readily shifted employment in strike situations as they probed the area economy for job possibilities. Using the family as a collective producer, strike-bound cigar workers could be found engaged in tenant farming, phosphate mining, citrus harvesting, and truck gardening (Interview with Provenzano, March 13, 1982, Tampa; U.S. Senate, 1911, pp. 433-435;

[12] A more extended discussion is in Gary R. Mormino and G.E. Pozzetta, "Immigrant Women in Tampa: The Italian Experience", Florida Historical Quarterly, 61, January, 1983, pp. 303-07. The 1900 and 1910 manuscript census schedules for Hillsborough County also reveal numerous instances of the employment pattern described above.

Kissimmee Valley, Nov. 11, 25, 1896; *Tampa Morning Tribune*, April 1, 12, 1908).

The early associative life of these groups also owed much to the collective presence of immigrant neighbors. The first clubs formed in the Spanish and Cuban communities clearly reflected the fissures created by the island struggle. Italians borrowed from both sides to forge an early, broad based association (*L'Unione Italiana*, 1894).[13] A process of sharing and cross fertilization similarly existed in the structuring of Ybor City's radical subsociety. Each of the immigrant groups possessed a leftist element, although the Spanish always were most active and numerous. By the early years of the twentieth century, there existed a network of speaking clubs, debating societies, and cultural centers representing the full spectrum of radical ideologies. Some were open to freethinkers of all nationalities; others were restricted to individual immigrant groups. The *Centro Obrero*, the Labor Temple, served as flagship center for immigrant workers. The cooperative effects of this phenomenon extended to the sharing of club libraries, the pooling of resources to finance visits of radical luminaries, occasional efforts to enter the local political arena, and the frequent sponsoring of public debates.[14] The possible integrative effects of this cooperation were diluted by the fact that the radical subsociety never constituted more than a small minority of the population and the long term trend was toward factionalism rather than increasing accord. Radicals served as lightening rods for the Anglo community, which attributed many of Ybor City's problems to them (often with violent consequences) (*El Internacional*, March 24, 1911; *Tampa Weekly Tribune*, June 22, 1899; March 5, 1903; Tampa Journal, Jan. 26, 1887).

As the twentieth century dawned, immigrants in Tampa faced a transitional period. The settlement of the struggle in Cuba, the trends toward consolidation in the cigar industry (as seen in the formation of a Manufacturer's Trust and broad-based workers' unions), and the "coming of age" of second generation ethnics called forth a different set of adaptations. This period also witnessed the Anglo community and greater American society play a more decisive role in shaping the social environment of Ybor City as both the intensity and frequency of their intrusions increased dramatically. The evolving ethnic community created a powerful set of institutions to cope with these changed conditions.

Union development reflected the new realities. With the war in Cuba

---

[13] The first president of *L'Unione Italiana* was Bartolomeo Filogamo, the bookkeeper of Pendas and Alvarez cigar factory. When Pendas a Spaniard, organized *Centro Espanol*, Filogamo assisted him, and the Spanish club served as a model for the 1894 creation of the Italian club. Messari, *La comunita*, pp. 149-52.

[14] *La Federacion*, February 16, 1900, describes a visit of Errico Malatesta; for evidence of various sharing activities, See, *El Internacional*, February 19, 1915, March 3, 10, 1916, October 6, 1916.

ended, long deferred working-class issues gained priority in the cigar workforce. Starting with the immigrant created and led union, *La Resistencia*, cigarworkers moved toward consolidation within the folds of the AFL locals of the Cigar Makers International Union (CMIU). These unions led workers in a series of protracted general strikes occurring in 1901, 1910, and 1920-21 which became benchmarks in the lives of Ybor City residents.[15] The local orientation of AFL structures, coupled with the presence of effective ethnic leaders and the continuing influence of the lector, led to the creation of a labor consciousness of such a broad and malleable nature that a disparate membership found common ground. That ethnic workers were able to stay out on protracted strikes and maintain their solidarity in the face of manufacturer opposition, vigilante justice, and economic deprivation attested, at least in part, to the effectiveness of union organization.[16]

Residents of Ybor City realized, however, that the most powerful institutions shaping their community were the ethnic clubs, not radical groups or unions. The Roman Catholic church, which nominally claimed the allegiances of many residents, failed to play a significant role. Church leadership responded ineptly to immigrant needs, in part because it was forced to battle against strongly entrenched, Old World anti-clerical attitudes.[17] More importantly, each of the major groups formed an ethnic club which, in addition to providing the usual range of services, added the unique benefits of a cooperative medical program. The first private hospitals in the state of Florida were begun by these Latin associations (Bryan, Tampa, p. 5; Long, Nov. 1965, pp. 217-34); Federal Writer's Project, Tampa). The foundation provided by these shared medical programs underwrote a vibrant and enduring club life that, in somewhat altered form, survives today.

The club provided Latins with opportunities to interact with their Anglo neighbors in other than conflict situations. This was particularly true of the contacts generated by various political campaigns, parades, club picnics,

---

[15] Durward Long, "Labor Relations in the Tampa Cigar Industry, 1885-1911", *Labor History*, 12, Fall, 1971, pp. 551-559; Long, "The Open-Closed Shop Battle in Tampa's Cigar Industry, 1919-21", *Florida Historical Quarterly*, 47, October, 1968, pp. 101-21; *Tampa Morning Tribune*, January 31, 1899. In each instance of a major strike, Anglo Tampa responded with vigilant activity, including deportations, lynchings, and a widespread physical intimidation.

[16] Interview with Jose Vega Diaz, August 24, 1980, Tampa. A reading of the columns of the major union newspaper of Tampa, *El Internacional* during the period 1904-1930 will also verify the observations.

[17] Interview with Sister Norberta, Sister Mary Lourdes, and Sister Mary Edith Mallard, September 13, 1982, St. Augustine. St. Augustine diocese records contain voluminous correspondence between the Bishop and various clerics working in Ybor City. One letter written to Amleto Giovanni Cicognani, Apostolic Delegate in 1935 concluded, "For 50 years and more, zealous, unselfish priests and sisters have exhausted themselves in trying to save these people, but their reward must be sought in heaven for they receive no earthly one". Bishop to Cicognani, August 25, 1935, St. Augustine Diocese Archives, St. Augustine.

theater performances, and sporting events, which typically attracted elements of the Anglo population.[18] Within Ybor City the clubs worked to sort out and solidify the various ethnic identities present in the community. The magnificent club buildings themselves illustrated this point. the construction of these multi-story, marble and granite structures (in the period 1897-1919) generated an element of rivalry between groups, each one of which attempted to outdo the other in terms of ostentation and display. Club construction became another legitimate expression of ethnic difference, rivalry and status.[19]

At the same time as the clubs worked to bring Anglo and Latin Tampa together, they served counter pruposes. By drawing ethnic groups inward toward a congenial local environment they insulated Latins from more open social contacts with others. There remained a tangible chasm between Anglo and Latin Tampa, as evidenced in, among other things, signs prominently displayed at Anglo bathing spots proclaiming "No dogs, Niggers, or Latins allowed".[20] During periods of crisis, of course, these gaps became even wider and the vigilante practices so often resorted to by native Tampans dramatically reminded Latins of both their composite identity in the eyes of the city's power structure and the common problems this generated. In the early years native Tampa generally welcomed immigrants as a skilled labor force underwriting the city's most important industry. Yet, they also exhibited rabid misgivings over the leftist ideologies finding favor in Ybor city and the popularity of labor militancy. In this context, the possibilities for harmonious relations between native and immigrant remained problematical.

The internal social relations of the Latin community itself were often characterized by disharmony. Points of division persisted and ethnic difference remain an important part of daily life. As Italians in greater numbers moved into the cigar industry, for example, (even if for brief periods of employment), they increasingly clashed with Cubans. The growing commercial and political power of Spaniards and Italians served to separate Cubans further within

[18] Middleton, p. 295; Interview with Manuel La Rosa, July 30, 1983, Tampa; *Tampa Morning Tribune*, May 21, 1927; *El Internacional*, May 3, 1902; March 26, 1920. By the early 1900s Latin baseball teams sponsored by the clubs were playing in city leagues and track teams were competing in races. The clubs were regular stops for Anglo politicians.

[19] Interview with Joe Maniscalco, April 3, 1980; Interview with Nina Ferlita, April 25, 1980; Interview with Angelina Comescone, July 18, 1979, Tampa. Many Italians described the erection of the Italian Club thusly, "Oh, when that [building]) was going up! We were all so excited, so thrilled. Most everybody didn't work because we'd go out and stand around and watch the building go up".

[20] Interview with John Pizzo, July 30, 1983, Tampa; "History of Ybor City as narrated by M. Jose Garcia", Federal Writer's Project, Tampa, 1936, p. 11. Garcia, a pioneer Cuban cigarworker, bitterly described old cigarworkers in 1936 refusing to attend a 50th anniversary banquet given in their honor by Tampa Mayor D.B. McKay. He did not go because for years Cubans were "considered little more than dogs by McKay and many others in prominent positions".

immigrant ranks and often underwrote the forging of sharply negative stereotypes of them (Interviews with Maella and Diaz, August 1, 1983, Marti-Maceo
Club, Tampa; "Life History of Fernando Lemos", p. 4; Ginesta, p. 3). Afro-
Cubans experienced a greater degree of segregation as the Jim Crow system
expanded and pushed them further to the periphery of Ybor City society.
Indeed, southern mores came to exert an increasing hold on the community as
seen, for example, in the decision of *Circulo Cubano* to ban blacks from
society ranks in 1902 (an action taken, in part, because of strident demands
made by Anglo Tampans) (*Tampa Morning Tribune*. May 5, 1903; January
20, 1905; "History of Circulo Cubano"; Muniz, *Los cubanos*, p. 116).

Divisions based upon subjective views of group difference also divided
the immigrant population. For years intermarriage between Cubans and
Italians was exremely rare and families on both sides strictly regulated dating
(Interviews with Grimaldi, Nov. 9, 1978; Antinori, March 5, 1982; Interviews
by Pollato and Kennedy, Tampa, 1939). Among other things, Cubans
complained of Italian ungratefulness for past assistance in breaking into the
cigar trades and derided their propensity for keeping cows, chickens, and
goats in their backyards. They also decried Italian frugality and absention,
seeing in these qualities the worst kind of parsimony. Cubans saw themselves
as the true builders of Ybor City because of their cigarmaking skills, and their
free spending, Havana-oriented folkways. Italians and Spaniards, on the
other hand, perceived Cubans as lazy spendthrifts who failed to share their
values of thrift and industry, and the pursuit of property ownership (Middleton,
p. 297; *Tampa Morning Tribune*, May 2, 1903; Sept. 20, 1905; Oct. 28, 1902;
U.S. Senate, 1911, pp. 192, 204-05). Occupying the bottom of the status
hierarchy, Cubans were the pariahs of immigrant Ybor City.

Even the growth and resiliency of the ethnic clubs played a paradoxical
role within the ethnic community. In one sense this signalled a move toward
homogenization as each club became structurally similar, but the process also
worked to isolate each group within its own baliwick. As each segment
carved out its own niche, responsive to its own specific needs, and as Ybor
City evolved into self-sufficient neighborhoods, the range of contacts reduced
rather than increased. The chances for more diffused and intensive intergroup
contact lessened, particularly so after factors pushing the groups together
began to disintegrate (the decline of union strength after 1920, the collapse of
the radical subsociety by World War I, the diminishing vigilante violence,
etc.). As a result each group developed its own solidarity. This meant that by
1920 points of contact tended to be more confined to the workplace, schools,
recreational areas, and the great main street for walks and parades, 7th
avenue.[21] Contacts were most often made at the secondary rather than primary

---

[21] "Life History of John Cacciatore", Federal Writer's Project, Tampa, n.d. *See*, Juliani,
pp. 51-52, for a discussion focusing on Italian-Jewish interactions at this stage.

level — important distinctions for such a compact community as Ybor City.

By the 1920s the city had undergone other profound changes. The Ten-Month Strike of 1920-21 seriously weakened the competitive advantage of Tampa factories in wider markets and the industry never regained its supremacy. Union capitulation in the strike, however, meant that owners could and did institute changes in the Tampa industry, including the introduction of tin molds to make cigars, followed soon by the use of cigar-making machines. The cigar machines were often operated by unskilled and unorganized American women who were recruited from small communities around Tampa.[22] The work force changed as the workplace itself was transformed. When Latin workers rallied for one last major challenge to their deteriorating world and precipitated a general strike in 1931 (led by the Tobacco Workers International Union, an affiliate of the Communist Party), they were completely crushed in little more than one week (Ingalls, Westport, CT, 1981, pp. 44-57; *Tampa Morning Tribune,* Dec. 7, 8, 1931). Owners then abolished the readers, replacing them with radios. The radical subsociety had been seriously weakened earlier after the 1910 strike and the repression of the World War I-Red Scare Era. With the defeat in 1931, whatever lingering influence it enjoyed passed away.

Native Tampa was making vigorous efforts to redirect the economic foundations of the city, looking toward a future based upon tourism and a diversified economy. The Great Depression destroyed any immediate hopes of these dreams. It also destroyed the cigar industry. Customers could no longer afford the high-priced, hand rolled cigars that had made Tampa famous. Factory after factory filed for bankruptcy and went out of business (Campbell, pp. 5-12). Cuban cigarworkers felt the pressure of these combined forces most acutely and began to desert the city for Havana, New York and elsewhere in search of cigar work. Italians meanwhile had been moving outside the confines of Ybor City in increasing numbers as their commercial strength in small businesses, trades, and farming permitted. Only the clubs remained strong because of the unique range of services offered. For the most part, however, the Latin community was feeling the tranforming effects of these profound changes occuring in its occupational structure, its residential patterns, and its institutional completeness.[23] What followed was a new era and a new set of interactive situations structured on very different foundations. When second and third generation Latins rediscovered the Catholic Church, for example, it ironically occurred in the suburbs, devoid of past meaning.

[22] Scaglione, pp. 26, 33-34, 63-64; Campbell, pp. 8, 10-11, 66-67. Long-time cigarworkers greeted all of these changes with consternation. Their protests fill the pages of *El Internacional*, the major cigarworker newspaper.

[23] Yancey, *et al.*, pp. 391-92, relate these variables to expressions of ethnicity in community settings.

CONCLUSION

The immigrant groups of Ybor City and Tampa were influenced by sets of centripetal and cetrifugal forces, alternately driving them apart and pulling them together. Unfolding over time was a pattern of interethnic adaptation which included a measure of sharing and rivalry, of cooperation and conflict, of contacts and social distancing. These dynamics operated along both formal and informal social and institutional lines, some drawn in the Old World, others sketched in the New World setting. Although these forces were at work during all periods under review, they existed in various combinations and intensities depending on a variety of factors. The Tampa experience suggests that there was not a simple continium at work, stretching from, on the one side, a less unified, more balkanized cluster of groups moving to a more unified, more "modern" and "Americanized" existence at the other end. What happened was much more complex than that, with many smaller dramas acted out within the larger sweep. Yet, the long term trend, at least to 1930, suggests that, if anything, the reverse is true. That is, once intrusions from the outside diminished and groups followed different routes to social mobility and group acculturation, they tended to grow further apart. During the early years, the groups possessed a set of common problems and enemies and, in some cases, a cluster of integrative institutions which by 1930 had largely fallen away. By the end of the period in question the groups were, in some important ways, more different from when they had first come together.[24]

With reference to the Italian experience in Tampa, the collective presence of other immigrant groups profoundly influenced the adaptations that took place. An economic structure essentially created by Cuban and Spanish immigrants largely shaped initial Italian work adjustments. Once settled, Italians often used Spaniards as their role models in the immigrant community, aiming at their status levels and finding many of their values compatible with their own. They desired the easy entrees that Spaniards possessed into Anglo society, believing that these were the roads to ultimate political and social position.

Italian institutional life also owed much to immigrant neighbors. Spanish club organization provided the model for *L'Unione Italiana*, a critically important institution for the community. Italian language newspapers frequently included Spanish language sections, a concession to the multiethnic environment in which they circulated. Immigrant unions, to which large numbers of Italians belonged, recognized fully the need for ethnic accord to achieve worker unity. Although Italians often devised their own strategies to cope with strikes and union policies they learned the art of

---

[24]MelvynDubofsky,"CommentonEducationandtheItalianandJewishCommunityExperience", in Scarpaci, *Interaction*, 59, hypothesizes that Jews and Italians in northeastern urban centers tended, over time, to follow similar lines.

compromise and borrowed from the experiences of their fellow union members. Tampa's radical subsociety similarly reflected the heterogeneous qualities of life in the city as it created organizations (some Italian) which aimed at pan-ethnic memberships and featured ideologies which accommodated different national backgrounds.

Italian social and recreational life was responsive to these wider trends as well. Ranging from drama programs offered by ethnic clubs to Italian linguistic adaptaions, the cross-currents of differing immigrant cultures were evident. Religion did not escape the influence of interactive forces. Anti-clericalism, which remained a minor current in many Italian American settlements, flourished in Ybor City, due in no small part to shared attitudes on those issues existing among Spanish and Cuban co-residents. Space limits further details which document similar development at work in the realms of politics, crime, and education. As Italians intersected with other immigrant groups, they found that their private and public lives were changed. Over time these various contact points proved to be important occasions for shaping loyalties, expanding relationships, and defining the different contexts of social intercourse.

What resulted from the coming together of these particular immigrant streams in Tampa was the creation of a distinctive community with a cultural landscape uniquely its own. To understand how it came to take the forms it did requires something more than an examination of each of its parts. In the case of this settlement — and presumably other multi-ethnic communities as well — the sum of its parts did not equal the whole. What must be added is a recognition of the role played by the broader, interactive qualities of group life.

27

Religion and Community Life Among Italian Americans: Some Comments and Observations

LUCIANO J. IORIZZO
Professor of History, Oswego College

IN the presentation on the church and the Italians in the Archdiocese of New York, the Rev. Stephen M. DiGiovanni examined an old problem from fresh material found in the newly opened archives of the Vatican and of the Sacred Congregation of the Faithful. Drawing freely from these materials, DiGiovanni allows us to get closer to the subject and assess the role of the Church more accurately. His narrative is straightforward, often insightful, and meticulously footnoted. Scholars, this commentator included, have gotten into the habit of footnoting at the end of paragraphs with multiple citations. From the viewpoint of both publisher and author, this method has advantages. But, the reader and researcher can often find it difficult to pinpoint a source with citations lumped together. The recent trend in footnoting can, but need not, lead to sloppiness in scholarship. DiGiovanni makes clear where his information came from. He is to be commended for his care. His interpretion, however, is another matter. When he says, for example, "the Church proved itself to be the only institution in America truly interested in the well-being of Italian immigrants", he demonstrates a lack of understanding of the wider aspects of Italian immigration. What of the efforts of the Italian American press, countless mutual benefit societies, the Unione Siciliana, The White Hand Society, the Society for Italian Immigrants, or the better agents in the *padrone* system, to name a few?

Interpretation aside, DiGiovanni makes many good points, *eg.* on the positions of conservative and liberal Catholics, on the "unique" Catholicism of Italians "not strongly bound up with national sentiment", and on the takeover of *padroni* services by Catholic clergy.

The heart of his presentation deals with the efforts of the "conservative"

Archbishop, Michael Corrigan, on behalf of the Catholic Italians in the Archdiocese of New York. Corrigan was numbered among those who "favored a more natural Americanization of the immigrants". This placed the maintenance of the immigrants' Catholic faith as the highest priority. Corrigan's "sincere efforts" brought mixed results, and DiGiovanni's exposition of them raised some questions.

We are told that political consideration partly motivated the Church's policy toward Italian Catholics in the United States. Does the author mean to say that permission to use individuals' dialects, while designed to strengthen their Catholic faith in America fits perfectly with the Vatican's refusal to encourage Italian nationalism among the immigrants? In other words, if Italian imigrants maintain their parochial loyalties to *campanilismo* they will continue to think of themselves as Romans, Neapolitans, etc. and not Italians? If this is so, what might the position of the Vatican had been towards Italian immigrants had church and state relations been more compatible in Italy? The motivation is important, especially since the author is claiming that the Church was the only institution truly interested in the welfare of the Italian immigrants.

The relating of the Vatican's plan for the pastoral care of Italians in the Americas is puzzling. We are told that the plan "was impractical from the onset". It "had not adequately considered the true religious state of the majority of the Italians". Are we to believe that the Vatican didn't know that "the Italian immigrants were far from a united people—politically or culturally" and that they wouldn't fit the plan which was designed "primarily for a church-going people, or at least for a people well-disposed toward the Church, having a modicum of religious education, common religious customs and heritage and a common language"? Hardly! After all, the Italian Catholics lived in the shadow of Rome, not half-way around the world in aboriginal seclusion. DiGiovanni, himself, earlier told us that the Church in Italy suffered from Garibaldi's victory and that it was aware of "the sorry spiritual and material state of the growing number of Italian immigrants". One is tempted to conclude that the plan, possibly, was deliberately made impractical, and then ask, why?

One wishes that DiGiovanni had spent more time detailing Corrigan's plan and assessing its effectiveness. We are told at the end that in many ways it didn't work. But, we also know that Corrigan "insisted that all New York seminarians... study Italian". We know too that he encouraged the religious under him to care for those in need: the "immigrant children who had no families", people caught up in the criminal justice system, the sick, the hungry, the newcomers in need, the unemployed, the homeless, and so on. It would be good to know just how effective Corrigan's church was in providing all these needed services. Development of this theme and that of the priest/padrone model would be very instructive. One hopes that the Rev. DiGiovanni will continue to take advantage of the opening up of Church archives and present his findings to the academic community at large.

As a practitioner of local history, I applaud the efforts of those who, like Professor La Gumina, seek to uncover the history of communities which have been neglected by scholars. We must resist the temptation however, to react to such works by saying that this is still another study of the Italians in such and such a community. The inference is that we don't need any more of these studies. On the contrary, any Italian American community which has not had its history recorded is probably worth doing. The stories may be completely familiar. But, after all, we really would not know that unless someone took the trouble to research the material. More than likely, no community history will be like all the others. So, there will be differences in both composition and detail. The value to studies such as La Gumina's is that they will enable scholars to test the theories and generalizations which abound on the history of Italians in America, a history which has been written, of necessity, while there was still much to learn of the individual communities of Italian Americans. The more we get of studies such as this one, the broader will be the base for histories on a national scale. Scholars will be able to provide better and more accurate syntheses.

La Gumina's survey of Italians on Long Island presents a number of interesting facets for the academician to ponder. A number of items touch upon subjects treated in larger studies. For example, the material on the *padroni* and on Italian labor suggest compatibility with the interpretation on those subjects found in Iorizzo and Mondello, *The Italian Americans*. It is hoped that La Gumina will probe those questions in depth. The success the San Rocco Group had in building an Italian parish with its own school over a twenty-six year period speaks to the persistence as well as to the commitment to the church its members exhibited. The struggle should be worth telling in detail. The conclusion that "Americans of Italian descent have been an integral part of the history of the nation's archetypical suburbia for the better part of a century" is an important one. Italian American history is usually viewed in urban terms and occasionally in a rural perspective. What La Gumina is suggesting is that Italian immigrants took part in the vanguard of a significant movement in American history, that is, the move to suburbia, a movement usually associated with middle class America. If this can be widely demonstrated, it would suggest, from still another vantage point, that the role of Italian immigrants in American history is not yet fully appreciated.

One hopes that Professor La Gumina will continue to work with this skeletal piece, flesh it out fully, and document it. Some charts, maps and graphs would help the reader's understanding of the piece. Defining Italian American, at times, would also help. For example, La Gumina writes about an aggregate number of Italian Americans on Long Island and in most states and cities in the United States. Is he talking about foreign born, foreign stock, third generation and fourth generation people? There are no footnotes so we can't tell if he used census material, which generally uses only first and second generation figures, or some other source. Sometimes, the context helps us to know what sources have been used. But, when we are told that "clearly Italians emerged as the largest single ethnic group in the work force" the reader wonders if the information came from an interview, a newspaper article, or from wherever. Thus, while one can appreciate the broad thrust, the lack of footnoting throughout makes it difficult to evaluate properly the details presented.

Professor Donald Tricarico's paper on the Italians in Greenwich Village is a sociologist's view which, while revealing a generous share of insightful observations and pertinent generalizations on Italian Americans, poses some problems for the historian.

Tricarico writes about a South Village Italian community which existed for over 100 years. Beginning in the second half of the nineteenth century its population peaked in World War I by which time "a new communal form had crystallized". New institutions took the place of old one like the mutual aid society and the padrone. At the center of the restructured community was the family. Today "a neighborhood-based" Italian American community is in eclipse while "selected aspects of the Italian heritage... became more prominent". As an ethnic quarter, the South Village is overshadowed by "the nearby Mulberry Street/East Side community".

The author is at his best when he supports his generalizations and observations with specifics. For example, there is ample evidence to demonstrate that South Village Italians developed a parish that was similar to its Irish counterpart. The fact that Italians still live in the South Village, though it is no longer an Italian neighborhood, is clearly drawn. Likewise the withering of the social neighborhood is plainly detailed. Tricarico adds, with no little insight, that the new neighborhood (So Ho) "has given Italians who stayed in the ethnic neighborhood a respectable address, an irony that mobile South Villagers have some trouble comprehending". One suspects that Italian Americans on the whole might well benefit from the improved image of the remaining South Villagers. The presentation comes together solidly in the last three pages when the author describes the South Village in eclipse. The conceptualization, the description, and the specifics work. Though this reviewer does not quarrel with his conclusion, it does raise some question about the meaning of ethnicity. If "ties had to be severed to consolidate status gains and prevent cultural backsliding" and if "the annual *festa Italiana* can furnish an occasion for the meaningful expression of ethnicity without disrupting (and perhaps even complementing) mainstream identities", what is the meaning of ethnicity? What does it mean if someone goes to an Italian festa miles away from his suburban, middle class neighborhood? If society were to decree tomorrow that ethnicity in American society would no longer have even "qualified acceptance" would "mobile Italian Americans" still participate in the festa? Maybe attending the festa is one way that some Italian Americans can atone for severing their ties with the old ethnic community. Is ethnicity something to be trotted out when the need arises, or does one live a life which reflects regularly the ethnic values that one cherishes?

Most of the difficulties this reviewer had with this presentation have to do with the unevenness of the writing, the lack of dates, the imprecise language, and the failure to develop points or ideas. These are mostly of the annoying kind, but detract from the overall effectiveness. A few examples should suffice. Tricarico talks of two Catholic parishes in the South Village. He refers to them as "the older one", "both parishes", "an early parish bulletin", (we're not sure if this was the older parish or the younger parish), "the two Italian parishes", again, "the older church", then "the other church". Certainly, somewhere along the way the churches could be identified by name! Some sort of map indicating the South Village, Mulberry Street, and the gerry-mandered districts referred to would have been helpful. The whole section on *Updating the Italian South Village* could have benefited from the inclusion of dates describing the changing process. From what time to what time is the author writing about? This reader would have liked to have had some explanation of the phrase "'families are not as close as they used to be'". What is the meaning of "neighborhood wakes have become second-rate affairs"? Tricarico could have specified what he meant by "new urban institutions" which replaced old immigrant ones. He could have spelled out the "ethnic family traditions" which "established a moral consensus which distinguished Italians from other groups". And, what was that moral consensus?

What is particularly disturbing in Tricarico's analysis is his frequent use of the word Mafia when talking about Italian criminals, syndicates, and the like. His sources for Mafia are "national law enforcement authorities" and F. Ianni's *A Family Business.* Ianni, himself, casts considerable doubt on the advisability of depending upon those government sources (p. 8).

Moreover, there is considerable literature on the subject which has come to question the reliability and accuracy of the government's position (D.C. Smith, Jr., *The Mafia Mystique*, 1975). Moreover, Ianni's position on the Mafia can hardly justify Tricarico's use of it. In speaking of the early Italian immigrants, Ianni states that "the immigrants did not form a new *Mafia* Despite all they brought with them and all they found discouragingly familiar here, three important elements of a *Mafia* were missing" (p. 54). Though by the mid-1920s the time was ripe for an Italian American Mafia, its "short melancholy life" came to an end (p. 59). This reviewer has no quarrel with the identification of Italian criminals, gangs, syndicates, etc. What is at issue is the use of the word Mafia (in place of those words) because it has, by official government sanction, become a synonym for organized crime and equates Italian Americans with organized crime. In short, use of the word Mafia encourages the maintenance of an erroneous stereotype.

Mormino and Pozetta present a careful, skillfully crafted, well-documented study of Italians and ethnic interaction in Tampa, Florida, a one-industry cigar-town. It is the kind of undertaking which few historians have tackled. In this study, the authors focus on Italians, Cubans, Spaniards and Afro-Cubans (all called Latins) and their relations with the host, Anglo society. By so doing they hope to "gain insight into the processes by which groups sorted out their New World orders for themselves" and "to explore the dynamics by which the wider context of ethnicity was arranged..."

The strength of this presentation comes from the wide range of source materials and the insights gained, especially from personal interviews, which enable the authors to illuminate the "ordinary patterns of life". For example, they point to Italians running shops catering to specific needs of the other Latins. They note that the contacts gained in these situations helped widen the social and economic horizons of Italian Americans. They demonstrate the adaptability of Italians in learning Spanish, acquiring cigar-making skills, etc. Further, the authors stress the crucial role played by ethnic clubs in building their communities. These innovative associations went beyond the normal range of self-helps and included cooperative hospital and medical programs which demonstrated unusual cohesion and farsightedness in the ethnic community. The Roman Catholic Church, which some scholars have cited as an important institution in the life of Italian Americans, "failed to play a significant role in Tampa".

One weakness of this presentation is that it often skirts the subject of interaction but seldom gets to the heart of the matter. It is a problem that plagues many scholars. For example, the authors cite interaction occasioned by Latino clubs and "political campaigns, parades,... picnics, theatre performances and sporting events". But, they really don't tell the reader much about these activities. In a footnote we learn that Latinos were playing sports in city leagues and that Anglo politicians regularly stopped at the clubs. But, what does that mean? What did the Anglos do when they stopped? Did they mix with the Latinos? Did they drink with them? Eat with them? Did they dance at their weddings; grieve at their funerals? Did they become godfathers to any of their children? Did the Anglos accept the Latinos as equals? Or did they simply stop, shake a few hands, and be off? The point is what did the politicians actually do at these meetings? And what of the athletes? Did they go their separate ways after the sporting events? What went on at the picnics? Did everyone mix, or did they keep to their own cliques? The deeper one is able to probe the knitty-gritty of life the better will be the exposition of the "ordinary patterns of life".

The use of interviews presents another problem. Mormino and Pozzetta rely on them, in part, in informing the reader that intermarriage was rare between Italians and Cubans. Assuming that a check of marriage records would bear out the impressionistic evidence, why did not more exogenous marriages take place? The authors give a number of reasons. Italians were ungrateful for Cuban assistance. They kept animals in their backyards. They were frugal. Cubans, on the other hand, were spendthrifts who did not value industry and property ownership? This reviewer remains unconvinced. Is it not more likely that these were surface excuses cloaked in stereotypes? Are these serious enough reasons to keep people apart for generations? Italians said much the same about Irish, that is they had the wrong values. They even added that they drank too much. The Irish looked down on the Italians who were considered strange greasers who were quick to use the knife. But, today the incidence of intermarriage among them is high.

Might not one of the most important reasons for the failure to marry between Cubans and Italians have been the impermanent nature of the Cuban population? The authors point out elsewhere that Cubans went back and forth to Cuba and often left Tampa for greener pastures during strikes. Thus, while the groups may have lived side by side for decades, the individuals did not. What chance for personal interaction was there under these conditions? Moreover, what of racial and color differences? Cannot interviewees be pushed for opinions on that score? Were Cubans too radical for Italians? As the author's quote one Italian in another context: "The cigarworkers were too crazy—too many radicals, too many strikes". None of these reasons appears to have been considered in the explanation of the phenomenon of rare intermarriage between Cubans and Italians.

Interviews are an important source for historians. But, though interviewees may not lie, they may not always give the complete picture. Might not the respondents have been reluctant to reveal themselves on such a deeply personal and sensitive issue as marriage? Sometimes it takes years to get an interviewee to level with the interviewer.

If intermarriage is the ultimate test of interaction, then interaction surely failed. In that sense the important point that Mormino and Pozzetta make, that groups "tended to grow further apart" and were "more different from when they had first come together", should come as no surprise. Yet, one wonders how close these groups actually were. Perhaps, there was more "forced" interdependence and conflict, a marriage of convenience as it were, rather than harmonious interaction and fusion right from the start. Might not a study of intermarriage between Italian/Spanish, Italian/Anglo, or Spanish/Anglo be more instructive on the question of interaction?

In sum, Mormino and Pozzetta have demonstrated in their presentation a solid grasp of a wide range of sources and information. Mature scholars, they have made a fine effort in a neglected dimension of immigrant history. One hopes they will continue their work and develop a full-blown treatment which will deal intensely with interaction among immigrant groups.

Religion and Community Life Among Italian Americans: Some Comments and Observations

RICHARD N. JULIANI
Villanova University

IN examining the preceding presentations, two basic questions can be raised. First, one needs to ask: what is the basic argument of each author? What is each writer essentially trying to tell us? Within that same question, we are also implicitly asking: is this, a new idea and is it supported by evidence or documentation that gives it some validity? Second, it is also necessary to ask: are these authors saying anything to one another? Do these presentations fit together in anyway?

Let me try to answer the second question first, because it is easier and can serve us as a device to get into the first question which requires a somewhat more detailed and complicated response. There are some interesting affinities between the Tricarico and LaGumina presentations. Initially, because of the obvious aspect of the metropolitan New York setting for the communities upon which they both focus, but also because of the opportunity both contain for the exploration of the continuing evolution of Italian American identity and social structure. On the other hand, I tend to link the DiGiovanni presentation and the Pozzetta-Mormino presentations together because both have attempted to focus on the interaction of Italian Americans and other kinds of people, certainly a critically important, but often neglected dimension of immigrant adjustment.

Let us rturn, at this point, to the other basic question, however, the issue of what each author wants to tell us, because that is the center of my response. The Tricarico presentation is, for me, the easiest to dispose of, because I have such high regard for it. Tricarico has attempted to trace the evolution of community structure among the Italians of Greenwich Village beyond the stage of mass migration by focusing upon the continuing kaleidescope of institutional rearrangements. His presentation of descriptive information, his conceptual analysis and his rhetorical skills are not only excellent, but especially impressive when considered against the constraints imposed by the necessity of a relatively brief presentation for this occasion.

My one major critical observation of Tricarico's work is not really a contention of any inadequacy with the work in itself, but rather certain implications it has for the research of scholars dealing with other communities. Tricarico calls attention to the problem of the relationship of upwardly mobile Italian Americans to their old neighborhood. He states:

> ...there have been limits on the ability of the community to absorb social and cultural changes. In particular, it has not been able to accommodate main-

stream, middle-class life-styles. Leaving the neighborhood has typically been perceived as entailing a status passage and a cultural leap.

My reaction to his observation here is that while this may be true for the case of the South Village, it is not necessarily applicable to Italian American neighborhoods in other American cities. In Philadelphia, for instance, a distinctively middle-class way-of-life is emerging that no longer requires Italian Americans to defect from the southeastern quarter or from the smaller satellite communities found within the city (such as in Chestnut Hill). Ironically, the gentrification of South Philadelphia converges with the flowering of middle-class life for Italian Americans.

Tricarico's conclusion implies a model for comparative analysis that would encourage us to examine the Italian American experience in various locales. But it does not provide a conceptual scheme that readily transfers to other places. It is, therefore, important to keep in mind that Tricarico is really concerned with the South Village case in particular, but not necessarily the Italian American neighborhood in general. Consequently, his final paragraph becomes more than just a bit troubling. He concludes:

> With the qualified acceptance of ethnicity in American society and the increasing respectability of Italian American ethnicity, the old neighborhoods have been regarded in a new light. For mobile Italian Americans, the neighborhood is able to mediate a symbolic connection to a cherished ethnic past; the annual festa Italiana can furnish an occasion for the meaningful expression of ethnicity without disrupting (and perhaps even complementing) mainstream identities. Although they have transcended the neighborhood socially and culturally, it can still be experienced on the level of "symbolic ethnicity".

Despite his disclaimer a few pages before, Tricarico has slipped in this passage into a subtle form of the "straight-line" model of assimilation. These lines suggest that one cannot remain an authentic part of the old neighborhood and yet enter the American middle class. Tricarico's use of the notion of "symbolic ethnicity" is particularly irritating in this regard because Gans has repeatedly invoked it when describing the behavior of middle class Italian Americans. According to this usage, whenever Italian Americans act as members of the middle-class, their ethnicity can never be anything more than "symbolic ethnicity". If there is a range of behaviors which represent "symbolic ethnicity", there must also be an alternative series of actions which expresses "authentic ethnicity". By implication, in the interpretation of Gans and Tricarico, "authentic ethnicity" consists of lower class and working class behavior as its content. In other words, even scholars may begin to create their own stereotype of "authentic" Italian American behavior which appears to me to have all too often the life style of Vinnie Barbarino as its content.

In short, Tricarico's generally fine analysis here has once again raised the still unresolved question of the relationship between social mobility and ethnic acculturation. But his work also places a burden upon the efforts of scholars working on the Italian American experience in other cities to show in their own work how closely these cases correspond to or diverge from the interpretation Tricarico has presented of the South Village.

In contrast to Tricarico, LaGumina examines the Italian American experience outside of the city itself, in the suburban communities and counties of Long Island. Also in contrast to Tricarico, rather than focus upon one concentrated area of settlement, LaGumina's discussion spans a broad geographical area. One might be tempted to add that LaGumina's presentation is also complemetary to that of Tricarico in yet another sense. And that is, while Tricarico focuses upon the transformation and attenuation of the old neighborhood, LaGumina examines the later locations of subsequent generations who abandoned places like the South Village. But LaGumina provides somewhat of a surprise if this is what we expect in the study of the suburban setting. LaGumina reveals two different sources of Italians for the Long Island communities that he is describing. For some Italians, it was, indeed, a second stage of settlement and a moment of mobility and assimilation after a previous period of life in the older city neighborhoods. But for many other Italians, the Long Island communities, La Gumina tells us, were areas of direct, first settlement in this country.

But the LaGumina presentation perhaps attempts too broad a survey of too many communities. While exceedingly rich in descriptive information, the work inevitably must make too great a sacrifice in regard to conceptual analysis. The reader searches in vain for some argument by the author that might provide greater cohesiveness to these details. The LaGumina work, however, does implicitly contain enough hints in this direction to suggest that the suburban experience of Italian community formation contained relatively stronger parallels to what Tricarico has offered in his analysis than we might have previously suspected. In short, LaGumina offers a large amount of factual data on the development of specific Italian American communities on Long Island, but it remains analytically underdeveloped. It is difficult to know, therefore, what is significant about the Italian American experience in these cases; whether we want to understand them for their own sake or in relation to the research by other scholars and in other locations. The mere reporting of information must be strengthened by a stronger effort toward some analytical explanation of these circumstances.

Father DiGiovanni has made an interesting effort to examine the attempts by Roman Catholic clergy within the Archdiocese of New York City to deal with the needs of the Italian immigrant population during the period from 1885 to 1902. One great strength of his work is his success in gaining access to much previously restricted material. Obviously, his own offical position within the Church has served him well in surmounting obstacles that have, at times, impeded the efforts of the rest of us. The same position however, may encourage a perspective about which the rest of us may be quite skeptical. For example, it is rather troubling to read DiGiovanni's observation that:

> In spite of the staunch provincialism; overwhelming poverty; distrust of the Church and anti-clerical sentiments of many of the Italian immigrants, the Church proved itself to be the only institution in America truly interested in the well-being of the Italian immigrants. (emphasis added)

His interpretation moreover, of how the Church came to be concerned with the Italian immigrant appears to understate, perhaps even omit, one crucial consideration, that is, the attention and somewhat successful efforts pursued by various Protestant missionary groups to meet the temporal and spiritual needs of Italians in the United States. (Tricarico remembers this point in his paper.) The basic question that this situation raises that still needs to be answered is: was the Catholic Church interested in the plight of Italian immigrants for their sake or for that of the Church as an institution?

In addition DiGiovanni consistently stresses the inadequacies of Italians — their prejudices and fears, their ignorance and poverty, their unwillingness to accept the Church — as the roots of their problems with the American Church. But he fails to give sufficient attention to the inadequacies of the American Church as a social institution and as a collection of individuals. For example, when he points out that "Many of these pastors had allowed the local Italian immigrants to worship in the basements of their churches, thus assuring the fact that they would be subject to the pastors' jurisdiction", DiGiovanni makes it seem almost as a kind gesture, rather than the manipulation and discriminatory act that it was. He fails to address the obvious question of why these Italian immigrants were not invited to hold their own worship services in the main church. In general, it is quite necessary to ask if the American Church really was ready to accept Italians as they were. It may be equally important to ask if the Church is even ready to accept Italian Americans as they are today, but more of that issue will be examined later.

DiGiovanni makes other, similarly startling assertions. He maintains, for instance, that:

> ...the work of the Church was grounded primarily in a desire to preserve their Catholic faith and not to inspire any nationalistic sentiments. The Church could not enter into nationalistic disputes or favor any one group over another in America.

While this may have been the official policy of the Vatican, it was not the actual practice of the Church in the American case. The Catholic Missionary Society of Philadelphia provides us with an interesting sample in the early years of the 20th century. The Society, exclusively concerned with the Italian population of the city, asked its Italians whom were served at the Madonna House, a settlement house in South Philadelphia, to observe St. Patrick's Day through a conspicuously Irish celebration. Whether by default in the manner suggested by DiGiovanni's interpretation or by more obvious policies such as indicated by the Madonna House program, the American Church was implicitly an Irish American Church. In contrast to Rudolph J. Vecoli's now familiar argument that the Irish hierarchy in the United States wanted Italian immigrants to practice Catholicism as if they actually were Irish Americans, we can go one step further. It now appears quite clear that the hierarchy and its social agencies wanted Italians not only to believe and to act as Catholics in an Irish manner. Rather, it appears that the intention was also that the Italians would become Americans in an Irish manner of everday attitudes and behavior. Irish American bishops, clergy and laypersons were attempting to transform Italians in their secular habits as well as their religious beliefs and practices.

But even today, the position of Italian Americans within the Catholic Church in the United States still remains problematic, despite the prominence and power of an individual such as Cardinal Bernardin. A recent newspaper article on the selection of four new archbishops for the American Church in the next year or two discusses the leading candidates — Roach, Quinn and Kelly — adding specifically that "Boston's Irish Catholics, who had trouble relating to the Portugal-born Cardinal Medeiros, would rejoice in an archbishop with a name like Kelly". There are two unavoidable implications in such an observation. First, we can ask the question of why do the worries of the Irish Catholics of any city take priority over those of the Italians, or of any other ethnic group? It is not sufficient to point out that the Irish probably represent the largest ethnic component among the Catholics of Boston. If the Catholic Church strives to be a universal church, this factor should not matter in the selection of an archbishop for any particular city. Neither should such considerations matter in the selection of a Pope for the Church as a whole. But the second implication of the newspaper item provides the answer to the question: the Catholic Church in the United States still is an Irish American Church in many respects, and the tensions with other groups will remain as long as consciousness of ethnic differences persists within the Catholic population.

Finally, before leaving the DiGiovanni presentation, let me use it to criticize this conference on a more general level. Despite the assets of this paper, of which there are several, I was anticipating a far broader examination of the position of Italian Americans within the Catholic Church in the United States as a part of this program. The DiGiovanni paper with its rather particularized focus in regard to time and place needs to be balanced by another presentation in which an assessment of far more general issues, both historical and contemporary in nature, is offered. This alternative would seem to be more congruent with the objectives of this conference.

In the final presentation, Pozzetta and Mormino claim to offer a somewhat distinctive approach by an examination of the interaction of ethnic minority groups with each other. There is, however, something of a defect with that claim. As the authors develop their analysis, it appears that they either forget their objective or they fail to understand what they have promised. Instead, they drift toward a slightly different subject. It is not so much the interaction of Italians with other groups that they are describing in their work, but rather how Italians fitted themselves into complementary institutional niches, particularly in the occupational and economic structure, of a pluralistic community. Pozzetta and Mormino are analyzing how the adjustment of Italians in Tampa, Florida from 1886 to 1930 represented a response to the prior presence and activity of other groups in the same city.

A major part of the problem here seems to be some confusion over what interaction precisely means. The functional adaptation and positioning of one group within a system   of opportunities that has already been approached by another group is not entirely the same issue as how these groups interact with each other. The sociological concept of interaction suggests more conscious, direct, and face-to-face contact between the groups involved. In contrast, Pozzetta and Mormino are examining a more indirect form of mutual adjustment to similar institutional opportunities. It is an important distinction if we seek to understand and to explain what it is to which any group is reacting. Otherwise, we may easily end up inappropriately blaming a particular group for the condition of some other, even though they may have had little or no contact with one another, but may have shared, nevertheless, the same institutions.

Another part of the problem is the choice of an appropriate research method by which to study interaction. It requires either direct observation or, at least, in the case of social relations in an earlier historical period than the present, first-hand accounts as documents of what actually occurred as these groups faced each other. In the absence of these kinds of materials, interaction may be a very inappropriate term to identify the processes that are being described.

Despite the criticisms that have been presented here, these papers altogether represent an encouraging continuation of serious research into the Italian experience in the United States. Tricarico has examined the enduring evolution of a specific Italian American community in the area of South Greenwich Village with great insight and imagination. His work is especially important for its consideration of the most recent phase of that case. LaGumina has added much useful knowledge to the history if Italian Americans in a series of Long Island localities. His work is unique and useful because of its focus on suburban circumstances, a social setting that has been far too often neglected by students of ethnic life. DiGiovanni has broken fresh ground in his extensive use of much new material from church archives. He is particularly provocative in his interpretation of the relationship of the Irish hierarchy and clergy to immigrant Italians in New York City at the end of the last century and the beginning of the present one. Pozzetta and Mormino have also contributed quite substantially by their analysis of the social and economic patterns of adjustment among the Italians of Tampa. Their work has considerable significance by its emphasis upon the complexity of integration in a multi-ethnic context. All of these papers provide strong indications not only that the study of the Italian American experience is still growing and developing, but that through such research as the work of these scholars this specialized field will also continue to enhance our understanding of America as a society in general.

28

Italian American Styles of Venture Entreprenuerism: A Proposed Study

Francis X. Femminella
S.U.N.Y. at Albany
Alfred Rotondaro
N.I.A.F., Washington, D.C.

The findings presented thus far in this conference appear to have been somewhat contradictory. On the one hand there seems to be evidence indicating the rapid (in the larger terms of generations) dissolution of ethnicity in the United States; and on the other hand the very same evidence gives other scholars reason to believe that, in fact, ethnicity persists. The assumptions underlining these interpretations have rarely been spelled out, but in view of their relevance, as Postiglione (1983) has recently shown, we shall in this paper, depart from the usual approach by explicating as carefully as possible the domain assumptions and process assertions underlying our work.

We have assumed, first of all, that in fact ethnicity does persist. Our reasons for this assumption will be presented at the end of the chapter, when we make some additional, hypothetical assertions. Secondly, we assume that this ethnicity reveals itself in styles of behavior that are overt and measurable and that exist across class, gender and geographical or regional lines. Finally, we assume that by investigating broad categories of behavior, these ethnic styles will be demonstrated.

This chapter is essentially to be viewed as a research note or study proposal, which we are presenting at this conference, not only to share our thinking with you, but to solicit your criticism and help. Overall the exploration we are beginning has three important elements: first, a review of several different bodies of literature; second, the creation of a data base from the collection of life histories through oral interviews; and third, the analysis of these data for patterns of ethnicity. To provide the background that would be required to understand the relationship between styles of venture entrepreneurism, education, achievement, and ethnicity, particularly Italian American ethnicity, the broad areas of pertient literature will have to be reviewed, and a brief outline will be sketched here. Later in the chapter we will address the significance of the study.

I

In a very real sense this chapter, and the idea of doing oral histories grew out of the enterprise of the director of the National Italian American Foundation and individuals who have become successful entrepreneurs. Invariably, in the course of introducing such individuals at various functions, conferences, dinners, etc., he would ask them to provide a short *Vita* or 'bio', of the kind that academicians and public speakers use regularly. To his consternation, he found that, very often, he received, not brief 'canned' resumes, but effusive presentations of life experiences centering around growing up in an Italian family and in an Italian or pointedly non-Italian neighborhood. Noting this we thought it might be useful for a variety of research functions to collect and preserve these stories and to search for patterns in them.

II

From the start we saw the uniqueness of these individuals. Some important characteristics were immediately observed. First, each of these persons was notably a high achiever. Second, their achievement came through the business world rather than the professions or the arts. Third, the persons that we were looking at and talking with all achieved through "risk-taking" in business. This last characteristic led us to seek some definitions.

First, a distinction had to be made between "venture entrepreneurism" and "managerial entrepreneurism". For our purposes venture entrepreneurism is that kind of business activity in which the essential feature is that there is high risk, that is, one engages in the investment of lots of money on the gamble that it will produce high profits. This is in contradistinction to managerial entrepreneurism, which refers to that kind of business activity relating to and including administration, bureaucracy and coordination. In practice, of course, venture entrepreneurs must also be good managers and the best are able to provide charismatic leadership. On the other hand, managerial entrepreneurs must also be willing to take risks, as can be found for example, in Lee Iacocca's risk taking at Chrysler Corporation.

Technovation is a creative financial process which includes inventors, managers and risk takers and is characteristic of today's high tech industries. Through conglomorates, technovation may exist in large corporations on the one hand or in very small businesses on the other hand. The plethora of microcomputer corporations and the production and service industries around them are good examples of this process.

While technovations are a relatively new notion, risk-taking in business is as old as profit-taking, and from the Marxist perspective that includes all of societal history: "Asiatic, ancient, feudal and bourgeois". Wherever private ownership existed and wealth became concentrated, there we had risk- and profit-taking.

The question of perspective is, of course, an important one and any discussion of Italians and capitalism must somewhere deal with this distinction between venture and managerial capitalism. Two bodies of literature that are most relevant since they focus on this area include: first, the monograph research of histories of the early Renaissance and second, the late 18th and early 19th century social theorists. Max Weber (1958), for example, who, very early, in a real sense, implied the venture/managerial distinction, provided a perspective that seemed to argue against the existence of capitalism in Italy before it's emergence as a unified nation. His definition of capitalism as "the ever renewed pursuit of profit through continuous enterprise" includes a profit orientation, repeated operations, sedentary nature and relative stability.

On the other hand when Weber speaks of the "spirit of capitalism", a less cautious kind of activity is implied since the idea here is of the individual's duty to increase his profit which was perceived as an end in itself. Rational capitalism including: the double entry bookkeeping (debit and credit) the use of trial balances, calculation, etc. were all found in Italy in the 1400s and the distinction was already made between "monk's time" and "merchant's time". The risk/reward trade-offs were also present, but what was probably very different was the shift in post reformation times from the previous use of profit in kinship and status seeking, (for example by getting one's children married into some noble family) to the use of profit for impersonal calculated production for more profit. Parenthetically, the *rentier*-speculator distinction of Pareto does not fit too precisely with our distinction, though the Paretian perspective is very useful for developing insights in this area of study. If the late 19th and early 20th century social theorists related entrepreneurial success to religious variables, mid-20th century American scholars concerned about explaining the nature of achievement in the United States related it to individual traits and personality.

III

The study of success and achievement in this country has an interesting history. Briefly the first studies viewed success as the direct result of talent and hard work. Psychological tests were used to create a data base. Some of these early scholars whom you will recognize are: Uris Bronfenbrenner

(1958), Alfred Baldwin, Bernard Rosen (1969), David C. McClelland (1958), and others, who using Henry A. Murray's Personological taxonomy related success to an individual's need for achievement — "N-ach". Fred L. Strodtbeck 1958) in his infamous, "Family Interaction, Values and Achievement" purported to add a cultural notion by comparing Italian and Jewish achievement, but this went nowhere.

The second stage or, period, if you will, was found among sociologists who related success to social structural notions, a) by linking their studies to American occupational organization and b) by studying education. The former included the meritocratic, Weberian oriented structural-functionalists, including the noted scholars Peter Blau (1967), Otis Dudley Duncan (1972), William H. Sewall (1965, 1969, 1970), David L. Featherman, and others. Among the structural-functionalists studying education are Sewall, Robert M. Hauser, David Goslin, Ted Youn, and others. A second group of scholars studying achievement and education emphasized the deterministic aspects of the social structure rather than the element of individual merit. These are the revisionists, whose argument emanates mainly from sociological conflict theory [Marx, (1906), Pareto and, Dahrendorf], includes such scholars as Gintes, Bowles (1976), Parenti, Katz, Tyack, Karier and Carnoy (1976).

Thus, three perspectives on achievement have arisen, constituting a simple typology.

— First — success is the result of an individual's inner needs and drives. Persons with high levels of achievement, N-ach, achieve highly; and those with low levels of N-ach achieve little, because they have little inner need for success.

— The second perspective — success is a function of fitting one's self into the proper niche (social structure), in a society, commensurate with one's abilities and training. Those who merit success — get it.

— Third — success is for the successful. The high achievers, *i.e.*, the wealthy and the powerful, structure the institutions of society to maintain themselves in power. The schools are a mechanism for the maintenance of class structure in a capitalist society, in that they filter out the poor, preventing them from socialization that would prepare them to function at higher levels of capitalist economy.

These are the main line perspectives of scholars trying to understand achievement in the United States. The data base for the "N-ach ' ers" as we pointed out, was obtained through psychological testing. For the "structuralists", the data base came from social system analysis, and in particular, through the use of block recursive models of the socioeconomic life cycle.

IV

Before describing the perspective of this chapter, we should point out that the data base for our research will be the recorded oral life histories, and their analysis, for patterns of risk-taking. By comparing any patterns found within an ethnic group with those found to be exhibited by persons of different ethnic groups, we will be able to determine whether, indeed, there are differential styles of venture entrepreneurism. We would explain the presence of these differential styles by asserting what we have said elsewhere about ethnic ideological themes and the occurrence of the process of impact integration.

1) Ethnic ideological themes are located deep in the ego-identities of members of an ethnic group and these themes inform the individual's perspectives and value orientations, and even overt behaviors, though these latter may be controlled particularly under external pressure, *i.e.*, the force of outside society.

2) Every immigrant group in the United States has experienced conflict. The host society acting territorily engenders in the immigrants their polar opposites. They create "estranged intruders" out of the raw material of hard working newcomers.

3) The conflict that each immigrant group experiences generates a synthesis in which the ethnic group and host group are impacted, that is, they become fused. But this integration of host and stranger, it must be understood, is not an homogenization. The newcomers retain selected aspects of their alien culture, even as they, by citizenship, acquire aspects of the domestic heritage.

4) The host culture contributes to a reshaping of the immigrant collectivity fostering the evolution of ethnic communities, that is, either for positive reasons of helpfulness, or negative reasons such as discrimination and prejudice, the collectivity of immigrants establishes interrelationships for mutual satisfaction, which become, as time passes, institutionalized. By this process the immigrant collectivity is transformed into an immigrant community. Over generations, the progeny of the immigrants may move out of the geographic immigrant community, but continue to identify themselves with — or be identified with — their ethnic group of origin. When those persons institutionalize shared interrelationships with others of their ethnic group, they become a non-physical community; and these new social structures, (non-physical ethnic communities), change the host society. Through this process United States culture emerges ever anew.

V

The most significant feature of this study lies in the fact that it provides a new and different perspective for studying achievement and success in this society.

On the one hand, it pulls together social, psychological and cultural theoretical positions. On the other hand, it addresses, in a unified way, social, psychological and cultural variables.

It has been our intention that this work should build on the work of earlier scholars, recognizing their insights, irrespective of their school of thought. From this study's perspective, the critical revisionists argument — those who possess power tend to want to preserve it for themselves, the structuralists argument — without innate talent and disciplined training, there is no success, and the "N-ach' ers" argument — success comes only to those who are driven to it, all are seen as having contributed insight and knowledge.

Finally, while we believe the oral histories will bear out the fruitfulness of our theoretical perspective, we feel that a faithful recording of these memories will be good in itself. We expect, therefore, to deposit them in appropriate collections so that they will be available for scholarly research.

29

Italian Americans and Politics

MICHAEL BARONE
The Washington Post

OFTEN what is not said is more important than what is: remember how Sherlock Holmes solved the case because of the dog that didn't bark in the night. So I think one of the most interesting indicators of the role Italian Americans play in the nation's politics came in 1982 in the Democratic primary race for governor of Ohio. It was not a contest which received much notice nationally. But the winner would—in a Democratic year, in an industrial state with high unemployment—be the heavy favorite to be elected governor of one of the nation's largest states. Who were the candidates? Former Lieutenant Governor Richard Celeste, whose father immigrated from southern Italy. Attorney General William J. Brown, whose family's name had originally been Barone. And Cincinnati Mayor Gerald Springer, who had been brought up in a Jewish family in New York. Two Italian Americans and one Jewish American, running in a state in the heartland of America.

All three candidates amassed significant constituencies. Yet seldom in the coverage of the primary was their ethnic background alluded to. There was relatively little speculation about how Italian American or, for that matter, Jewish voters in Ohio would vote, although there are sizeable numbers of both groups in different parts of the state. As it turned out, Richard Celeste won the primary and was elected governor in November. In the same year, Mario Cuomo was elected governor of New York: so two of the nation's seven largest states have governors who are the sons of Italian immigrants. A decade or two ago, this would have been hailed in many quarters as a stirring victory for Italian Americans; and by many it is today. But more frequent are the comments which speculate on the future presidential prospects of these two governors, particularly Mr. Cuomo. His Italian background is considered a political asset. Even more important are his self-evident ability and his capacity to articulate certain positions as well as any American politician today.

It has only been a long generation since Italian Americans have had such political success. The first Italian American governor and senator, John Pastore of Rhode Island, was first elected to those offices in 1946 and 1950. The first Italian American cabinet member, secretary of Health, Education and Welfare Anthony Celebrezze, was appointed by President Kennedy in 1962. Italian American congressmen were rare as late as the 1960s.

But today the story of the rise of Italian Americans in politics must be counted a history of success, not failure. Politicians with Italian names were once suspected by many voters to have criminal connections. But key roles in uncovering the greatest scandal in recent American politics, Watergate, were played by two Italian Americans, Judge John Sirica and Congressman Peter Rodino. Today the number of high officials of Italian descent is hard to count. They include men with names like Patrick Leahy, Senator from Vermont, and Thomas Downey, Congressman from New York, as well as Pete Domenici, Senator from New Mexico, and Alfonse d'Amato, Senator from New York. Italian American success has become commonplace enough that it is no longer considered worthy of note — as in the case of the dog who didn't bark, the governor's primary in Ohio.

How did this happen? What made it difficult for Italian Americans to move ahead in politics for so long, and what has made it so easy, relatively, for them to succeed in the late 1970s and 1980s? For the answers to these questions, we need look at the political habits of Americans of Italian descent, going back to the first large wave of Italian immigrants which can be dated, with precision, to the year 1880.

The first generations. The vast bulk of Italian immigrants in the period 1880-1924 were from southern Italy, mostly from the territory which was, until Garibaldi's successes of 1860, the *Regno* of the Two Sicilies. The basic outlook of people in this part of Italy has been described by Edward Banfield as "amoral familism". Loyalty extends to the family and, to a very limited extent, to the village — and no farther. There is no trust in the good intentions of strangers and certainly none in the state or its agents. Nor is it thought that the state has legitimate claims on the ordinary person. Even toward the church there is little loyalty: especially among the men, there is a fundamental anticlericalism.

These first waves of Italian immigrants tended to settle in what have been described as "urban villages". People from one village would cluster on one block or street, and would remain there for generations. Staying in school, moving up in socioeconomic status, making large amounts of money — all were discouraged, on the theory that they would break up the family, the one connection people could, in the long run, rely on. Many Italians intended to, and did, return home as they earned enough money—the first immigrant group to follow this pattern, which since has become common among Greeks and now some Latin Americans. Italian American incomes remained low; well into the 1940s they remained below the national average, though Italian Americans were concentrated in East Coast and Great Lakes metropolitan areas, which then had income levels far above the national average. Italian Americans' participation in the Catholic Church was limited; all the positions seemed to be taken by Irish, and the instinctive anticlericalism of the early immigrants prevailed. Thier children were educated, to the extent they were educated, in public rather than parochial schools.

And Italian American participation in politics was limited. They did vote, and some did even run for public or party office. But not very many. They encountered in the Democratic Party what they encountered in the Roman Catholic Church: coteries of Irish Americans adept at organizational politics and uninterested in working with Italian Americans. As a result, Italian Americans in many communities became Republicans—sometimes with the encouragement of astute Yankee Republican politicos. A prime example is New Haven, Connecticut, where Italian American Republicanism survived the New Deal, was strong enough to elect a mayor in some wards. Many of the first notable Italian American politicians had backgrounds and political affiliations atypical of most Italian American immigrants. Fiorello La Guardia, born to a Protestant father and a Jewish mother, raised in Arizona, a Republican allied with the heavily Jewish American Labor Party, is the best known instance. Others include prominent New York Republicans like Edward Corsi, immigration commissioner under Hoover and mayoral candidate in 1950, and John Marchi, a key state senator and mayoral candidate in 1969 and 1973; both are of northern Italian descent and are from professional families.

The first generations of Italian Americans not only produced relatively few politicans, they also showed relatively little ethnic solidarity. The immigrants' loyalty, after all, was to family and, perhaps, village; "Italy" was a distant abstraction, and for many a relatively recent historical phenomenon. Their own language was a form of dialect, in most cases far more dissimilar to standard literary Italian than, say, Salvadorian or Peruvian Spanish is to standard literary Spanish today. So why should they vote for someone just because his last name ended in a vowel? The shrewder course was to barter your vote for something worthwhile.

And that, apparently, is what a great many Italian Americans, and members of many other ethnic groups as well, did during the 1920s, 1930s, and 1940s. They accepted baskets of coal and city jobs from machine politicians (not all of them Democrats), and gave them their votes instead. Nationally, Italian Americans collected together never showed overwhelming allegiance to either party, as the Irish Americans did to Democrats for so many years and blacks do to Democrats today. Their preferences were rather the result of a very large number of local decisions and accommodations. And that was true even when Italian candidates were running. La Guardia, for example, had a lower than average percentage of the Italian vote the last time he ran; he did better with Yankees and Jews.

The third generation. As Daniel Patrick Moynihan and Nathan Glazer put it in *Beyond the Melting Pot*, after World War II, "as Italians emerged from the grip of neighborhood and family which had maintained the peculiar cast of south Italian culture, they did not enter directly into an unmodulated and abstract Americanism... The Italian migrant to the suburbs found in the new, ethnically mixed Roman Catholic church of the suburbs an important expression of his new status as a middle-class American." The rising tide of the American economy, plus the hard work and savings and struggle of thousands of Italian American families, had lifted the bulk of Italian Americans into the middle class. By the 1950s, they had reached the average national income levels — at a time when real incomes were rising rapidly. That means that Italian American incomes were rising at quite precipitous rates. The success which the first and second generations feared would break up the famiy was occurring. So was movement within metropolitan areas. (Only a small percentage of Italian Americans, even today, is found outside major metropolitan areas). True, Italian Americans, together with a few other ethnic groups, have shown a strong attachment to their old neighborhoods and are much more likely than many ethnic groups (Irish and Jews especially) to remain in them. But Italian American numbers were growing rapidly, and as the housing market suddenly boomed in 1946 after nearly two decades of stagnation they moved out.

Rising incomes, geographical dispersion — these have not left the old-fashioned political machines much to work with. Ironically, the first Tammany Hall leader of Italian descent, Carmine De Sapio, came to power just as these trends were taking hold. Italians remained in De Sapio's personal stronghold of Greenwich Village. But not enough to defeat his Reform opponent for district leader in an increasingly gentrified area in 1961 — none other than New York's current mayor, Edward Koch. Meanwhile, the sons and daughters of De Sapio's constituents were on their way to Long Island, Westchester, various parts of northern New Jersey, and points west. There was no feasible way to make them into a coherent bloc.

Moynihan and Glazer, writing in 1963, conclude that Italian Americans had already moved into an ethnically more or less undifferentiated Catholic bloc. They cited large rates of intermarriage between Italian and other Catholics, together with low rates of marriage to non-Catholics; they might have cited as well the large families so typical of Catholics in that period. A Catholic affiliation did have political consequences, but they were mixed. Catholics, and Italian Americans, supported John Kennedy in numbers that seem unbelievable today—78% of the vote! But they also supported Republican candidates in national and state contests. These included Dwight D. Eisenhower in the 1950s and governors like Thomas Dewey and Nelson Rockefeller in New York. But they also included some Republicans whose politics were considered more conservative. Like many Catholics, Italian Americans in this third generation period tended to be liberals on economic issues; they wanted the New Deal maintained and extended. But they were conservative on other issues: anti-Communist in foreign affairs, and in local affairs on anything which threatened direct taxes. As Moynihan and Glazer put it, they had "the ideological outlook of small homeowners, which many Italian Americans were or aspired to be; this involved opposition to high taxes, welfare progress, and the like. The comptroller of the city during Wagner's first two administrations, Laurence Gerosa, exemplified this point of view perfectly. He was against 'frills' in the building of schools (art, murals), in favor of a conservative financial policy, and without any views on the general problems of the city. Such views are hardly necessary when one's major concern is the neighborhood and its homeowners." The rather patronizing tone of the reference to homeowners may come naturally to men studying New York, our one major city with a majority of renters, then and now; in fact, homeownership became the ideal and then the practice of Italian Americans in most other cities during this period or before, and it did in the New York suburbs as well, where homeownership is as common as it is in suburbs of other cities.

Today's Italian Americans. The third generation of Italian Americans lived at a time when the United States, though ethnically still heterogeneous and spilt politically still largely on economic lines, was in its cultural attitudes and behavior a strikingly homogeneous country. Italian Americans may have partaken of a Catholic lifestyle, as *Beyond the Melting Pot* argues, but beyond a few particulars (fish on Friday, larger families) that lifestyle was one whose practitioners ached to belong to the great American middle class and strove, largely successfully, to do so. In the 1960s and 1970s, I have argued elsewhere, the United States became ethnically and economically less heterogeneous; because of increasing tolerance and the rise in real incomes, ethnic and economic differences tended to matter less and less in people's lives and in their politics. This tendency was accelerated, in the case of Italian Americans, by the erosion of Catholic particularity: the Vatican II reforms that got rid of fish on Friday, Latin in the mass, and the concomitant changes in attitudes that sharply reduced the number of new priests and made the church's prohibition of contraception a dead letter made the experience of being a Catholic much less distinctive in the America of 1980 than it was in the America of 1950.

At the same time as the nation has become ethnically and economically more homogeneous, it has become culturally more heterogeneous. And

Italian Americans have as well. The stereotypical Italian American voter is a middle-aged man, living in a comfortable but not lavish house in Nassau County, New York, with his wife and perhaps one almost-grown child, working at an above-average wage or salary job, and voting Republican (or Conservative) at least as often as he votes Democratic (and never Liberal). On non-economic issues his stands are almost all conservative: for a more aggressive foreign policy, against abortion, for a crackdown on crime, dubious about civil rights quota programs. He has some interest in Italian American candidates for major office, but does not automatically support them: he was just about as likely to support Lewis Lehrman as Mario Cuomo in the 1982 New York gubernatorial race. On national issues, he is not for cutting all economic programs to help the poor, and he is certainly against cutting Social Security and programs which benefit the middle class. But he is not at all likely to support big spending programs either. He almost certainly voted for Ronald Reagan in 1980, and supported Jimmy Carter in 1976 only because aid to New York City was a raging issue then (Italian Americans in states other than New York were just as likely to back Gerald Ford). He voted for Richard Nixon in 1972; in 1968 he was spilt: He may have said some approving things about George Wallace, but he never seriously considered voting for him.

This voter seems recognizable—almost a kind of Archie Bunker, except he is better off and not bigoted: the experience of being from a group that has suffered some discrimination itself does have an impact. But he is not the whole story of Italian Americans today. His cousin, who is in the building business, is a staunch Republican: he supports their economic policies, and it also helps on Long Island to be a backer of Joseph Margiotta's machine. Another cousin, from another part of the family, works in a factory in Queens: a labor Democrat. His oldest son went to law school and is starting a practice; he was something of a liberal, interested in legal aid to the poor, but may be getting a little more conservative, having just gotten married and beginning, at age 30, to think of starting a family himself. His brother's son is a graphics art designer in Manhattan, one of the group of Italian Americans who designs all the nation's bookjackets: doing all right financially, but the less one knows about his personal life the better. A liberal Manhattan voter, he may even have supported John Lindsay—a *bête noire* of Italian American. His aunt the nun has always gone with the Democrats—from childhood attachment to the New Deal. And who knows what the cousin's kid who moved to California thinks about politics?

Italian Americans today have achieved all the success and are enjoying all the cultural variety that is typical of Americans generally. And their political behavior is showing the same kind of variety. Fortunately for our democracy, many of the differences in lifestyle do not carry over into politics: we live and let live pretty well generally. Nevertheless, politics is characterized increasingly about disputes which are more symbolic than real. Ronald

Reagan Republicans and Tip O'Neill Democrats have reached a *de facto* agreement on how much domestic programs should be cut and to what extent they should still be funded. But political battles rage and rhetoric is shouted on the theory that these issues are still in dispute and the outcome uncertain. The different issues—economic, cultural, foreign—which account for the gender gap cover materials on which, for the most part, the two major parties are not far apart. But voters on both sides of the barricades have a psychological stake in believing they are.

In this confused and confusing politics, you will not find Italian Americans in any one place. Their heritage did not in any case dispose them to vote as a unit, and in today's politics of cultural variety neither they nor most other identifiable groups are going to do so. One of the prices of the success that Italian Americans have achieved is the fact that they lack this coherence and self-consciousness as a group. Returning to the Ohio governor primary of 1982, many if not most of the Italian American Democratic voters in that state probably did not even know that they had two Italian American candidates to choose from. And how many voters not of Italian descent were aware in the general election that Richard Celeste was an Italian American? Italian Americans are winning recognition and public office because of their individual qualities and stands on issues, not because of their ethnic origin.

30

The Role of Italian Americans in the Cultural and Political Relations Between Italy and the U.S.

RICHARD GARDNER
Henry L. Moses Professor of Law,
Columbia University and former U.S. Ambassador to Italy

WHEN I was aked to be a speaker in this distinguished group, my first reaction was "Why me? I'm not an Italian American". Then I thought I'm married to an Italian American so maybe that helps. It then occurred to me that maybe I'd be allowed to count myself as an Italian American by adoption. I feel that way, I really do. I love Italy and I feel very much at home in the Italian American community and so I was really very honored to be asked to come here and I want to take fifteen minutes to speak to you from the heart.

I want to take the first five minutes or so to celebrate what has been going on, and the next ten minutes or so to talk about thé future because we can't just rest on our laurels and be satisfied — we have to make things better than they are in relations between these two great countries.

My word of celebration is about the tremendous things that have been undertaken in the last few years by the Italian American community to make relations better between our two countries. I want to bear witness, as former Ambassador, that I could not have done my job without the help of all of you and some of the people I am going to mention, and if I forget to mention somebody by name it is probably unintentional but I am just going to pick out, by way of paying tribute, because I think people should know what has been done. Some of the people who have meant particularly much to me and still do in support of better understanding between Italy and the U.S. First and foremost, of course, there is the Italian American Foundation and I think that what Frank Stella and Gino Paolucci have done, and John Volpe and

Fred Rotondaro, and Furio Colombo, and many other collaborators is absolutely miraculous.

It started eight years ago and you have gotten so many things going. I recall the dinners that have been held and the international relations forums in which you have brought some of the major protagonists from the two countries. I think of the things you are doing to promote student exchange and educational exchange between our two countries. I think of the six-week educational program you just had for fifteen Italian students who came to this country. I think of the work you are doing to help Italian students come to the U.S. as well as Italian teachers. And there is a very important new project I know you have put forward to the endowment for democracy that is about to be set up which will involve training and educational programs for Italian labor leaders, for poliotical leaders, educators, and so on. This is fantastic. I think you represent one of the key pillars in the arch of cooperation between the two countries.

I think of people in the world of business in the Italian American community — Gino of course, I mentioned Virgil Dardi, Dominic Scaglione, Mario Perillo of Perillo Tours, I've just picked out some of the names of people who have done wonders in promoting economic and commercial relationships.

In politics, believe me, an ambassador needs support back from home base. We have what I used to call the "gang of four". You think the gang of four has something to do with China? No, my gang of four, the four I could always count on in American politics to help me when I had a problem with Brzezinski or Vance, or somebody, was Peter Rodino, Fran Annuzio, Silvio Conte and Dante Fascell. Believe me, when I called up, those four congressmen never failed me. If I said, Dante or Peter, the latest crazy thing to come out of the White House is to close the consulate in Turin which has been there 103 years, they would go to work like the four horsemen of the Apocalypse, and they would descend on the White House and people would really feel the heat there. Unfortunately, they did close the Turin consulate but they reopened it this year. Governments do dumb things. Can you imagine? We had a consulate in Turin for 103 years and to save $200,000 a year they closed that consolate. I told Phil Klutsnick, consular district, but to save $200,000, they closed the consulate. Of course, they didn't save $200,000. They had to move all its work to Genoa and it cost $150,000 to build up the Genoa consulate and now it has cost one half-million dollars to reopen the consulate and hire a whole new staff. But anyway, the four horsemen of the Apocalypse struck and finally reopened the consulate.

Then the Carter administration held a meeting in Guadalupe without inviting Italy. (I'm being very bipartisan here. We've got a wonderful Republican Frank Stella here and I'm criticizing the Carter administration. I'll get around to the present administration later). Anyway, they held a Guadalupe meeting without Italy. We reached the four horsemen of the Apocalypse again, and that never reoccured under the Carter Administration and I hope it never will.

So, there is tremendous support in the Congress, and I just mentioned four and of course there are many others — these are the people that have been working there for many years and now we have new faces in American politics like Mario Cuomo, and Alfonse D'Amato, Geraldine Ferraro, and many others, and they are making their mark and providing enormous support.

I think a word should also be said about the law.We have an International Association of Jurists — Italy-U.S.A. and Judge Ed Re whom many of you know has been the man who has organized the American lawyers all over the country to work with a great jurist in Italy, Oronzo Meltignano and they have had conferences every year in the U.S.A. and Italy on matters that include extradition, the rights of women, terrorism, and so on. I think also of journalism, and someone like Leo Wollenborg — a great Italian American who has been living in Italy, in Rome. He is, perhaps the sagest commentator on relations between the two countries in the world of journalism and he has a book coming out which I recommend to you. It is called *Stelle, Striscie e Tricolore*, (Stars and Stripes and Tricolor), and it is a definitive history of Italian American relations from WW II to the present. It is a very important book and it is coming out in Italian, published by Mondadori, and I hope an American publisher will publish it in English.

Then there is John DiSciullo and the contribution of an unsung hero like John is not very well known to the American public. For 25 years he was "Mr. Italy" in the Department of State. He served in Palermo, as Consul General in Genoa, ran the Italian desk, ran the Southern European desk in the State Department and he was brilliant — he really knew the country. And when certain professors in American universities said "why don't we bring the Communists into the Italian government. Wouldn't that be a wonderful idea? John DiSciullo said, "No. We shouldn't support that. Let the Italian people do whatever they please, but in no way should the U.S. encourage that". When I became ambassador, he said to me, "Mr. Ambassador, don't worry. The communists will not get into the Italian government as long as John DiSciullo is in the Department of State". I said, "What happens when you leave?" He said, "Well, by that time they'll be on their way down". And he was right. He was a source of enormous strength throughout that whole period and he was my senior political advisor when I was in Italy.

Joe LaPalombara, in the field of education, is another example. I couldn't find in the USIA, a person who could bring total fluency in Italian, expertise on Italian culture and contemporary society and someone who could go out and represent us with pride in Italian universities. I said to the Secretary of State, "Please let me bring Joe LaPalombara from Yale to work with me" and I got permission to do that and he represents such a great asset for our country .

Those are just some of the names that have reasonance to me from my personal experience. If I've left somebody out it's just because these are the ones that happen to have come into my horizon and have made such a contribution.

Italian Americans have made, and are obviously making, a major contribution in relations between our two countries. What of the future? Allow me ten minutes to talk about that. What can we do, what can Italian Americans and adopted Italian Americans and the people who care about Italy do to make things better than they are? I want to touch five areas briefly and just mention the chapter headings. You'll have to fill in the chapters because all of you are doing work in these various fields.

I'll mention the five chapter headings: 1) the mass media; 2) education and cultural exchange between the two countries; 3) the teaching of the Italian language and Italian studies in the U.S. and vice versa — English language and American studies in Italy; 4) having more Italian Americans personally involved in U.S. diplomacy with Italy; and 5) U.S.-Italian economic relations. This is my personal agenda of where we can all work and produce results in the years ahead.

First, the mass media. We have here Mr. Barone from the *Washington Post*. I don't want to trespass on his domain. He may wish to comment on some of the things I'm going to say. I'll tell you a little story. In June 1980, in Venice, we had an economic summit where seven leaders of the world's great industrial democracies met: I was the ambassador at the time and was present. Of course, at all these meetings, they have photo opportunities to gather the great men and women and they took a picture of the seven leaders. The next day I saw the *International Herald Tribune*, there were pictures of the seven, President Carter with Schmidt, Thatcher, Giscard and of course Francesco Cossiga and the caption read "and an unidentified Italian". Italy is the unidentified personality. There's Schmidt, and there's Thatcher, there's Giscard — I take nothing away from them, but Francesco Cossiga, a great Italian leader, a courageous prime minister, he took the personal decision that those missiles were going to Comiso, he faced down the communists on that issue. He paid the price on Italian terrorism when he was Minister of the Interior. Fortunately, he is back now as President of the Italian Senate. How is he rewarded by the American media? He is "an unidentified personality". When he came to the U.S. on a state visit in January 1980, *The New York Times* relegated him to the fifth page of the financial page and was about half an inch. But when Schmidt, Giscard, and Margaret Thatcher came it was page one and a picture too. So we've got a long way to go. I haven't given up on the American press. I want to see what the *Washington Post* does when Bettino Craxi comes. I want to see what *The New York Times* does. It's a very important visit. It is the first socialist prime minister in Italian history. A man who has changed the road map of Italian politics by taking the socialist party from alliance with the communists into a tri-party coalition that is firmly pro-western. How is the American media going to note that fact?

I've been told to speak frankly, I'm no longer diplomat so I can be undiplomatic. The fault is not just the American press, I think we have to talk frankly to our friends in the Italian government. We have some very distinguished representatives of the Embassy here. Compare the job that is done in terms of press and public relations by our major allies in Washington and New York. Compare what the British do, what the French do, what the Germans do, what the Japanese do, and compare that to what Italy does. Every American newspaper and every American television network is lobbied by those other countries effectively — they have a massive attack, but Italy has been absent. It's not because the press offices aren't good people. They don't have secretaries, they don't have staff, they're not given any support. So the first thing our friends in Italy would like to see is the Italian government devote more resources to press as culture, at least as other major allies do. I hope you will take that message back to Ambassador Petrignani, Mr. Ferrero, and more important, to the Farnesina and to the Prime Minister because I think that's one of the most important things to be done.

Now, second: education and cultural exchange. Here I am going to get around to the Reagan Administration. No administration has done enough to support, in budgetary terms or in people terms, the exchange of scholars, students, and leaders between Italy and the U.S. (or generally with other countries). The Carter Administration increased from 30 to 50 the number of young Italian leaders brought here under the international visitors program — young trade union leaders, political, journalistic leaders — and I had to fight and pound the table in Washington to get it from 30 to 50 and now it's back to 35 again. The first year of the Reagan Administration Mr. Wicks announced a sixty percent cut in educational and cultural exchange programs which would have wiped out programs entirely in many countries and cut them severely in countries like Italy. Even in the Carter Administration this nonsense was going on. One of the first recommendations that reached my desk as Ambassador was close the USIA libraries. Too expensive. We avoided the sixty percent cut that Mr. Wicks proposed because many people in this room and others were so outraged that they spoke out against it. But even maintaining the program as it is we have a $100 million total U.S. effort in educational and cultural exchange. This year our national defense budget will be $320 billion. Of course we have to be strong, but the power of ideas in the modern world is crucial. Can you think of any countries we've lost in the last thirty years because we haven't had enough aircraft carriers or submarines. How many countries have we lost because we didn't communicate with their people and their emerging elites, because we didn't speak their languages or understand their political, economic and social systems.

I think there is an imbalance here. The Fulbright program for exchange of scholars and students is down from 7600 people in 1965 to 5000. The foreign leaders coming here each year for short visits under the visitor program is down to 1700 from a high of 2400. The number of books being sent abroad under U.S. government auspices is down from 10 million to 500,000 copies per year. The number of libraries down from 254 to 132, and so on. This is really tragic. I think we ought to make our political muscle evident in demanding an increase in these programs for Italy and for the world. There is no better investment of the American taxpayers' dollar, and you can double the whole thing each year for the cost of two F 15 aircraft.

The third issue is the study of Italians in this country and of English and American studies in Italy. We started that during my term as ambassador, bringing 30 to 40 Italian teachers of English here every year to improve their skills and teaching methods and go back and do more in our school systems. So much more can be done. We don't have enough specialists in the United States, in our primary and secondary schools and universities, to teach Italian history, culture, and contemporary, political and economic life. The demand is far ahead of the supply. State systems, local systems need help. They are not getting enough of it from the federal government. Nor is the Italian government doing enough to support American studies and the teaching of English in its schools. There is still less than one Italian out of twenty who can speak English well. In this country, I guess, it is one American out of two thousand that can handle Italian. This is a tragic mistake and reflects neglect which should be corrected. Many people here at Columbia are making a contribution on this local scene. I'm proud that Columbia University has a very strong group. Giovanni Sartori of course is our jewel. He is a jewel in the crown of great Italian political scientists who heads our Italian studies. Furio Colombo, Maristella Lorch, Professor Rekey and others have been doing wonderful work. Many of you are in the university and college systems around New York and the country at large: but much more needs to be done.

Fourth, Italian Americans in U.S. diplomacy. I mentioned John DiSciullo but he retired in 1981. Where are the Italian specialists for the 80s and 90s in the State Department? In the U.S. Trade Representative's office? In the White House? I don't see them. A great generation of experts — American experts on Italy — has departed from the scene and I do not see the next generation. Of course, you don't have to be an Italian American to serve in the State Department on Italian matters, but it sure helps because the supply of non-Italian Americans who know Italian and know Italy is very sparce. I think more attention to training American diplomats in the broader sense throughout the U.S. government on Italy is a key priority to meet. So many Americans arrive in Italy to serve the State Department and know nothing about Italy. I conducted a little straw poll as Ambassador and I asked in the cultural and educational section of our Embassy, what they knew about

Mazzini, Croce, Don Sturzo, Turati, Gramsci. Most hadn't read anything they'd ever written. And you may say why I bring that up, that's history. Ladies and gentlemen, history is very important in a country like Italy. If you don't understand the historical context of certain political and social ideas, you don't understand contemporary Italy. If you haven't read Sturzo, Gramsci and Croce, you don't understand the dialogue. And very few of our representatives understand.

Fifth, and I'll close with this, is the U.S. -Italian economic relationship. Here I have in mind two-way trade which is good; but could still be better. It is very sad that the U.S. has done so little to implement the Memorandum of Understanding of six years ago for the two-way flow of defense procurement. Italy buys our defense articles and we buy some of theirs for the mutual strengthening of NATO but so far its a one way street. We say let's standardize equipment between the armed forces of Italy, France, Germany and the U.S. and modernize NATO's equipment. It sounds great but it turns out that what the Pentagon has in mind is everybody buy American equipment. Can't we find something the Italians make in the military field? I had about 12 items so I went to the Secretary of Defense, Frank Carlucci, a good Italian American and he said "Give me an example." I said "I'll take something that's not threatening to American industry. The Beretta pistol. Beretta makes a better pistol at the price than any American, even better than Colt Industries. Now can't we buy Beretta pistols to show we're serious". Two years later not one Beretta pistol has been bought by the Department of Defense.

The Italians are very sensitive about this. They say, you haven't honored your obligation. You want us to be good allies. We put the missiles in Comiso. We support you. We sent our Italian soldiers to Lebanon, and you can't even buy the Beretta pistol. I think this is something that deserves more attention from the community.

We can cooperate more in energy, helping Italy deal with its very serious energy problem by promoting solar energy, using our technology particularly in the Italian south, also for bio-mass and coal which Italy has to use increasingly as a substitute for oil.

Finally, the Mezzogiorno where we ought to be helping to promote the earnings and the income of the people in that area, in a way that is mutually beneficial for our country. Tourism — too little has been done by the Italian government and by groups here to promote tourism in the Italian south. It's almost a secret. Everybody knows Venice and Florence and Rome, but the south of Italy — you and I, in this group, know the beauties of it — its almost a secret, a conspiracy, not to tell the Americans about Capodimonte, about Monreale about Agrigento and Piazza Armerina and Siracusa. Nobody thinks of going there. Why doesn't the Italian government invest some money in the promotion of the Mezzogiorno as a tourist attraction, promoting some cultural and historical itineraries. Much could be done. And then, industry and agriculture. The agriculture of the Mezzogiorno has been so long neglected. Italy has an import deficit on meat alone of $6 billion a year because of neglect of livestock in the south. They import the cows and the lambs — they ought to be importing American feed grains and developing their own livestock that would give business to American farmers and cut by 2/3 the import bill of Italy. Finally, joint ventures in the industrial field between American and Italian entrepreneurs. I am convinced that there is a great scope for work there, Frank, and I know you've given thought to that and Gino has, but a lot more can be done. Let's face it, American businessmen have to be informed. Ireland is on the phone every day with American businessmen to attract investment in Ireland. But as far as the Mezzogiorno is concerned it's a secret. We've had ministers come from Italy and they say "Why don't you invest in the Mezzogiorno?". I've heard businessmen say to them "Is there a book in English that tells us what incentives you offer? What the tax position is?" "Oh, we're preparing one". We've been waiting for years, Dr. Ferrero, for a book telling in English what an American businessman can expect in the Mezzogiorno. Maybe you can use your good influence to hasten the publication of that book, and open a Mezzogiorno office in the U.S., in New York, to do something for the people of that part of Italy.

Ladies and gentlemen, I've taken off my gloves and I've not been diplomatic, but I felt I had to get this off my chest. Thank you for giving me the opportunity.

References

CHAPTER 1: A Sociodemographic Profile of Italian Americans

Femminella, F.X. and J.S. Quadagno
1976 "The Italian American Family" in *America: Patterns and Variations*. Edited by Charles H. Mindel and Robert W. Habenstein. New York: Elsevier.

Firey, W.
1947 *Land Use in Central Boston*. Cambridge, MA: Harvard University Press.

Glazer, N. and D.P. Moynihan
1983 *Beyond the Melting Pot*. Cambridge, MA: M.I.T. Press.

Greeley, A.M.
1974 *Ethnicity in the United States*. New York: Wiley.

Lieberson, S.
1963 *Ethnic Patterns in an American City*. New York: The Free Press.

Lopreato, J.
1970 *Italian Americans*. New York: Random House.

McKenny, N., R. Farley, and Michael Levin
1983 "Direct and Indirect Measures of Ethnicity: How Different Definitions Affect the Size and Characteristics of Various Ethnic Groups", paper published at American Statistical Society meetings. Toronto, Canada.

Rosenwaite, I.
1973 "Two Generations of Italians in America: Their Fertility Experience". *International Migration Review 7(Fall)*.

Sowell, T.
1981 Ethnic America. New York: Basic Books, Inc.

U.S. Bureau of the Census
1983 "Ancestry of the Population by State: 1980", *Supplementary Report*, PC80-SI-10. Washington, D.C.: U.S. Government Printing Office.

_____
1982 "Ancestry and Language in the United States: November 1979", *Current Population Reports*, Series P-23, No. 116. Washington, D.C.: U.S. Government Printing Office.

_____
1975 *Historical Statistics of the United States, Colonial Times to 1970*, Bicentennial Edition. Washington, D.C.: U.S. Government Printing Office.

1973 "Characteristics of the Population by Ethnic Origin: March 1972 and 1971", *Current Population Reports*, P-20, No. 249. Washington, D.C.: U.S. Government Printing Office.

1971 *People in the United States in the 20th Century*. Washington, D.C.: U.S. Government Printing Office.

1945 Sixteenth Census of the United States: 1940, "Different Fertility: 1940 and 1910", Washington, D.C.: U.S. Government Printing Office.

CHAPTER 2: Italian Migration to the United States, 1966-1978.
The Transition Period and a Decade Beyond Public Law (89-236).

Crispino, J.A.
1980 *The Assimilation of Ethnic Groups: The Italian Case*. Center for Migration Studies. P. v.

Salt, J.
1981 *International Labor Migration in Western Europe: A Geographical Review*. Reprinted in *Global Trends in Migration*. Edited by Mary Kritz, Charles B. Keely, and Silvano Tomasi. Center for Migration Studies. Pp. 133-157.

Velikonja, J.
1977 *Italian Immigrants in the United States in the Sixties*. Reprinted in *The Italian Experience in the United States*. Edited by Silvano M. Tomasi and M.H. Engel, New York Center for Migration Studies. Pp. 23-38.

CHAPTER 5: Italian Americans and the Media: An Agenda for a Positive Image

Commission on Civil Rights
1979 *Window Dressing in the Set: An Update*. U.S.G. Printing Office, Washington, D.C., Jan.

1979 Testimony by Richard Gambino, *Civil Rights Issues of Euro-Ethnic Americans in the United States: Opportunities and Challenges*, Chicago, Ill., Dec. 3.

Commission for Social Justice, Order of the Sons of Italy and the
National Italian American Foundation
1983 *Italian Americans and the Media: Building a Positive Image*, Sheraton Center, New York City, April 9.

Franchine, P.
1982 "New Approaches to Student Behavior Help Reduce Ethnic Tensions in Schools" in *Heritage*, Illinois Consultation on Ethnicity in Education, Vol. VI, #1, Oct.

1981 "Ethnics and the Media, in *14Chicago Tribune*, April 27.

Giordano, J.
1981 "What TV Teaches Children", Families Column in *Attenzione Magazine*, December.

1973 Ethnicity and Mental Health.

Giordano, J. and G. Giordano
1978 *Ethno-Cultural Factors in Mental Health*. N.Y.: Center of Ethnicity, Human Behavior and Communications, A.J.C.

Golden, D. S.
1982 "The Fate of La Famiglia: Italian Images in American Films", in *Kaleidoscopic Lens: How Hollywood Views Ethnic Groups*, Commission for Social Justice, Order of the Sons of Italy, New York.

Heritage News Service
1981 "Ethnic Groups and the Media", Chicago, March, 1981.

Illinois Consultation on Ethnicity in Education
1982 *Hard Times and Beyond: New Roles for Ethnic Leaders in School-Community Relations*, Chicago, June 4.

Klein, J. W.
1980 *Jewish Identity and Self-Esteem: Healing Wounds Through Ethnotherapy.* New York: Center on Ethnicity, Human Behavior and Communications.

Lichter, L. and R. S. Lichter
1982 *Italian American Characters in Television Entertainment*, Commission for Social Justice, Order of the Sons of Italy, New York.

McGoldrick, Pearce and Giordano
1983 *Ethnicity and Family Therapy*, Guilford Press, New York.

Miller, R. M., ed.
1980 *The Kaleidoscopic Lens: How Hollywood Views Ethnic Groups*, Ozer Publisher, Englewood, NJ.

Order of the Sons of Italy
1982 *Survey of Forbes 800 Corporations*, Sept.

National Institute of Mental Health
1983 *Television and Behavior*. Washington, DC.

Steiner, L.
1983 "Conference Takes Aim at TV Stereotypes", in *The Milwaukee Journal*, April 20, 1983.

Unger, A.
1983 *Minorities in the Media*, in *The Christian Science Monitor*, May 9, 10.

Washington, B.
1983 "The Ethnic Roots of Parenting", in *Chicago Sun Times*. August 8.

CHAPTER 6: Italian Americans in Contemporary America.

Acocella, N.
1979   "Politics: Who Are We Now?" in *Attenzione*, July, p. 22.

Albini, J.L.
1971   *The American Mafia: Genesis of a Legend.* New York: Appleton Century Crofts.

Barbaro, F.
1974   "Ethnic Affirmination, Affirmative Action and the Italian American", in *Italian Americana*, I Autumn.

Chicago Tribune
1976   August 22 and September 14.

Discala, S.
1977   "The Boston Italian American Community", in *The United States and Italy: The First Two Hundred Years*, Humbert S. Nelli, ed., New York, p. 229.

Glazer, N. and D. P. Moynihan
1970   *Beyond the Melting Pot: The Negroes, Puerto Ricans, Jews, Italians, and Irish of New York City*, 2nd. ed., Cambridge, MA, pp. 204-206.

Greeley, A. M.
1974   *Ethnicity in the United States: A Preliminary Reconnaissance*, New York, p. 51.

Lopreato, J.
1970   *Italian Americans*, New York, p.85-86.

Ianni, F.A.J.
1961   "The Italian American Teenager", *Annuals of the American Academy of Political and Social Science*, November, p. 77.

Louisville Courier-Journal
1983   U.S. Census of Population: 1970, *Characteristics of Population*, Vol. I, Pt. 1, Sect. 2, pp. 1087-1088, June 5.

Miranda, E.J.
1977   "The Italian Americans: Who, What, Where, When, Why", in *Identity*, I July, p. 15.

Nelli, H.S.
1976   *The Business of Crime: Italians and Syndicate Crime in the United States*, New York.

1983   Los Angeles *Times*, Sept. 10.

CHAPTER 7: The Search for an Italian American Identity: Continuity and Change

Afron, M.J.
1977   "The Italian American in American Films, 1918-1971", *Italian Americana* (herafter cited *IA*) 3, Spring/Summer. Pp. 233-55.

Arnaudo, D.L.
1983 "The Status of Italian American Families" (mimeograph).

Arnold, M.
1972 "The City's Italian American Needy: Too Proud to Take Aid They 'Earned'," *The New York Times*, September 29.

Barbaro, F.
1974 "Ethnic Affirmation, Affirmative Action and the Italian American", *IA*, 1, Autumn. Pp. 41-54

Bell, D.
1962 "Crime as an American Way of Life", *The End of Ideology* (rev. ed.), New York: Collier Books.

Brizzolara, A.
1980 "The Image of Italian Americans on U.S. Television", *IA*, 6 Spring/ Summer. Pp. 60-67.

Byrne, D.
1983 "Ethnic Roots Deep in City Suburbs", *Sunday Sun-Times*, Chicago, February 6. P. 1-6.

Calandra, J.D.
1978 *A History of Italian-American Discrimination at CUNY.* A report by Senator John D. Calandra, Chairman, Italian American Legislative Caucus, Albany: N.Y. State Senate, January.

Cannistraro, P.V.
1976 "Gli Italo-Americani di fronte all' ingresso dell'Italia nella Seconda Guerra Mondiale", *Rivista di Storia Contemporanea*, VII. P. 862

Casalena, J.
1975 *A Portrait of the Italian American Community in New York City*, Vol. 1, New York: Congress of Italian American Organizations, Inc. Pp. 71.

Child, I.
1943 *Italian or American? The Second Generation in Conflict.* New York: Yale University Press.

Cocchiara, G.,
1981 *The History of Folklore in Europe* (trans. by John N. McDaniel). Philadelphia: Institute for the Study of Human Issues. P. 293.

Commission for Social Justice, Order Sons of Italy in America
n.d. *A Survey of Italian American Representation in the Top 800 Companies in the United States* (n.p.).

Covello, L.
1967 *The Social Background of the Italo-American School Child.* Leiden: E.J. Brill.

Crispino, J.A.
1980 *The Assimilation of Ethnic Groups: The Italian Case.* Staten Island, NY: Center for Migration Studies.

DeConde, A.
1971 *Half Bitter, Half Sweet: An Excursion into Italian American History.* New York: Charles Scribner's Sons. Pp. 225-48.

DiDonato, P.
1960 *Three Circles of Light.* New York: Julian Messner.

1939   *Christ in Concrete.* Indianapolis: Bobbs-Merrill Co.

Diggins, J.P.
1972   *Mussolini and Fascism: The View from America.* Princeton: Princeton University Press. P. 108.

Erikson, E.H.
1975   "Identity Crisis in Autobiographic Perspective", in *Life History and the Historical Moment*, New York: W.W. Norton. P. 43

1968   *Identity: Youth and Crisis*, New York: W.W. Norton.

1963   *Childhood and Society*, 2nd. ed. New York: W.W. Norton.

Ets, M. H.
1970   *Rosa: The Life of an Italian Immigrant.* Minneapolis: University of Minnesota Press.

Ewen, S.
1976   *Captains of Consciousness: Advertising and the Roots of Consumer Consciousness.* New York: Harper and Row.

Fondazione Giovanni Agnelli
1980   *The Italian Americans: Who They Are, Where They Live, How Many They Are.* Turin.

Fonzi, G.
1971   "The Italians are Coming!", *Philadephia Magazine*, December. Pp. 98-181.

Gallo, P., ed.
1977   *The Urban Experience of Italian Americans.* Proceedings of the Eighth Annual Conference of the American Italian Historical Association, Staten Island, NY: A.I.H.A.

Gambino, R.
1974   *Blood of My Blood: The Dilemma of the Italian Americans.* Garden City, NY: Doubleday & Co.

Gans, H.
1962   *The Urban Villagers: Group and Class in the Life of Italian Americans.* Glencoe, IL: Free Press.

Gleason, P.
1983   "Identifying Identity: A Semantic History", *Journal of American History*, March. Pp. 928-29.

1980   "American Identity and Americanization ", in *Harvard Encyclopedia of American Ethnic Groups*, Cambridge, MA: Harvard University Press. Pp. 31-58.

1972   " 'The Godfather': Triumph for Brando", *Newsweek*, March 13. Pp. 56-61, (cover story).

Golden, H.
1959   *Only in America.* New York: Permabooks. Pp. 139-140.

Greeley, A.
1975   "An Irish-Italian?", *IA*, 1, Spring. P. 245.

Greenbaum, W.
1974 "America in Search of a New Ideal: An Essay on the Rise of Pluralism", *Harvard Educational Review*, 44 (August). Pp. 411-40.

Hall, S.S.
1983 "Italian Americans: Coming Into their Own", *The New York Times Magazine*, May 15, 28ff.

Hansen, M.L.
1938 *The Problem of the Third Generation Immigrant*, Rock Island, IL: Augustana Historical Society.

Herberg, W.
1955 *Protestant, Catholic, Jew: An Essay in Religious Sociology.* Garden City, NY: Doubleday.

Howells, W.D.
1909 "Our Italian Assimilators", *Harper's Weekly*, Vol. 53, April 10. P. 28.

Hutchinson, E.P.
1956 *Immigrants and Their Children: 1850-1950.* New York: Wiley.

1983 "Italian-Americans and the Media: Building a Positive Image", *La Follia di New York.* April. Pp. 10-11.

Juliani, R.N.
1978 "The Image of the Italian in American Film and Television". In *Ethnic Images in American Films and Television.* Edited by Randall M. Miller. Philadelphia: The Balch Institute.

1970 "Little Italy's Procession of St. Gabriel", *The Sun Magazine* (Baltimore, Maryland), October 4. Pp. 6-9.

Lichter, R.S. and L.S.
1982 "Italian Characters in Television Entertainment", (mimeograph) prepared for the Commission for Social Justice, Grand Lodge of the State of New York, Order Sons of Italy in America.

Lopreato, J.
1970 *Italian Americans.* New York: Random House.

Mancini, A.
1971 "Ethnic Travel: When You Find Your Roots You Eat Them", *The New York Times*, August 1.

Mangione, J.
1979 *Mount Allegro* (various editions).

Mann, A.
1979 *The One and the Many: Reflections on the American Identity.* Chicago: University of Chicago.

Migone, G.G.
1979 *Gli Stati Uniti e il Fascismo.* Milan: Feltrinelli.

Montgomery, P.L.
1970 "Thousands of Italians Rally to Protest Ethnic Slurs", *The New York Times*, June 30.

Monte, J.L.
1978 "Correcting the Image of the Italian in American Film and Television". In *Ethnic Images in American Films and Television.* Edited by Randall M. Miller. Philadelphia: The Balch Institute.

Mormino, G.
1982	"Little Italy and the Bijou: Italian Americans and the Movies" (unpublished paper).

N.I.A.F. (National Italian American Foundation)
1977	*Washington Newsletter*, 1, January/February.

Owen, C.A. *et. al.*
1981	"A Half-Century of Social Distance Research: National Replication of the Bogardus' Studies", *Sociology and Social Research*, 66, October. Pp. 80-98.

Pane, R.U., ed.
1983	*Italian Americans in the Professions*, Proceedings of the Twelfth Annual Conference of the American Italian Historical Association, Staten Island, NY: A.I.H.A.

1978	"Seventy Years of American University Studies on the Italian Americans: A Bibliography of 251 Doctoral Dissertations Accepted from 1908 to 1977", *IA*, 4, Spring/Summer. Pp. 244-73.

Papaleo, J.
1978	"Ethnic Pictures and Ethnic Fate: The Media Image of Italian Americans", in *Ethnic Images in American Films, 1918-1971*. Philadelphia: The Balch Institute.

Parenti, M.
1978	"The Italian American and the Mass Media" in *Ethnic Images in American Film and Television*, Philadelphia: The Balch Institute.

Pedatella, A.
1983	"Letters", *La Follia di New York*. Februrary.

Pileggi, N.
1971	"Risorgimento: The Red, White and Greening of New York", *New York*, June 7. Pp. 26-36.

1969	"Little Italy, Study of an Italian Ghetto", *New York*, 1, August 12, 1969. Pp. 14-23.

Pollenberg, R.
1980	*One Nation Divisible: Class, Race and Ethnicity in the United States Since 1938*. New York: Penguin Books.

Posen, S.I. and J. Sciorra
1983	"Brooklyn Dancing Tower", *Natural History*, 92, June. Pp. 30-37.

Prezzolini, G.
1984	*Diario, 1900-1941*. Milan: Rusconi. P. 470. (Note of February 21, 1931) quoted in Nadia Venturini, "Le comunitá Italiane negli Stati Uniti fra storia sociale e storia politica", *Rivista di Storia Contemporanea*, Spring XIII. P. 192

Puzo, M.
1972	*The Godfather Papers and Other Confessions*, New York: Putnam. Pp. 32-69.

1982	"Public Opinion of Ethnics Surveyed", Roper Organization. March 1982.

Rolle, A.
1980	*The Italian Americans: Troubled Roots*, New York: The Free Press. P. 43.

Ruffini, G.
1983 "Employment Equity and Euro-Ethics", *The Civil Rights Quarterly*, U.S. Commission on Civil Rights, 14. Summer. Pp. 40-44.

1981 "A Rule of Law", *Attenzione*, July/August. Pp. 60-64

Salvemini, G.
1977 *Italian Fascist Activities in the United States*. New York: Center for Migration Studies.

Sammartino, P.
1983 "National Italian American Organizations". In *The Family and Community Life of Italian Americans*, Proceedings of the Twelfth Annual Conference of the American Italian Historical Association. Edited by R.N. Juliani. Staten Island, New York: A.I.H.A. Pp. 161-164.

Shipler, D.
1972 "The White Niggers of Newark", *Harpers Magazine*, August. Pp. 77-83.

Silversteen, N.
1974 "The Godfather: A Year Later", *IA*, 1, Autumn. Pp. 105-116.

Sinicropi, G.
1975 "The Saga of the Corleones", *IA*, 2, Autumn. Pp. 79-91.

Simons, W. *et. al.*
1981 "Bloomfield", *IA*, 7, Fall/Winter. Pp. 102-116.

Smith, D.
1976 "Sons of the Godfather", *IA*, 2, Spring. Pp. 191-208.

Szczepanski, K.
1979 "The Scalding Pot: Stereotyping of Italian American Males in Hollywood Films", *IA*, 5, Spring/Summer. Pp. 196-204.

Tomasi, S., ed.
1977 *Perspectives in Italian Immigration and Ethnicity. New York: Center for Migration Studies.*

1980 *National Directory of Research Centers, Repositories and Organizations of Italian Culture in the United States*, Turin: Fondazione Giovanni Agnelli.

Tricarico, D.
1983 "The Italians of Greenwich Village: The Restructuring of Ethnic Community", in *The Family and Community Life of Italian Americans*, Proceedings of the Twelfth Annual Conference of the American Italian Historical Association. Edited by Richard N. Juliani. Staten Island, NY: A.I.H.A. Pp. 133-46.

U.S. Bureau of the Census,
1983 *1980 Census of Population. Ancestry of the Population by State: 1980*, Washington, D.C.

U.S. Commission on Civil Rights
1980 *Civil Rights Issues of Euro-Ethnic Americans in the United States: Opportunities and Challenges*, Washington, DC: U.S. Commission on the Civil Rights, 1980. *See*, "Sixth Session: Employment and Ethnicity". Pp. 373-508.

Vecoli, R.J.
1983a "The Formation of Chicago's 'Little Italies' ", *Journal of American Ethnic History*, 2: Spring. Pp. 5-20.

1983b "The Italian Immigrants in the Labor Movement of the United States from 1880 to 1929", in *Gli Italiani fuori d'Italia*, Edited by B. Bezza. Milan: Franco Angeli. Pp. 257-306.

1981   "The Italians", in *They Chose Minnesota*. Edited by June Holmquist.St. Paul: Minnesota Historical Society. Pp. 449-71

1978a "Louis Adamic and the Contemporary Search for Roots", *Ethnic Studies*, Monash University, Australia, 2:1978. Pp. 29-35

1978b "The War and Italian American Syndicalists", (unpublished paper).

1978c "The Coming of Age of the Italian Americans", *Ethnicity*, 5:1978. Pp. 119-47.

1977a "Cult and Occult in Italian American Culture", in *Immigrants and Religion in Urban America*. Edited by R.M. Miller and T.D. Marzik. Philadelphia: Temple University Press. Pp. 25-47

1977b "Italian American Workers, 1880-1920", in *Perspectives in Italian Immigration and Ethnicity*. Edited by S.M. Tomasi. New York: Center for Migration Studies. Pp. 25-49

1970   "The Italian American Literary Subculture: an Historical and Sociological Analysis", in *The Italian American Novel*, Proceedings of the Second Annual Conference of the American Italian Historical Association. Edited by John M. Cammett. Staten Island, NY: A.I.H.A. Pp. 6-10.

1969   "Prelates and Peasants: Italian Immigrants and the Catholic Church', *Journal of Social History*, 2:Spring. Pp. 217-68

1965   *The People of New Jersey*, Princeton, NJ: D. Van Nostrand Co.

1964   "Contadini in Chicago: A Critique of The Uprooted", *Journal of American History*, LI, Dec. Pp. 404-417.

Venturini, N.
1984   "From Roosevelt and Mussolini to Truman and De Gasperi: The Politics of Italian American Leadership, 1930-1950", (unpublished master's thesis). University of Minnesota.

Ventresca, F.B.
1980   "Italian Americans and the Ethiopian Crisis", *IA* Fall/Winter, 6. Pp. 4-28.

Ware, C.F.
1935   *Greenwich Village, 1920-1930*. New York: Harper.

Ware, C.F. editor
1940   *The Cultural Approach to History*. New York: Columbia University Press. P. 63.

White, T.
1982 *America in Search of Itself: The Making of the President 1956-1980.* New York: Harper and Row.

Whyte, W.F.
1943 *Street Corner Society: Social Structure of an Italian Slum.* Chicago: University of Chicago.

Wonk, D.
1983 "Sons of Contessa Entellina", *Dixie. The Times-Picayune.* New Orleans. October 16, 1983. Pp. 10-15.

CHAPTER 9: The State of Italian American Research Since 1976: Sources, Methodolgies and Orientations in Italy.

Aga Rossi Sitzia, E. *et al.*
1979a "Gli Stati Uniti e la divisione dell'Europa", *Storia contemporanea,* 10(6):1157-1177.

_____
1979b *Il rapporto Stevenson: documenti sull'economia italiana e sulle direttive della politica americana in Italia nel 1943-1944.* Roma: Carecas.

_____
1976 *Italia e Stati Uniti durante l'amministrazione Truman.* Milano: Franco Angeli.

Agnelli, G. Foundation
1980 *The Italian Americans: Who They Are, Where They Are, How Many They Are.* Torino: Fondazione G. Agnelli.

_____
1979 *Italia e USA: giudizi incrociati. Italy and USA: Mutual Judgments,* (Florence Conference, May 1978). Torino: Fondazione Giovanni Agnelli.

Arlacchi, P.
1980 *Mafia, contadini e latifondo nella Calabria tradizionale.* Bologna: Il Mulino.

Assante, F., ed.
1978 *Il movimento migratorio italiano dall'Unità nazionale ai giorni nostri,* 2 vol. Genève-Napoli: Librairie Droz.

Avagliano, L.
1976 *L'emigrazione italiana.* Napoli: Ferraro.

Bairati, P. ed.
1978 *Storia del Nord America.* Firenze: La Nuova Italia.

Barie, O.
1978 *Gli Stati Uniti nel ventesimo secolo.* Milano.

Bartile, A., A. Dell'Omodarme, eds.
1981 *Italia e Stati Uniti d'America. Concordanze e dissonanze.* Roma: Il Veltro.

_____
1980 *Immagine culturale dell'Italia all'estero.* Roma: Il Veltro.

Bettini, L.
1976 *Bibliografia dell'anarchismo, V.I., tomo 2: Periodici e numeri unici anarchici in lingua italiana pubblicati all'estero (1872-1971).* Firenze: C.P. Editrice.

Bezza, B., ed.
1983   Gli italiani fuori d'Italia. Gli emigrati italiani nei movimenti operai dei Paesi di adozione (1880-1940). Milano: Franco Angeli.

Bock, G., et. al.
1976   La formazione dell'operaio massa negli USA: 1898-1922. Milano: Feltrinelli.

Boelhower, W.
1982   Immigrant Autobiography in the United States. (Four versions of the Italian American self). Verona: Essedue ed.

Bologna, S. et al.
1977   Operai e stato. Lotte operaie e riforma dello stato capitalistico tra rivoluzione d'ottobre e New Deal. Milano: Feltrinelli.

Bonazzi, T.
1976   "La situazione attuale degli studi di storia americana in Italia", in Gli Studi Americani in Italia. Atti del primo convegno di studio, Pisa.

Borzomati, P. ed.
1982   L'emigrazione calabrese dall'Unità ad oggi. Roma: CSER.

Briani, V.
1978   La legislazione emigratoria italiana nelle sue successive fasi. Roma: Istituto Poligrafico dello Stato.

————
1977   La stampa italiana all'estero dalle origini ai nostri giorni. Roma: Istituto Poligrafico dello Stato.

Brunello, P.
1982   "Agenti di emigrazione, contadini e immagini dell'America nella provincia di Venezia", Rivista di storia contemporanea, 1:95-122.

Calice, N.
1982   "Il fascismo e l'emigrazione lucana negli USA", Studi storici, 23(6):881-896.

Calvi, G.
1982   "Donne in fabbrica", Quaderni storici, 51:817-851.

————
1980   "Da paesani a cittadini: gli italiani immigrati negli Stati Uniti (1900-1920), Rivista di storia contemporanea, 4:535-551.

————
1979   Società industriale e cultura operaia negli Stati Uniti (1890-1917), Roma: Bulzoni.

Canavero, A.
1979   "Tommaso Gallarati Scotti and His Role in Italian Foreign Policy after World War II", Journal of Italian History, 2(1):32-51.

Cannistraro, P.V.
1976   "Gli italo-americani di fronte all'ingresso dell'Italia nella seconda guerra mondiale", Storia contemporanea, 7:855-864.

Cannistraro, P.V. and G. Rosoli
1979   Emigrazione, Chiesa e fascismo. Lo scioglimento dell'Opera Bonomelli (1922-1928). Roma: Studium.

Caroli, B.B.
1976   "The United States, Italy and the Literacy Test", Studi Emigrazione, 13(41):3-22.

Carpignano, P.
1976   "Immigrazione e degradazione: mercato del lavoro e ideologie della classe operaia americana durante la 'Progressive Era'". In *La formazione dell'operaio massa negli USA: 1898-1922*. Edited by G. Bock. Milano: Feltrinelli. Pp. 189-238.

Centro di Studi Americani
1981   *Catalogo unico dei periodici americani in Italia. Union Catalog of American Periodicals in Italy*. Roma: CSA, 1978-1981.

Cerase, F.P.
1976   *Sotto il dominio dei borghesi. Sottosviluppo ed emigrazione nell'Italia meridionale*. Roma: Carucci.

Cetti, L.
1983   "Donne italiane a New York: lavoro e attivita sindacale", *Economia e Lavoro*, 17(1): 159-164.

Cinel, D.
1982   "Apprendistato per le migrazioni internazionali: le migrazioni interne in Italia nel sec. XIX", *Comunità, 184:181-203*.

1981   *"Emigrazione di ritorno e movimenti contadini nell'Italia di fine Ottocento"*, *Comunità*, 183:192-211.

Ciuffoletti, A. and M. Degl'Innocenti
1978   *L'emigrazione nella storia d'Italia, 1868-1975. Storia e documenti*. Firenze: Vallecchi, V.I. V.II.

Codignola, L., ed.
1982   *Terre d'America e burocrazia romana. Simon Stock, Propaganda Fide e la colonia di Lord Baltimore a Terranova, 1621-1649*. Venezia: Marsilio.

1979   *Canadiana. Storia e storiografia canadese*. Venezia: Marsilio.

1978   *Canadiana. Aspetti della storia e della letteratura canadese*. Venezia: Marsilio.

Conferenza Nazionale Dell'Emigrazione
1975   *L'emigrazione italiana nelle prospettive degli anni ottanta. Atti della Conferenza Nazionale dell'Emigrazione*. Roma.

1974   *Aspetti e problemi dell'emigrazione italiana. Elementi di documentazione preliminare*. Roma.

Conti, F.G.
1976   "Il problema politico dei prigionieri di guerra italiani nei rapporti con gli alleati (1943-1945)", *Storia contemporanea*, 7(4);865-920.

Dada, A.
1982   "I radicali italo-americani e la società italiana", *Italia contemporanea*, 146-147:13-140.

1979   "Contributo metodologico per una storia dell'emigrazione e dell'antifascismo italiani negli Stati Uniti", *Annali dell'Istituto di Storia*. Firenze, 1:197-218.

Damiani, C.B.
1978   "L'emigrazione italiana negli Stati Uniti durante il periodo fascista", *Affari Sociali Internazionali*, 6:105-124.

De Felice, R., ed.
1982 "Prezzolini, la guerra e il fascismo", *Storia contemporanea*, 13(3):361-426.

———
1979 *Cenni storici sull'emigrazione italiana nelle Americhe e in Australia*. Milano: Franco Angeli.

Della Terza, D.
1982 "L'immagine dell'Italia nella cultura americana, 1942-1952", *Belfagor*, 37(5):513-532.

Dell'Orefice, A., ed.
1978 *Tendenze dell' emigrazione italiana: ieri, oggi*, Incontro promosso dalla Società Italiana degli Economisti (Napoli-Salerno, 1 giugno 1976). Genève-Napoli: Librairie Droz.

De Marco, W.
1980 "Boston's Italian Enclave, 1880-1930", *Studi Emigrazione*, 17(59):331-359.

De Rosa, L.
1980 *Emigranti, capitali e banche (1896-1906)*. Napoli: Giannini-Edizione del Banco di Napoli.

Di Giovanni, S.M.
1983 *Michael Augustine Corrigan and the Italian Immigrants: The Relationship between the Church and the Italians in the Archidiocese of New York, 1885-1902*. Dissertatio ad Doctoratum. Roma: Pontificia Universitas Gregoriana.

Di Pietro, R.J.
1976 "Language as a Marker of Italian Ethnicity", *Studi Emigrazione*, 13(42): 202-218.

Di Nolfo, E.
1978 *Vaticano e Stati Uniti, 1939-1952 (Dalle carte di Myron C. Taylor)*. Milano: Franco Angeli.

Dinucci, G.
1979 "Il modello della colonia libera nell'ideologia espansionistica italiana. Dagli anni "80 alla fine del secolo", *Storia contemporanea*, 10(3):427-479.

Fasce, N.
1981 "Dentro e fuori la comunità etnica: testimonianze orali di immigrati italiani in USA nel primo Novecento", *Movimento operaio e socialista*, 4(1-2):33-48.

Fillippone-Thaulero, G.
1979 *La Gran Bretagna e l'Italia. Dalla Conferenza di Mosca a Potsdam, 1943-1945*. Roma: Edizioni di storia e letteratura.

Fiori, G.
1983 *L'anarchico Schirru: condannato a morte per l'intenzione di uccidere Mussolini*. Milano: Mondadori.

Formez-CSER
1976 *Repertorio delle ricerche sull'emigrazione in Europa*. Roma: Formez.

Franzina, E., ed.
1983 *Un altro Veneto. Saggi e studi di storia dell'emigrazione nei sec. XIX eXX*. Albano, Francisci.

———
1982 *La classe, gli uomini e i partiti, Storia del movimento operaio e socialista in una provincia bianca: il Vicentino (1873-1948)*. Vicenza: Odeonlibri.

1979 *Merica! Merica! Emigrazione e colonizzazione nelle lettere dei contadini veneti in America Latina, 1876-1902.* Milano: Feltrinelli.

1978 "Sui profughi d'Italia: emigrati e immigrati nella storiografia più recente (1975-1978)", *Movimento operaio e socialista*, 4:413-425.

1976 *La grande migrazione. L'esodo dei rurali del Veneto durante il secolo XIX.* Venezia: Marsilio.

Gould, J.D.
1980 "European Inter-Continental Emigration. The Road Home: Return Migration from the U.S.A.", *Journal of European Economic History*, 9(1):41-112.

Haupt, G.
1976 "Il ruolo degli emigrati e deella diffusione delle idee socialiste all'epoca della Seconda Internazionale". In *Anna Kuliscioff e l'età del riformismo.* Roma.

Killinger, C.
1981 "Gaetano Salvemini e le autorità americane. Documenti inediti del FBI", *Storia contemporanea*, 12(3):403-439.

Kowalsky, N. and J. Metzler
1983a *Inventory of the Historical Archives of the Sacred Congregation for the Evangelization of Peoples or "De Propaganda Fide".* Rome: Urbaniana University Press.

1983b *In Their Own Words.* European Journal of the American Ethnic Imagination. Venice: Cafoscarina, 1(1), Summer.

Izzo, L.
1977 "Appunti per una storia del movimento migratorio della Calabria (1861-1971)." In *Fatti e idee di storia economica nei sec. XII-XX. Studi dedicati a F. Borlandi*, Bologna.

Lange, P.
1977 *Studies on Italy, 1943-1975. Selected bibliography of American and British materials in political science, economics, sociology and anthropology.* Torino: Fondazione G. Agnelli.

Lazzarini, A.
1981 *Campagne venete ed emigrazione di massa (1866-1900).* Vicenza: Istituto per le Ricerche di Storia Sociale e di Storia Religiosa.

Lerda, G.V.
1981a *Il populismo americano.* Geneva: Mondini & Siccardi.

1981b "Letterature d'America". Special on Italian American Literature. 2(9-10). Roma: Bulzoni.

Levy, C.
1981 "Malatesta in Exile", *Annali della Fondazione L. Einaudi*, 15:245-280.

Lewanski, R. and R.C. Lewanski
1979 *Guide to Italian Libraries and Archives.* New York: Council for European Studies.

Loatman, R.J., Jr.
1977 "'Contadini' in the New World 'Paese'", *Studi Emigrazione*, 14(45):68-84.

Lodolini, E., ed.
1976 *Guida delle fonti per la storia dell'America Latina estistenti in Italia*. Roma: Direzione generale degli Archivi di Stato.

Loverci,F.
1979 "Italiani in California negli anni del Risorgimento", *Clio*, 15(4): 469-547.

1977 "Il primo ambasciatore italiano a Washington: Saverio Fava", *Clio*, 13(3): 239-275.

Lupi, C.
1981 "Qualche consiglio per chi parte: le guide degli emigranti (1855-1927)", *Movimento operaio e socialista*, 4(1-2):77-89.

Luraghi, R. *et al.*
1978 *Italia e Stati Uniti dall'indipendenza americana ad oggi (1976-1976)*. Atti del I Congresso internazionale di storia americana (Genova, 26-29 maggio 1976). Genova: Tilgher.

Mannucci, L.V.
1981 *Le radici ideologiche degli Stati Uniti*. Lecce: Milella.

Margariti,A.
1979 *America! America!* Casalvelino Scalo: Galzerano.

Margiocco, M.
1981 *Stati Uniti e PCI, 1943-1980*. Bari: Laterza.

Martellone, A.M.
1980 *La "questione" dell'immigrazione negli Stati Uniti*. Bologna: Il Mulino.

Massara, G.
1984 *Americani*. Palermo: Sellerio.

1976 *Viaggiatori italiani in America (1860-1970)*. Roma, Edizioni di Storia e Letteratura.

Micelli, F., *et al.*
1982 "Emigrazione e società in Friuli fra '800 e '900", *Qualestoria*, 10(3):3-132.

Migliorino, E.G.
1976 "Il proletariato italiano di Filadelfia all'inizio del secolo", *Studi Emigrazione*, 13(41):23-40.

Migone, G.G.
1980 *Gli Stati Uniti e il fascismo. Alle origini dell'egemonia americana in Italia*. Milano: Feltrinelli.

Miller, J.E.
1980 "La politica dei 'prominenti' italo-americani nei rapporti dell'OSS", *Italia contemporanea*, 32(139):51-70.

1976 "Carlo Sforza e l'evoluzione della poitica americana verso l'Italia, 1940-1943", *Storia contemporanea*, 7(4):825-854.

Ministero degli Affari Esteri
1982 *Traduzioni dall'italiano nella biblioteca del Congresso di Washington, 1977-1981*. Ministero degli Affari Esteri: Direzione delle Relazioni Culturali.

Ministero per i beni Culturali e Ambientali
1983 *Guida generale degli Archivi di Stato italiani*. V.II (F-M). Roma: Ufficio Centrale per i Beni archivistici.

———
1981 V.I (A-E).

Molinari, A.
1981 "I giornali delle comunità anarchiche italo-americane", *Movimento operaio e socialista*, 4(1-2):117-130.

Mormino, G.
1982 "The Church Upon the Hill: Italian Immigrants in St. Louis, Missouri, 1870-1955, *Studi Emigrazione*, 19(66):203-224.

Nelli, H.S., ed.
1977 *The United States and Italy: The First Two Hundred Years*, (Proceedings of the IX Conference of the AIHA, Washington, D.C., October 8-10, 1976). New York: The American Italian Historical Association.

Nobile, A.
1977 "Gli anni del 'grande esodo': emigrazione e spopolamento in Calabria (1881-1911)", in *Aspetti e problemi di storia della società calabrese nell'età contemporanea*, Atti del I Convegno di studio (Reggio Calabria, 1-4 novembre 1975). Reggio Calabria: Editori Meridionali Riuniti.

Ortoleva, P.
1981 "Una voce dal coro: Angelo Rocco e lo sciopero di Lawrence del 1912", *Movimento operaio e socialista*, 4(1-2):5-32.

Ostuni, M.R.
1981 "Fonti e spunti di ricerca per la storia dell'emigrazione italiana", *Movimento operaio e socialista*, 4(1-2):131-143.

———
1980 "I fondi archivistici del Commissariato generale dell'emigrazione II e della Direzione generale degli italiani all'estero", *Studi Emigrazione*, 17(59): 360-372.

———
1978 "Il fondo Commissariato Generale dell'Emigrazione", *Studi Emigrazione*, 15(51):411-440.

Ottaviano C.
1982 "Antonio Labriola e il problema dell'espansione coloniale", *Annali della Fondazione Luigi Einaudi*, 16:305-328.

———
1981 "Quando l'Italia esportava idee. La diffusione degli scritti di Achille Loria fra gli intellectuali americani", *Annali della Fondazione Luigi Einaudi*, 15:281-321.

Pane, R.
1982 "L'esperienza degli emigrati calabresi negli Stati Uniti, in *L'emigrazione calabrese dall'Unità ad oggi*. Edited by P. Borzomati. Roma: CSER.

Papa, E.R.
1982 *Per una biografia intellettuale di F.S. Merlino. Giustizia e sociologia criminale. Dal "socialismo anarchico" al "riformismo rivoluzionario" (1878-1930)*. Milano: Franco Angeli.

Pellegrini, V.
1983 "Le fonti per la storia del Mezzogiorno nell'Archivio storico-diplomatico del Ministero degli Affari Esteri", in *Le fonti archivistiche per la storia del Mezzogiorno nell'età moderna e contemporanea. Ricerca storica ed occupazione giovanile.* Lecce: Milella.

Piselli, F.
1981 *Parentela ed emigrazione. Mutamenti e continuità in una comunità calabrese.* Torino: Einaudi.

Pozzetta, G. *et al.*
1981 "Le Little Italies negli Stati Uniti tra '800 e '900", *Storia Urbana*, 5(16):3-145.

Romano, S.
1979 "Storia d'Italia e cultura italiana all'estero: nota di lavoro", *Storia contemporanea*, 10(2):377-385.

Romero, F.
1981 *Il sindacato come istituzione. La regolamentazione del conflitto industriale negli Stati Uniti, 1912-1918.* Torino: Rosenberg & Sellier.

Rosoli, G.
1979 "Chiesa e comunità italiane negli Stati Uniti, 1880-1940", *Studium*, 1:25-47.

_____ (ed.)
1978a *Un secolo di emigrazione italiana, 1876-1976.* Roma: Centro Studi Emigrazione.

_____
1978b "L'emigrazione italiana negli Stati Uniti: un bilancio storiografico", *Affari Sociali Internazionali*, special issue. Pp. 75-103.

_____
1978c "Lo stato della ricerca sull'emigrazione in Italia e nei Paesi mediterranei", *Quaderni Mediterranei*, 3:11-62.

_____
1977 "Sources and Current Research in Italy on Italian Americans". In *Perspectives in Italian Immigration and Ethnicity.* Edited by S.M. Tomasi. Staten Island: Center for Migration Studies. Pp. 133-162.

Russo, F.
1981 *Il sindacato come istituzione. La regolamentazione del conflitto industriale negli Stati Uniti, 1912-1918.* Torino: Rosenberg & Sellier.

Salvadori, M.
1978 "Antifascisti italiani negli Stati Uniti". In Atti del I Congresso internazionale di storia americana: *Italia e Stati Uniti dall'Indipendenza americana ad oggi (1976-1976).* Genova: Tilgher.

Salvetti, P.
1984 "Una parrocchia italiana di New York e i suoi fedeli: Nostra Signora di Pompei (1892-1933)", *Studi Emigrazione*, 21(73):43-65.

_____
1982 "La comunità italiana di S. Francisco tra italianità e americanizzazione negli anni '30 e '40", *Studi Emigrazione*, 19(65):3-40.

Sartori, C.
1979 "Giuseppe Volpi di Misurata e i rapporti finanziari del gruppo SADE con gli USA (1918-1930)", *Ricerche storiche*, 9(2-3): 375-438.

Scarzanella, E.
1977 "L'emigrazione veneta nel periodo fascista", *Studi storici*, 18(2): 171-199.

Sori, E.
1979 *L'emigrazione italiana dall'Unità alla seconda guerra mondiale.* Bologna: Il Mulino.

Spadolini, G., *et al.*
1982 "Gaetano Salvemini tra storia e politica", Archivio trimestrale, 8(3-4).

Spini, G. *et al.*
1976 Italia e America dal settecento all'età dell'imperialismo. Italia e America dalla grande guerra a oggi. 2 vol. Venezia: Marsilio.

Surdi, A.P. and C. Penteriani, eds.
1981 *L'immagine degli Stati Uniti attraverso le testimonianze dell'esperienza italiana in America, 1850-1914.* Introduzione di Giuseppe Massara. Roma: Centro di Studi Americani.

Tagliarini, F., ed.
1976 *Le relazioni economiche fra l'Italia e gli Stati Uniti d'America. Esperienze, sviluppi e prospettive.* Roma: Il Veltro.

Tirabassi, M.
1982 "Prima le donne e i bambini: gli "International Institutes" e l'americanizzaione degli immigrati", *Quaderni storici*, 17(51):853-880.

Tomasi, S.M.
1982 "L'assistenza religiosa agli italiani in USA e il Prelato per l'emigrazione italiana: 1920-1949", *Studi Emigrazione*, 19(66): 167-190.

_____
1980 *National Directory of Research Centers, Repositories and Organizations of Italian Culture in the United States.* Torino: Fondazione Giovanni Agnelli.

_____
1979 "Emigration Studies in Italy, 1975-1978", *International Migration Review*, 13(2):333-346.

Tosi, L.
1983 *L'emigrazione italian all'estero in eta giolittiana. Il caso umbro.* Firenze: Olschki.

Traldi, A.
1976 "La tematica dell'emigrazione nella narrativa italo-americana", *Comunita*, 30:145-173.

Treves, A.
1976 *Le migrazioni interne nell'Italia fascista. Politica e realtà demografica.* Torino: G. Einaudi.

Valiani, L.
1982 "L'emigrazione antifascista e la seconda guerra mondiale", *Nuova Antologia*, 117(2143):47-56.

Vannicelli, M.L.
1982 "L'opera della Congregazione di Propaganda Fide per gli emigrati italiani negli Stati Uniti (1883-1887)". In *L'emigrazione calabrese dall'Unità ad oggi.* Edited by P. Borzomati. Roma: CSER. Pp. 135-151.

_____
1978 *Per una storia della comunità cattolica italiana negli Stati Uniti d'America dal 1860 al 1900.* Tesi di laurea. Università degli studi di Roma, A.A. 1977-78.

Vanzetti, B.
1977   *Autobiografia e lettere inedite*. A cura di Alberto Gedda. Firenze: Vallecchi.

Varsori, A.
1982   *Gli alleati e l'emigrazione democratica antifascista (1940-1943)*. Firenze: Sansoni.

Varsori, A.
1980a   "L'antifascismo e gli Alleati: le missioni di Lussu e Gentili a Londra e Washington nel 1941-42", *Storia e politica*, 19(3): 457-507.

1980b   "La Mazzini Society", *Nuova Antologia*, 115(2136): 106-124.

1976   "La politica inglese e il conte Sforza", *Rivista di Studi Politici Internazionali*, 43:31-57.

Vaudagna, M.V.
1981a   *Corporativismo e New Deal. Integrazione e conflitto sociale negli Stati Uniti (1933-1941)*. Torino: Rosenberg e Sellier.

1981b   *Il New Deal*. Bologna: Il Mulino.

Vecoli, R.J.
1982   "Italian Religious Organizations in Minnesota", *Studi Emigrazione*, 19(66): 191-201.

Vezzosi, E., ed.
1983   *Le relazioni Italia-Stati Uniti dal 1943 al 1953. Storia-Economia-Cultura* (Firenze, 8-10 maggio 1980). Incontro internazionale organizzato dall'Istituto storico-politico della Facoltà di Scienze politiche "C. Alfieri" e dall'United States International Communication Agency. Firenze.

Villari, F. ed.
1977   *New Deal. Teoria e politica*. Roma: Editori Riuniti.

Villari, R.
1980   "Storici americani e ribelli europei", *Studi storici*, 21(3):487-502.

CHAPTER 10: The State of Canadian Italian Research Since 1975

Anderson, B. and J.S. Frideres
1981   *Ethnicity in Canada*. Toronto: Butterworths.

Anisef, P.
1975   "Consequences of Ethnicity for Educational Plans among Grade 12 Students". In *Education of Immigrant Children*, Edited by A. Wolfgang, Toronto: O.I.S.E.

Ares, R.
1975   *Les positions Artniques, linguistiques et religieuses des Canadiens francais a la suite du recensement de 1971*. Montreal: Bellarmin.

Augimeri, M.C.
1978   *Italian Canadians: A Cross Section: A National Survey of Italian-Canadian Communities*. Ottawa: National Congress of Italian Canadians.

Battistelli, F.
1975 L'Autonomia cuturale come strumento di assimilazione: i mass media italiani nella communita immigrata di Toronto", *Rassegna Italiana di Sociologia*, 16 (3).

Berry, J.W., R. Kalin, and D.M. Taylor
1977 *Multiculturalism and Ethnic Attitudes in Canada*, Ottawa: Ministry of Supply and Services.

Briani, V.
1975 *Il Lavoro Italiano Oltremare*, (X: Il Nuovo Sbocco Canadese). Rome: Ministero degli Affari Esteri.

Caroli, B.B., R.F. Harney and L.F. Tomais, eds.
1978 *The Italian Immigrant Woman in North America*. Toronto: The Multicultural History Society of Ontario.

Chandler, S.B. and J.A. Molinaro, eds.
1979 *The Culture of Italy: Medieval to Modern*. Toronto: Griffin House.
Colalillo, G.
1979 Patterns of Socialization among Italian Adolescent Girls", *Journal of Baltic Studies*, 10 (1).

D'Ambrosio, L.G. and E.A.M. D'Ambrosio
1980 *Cultural Retention of Italo-Canadian Youth*. Toronto: C.I.P.B.A.

D'Antini, B.
1975 *The Quiet Desperation of the Immigrant*. Toronto: Ministry of Culture and Recreation.

Danziger, K.
1979 "Attitudes to Parental Control and Adolescents' Aspirations: A Comparison of Immigrants and Non-Immigrants". In *The Canadian Family*, Edited by K. Ishwaren. Toronto: McGraw-Hill Ryerson.

———
1977 *Sources of Instability in the Distribution of Control among Italian Immigrant and Non-Immigrant Families in Canada*. Toronto: York University, Department of Psychology Report No. 56.

———
1976 "The Acculturation of Italian Immigrant Girls". In *The Canadian Family*, Toronto: Holt Rinehart and Winston of Canada, Ltd.

———
1975 "Differences in Acculturation Patterns of Socialization among Italian Immigrant Families". In *Socialization and Social Values in Canadian Society*, edited by E.Zureik and R.M. Pike.

Darroch, A.G.
1980 "Another Look at Ethnicity, Stratification and Social Mobility in Canada". In *Ethnicity and Ethnic Relations in Canada*, edited by J.E. Goldstein and R.M. Bienvenu, Toronto: Butterworths.

Day, R.D.
1981 "Ethnic Soccer Clubs in London, Canada: A Study of Assimilation", *International Review of Sport Sociology*, 16 (1).

Denis A.B.
1978 "The Relationship between Ethnicity and Educational Aspirations of Post-Secondary Students in Toronto and Montreal". In *Ethnic Canadians*, edited by M.L. Kovacks, Culture and Education, Regina.

Di Giacomo, J.L.
1982 *They Live in the Moneta: An Overview of the History and Changes in Social Organization of Italians in Timmins, Ontario.* York-Timmins Project, Report #2, Toronto: I.B.R., York University.

Di Santo, O.
"Forze Nuovo", *Polyphony*, 4 (1).

Doughty, H.A., D.R. Skidmore, A.J.C. KING and I.R. Munroe
1976 *Canadian Studies: Culture and Country.* Toronto: Wiley Publishers of Canada Ltd.

Driedger, L.. and R.A. Mezoff
1981 "Ethnic Prejudice and Discrimination in Winnipeg High Schools", *Canadian Journal of Sociology*, 6 (1)

Franocchia, F.
1977 "Italiani in Canada: Il caso di Montreal", *Bolletino della Societa Geografica Italiana*, 10.

Ferguson, E.
1977 *Immigrants in Canada.* Toronto: University of Toronto Press.

F.I.L.E.F.
1981 "Il drama dell'identita' dei giovani italo-quebechesi", *Emigrazione*, 12.

Frideres, J., J. Di Santo, S. Goldenbeg, S. and J. Horna
1978 *The Process of Citizenship Acquisition.* Ottawa: Secretary of State.

Germano, G.
1978 *The Italians of Western Canada.* Florence: Giunti.

Grohovaz, G.
1982 "Toronto's Italian Press after the Second World War", *Polyphony*, 4 (1).

Grygier, T.
1975 "Integration of Four Ethnic Groups in Canadian Society: English, German, Hungarian, Italian". In *Sounds Canadian: Languages and Culture in Multi-ethnic Society*, edited by P. Migus, Toronto: Peter Martin Associates.

Harney R.F.
1979a "The Italian Community in Toronto", in *Two Nations, Many Cultures*, edited by J.L. Elliott, Toronto: Prentice Hall Of Canada.

1979b "Montreal's King of Italian Labor: A Case Study of Padronism", *Labor*.

1979c "Italians in Canada". In *The Culture of Italy: Mediaeval to Modern*, edited by Chandler and Molinaro, Toronto: Griffin House.

1979d "Toronto: Little Italy Now", *Attenzione*, Toronto, December.

1978a   Men Without Women: Italian Migrants to Canada, 1885-1930". In *The Italian Immigrant Woman in North America*, edited by B.B. Caroli *et. al.*, Toronto: Multicultural History Society of Ontario

1978b   "Boarding and Belonging: Thoughts on Sojourner Institutions", *Urban History Review*, 2 (78).

1978c   *Italians in Canada*, Toronto: The Multicultural History Society of Ontario.

1977a   "The Commerce of Migration", *Canadian Ethnic Studies*, 9 (1).

1976   "Frozen Wastes: The State of Italian-Canadian Studies". In *Perspectives in Italian Immigration and Ethnicity*, edited by S.M. Tomasi, New York: Center for Migration Studies.

1976   "From Bokhara to the Soo: The Advantage of Italian Emigration", *Mosaico*, March.

1975a   "Chiaroscuro: Italians in Toronto 1885-1915", *Italian Americana*, Spring.

1975b   "Ambiente and Social Class in North American Little Italies", *Canadian Review of Studies in Nationalism*, 2 (2).

Jansen, C.J.
1981a   *Education and Social Mobility of Immigrants: The Case of Italians in Vancouver.* Toronto: I.B.R., York University.

1981b   *The Italians of Vancouver: Case Study of Internal Differentiation of an Ethnic Group.* Toronto: I.B.R., York University.

1981c   "Problems and Issues in Post-War Immigration to Canada and Their Effects on Origins and Characteristics of Immigrants", paper presented at Canadian Population Society Meetings, Dalhousie University, Halifax.

1979   "Italo-Canadians, Politics and Parties: Role of Vancouver Italians in 2 Elections", paper presented at Canadian Ethnic Studies Association Conference, Vancouver.

1978a   "Community Organization of Italians in Toronto", in *The Canadian Ethnic Mosaic*, edited by L. Driedger, Toronto: McClelland and Stewart.

1978b   "The Italian Dilemma over Multiculturalism and Separatism", paper presented at Canadian Sociology and Anthropology Meetings, London, Ont.

Jansen, C.J. and J. Gallucci
1977 *A Study of Multiculturalism and Italian Media.* Toronto: Wintario Citzenship and Multicultural Program.

Jansen, C.J. and L.R. La Cavera
Fact-book on Italians in Canada. (First Edition), Toronto: York University.

Kalback, W.E. and W.W. McVey
1979 *The Demographic Bases of Canadian Society.* (2nd ed.), Toronto: McGraw-Hill Ryerson Ltd.

La Vigna, C.
1979 "Women in the Canadian and Italian Trade Union Movements at the Turn of the Century: A Comparison. In *The Italian Immigrant Woman in North American Society*, edited by Caroli *et. al.*, Toronto: Multicultural History Society of Ontario.

Macvey, J.
1980 "Entity vs. Process Approaches to Ethnic Relations and Ethnic Identity: A Case Study of Ethnic Soccer Clubs in Toronto's Italian Community", *Canadian Ethnic Studies*, 12 (3).

Mastrangelo, R.
1979 *The Italian Canadians.* Toronto: Van Nostrand Reinhold Ltd.

Maykovich, M.K.
1975 "Ethnic Variation in Success Value". In *Socialization and Social Values in Canadian Society*, edited by E. Zureik and R.M. Pike, Toronto: McClelland and Stewart Ltd.

Menniti, P.
1981 "Scenes of Two Cultures—The Need for Italian Canadian Textbooks", *Canadian Journal of Italian Studies*, 4 (1-2)

O'Bryan, K.G., J.G. Reitz and Kuplowska, O.M.
1976 *Non-Official Languages.* Ottawa: Ministry of Supply and Services.

Paci, F.
1978 *The Italians.* Toronto: Oberson Press.

Painchaud, C. and R. Poulin
1981 *Le phenomene migratoire italien et la formation de la communaute italo-quebecoise.* Pro-developpemet italo-canadien, Ottawa.

Parry, H.
1979a "The Metonymic Definition of Female and the Concept of Honour among Italian Immigrant Families in Toronto". In *The Italian Immigrant Woman in North America*, edited by Caroli *et.al.*, Toronto: Multicultural History Society of Ontario.

1979b "Family Attitudes among Italians in Toronto", paper presented at Open Symposium on Community Health, Addenbrook's Hospital, Cambridge, England.

Pautasso, L.
1979 "La Donna Italiana durante il Periodo Facista in Toronto 1930-1940". In *The Italian Immigrant Woman in North America*, edited by Caroli *et. al.*, Toronto: Multicultural History Society of Ontario.

Porter, J.
1972 *The Vertical Mosaic.*

Principe, A.
1980 "The Italo-Canadian Anti-Fascist Press in Toronto 1922-1940", *Nemla Italian Studies*, 4.

Ramirez, B.
1982 "L'Immigration Italienne", *Critere*, no. 33.

_____
1981 "Montreal's Italians and the Socio-Economy of Settlement 1900-1930: Some Historical Hypotheses", *Urban History Review*, 1.

_____
1980 *The Italians of Montreal 1900-1921.* Montreal: Les Editions du Courant.

Rayfield, J.R.
1976 "Maria in Markham Street: Italian Immigrants and Language Learning in Toronto", *Ethnic Glyphony*, 3 (1).

Reitz, J.G.
1981 "Language and Ethnic Community Survival". In *Ethnicity and Ethnic Relations in Canada*, edited by J.E. Goldstein and R.M. Bienvenu, Toronto: Butterworths.

_____
1980 *The Survival of Ethnic Groups.* Toronto: McGraw-Hill Ryerson Ltd.

Richmond, A.H.
1970 *Ethnic Variation in Family Income and Poverty in Canada.* Toronto: I.B.R., York University.

Richmond, A.H. and J. Goldlust
1979 *Family and Social Integration of Immigrants in Toronto.* Toronto: York University.

Richmond, A.H. and W. Kalback
1980 *Factors in the Adjustment of Immigrants and their Descendents.* Ottawa: Statistics Canada.

Sheffe, N.
1976 *Many Cultures, Many Heritages.* Toronto: McGraw-Hill.

Simone, N.
1981 *Italian Immigrants in Toronto 1890-1930.* Toronto: Department of Geography, York University.

Sturino, F.
1980 "Family and Kin Cohesion among Southern Italian Immigrants in Toronto". In *Canadian Families: Ethnic Variations*, edited by K. Ishwaren, Toronto: McGraw-Hill Ryerson Ltd.

1978   "A Case Study of a South Italian Family in Toronto 1935-1960", *Urban History Review*, 2 (78).

Tomasi, L.F.
1977   "The Italian Community in Toronto: A Demographic Profile", *International Migration Review*, 11 (4).

Toscano, S.
1975   "Teaching English, Italian Style". In *Education of Immigrant Children*, edited by A. Wolfgang, Toronto: O.I.S.E.

Troper, H. and L. Palmer
1976   "St. Leonard", *Issues in Cultural Diversity*. Canadian Critical Issues Series, Toronto: O.I.S.E.

Trovato, F.
1981   "Canadian Ethnic Fertility", *Sociological Focus*, 14 (1).

Trovato, F. and T.K. Burch
1980   "Minority Group Status and Fertility in Canada", *Canadian Ethnic Studies*, 12 (3).

Wilkenson, D.
1981   "Education and the Social Mobility of Three Ethnic Groups: A Canadian Case Study", *Canadian Ethnic Studies*, 13 (2).

Wolfgang, A.
1979   "The Teacher and Non-verbal Behavior in the Multicultural Classroom". In *Non-verbal Behavior: Applications and Cultural Implications*, edited by A. Wolfgang, Toronto: O.I.S.E.

Yeo, W.G.
1979   "Canada's Curious Use of Italian Place Names (1850s-1910s)", *Canadian Geographic*, 98 (1).

Ziegler, S.
1980a   "Report from Canada: Adolescents Inter-ethnic Friendships", *Children Today*, March-April.

1980b   "School for Life: The Experience of Italian Immigrants in Canadian Schools", *Human Organization*, Fall.

1980c   "Measuring Inter-Ethnic Attitudes in a Multi-Ethnic Context", *Canadian Ethnic Studies*, 12 (3).

1977   "The Family Unit and International Migration: The Perceptions of Italian Immigrant Children", *International Migration Review*, 11 (3).

Zucchi, J.
1981   "The 'Annuario Italiano': A Toronto Italian City Directory", *Polyphony*, 3 (1).

CHAPTER 11: Italian Americans in the East and West: Regional Coverage in Italian American Studies, 1975-1983.

Bentley, G.
1981   *Ethnicity and Nationality. A Bibliographical Guide.* Seattle: University of Washington Press.

Bianco, C.
1974   *The Two Rosetos.* Bloomington: Indiana University Press.

Briani, V.
1979   *Italian Immigrants Abroad: A Bibliography on the Italian Experience outside Italy in Europe, The Americas, Australia, and Africa.* Emigrazione e Lavoro Italiano All-Estero: Repertorio Bibliografico.

Brown, H.
1980   *Wyoming: A Geography.* Boulder, CO: Westview Press.

Brown, K.M.
1980   "Ethnicity in Urban America", in *Impact of Urbanization and Industrialization on the Landscape.* Edited by D.R. Deskins, Jr. Michigan Geographical Publications No. 25.. Ann Arbor: University of Michigan. Pp. 38-64.

Brye, D.L., ed.
1983   *European Immigration and Ethnicity in the United States and Canada. A Historical Bibliography.* Santa Barbara, CA.: ABC-CLIO Information Service.

Campisi, P.J.
1947   "A Scale for the Measurement of Acculturation". Unpublished doctoral thesis. University Of Chicago.

1942   "The Adjustment of Italian Americans to the War Crisis". Unpublished M.A. thesis. University of Chicago.

Caroli, B.
1977   "Italian Settlement in American Cities", in *The United States and Italy: The First Two Hundred Years.* Edited by H. Nelli. Staten Island: American Italian Historical Association. Pp. 154-161.

Comeau, M.L.
1981   *Arizona: A Geography.* Boulder, Co.: Westview Press.

Cordasco, F.
1978   *Italian Americans. A Guide to Information Sources.* Detroit: Gale Research Co. Pp. 109-127, (181 regional items).

1974   *The Italian American Experience. An Annotated and Classified Bibliographical Guide.* New York: Burt Franklin and Co. (64 regional items).

D'Aniello, C. and Porcari, S.
1983   "Current Bibliography of Italian American Studies, 1980", *Italian Americana*, 7(2): Spring/Summer. Pp. 93-110.

Della Cava, O.
1971   "Italian American Studies: A Progress Report", in *Perspectives in Italian Immigration and Ethnicity.* Edited by S.M. Tomasi. New York: Center for Migration Studies. Pp. 165-172.

Graebner-Anderson, A.
1979   *The Business of Organized Crime, A Cosa Nostra Family.* Stanford, CA.: Hoover Institution Press.

Iorizzo, L.
1970 "The Padrone and Immigrant Distribution", in *The Italian Experience in the United States.* Edited by S.M. Tomasi and M.H. Engel. Staten Island: Center for Migration Studies. Pp. 43-75.

Light, T.C. and Jeansome, G.
1982 *A Guide to the History of Louisiana.* Westport, CT. and London: Greenwood Press.

Miller, W.C.
1976 *A Comprehensive Bibliography for the Study of American Minorities,* Volume 1, "Italian Americans". New York: New York University Press. Pp. 423-457.

Nelli, H.
1980 "Italians", in *Harvard Encyclopedia of American Ethnic Groups.* Edited by S. Ternstrom. Cambridge: Harvard University Press. Pp. 545-560.

1976 *The Business of Crime: Italians and Syndicate Crime in the United States.* New York: Oxford University Press.

1970 "Italians in Urban America", in *The Italian Experience in the United States.* Edited by S.M. Tomasi and M.H. Engel. Staten Island: Center for Migration Studies. Pp. 77-102

1970 "The Italians in Chicago: A Study in Ethnic Mobility". New York: Oxford University Press.

Raitz, K.B.
1979 "Themes in the Cultural Geography of European Ethnic Groups in the United States", *Geographical Review,* 1979, 69(1): 79-94.

Rolle, A.F.
1968 *The Immigrant Uprised.* Norman: University of Oklahoma Press.

Russo, P.
1983 *Catalogo Collettivo della Stampa Periodica Italo Americana (1836-1980),* Edizione Provisoria, Roma: Centro Studi Emigrazione.

Sibley, D.
1981 *Outsiders in Urban Societies.* Oxford: Blackwell.

Thompson, B.
1973 "Newcomers to the City: Factors Influencing Initial Settlement and Ethnic Community Growth Patterns: A Review", *East Lakes Geographer,* 8: Dec. Pp. 50-78.

Vecoli, R.J.
1963 "Chicago's Italians Prior to World War I: A Study of Their Social and Economic Adjustment". Unpublished doctoral thesis. University of Wisconsin.

Velikonja, J.,
1977 "Territorial Spread of the Italians in the United States", in *Perspectives in Italian Immigration and Ethnicity.* Edited by S.M. Tomasi. New York: Center for Migration Studies. Pp. 67-83.

1972 "Contributo Italiano al Carattere Geografico di Tontitown, Arkansas e Rosati, Missouri", *Gli Italiani negli Stati Uniti*. Istituto di Studi Americani. Università degli Studi di Firenze, Firenze. Pp. 423-452.

1963 *Italians in the United States. Bibliography*. Occasional Papers, No. 1, Department of Geography, Southern Illinois University, Carbondale, Il, (233 regional items).

Ward, D.
1982 "The Ethnic Ghetto in the United States: Past and Present", *Transactions, Institute of British Geographers*, N.S. 7: 257-275.

Wasserman, P. and Kennington, A.E.
1983 *Ethnic Information on Sources of the United States*. Second Edition, V.1, "Ethnic People: Afhgans — Italians". Detroit: Gale Research. (Italians, pp. 617-654).

CHAPTER 13: The Future of Italian American Studies: An Historian's Approach to Research in the Coming Decade

Arlacchi, P.
1983 *Mafia, Peasants and Great Estates, Society in Traditional Calabria*. New York: Cambridge University Press.

Baily, S.L.
1983 "The Adjustment of Italian Immigrants in Buenos Aires and New York, 1870-1914", *American Historical Review*, 88(2):281-305. April.

1982 "Chain Migration of Italians to Argentina, Case Studies of the Agnonesi and the Sirolesi", *Studi Emigrazione*, 19:73-91.

Barton, J.J.
1975 *Peasants and Strangers, Italians, Rumanians and Slovaks in an American City, 1890-1950*. Cambridge: Harvard University Press.

Bayor, R.H.
1978 *Neighbors in Conflict, the Irish, German, Jews and Italians of New York City, 1929-1941*. Baltimore: Johns Hopkins.

Bell, R.M.
1981 "Migration: Chain or Cluster, The Case of a Northern Italian Village". Paper read before the Mediterranean VI Conference at the Italian American Institute in Rome. July.

1979 *Fate and Honor, Family and Village, Demographic and Cultural Change in Rural Italy since 1800*. Chicago: University of Chicago Press.

Bodner, J., R. Simon and M.P. Weber
1982 *Lives of Their Own, Blacks, Italians and Poles in Pittsburgh, 1900-1960*. Urbana: University of Illinois Press.

Boissevain, J.
1975 *The Italians of Montreal, Social Adjustment in a Plural Society*. New York: Arno Press.

1974   *Friends of Friends, Networks, Manipulators and Coalitions.* Oxford: Basil Blackwell.

Briggs, J.W.
1978   *An Italian Passage, Immigrants to Three American Cities, 1890-1930.* New Haven, CT: Yale University Press.

Choldin, H.M.
1973   "Kinship Networks in the Migration Process", *International Migration Review*, 7(2):163-175, Summer.

Cinel, D.
1982   *From Italy to San Francisco, The Immigrant Experience.* Stanford, CA: Stanford University Press.

Cohen, M.
1982   "Changing Education Strategies among Immigrant Generations", *Journal of Social History*, 15(3):443-466. Spring.

Cordasco, F.
1981   *American Ethnic Groups.* Metuchen, NJ: Scarecrow Press.

1974   *The Italian American Experience.* New York: B. Franklin.

Cordasco, F. and S. LaGumina
1972   *Italians in the United States.* New York: Oriole Editions.

D'Aniello, C. and S. Porcari
1983   "Current Bibliography of 'Italian American' Studies, 1980-....", *Italian Americana*, 7(2):93-110.

DeMarco, W.
1981   *Ethnics and Enclaves: Boston's Italian North End.* Ann Arbor, MI: VMI Research Press.

Douglass, W.A.
1984   Emigrants in a Southern Italian Town: An Anthropological History". New Brunswick, NJ: Rutgers University Press.

Frederickson, G.
1981   *White Supremacy, A Comparative Study in American and South African History.* New York: Oxford University Press.

Garbaccia, D.R.
1984   "From Sicily to Elizabeth Street: Housing and Social Change among Italian Immigrants, 1880-1930". Albany: New York Press.

1982   "Sicilians in Space", *Journal of Social History*, 16(2):53-68. Winter.

Grew R.
1980   "The Case for Comparing Histories", *American Historical Review*, 85(4): 763-778. October.

Harney R.F. and J.V. Scarpaci
1981   *Little Italies of North America.* Toronto: Multicultural History Society of Ontario.

Ianni, F.
1958   "Time and Place as Variables in Acculturation Research", *American Anthropology*, 60(1):39-46. February.

Kessner, T.
1977   *The Golden Door, Italian and Jewish Immigrants: Mobility in New York City,*
       1880-1915. New York: Oxford University Press.

MacDonald, J.S. and L.D. MacDonald
1970   "Italian Migration to Australia", *Journal of Social History*, 3(3):249-275.
       Spring.

1964   "Chain Migration, Ethnic Neighborhood Formation and Social Networks",
       Milbank Memorial Fund Quarterly, 13(42):82-95.

Morner, M., J. Fawaz de Viñuela and J.D. French
1982   "Comparative Approaches to Latin American History", *Latin American*
       Research Review, 18(3):55-90.

Pascoe, R.
forth- "Study of Italians in Boston, Milwaukee, Denver and San Francisco".
coming

Piselli, F.
1981   *Parentela ed emigrazione, mutamenti e continuita in una comunità calabrese.*
       Torino: Guido Einaudi Editore.

Price, C.
1969   "The Study of Assimilation". In *Migration.* Edited by J.A. Jackson. London:
       Cambridge University Press. Pp. 181-237.

Ramella,
forth- Study of Emigrants from Biella.
coming

Skocpol, T.
1979   *States and Social Revolutions, A Comparative Analysis of France, Russia and*
       China. New York: Cambridge University Press.

Skocpol, T. and M. Sommers
1980   "The Uses of Comparative History in Macrosocial Inquiry", *Comparative*
       Studies in Society and History, 22(2):174-197, April.

Sturino, F.
1981   "Inside the Chain: A Case Study of South Italian Migration to North America,
       1880-1930", Ph.D. dissertation, University of Toronto.

Tricarico, D.
1984   "The Italians of Greenwich Village: The Social Structure and Transformation
       of an Ethnic Community". Staten Island: Center for Migration Studies.

Vecoli, R.J.
1964   "Contadini in Chicago: A Critique of the Uprooted", *Journal of American*
       History, 51(3):404-417. December.

Yans-McLaughlin, V.
1982   *Family and Community, Italian Immigrants in Buffalo, 1880-1930.* Urbana:
       University of Illinois Press.

CHAPTER 14: Comments on the Paper by Samuel L. Baily

Langer, W.
1958   "The Next Assignment", *American Historical Review*, 63:284-285.

Mangione, J.
1978   *An Ethnic at Large.* New York.

Rolle, A.
1981   *The Italian Americans: Troubled Roots.* New York.

CHAPTER 15: Circles of the Cyclopes: Schemes of Recognition in Italian American Discourse

Acconci, V.
1973   *Pulse (For My Mother).* Paris: Michel Durant.

Anderson, J.
1976   *Language, Memory, and Thought.* Hillsdale, NJ: Lawrence Erlbaum Associates.

———
1980   *Cognitive Psychology.* San Francisco: W.H. Freeman and Company. Pp. 128-160.

Bakhtin, M.
1981   *The Dialogic Imagination: Four Essays by Mikhail Bakhtin*, trans. Karl Emerson and Michael Holquist. Austin: TX: University of Texas Press. Pp. 50-51.

Bowlhower, W.
1982   *Immigrant Autobiography In the United States: Four Versions of the Italian American Self.* Verona: Essedue Edizione.

Green, R.B.
1974   *The Italian-American Novel: A Document of the Interaction of Two Cultures.* Rutherford, NJ: Fairleigh Dickinson University Press.

D'Angelo, L.
1977   *A Circle of Friends.* Garden City: Doubleday.

———
1971   *What the Ancients Said.* Garden City: Doubleday. Pp. 11,14.

———
1968   *How to Be an Italian.* Los Angeles: Price/Stern/Sloan.

Diacono, M.
1975   *Vito Acconci: dal testo-azione al corpo come testo.* New York/Norristown/Milano: Out of London Press. Pp. 162-170.

Dimock, JR.
1969   "The Name of the Odysseus", in *Essays on the Odyssey.* Edited by Charles H. Taylor, Jr. Bloomington: Indiana University Press. Pp. 54-72.

Ellmann, R.
1979   *Ulysses on the Liffey.* New York: Oxford University Press. P. 112.

Fante, J.
1939   *Ask the Dust.* New York: Stackpole Sons.

Homer,
1952   *The Odyssey.* Translated by Samuel Butler. Chicago: Encyclopedia Brittanica
        Pp. ix, 111-116, 367.

Mangione, J.
1981   *Mount Allegro: A Memoir of Italian American Life.* New York: Columbia
        University Press. Pp. 287-309.

Pater, W.
1908   "Style", in *Appreciation, with an Essay on Style.* London: Macmillan. P 10.

Stewart, S.
1978   *Nonsense: Aspects of Intertextuality in Folklore and Literature.* Baltimore:
        Johns Hopkins University Press.

Viscusi, R.
1982   "The Text in the Dust: Writing Italy Across America", *Studi emigrazione,*
        19 (Marzo). Pp. 127-130.

CHAPTER 17: Italian American Experience through Literature and the Arts

Journalists and Authors:

Caputo, P.
1983   *Del Corso's Gallery.* New York: Holt Rinehart & Winston.

1980   *The Horn of Africa.* New York: Holt Rinehart & Winston.
1981   Paperback edition, New York: Dell.

1977   *A Rumor of War.* New York: Holt, Rinehart & Winston.

Gallico, P.
1974   For a bibliography of his 36 novels, *See,* Rose Basile Green's *The Italian
        American Novel.* Rutherford, NJ: Fairleigh Dickinson University, pp. 393-394.

Giovannitti, L.
1977   *The Nature of the Beast.* New York: Random House.

1973   *The Man Who Won the Medal of Honor.* New York: Random House.

1965   *The Decision to Drop the Bomb,* (with Fred Freed). New York: Coward
        McCann.

1957   *The Prisoners of Combine D.* New York: Henry Holt.

1948   *Sidney Hillman: Labor Statesman.* New York: Amalgamated Clothing
        Workers of America.

Grizzuti Harrison, B.
1980   *Off Center.* New York: The Dial Press.

1975   *Visions of Glory: A History and a Memory of Jehova's Witnesses.*

1973 *Unlearning the Lie Sexism in School.* New York: Liveright.

1974 Paperback edition, New York: Morrow.

Hall, S.

1983 "Italian Americans, Coming Into Their Own", *The New York Times Magazine*, May 15.

Rovere, R.

1984 *Final Reports: Personal Reflections on Politics and History in Our Time.* Foreword by Arthur Schlesinger, Jr., New York: Doubleday.

1976 *Arrivals and Departures: A Journalists' Memoirs.* New York: MacMillan.

1968 *Waist Deep in the Big Muddy: Personal Reflections on 1968.* Boston: Little, Brown, 1968.

1965 *The Goldwater Caper.* New York: Harcourt.

1962 *The American Establishment and Other Conceits, Enthusiasms, and Hostilities.* New York: Harcourt.

1959 *Senator Joe McCarthy.* New York: Hanscourt.

1956 *Affairs of States: The Eisenhower Years.* New York: Farrar, Straus

1951 *The General and the President,* (with A.M. Schlesinger, Jr.).New York: Farrar, Straus.

1947 *Howe and Hummel: Their True and Scandalous History.* New York: Farrar, Straus, reprinted, Publishing Center for Cultural Resources, 1979.

Talese, G.

1980 *Thy Neighbor's Wife.* New York: Doubleday, (published by Mondadori in Milan in 1980 in Italian translation with title *La donna d'altri*).

1971 *Honor Thy Father.* New York Publishing, (An inside look at the life of Mafia boss Joseph Bonanno and his organization).

1970 *The Kingdom and the Power.* New York: World Publishing, (An Insider's Portrait of *The New York Times*).

1965 *The Overreachers.* New York: Harper.

1964 *The Bridge, (The building of the Verrazzano Bridge),* New York: Harper.

1961 *New York: A Serendipiter's Journey.* New York: Harper.

_____
    Fame and Obscurity. New York: World Publishing.

Italian American Writers:

Canzoneri, R.
1976   *A Highly Ramified Tree.* New York: The Viking Press.

_____
1970   *Barbed Wire and Other Stories.* New York: The Dial Press.

_____
1969   *Men With Little Hammers.* New York: The Dial Press.

_____
1968   *Watch Us Pass* (poems).Columbus: Ohio State University Press.

_____
1965   *I Do So Politely: A Voice from the South.* Boston: Houghton Mifflin.
Cuomo, G.
1983   *Family Honor: An American Life.* New York: Doubleday.

_____
1982   *Living Wage.* New York.

_____
1976   *Pieces of a Small Bomb.* New York: Doubleday.

_____
1974   *Geronimo and the Girl Next Door* (poetry). New York: Bookmark.

_____
1971   *The Hero's Great Great Great Great Great Grandson.* New York: Atheneum.

_____
1970   *Sing Choirs of Angels* (short stories). New York: Doubleday.

_____
1968   *Among Thieves.* New York: Doubleday.

_____
1964   *Bright Day, Dark Runner.* New York.

_____
1963   *Jack Be Nimble.* New York: Doubleday.
D'Agostino, G.
1952   *The Barking of a Lonely Fox.* New York: McGraw Hill.

_____
1947   *My Enemy the World.* New York: The Dial Press.

_____
1942   *Hills Beyond Manhattan.* New York: Doubleday.

_____
1940   *Olives in the Apple Tree.* New York: Doubleday.
DeLillo, D.
1982   *The Names.* New York: Alfred A. Knopf.

1980   *Ratner's Star.* New York: Alfred A. Knopf, 1976, paperback, New York: Vintage

1977   *Running Dog.* New York: Alfred A. Knopf.

1977   *Players.* New York: Alfred A. Knopf.

1973   *Great Jones Street.* Boston: Houghton Mifflin.

1972   *Americana.*   Boston: Houghton Mifflin.

1971   *End Zone.* Boston: Houghton Mifflin.

diDonato, P.
1970   *Naked Author.* New York: Phaedra.

1962   *The Penitent* (biography). New York: Hawthorn Books.

1960   *Three Circles of Light.* New York: Julian Messner.

1961   Italian Translation. *Tre cerchi di luce*, Milano: Rizzoli.

1958   *This Woman* (play). New York: Ballantine.

1950   *Immigrant Saint: The Life of Mother Cabrini.* New York: McGraw-Hill.

1938   *Christ in Concrete.* Cleveland: Bobbs-Merrill.
1941   Italian translation, *Cristo fra i muratori.* Milan: Bompiani.

DiMona, J.
1983   *Coroner.* Thomas T. Noguchi with Joseph DiMona, New York: Simon & Schuster.

1980   *To the Eagle's Nest.* New York: William Morrow.

1978   *The Ends of Power.* R.H. Haldeman with Joseph DiMona, New York: Times Books.

1977   *The Benedict Arnold Connection.* New York: William Morrow.

1974   *Frank Costello: Prime Minister of the Underworld.* George Wolf with Joseph DiMona, New York: William Morrow.

1973   *Last Man at Arlington.* New York: A. Fields.

1972 *Seventy Sutton Place.* New York: Dodd Mead.

1972 *Great Court-Martial Case.* New York: Grosset & Dunlop.

1968 *This Was Burlesque.* Ann Corio with Joseph DiMona, New York: Grosset & Dunlop.

Fante, J.
1982 *Dreams From Bunker Hill.* Boston: Houghton Mifflin.
Paperback, New York: Black Sparrow, 1983.

1977 *Brotherhood of the Grape.* Boston: Houghton Mifflin.

1952 *Full of Life.* Boston: Little Brown.

1940 *Dago Red* (short stories). New York: The Viking Press.

1939 *Ask the Dust.* New York: Stackpole Sons.

1938 *Wait Until Spring. Bandini,* New York: Stackpole Sons.

Published many short stories in magazines and also wrote about one dozen screen plays.

Mangione, J.
1981 *Mount Allegro: A Memoir of Italian American Life.* New York: Columbia University Press; New York: Hill & Long, 1963; New York: Crown Publishers, 1972; New York: Alfred A. Knopf, 1952; Boston: Houghton Mifflin, 1943.

1978 *An Ethnic At Large: A Memoir of the Thirties and Forties.* New York: Putnam.

1975 *Mussolini's March on Rome.* New York: Watts.

1972 *The Dream and the Deal: The Federal Writer's Project 1935-1943.* Boston: Little Brown.

1969 *America is Also Italian.* New York: Putnam.

1968 *A Passion for Sicilians: The World Around Danilo Dolci.* New York: Morrow.

1966 *Life Sentences for Everybody.* New York and London: Abelard-Schuman.

1965 *Night Search.* New York: Crown.

1950 *Reunion in Sicily.* Boston: Houghton Mifflin.

1948   *The Ship and the Flame.* New York: WYM-Current Books.
Morreale, B.
1977   *Monday, Tuesday... Never Come Sunday.* Plattsburgh, NY: Tundra Books.

1973   *A Few Virtuous Men: Li Cornuti.* Plattsburgh, NY: Tundra Books.

1958   *The Seventh Saracen.* New York: Coward-McCann.
Pasinetti, P.M.
1979   *Il Centro.* Milano: Bompiani.

1975   *D'allestrema America.* Milano: Bompiani.

1973   *Suddenly Tomorrow: A Novel.* New York: Random House.

1971   *Domani improvvisamente.* Milano: Bompiani.

1970   *From the Academy Bridge: A Novel.* New York: Random House.

1968   *Il ponte dell'Accademia.* Milano: Bompiani.

1967   *The Crown.* New York: Putnam.

1966   *Excursion.* New York: Putnam.

1965a   *The Smile on the Face of the Lion.* New York: Random House.

1965b   *Glover.* New York: Putnam.

1964   *La confusione.* Milano: Bompiani.

1960   *Venetian Red.* New York: Random House.

1959   *Rosso veneziano.* Rome: Colombo.
Pollini, F.
1976   *The Hall.* New York: Quartet.

1975   *Dubonnet.* New York: Quartet.

1968   *Pretty Maids All in a Row.* New York: Delacorte.

1967a   *Three Plays.* Sudsbury, Suffolk, England: Spearman.

1967b   *The Crown.* New York: Putnam.

1966   *Excursion.* New York: Putnam.

1965   *Glover.* New York: Putnam.

1962   *Night.* Boston: Houghton Mifflin.

1953   Rose Basile Green, New York: Henry Holt.

Puzo, M.

1984   *The Sicilian.* New York: Linden Press/Simon & Schuster.

1978   *Fools Die.* New York: Putnam.

1977   *Inside Las Vegas,* New York: Grosset & Dunlap.

1972   *The Godfather Papers and Other Confessions.* New York: Putnam.

1969   *The Godfather.* New York: Putnam.

1966   *The Runaway Summer of Davie Shaw.* New York: Platt & Munk.

1965   *The Fortunate Pilgrim.* New York: Atheneum.

1955   *Dark Arena.* New York: Random House.

He also has written a number of screenplays including *Godfather I* and *II* and *Superman I* and *II* and others, as well as many short stories, articles and reviews appearing in magazines and periodicals. He was the subject of a cover story in *Time,* August 18, 1978.

Tucci, N.

1977a *The Sun and the Moon.* New York: Knopf.

1977b   *Confessioni involontarie.* Milano: Mondadori.

1968   *Gli Atlantici.* Milano: Garzanti.

1964   *Unfinished Funeral.* New York: Simon & Schuster.

1962   *Before My Time.* New York: Simon & Schuster.

1956   *Il segreto.* Milano: Garzanti.

Vivanti, A.

1979   *Run to the Waterfall.* New York: Charles Scribner's Sons.

1975   *English Stories.* Boston: Little Brown.

1969   *Doctor Giovanni.* Boston: Little Brown.

1967   *The French Girls from Killini* (short stories). Boston: Little Brown.

1959   *A Goodly Babe.* Boston: Little Brown.

1951   *Poesie.* Venice: Perrari.

Mystery Writers:

Avallone, M.A.
For a complete list of pseudonyms and lists of his publications through 1981, *See,* *Contemporary Authors, New Revision Series,* Vol. 4, Detroit: Gale Research Co.,1981. Also useful information is found in the 1982-83 edition of *Who's Who in America.*

Bova, B.W.
For a complete list of his publications *See,* the 1982-83 edition of *Who's Who in America.*

Hunter, E.
For a complete list of his publications, *See,* the 1982-83 edition of *Who's Who in America* and *Contemporary Authors, New Revision Series,* Vol. 5, Detroit:Gale Research Co., 1981.

Pronzini, J.
See, Contemporary Authors, New Revised Edition, Vol. 1 for a complete bibliography of his works.

Biographers:

Winwar, F. (Francesca Vinciguerra)
1967   *All About Napoleon Bonaparte.* Philadelphia: W.H. Allen.

1961a   *The Land of the Italian People.* Philadelphia: Lippincot, 1961, revised edition published as *The Land and People of Italy.*

1961b   *Jean-Jacques Rousseau: Conscience of an Era.* New York: Random House.

1959a   *The Haunted Palace: A Life of Edgar Allen Poe.* New York: Harper.

1959b   *Cupid: The God of Love.* New York: Random House.

1957   *Italy and Her People.* New York: Lutterworth

1957a   *The Monument in Staten Island, Meucci, Garibaldi and the Telephone.* Chicago: E. Clemente.

1957b   *Elizabeth: The Romantic Story of Elizabeth Barrett Browning.* New York: Random House.

1956   *Wingless Victory: A Biography of Gabriele d'Annunzio and Eleonora Duse.* New York: Harper.

1954a *The Last Love of Camille.* New York: Harper & Bros.

1954b *Queen Elizabeth and the Spanish Armada.* New York: Random House.

1953a *Napoleon and the Battle of Waterloo.* New York: Random House.

1953b *The Eagle and the Rock.* New York: Harper & Bros.

1950 *The Immortal Lovers: Elizabeth Barrett and Robert Browning.* New York: Harper.

1940 *Oscar Wilde and the Yellow Nineties.* New York: Harper.

1948a *The Saint and the Devil: A Biographical Study of Joan of Arc and Gilles de Rais.* New York: Harper.

1948b *Joan of Arc.* New York: Bantam.

1945 *The Life of the Heart: George Sand and Her Times.* New York: Harper.

1943 *The Sentimentalist.* New York: Harper & Bros.

1941 *American Giant: Walt Whitman and His Times.* New York: Harper.

1938a *Farewell the Banner: "Three Persons and One Soul"— Coleridge, Wordsworth and Dorothy.* New York: Doubleday.

1938b *Puritan City: The Story of Salem.* New York: R.M. McBride.

1937 *Gallows Hill.* New York: Henry Holt.

1935 *The Romantic Rebels.* Boston: Little Brown.

1933 *Poor Splendid Wings: The Rossettis and Their Circle.* Boston: Little Brown.

1930 *Giovanni Boccaccio, The Decameron.* New York: Limited Editions Club. Reprinted, New York: The Modern Library, 1955.

Children's Books:
Angelo, V.
1966 *The Tale of a Donkey.* New York: The Viking Press.

1963 *The Merry Marcos.* New York: The Viking Press.

1961 *Angelino and the Barefoot Saint.* New York: The Viking Press.

1960   *The Candy Basket.* New York: The Viking Press.

1959   *The Honey Boat.* New York: The Viking Press.

1958   *The Acorn Tree.* New York: The Viking Press.

1955   *Big Little Island.* New York: The Viking Press.

1949   *The Bells of Bleeker Street.* New York: The Viking Press. Reprinted 1969.

1944   *The Rooster Club.* New York: The Viking Press.

1943   *Look Out Yonder.* New York: The Viking Press.

1942a   *A Battle in Washington Square.* Golden Cross Press.

1942b   *Hill of Little Miracles.* New York: The Viking Press.

1940   *Paradise Valley.* New York: The Viking Press.

1939   *The Golden Gate.* New York: The Viking Press. Reprinted, New York: Arno Press, 1975.

1938   *Nino.* The Viking Press.

de Paola Tomie (Thomas Anthony)

1981   For a complete listings of books written and illustrated by de Paola, *See, Contemporary Authors. New Revision Series,* Vol. 2. Detroit: Gale Research Co.

Lionni, L.

1983   *Who? What? Where? When?* (four separate volumes). New York: Pantheon.

1979   *Geraldine the Music Mouse.* New York: Pantheon.

1977a   *I Want to Stay Here.* New York: Pantheon.

1977b   *A Parallel Botany.* New York: Pantheon.

1976   *Pezzettino.* New York: Pantheon.

1975a   *In the Rabbit Garden.* New York: Pantheon.

1975b   *A Color of His Own.* Abelard. New York: Pantheon.

1973   *The Greentail Mouse.* New York: Pantheon.

1972   *Il taccuino di Leo Lionni.* Milano: Electra.

1971   *Theodore and the Talking Mushroom.*New York: Pantheon.

1969   *Alexander and the Wind-Up Mouse.*New York: Pantheon.

1970   *Fish is Fish.*New York: Pantheon.

1968a   *Alphabet Tree.* New York: Pantheon.

1968b   *The Biggest House in the World.* New York: Pantheon.

1964   *Tico and the Golden Wings.* New York: Pantheon.

1961   *On My Beach There Are Many Pebbles.* New York: Obolensky.

1960   *Inch by Inch.* New York: Obolensky, 1960

1959   *Little Blue and Little Yellow.* New York: Obolensky.

Politi, L.
All books published by Scribner in New York, except as indicated:

1973   *The Nicest Gift*

1971   *Emmet.*

1969   *Mieko.* Golden Gate.

1966   *Tales of the Los Angeles Parks.* Best-West Publications.

1965   *Piccolo's Prank* .

1963a   *Bunker Hill, Los Angeles Reminiscences of Bygone Days.* Desert-Southwest.

1963b   *Rosa.*

1962a   *Lito and the Clowns.*

1962b   *All Things Bright and Beautiful.*

1960a   *Moy Moy.*

1960b   *Boat for Peppe.*

1959   *Saint Francis and the Animals.*

1957   *Butterflies Come.*

1953   *Mission Bell.*

1951   *Little Leo.*

1949   *Song of the Swallows.*

1948   *Juanita.*

1947   *Young Giotto.* New York: Horn.

1946   *Pedro, the Angel of Olvera Street.*

1938   *Little Pancho.* New York: Viking.

Social and Psychological Sciences:
Arieti, S.
1959-   *American Handbook of Psychiatry.* New York: Basic Books.
1975

1955   *Interpretation of Schizophrenia.* New York: Basic Books.
Buscaglia, L.
1983   *New York Times Book Review.* April 17.

1982a   *Love.* Thorofare, NJ: Charles B. Slack, 1972, paperback editions, New York: Fawcet Crest, 1978, New York: Ballantine Books, 1982.

1982b   *Time.* November 15, p. 83.

1982c   *Living, Loving and Learning.*

1981   *Time.* November 15, p. 83.

1978   *Personhood.*

        The Fall of Freddie the Leaf. Thorofare, NJ: Charles B. Slack.

        The Way of the Bull, Because I am Human and *The Disabled and Their Parents*, published by Charles B. Slack and distributed by Holt, Rinehart & Winston, New York.

Robertiello, R.C.
For a complete list of publications, *See, Contemporary Authors*, Vol. 21-22, Detroit: Gale Research Co., *See also, Obituary* in *The New York Times*, 8/10/81; *See Contemporary Authors, New Revision Series*, Vol. 3 for more information and list of publications.

Rossi, P.H.
See, Contemporary Authors. New Revision Series, Vol. 2 for a list of his books.

Religion:
Politella, J.
1968   *Mystical Foundation of World Religions*. Iowa City: Sernoll.

1967   *Taoism and Confucianism: The Way of Heaven and the Way of Man*. Iowa City: Sernoll.

1966a   *Hinduism: Its Scripture, Philosophy and Mysticism*. Iowa City: Sernol.

1966b   *Buddhism: A Philosophy of the Spirit and A Way to the Eternal*. Iowa City: Sernoll.

1964   *Mysticism and the Mystical Consciousness Illustrated from World Religion*. Kent, Ohio: Kent State University Press.

1963   *Seven World Religions*. Kent, Ohio: Kent State University Press, Volume 1, 1950, Volume II.

1938   *Platonism, Aristotelianism and Kabbalism in the Philosophy of Leibniz*. Philadelphia: University of Pennsylvania Press.

Politics:
Califano, J.A.
1981   *Governing America: An Insider's Report from the White House and the Cabinet*. New York: Simon & Schuster.

1979   *The Media and Business*, (with Howard Simon). New York: Praeger.

1976   *The Media and the Law*, (with Howard Simons). New York: Praeger.

1975   *A Presidential Nation*. New York.

1969   *The Student Revolution: A Global Confrontation*. New York: Norton.
Caro, R.
1982   *The Years of Lyndon Johnson: The Path to Power*. New York: Knopf.

1974   *The Power Broker: Robert Moses and the Fall of New York*. New York: Knopf and New York: Vintage Books, 1975.

Literary Criticism:

Bruccoli, M.J.

For lists of publications, *See Contemporary Authors*, Vol. 11-12, Detroit: Gale Research Co. and the 1982-83 edition of *Who's Who in America.*

Monaco, J.

See, Contemporary Authors, Vol. 69-72.

Poetry:

Ciardi, J.

1980   *A Browerser's Dictionary and Native's Guide to the Unknown American Language.* New York: Harper.

——————

1977   Reprint *The Divine Comedy.* New York: Norton.

——————

1970   *The Paradiso,* New York: New American Library.

——————

1961   *The Purgatorio,* New York: New American Library.

——————

1954   *The Inferno.* New Brunswick: Rutgers University Press.

For a detailed list of Ciardi's publications, *See, Contemporary Authors, new Revision Series* Vol. 5.

Corso, G.N.

1962   *Long Live Man.* New York: New Directions.

——————

1960   *Happy Birthday of Death.* New York: New Directions.

——————

1958   *Gasoline.* Introduction by Allen Ginsburg. San Francisco: City Lights, 1958

——————

1955   *The Vestal Lady on Brattle, and Other Poems.* Cambridge, MA: R. Bruckenfeld.

For a list of his publications, *See, Contemporary Authors*, Vol. 7-8.

Ferlinghetti, L.

1983   For lists of his publications *See, Lawrence Ferlinghetti: Poet at Large,* by Larry Smith, Carbondale: Southern Illinois University Press.

——————

1981   *Endless Life: Selected Poems,* New York: New Directions.

——————

1958   *A Coney Island of the Mind.* New York: New Directions.

Giovannetti, A.

——————

1962   *The Collected Poems of Arturo Giovannitti.* With an Introduction by Norman Thomas. Chicago: E. Clements & Sons. Reprint, New York: Arno Press, 1975.

——————

1919   *The New Era in American Poetry.* New York: Henry Holt & Co.

1914   *Arrows in the Gale.* With an introduction by Helen Keller. Riverside, CT: Hillacre Bookhouse.

Marinoni, R.Z.

1967   *Whoo-Whoo, the 'Howl' of the Ozarks Says: Think and Wink!.* Fayetteville: Ozark Series Press.

1966   *Lend Me Your Ears: A Beakful of Humorous Verse.* Fayetteville: Ozark Series Press.

1963   *The Green Sea Horse.* Francestown, NH: Golden Quill Press.

1961   *The Ozarks and More of Its People.* Fayetteville: Ozark Series Press.

1956a   *Radici al vento (Roots to the Sky)* (bilingual edition).Milano:Mario Bazzi.

1956b   *The Ozarks and Some of Its People.* Fayetteville: Ozark Series Press.

1954   *Timberline.* Cedar Rapids, Iowa: Torch Press.

1941   *Sunny Side Up.* New York: Atheneum.

1938   *Side Show.* Philadelphia, David McKay.

1931   *North of Laughter.* Atlanta: Oglethorpe University Press.

1930   *In Passing.* New York: Parnassus.

1929   *Red Kites and Wooden Crosses.* Chicago: Packard.

1927a   *Pine Needles.* New York: Parnassus.

1927b   *Behind the Mask.* New York: H. Harrison

Sorrentino, G.

1981   *Selected Poems, 1958-1981.* Santa Barbara: Black Sparrow Press.

1980   *Aberration of Starlight.* New York: Random House.

1979   *Mulligan Stew.* New York: Grove Press.

1960   *The Darkness Surrounds Us.* Jargon Society.

Tusiani, J.

1979   For an exhaustive listing of Tusiani's works, *See, Joseph Tusiani's: A Bibliography*, compiled and edited by Pasquale Perretta. New York: Fordham University.

1978 *Gente Mia and Other Poems.* Stone Park, IL: Italian Cultural Center.

1974a *The Age of Dante.*

1974b *From Marino to Morinetti.*

1971 *Italian Poets of the Renaissance.* New York: Baroque Press.

1970 *Tesso's Jerusalem Delivered.* Rutherford, NJ: Fairleigh Dickinson University Press.

1964 *The Fifth Season: Poems.* New York: Obolensky.

1962 *Rind and All: Fifty Poems.* New York: The Monastine Press.

1960 *The Complete Poems of Michelangelo.* New York: Noonday Press.

The Theater:
Carlino, L.J.
1980 *Cages, Telemacus Clay,* and *Doubletalk, The Great Santini* and *Ressurrection, New York Times,* November 2, p. 19.
Fratti, M.
1982 For a full discussion of Fratti Theatre and information on his life *See:* Jane F. Bonin: *Mario Fratti.* Boston: Twayne Publishers.
Innaurato, A.
1980 *Bizzare Behavior: Six Plays by Albert Innaurato.* New York: Avon Books; (Contains: *Gemini, Ulysses in Traction, The Transfiguration of Benno Blimpie, Urlicht, Wisdom Amock, Earth Worms*).
Manteo, A.
1984 *See,* article by Harold C. Schoenberg in *The New York Times,* January 20.

1983 *Smithsonian,* August, cover and pp. 68-74.

Mastrosimone, W.
1982 *Extremities, The New York Times,* December 23; January 2, 1983.

1980 *The Wool Gatherer, The New York Times,* June 6.
Pintauro, J.
1982 *Cacciatore I, II* and *III,* Orchid, *New York Times,* March 11, p. C17.

Broadway Musicals:
Bennett, M.
1983 *Time,* October, 10, p. 55.

Corsaro, F.
1978   *Maverick: A Director's Personal Experience in Opera and Theater*, New York: Vanguard.

Warren, H. (Salvatore Guaragna)
1981   *The New York Times*, September 23, p. D23.

Ballet:

Barker, B. McKin
1981   "The American Careers of Rita Sangalli, Giuseppina Morlacchi and Maria Bonfanti: Nineteenth Century Ballerinas", unpublished Doctoral Dissertation, New York University.

Croce, A.
1982   *Going to the Dance*. New York: Knopf.

_____

1977   *Afterimages*. New York: Knopf.

Music:

Schiavo, G.
1947   *Italian American History, Vol. 1*. New York: The Vigo Press, p. 46.

Le Selva, V.
1983   *New York Times*, July 24, Arts and Leisure Section.

Toscanini, A.
1979   *New York Times*, September 2, Sec. 2, p.1.

Composers:

Corigliano, J. Jr.
1982   Bernard Holland, "Highbrow Music to Hum", *The New York Times Magazine*, January 31.

Del Tredici, D.
1983   Tim Page, "The New Romance and Tonality" *The New York Times Magazine*, May 29.

_____

1980   John Rockwell, "Del Tredici — His Success Could Be a Signpost", *The New York Times*, October 26, p. D23.

Jazz, Rock, Pop Music:

Corea, C. (Armando)
1983   Chick Corea is Thinking a Lot about Mozart Now", *The New York Times Magazine*, June 2, Arts and Leisure Sec. p. 15.

Band Music:

Falcone, L.
1973   Myron Delford Welch's "The Life and Work of Leonard Falcone with Emphasis on His Years as Director of Bands at Michigan State

University, 1927-1957", unpublished Ph.D dissertation, University of Illinois.

Scala, F.
1973   Paul Joseph Le Clair's, "The Francis Scala Collection: Music in Washington, D.C. at the Time of the Civil War", unpublished Ph.D dissertation, Catholic University of America.

Venetozzi, T.
1954   John Thomas Venetozzi's "Band Works of Tommaso Venetozzi, Edited and Rescored", unpublished doctoral dissertation, Florida State University.

Vivatieri, F.
1982   James Richard Gay's, "The Wind Music of Felix Vivatieri, Dakota Territory Bandmaster", unpublished dissertation, Northern Colorado University.

Art:

Fairman, C.E.
1925   *Congressional Record — House*, January 29, 1930, p. 2630.
Another article by the same author on the subject appeared in the *Congressional Record* of January 18, p. 2606, 2608.

Painting:

Guglielmi, O.L.
1980   *O. Louis Guglielmi, A Retrospective Exhibition.* Essay by John Baker, New Brunswick, NJ: Rutgers University Art Gallery. Louis Guglielmi, A Retrospective Exhibition.

Rodia, S.
1983   For a colored picture of the Watts Towers, *See*, The *Smithsonian* magazine, August, p. 84.

Stella, J.
1971   John I. H. Baur, *Joseph Stella*, New York: Praeger.

CHAPTER 20: Generoso Pope and the Rise of Italian American Politics, 1925-1936.

Ascoli, M.
1967   "Salvemini negli Stati Uniti", *La Voce Repubblicana.* December 20-21.

1941   *Gaetano Salvemini Papers.* June 24. Rome.

Aquilano, B.
1925   *L'Ordine dei Figli d'Italia.* New York. P. 99.

Arents Research Library
n.d.   *Edward Corsi Papers*, box 27, "Correspondence of Others". Syracuse University,

Balch Institute for Ethnic Studies
1927   *Leonard Covello Papers*, box 98, folder 10, "Leaders—1927". Philadelphia.

1932   Folder 31, "Freschi".

Bayor, R.H.
1978 *Neighbors in Conflict: The Irish, Germans, Jews, and Italians of New York City, 1929-1941.* Baltimore. Pp. 126-33, 137, 145-46, 212 (note 70).

Bonnano, J. with S. Lalli
1983 *A Man of Honor: The Autobiography of Joseph Bonnano.* New York. Pp. 59-143.

Censimento Della Popolazione del Regno al 10 Febbraio 1901
1901 Rome. P. 8.

Cannistraro, P.V.
1977 "Fascism and Italian Americans", in *Perspectives in Italian Immigration and Ethnicity.* Edited by S.M. Tomasi. New York. Pp. 51-66.

Castronovo, V.
1970 *La Stampa italiana dall'unità al fascismo.* Bari. Pp. 252, 422-23, 426-27.

Clark, E.
1935 "The Italian Press, New York", *The New Republic,* November 6. Pp. 356-57.

Colonial Sand and Stone Company, Inc.
1966 *Annual Report.* P. 3.

Congressional Quarterly
1975 *Guide to U.S. Statistics.* Washington, D.C. P. 768.

Cook, F.J.
1972 "The Purge of the Greasers", in *Mafia, U.S.A.* Edited by Nicholas Gage. Chicago. Pp. 80-99.

Diggins, J.P.
1972 *Mussolini and Fascism: The View from America.* Princeton. Pp. 78-79, 282, 303.

Fink, G.M., ed.
1974 *Biographical Dictionary of American Labor Leaders.* Westport. Pp. 316, 380-81.

Flamma, A., ed.
1936 *Italiani di America.* New York. Pp. 271, 183, 188-89.

Fortune
1940 November. P.112.

Gambino, R.
1974 *Blood of My Blood: The Dilemma of the Italian Americans.* Garden City. Pp. 318-20.

Gerson, L.
1964 *The Hyphenate in Recent American Politics and Diplomacy.* Lawrence, Kansas.

Henderson, T.M.
1976 *Tammany Hall and the New Immigrants.* New York. Pp. 42-47, 128-29, 179-80, 242-43, 277, 287-94.

_____

1979 "Immigrant Politician: Salvatore Cotillo, Progressive Ethnic", *International Migration Review,* 13, Spring. Pp 84-87.

Il Giornale D'Italia
1937 Rome. June 16.

Il Corriere Della Sera
1937   Milan. June 12.
Il Progresso Italo-Americano
1950   April 29.

_____

1942   June 9.

_____

1937   June 6-18.

_____

1936   February 6, 20; March 25.

_____

1935   June 14; July 6, 7, 14, 18, 21; August 23.

_____

1933   November 5,6.

_____

1932   June 4.

_____

1931   January 6; April 5, 7, 8, 12, 16, 18-20, 23; May 15-17.

_____

1929   June 27, 30; July 2, 4-6, 14.
Il Mondo
1942   June. P. 11, 12.

_____

1941   July.

Immigration History Research Center
ca. 1941   "Generoso Pope, His Paper and His Politics". Undated typescript. *Cupelli Papers*, box 1, folder "Pope". University of Minnesota.

Iorizzo, L.J.
1970   "The Padrone and Immigrant Distribution", in *The Italian Experience in the United States*. Edited by S.M. Tomasi and M.H. Engel. New York. Pp. 43-75.

_____

n.d.   "A Reappraisal of Italian Leadership", in *Gli italiani degli Stati Uniti. Pp. 207-32.*

Kanawada, L.V., Jr.
1982   *Franklin D. Roosevelt's Diplomacy and American Catholics, Italians, and Jews.* Ann Arbor. Pp. 74, 77-81, 86, 87.

Kern, P.J.
1938   "Fiorello La Guardia", in *The American Politician*. Chapel Hill. P. 9.

Kessner, T.
1977   *The Golden Door: Italian and Jewish Immigrant Mobility in New York City, 1880-1915.* New York. Pp. 15, 17, 127-60.

L'Agente Elettorale
1935   Charles Poletti Papers, folder "Ingegnieros". Columbia University.

La Stampa Libera
1933   November 1, 5, 7, 9-11; December 2.

Lehman, H.
1932   *Herbert Lehman Papers.* Columbia University. Special File #720, "Pope". December 19.

1931   *Herbert Lehman Papers.* Columbia University. Special File #720, "Pope". May 8.

Lynch, D.T.
1932   *Criminals and Politicians.* New York. Pp. 87-94.

Mangano, A.
1917   *Sons of Italy: A Social and Religious Study of the Italians in America.*New York. Pp.123, 129.

Mann, A.
1933   *La Guardia Comes to Power, 1933.* Philadelphia and New York. Pp. 78, 134, 137-38.

1959   *La Guardia: A Fighter Against His Times.* Philadelphia and New York. Pp. 279, 314-20.

Mitgang, H.
1963   *The Man Who Rode the Tiger: The Life and Times of Judge Samuel Seabury.* Philadelphia and New York.

Moody's Manual of Investments
1928   New York. P. 392.

Muste, A.J.
1932   Letter to *The New Republic.* January 27. P. 298.

National Archives and Records Service
1906   "List or Manifest of Alien Passengers", *SS Madonna.* May 17. T-715, Roll 711. P. 57. U.S. Department of Justice, Immigration and Naturalization Service. Washington, D.C.

n.d.   Franklin D. Roosevelt Library, Hyde Park. "Foreign Language Citizens Committee". PPF 603; "Federation of Italian American Democratic Organizations". PPF 3778, 233A.

n.d.   Record Group 59, Department of State, 811.00F/227; 765.84111/79; 800.01811.

n.d.   Italian Records, T586, roll 430, 429.

Nelli, H.
1964   "The Italian Padrone System in the United States", *Labor History,* V, 2, Spring. Pp. 153-67

1983   *From Immigrants to Ethnics: The Italian Americans.* New York. Pp. 97, 124.

1976   *The Business of Crime: Italians and Syndicate Crime in the United States.* New York. Pp. 199-205, 245-48.

New York State, Joint Legislative Committee to Investigate the Administration of Various Departments of the Government of the City of New York.
1931-32 Report. July - December, 24 vols., New York Public Library.

New York Times
1951   April 10.

_____

1950   April 29.

_____

1931   May 15; December.

_____

1930   April 3.

_____

1929   February 6; July 4, 6.

_____

1928   September 30.

_____

1926   May 11.

_____

1906   May 16.

Peel, R.V.
1935   *The Political Clubs of New York City.* New York. Pp. 254 (note 7), 256, 265 and Appendix.

Peterson, J.
1935   *Sixty-Five Years of Progress and a Record of New York City's Banks.* New York. P.54.

Polk's Bankers Encyclopedia
1925   62nd ed. Detroit and New York. P. 1688.

Pope, G.
1932   Papers to Lehman. November 8.

_____

1931   April 29.

Rand McNally Bankers Directory and Bankers Register
1926   100th ed. Chicago. January. P.2174.

_____

1923   95th ed.Chicago. July. P. 2517

Reid, E.
1953   *The Shame of New York.* New York. Pp. 151-78.

Rosoli, G., ed.
1978   *Un secolo di emigrazione italiana, 1876-1976.* Rome.

Russo, P.
1972   "La stampa periodica italo-americana", in *Gli italiani negli Stati Uniti.* Florence. Pp. 493-546.

Salvemini, G.
1977   *Italian Fascist Activities in the United States.* Edited by Philip V. Cannistraro. New York. Pp.5-9, 208.

n.d.   "Transmission Belts". Unpublished typescript.

n.d.   *Michele Cantarella Papers*. (Mimeograph in author's possession).

1938   *The New Italian*. August - September.

U.S Department of Justice
1941   Reports. Generoso Pope file. Federal Bureau of Investigation (FBI). April 13; October 3, 4.

1943   November 8.

1941   May 10; July 8, 19, 31; August 1, 21.

1940   Papers. J. Edgar Hoover to Henry Morgenthau, Jr. July 2.

U.S. Department of Justice, Immigration and Naturalization Service
1915   "Certificate of Naturalization", no. 640585. December 13.

1914   "Petition of Naturalization", vol. 34, no. 7559. August 7.

1912   "Declaration of Intention", no. 1641. April 29.

WPA Federal Writer's Project
1938   *The Italians of New York*. New York. P. 97.

Who's Who in America
1972   1970-71, vol. 36. Chicago. P. 1434.

Whythe, W.F.
1955   *Street Corner Society: The Social Structure of an Italian Slum*. Chicago. P. 200.

CHAPTER 21: "La Questione Sociale", an Anarchist Newspaper in Paterson, N.J. (1895-1908).

Altarelli, C.C.
1911   *History and Present Conditions of the Italian Colony of Paterson, N.J.* duplicated. P. 3.

Borghi, A.
1930   Errico Malatesta in 60 anni di Lotte anarchicie. New York. P. 136f.

Fabbri, L.
1936   *La Vida de Malatesta*. Barcelona. Pp. 138, 145, 146f.

Fedeli, U.
1956   *Giuseppe Ciancabilla; Luigi Galleani, Quarant'anni de Lotte Rivoluzionaire (1891-1931)*. Edizione "L'Antistato". Cesena. Pp. 108, 111.

Galleani, L.
1930   *Medaglione: Figure e Figuri*. Bibilioteca de L'Adunato dei Refrattari. Newark, N.J. P. 95

1907 *Cronaca Sovversiva*. Barre, Vermont. May 18.

Ghio, P.
1903 *L'anarchisme aux Etats-Unis*. Librarie Armand Colin, Paris. P. 141.

Goldman, E.
1970 *Living My Life*. AMS Press, New York. P. 150.

La Questione Sociale (LQS), Paterson, N.J. 1895-1908.

Malatesta, E.
1899 "Il Nostro Programma", in *LQS*. Sept.

Masini, P.C.
1969 *Storia degli anarchici italiani de Bakunin a Malatesta*. Rizzoli editore, Milan. P. 227.

Nettlau, M.
1924 *Errico Malatesta: The Biography of an Anarchist, a Condensed Sketch*, Jewish Anarchist Federation, New York City. P. 59.

N.Y. Times, March 22, 24, 1908.

Paterson Daily Press, (PDP), April 25, 26, 1902; May 6, 1902; June 7, 1902.

Paterson Morning Call, March 23, 24, 1908.

Paterson Evening News, Aug. 3, 1900.

Petacco, A.
1969 *L'Anarchico, che venne dall'America*. Mondadori, Milan. P. 13f.

Richards, V.
1965 *Errico Malatesta, His Life and Ideas*. Freedom Press, London. P. 224.

Wishart, A.W.
1905 *The Case of William McQueen, Reasons Why he Should be Liberated.* Trenton, N.J.

CHAPTER 23: Michael Augustine Corrigan and the Italian Immigrants:
The Relationship Between the Church and the Italians in the Archdiocese
of New York 1884-1902

Billington, R.
1964 *The Protestant Crusade: 1800-1860, A Study in the Origins of American Nativism*. Chicago.

Chapman, C.G.
1971 Milocca: A Sicilian Village, Cambridge, p. 27.

DiGiovanni, S.
1983 *Michael Augustine Corrigan and the Italian Immigrants: The Relationship Between the Church and the Italians in the Archdiocese of New York, 1885-1902*, (unpublished doct. dissert.). Romae, pp. 403-430.

Dore, G.
1964 La Democrazia italiana e l'Emigrazione in America, Brescia, p. 56.

Foerster, R.
1919 *e Italian Emigration in Our Times*. Cambridge, MA., p. 474.

Francesconi, M.
1969   Inizi della Congregazione Scalabriniana (1995-1888). Roma.

Halperin, W.
1951   Leo XIII and the Roman Question, in Leo XIII and the Modern World (Gargan, E., ed.,) NY.

Iorizzo, L.
1970   The Padrone and Immigrant Distribution, in The Italian Experience in the United States (Tomasi, S. and M. Engel, eds.), NY, pp. 52-58.

Lynch, B.,
1888   The Italians of New York, in The Catholic World, XLVII, 1888, pp. 70, 67-73

Martina, G.
1978   La Chiesa nell'Età del Totalitarianismo, Brescia, pp. 9-14.

Perotti, A.
1959   La Società Italiana di fronte alle prinme migrazioni di massa, in Studi Emigrazione, Febbraio-Giugno, Anno V, n. 11-12, 15, nt. 3.

Rosoli, G.
1979   Chiesa e communità Italiane negli Stati Uniti [1880-1940], in Stadium, Roma I-1979 , 28.

Shaugnessy, G.
1925   Has the Immigrant Kept the Faith?. NY, pp 166-172.

Soderini, E.
        Leo XIII and the United States of America, (undated manuscript) in AUND Eng. trans. of Ital. orig.).

Williams, P.
1966   South Italian Folkways in Europe and America, New York, 146ff

CHAPTER 24:The Greenwich Village Italian Neighborhood:
The Emergence and Eclipse of an Ethnic Communal Form

Barth, F.
1969   Ethnic Groups and Boundaries, Boston: Little Brown.

Covello, L.
1967   The Social Background of the Italo-American Schoolchild. Leiden, Netherlands: E.J. Brill.

Crispino, J.
1980   The Assimilation of Ethnic Groups: The Italian Case. Staten Island: The Center for Migration Studies.

Gans, H.
1982   "Symbolic Ethnicity: The Future of Ethnic Groups and Culture in America", in Minority and Majority (eds. Yetman and Steele), New York: Allyn and Bacon.

Glazer, N. and D.P. Moynihan
1970   *Beyond the Melting Pot.* Cambridge: M.I.T. Press.

Horowitz, D.
1975   "Ethnic Identity", in *Ethnicity: Theory and Experience*, (eds.N. Glazer and D.P.Moynihan) Cambridge: Harvard University Press, pp. 111-140.

Ianni, F.
1972   *A Family Business.* New York: Mentor.

Irwin, J.
1977   *Scenes.* Beverly Hills, CA: Sage.

Kramer, J. and S. Leventman
1969   *Children of the Gilded Ghetto.* New York: Archon Books.

Laidlaw, W.F. (ed.)
1935   *Population of the City of New York, 1890-1930.* New York: Cities Census Commission.

Muraskin, W.
1974   "The Moral Basis of a Backward Sociologist: Edward Banfield, the Italians, and the Italian-Americans", *American Journal of Sociology*, Vol. 79, No. 6 (May), pp. 1484-1496.

Nelli, H.
1974   *Italians in Chicago, 1880-1930*, New York: Oxford, 1970. New York City Department of Planning, *Little Italy Risorgimento.*

Royce, A.P.
1982   *Ethnic Identity: Strategies for Diversity.* Bloomington: University of Indiana Press.

Russo, N.J.
1970   "Three Generations of Italians in New York City: Their Religious Acculturation, in *The Italian Experience in the United States* (eds., S.M. Tomasi and M. Engel), Staten Island: Center for Migration Studies, pp. 195-209.

Sandberg, N.
1974   *Ethnic Identity and Assimilation: The Polish American Case*, New York: Praeger.

Steinberg, S.
1981   *The Ethnic Myth: Race, Ethnicity, and Class in America.* New York: Atheneum.

Suttles, G.
1972   *The Social Construction of Communities.* Chicago: University of Chicago Press.

───────────

1968   *The Social Order of the Slum.* Chicago: University of Chicago Press.

Tomasi, S.M.
1970   "The Ethnic Church and the Integration of Italian Immigrants in the United

States", in *The Italian Experience in the United States*, (Tomasi and Engel, eds.), New York: The Center for Migration Studies.

Tricarico, D.
1984 "The 'New' Italian-American Ethnicity" (forthcoming *The Journal of Ethnic Studies*),.

Vecoli, R.
1969 "Prelates and Peasants: Italian Immigration and the Catholic Church", *Journal of Social History*, Vol. 2 (Spring), pp. 217-268.

Ware, C.
1965 *Greenwich Village, 1920-1930*. New York: Harper.

Yancey W., E. Ericksen and R. Juliani,
1976 "Emergent Ethnicity: A Review and Reformulation", *American Sociological Review*, Vol. 41 (June), pp. 391-403.

CHAPTER 25: Italian Americans on Long Island: The Foundation Years

Amityville Record
1900- Passim.
1976

Carucci, M.
1982 "The Sand Pits of Port Washington", *Long Island Heritage*, October 1982.

Femminella, F.X.
1968 *Ethnicity and Ego Identity*. Ph.D. Thesis, New York University.

Glen Cove *Echo*
1913- Passim.
1960

Glen Cove *Record*
1934- Passim.
1976

LaGumina, S.
1982 "Francis B. Spinola, Nineteenth Century Patriot and Politician", paper delivered at Annual Conference of American Italian Historical Association, St. John's University, New York.

1980 "The History of Westbury's Italian American Community", *Ethnicity in Suburbia: The Long Island Experience*, Salvatore La Gumina, ed., Garden City.

Mathias, E.L.
1983 "Sardinian Born and Bread", *Natural History*, January, pp. 54-62.

Newsday
1972 Long Island *Magazine* June 4.
1976

New York State Manuscript Census
1915　Nassau County.

1925　Nassau County.

Oyster Bay *News* and *Guardian*
1899-　Passim.
1920

Port Washington *News*
1904-Passim. 1980

Pyrke B.
1943　A. "Long Island's First Italian, 1639", *Long Island Forum*, August, pp. 143-45;
　　　September, pp. 169-76.

Rockaway *News*
1905-Passim.
1925

St. Rocco's
1937　*First Souvenir Journal of St. Rocco's Parish*. Established January 18.

Seyfried, V.A.
1966　*The Long Island Railroad: A Comprehensive History. The Age of Expan-
　　　sionism, 1833-1880*. Garden City.

United States Census, Schedule of the Population Tracts
1900　Nassau and Suffolk Counties.

Westbury *Times*
1936-　Passim.
1978

Williams, G.L.
1983　"Sand Mining in Port Washington: Its Impact on the Community", *Long
　　　Island Forum*, February, pp. 32-8.

Winsche, R.A.
1964　"Echos of Belmont Park", *The Nassau County Historical Society Journal*, Vol.
　　　XXV (Spring) No. 2, pp. 15-33.

Chapter 26: Concord and Discord: Italians and Ethnic Interaction in Tampa, Florida,
1886-1930

Bagley, S.
1948　"The Latin Clubs of Tampa, Florida". Unpublished M.A. thesis. Duke Uni-
　　　versity.

Bayor, R.
1978　*Neighbors in Conflict: The Irish, Germans, Jews, and Italians of New York
　　　City, 1929-1941*. Baltimore.

Bryan, L.M.
n.d.　"Fifty Years of Group Medicine in Tampa". P. 5.

Campbell, S. and W.P. McLendon
1939   *The Cigar Industry of Tampa, Florida.* Gainesville. Pp. 8, 10-12, 66-67, 5-12.

Cordero, E.A.
1982   "Preliminary Research Report, The Afro-Cuban Community in Tampa, Florida". Unpublished honor's paper, USF.

del Rio, E.
1950   *Yo fui uno de los fundadores de Ybor City.* Tampa. P. 11.

Dubofsky, M.
1975   "Comment on Education and the Italian and Jewish Community Experience", in *The Interaction of Italians and Jews in America.* Proceedings of the 7th Annual Conference of the American Italian Historical Association. Edited by J.A. Scarpaci. P. 59.

Federal Writer's Project
n.d.   Interview with Enrique Pendas. P.K. Yonge Library of Florida History. University of Florida, Tampa.

_____

n.d   "Ybor City: General Description".Tampa. Pp. 177, 186

_____

1936   *Seeing Tampa: A Guide and Handbook of Information to the City and its Suburbs.* American Guide Series. Tampa. P. 42.

_____

n.d.   Interview with Fermin Souto. Tampa. Pp. 3-5.

_____

n.d.   "History of Centro Asturiano". Tampa. Pp. 2-5.

_____

1939   Interview with Jose Ramon Sanfeliz. Tampa. P. 7.

_____

n.d.   "Life Histories of Cuban Cigar Workers".

_____

n.d.   "Fifty years of Group Medicine in Tampa". P. 5.

_____

n.d.   "History of Circulo Cubans". Tampa.

_____

1936   "History of Ybor City". Tampa.

_____

1939   Interviews by A. Pollato and S. Kennedy. Tampa. P. 4.

_____

n.d.   "Life History of John Cacciatore". Tampa.

Florida Historical Quarterly
1983   "Immigrant Women in Tampa: The Italian Experience". January 61. Pp. 303-07.

_____

1978   October, 57.

_____

1975   April, 53.

1963   April, 41.

Gallo, J.G.
1936   *El tabaquero cubano*. Havana.

Ginesta, D.
n.d.   "Life Histories of Cuban Cigar Workers". P. 3.

Gomez, R.A.
1962   "Spanish Immigrants in the U.S", *The Americas*, 19, July. Pp. 59-77.

Ingalls, R.P.
1981   "Radicals and Vigilantes: The 1931 Strike of Tampa Cigarworkers", *Southern Workers and Their Unions, 1888-1975*. Edited by Gary Fink and Merl Reed. Westport, CT. Pp. 44-57.

Juliani, R. and M. Hutter
1975   "Research Problems in the Study of Italian and Jewish Interaction in Community Settings" in *The Interaction of Italians and Jews in America*. Edited by Jean A. Scarpaci. American Italian Historical Association. P. 42-56.

Kissimmee Valley
1896   Nov. 11, 25.

Leon, J.M.
1962   "The Cigar Industry and Cigar Leaf Tobacco in Florida During the Nineteenth Century". Unpublished M.A. thesis. Florida State University. Pp. 76-83.

Long, D.
1971a   "The Making of Modern Tampa: A City of the New South, 1885-1911", *The Florida Historical Quarterly*, 56, April. Pp. 333-45.

1971b   "Labor Relations in the Tampa Cigar Industry, 1885-1911", *Labor History*, 12, Fall. Pp. 551-559.

1968   "The Open-Closed Shop: Battle in Tampa's Cigar Industry, 1919-21". *Florida Historical Quarterly*, 57, October. Pp. 101-21;

1965   "An Immigrant Cooperative Medicine Program in the South", *Journal of Southern History*, 31, November. Pp. 217-34.

Massari, A.
1965   *The Wonderful Life of Angelo Massari*. New York. P. 107.

1959   *La comunita italiana di Tampa*. New York. P. 297.

Messina, C.
1977   *S. Stefano Quisquina: Studio critico*. Palermo.

Mormino, G.R.
1982   "Tampa and the New Urban South: The Weight Strike of 1899", *Florida Historical Quarterly*, 60, January. Pp. 337-56.

Mormino, G.R., and T. Pizzo
1983   *Tampa, The Treasure City*. Tulsa. Pp. 60-76.

1971   *The Florida Historical Quarterly*, 59, July. Pp. 31-44.

Mormino, G.R. and G.E. Pozzetta
1983 "Immigrant Women in Tampa: The Italian Experience", *Florida Historical Quarterly*, 61. January. Pp. 303-307.

Muniz, J.R.
1976 *Los cubanos en Tampa*. Translated as *The Ybor City Story: 1885-1954* by E. Fernandez and H. Beltran. Tampa. Pp. 6-14, 28, 58, 89.

1963 "Tampa at the Close of the Nineteenth Century", in *The Florida Historical Quarterly*, 41 April. Pp. 335-336.

Perez, L.A., Jr.
1975 "Reminiscences of a Lector: Cuban Cigar Workers in Tampa", *Florida Historical Quarterly*, 53, April. Pp. 443-44.

1978 "Cubans in Tampa: From Exiles to Immigrants, 1892-1901", in *Florida Historical Quarterly*, 57, October. Pp. 129-140.

Rabb, J.W.
1938 "Trade Jargon of the Cigar Industry of Tampa". Tampa. P. 7.

Rerrick, R.
1902 *Memoirs of Florida*, 2 vols. Atlanta. Pp. II, 222.

Scaglione, P.C.
1933 "The Cigar Industry in Florida". Unpublished M.A. thesis. University of Florida. Pp. 7-10, 26, 33-34, 63-64.

Stelzner, H.G., and D. Bazo
1965 "Oracle of the Tobacco Ranch", *Southern Speech Journal*, 31. Pp. 124-31.

Steffy, J.M.
1975 "The Cuban Immigration to Tampa, Florida, 1886-1898". Unpublished M.A. thesis. University of South Florida. Pp. 14-15, 44-45, 46-49, 46, 143.

Tampa City Directories
1900-30 Special Collections. USF Library. Tampa.

Tampa Journal
1887 Jan. 26.

Tampa Morning Tribune
1977 Sept. 14.

1931 Dec. 7, 8.

1927 May 21.

1911 January 26; September 23, 28-30; December 18.

1910 December 20.

1908 April 1, 12.

1905 January 20; September 20.

1903   May 2, 5.

1899   January 31.

1896   July 30.

1895   June 23; October 29; Dec. 27.
Tampa Times
1977   Sept. 14. D. 1
Tampa Weekly Tribune
1899   June 22.
University of Florida
1983a   Interview with Francesco Rodriguez. July 15. Tampa.

1983b   Interview with Juan Maella. August 1. Tampa.

1982   Interview with Tina Assunta Provenzano. March 13. Tampa.

1979   Interview with Paul Longo. June 1. Tapes at Oral History Collection.

1976   Interview with Sirio Bruno Coniglio. May 2. Clearwater, Oral History
        Collection.
U.S. Census
1902   *Population*, 1900, Vol. II, Table 27. Washington. P. 214

1912   *Population Florida*, Thirteenth Census, 1910. Tables 2, 4. Washington.
        Pp. 330-32.
U.S. Congress, Senate
1911   *Reports of the Immigration Commission, Immigrants in Industries*, "Cigar
        and Tobacco Manufacturing". Pp. 87, 192, 204-205.

1980   Interview with Mary Italiano. April 16.
Westfall, G.
1977   "Don Vicente Martinez Ybor: The Man and His Empire". Unpublished Ph.d.
        dissertation. University of Florida. Pp. 55-75.

n.d.   "Early Days of Ybor City as Narrated by Fernando Lemos". Federal
        Writer's Project. Tampa. Pp. 118, 130, 82-85, 116-117.

CHAPTER 28: Italian American Styles of Venture Entrepreneurism:
A Proposed Study

Anon
1981 "Women: The New Venture Capitalists", *Business Week*. Nov., Vol. 2712 (Industrial Edition).

Bacharach, S. and E.J.
1981 *Power and Politics in Organizations*. San Francisco: Jossey-Bass Publishers.

Bekey, M.
1981 "Born and Bred Entrepreneurs", *Venture*, 3:3 March, pp. 36-46.

Blau, P.M. and O.D. Duncan
1967 *The American Occupational Structure*. New York: John Wiley and Sons.

Bowles, S. and H. Gintis
1976 *Schooling in Capitalist America*. New York: Basic.

Carnoy, M. and H.M. Levin, eds.
1976 *The Limits of Educational Reform*. New York: McKay.

Coleman, J.S., E.D. Campbell, C.J. Hobson, J. McPartland, J. McPartland, A.M. Mood, F.D. Weinfield and R.L. York.
1966 *Equality of Educational Opportunities*. Washington, D.C.: U.S. Government Printing Office.

Dizard, J.W.
1982 "Management; Venture-Capital; Personality Analysis. *Fortune*, Vol. 106, No. 7, pp. 106-114.

Dobb, M.
1946 *Studies in the Development of Capitalism*. 1946. London: George Routledge.

Duncan, O.D., D.L. Featherman, B. Duncan
1972 *Socioeconomic Background and Achievement*. New York: Seminar Press.

Erikson, E.H.
1959 "Identity and the Life Cycle". In *Psychological Issues*. George S. Klein, ed. New York: International Press. Pp. 1-176.

Fanfani, A.
1939 *Catholicism, Protestantism and Capitalism*. New York: Sheed & Ward.
(1935)

Femminella, F.X.
1983 "The Ethnic Ideological Themes of Italian Americans". In *The Family and Community Life of Italian Americans*. Richard N. Juliani, ed. New York: AIHA. Pp. 109-120.

Grossman, R. "Why Venture Capital Won't Work for the Japanese". Nov. 29, 1982. *Business Week*, No. 2767, p. 97.

Harrington, M.
1975 (The Twilight of Capitalism.), New York: Simon & Shuster.

Hoban, J.P. Jr.
1976 *Characteristics of Venture Capital Investments*. Ph.D. Thesis, University of Utah.

Kelly, G.A.
1955   *A Theory of Personality: The Psychology of Personal Constructs*. New York: W.W. Norton.

Kramer, M.
1980   *The Venture Capital of Higher Education. The Private and Public Sources of Discretionary Funds*. San Francisco, CA: Jossey-Bass.

Marx, K.
1906 (1867). *Capital*. New York: Random House.

McClellan, B.
1958   Bronfenbrenner and Stodbeck. *Talent and Society*. New York: D. Van Nostrand Co.

Perlo, V.
1976   *Economies of Racism, U.S.A*. New York: International Publishers.

Perrow, C.
1967a   "A Framework for the Comparative Analysis of Organizations", *American Sociological Review*. 32(2):194-208.

Perry, T.S.
1982   "Six Steps to Becoming a Successful Entreprenuer", *Spectrum*. 19:12. Pp. 46-50.

Postiglione, G.A.
1983   *Ethnicity and American Social Theory*. Lanham, MD: University Press of America.

Rosen, B.C., H.J. Crockett and C.Z. Nunn
1969   *Achievement in American Society*. Cambridge, MA: Schenkman Publishing Co.

Sartori, G.
1983   "The Market, Planning, Capitalism and Democracy". In *This World*. Spring/Summer, No. 5, pp. 55-83.

Sewell, W. and A.O. Haller
1965   "Educational and Occupational Perspectives of Farm and Rural Youth". In *Rural Youth in Crisis: Facts, Myths, and Social Change*. Lee G. Burchinall, ed. Washington, D.C.: U.S. Government Printing Office. Pp. 149-169.

Sewell, W., A.D. Haller and G. W. Ohblendorf
1970   "The Educational and Early Occupational Attainment Process: Replication and Revision". In *American Sociological Review*. Dec., pp. 1014-1027.

Sewell, W., A.O. Haller and A. Portes
1969   "The Educational and Early Occupational Attainment Process". *American Sociological Review*. February. Pp. 82-92.

Sewell, W. and R.M. Hauser, *et al.*
1975   *Education, Occupation and Earnings*. New York: Academic Press.

Sowell, T.
1983   *The Economics and Politics of Race*. New York: William Morrow and Co.

Tawney, R.H.

1948   *Religion and the Rise of Capitalism.* New York: 2nd Mentor Ed. Harcourt,
1926   Brace & Co.

Teague, B.W.
1980   "Venture Capital — Who Gets It and Why", *Inc.* June 2:6. Pp. 70-74.

Vesper, K.H.
n.d.   "New Venture Ideas", *Harvard Business Review.* July/Aug. 57:4. Pp.
        164-170.

Weber, M.
1958   *The Protestant Ethnic and the Spirit of Capitalism.* (Translated by T.
        Parsons, 1958).1904-1905. New York: Chas. Scribner & Sons.

Wetzel, W.E. Jr.
1981   "Technovation and the Informal Investor", *Technovation.* Netherlands: Feb.
        1:1. Pp. 15-30.

Appendix

Program of the International Conference on the Italian Experience in the United States held at Columbia University in 1983.

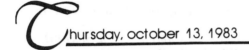 hursday, october 13, 1983

8:00 a.m.   Registration

8:30   Welcome: Giovanni Sartori, *Albert Schweitzer Professor,*
            Columbia Univ., and Director of the Center for Italian Studies

8:45   Opening Remarks:
            His Excellency Rinaldo Petrignani, *Ambassador of Italy*

9:00   DATA AND PERCEPTIONS

Chair   Silvano M. Tomasi, *President Center for Migration Studies, New York*

            1. *A NATIONAL SOCIODEMOGRAPHIC PROFILE OF ITALIAN*
            AMERICANS BASED ON THE 1980 U.S. CENSUS

            Nampeo McKenney and Michael Levin, *Ethnic and Racial Statistics*
            Program, Population Division, U.S. Bureau of the Census and
            Alfred J. Tella, *Special Advisor to the Director, U. S. Bureau of the Census*

            2. *ITALIAN MIGRATION TO THE U.S., 1968-1978:*
            THE TRANSITION PERIOD AND A DECADE BEYOND

            John F. Seggar, *Professor of Sociology, Brigham Young Univ., Utah*
Comment   William D'Antonio, *Executive Officer, A.S.A., Washington, D.C.*
            Joseph Lopreato, *Professor of Sociology, Univ. of Texas, Austin*

            3. *MEDIA PERCEPTION OF TODAY'S ITALIAN AMERICANS*

            Stephen Hall, *New York Times*
            and Joseph Giordano, Director, Louis Caplan, Center on Group Identity
            and Mental Health, American Jewish Committee

4. ITALIAN AMERICANS IN THE 1970s and 1980s

Humbert S. Nelli, *Professor of History, University of Kentucky*

5. THE SEARCH FOR AN ITALIAN AMERICAN IDENTITY

Rudolph J. Vecoli, *Professor of History, University of Minnesota and Director, Immigration History Research Center*

Comment   Furio Colombo, *Professor of Italian Studies, Columbia/Barnard*
Virginia Yans-McLaughlin, *Professor of History, Rutgers University*
Richard D. Alba, *Associate Professor of Sociology, SUNY, Albany*

11:00   RESOURCE AND THEORIES

Chair   Francis X. Femminella, *Prof. of Sociology and Education, SUNY Albany*

*6. THE STATE OF ITALIAN AMERICAN RESEARCH
SINCE 1976: SOURCES, METHODOLOGIES AND
ORIENTATIONS IN ITALY AND THE UNITED STATES*

Gianfausto Rosoli, *Editor, Studi Migrazione, CSER, Rome* and Robert Harney, *Professor of History, University of Toronto*

*7. ONGOING RESEARCH
ON ITALIAN AMERICANS IN THE U.S.: A SURVEY*

Diana Zimmerman, *Librarian, Center for Migration Studies, New York*

*8. NEEDED THEORETICAL AND COMPARATIVE
STUDIES ON THE ITALIAN AMERICAN EXPERIENCE*

Samuel L. Baily, *Professor of History, Rutgers University*

Comment   Bruno Arcudi, *Professor of Romance Languages, State University of N.Y. at Buffalo*, and *Editor, Italianamericana*

Andrew Rolle, *Cleland Professor of History, Occidental College*

Luncheon program

Presiding His Excellency Rinaldo Petrignani, *Ambassador of Italy*
Speaker   The Honorable Mario Cuomo, *Governor of New York*

2:30   DIMENSIONS/THE ITALIAN AMERICAN EXPERIENCE I
Chair   Betty Boyd Caroli, *Prof. of History, Kingsboro Community College, C.U.N.Y*

*9. ITALIAN AMERICAN EXPERIENCE
THROUGH LITERATURE AND THE ARTS*

Robert Viscusi, *Professor of English, Brooklyn College*
Robert Volpe, *International Art Consultant, New York*

10. *ITALIAN AMERICAN EXPERIENCE REFLECTED IN THE ITALIAN AMERICAN PRESS, 1836-1980*

Pietro Russo, *Professor History, University of Florence, Italy*

Comment   Jerre Mangione, *Director, Italian Studies Center, University of Pennsylvania;* Remigio Pane, *Professor of Romance Languages, Rutgers University;* Joseph Velikonja, *Professor of Geography, University of Washington*

4:00   DIMENSIONS/THE ITALIAN AMERICAN EXPERIENCE II

Chair   Giovanni Ferrero, *Counselor for Labor and Emigration, Italian Embassy, Washington, D.C.*

11. *ITALIAN AMERICANS BETWEEN THE TWO WARS*

Philip V. Cannistraro, *Professor of History, Drexel University*

12. *"LA QUESTIONE SOCIALE" AND ANARCHIST WORKING-CLASS NEWSPAPERS, PATERSON, NEW JERSEY*

George W. Carey, *Professor of Urban Studies, Rutgers University*

13. *ITALIAN WORKING WOMEN 1930-1950: WORK AND SCHOOL LIFE*

Miriam Cohen, *Professor of History, Vassar College*

Comment   Josef J. Barton, *Professor of History, Northwestern University* Ronald Bayor, *Professor of Social Sciences, Georgia Institute of Technology*

7:00   RECEPTION

Hosted by Professor Lia Beretta, Director

Exhibit of Recent Books of Italian Interest Published in the U.S.A.

Italian Cultural Institute of New York
686 Park Avenue
New York City, New York 10021   Telephone: (212) 879-4242

Friday, october 14, 1983

8:30   DIMENSIONS/THE ITALIAN AMERICAN EXPERIENCE III

Chair   Lydio F. Tomasi, *Executive Director, Center for Migration Studies, N.Y.*

14. *ITALIAN AMERICANS AND RELIGION*

Stephen Di Giovanni, *Gregorian University, Rome*

15. *ITALIAN AMERICAN COMMUNITIES* *IN GREENWICH VILLAGE, N.Y.C.; L.I., N.Y.; & TAMPA, FL*

Panelists   Donald Tricarico, *Prof. of Social Science, Queensboro Community College;* Salvatore J. LaGumina, *Prof. of History, Nassau Community College;* George E. Pozzetta, *Prof. of History, Univ. of Florida* and Gary R. Mormino, *Prof. of History, University of South Florida*

Comment   Silvano M. Tomasi, *Editor, International Migration Review*
Luciano J. Iorizzo, *Professor of History, Oswego College*
Richard Juliani, *Professor of Sociology, Villanova University*

10:30   DIMENSIONS/THE ITALIAN AMERICAN EXPERIENCE IV

Chair   Frank Stella, *President, The National Italian American Foundation, Washington, D.C.*

16. *ITALIAN AMERICAN STYLE* *OF VENTURE ENTREPRENEURISM*

Panelists   Francis X. Femminella, *S.U.N.Y., Albany*
and Fred Rotondaro, *N.I.A.F., Washington, D.C.*

17. *"ITALIAN AMERICANS AND POLITICS"*

Michael Barone, *The Washington Post*

18. *"THE ROLE OF ITALIAN AMERICANS IN THE CULTURAL* *& POLITICAL RELATIONS BETWEEN ITALY & THE U.S."*

Richard Gardner, *Henry L. Moses Professor of Law,*
Columbia University and former U.S. Ambassador to Italy

Comment   Giovanni Sartori, Albert Schweitzer *Prof., Columbia University,*
Alexander de Conde, *Professor of History, University of California,*
Santa Barbara

Conference Sponsors:

The Italian Embassy of Washington, D.C., Italian Consulate General of New York, The Italian Cultural Institute of New York, The Center for Migration Studies of New York, Inc., and Columbia University Center for Italian Studies.

Conference Coordinating Committee:

Lia Beretta, Betty Boyd Caroli, Giovanni Ferrero, Salvatore LaGumina, Remigio Pane, Giovanni Sartori, Maggie Sullivan and Lydio F. Tomasi

---

Index